220.6
R44 Riedel, Eunice.
         The book of the Bible.

The Book
of the Bible

Dürer's Adam and Eve.

The Book of the Bible

*Eunice Riedel, Thomas Tracy,
and Barbra D. Moskowitz*

WILLIAM MORROW AND COMPANY, INC.
New York   1979

To LH: *"And he will take . . . your asses, and put them to his work"* (1 Sam 8:16).

Library of Congress Cataloging in Publication Data

Riedel, Eunice.
  The book of the Bible.

  1. Bible—Criticism, interpretation, etc.—
Miscellanea.   I. Tracy, Thomas, 1954- joint author.
II. Moskowitz, Barbra D., joint author.   III. Title.
BS538.R53   220.6   79-16740
ISBN 0-688-03527-2

Printed in the United States of America

First Edition
1 2 3 4 5 6 7 8 9 10

Contents

TWO: PROMISES! PROMISES!
—STRUGGLING FOR THE PROMISED LAND

THREE: I LOOKED OVER JORDAN AND WHAT DID I SEE?

FIVE: MATTERS OF THE MIND

SIX: THE DARK SIDE

EIGHT: ABOUT THE GOOD BOOK

Acknowledgments

A book of this scope could never have been written without the aid and constructive criticism of many people. It would be impossible to list all of them here, but we are especially indebted to the Israel Government Tourist Office; the Oriental Institute, University of Chicago; the Jerusalem Biblical Zoological Garden; the Jewish Institute of Religion-Hebrew Union College; Union Theological Seminary; Dr. Byron E. Shafer, Fordham University; Dr. Ernest Y. Weiss, Jewish Teachers Seminary; and Dr. John Gager, Princeton University. Although all of these institutions and individuals were of great assistance, the editors alone are responsible for the contents of this volume.

Introduction

Both read the Bible day and night,
But thou read'st black where I read white.
—WILLIAM BLAKE

(who as a child was punished by his mother for claiming to have seen the prophet Ezekiel under a tree in an English field)

With the translation of the Amarna tablets at the turn of the century, excitement grew over what appeared to be confirmation of the invasion of Canaan by the Hebrews. The tablets, which a peasant woman from the Egyptian village of Amarna had accidentally discovered in 1887, were diplomatic reports from minor potentates of city-kingdoms throughout Palestine to their Egyptian overlords. In these letters, dated from the 14th century BC, scholars found references to people called the "Hapiru" who were overrunning cities in eastern Palestine.

Suddenly, linguistic arguments became particularly urgent. Should "Hapiru" be read as "Hebrews" or as "Habiri" ("allies")? Is the word a proper name of a people—or does it mean simply "strangers" or even "robbers"? Is the name of one of the warlords, "Ilimelec," the same as "Elimelech" in Ruth (1:2, 3); indeed is it an exclusively Hebrew name? Should a certain line read "They have taken the fortress of Jericho" or "They have been swift to seize"? Though few scholars would admit it, this battle over points of grammar was fought as if the "truth" of the Bible were at stake.

As with many previous archaeological and literary finds that people hoped would confirm or deny the historical authenticity of the Bible, the Amarna tablets remain tantalizingly inconclusive. No sect or religion was shown to be more historically, or for that matter spiritually, correct than any other: certainly the Bible was not proven to be fact or fancy, wrong or right. What is certain is that this cache of ancient letters generally substantiated the Old Testament narrative of the conquest of Canaan. The conquering Hapiru could well have been people similar to the nomadic tribes of Israel; in fact they probably were, if, together with the evidence from the tables, we choose to give the Bible the benefit of the doubt and consider it to be a basically sound history.

No doubt arguments will crop up each time someone claims verification of a biblical event or personage. In the 1950s, after the discovery of the Dead Sea Scrolls, outrageous claims were made that the scrolls alluded to Jesus. Although this theory has been thoroughly discredited, most scholars agree that certain rites mentioned in the scrolls and some catchwords that the authors of the scrolls employ are prominent in the New Testament and early Christian church.

The Bible is historically elusive: some of what the Bible reports has been confirmed, generally or in detail; some has been refuted. The Bible is, after all, a book of faith, a spiritual book whose merit does not depend on its factual accuracy as much as on its moral truth. To read it as we would read a modern history is to misconstrue it, to take it for what, in its entirety, it is not. This is not to say it lacks historical value: indeed most of what is known about the ancient history of Palestine derives directly from the Bible with the support of archaeological evidence. What can be said of the Bible as history is that it is the record of a faith as the believers chose to preserve it— and that is the way the Bible is still read. Among Christians and Jews, each religion, each sect, reads the version and translation of the Bible it chooses.

Only when we realize that the Bible is unassailable for its spiritual worth, a book that has been so valued for thousands of years by the world's greatest philosophers, theologians, and writers, can we appreciate its other qualities with fairness. It contains practical advice, observations on nature and on the mores of various peoples during various periods, many secular stories, some songs, some wise sayings. It is, in short, a compendium, an encyclopedia of information put together by people who believed in a single God, the same God.

Much of this information, or where it can be found in the Bible, is in this book. But there is much else here as well: the trivia (how many words are there in the Bible?); the controversies that rage and have raged over the Bible (who wrote it?); archaeological finds; the stuff of miracles, dreams, and prophecies; how the Bible wants you to live your life (you might be surprised); and details about kings, angels, devils, and prophets.

This book does not pretend to interpret or to have the last say on any aspect of the Bible. Nor is it written to project or support any particular religious viewpoint. Instead we have tried to bring a fresh approach in hopes it will lead you to your own discoveries.

For God is not the author of confusion. . . .
(1 Cor 14:33)

Ancient Palestine

0   25   50
Miles

MEDITERRANEAN
SEA

PHOENICIA

Sidon

Damascus

▲ Mt. Hermon

Tyre

Dan

UPPER
GALILEE

Lake Huleh

BASHAN

Mt. Meron ▲

Hazor
Capernaum

LOWER
GALILEE

Sea of Galilee

Mt. Carmel ▲

Nazareth

Hamath

Kishon R.

Plain of
Esdraelon

Mt. Tabor ▲

Yarmuk
River

Dor

Megiddo

Valley of Jezreel

Taanach

Beth-shean

Mt. Gilboa ▲

Jordan River

G
I
L
E
A
D

Jabbok River

SAMARIA

Samaria

Mt. Ebal ▲
Shechem
Mt. Gerizim ▲

Caesarea

Plain of Sharon

Aijalon River

Shiloh

AMMON

Rabbah

Joppa

Bethel

Jericho

Gezer

Ashdod

Jerusalem

▲ Mt. Nebo

Ashkelon

Plain of Philistia

Bethlehem

Lachish

Dead Sea

Gaza

Hebron

JUDAH

En-gedi

Arnon River

MOAB

Beersheba

Kir-hareseth

Sodom?
Gomorrah?

Zoar

NEGEV

EDOM

Kadesh-barnea

One

That Was the World That Was

Upper left: Model of the Tower of Babylon. *Upper right:* Statue of Baal found at Megiddo. C. 1200 BC. *Bottom:* Stone statuettes of Mesopotamian gods. C. 2900–2800 BC. COURTESY OF THE ORIENTAL INSTITUTE, UNIVERSITY OF CHICAGO.

In the Beginning—Famous Firsts

First Voodoo: The Egyptian Execration Texts were pottery bowls or figurines on which the names of enemy kings, peoples, or cities were inscribed, along with a curse ("execration"). The pottery was then smashed and formally buried in the belief that destroying the name would make the curse fall on the actual people or town involved. The Execration Texts date from the 20th to the 18th centuries BC, and the later ones were the most elaborate—depicting people as captives in crouched positions, with their hands tied behind them. Among the place names found on the Execration Texts were Jerusalem, Beth-shean, Tyre, and many other cities prominently mentioned in the Bible.

First "Back-to-the-Land" Movement: The Rechabites, a tribe allied to the Israelites, fostered a reform movement that urged a return to nomadic ideals and lifestyle. The Rechabites lived in tents instead of houses and did not farm or keep vineyards (and would not drink wine). They voiced these ideals quite loudly during Jeremiah's time, inciting Israelites to disdain luxury and to return to the desert ways of their ancestors as a means of getting closer to God. Indeed, God approved of the Rechabites and said, "A son of Rechab shall not want a man to stand before me forever" (Jer 35:19).

First Food Poisoning: After the Israelites complained that they had no meat to eat during the Exodus, God sent a great wind from the sea that swept quail into and around the camp. The people gathered more than ten quail each and began to eat the meat. "And while the flesh was yet between their

3

teeth, ere it was chewed" God sent a plague to kill the Israelites because they had "lusted" (Num 11:18, 32–33).

First Furniture Stripper: In 597 BC, Nebuchadnezzar stripped all the gold cult objects from the Temple in Jerusalem, keeping the gold for his treasury, and leaving the bare wood (2 Kings 24:13).

First Piggy Bank: Israelites brought money to the high priests in Jerusalem for the upkeep of the Temple. In the days of King Joash, however, so much of the treasury disappeared after it left the hands of the people that the Temple was in bad shape.

Joash therefore set up an early-style piggy bank—he ordered "a chest, and bored a hole in the lid of it." This prevented the priests from stealing the funds, so that Joash was able to pay the builders and craftsmen to fix the Temple (2 Kings 11–12; 2 Chr 23–24).

First Sermon Snoozer: Eutychus fell asleep while he was sitting in a window listening to Paul preach a long sermon. Fortunately, although he fell out of the window and was at first taken for dead, Paul was able to revive him (Acts 20:9).

First Pseudonym: Queen Esther may have been the first to use a pseudonym. The Bible says Hadassah used the name Esther in the court of King Ahasuerus. Hadassah means "myrtle," but it may also be derived from the name of the goddess Ishtar (Est 2:7).

First Coup d'État: Absalom led an attempt to overthrow his father, King David. He and his followers actually chased David out of the palace, but the coup failed after Absalom was defeated in battle and slain (Sam 15–18).

First Women Construction Workers: The daughters of Shallum helped rebuild part of Jerusalem in the days of the return from Babylon (Neh 3:12).

First Recorded Dream: Abimelech was told in a dream to return Sarah to her husband, Abraham (Gen 20:3–8).

First Birthday Party: Birthdays were evidently celebrated quite early in history. The pharaoh of Egypt during Joseph's time in prison celebrated his birthday with a "feast unto all his servants." It was on this day that he fulfilled the prophecies of Joseph's interpretation of the butler's and baker's dreams (Gen 40:20–22).

First Price Control: Elisha predicted that "Tomorrow about this time shall a measure of fine flour be sold for a shekel, and two measures of barley for a shekel" (2 Kings 7:1).

First Land Purchase: Abraham bought the Cave of Machpelah from Ephron the Hittite, as a tomb for his wife, Sarah (Gen 23:3-20).

First Drunk: After finding dry land and letting the animals out of the ark, Noah settled down to husbandry. He planted the first vineyard and prepared the first wine. He then became completely inebriated and passed out in his tent (Gen 9:21).

First Commandment in the Bible: "Be fruitful and multiply" (Gen 1:27).

First War: The War of the Kings of the North is the first war mentioned in the Bible (Gen 14:1-24). Its authenticity was questioned for a long time, but archaeological evidence now suggests that the events may have taken place about the 20th century BC.

Four kings of the north—led by Chedorlaomer, king of Elam—invaded the territory of five kings in the valley of the Dead Sea. All nine kings are named in the Bible but none have been positively identified yet by historians. The northern kings were probably from the Tigris-Euphrates area, and the southern kings were probably Amorites.

The Bible lists the towns of the five southern kings as Sodom, Gomorrah, Admah, Zeboim, and Bela (Zoar), and says they had been paying tribute to Elam for twelve years. In the thirteenth year they failed to pay tribute, which was equivalent to revolt. Therefore, Chedorlaomer, allied with three other kings, formed a punitive expedition. But as the four northern kings came by way of Damascus along the King's Highway and bypassed the Dead Sea, going considerably out of their way to the Red Sea, the expedition may have had the double purpose of spying out the copper mines between these two seas.

After reaching the Red Sea, the four northern kings doubled back to the Dead Sea valley to attack the five rebel kings. The kings of Sodom and Gomorrah hid in bitumen pits while their people fled to the hills. After sacking the cities, the northern kings started home with captives and booty. But one of their prisoners from Sodom was Lot, Abraham's nephew, so Abraham gathered 318 servants and pursued the four kings up the Jordan Valley. Near Damascus, Abraham divided his small force into several groups that attacked in the night from different directions, rescuing Lot and the other captives as well as retrieving the spoils.

What supports this biblical story is that Elam was a combative little kingdom whose wars with other states in the Tigris-Euphrates area are mentioned in Sumerian, Babylonian, and Assyrian sources. About the 20th century BC it deposed the Sumerian dynasty at Ur and took over Babylonian territory. During the same period numerous settlements in the Dead Sea area—and some sites elsewhere along the route of the northern kings—were suddenly abandoned.

First Hebrew King: Abimelech, who was half Gideonite and half Israelite, approached the people of Shechem with the proposition that it would be better for them to have one ruler—namely, himself—than seventy rulers (his brothers). The people of Shechem agreed with him and he slew the other leaders. "And all the men of Shechem ... made Abimelech king" (Judg 9:1–6).

First Beauty Contest: When Xerxes I (486–465 BC) divorced his first wife, Vashti, all the beautiful virgins of Persia were called to the capital to compete for the job of queen. After a preliminary selection, contestants chosen as the most beautiful were put in charge of a eunuch named Hegai. For a whole year Hegai instructed them on how to use oil of myrrh and other beauty preparations. Then the girls were dressed to meet the king. Each girl spent one night with the king and then went to the care of another eunuch, where they waited nervously to see if the king had liked them well enough to call them back. The contest ended when the king set the royal crown on Esther's head (Est 2).

First Christian Martyr: Stephen was the first man killed for preaching about Jesus. He was stoned to death in Jerusalem (Acts 6:7—8:3).

First Book Burning: The prophet Jeremiah had dictated to his scribe prophecies of disaster for Jerusalem and King Jehoiakim. When the scroll reached the king it was winter, and Jehoiakim sat before a fire in his hearth while his scribe read Jeremiah's predictions. As soon as the scribe read three or four "leaves" (columns), Jehoiakim ordered him to cut that section out of the scroll with his penknife and toss it into the fire. This contemptuous treatment continued until the entire scroll had been consumed in the flames (Jer 36:21–23).

Confusing Bible Terms

ISRAEL:
1. Was the name given to Jacob by an angel.
2. Israel, children of Israel, all Israel, or Israelites were collective terms for the twelve Hebrew tribes.
3. When the kingdom split after the reign of Solomon, it became the southern Kingdom of Judah and the northern Kingdom of Israel. Israel in these passages therefore usually refers only to the north, although the earlier meaning of all the tribes occasionally still occurs.

JUDAH:
1. The patriarch Judah, fourth son of Jacob.
2. The tribe descended from Judah.
3. The Kingdom of Judah, the southern kingdom after the united nation split in two, following the death of Solomon.
4. After the northern kingdom disintegrated, Judah was used to mean all Hebrews left in the promised land.

JEW:
The word Jew is of Latin and Greek derivation. Originally it was from the Hebrew patriarch Judah and was first used to mean the tribe of Judah, the country of Judah, or the southern kingdom and its inhabitants. After the return from Babylon, Jew was applied to any Hebrew.

HEBREW:
1. The first person in the Bible called a Hebrew is Abraham, and the name was thereafter occasionally applied to other Israelites.
2. The language of the Israelites. Hebrew is a Semitic language that the Bible never calls Hebrew but "the language of Canaan." Except for sections written in Aramaic, most of the Old Testament was written in Hebrew.

You Don't Say—Understatements in the Bible

1. In describing the physical state of the men of Shechem after they had undergone circumcision, the Bible states that "they were sore" (Gen 34:25).

2. Jesus taught the Apostles that when they entered a house, "there abide till ye depart from that place" (Mark 6:10).

3. After forty days in the wilderness where he ate nothing, Jesus "afterward hungered" (Matt 4:2; Luke 4:2).

4. "For my thoughts are not your thoughts, neither are your ways, saith the Lord" (Isa 55:8).

5. In the sermon on the Mount, Jesus stated that "A city that is set on a hill cannot be hid" (Matt 5:14).

What Happened—A Short History

THE PATRIARCHS (2000–1250 BC)

A crossroads between the cultures of the Nile and the Tigris-Euphrates, ancient Palestine was trampled by empires arising in Egypt and Mesopotamia, by Armenoid people from the north, and by Semites from deserts to the east and south. (The latter two groups probably intermingled to become the Canaanites.) City-states that wanted to attain power in Palestine quickly learned to fortify themselves against sacking and destruction by Egyptians.

The Hebrews were possibly a seminomadic people from the deserts surrounding Mesopotamia, some of whom migrated to Palestine in Abraham's time. The Bible says Abraham was born in Ur, in the Tigris-Euphrates valley, and the names of his relatives are also the names of Mesopotamian cities. There is some evidence that he existed. He is said to have wandered south through what is now Israel to Egypt, and returned north to die at Hebron. Abraham made a covenant with God in which God promised to multiply his seed and give him Canaan for his children. Muslims call him Friend of God and also consider him an ancestor, and the Cave of Machpelah where he and his son Isaac are buried is a shrine for them as well as for Jews.

Abraham's grandson Jacob was given the name Israel ("one who has striven with God") after he wrestled with an angel on the banks of the Jabbok River. Later, during a famine, he migrated to Egypt, where he died

8

(he too was buried at Hebron). His ten sons and two of his grandsons became ancestors of the twelve tribes of Israel.

Although Egypt was a major power, the Hyksos—a mysterious people with Semitic names who swept down with chariots from the north—took much of Palestine and then conquered Egypt. The Egyptians couldn't shake off the Hyksos until about 1570 BC. Probably it was during this Hyksos period that Jacob's son Joseph rose to such prominence in Egypt.

EXODUS (13TH CENTURY BC)

After expelling the Hyksos, the Egyptians regained power. In the 1400s— under Tuthmosis III and Amenophis II—they conquered Canaan and southern Syria. (In northern Syria the Hittites ruled.) It was a messy situation. Local Canaanite kings, who were allowed to keep their thrones if they paid tribute, sometimes rebelled. They also squabbled over the bound- aries of their city-kingdoms. Egypt's other headaches included hostile tribes in the highlands of Palestine and nomadic desert raiders. The Hittites remained a threat until Rameses II made a peace treaty with them about 1270 BC, but by then Egypt was losing its grip on Palestine.

Because of oppression by Rameses II (1299–1232), Moses led the escape from bondage in Egypt. The Israelites first wandered in the desert of Sinai for a generation, but of their camps listed in the Bible only Kadesh-barnea (south of modern El Arish), a crossroads oasis where they camped a long time, has been positively identified. From here Moses circled the Dead Sea, sometimes battling hostile local inhabitants, to the Jordan River. Moses climbed Mount Nebo to view the promised land, but he died before his people crossed the Jordan into Canaan.

CONQUEST OF CANAAN (13TH TO 12TH CENTURIES BC)

Joshua led the children of Israel across the Jordan. The exact site of the first camp they established in the promised land is not known, but it was called Gilgal. Here some Israelites were circumcised, and Gilgal remained so symbolic that Saul was later crowned here. The Israelites were vulnerable in the valley and needed to command the strategic mountain ridges. After Joshua sent spies to reconnoiter, he besieged and burned the closest city, Jericho. Climbing higher in the hills, he conquered Ai (location not certain) and then took Gibeon by treaty. In turn the kings of southern and then northern Canaan became alarmed and vainly tried to stop the Israelites. By the time Joshua died, Israel had the highlands of Palestine from Galilee in the north to Kadesh-barnea in the south.

With the conquest of Canaan theoretically complete, the tribes of Israel scattered to settle their lands. However, only the hills of Canaan were theirs. The Israelites had inferior weapons and had conquered with guer- rilla tactics that were effective only in highlands. They were no match for fortified Canaanite cities and their chariots which controlled the plains. From the east, desert nomads raided Israelite crops and livestock. Some tribes were badgered by Mesopotamians, Moabites, Ammonites, Amalekites, or others. Things were especially bad in the north, where Deborah rallied local tribes for an important defeat of a Canaanite coalition. Yet settlement had severed tribal bonds so that many tribes had not responded to her urgent call.

A new menace appeared in the Sea People—believed to have come from Asia Minor and the Aegean islands—whom the Israelites called Philistines. The Philistines, with their superior iron weapons, were expert warriors whom the Egyptians had hired to guard the coast of Palestine. As Egyptian power declined the Philistines took over the coast for themselves and began to infiltrate the hills. About 1050 BC they slaughtered an Israelite force and captured the Ark of the Covenant.

Up until this time the tribes of Israel had been rather informally ruled by "judges" but had no central administration. Realizing that to defend themselves against the Philistines they needed a united front under strong military leadership, they established a monarchy to rule "all Israel."

THE UNITED MONARCHY (c. 1025–928 BC)

Saul was anointed king. Yet so many Jews—especially the prophet Samuel—had reservations about an earthly king that Saul continued to farm until a military threat drove him to rally all the tribes of Israel for the first joint war since the time of Joshua. Although the Israelites fought under him against Ammonites, Moabites, Philistines, and others encroaching on their territory, they frequently criticized Saul and worried about whether he was following God's word. Finally, when Saul disobeyed Samuel, the prophet declared that God had rejected Saul as king, and Samuel anointed David to be the new king.

Like Saul, David did not rule immediately after being anointed. He became a folk hero after defeating the giant Goliath and roaming the countryside with an armed band. Saul honored and loved David at times, yet so often threatened to kill him that David eventually fled to the Judean hills. Here, despite hiring himself and his band out as mercenaries to the hated Philistines, David became an even more romantic figure as he massacred nomadic raiders and other enemies. In a battle about 1006 BC, Saul was wounded by the Philistines and fell on his sword to avoid falling into enemy hands.

David at age thirty was made king over "all Israel." Because his capital at Hebron in the south was too partisan for a national administration, David immediately conquered Jerusalem for a new capital. This was a brilliant move, because Jerusalem was centrally located, had remained an independent enclave without historic or emotional association for either north or south, offered natural defenses, and was strategically situated to control major highways. While Saul had united the nation and made its lands safe for a farming and herding life, David expanded the kingdom to play a larger role. His conquests stretched Israel from Dan to the Brook of Egypt—except for a coastal strip occupied by Philistines—so that Israel had control of most of the Via Maris (the coastal highway) and the King's Highway (east of the Jordan and the Dead Sea). In the south he gained access to the Red Sea by taking Edom on the Gulf of Akaba. Israel now controlled all the trade routes from Damascus to Egypt. David's private life was marred when his son Absalom tried to mount a rebellion against him. Although this failed and Absalom was killed, the grief-stricken king began to withdraw from public life and finally abdicated to Solomon.

David's conquests had made Israel the dominant power between the Nile and the Euphrates, and Solomon began to develop the trade routes. Israel became an international center, profiting culturally and economically from contact with foreign states. As wealth flowed in, Solomon built Israel's first grand buildings with the aid of Phoenicians, developed a navy with expertise from Tyre, and collected an army of chariots with Egyptian advice. Such gigantic projects required skilled administration, and Solomon efficiently organized his kingdom to obtain taxes and forced labor. These tax and labor burdens, plus Solomon's unabashed admiration for foreign knowledge, created unrest. Solomon was sufficiently revered for his wisdom and skill to hold Israel together in his lifetime, but when he died in 928 his son could hold only Judah (the south). The north declared itself a separate kingdom of Israel and anointed its own king.

In All His Glory

Solomon was so great that the Bible doesn't say anyone "greater than Solomon is here" until the New Testament (Matt 12:42). Solomon began life as a love child, having been conceived by the passionate lovers David and Bathsheba (2 Sam 12:24-25; 1 Kings 1-11; plus incidental mentions). He was not entitled to the throne, but Bathsheba got it for him. Everything said about him after that was in superlatives:

1. He was "wiser than all men."
2. He knew 3000 proverbs.
3. He knew 1005 songs.
4. He organized Israel's first (and only) navy.
5. He had 1000 wives and concubines.
6. He made silver and gold as plentiful as stones.
7. He spent seven years building the Temple that made

11

Jerusalem a permanent shrine (he spent thirteen years building his own palace).

8. Statistics on his reign are inflationary—40,000 stalls for his horses, 80,000 woodsmen, so many workers he needed 3300 overseers—yet his officers "lacked nothing" and his subjects were so happy they just ate, drank, and made merry.

9. He offered a prayer forty-seven verses in length (1 Kings 8:15–61).

10. He is credited with writing three books of the Old Testament himself (only Moses is credited with more)—Proverbs, Ecclesiastes, and Song of Songs.

The First Gift Horse?

Solomon, trying to be neighborly, gave King Hiram of Tyre what he thought was a nice present—twenty cities in Galilee. Hiram eagerly left Tyre to inspect his new possessions and was so disappointed he berated Solomon, asking what kind of cities Solomon thought they were. Obviously they did not measure up to Tyre, or Hiram preferred ports, or they just didn't see eye to eye on what constituted a nice city. Hiram nicknamed them all Cabul ("worthless"), and the Bible never mentions his visiting them again (1 Kings 9:11–13).

Did Solomon Export Wisdom?

One of the favorite Solomon stories is of his wise judgment when two women came before him to claim the same infant. Solomon offered to cut the child in half with a sword. The woman who preferred to give the baby up rather than see it slaughtered was proclaimed the true mother by Solomon (1 Kings 3:16–28).

Here's the same story from India: A woman took her child to a pool to wash it. After it was clean, she put it on the bank while she took a dip. Another woman, pretending to coddle the infant, walked off with it. When the mother chased her, the woman claimed the baby was hers. The women took the baby to Buddha's judgment hall. Buddha had a line drawn on the ground and placed the baby across it. One woman was to grab the baby's arms and the other the legs, and whichever woman dragged the baby over the line first was to win. But when the women began to tug, the baby cried, and one woman let go. "Whose hearts are tender toward babes?" asked Buddha, and everyone knew that the woman who could not bear to see the infant suffer was the true mother.

Buddha lived about 563–483 BC, while Solomon is believed to have died about 932 BC, and the Books of Kings record events only through 560 BC—so obviously the tale could not have originated with Buddha. Yet variants of this story are found from Persia to China, and some may predate Solomon too.

DIVIDED KINGDOM: ISRAEL, THE NORTHERN KINGDOM (928–732 BC)

Divided, Israel and Judah were reduced from a great power to petty states. For more than forty years they scrapped over their common boundary—a mere ten-mile strip—while foreign powers rose on their other borders.

Israel soon collapsed. After its first king, Jeroboam, died, two of Israel's next four kings were murdered and one enjoyed the throne only seven days before committing suicide. In 882–871 one of Israel's great kings ruled— Omri. His reign was so prosperous and constructive that long after he died Israel was still called the Land of Omri. To strengthen his kingdom, Omri made peace with Judah and alliances with Phoenicians and other neighbors. He abandoned Israel's capital in the hills and built a new capital, Samaria, strategically located to control the Via Maris.

After Omri's death, Arameans headquartered in Damascus attacked, and by 810 Israel been reduced to an Aramean vassal. When the power of Damascus declined, in the late 700s, Israel had a brief comeback under King Jeroboam II. But after his death the next five kings were murdered during internal power plays. Assyrians now moved in relentlessly, until by 732 all that was left of Israel was a few miles surrounding Samaria—and that was lost to Assyria in 722.

The Assyrians had a policy of shuffling about conquered populations to destroy opposition, so they deported more than 27,000 inhabitants of Israel to Nineveh and other parts of the Assyrian Empire. These people, who apparently lost their cultural identity after resettlement and never returned, became known as the ten lost tribes of Israel. The Assyrians then repopulated Israel with subjugated people from Hamath, Babylonia, and the Arabian desert. These—mixed with Israelite shepherds and herders the Assyrians had not bothered to relocate—became known as Samaritans.

DIVIDED KINGDOM: JUDAH, THE SOUTHERN KINGDOM (928–587 BC)

Only four years after the division of the kingdom, Judah was threatened by an invasion from Egypt and then began to lose control of the King's

Highway and other vital areas. In 786 Jerusalem was sacked by Israel. Prosperity returned under King Uzziah (783–742), who reconquered Judah's lost territories and reestablished trade routes on the coast, to the Red Sea, and along the King's Highway.

When the Assyrians attacked Israel in 734, Judah saved itself by sending tribute to the Assyrian king and therefore did not suffer the deportation of its population, as Israel had. But in 705 Judah rebelled by not sending tribute. Miraculously, although Assyria sent troops to destroy forty-six cities, Jerusalem was spared. Nevertheless, Judah remained a vassal and was forced to adopt Assyrian cults.

Assyrian power had so declined by the time of Josiah (639–609) that Israelite worship was reestablished. Josiah then stupidly attacked a passing Egyptian army, so that Egypt took over Judah in retaliation.

In 605 the Babylonian Empire made Judah a vassal. Once again Judah rebelled. As the Assyrians had done to the people of Israel, the Babylonians now (597) deported 10,000 of Judah's citizens to Babylonia. Ten years later Judah rebelled again. This time Jerusalem was attacked. The city fell in 587 after a long siege, and the Babylonians smashed the walls, looted the city, and burned it down. The population—perhaps as many as 50,000—either was slaughtered, or deported to Babylonia, or it fled to Egypt and other countries on the Mediterranean. This dispersal of Jews became known as the Diaspora. As had happened in Israel, only peasants and herders were left.

PERSIAN EMPIRE (539–333 BC)

The people of Judah in exile did not lose their identity as the people from Israel had, because soon after they were deported the Babylonian Empire began to fail. Jews kept their religion alive by establishing synagogues and producing religious literature. In 539 Babylon was conquered by the new power, the Persian Empire, which allowed Judeans to return home. Although the first Jews returned to Jerusalem in 537, their land was devastated and other peoples who had meanwhile moved in were hostile. The Jews had a difficult time reestablishing themselves. The Temple—called the Second Temple—was not finished until 515, and even then it was so poor that old people who remembered the first Temple wept. Recovery was so sluggish that Jerusalem's defenses weren't rebuilt until 440. Israel never reunited, and Judah remained a pawn battered about by greater empires.

Even God Loved Cyrus

Cyrus the Great had such a reputation for magnanimity toward the people he conquered that former enemies often praised him. He

14

said of himself that the god Marduk had looked all over every land for an upright king before choosing Cyrus and taking him "by the hand" to be ruler of the entire world. The Jews had an equally benevolent view. In calling Cyrus the Lord's "anointed," Isaiah records that God said of Cyrus, "He is my shepherd . . . whose right hand I have holden" (Isa 44:28; 45:1).

THE GREEKS: EGYPTIAN PTOLEMAIC, SYRIAN SELEUCID (332–167 BC)

Now the Persian Empire began to crumble and power passed to the Greek-speaking Macedonians. Alexander the Great moved against Persia in 334 BC and by 332 he had swept down the coast of Palestine into Egypt. In 323, when Alexander died at age thirty-three, his kingdom was the largest ever known, stretching into India. But as his son had not yet been born and his brother was demented, Alexander's generals began a power struggle for his kingdom. The generals that harassed Palestine were Ptolemy (from Egypt) and Seleucus (from Syria). Their lands were so vast that the Seleucids carelessly bartered India for a corps of war elephants and for a long time did not contend Ptolemaic control of Palestine. But as time went on, Syrian and Egyptian armies began to struggle over Palestine. After 219 the Seleucids captured cities on the Sea of Galilee and elsewhere in the north, and then moved into the Judean hills. Although in 217 the Ptolemaics scored a victory on the coast with 70,000 foot soldiers, 5000 horsemen, and 73 war elephants, by 201 the Seleucids were back to stay.

MACCABEANS, or Hasmoneans (167–64 BC)

Although Palestine was gradually being hellenized—geographic names were changed (Amman to Philadelphia, Beth-shean to Scythopolis, etc.) and administration was under the Greek city-state system—Jews had been allowed to continue their own worship. Aping Greeks became fashionable among some Jews, creating divisiveness with the more conservative, but hellenization was not forced.

Now, however, the new Roman power was pressing the Seleucids from the northwest, permitting them to rule only if they paid heavy tribute. Seleucids were so pressed for money that one Seleucid king was killed in 187 trying to rob a temple at Elam. When Seleucid power passed to Antiochus IV he plundered Jerusalem's Temple, sold the office of its high priest to the highest bidder, established a gymnasium to teach Greek culture and games next to it, and finally outlawed Jewish worship and practices, dedicating the Temple to worship of Zeus. A garrison—the hated Acra—kept the peace in Jerusalem, so in 167 the revolt broke out in a little town to the west, where an old man named Mattathias killed the Seleucid minister sent to enforce worship of Zeus. Mattathias and his five sons fled to the Gophna hills. These five sons founded a ruling dynasty—called Maccabean or Hasmonean—that was to dominate Jewish history for more than a century.

The Maccabeans began by making guerrilla raids from the Gophna hills to destroy pagan altars, but after defeating Greek troops in 166 they gained 3000 adherents, who crushed a large Greek army the following year. They became heroes in 165 by relighting the menorah to reestablish worship in the Temple (commemorated today with the Festival of Lights). The Maccabeans went on to rescue Jews who were being persecuted throughout Palestine, and then to conquer and to rule the Holy Land. By the turn of the century they controlled from Dan to the Brook of Egypt, most of the coast, and held land east of the Jordan that gave them the King's Highway. As Seleucid power declined, Maccabeans gradually gained independence for their kingdom.

Yet wholehearted support from the Jewish community eluded the Maccabeans. Their holy war was soon perverted by employing mercenaries. Although they had rebelled against hellenization, they became hellenizers. Though they had fought for religious freedom, they usurped the high priesthood for themselves and forced Judaism on conquered subjects. Their reign therefore bred contention, with Pharisees and Sadducees almost at civil war, and at least one conservative sect (who left the Dead Sea Scrolls) withdrawing to the desert. In the end the Maccabeans were conspiring against and murdering each other.

ROMAN EMPIRE (64 BC on)

In 64 BC, when the Roman army marched from Damascus to Jerusalem, one Maccabean faction seized the lower city and opened the city gates to welcome the Romans, while another faction barricaded themselves on the Temple Mount to resist. Jerusalem fell to Rome on the Sabbath, the walls breached with siege machines and catapults during worship, and more than 10,000 people died.

Herod, though only a child, was made governor of Galilee while his older brother, Phasael, governed Jerusalem. In the chaos that erupted after Julius Caesar was murdered in 44 BC, Parthians invaded Palestine. The Maccabeans, hoping to regain power, accompanied them to Jerusalem and had the gates opened for them. As a reward, the Maccabeans were given Jerusalem to rule. Phasael was captured and committed suicide, but Herod escaped to Rome, where he was given a hero's welcome. In 40 BC Rome appointed him king of the Jews. His land was supposed to run from Galilee to Idumea, but with the Maccabeans in charge none of it was his. When Herod left Rome he didn't dare land in his kingdom. He debarked on the coast northwest of Galilee, and working south, he conquered his kingdom bit by bit, not taking Jerusalem until 37 BC.

Herod considered himself Jewish, though he was an Edomite by birth. He married a Maccabean (he later killed her and three of his sons for engaging in Hasmonean conspiracies against him). He rebuilt historic Hebrew centers such as Samaria and embellished religious sites such as Hebron. On Jerusalem he lavished special care, erecting his palace there and reconstructing the Temple with an enlarged esplanade, walls, and porticoes. Yet the Jews remained hostile.

Herod's image was no better among Christians, because before his death, in 4 BC, Jesus was born. Although there is no historic evidence for this, tradition says Herod was infuriated to hear that a baby was being called by his own title, "king of the Jews." Being unable to identify the infant, he ordered all boys under age two killed, forcing Mary and Joseph to flee to Egypt with their child.

In his will, Herod requested that his kingdom be divided among three of his sons. Although Rome allowed this division, it appeased Jews who protested the reign of Herod's line by titling Herod's sons "ethnarchs" and "tetrarchs" instead of kings.

It was a short-lived regime. Archelaus, who received Judea and Samaria, was so inept and antagonistic that Rome dumped him after ten years. Herod Antipas, the son who got Galilee and Perea (northeast of the Dead Sea), clung to his share until AD 37, when he too was replaced by Rome. Only Philip ruled his territory, in southern Syria, until he died (AD 34). The Bible remembers Herod Antipas as the man who had John the Baptist beheaded (Matt 14:1–12) and who questioned Jesus at the time of his accusation (Luke 23:7–15), but it barely mentions Philip (Luke 3:1) and only alludes to Archelaus (Luke 19:12 ff.).

After removing Archelaus from office, the Romans appointed a series of procurators, or more accurately prefects, to rule Judea. The fifth of these was Pontius Pilate (about 26–37). Although Pilate's term was one of the most stable, it was riddled with misunderstandings with the Jewish religious community. He often tried to appease them after he had upset them. The most infamous example of this policy is the gospel account of Jesus' sentencing, in which Pilate orders crucifixion after accusations by "priests, elders, and scribes" (Matt 27; Mark 15; Luke 23; John 18–19).

The Roman stranglehold on Palestine together with enforced exile led to additional scattering—Diaspora—of the Jewish people to cities such as Alexandria, Babylon, and Rome. The Apostles, many of whom were being arrested in Jerusalem for preaching, journeyed to these cities to preach. Some Apostles, such as Peter and Philip, stayed close to home, venturing only as far as Samaria or the Phoenician coast. But one, Paul (AD 1–67), went farther, to Greece and Rome, and broadcast the seeds of Christianity in centers of Western culture.

Imported Idols

1. Moses made a serpent of brass to which incense was burned (Num 21:9; 2 Kings 18:4).
2. The Israelites in the desert made a golden calf (Ex 32:4; Psa 106:19).
3. King Jeroboam of Israel made images of gods, molten images, and set up two golden calves (1 Kings 14:9).

An Egyptian Prayer

When thou embarkest on the lake of truth—May thy mainsail not fly loose. May there not be lamentation in thy cabin ... May thy mainstays not be snapped. Mayest thou not run aground. ...

Give Me That Old-time Religion

As picturesque and romantic as the terms "Fertile Crescent" and "Cradle of Civilization" may seem, they are nevertheless apt. The amazing productivity of the area between the Tigris and Euphrates rivers awed every ancient visitor from Herodotus to Alexander, and even today the extensive ruins of the cities of Ur and Babylon are astonishing reminders of the expertise of the first urban planners.

The phrase Fertile Crescent is easily understood if one imagines an upside-down U superimposed on the map of the Middle East. The right tip is at the head of the Persian Gulf; the peak of the arch is what is today Iraq; the left arm runs along the eastern shore of Palestine. This sequence— starting at the Persian Gulf, moving up and over, and finally coming down through Israel—is roughly the path of Mesopotamian civilization as it moved from east to west.

NOTE: A good source for documents discussed in the following pages is *The Ancient Near East*, edited by James B. Pritchard, published in paperback in two volumes by Princeton University Press.

THE SUMERIANS

Mesopotamian civilization began on the headwaters of the Persian Gulf with the Sumerians. No one knows where the Sumerians came from. They were not Mesopotamia's original inhabitants because they used non-Sumerian place names for cities they inhabited.

Unlike the Babylonians, Assyrians, Accadians, and almost all the other Mesopotamians that followed, the Sumerians were non-Semites; that is,

19

they spoke a language unrelated to those in the area. In fact their language appears to be unrelated to any other. Though the Sumerian language seems to have developed in isolation, it became one of the world's most influential, for it was probably the first to be written. Sumerian in its oldest form (c. 3100 BC) is poorly understood, in part because of the scarcity of samples, yet it is clear that its earliest uses were unglamorous: the first written records are business accounts. If man developed writing to express himself, then what the Sumerian wanted to express was what was owed him and what he possessed. From a later stage of the language (2500–2300 BC), generally known as classical Sumerian, more examples have been found, and they include religious, royal, and private inscriptions of many types.

Presumably the Sumerians were the inventors of cuneiform writing—impressions made in the writing medium by a tool with a wedge-shaped tip. After the Sumerians were conquered, cuneiform writing and the Sumerian language were adapted by the Babylonians and Assyrians for court and learned documents—the reverse of the situation in which subject peoples are forced to use the language of their conquerors. Up to the time of Ashurbanipal (705–681 BC), the Assyrian scholar-king who possessed one of the great libraries of antiquity, Sumerian was maintained artificially as the language of the educated, much as Greek was by the Romans, and Latin by the patristic fathers. Ashurbanipal himself boasted that he had learned this "sweet and difficult" tongue.

The Original Flood: The Bible's most direct legacy from the Sumerians is the stories of the Creation, the antedeluvian patriarchs, and the Flood. The Sumerians kept a king list which distinguished between the monarchs "before the Flood" and those "after the Flood." Just as the biblical patriarchs who antedated the Flood were particularly long-lived, the Sumerian kings who reputedly lived before the deluge had lives and reigns thousands of years long. Eight kings ruled a total of 241,200 years!

Sumerian religious literature provides a strikingly familiar story of the creation of the world. According to this version, the universe was created by a conclave of gods under whose direction man, vegetation, and four-legged animals of the plain "were brought artfully into existence." In the text, about a hundred lines after the Creation story, the following verses can be found:

> ... a flood will sweep over the temples
> To destroy the seed of humanity ...
> This is the decision of the council of gods,
> commanded by Anu and Enlil ...
> All the windstorms, exceedingly violent,
> attack as one,
> At the same time that the flood sweeps over the temples.
> After the seven days and nights that
> The flood had swept over the land,

> And the huge boat had been tossed about by
> > storms on the great waters,
> > Utu emerged. . . .

With these lines and the king list, scholars had proof that the Book of Genesis was not created in a cultural vacuum, but in the long tradition of Mideastern mythology which stretched back at least as far as the Sumerians.

While these texts demonstrated an unsuspected cultural link between the Flood myth of the Bible and of the Sumerians, an even greater surprise was the sensational finds that C. L. Woolley made while excavating the ancient Sumerian city of Ur.

A Sumerian Pyramid: Ur first came under the archaeologists' spades in the 1850s, when J. E. Taylor investigated a huge and ancient heap of bricks on the alluvial plain near the Euphrates River. His was the era of the archaeological treasure hunt, when expeditions looked only for impressive statues and reliefs, golden artifacts, and other museum pieces. As was the practice in those days, Taylor began work on the ancient mound by starting at the top and tearing it down layer by layer. He found little—some cuneiform-inscribed cylinders that no one could read—and he did more harm to the ruin than thousands of years of weathering.

The mound was the remains of an ancient ziggurat, a step pyramid somewhat like those of the Egyptians or even those of the Aztecs and Maya. It was built of burnt and sun-baked brick and mortared with sticky asphaltic bitumen, for which it had acquired the Arab name *Tell al Muqayyar*, "mound of pitch" (see the tower of Babel, Gen 11:3).

In the years after Taylor's expedition, the ziggurat continued to be dismantled by the Arabs, who took its bricks for buildings of their own. Eventually the cuneiform cylinders that Taylor brought out were translated. They revealed that the structure was originally built by a king Ur-Nammu and restored by Nabonidus, a Babylonian king. In 1923, C. L. Woolley and a team of English and American archaeologists set out with the hope that this mound was on the site of Ur, the Ur of the Chaldees from which Abraham, the first Hebrew, is said to have come (Gen 11:31). In the area around the ziggurat, Woolley found a city with such amenities as two-story houses, factories which produced twelve different styles of clothing, and legal courts which detailed records of fines paid and sentences meted out. If Abraham came from this city, he was probably no wandering shepherd; more likely he was urbane and sophisticated. Moreover he probably did not speak a Semitic language, unlike the Hebrews who followed him.

Proof of the Flood: From 1926 to 1929 Woolley excavated the graves of Sumerian nobles. Trying to see how deep the layers of artifacts might be, Woolley continued to dig in the deepest grave and soon discovered pottery shards and inscriptions centuries older than the grave. As he went down he

21

noticed that the pottery style remained unchanged, indicating that the cultural traits of the Sumerians had developed early and been stable for many years. Then he hit water-laid sand and clay.

Initially he paid little attention, thinking only that he had discovered the original soil of the Tigris-Euphrates plain. But more accurate calculations showed that the level was too high above the plain to be from normal seasonal flooding. On a hunch Woolley dug deeper—through nine feet of mud and sand. Then the layer of water-laid silt suddenly stopped and—what no one would have imagined—the potsherds started again, only this time they were of an epoch far older than those found in the previous layer. There was only one conclusion: The area had once suffered an immense, sudden flood; people were there to witness it, and they could not or did not return to the flooded area for a very long time. As a check, Woolley dug shafts all over Ur. Others did the same throughout Mesopotamia. The conclusion was unchanged. During the Sumerian period the area had been subject to one or more inundations with fronts perhaps one hundred miles wide. Many people considered Woolley's findings to be evidence that the myth of the Flood was based on historical fact.

A Sad Sumerian Story

The eagle and the serpent were good friends until the eagle got it into his head one day to swoop down and eat the serpent's young. The serpent was outraged and appealed to the sun god.

"Hide under a dead animal," advised the sun god, "and when the eagle comes down to devour it, spring out and eat its feathers."

The serpent did as the god advised and left the defeathered eagle hopping helplessly about, unable to fly. Now it was the eagle's turn to appeal to the sun god.

"I will give you back your feathers," said the god, "only on condition you help mankind." Naturally, the eagle agreed. The god arranged for the helpless bird to be found by a man who was sad because he had no son. While he nursed the eagle back to health, he told the bird how he wished he could fly, so he could go to heaven to get the plant of life that would give him a child. The eagle promised that as soon as his feathers were regrown he himself would carry the man to heaven to fetch the sacred plant.

Finally the great day came and the eagle mounted to the sky with the man on his back. Unfortunately, the man was unused to such heights, and the eagle's way of climbing by spiraling made his head reel. The poor man lost his grip, slipped off, and plunged to his death on earth.

THE BABYLONIANS

Strictly speaking there was no "Babylonian" people. "Babylonian" is the designation given to whichever nation happened to hold sway in Babylon, a city with a long history of coups and conquests. Among the nations that ruled the city were the Sumerians, Accadians, Amorites, Assyrians, Chaldeans, and Persians.

The authors of the Bible were more aware than we of these distinctions—only Ezekiel uses the general term Babylonians and then only twice (Ezek 23:15, 17). Though their statements of Babylonian history are often distorted (in Daniel, for example, Darius is said to have reigned before Cyrus) the Bible's authors were more correct in thinking of Babylon as a city-state rather than as the seat of an empire as we are apt to do. It is as a city that Babylon captured the prophetic and apocalyptic imagination—first as the city of Babel, in which the tower (probably the ziggurat) was built; then as the corrupt city that is the symbol of what Jerusalem was in danger of becoming; and finally as the whorish city of Rahab in Revelation. Of all the kings who ruled Babylon, Nebuchadnezzar and Cyrus are the most central to the Old Testament; the former for bringing the Israelite captives to Babylon, the latter for freeing them.

Historically the first non-Sumerians to control the lands about Babylon were the Accadians. Probably they were nomadic shepherds from the deserts surrounding the northern half of the Tigris-Euphrates valley. Some historians paint scenarios that portray covetous Accadians gradually encroaching on the flourishing fields of the Sumerians. Such scenes are speculation, but it is known the Sumerians and Accadians were neighbors for many years—long enough for the Sumerian language to borrow a number of Semitic words from the Accadians. Eventually an Accadian kingdom was established in the northern half of Mesopotamia, and under the leadership of King Sargon (2350–2300 BC) the Accadians conquered the Sumerians, taking the land from above Babylon all the way to the Persian Gulf, where the victorious Sargon "washed his weapons."

The Baby in the Bulrushes: This is not the Sargon of the Bible, but his ancient precursor. A more accurate transliteration of this Sargon's Semitic name is Sharrum-kin, which means "the king is legitimate." It is a rather telling title in light of the following story, a late Accadian legend about Sargon's birth which has an obvious and very striking affinity with a very well-known Bible tale, the story of Moses' birth.

> Sargon, mighty king, king of Agade, am I.
> My mother was of mixed blood; I never knew my father . . .
> My city is Azupiranu, on the banks of the Euphrates.
> My mother conceived and she secretly bore me.
> She put me into a basket of rushes, and sealed its lid with tar.
> She cast me into the river which did not drown me.
> The river swept me to Akki, the drawer of water.

Akki, the drawer of water, scooped me up in his pitcher.
Akki, the drawer of water, raised me as his son.
Akki, the drawer of water, appointed me his gardener.
While I was a gardener, Ishtar bestowed her love on me,
And for four years I was king.

That this legend, like the Sumerian account of the Flood, has been preserved in variant form in the Bible suggests that Mesopotamia was the origin of the Hebrew people, as the story of Abraham indicates.

Building the Ark: Most memory of early life in Babylonia was lost before the Bible was written, but place names occasionally turn up as the last vestiges of the Hebrew people's recollection of their homeland. The city of Agade, which Sargon boasts of ruling, appears in the list of Nimrod's cities, as do other Mesopotamian cities in thin disguises: "And the beginning of his kingdom was Babel, and Erech and Accad, and Calneh in the land of Shinar" (Gen 10:10). A modern translation of this passage might read, "His kingdom was Babylon, and Warka (Uruk) and Agade and Nippur in the land of Mesopotamia"—though the identification of Calneh with Nippur is still controversial.

Uruk and Nippur were originally Sumerian. As for Nimrod, his name perhaps derives from the Sumerian *Nin-marrada,* "lord of Marad," a town near Kish. Throughout antiquity his name occurred in the form "Nimrud" as part of the names of Mesopotamian towns such as Tell Nimrud. Nothing is known of him as a historical figure; it is suspected that he was a deity, perhaps connected with Gilgamesh.

Gilgamesh is the epic hero whose story provides the most direct connection between the literary traditions of Mesopotamia and those of the Bible. We have already seen that the Sumerians had their own version of the story of the great Flood and the Creation. This tale was evidently adapted and enlarged upon by the Semitic peoples who conquered the Sumerians, and this enlarged version became the *Epic of Gilgamesh.*

The hero of the section of the epic concerned with the Flood is Utnapishtim. Ea, one of the supreme gods, commands Utnapishtim to tear down his house and "build a ship!" To preserve life and "keep the soul alive," he must give up his earthly possessions and take aboard his ship "the seed of all living things." The ship he is ordered to build must have been ungainly if not unseaworthy, because the length, width, and height were to be of equal dimension—a perfect cube! It was about three times the height of Noah's ark, with six decks instead of three. Utnapishtim goes on to tell what he does after hammering in the water plugs and caulking the boat with pitch:

I ordered my family and relatives onto the ship.
Along with the beasts of the field and the wild animals.

...

Six days and six nights
the flood wind blew and the storm swept the land.

...

On Mount Nisir the ship grounded.

...

When the seventh day arrived,
I released a dove.

This version of the Flood and the biblical account (Gen 6–9) correspond at point after point. A god singles out a hero to be saved. The hero is commanded to build a boat of a specific plan, and to take his family and a selection of animals aboard. After the cataclysmic inundation destroys all life, the boat settles on a mountain and the hero sends forth birds on the assumption that they will return if the waters have not receded.

Obviously Utnapishtim's story is the direct literary ancestor of Noah's. Apart from other similarities, a final proof is that in the Hebrew the word used for pitch is *kofer*. This is the word used in the Babylonian tale, and *kofer* appears nowhere else in the Bible.

The hero Utnapishtim may have been based on a historical figure. His father in the *Epic of Gilgamesh*, Ubar-Tutu, is mentioned on one of the tablets kept by Babylonians to record the reigns of their kings. In fact, Gilgamesh appears on the king list of the early Sumerian city of Uruk. He is said to have been "high priest of the land" and he reigned for 126 years.

If these names were preserved in the Accadian epic, why did the Bible, which keeps so many of the details of the original flood story, change the name of the hero to Noah?

Biblical Ancestors: One clue comes from the Mari Letters, clay tablets inscribed with communications between the kings of the ancient city of Mari and their frontier commanders like Babylon. Mari was an ancient city-state of the Mesopotamian plain. It was rediscovered in 1933, about 3500 years after it had been sacked and burned by the armies of Babylon under the command of Hammurabi.

From the ruins archaeologists carted away over 20,000 documents written in a West Semitic dialect (Amoritic) closely related to patriarchal Hebrew. In many of the Mari texts the name of Noah is given as the name of a god. More significant for Bible historians, however, were the many references to a tribe called the Bana-yamina, "the sons of the south." Almost without exception, archaeological linguists have translated the name of this people as the Benjamites, one of the twelve tribes of Israel. The letter from one advance scout reads:

> Yesterday I left Mari and spent the night at Zuruban. All the
> Benjamites lit signal fires. From Samanum to Ilum-Muluk,
> from Ilum-Muluk to Mishlan, all the cities of the Benjamites

of the Terqua district lit signal fires in response, but so far I haven't figured out the meaning of those signals.

Another writes to his commander about the Hapiru, a tribe which may well have been the Hebrews:

> The next day we got the following report of the enemy: "Yapah-Adad has prepared the settlement Zallul on this bank of the Euphrates River, and with two thousand Hapiru troops is dwelling in that city."

And from the Mari documents came names that had previously been known only from the Bible—Serug, Nahor, Terah—names from the generations following Noah. In the Mari tablets it becomes clear that these are the names of cities of the northern Mesopotamian plain. As these documents were deciphered, the sense of locale, the feeling of glimpsing day-to-day affairs in the homeland of the first Hebrews became increasingly stronger.

After Sargon's conquest of the Sumerians, the rule of Babylonia teetered between the Accadians and the insurgent Sumerians, was then held briefly by the Guti, an eastern people about whom the Bible evidently says nothing, and then fell to Hammurabi.

The Law and Hammurabi: When Hammurabi came to power in Babylon (c. 1728 BC) he had many potent neighbors to contend with, most notably the Assyrians. This people, which derives its name from the worship of the god Assur, is alluded to in the Bible as Ashur, the son of Shem (Gen 10:22). To make the matter thoroughly confusing, the name of the Assyrian capital was Ashur, a city on the west bank of the Tigris.

The Assyrians and the Babylonians had few cultural differences. They both spoke Accadian—although two different dialects—and both had essentially the same religion, except that Marduk, not Assur, was the chief deity of the Babylonians. (Marduk is called Merodach in the Bible. See Jer 50:2.) Hammurabi seems to have had little trouble with the Assyrians. When he took the throne the Assyrians had been weakened by the recent death of their king, and by the end of Hammurabi's rule he was claiming sovereignty over them.

Hammurabi's best-known achievement is his law code. Hammurabi's Code was not the first in Babylonia—that is another honor that goes to the Sumerians—but it was perhaps the most extensive. Its influence can be seen in the Bible's two books of legal codes, Deuteronomy and Leviticus. Although the wording of the codes is often different, the spirit is frequently the same. Perhaps this has something to do with divine inspiration: Just as Moses got his laws from Jehovah, Hammurabi reportedly got his from Marduk. The first of Hammurabi's laws is really the injunction not to bear false witness (Deut 5:20), except that it specifies murder charges:

> If a seignor [a free citizen] accused another seignor of murder but has not proved it, the accuser shall be put to death.

Some laws are much closer in phrasing: The law of Deuteronomy (24:7) that reads

> If a man be found stealing any of his brethren of the children of Israel ... then that thief shall die

is closely paralleled by one of Hammurabi's:

> If a seignor steals the son of another seignor, he shall be put to death.

The Lost Tribes: Hammurabi's descendants ruled Babylon for five generations until they were conquered (c. 1530 BC) by the Hittites, a people from the regions northeast of Mesopotamia. The Hittites were the first people in Mesopotamia to speak a form of Indo-European, the family of languages from which Greek, Latin, and ultimately English descend. The Hittites were renowned for their ferocity and for being the first to discover the smelting of iron, a technique they kept secret in order to ensure a monopoly on the metal.

In the early sections of the Old Testament the Hittites are known as the sons of Heth (Gen 23:7). But the Bible mentions contact with the Hittites only in Canaan, suggesting that the Hebrews left Mesopotamia before the Hittite conquest of Babylon.

According to the Bible, Abraham was in Haran when the Lord commanded him to leave for Canaan (Gen 11:31–12:1). Haran is on the Balih River, a northern tributary of the Euphrates, and was in ancient times surrounded by the cities mentioned earlier—Serug, Nahor, and Terah. This is a land that the Hebrews knew intimately, for the place names of its small towns survive in their literature. It may well be their homeland. Not a hundred miles from Haran flows the Khabur River. Its ancient name was the Haburu.

Approximately one thousand years after Abraham and his followers left Mesopotamia, Hebrews returned in captivity. Tiglath-pileser was the first to take Hebrew prisoners back to Mesopotamia when he conquered Israel (with the exception of Samaria) in 732 BC (2 Kings 15:29). The period of the Exile did not effectively end until Cyrus, the Persian king whose empire would stretch from India to Greece, marched into Babylon and freed the captives in 539 BC.

Almost nothing is known of the fate of those Tiglath-pileser took to Assyria. In his annals *The Campaigns Against the West and Against Syria and Palestine* he merely notes that "Israel, all its inhabitants and their possessions I led to Assyria." Ten years later, Sargon II reported taking 27,290 Samaritans captive. They too disappeared into the east, and in the absence of any knowledge about their fortune there, they became traditionally known as "the ten lost tribes of Israel"—a band from which people the world over have claimed descent.

More Laws from Hammurabi

Any citizen who commits a robbery and is caught shall be put to death.

If a fire starts in a citizen's house and another citizen steals goods from that house while pretending to extinguish the fire, that citizen shall be thrown into the fire.

If a citizen is accused of witchcraft, he shall go to the river and throw himself in. If he drowns the accuser receives his property. If he survives, the accuser is put to death and the accused receives the accuser's property.

If a citizen steals property or livestock from the church, he shall pay thirty times its worth. If he steals from another citizen he shall pay ten times. If he does not have the money to pay, he shall be put to death.

If a trader borrows money from a merchant to buy the merchant's goods to sell abroad, and the trader has not made a profit, the trader shall repay the merchant twice the money he borrowed.

If a trader has all his merchandise stolen by thieves while he was on the road, he shall swear so by god; then he may go free.

If a woman selling wine has cheated her customers by watering her wine she shall be thrown into the river.

If a citizen points the finger at (i.e., accuses of adultery) a nun or the wife of another citizen, but cannot prove his accusation, half of his hair shall be cut off in the presence of the judges.

If a woman gives herself an abortion, she shall be prosecuted, convicted, impaled, and left unburied.

If the wife of a citizen has been caught sleeping with another citizen, they shall be bound and thrown into the river.

If a citizen married a woman and she has come down with a fever, and he has made up his mind to marry another woman, he may marry her, but his first wife shall stay in his house and be supported by him.

If a citizen has intercourse with his daughter that man shall leave the city.

If a citizen has intercourse with his mother after the death of his father, both shall be burned.

If a citizen has children by his wife and by his slave, and during his lifetime counted his children by the slave among his children, then upon his death his estate shall be divided equally among his children by his slave and those by his wife.

If a son strikes his father, they shall cut off his hand.

If the adopted son of an official has said to his mother or to his father, "You are not my parent," they shall cut out his tongue.

If a citizen puts out the eye of one of the nobility, they shall put out his eye.

If a citizen knocks out the tooth of a citizen, they shall knock out his tooth.

Love Thy Neighbor—The Babylonian

"Babylon the great, the mother of harlots and abominations of the earth" (Rev 17:5).

"I will punish the king of Babylon and that nation . . . and will make it perpetual desolations" (Jer 25:12).

"The broad walls of Babylon shall be utterly broken" (Jer 51:58).

"Babylon is taken . . . her idols are confounded, her images are broken in pieces" (Jer 50:2).

"Her mighty men are taken, every one of their bows is broken" (Jer 51:56).

"Her princes . . . shall sleep a perpetual sleep, and not wake" (Jer 51:57).

"Everyone that goeth by Babylon shall be astonished, and hiss" (Jer 50:13).

"Thus shall Babylon sink, and shall not rise" (Jer 51:64).

"Babylon the great is fallen, is fallen, and is become the habitation of devils, and the hold of every foul spirit, and a cage of every unclean and hateful bird" (Rev 18:2).

THE CANAANITES

Before the 20th century little was known of the Canaanite religion outside of a few facts gleaned from the Bible and confirmed by archaeology. With the discovery of a Canaanite temple library at Ras Shamra, knowledge of Canaanite religious practice and theology increased thousandfold.

Ras Shamra lies on the coast of Syria, north of what was the ancient Kingdom of Israel. In 1928 a farmer tilling his field plowed open an underground passageway leading to a vaulted tomb. The discovery prompted a team of French archaeologists to excavate a nearby mound which turned out to be the site of the ancient city of Ugarit. Between the ruins of two temples was found the library and house of the high priest of the city. In the library, tablets covered with an unfamiliar cuneiform alphabet were discovered. Upon deciphering, the language, now known as Ugaritic, proved to be very close to Mosaic Hebrew.

Some of the tablets record the epic adventures of various Canaanite deities. Though the tablets were inscribed during the first half of the 14th century BC, the stories are probably much older sice they abound in linguistic archaisms and are part of a traditional religious literature.

Father Bull and Baal: At the head of the Canaanite pantheon is El, the supreme deity. Like one of the Titans in early Greek mythology, El is violent and incestuous: He kills his brother and his favorite son, decapitates his daughter, castrates his father and himself, and takes his three sisters for wives. Variously called the "father of years," the "father of man and gods," and the "father bull," El is the divine progenitor, creator of all beings on heaven and earth.

Despite his supremacy, El is not the god most frequently mentioned in the Ras Shamra texts. Baal, a younger god, was apparently far more popular. A god of weather and of agriculture, Baal is frequently depicted wielding a thunderbolt in the style of the Greek Zeus. Like many of the Canaanite gods his lineage is uncertain: He is called the "son of Dagon" (the god of agriculture; in Hebrew *dagan* means "grain") or "the son of El." More adventurous than El, whose exploits are rather tame abominations in comparison, he is the protagonist of a series of heroic poems which describe his conquest of the Prince of the Sea and his capture by Mot, the god of death and sterility. He is rescued by his sister, Anath, a goddess of sex and war, and a virgin who nevertheless is perpetually pregnant. As in the Greek myth of Demeter and Persephone, the rescue of the divinity from the world of death wipes famine and drought from the land and restores fertility.

These gods and goddesses and the myths in which they were the main characters possessed a strong magnetism for the Hebrews who settled in Canaan. Compared to the austere monotheistic faith of the Hebrews, the practices and pantheon of the Canaanites were temptingly lively and sensuous. In Canaan, temple prostitution was common, as it was in Mesopotamia, and sexual license was allowed and probably encouraged during the celebration of fertility rites. So insistently seductive was the cult that one of the Bible's main themes, given in the exhortations of prophets from Moses to Micah, is that the Hebrew people reject all Canaanite practices, particularly idolatry, which was pernicious and widespread.

Graven Images: The term idolatry is often used in the Bible as a catchall word to designate the religious cults of Canaan; but more narrowly speaking, idolatry is the belief that a material object may possess a spirit unique to it. By this definition almost all of ancient Israel's neighbors except for the Persians practiced idolatry. Certainly the Hebrews had been influenced by pagan practice ever since Rachel stole her father's images (Gen 31:19) and Aaron conceded to making the golden calf. But when they settled in Canaan, contamination became particularly hard for the Hebrews to avoid.

This was not only because of prolonged exposure to the Canaanites but more specifically because of mixed marriages and the widespread belief that the local deities held a kind of proprietorship of the land.

The idols themselves came in so many forms that there are more than a dozen Hebrew words used in the Bible for the images. The idols most commonly adopted by the Hebrews were the teraphim: small household figurines used throughout the ancient Middle East to invoke fertility, as good-luck charms, or as part of an ancestor cult. From excavated texts there is some evidence that the family that had the teraphim was predominant in the clan and held the property rights, which suggests there may have been more than religious zeal behind Rachel's eagerness to steal her father's figurines.

Though Josiah condemns them (2 Kings 23:24), there was undoubtedly some toleration of the teraphim by religious leaders. The teraphim excavated from Hebrew towns show one remarkable characteristic which may explain this acceptance—most of the statuettes are abstract portrayals of women. There is no indication that any attempt was made to create an image of Yahweh, definitely a "he" in the Bible.

The idols that were not tolerated by the prophets are those such as the Asherah (a.k.a. Asherim or Ashtaroth), which are seen as the religious objects of another culture and faith (see 1 Kings 11:33). The Asherah figurines were named after Asherah, the consort, wife, and daughter of El. A goddess with an international reputation, she was known to the Canaanites as Astart and to the Greeks as Astarte, and is related to the Babylonian Ishtar. As an idol Asherah could be represented as anything from a pillar of wood to a lewd female figurine, as befits a goddess of the temple prostitutes. Sometimes she is depicted riding upon a lion and often she has a lily in one hand and a serpent in the other.

Like Asherah, Baal was often represented merely by an upright object, usually a stone pillar, but could be elaborately anthropomorphized. One gold-plated statuette of Baal depicts him as a lithe man sitting upon a throne and wearing the tall cap characteristic of the Canaanite gods.

Canaanite idols could be made of almost anything—wood, ivory, bone, clay, stone, or metal (see Isa 44:9–17). For some reason, no one knows precisely why, cast metal images ("molten gods" [Ex 34:16]) and carved images ("graven images" [Deut 12:3]) were particularly abhorrent to the Hebrew prophets. The special taboo on these types of idols may be related to the prohibition against using stone worked by metal in the construction of an altar. It could be that any use of metal was strongly associated with weapons of war and would thus be unsuitable for a holy place. Or perhaps metal and the labor of making an image were thought to be too valuable to squander.

Taboos: Although it is the most frequently cited, idolatry is not the only Canaanite practice that the prophets railed against. Their contempt for specific rites could have grown only through long observance. For instance, the biblical prohibition "Thou shall not seethe [boil] a kid in its mother's milk" (Ex 23:19; 34:26) is probably directed at a Canaanite rite. In fact, there appears to be some confirmation of this ritual in the lines, reconstructed from a Ugaritic text, that describe a sacrifice:

> They cook a kid in milk,
> A young goat in butter.

Some scholars suggest that this practice forms the basis for the rabbinical prohibition against eating meat and milk together.

Another aspect of Canaanite worship that appears to have been rejected by the Hebrews is the placement of holy places in a "grove," meaning either a grove of trees or a grove of Asherah poles (Deut 16:21).

Names for Gods: Despite all the precautions that Hebrew religious leaders took to shut out Canaanite religion, much assimilation took place throughout the long period of contact. In fact, the earliest foundations of both religions are rooted in the same traditions. The name of the Canaanite god El, from the Semitic stem *el,* meaning "god" or "deity," was adopted from or is cognate with a number of words that the earliest Hebrews used to denote their god. The plural form *Elohim* is one of the names used throughout the first books of the Old Testament for the deity. The root word appears in the phrase *El Shaddai,* "god of the mountains," which reflects the almost universal belief that the supreme gods live on high places. *El* again turns up in the names of the angels Michael, "who is like God?" and Gabriel, "man of God," as well as in names such as Samuel, "the name of God."

Names of Hebrews were also frequently compounded with a *baal* stem: for example, Eshbaal, "man of Baal," and Meribbaal, "contender with Baal." Such names were considered deplorable by the more devout and were often changed by altering the *baal* suffix into *bosheth,* the Hebrew word for shame. Thus Eshbaal became Ish-bosheth; Meribbaal, Mephibosheth; and so on. The idea of putting *bosheth* into Canaanite-like names can be seen in one form of Asherat's name: Ashtoreth was probably altered from a more primitive form, Ashtoroth. By bringing the vowels of her name closer to those of *bosheth,* the Hebrews created a soubriquet, a nickname signifying distaste for the goddess.

On occasion the Canaanite influence shows up directly in biblical imagery. For example, the beast described in the following lines from Ras Shamra

> Have I not quieted the dragon
> And crushed the crooked snake
> Terrible beast with seven heads

is Lotan, whose name is identical, in the original languages, with Leviathan. Undoubtedly Lotan is a close relation of the seven-headed beast of Revelation.

A Great and Wonderful House: Another parallel between the Bible and the Ras Shamra texts can be seen by comparing the passages in which the Lord commands Solomon to build the Temple (2 Chr 1-2) with the following lines addressed to Baal:

> A house will be built for you.
> Including a court . . .
> The mountains will bring you much silver
> The hills, the finest gold
> To build a house of silver and gold
> A house of lapis lazuli.

The two accounts share the conviction that the time has come for the faithful to build a house of worship for their god—a house so magnificent its construction demands virtually all the land's reserves of silver and gold.

During the time of Ahab and Jezebel, Baal worship came close to becoming the religion of Israel. Jezebel brought in 450 baalic priests from Phoenicia, her homeland, in order to set up a cult center in Samaria, the capital. The practice of Baal worship was so widespread that King Ahab of Israel was accused of having taken up idolatry at his wife's insistence. After her gruesome death at the hands of reformers, the prophets continued to vilify her, and many other Hebrew kings were accused of practicing Canaanite religion. As late as the writing of Revelation, the Bible's authors would lament that Israel ever had to suffer "that woman Jezebel" (Rev 2:20).

Too Short to Rule

One Canaanite story recounts how a replacement for Baal was chosen after the god fell in battle. Asherah, El's consort, wants one of her sons to rule in Baal's place and suggests them one by one. Says Lady Asherah, the Sea Goddess, "Let's try Yadi Yalhan as king." El, the Kind One, replies, "He's too weak, never could run with Baal and can't throw the javelin with Dagon's son, Splendid Crown." Lady Asherah, the Sea Goddess answers him saying, "Let's give Ashtar the Tyrant a chance, let him be king." Hearing this, Ashtar the Tyrant heads for Zaphon to sit on Strong Baal's throne, but his feet don't reach to the footstool and his head doesn't reach to the top. So Ashtar the Tyrant says, "I don't want to rule in Zaphon anyway," and he hops down from Strong Baal's throne.

All thrones had footstools, even God's (Isa 66:1). Frequently the earth or God's enemies are called his "footstool" (Acts 7:49; Matt 22:44; Mark 12:36; Luke 20:43; Acts 2:35; Heb 1:13).

Thou Shalt Not Make unto Thee Any Graven Image

The tribe of Dan set up a graven image (Judg 18:30).

Rachel took her father's images when she left to get married (Gen 31:19, 34).

Micah's mother made a graven image and a molten image (Judg 17:4).

Micah made teraphim (Judg 17:5).

Maachah, mother of King Asa of Judah, made an idol in a grove (1 Kings 15:13).

The princes of Judah served idols and groves (2 Chr 24:18).

King David and his wife Michal had an idol (1 Sam 19:13, 16).

King Solomon built sanctuaries for Ashtoreth, Milcom, and other gods (2 Kings 13:13).

King Ahab of Israel served foreign gods (1 Kings 21:26).

King Manasseh of Judah set up a graven image (2 Kings 21:7; 2 Chr 33:19).

King Ahaz of Judah made molten images (2 Chr 28:2).

King Amon of Judah worshiped idols and carved images (2 Kings 21:21; 2 Chr 33:22).

Jerusalem and Samaria were full of idols (Isa 10:11).

The people of Israel and Judah put idols "under every green tree" (1 Kings 14:23; 2 Kings 17:10; 21:11; 2 Chr 14:5-8; 31:1; Ezek 8:10).

Love Thy Neighbor—The Canaanite

"Thou shalt drive out the Canaanites" (Josh 17:18).

"The word of the Lord is against you; O Canaan" (Zeph 2:5).

"There shall be no more the Canaanite in the house of the Lord" (Zech 14:21).

THE EGYPTIANS

Even though Hebrew contact with Egypt has been long and extensive, and began with total immersion in Egyptian culture during the period of the bondage, surprisingly little profound influence can be detected in Hebrew culture or religious thought. Part of the reason for this was the Egyptian clergy's almost total lack of missionary zeal. Unlike the Hebrews, the

Egyptians were syncretic; they adopted other gods as their own, casually combining foreign with familiar. From the Canaanites, for example, Astarte and Anath were introduced to the Egyptian pantheon and Baal was likened to the Egyptian deity Seth, brother and murderer of a chief god, Osiris.

The Egyptian gods were innumerable, since there was a god for everything—for crocodiles, fish, birds, and cats. Egyptian theology was complex, even to the point of contradiction. The sky, for example, could be represented as a cow, a vulture, or a human. Rather than causing confusion, this variety and plentitude were thought to contribute to enlightenment and were considered to be variant ways of seeing the same thing. Such rampant creativity led to localized schools of theology, the main centers being at Thebes, Memphis, and Heliopolis. Often even small towns introduced their own concepts and gods. One popular practice was to combine the name of a local deity with that of some nationally known god to create a hybrid such as Re-Atum or Aton-Re. Without a doubt, this fluidity and kaleidoscopic variety gave Egyptian religion the flexibility and toleration that allowed the Hebrews to practice their own religion with some freedom.

The one break in this tradition of tolerance came in the reign of Amenophis IV (1379–1362 BC) and even then the pressure to change was directed at the doctrines of the Egyptians themselves and not those of the Hebrews who were in Egypt at the time. Amenophis tried to change radically the theology of the Egyptians by introducing one universal and supreme god, a revolution that has often been termed the first monotheism.

The god he chose to acknowledge was Aton-Re, an incarnation of the sun god, Re. In itself this would not have done much to incur the enmity of the priests, but he also rejected the theology of Memphis and Heliopolis and set up a religious center at Amarna in Middle Egypt, thus undermining the clergy's power. Although some scholars do consider this move to be self-serving and manipulative, there is some reason to believe that the pharaoh was sincerely motivated. For example, he changed his name to Akhenaten, "it is well with Aton," a flourish which a true schemer probably wouldn't think of. And in the spirit of his peace-loving god, he was known to have lost kingdoms because he refused to go to war. In one way, however, his religion was not truly monotheistic: He continued the Egyptian practice of allowing the court and clergy to worship him as a god.

After his death his kingdom lapsed into a period of anarchy which probably ended during the reign of Akhenaten's son, Tutankhamun, the boy king who has become famous for the treasure of his tomb. Nine years old when he took the throne, Tutankhamun was the puppet of Nefertiti, Akhenaten's wife, and of Eye, one of the more powerful priests. Under the control of this pair, the little pharaoh restored the former gods.

Our Father, Who Art in Amarna: The Hebrews were in Egypt during Amenophis IV's religious revolution and might have incorporated elements of this "monotheism" into their worship of Yahweh. Many parallels have been pointed out over the years; whether or not they represent direct influence is, as always, a matter of doubt. It is interesting that Aton-Re, like Yahweh, was addressed as "Father which art in heaven." He was also considered to be invisible and yet present everywhere, the creator of the heavens and earth, viewing every one of his creations with tenderness and mercy. Many similarities have been noticed between Psalm 104 and a hymn of Akhenaten's that has been preserved on a papyrus from the 14th century BC. For example, in both the hymn and the psalm, the deity, the creator of the world, is a light- and life-giving source, wrapped in vestments of sunny brilliancy.

The two songs also offer some startling similarities in wording. The line from the Egyptian hymn "How manifold it is, what thou hast made!" seems to have a counterpart in the biblical line "O Lord, how manifold are thy works!" from verse 24 of the psalm. On a larger scale, the following passage from the hymn

> The world came into being by your hand,
> According as thou hast made them,
> When you rise they live,
> When you set they die

expresses the same sentiment with the same imagery as:

> That thou givest them they gather: thou openest thine hand,
>   they are filled with good.
> Thou hidest thy face, they are troubled: thou takest away
>   their breath, they die, and return to their dust

—from verses 28 and 29. Whatever the relation of the Egyptian hymn to the psalm—perhaps an ancient Near Eastern prayer is their common ancestor—the similarities are undeniable.

Egyptian Proverbs: Another instance of parallelism is found between an Egyptian instructional text and Proverbs 22:17–24:22. Here are some side-by-side extracts:

The Instruction of Amen-em-opet	*Proverbs*
Lend thine ears, hear the words that are said,	Bow down thine ear, and hear the words of the wise, and apply thine heart unto my knowledge (22:17)
Lend thine heart to understand them.	
To put them in thine heart is worthwhile.	
Take care not to rob the oppressed.	Rob not the poor, because he is poor: neither oppress the afflicted in the gate (22:22)
Do not associate with the angry man,	Make no friendship with an angry man

36

Nor converse with him.   and with a furious man thou shalt not
go (22:24)

While this instruction and the hymn to Aton-Re are the most fruitful Egyptian texts for those who want to hunt up biblical parallels, other works of Egyptian religious literature yield tantalizing finds. For example, one can easily, perhaps too easily, hear echoes of Genesis (1:31), "And God saw every thing he had made, and behold, it was very good," in the following line from an Egyptian myth about the creation of the world: "And so, after he had made everything, including the divine order, Ptah was content." Another Egyptian text, a royal decree purportedly set in the 28th century BC, reports a seven-year famine in Egypt—a plague resembling that in Gen 41:27. Part of this Egyptian text reads:

> ... those in the palace were heartsick over a great evil, because the Nile had not flooded for seven years. Grain was scarce, fruits were dried up, and every type of food was lacking.

However, the most obvious influence that Egyptian culture had on the Bible, and one which lends credence to the story of the bondage, can be seen in the names of some of the early personages and patriarchs. "Moses," for example, is probably from the Egyptian *mesu,* meaning "child," and "Potiphar" (Gen 37:36) means "gift of the god Re." There are problems with some of these names, however. The sons of Joseph have only Hebrew names, not what one would expect of the children of the pharaoh's vizier. And the Egyptian name given to Joseph, Zaphnath-paaneah, has not been conclusively translated.

Borrowed Baubles: Despite the strong undercurrents from Egyptian literature and culture present in the Bible, there was exceedingly little that could be called Egyptian in the religious practices of the Hebrews—a lack which is surprising, considering how prevalent Canaanite and Assyrian practices became among the Hebrews. One quasi-religious practice borrowed from the Egyptians did become popular, however. That was the keeping of amulets. Amulets, small oval-shaped gems engraved with scarab (beetle) or other designs, were kept by the Egyptians as charms to ward off sickness, witchcraft, or accident. The large number of Egyptian amulets recovered in Palestine indicates the practice was widespread. Hebrews were reluctant to manufacture the charms themselves because of the prohibitions against making graven images, so Israelite-made amulets are rare.

Other aspects of Hebrew religious practice and theology that were allegedly borrowed from the Egyptians—the rite of circumcision and the worship of bull idols (in the form of the golden calf or Jeroboam's calves [1 Kings 12:28])—were common to many Near Eastern religions.

In and Out of Egypt: That Egyptian influence on the Israelites seems uneven—strong in a few specific texts and practices, almost absent in the Israelite religion and culture as a whole—may be a corollary to the ambiguous attitude that Israel has had toward Egypt, a love-hate relationship that began with the patriarchs. Even when Moses was leading his people away from slavery some of the hungry wanderers lamented leaving Egypt and its abundant food (Ex 16:3; Num 11:8). These mixed feelings extend throughout Israel's history because Egypt, for all that the Hebrews could not tolerate about it, could be counted on as a place of refuge from famine or the internal troubles of Palestine—witness the sojourn of Joseph, the exile of Jeremiah (Jer 43:6–7), and the flight of Mary and Joseph (Matt 2:13). Probably the religious leaders among the Hebrews found the Egyptian wisdom literature and the hymns to the universal god Aton-Re as congenial as the climate and the soil, but the bizarre Egyptian gods as intolerable as service to a number of masters.

One particularly dramatic set of documents, the Elephantine Letters, has shown that Egypt could on occasion allow the Hebrews a home more comfortable than one might expect. One letter (c. 419 BC) petitions the governor of Judah for authorization to rebuild a temple to Yaho (Yahweh) at Elephantine, Egypt. The original temple, dating from sometime before 525 BC, had been destroyed by invading Persians, not by Egyptians. The letter, from one of the Hebrew community's elders, reports that this temple had existed at Elephantine since the time of the pharaohs.

Egypt for its part seems to have been largely indifferent to the Israelites scampering in and out of its borders; as long as they didn't make trouble they were welcome. The only known mention of Israel by the Egyptian royal court is brief and imperious. The pertinent part of this record, engraved on a stela to commemorate the victories of Merneptah (1236–1223 BC), son of Rameses II, reads:

> Israel is desolate; it has no offspring.
> Syria has become a widow for Egypt.
> All the united lands, they are pacified.

Love Thy Neighbor—The Egyptian

"Thou shalt not abhor an Egyptian" (Deut 23:7).

"The Egyptians are men, and not gods" (Isa 31:3).

"Woe to them that go down to Egypt" (Isa 31:1).

"The Lord doth put a difference between the Egyptians and Israel" (Ex 11:7).

"The land of Judah shall be a terror unto Egypt" (Isa 19:17).

"Defile not yourselves with the idols of Egypt" (Ezek 20:7).

"They committed whoredoms in Egypt" (Ezek 23:3).

"They had made them a molten calf, and said, This is thy God that brought thee up out of Egypt" (Neh 9:18).

"Thou shalt not . . . remember Egypt any more" (Ezek 23:27).

None Other Gods

"And the children of Israel . . . followed other gods, of the gods of the people that were round about them, and bowed themselves unto them, and provoked the Lord to anger. And they forsook the Lord, and served Baal and Ashtaroth" (Judg 2:11–13).

"We have forsaken the Lord, and have served Baalim and Ashtaroth" (1 Sam 12:10).

"And they left all the commandments of the Lord their God, and made them molten images . . . and served Baal" (2 Kings 17:16).

King Manasseh "reared up altars for Baal" (2 Kings 21:3).

King Ahab "reared up an altar for Baal in the house of Baal, which he had built in Samaria" (1 Kings 16:32).

"The prophets prophesied by Baal, and walked after things that do not profit" (Jer 2:8).

"They have offered incense unto Baal, and poured out drink offerings unto other gods" (Jer 32:29).

"They taught my people to swear by Baal" (Jer 12:16).

"They have built also the high places . . . for burnt offerings unto Baal" (Jer 19:5).

"They have forgotten my name for Baal" (Jer 23:27).

"They have forsaken me, and have worshipped Ashtaroth" (1 Kings 11:33).

Only "seven thousand men . . . have not bowed the knee to the image of Baal" (1 Kings 19:18; Rom 11:4).

A Happy Egyptian Story

The sad and weary pharaoh wandered the palace unable to find a way to lighten his heart. So he called his magician Zazamankh, who advised that the king take a boat onto the lake to view birds, sweet fields, and grassy shores. Zazamankh ordered oars of ebony inlaid with gold, and for rowers he called for twenty beautiful virgins dressed in nets.

The boat trip was going splendidly, and the king was just

39

beginning to feel good, when suddenly one of the girls stopped rowing because her malachite jewel had dropped overboard. "Row on," said the pharaoh. "I will replace it."

But the girl refused. She didn't want a new jewel; she was attached to her old one. Since she was ruining the trip, the king sent for his magician again. Zazamankh made a magic speech that caused the water in half the lake to flow to the opposite side of the lake. From the dry lake bed he picked up the girl's jewel, and then rearranged the water. The day was saved, and as a reward the king gave Zazamankh a loaf, a jar of beer, and a jar of incense.

National Brotherhood Week

The Bible's attitude toward neighbors sounds harsh: "Thou shalt utterly destroy them; namely, the Hittites, and the Amorites, the Canaanites, and the Perizzites, the Hivites, and the Jebusites; as the Lord thy God hath commanded thee" (Deut 20:17). Yet the Hebrews were not unique. Ancient documents from Mesopotamia to Egypt abound in joyous references to annihilating neighbors— frequently the very same peoples the Bible mentions. For example, in the Amarna Letters, the Amorites were said to be troublesome foes of the house of Egypt's pharaoh and deserved annihilation. The pharaoh was assured that "their fortress burns in flames" and that "all the land of the Amorites" would soon belong to Egypt. Officials writing these letters promised to bind all the Amorites ("a chain of bronze exceedingly heavy shall shackle their feet") "and not leave one among them."

The Neighbors—Who Was Who

Amalekites: A marauding nomadic tribe of the Negev and Sinai Peninsula that first attacked the Israelites during the wandering after the Exodus. They continued to be a nuisance during the settlement of Canaan and were last mentioned during the reign of King Hezekiah of Judah (727-698 BC).

"And the Lord said unto Moses ... I will utterly put out the remembrance of Amalek from under heaven" (Ex 17:14).

"The Lord will have war with Amalek from generation to generation" (Ex 17:16).

"Amalek was the first of the nations; but his latter end shall be that he perish forever" (Num 24:20).

Ammonites: Semitic nomads who settled in Ammon—east of the Jordan River and the Dead Sea—about the same time the Hebrews moved into Canaan in the 13th century BC. Their capital was Rabbah-ammon (today Amman, Jordan). Despite frequent hostilities between Ammonites and Hebrews, they were apparently related peoples. The Bible says Ammonites are descended from Lot and mentions intermarriages with Hebrews. After Ammonite power gave way under Assyrian and Persian pressure, Jews began to move into the area. Presumably the Ammonites were eventually absorbed by the Hebrews and by the Arabs.

"And I will make Rabbah a stable for camels, and the Ammonites a couching place for flocks. . . . that the Ammonites may not be remembered among the nations" (Ezek 25:5, 10).

Amorites: The name Amorites comes from the Accadian Amurru ("people of the west"). It is believed that the Amorites arrived in Mesopotamia from

41

the west. They were originally a Semitic people that quickly mixed with Hittites and other non-Semites.

The best early records of the Amorites come from their capital at Mari, on the Middle Euphrates; from here they carried on aggressive campaigns that included the destruction of Ur. They set up a number of Amorite kingdoms, including the Babylonian dynasty that produced Hammurabi, but after Babylon fell to the Hittites, about 1550 BC, the Amorites temporarily disappeared from ancient records. When they reappeared—in the Bible, Amarna Letters, and other documents—the Amorites were in Palestine. In Abraham's time they are mentioned as far south as En-gedi on the Dead Sea, but during Joshua's lifetime their strongholds were in the north, around the Sea of Galilee. They preferred mountains—their chief deity, Amurru, was a mountain god (his consort was the ubiquitous goddess Asherah). They occupied the hill country of Bashan (east of the Sea of Galilee) and Galilee and into the mountains of Lebanon, but their cities mentioned in the Bible also included Eglon, Lachish, Jarmuth, Hebron, and Jerusalem—all in the south. It was because of the Amorites that the Hebrews had such a precarious hold on the north of Canaan; the Amorites ran trade routes between the Hittites and Egyptians, obtained Hittite aid in defending themselves against Egypt, and preferred to be under Hittite rather than Israelite sway.

"The Lord God of Israel hath dispossessed the Amorites" (Judg 11:23).

"Destroyed I the Amorite ... whose height was like the height of the cedars, and he was strong as the oaks; yet I destroyed his fruit from above, and his root from beneath." (Amos 2:9).

Arameans: A group of tribes of obscure origin who settled between Damascus and Babylon by 2000 BC and then spread out into many directions. The Bible says they were descendants of Shem, and scholars believe they came from the Tigris-Euphrates area or the Arabian desert and may have been related to Amorites. Early records mention them as raiders, but later they became such great traders along the caravan routes that the Aramaic language became the chief tongue in Middle East trade. The Arameans never founded a united empire, but some of their little kingdoms—such as Aram-damascus and Aram-zobah—were powerful between the 11th and 8th centuries BC. They were sometimes allies and sometimes enemies of the Hebrews. After Tiglath-pileser took Damascus in 732 BC and Sargon II defeated Hamath in 722 BC, many Arameans were deported to other areas. Their language survived for many centuries, and small groups of Arameans continued to be important in trade. (Some Bibles render Aram as Syria and Arameans as Syrians.)

"Damascus is waxed feeble, and turneth herself to flee, and fear hath seized on her; anguish and sorrows have taken her" (Jer 49:24).

"I will kindle a fire in the wall of Damascus, and it shall consume the palaces" (Jer 49:27).

Assyrians: People of Semitic and Hurrian background who built an empire on the Tigris River. Their great cities—especially Assur and Nineveh—rivaled Babylon, and the histories of the Assyrian and Babylonian kingdoms intertwined. Assyrian power was most devastating to the Hebrews between the 9th and 7th centuries BC: Shalmaneser III (858–824 BC) made several attacks on Israel; Tiglath-pileser III (745–727 BC) conquered most of the Kingdom of Israel; Shalmaneser V (726–722 BC) besieged Samaria, and either he or Sargon II (721–705 BC) took the city and began to deport its population to Mesopotamia; finally, moving south, the Assyrians attacked Judah, and Sennacherib (704–681 BC) exacted crippling tribute from Jerusalem.

"I will break the Assyrian in my land, and upon my mountains tread him under foot" (Isa 14:25).

"Waste the land of Assyria with the sword" (Mic 5:6).

"Destroy Assyria ... make Nineveh a desolation, and dry like a wilderness" (Zeph 2:13).

Babylonians: Babylon ("gate of the gods"), an ancient city-state on the Euphrates River, had two periods of power, both of which affected Palestine. Like surrounding cities, it was developed in historic times by Sumerians, who were not Semites, but it was ruled at various times by Semitic people too. Babylonia began to rise to power about 3000 BC, flourished under the Semitic Dynasty founded by Sargon I (c. 2371–2316 BC), and reached its first peak under the great Amorite leader Hammurabi (1728–1686 BC). Soon after, the Assyrians rose to power, putting Babylon in eclipse. The Chaldeans, seminomads of Aramean origin, began to arrive from the north and lay the groundwork for a resurgence at the end of the 8th century BC. Under Nebuchadnezzar II (605–562) Babylonia again became the most important empire in Mesopotamia. It was under Nebuchadnezzar that Jerusalem fell and its population was deported to Babylonia; freedom to return to Judah came only after Cyrus the Great brought Babylon under Persian rule in 539 BC.

Canaanites: Canaanite was the name the Hebrews applied to all the various (mostly Semitic) inhabitants of the promised land, many of whom are believed to have come from northeastern Arabia and settled in the area by 3000 BC. Relationships between Amorites and Canaanites are suggested by scholars, but the Bible describes them as different peoples. Moreover, the Bible lists several subgroups of Canaanites that are poorly understood today—Girgashites, Hivites (mostly in the north near Tyre), Jebusites (who held Jerusalem until the time of David, and who also are still mentioned as a separate tribe by Ezra and Nehemiah), and Perizzites (mentioned from the time of Abraham to the time of Solomon; some scholars theorize this was not a tribe but a term used to designate Canaanites who did not live in fortified cities). Canaanite technology was more highly advanced than the

Israelite, as shown by the temples, palaces, tombs, and walled cities that have been excavated. Their pantheon was headed by El, and fertility cults revolved about his son Baal and one to three goddesses of sex and war (Anath, Astarte, Asherah). Cultic objects included bulls, serpents, and doves. Sacred prostitution and orgies took place in groves and temples, and firstborn humans and animals were sacrificed. The Canaanites were gradually absorbed by the Hebrews and other invaders.

"Cursed be Canaan" (Gen 9:25).

"There shall be no more the Canaanites in the house of the Lord" (Zech 14:21).

"All the inhabitants of Canaan shall melt away" (Ex 15:15).

Edomites: Seminomadic Semites who by the 13th century BC had settled in Edom (between the Dead Sea and the Gulf of Akaba). The Bible says they were descended from Esau. Edomites engaged in chronic war with the Israelites and from time to time were under Hebrew domination. Their land was coveted because it contained copper and iron mines. After Babylonians conquered Edom in the 6th century BC, the Edomites were pushed west into southern Judah by invading nomads. The Maccabeans forced them to become converts to Judaism. Under Roman rule their land was called Idumea, and the most famous Idumean was Herod the Great.

"Edom shall be a possession" (Num 24:18).

"Edom shall be a desolation" (Jer 49:17).

Gittites: Inhabitants of Gath, a royal Philistine city near Lachish; its site has not yet been positively identified. Goliath was born at Gath, and Gittites formed David's bodyguard.

"The beauty of Israel is slain. . . . Tell it not in Gath, publish it not in the streets of Askelon; lest the daughters of the Philistines rejoice" (2 Sam 1:19–20).

Hittites: An Indo-European people who entered Asia Minor about 2000 BC and who formed a cultural bridge between Mesopotamia and Europe. Their powerful kingdom flourished from about 1600 to 1200 BC in Asia Minor and Syria. Their advance south was checked by Egypt, and east by the Mitanni. Nevertheless, there was much cultural exchange with the Tigris-Euphrates area, and about 1550 the Hittites destroyed Hammurabi's Babylonian capital. Their power was broken by the Assyrians. Archaeologists now tend to believe the Bible's mention of Hittites in Canaan: in Hebron at the time of Abraham, in southern Palestine in the time of Moses, among David's followers, among Solomon's forced laborers. The Bible also mentions that Hebrews intermarried with Hittites. Among Hittite contributions to the Middle East are an early law code, iron smelting, and the introduction of the war chariot.

"I will send hornets before thee, which shall drive out the Hivite, the Canaanite, and the Hittite" (Ex 23:28).

"And the children of Israel dwelt among the ... Hittites. ... And they took their daughters to be their wives. ... And the children of Israel did evil in the sight of the Lord" (Judg 3:5–7).

Hyksos: The Hyksos (from Egyptian, meaning "rulers of foreign lands") were a Semitic people (possibly Amorites) from the north (probably Mesopotamia) who about 1720 BC swept into Syria and Palestine with war chariots. In Palestine their capital was at Hazor, but their remains have been found at dozens of important archaeological sites in Palestine. Then they invaded Egypt, disregarding the capital at Thebes and building a new center for their powerful kingdom at Avaris-Tanis in the Nile delta. Their contributions included beaten-earth fortresses surrounded by moats (remains have been found at Shechem, Lachish, and Jericho) and the introduction of the composite bow. Their worship centered on Baal, and cultic objects included fertility goddesses, serpents, and doves. In about 1570 BC the Hyksos were driven from Egypt into southern Palestine. They must have dispersed and/or integrated with native populations, because by the time of the Egyptian campaigns in Palestine (1468–1431 BC) the Hyksos are no longer mentioned in military records.

Kenites: A nomadic tribe of metalsmiths who were friendly to the Hebrews, accompanied the Israelites into the promised land, and intermarried with them.

"The Kenite shall be wasted" (Num 24:22).

Midianites: The Bible describes the Midianites as nomadic, camel-riding traders of the desert south and east of the promised land. In both the Bible and Arab sources they are said to be descendants of Abraham through one of the sons he exiled to the east. Although they were so friendly in the time of Moses that he took refuge with them and married the daughter of one of their priests, after the conquest of Canaan they made annoying raids on Israelite settlements. The Midianites were probably absorbed by Arab tribes.

"Thou shalt smite the Midianites" (Judg 6:16).

"And the Lord spake unto Moses, saying, Vex the Midianites, and smite them" (Deut 25:16–17).

Moabites: A Semitic people who settled east of the Dead Sea about the 14th century BC. The Bible says Moabites, like Ammonites, were descended from Lot. The only example of a written document from Moab—the Stela of Mesha, dating from about 850 BC—reveals that the language was very similar to the Hebrew of the period. Hostility between Moabites and

Israelites alternated with periods of friendship, and Moab ultimately suffered a fate similar to Israel's under Assyrian, Persian, and Babylonian conquest.

"There shall be no more praise of Moab ... let us cut it off from being a nation" (Jer 48:2).

Philistines: The Philistines were one of the non-Semitic "Peoples of the Sea" who settled the coast of Palestine in the 12th century BC. Most scholars believe they came from Aegean islands—notably Crete—but because they brought iron-making techniques and war chariots they may first have migrated to Asia Minor or otherwise been in contact with Hittites. The biblical reference to Philistines in the Beersheba area in patriarchal times has not been substantiated by archaeologists.

Philistine sailing ships unsuccessfully attempted to invade the Nile delta about 1220 BC and during the reign of Rameses III (1195–1164 BC). Egyptian reliefs of these defeats show the Philistines as tall and shaven, wearing skirts and elaborate feathered headdresses. At least two other Sea Peoples are depicted with them. The Sea People then settled the coast of Palestine, where they assimilated with the Canaanites. They maintained strong ties with Egypt, and were probably paid by Egypt to guard the coast. Philistine power was concentrated in five fortified cities defended by chariot corps—Ashdod, Ashkelon, and Gaza on the coast, and Gath and Ekron inland. From these they carried on sea trade and established military outposts to guard roads to the caravan routes to the east. As the Hebrews were never able to conquer them, Philistine control of the southwest coast was not weakened until Egyptians and Assyrians began to vie for control of the coastal highway in the 8th to 7th centuries BC.

The Philistine god was Dagon ("little fish"), who had a man's head and hands but the tail of a fish; the Philistines also worshiped Ashtaroth.

The Greeks called this part of the coast Philistia, and the name Palestine is also derived from the Philistines.

"The Syrians before, and the Philistines behind; and they shall devour Israel with open mouth" (Isa 9:12).

"Behold, I will stretch out mine hand upon the Philistines ... and destroy the remnant of the sea coast" (Ezek 25:16).

Phoenicians: Phoenicians were Canaanites, but the Bible never uses the former name for them. Phoenicians had been in Palestine since the dawn of history and evidence of their trade with Egypt by at least 2800 BC has been found by archaeologists at Byblos. When the Israelites entered the promised land under Joshua, the Canaanites had centers at Jericho, Jerusalem, and elsewhere. Gradually, however, they were pushed to a narrow coastal strip north of Mount Carmel, and from the 12th century BC on they engaged in vigorous seagoing trade. Their chief coastal cities—Tyre and Sidon—were so well fortified that not even the Assyrians could capture them. Although at length (6th century BC) the Phoenicians submitted to the Persians, they retained their autonomy and were not conquered until Alexander the Great laid a long siege at Tyre in 333–332 BC.

In the Bible the Phoenicians were either called by the general term Canaanites or were identified with their chief cities such as Tyre and Sidon (or Zidon). The name Phoenician—given by the Greeks—is of obscure origin. It comes from a root meaning "red" and one theory is that it referred to the purple and red cloth they exported. The biblical view of Phoenicians is derogatory not only because of their religious practices but because they readily absorbed foreign influences from all the countries they visited (certainly all of the Mediterranean and perhaps the British Isles, South Africa, and the East Indies).

"Howl ye ships of Tarshish: for your strength is laid waste. And it shall come to pass . . . that Tyre shall be forgotten" (Isa 23:14–15).

Semites: The Bible uses the term Semites to designate descendants of Noah's son Shem, but scholars use it to cover a large number of ancient peoples whose languages are related and believed derived from a common tongue, Semitic. At the dawn of history, Semites were seminomads who scattered from the Arabian peninsula as early as 2500 BC and settled throughout the Fertile Crescent. They were dominant in Babylon under Sargon and Hammurabi, and the Hebrew group that migrated south to the Nile delta eventually took over most of Palestine. Included in this wide-ranging group are Accadians of Babylonia; Arabs; Arameans and the related Hebrews; Assyrians; and Canaanites (including Ammonites, Amorites, Edomites, Moabites, Phoenicians, and various subgroups mentioned in the Bible).

Curious Words of Biblical Origin

Bible: "Bible" originated with the word Byblos, the Greek name for the Phoenician city from which papyrus, the first paper, was imported to Greece. The name of the city was adapted to mean papyrus itself and eventually *biblia* was used by both the Greeks and Romans for "little books." Thus the Scriptures, a collection of little books, came to be known as the Bible in Old French, whence it came down to us.

Armageddon: The word derives from Har Megiddon, "the mountain of Meggido." This area had been the site of many battles in the Old Testament (Judg 5:19; 2 Kings 9:27; 23:29) and the author of Revelation believed the final conflict, the battle of the Apocalypse, would take place on the plain that lies around the mountain (Rev 16:16).

Jeroboam, Rehoboam: Jeroboam, the first king of Israel, and Rehoboam, the first king of Judah, have given their names to two sizes of wine bottles. A rehoboam holds about five quarts and a jeroboam slightly more than three. Precisely what the connection is between the kings and the bottles no one knows.

Philistine: The Philistines and the Israelites were neighbors who became long-standing enemies because each wanted what the other had. The Philistines occupied the coast of Palestine, monopolizing the sea trade, while the Israelites had control of fertile farm lands in the interior through which the overland trade routes ran. "Philistine" has come to mean a boorish and uncultured person because the Philistines believed in Canaanite religion and because they stole the Ark of the Covenant.

Beulah Land: In English the phrase "Beulah Land," like "promised land," has come to mean any paradise, a faraway realm where dreams come true. Among U.S. pioneers, the more religious would paint both phrases on their wagons as they journeyed out west in search of a new home. The term "Beulah Land" originates in Isaiah (62:4); "Thou shalt no more be termed Forsaken; neither shall thy land any more be termed Desolate: but thou shalt be called Hephzibah, and thy land Beulah: for the Lord delighted in thee, and thy land shall be married." There's a bit of conscious wordplay here on the part of Isaiah, for *beulah* means "married" in Hebrew.

Adam's Apple: According to folk anatomy, the Adam's apple is a remnant of man's first sin—a piece of the forbidden fruit stuck in the throat.

Lazar: A lazar is anyone smitten with a repulsive disease, usually leprosy. The word directly derives from Lazarus, the name of the leprous beggar that Jesus cured (Luke 16:19–25). Similarly, a lazaretto is a leper's house, specifically an isolation ward for lepers.

Job's Comforter: Anyone who pretends to be empathizing with you and makes you feel worse is a job's comforter. Job's friends had been scolding the wretched man, telling him his troubles were the result of sin. He answered them with "I have heard many such things: miserable comforters are ye all" (Job 16:2).

Proof of the Past

The Flood: Excavations by C. L. Woolley at the ancient Sumerian city of Ur and nearby sites show that extensive and catastrophic floods had plagued the Tigris-Euphrates valley about 4000 BC.

The Tower of Babel: Examination of the ancient Babylonian step pyramid, the Entemanamki ziggurat, confirms that the "tower" was built "with brick for stone" and "slime [asphalt] for mortar," as the Bible reports (Gen 11:2).

The Name of Abraham: Clay tablets from the reign of the Babylonian king Ammizaduga (First Dynasty) mention names resembling "Abraham," evidence of the patriarch's Mesopotamian origins.

The Nuzi Tablets: Clay tablets from the city of Nuzi, in northern Mesopotamia, record customs resembling those of the patriarchs. Among these customs are adoption, transferral of birthright, respect for a deathbed blessing, and the taking of a servant girl to bear children if the wife is infertile.

The Mari Letters: Correspondence between border guards and the king of Mari, a city-state in Mesopotamia, refers to Hapiru and Benjamite raiders, suggesting the presence of early Hebrew tribes in the area during the second millennium BC.

The Amarna Letters: Letters from vassal princes to Pharaoh Akhenaten record the destruction of Canaanite cities by a certain group called the Hapiru, perhaps the Hebrews, c. 1388–1362 BC.

49

The Stela of Merneptah: First-known mention of Israel, in an inscription commemorating a victory by the son of Rameses II over some of the nations in Palestine. Circa 1220 BC, the stela confirms that Israel was known as a nation at the time.

Bethel, Debir, Lachish, and Hazor: Cities in northern Palestine which show signs of being sacked and burned at about the same time, before 1200 BC, indicate the basic truth behind the biblical history of the destruction of Canaanite fortified cities.

Shiloh: American archaeologist W. F. Albright has confirmed the Bible's assertion that Shiloh was settled by the Israelites at the time of the conquest of Canaan (13th century BC) and destroyed by the Philistines about 1050 BC.

Megiddo: Distinctive imperial architecture, which is similar to that at Hazor, Gezer, and other sites, supports the Bible's statement that "Solomon ... built the wall of Hazor, Megiddo and Gezer" (1 Kings 9:15). Characteristic of the Solomonic fortifications were the casemate wall, a wall with rooms inside for armories or general storage, and the chambered gate, a straight narrow passageway through the middle of three rooms. This gate, which seems designed specifically for chariots, may be evidence of the tradition that Hazor, Gezer, and Megiddo were among the chariot cities (2 Chr 9:25). This chambered gate also fits Ezekiel's description of Solomon's Temple (Ezek 40): "And the little chambers of the gate eastward were three on this side and three on that side."

The Pool of Siloam: In 1880 archaeologists rediscovered the ancient water system of Jerusalem. Perhaps first built in the time of David, or before that by the Jebusites (2 Sam 5:8; Isa 22:11), tunnels carried water from the spring of Gihon to the pool of Siloam inside the city walls. In one tunnel was found an inscription describing the act of chiseling the shaft and commemorating the feat. The tunnel is almost certainly the one that Hezekiah ordered built to ensure a water supply that would be safe from the Assyrian army that was on its way to Palestine (2 Kings 20:20; 2 Chr 32:30). The message inscribed in the tunnel was never completed and it is often conjectured that the inscriber broke off his work because he had been notified that the Assyrian army was at the city gates.

Beth-shean: According to the Bible, Saul's body was hung from the walls of Beth-shean by the Philistines and his armor was hung in the temple of Ashtoreth. Archaeologists have proven that the city was occupied by the Philistines before 815 BC and that the goddess Ashtoreth (Astarte) was worshiped there (1 Sam 31:20).

Inscription of Pharaoh Sheshonq (Shishak): The Egyptian pharaoh Sheshonq, known in the Bible as Shishak, preserved the record of his campaign in Palestine in inscriptions (c. 900 BC) on the wall of a temple in Karnak. The record supports the biblical contention that he did not take Jerusalem, but levied a heavy tribute instead (2 Chr 12:4, 7).

The Moabite Stone: Mesha, the Moabite king who successfully rebelled against Ahab (2 Kings 3:4 ff.), memorialized his victory in an inscription on a black basalt stela. The stone's inscription mentions Omri and his son (Ahab) and reports the seizure of an altar to Yahweh.

The Horns of the Altar: The mention of horns in First Kings, "Joab fled unto the tabernacle . . . and caught hold on the horns of the altar," puzzled people for centuries until altars began to be discovered with triangular, hornlike projections rising from each corner of the altar's top surface.

Samaria: Omri moved the capital of Israel to Samaria, a previously unoccupied hill (1 Kings 16:24), and during the time of Ahab and Jezebel the court there was said to be heavily influenced by the Phoenicians (1 Kings 16:32). Digs on the site have substantiated these general facts and provided confirmation of some details of the Bible's reports. Ahab's "ivory house" (1 Kings 22:39) was corroborated by fragments of Phoenician ivories that have been recovered, as have Jeroboam II's "houses of ivory" and "beds of ivory" (Amos 3:15; 6:4) by similar fragments from a later date.

Arad: A temple from the time of Solomon was found that displays many of the architectural peculiarities of the earliest temples. The altar for burnt offerings was a square of 5 cubits, exactly as the Bible says it should be (Ex 27:1; 2 Chr 6:13), and it is built of earth and unhewn stones to accord with the prohibition in Exodus (20:25). Also found were pottery shards with the names of two priestly families known from the Bible, Pahur and Meremoth (Ezra 10:22, 36).

The Obelisk of Shalmaneser III: The Assyrian king Shalmaneser III had a stone pillar inscribed to record his victories (c. 841 BC). Noted on the stela is the tribute from one Jaua of Bit-Humri, who is shown groveling before the king, while attendants bear gifts of gold, silver, tin, and wood. The attendants are clearly Israelites: They wear beards (Lev 19:27) and fringed garments (Deut 22:12). And this "Jaua of Bit-Humri" is none other than Jehu of the house of Omri, a.k.a. King Jehu of Israel—or his ambassador— whose embarrassing tribute payment is not mentioned by the authors of the Bible.

Sennacherib and Lachish: In his palace near Nineveh, Sennacherib (704–681 BC) had his successful invasion of Palestine immortalized in friezes which decorated thousands of feet of the palace's walls. One of these sculptures depicts his siege of Lachish (2 Chr 32:9) with such precision that it distinguishes the bearded Israelites from the shaven Assyrians. In Nineveh archaeologists unearthed the literary records of his conquest—prisms of clay inscribed with cuneiform. In these, Sennacherib boasts of shutting Hezekiah up in Jerusalem like a "bird in a cage," and of collecting 30 talents of gold and 800 talents of silver from the king as tribute. This figure exactly matches the Bible's account of the tribute paid, except that the Bible says the silver amounted to only 300 talents. Clearly one or both of the parties are lying to save face (2 Kings 18:14).

Nebuchadnezzar's Annals: In 1955, while translating Babylonian cuneiform texts, D. J. Wiseman discovered a startling passage on one of the clay tablets:

> In the seventh year [of Nebuchadnezzar's reign—c. 599 BC] the king prepared his army and advanced on Syria and Palestine, laying siege to the city of Judah. On March 16 he conquered it, took King Jehoiachin prisoner and replaced him with a king of his own choosing [Zedekiah]. He demanded great tribute and sent it to Babylon.

The following is the Bible's version (2 Kings 24:11–17):

> And Nebuchadnezzar king of Babylon came against the city and his servants did besiege it. And Jehoiachin the king of Judah went out to the king . . . and the king of Babylon took him in the eighth year of his reign. And he [Nebuchadnezzar] carried out . . . and cut in pieces all the vessels of gold which Solomon king of Israel had made in the temple. . . . And he carried away Jehoiachin to Babylon. . . . And the king of Babylon made Mattaniah his father's brother king in his stead, and changed his name to Zedekiah.

Still more remarkable was one inscription found on one of the 300 tablets recording the accounts of the royal stores of Nebuchadnezzar. Among the tedious lists was the following: "10 measures of oil for Jehoiachin king of Judah, 2½ for the king's sons, 4 for his eight men." The humble inscription is amazing proof of this verse from Jeremiah:

> And for his diet [i.e., Jehoiachin's diet], there was continual diet given him of the king of Babylon, every day a portion until the day of his death, all the days of his life (52:34).

Lachish: Archaeologists digging at the main gate of 6th-century-BC (c. 588 BC) Lachish found eighteen potsherds on which messages were inscribed. Most of the messages are military dispatches from outposts to the head-

52

quarters at Lachish. The scouts were watching for the advancing armies of Nebuchadnezzar. One of the shards, probably the last to be received, reports that fire signals from the neighboring town of Azekah could no longer be seen—the city had been taken and Lachish was next. The archaeologists also discovered a layer of ashes several yards thick at the remains of the city's walls. Undoubtedly Nebuchadnezzar's siege strategy was to set huge bonfires against the walls and keep them lit until the superheated stones collapsed. It worked at Lachish; the pile of ashes was higher than the remains of the walls.

Elephantine Papyri: Although they come from the period of the Persian occupation of Egypt (c. 419 BC), the papyri mention that a Jewish community on Elephantine, an island in the upper reaches of the Nile, had been in existence since the days of the pharaohs. The community there had a temple dedicated to Yahu (Yahweh), and even a military garrison. Though exiles, they kept in touch with Jerusalem through letters.

The Pool of Bethesda: Jesus was said to have healed at the pool of Bethesda, which the Bible describes as having five porches (John 5:2). For years the site of the pool was unknown. In 1888 the remains of a bath were discovered beneath the Church of St. Anne in Jerusalem. It had five porches or colonnades: four surrounding and a fifth dividing the two pools. This central colonnade is where the handicapped would come to be healed.
   Among the Dead Sea Scrolls was found a copper scroll listing the purported sites of buried treasure. The scroll claims that treasure was hidden in the smaller pool at Bethesda, confirming that the baths had two pools. No treasure, however, has been found.

The Pilate Inscription: A stone slab, apparently commemorating the construction of a Roman theater, has the name of Pontius Pilate inscribed upon it. The slab would seem to be contemporary to Pilate, AD 26-36.

The Antonia Pavement: Under the Antonia tower in Jerusalem a large paved area from the Roman period has come to light. One section is a roadway or track scored to give the horses' hooves better traction, and on one of the paving blocks a gaming board of some kind is inscribed. The area was thought to be Gabbatha, the courtyard in which Jesus was brought before the crowd and sentenced by Pilate, but that conclusion is now disputed.

The Remains of a Crucified Man: In 1968 a bulldozer unearthed the grave of a victim of crucifixion in Jerusalem from the 1st century AD. The man's name, inscribed on the urn in which his bones rested, was Jonathan. Unlike Jesus in representations of his crucifixion, this man seems to have been put

53

on the cross in a sitting position, a nail driven through both ankles, and a nail piercing each forearm.

Reports of Jesus and the Early Christians: Outside of the Bible, the earliest references to Jesus and the first Christians come from Roman historians. Suetonius (c. AD 110) reports that in the ninth year of the reign of the Emperor Claudius (AD 49), Jews were expelled from Rome for rioting having to do with "Chrestus." It is often assumed that "Jesus Christ" is meant by this "Chrestus" and that a riot was caused by a dispute over whether or not Jesus was the Christ. If this is so, then Christianity had begun to take hold in Rome less than twenty years after the death of Jesus.

Tacitus, another Roman historian, shows familiarity with one portion of the gospel story, the death of Jesus in the time of Pontius Pilate. The following lines are from Tacitus' *Annals,* published sometime around AD 115; they describe events that took place in AD 64: "In place of himself Nero accused and punished with skillful malice, people who the masses hated for their crimes, called Christians. Christ, the person from whom the name came, had been put to death during the rule of Tiberius by the procurator Pontius Pilate. This evil belief, which had been arrested for a time, started again in Judea, where it first began, and in Rome as well. . . ."

Two

Promises! Promises!—Struggling for the Promised Land

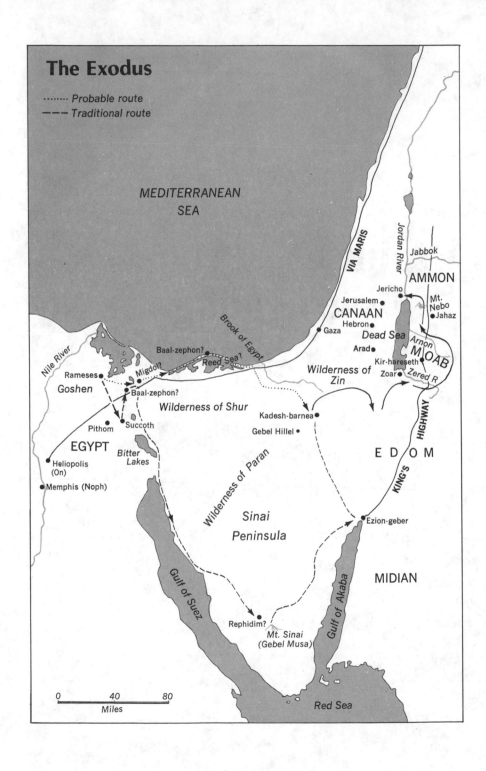

The Exodus

········ Probable route
‒‒‒‒ Traditional route

MEDITERRANEAN
SEA

VIA MARIS

Jordan River

Jabbok

AMMON

Brook of Egypt

Jericho

Jerusalem
CANAAN
Hebron
Gaza

Mt.
Nebo
Jahaz

Dead Sea

Arnon

Nile River

Baal-zephon?

Reed Sea?

Arad

MOAB

Rameses
Goshen

Migdol?

Baal-zephon?

Wilderness of Shur

Kir-hareseth
Zoar

Zered R.

Wilderness of
Zin

HIGHWAY

Pithom

Succoth

Kadesh-barnea
Gebel Hillel

E D O M

EGYPT

Bitter
Lakes

KING'S

Heliopolis
(On)

Wilderness of Paran

Memphis (Noph)

Sinai
Peninsula

Ezion-geber

MIDIAN

Gulf of Suez

Gulf of Akaba

Rephidim?

Mt. Sinai
(Gebel Musa)

0   40   80
Miles

Red Sea

What and Where Was the Promised Land?

In the covenant with Abraham, God promised the descendants of the first patriarch a vast area from the Brook of Egypt to the Euphrates River (Gen 15:18). These boundaries were achieved only once by the Hebrew people, during the days of King Solomon.

After the covenant with the children of Israel at Sinai, however, the boundaries of the promised land shrank considerably. The Bible says Moses could see the entire area of land that the children of Israel were to occupy from his perch on Mount Nebo (Deut 34:1-4).

A Land by Any Other Name

Palestine: "Palestine" was adapted from "Philistine," the name of the people that lived along the southern coast of the region. In the 2d century AD, the Romans called their province, which contained both Syria and Palestine, Syria Palaestina. In World War I, when the British attained their mandate to govern the area, they called the land Palestine.

The Land of Milk and Honey: This term comes from God's description of the land he will give the Israelites as a home. No particular boundaries for the country are given for this paradisical homeland but it is usually thought to cover the same territory as the "promised land." Exodus gives this description: "I am come down to deliver them . . . unto a good land and a large, unto a land flowing with milk and honey; unto the place of the Canaanites, and the Hittites, and the Amorites, and the Perizzites. . . ."

The Holy Land: Since this tiny region is a focal point for three major religions—Judaism, Christianity, and Islam—the area has become known as the Holy Land. The city of Jerusalem, in particular, contains many places sacred to each of these religions.

United Kingdom, Kingdom of Israel, Kingdom of Judah: The "United Kingdom" is the term used by most biblical authorities to describe the lands held under the reigns of Saul, David, and Solomon. This kingdom expanded from Saul's time, when it stretched only from the Dead Sea to Mount Hermon, to Solomon's, when it reached its greatest extent—from the Brook of Egypt to the Euphrates in the north. These are exactly the boundaries of the "promised land" given in Genesis (15:18).

After Solomon's reign, the kingdom split up on account of internal strife. Basically the people in the south, the Judeans, had been ruling over those in the north, the Israelites. The Israelites rebelled after Solomon's death and established an independent kingdom in the north, Israel. The southern kingdom was Judah.

House of Omri: Omri was one of the great kings of Israel. His reputation among foreign nations was so great that Israel, even after his death, was referred to as the "house of Omri."

Canaan: "Canaan" designated the same general territory as the term "promised land." This was an expanse larger than the kingdoms of Israel and Judah combined. It approximated the size of Solomon's kingdom.

The word Canaan probably means the "land of indigo," a reference to the royal-purple dye that a native mollusk provided. Canaanites were the people that the Israelites gradually displaced or absorbed.

Zion: Originally, "Zion" (fortress or citadel) referred to the southern tip of the ridge located between the Tyropoeon and Kidron valleys in the Jebusite city that became Jerusalem. The application of the name spread along with the expansion of the city, and came to mean the southern portion of the city's western ridge. "Zion" has also been applied to the Holy Land in general, as in the term "Zionism."

The Exodus

The exact time and route of the Exodus may never be known, because the brief biblical version seems to be the only record. It is unlikely the Egyptians ever recorded this escape. It was quite common for seminomads in time of famine to go temporarily to Egypt or Mesopotamia, where there were large cultivated grain fields. Although the Egyptians were annoyed enough to send chariots in pursuit, the escape of a small group of slaves would not have had much economic importance.

Many scholars believe that Moses left Egypt under Rameses II (1304–1237 BC). The Bible says that the Israelites, who had come into Egypt as shepherds, were forced by a new pharaoh to build his treasure cities of Pithom and Rameses and to cultivate the surrounding fields (Ex 1:11, 14). It is likely the Hebrews were constructing the new capital, which Rameses moved to the northeast delta to make it more convenient for his northern military campaigns. His father, Sethos I, had conquered Palestine, and Rameses intended to push farther north, to Syria. Moses may even have used the disastrous defeat of Egyptian forces in 1286 BC, when Rameses had tried to wrest Syria from the Hittites, as an opportunity to escape. Rameses, however, had an unusually long reign of sixty-seven years, and as he grew older the unrest caused by foreigners settling in the delta and harrying the coast might have afforded Moses the opportunity to lead his people out of Egypt.

The first recorded mention of Israel as a tribe of Palestine—in an inscription from the time of Rameses' son (1220 BC)—has sometimes been taken as additional proof that the Hebrews had left under Rameses. More recent discoveries, however, indicate that not all Israelite tribes went to Egypt during the famine—some are believed to have settled in Palestine before the Exodus—and not all the Hebrews in Egypt left with Moses.

The Escape: Moses was not a warrior. When he sought the release of his people from bondage he never resorted to violence but waited for the plagues sent by God to frighten the Egyptians. Finally, when the tenth plague killed the firstborn of Egypt, including the pharaoh's son, the pharaoh relented and told Moses he could leave. To avoid trouble, Moses rushed his people into immediate departure—they had no time to prepare food and even had to pack "their dough before it was leavened" (Ex 12:34,

39). Fleeing in the moonlight, they circumvented the main route—the Via Maris—north to Canaan, because it was guarded by Egyptian fortresses.

Which Way Did Moses Go? The Bible says Moses led his people by way of the Yam Suf—the Reed Sea, which is incorrectly translated as "Red Sea" in some Bibles.

For many years the "Reed Sea" was thought to be the Bitter Lakes of Egypt, a marshy area north of the Gulf of Suez through which the Suez Canal was later cut. Here the pharaoh's chariots could have become mired as waters from the Gulf of Suez rose. Traditionally it was thought that the Israelites had trudged south on the Sinai Peninsula about 300 miles to Mount Sinai—the 7497-foot Gebel Musa. This area would have been known to the Israelites; it contained the Egyptian turquoise and copper mines, exploited until the 11th century BC, which used captives from Palestine and Syria as forced labor. Inscriptions in an early Semitic script, still not entirely deciphered, have been found near the mines. From Mount Sinai the Israelites would have turned north to trudge another couple of hundred miles to the oasis of Kadesh-barnea (south of modern El Arish). Of all the Israelite camps in the wilderness listed in the Bible, only Kadesh-barnea has been positively identified. It was a crossroad of ancient travel routes and is still used by nomads today. The Israelites stayed here a generation.

A more recent theory holds that Moses would never have taken his people on such a roundabout route. It would have involved a southern detour from Goshen and miles of difficult march within the borders of Egypt and past fortresses guarding the Bitter Lakes. Also, the southern Sinai is inhospitable volcanic land that has never supported much of a population. Moses may therefore have taken the more sensible course of getting out of Egypt as quickly as possible by exiting immediately through the northeast delta. Two Egyptian fortresses here—Migdol and Baal-zephon—are mentioned in the Bible. To avoid the guarded Via Maris, the Israelites would have gone out onto a narrow isthmus that juts into the Mediterranean from the northern edge of the Sinai Peninsula, and tides here could have caught the pharaoh's chariots. Kadesh-barnea would have been reached by a shorter route, and the mountain on which Moses received the Ten Commandments could have been Gebel Hillel (some thirty miles west of the oasis).

Joshua and Caleb Become Impatient: During the thirty or forty years that Israel was camped at Kadesh-barnea, Moses had sent spies into the land of Canaan to report on whether the people lived in tents or in strongholds, and whether the land was fruitful. When the spies reported that fortified cities and a great people had to be overcome before they could move into the land of milk and honey, many Israelites were afraid, and some even wanted to return to Egypt. On top of that, Joshua and Caleb were impatient to go "at once" and wanted to go straight north into Canaan, while Moses seemed bent on taking a longer way around—via the Dead Sea—to enter Canaan from the east.

Annoyed with all the bickering, Joshua and Caleb headed north on their own with armed men, not even bothering to take the Ark of the Covenant. Ahead was Arad, a fortified Canaanite city whose inhabitants were trained to repel nomads and keep other invaders from penetrating into Canaan. When they saw the Israelites coming, they rounded up allies among the Amalekites. The Israelites were at a disadvantage because they had to climb uphill toward Arad and also because, while they had acquired weapons during their years in the wilderness, they were not yet trained in combat. The people of Arad easily routed them, taking some prisoners, and the remaining Israelites fled back to Kadesh-barnea (Num 13:16-33;14:1-45; Deut 1:38-46).

Amorites Attack: Moses had wanted to go from Kadesh-barnea directly east to the King's Highway and then take this road north to Canaan. But the highway ran through the kingdoms of Edom and Moab, which refused the Israelites passage through their lands. Moses had to take a detour that more than doubled the marching distance—going all the way south to the Red Sea and then turning north through wilderness to skirt Edom and Moab. They reached the Arnon River—the northern border of Moab—and beyond it lay the land of the Amorites. Moses now asked the Amorite king Sihon for permission to take the King's Highway north, promising not to touch Amorite wells or vineyards. Sihon's reply was to bring his warriors to Jahaz (southeast of Medaba), where the Israelites waited. The Israelites defeated the Amorites, taking possession of their land from the Arnon River north to the river Jabbok, but instead of moving into the fortified cities they destroyed them, killing the men, women, and children. They then moved on toward Canaan, taking cattle and other spoils.

Moses had led his people to the edge of Canaan, but God decreed he was to die here without ever setting foot across the Jordan into the promised land. He did, however, climb Mount Nebo (just northwest of Jahaz) to see it all before his death (Num 21:21-31; Deut 2:24-37; Judg 11:17-22).

Barefoot in the Bible

1. Isaiah walked barefoot three years (Isa 20:2-3).
2. David, driven from his throne, climbed Mount Olivet barefoot (2 Sam 15:30).
3. Egyptian prisoners were barefoot (Isa 20:4).
4. Captives from Judah were barefoot (2 Chr 28:15).

5. Moses was barefoot before God (Ex 3:5).

6. Jesus was barefoot several times (Luke 7:38; 24:40; John 12:3).

7. Men who would not follow levirate law took off one shoe (Deut 25:9).

8. Joshua took off his shoes at Jericho (Josh 5:15).

9. Boaz was barefoot (Ruth 3:4, 8).

10. Disciples of Jesus went without shoes (Luke 10:4; 22:35).

11. Mephibosheth went barefoot as a sign of mourning after David was driven from Jerusalem (2 Sam 19:24).

12. The prodigal son lost his shoes (Luke 15:22).

13. The psalmist threw his shoes over Edom (Psa 60:8; 108:9).

The Holy War

All wars in biblical times were holy wars. They were begun either by command of the gods or with their approval. The gods gave victory to their own people—and if people were defeated it was because they had angered their gods. Victory celebrations included thanksgiving to the gods and often a share of the booty for the temples.

One reason Tuthmosis III (1504–1450 BC) of Egypt left such a good record of his military campaigns was that he inscribed those annals on the walls of the temple of Karnak in recognition of the fact that the victories were given by Amon-Re.

The Assyrians tended to confuse the power of their kings with the power of the gods. Tiglath-pileser III (745–727 BC) liked to boast of how he frightened enemies: One king fled at the mere sound of the Assyrian army and was not seen again, while another ran so fast he left his wife and children behind. Tiglath-pileser claimed that he overwhelmed King Menahem of Israel like a snowstorm, so that Menahem fled "like a bird, alone, and bowed at my feet."

Cyrus of Persia believed he was ordered into battle by the Babylonian god (Marduk), who marched at his side like a "real friend," and who gave him victories because he had such an upright heart. Cyrus was careful not to antagonize foreign gods and in his conquests he left foreign idols in their native temples because he thought they'd be happier that way.

GOD TAKES CANAAN

What made the Israelite wars unique was that for so long they remained so pure. Eventually this pristine quality was subverted, but it has been preserved with clarity in the Bible.

In the earliest days there was no army, because the people as a whole voluntarily took up arms. The Israelites did not fight for God; it was God who fought for Israel. All the battles they undertook were God's battles— "Fight the Lord's battles," Saul told David (1 Sam 18:17). The enemies they fought were God's enemies—it was God, for instance, and not the Israelites who was to war with the Amalekites from generation to generation (Ex 17:16). The Hebrews were troops of God, the armies of God, or simply the people of God, and it was God who gave them "dominion over the mighty" (Judg 5:13; 20:2; 1 Sam 17–26).

No battle was undertaken until God was consulted and decreed it should be fought (Judg 20:23). When people took a battle into their own hands—as when the Israelites tried to take Canaan too soon—they were defeated.

God ordered and approved battles, and marched in the vanguard, God was "a man of war" who "goeth with" the Israelites into battle. "Is not the Lord gone out before thee?" Deborah asked Barak (Ex 15:3; Deut 20:4; Judg 4:14). In addition to the cloudburst during Deborah's War, hailstones, earthquakes, mysterious plagues, and other calamities were sent by God to panic enemies and make them flee.

Because God was present, the battleground was holy—as in the Temple, sacrifices had to be offered (1 Sam 7:9) and the camp and everyone in it had to be made ritually clean (Deut 23:10–15).

Once the battle started, the symbol of God's presence was the Ark of the Covenant. The Ark was carried across the desert in the time of the wanderings and across the Jordan into Canaan. It was paraded around the walls of Jericho and taken into the other battles of the conquest. One of the nadirs of Israelite history was when the Philistines captured the Ark at Shiloh.

Over and over the Israelites were assured that they should not fear chariots or other formidable weapons of their enemies because victory was certain. Before the battle God had already "delivered the enemy into their hands" (Judg 3:28; 4:7; 7:9, 15). What was required was that the people retain faith. When they lost faith and became fearful they angered God and lost the battle. For this reason, halfhearted soldiers were not allowed to take part in war and were sent home (Deut 20:8).

GOD ORDAINS DEFEAT

The first debasement in the concept of war came under Saul. Many Israelites worried that a monarch would usurp God's place and were therefore reluctant to let Saul rule except in time of crisis. These fears were justified, because under Saul the Israelites ceased to rely on God and began to say that the king would "go out before us, and fight our battles" (1 Sam 8:20). Saul himself agonized, and the prophet Samuel accused him of not obeying God (1 Sam 13:8–14, 15, 28). After Samuel's death Saul doomed himself by consulting a witch instead of God before battle.

Under David war became even less God's work. Although the sacrifice and cleansing rituals were still observed, and the Ark was carried into battle, the voluntary army was replaced by foreign mercenaries, and David even had the army make a military census of his kingdom so that no one would escape the draft (1 Sam 24:1–10). Also, while some of the spoils were being consecrated to God, some were being diverted to pay for the mercenaries and other expenses of the monarchy. In addition, victory now began to be credited to men. David's general Joab claimed credit for taking the city of Rabbah and David himself wore the crown of Rabbah's king (2 Sam 12:27–30).

During Solomon's reign there was little warfare, and when battles began anew under the divided kingdom the picture was much changed. For one thing, war from then on was almost always defensive, and perhaps it was harder to keep the faith. God was no longer directly consulted about war or expected to lead the army. When King Ahab of Israel asked a prophet who should order a battle, the prophet replied "Thou" (1 Kings 20:13–14). Kings were making the decisions in regard to war, and no longer consulted God directly. At most they consulted God indirectly through a prophet. But there were many prophets, and in addition to kings disagreeing with prophets over the conduct of war, prophets disagreed with each other, so that kings were choosy about which prophet to believe. A prophet who foretold disaster in battle was thrown into prison and another one was consulted (1 Kings 22:5–28). The prophet Elisha even refused to consult God about the Moabite war for King Jehoshaphat, and the king had to take the word of a minstrel (2 Kings 3:11–19).

Although Isaiah tried to revive the concept of a holy war and railed against relying on military preparations and Egyptian aid instead of God, war was increasingly profaned. According to the prophets, lack of proper respect for God was what cost the Israelites the Holy Land. God ceased to protect the people, so the kingdoms of Israel and Judah were doomed (2 Kings 23:27). Jeremiah said God became angry enough to fight against the chosen people and to command the fall of Jerusalem (Jer 21:4–7; 34:22).

---

14 Threats Made by God

1. "I shall bruise thy head" (Gen 3:15).
2. "I will put my hook in thy nose" (2 Kings 19:28).
3. "I will smite thy bow out of thy left hand, and will cause thine arrows to fall out of thy right hand" (Ezek 39:3).
4. "I will also send wild beasts among you" (Lev 26:22).
5. "I will send the pestilence among you" (Lev 26:25).

6. "Behold, I will send serpents" (Jer 8:17).

7. "I will send upon you famine" (Ezek 5:17).

8. "I will break in pieces the chariot and his rider" (Jer 51:21).

9. "I will fill all the inhabitants of this land ... with drunkenness" (Jer 13:13).

10. "I will roll thee down from the rocks" (Jer 51:25).

11. "Also will I make thee sick" (Mic 6:13).

12. "I will make thee a terror, and thou shalt be no more: though thou be sought for, yet shalt thou never be found again" (Ezek 26:21).

13. "Ye shall eat flesh. . . . until it come out at your nostrils" (Num 11:18–20).

14. God will "toss thee like a ball into a large country" (Isa 21:18).

First Steps in the Promised Land

Four ceremonies were demanded of the Israelites when they entered the promised land:

1. the cursing of different people who were the enemies of the Israelites;

2. the erection of an altar on Mount Ebal;

3. the erection of twelve stone monuments on Mount Ebal with the Law engraved upon them;

4. the reading of the Law and the reacceptance of the covenant by the Israelite people.

Conquest of Canaan

On the death of Moses, Joshua took command of the Israelites and led 40,000 men across the Jordan. Their first camp in Canaan was on the plain of Jericho at Gilgal. Gilgal, which the Hebrews considered a sanctified city, was later the site of Saul's coronation. It has not been positively identified, however.

The Bible depicts the war against Canaan as a well-planned, well-executed military campaign in which the Israelites first took strategic ridgetops, then the Judean hills to the south, and finally the Galilee area in the north. For the most part archaeology tends to support these accounts of widespread destruction in Canaan in the 13th century BC, but the biblical version is highly simplified. Undoubtedly there were many more battles than the Bible describes—some of them defeats, some unrecorded skirmishes. And there must have been pockets of people whom the Hebrews never fought and who were peacefully assimilated. Shechem, for instance, had been a non-Canaanite enclave, and was probably incorporated by treaty rather than by violence. Even after the conquest there remained nomads and settlements not truly controlled by Israel that managed to coexist without friction. The ruined towns were not all necessarily attributable to the Israelites; during that period the Philistines along the Gaza coast made forays inland, and the Egyptians, who were rapidly losing power in Canaan, occasionally battled to regain control.

JERICHO COLLAPSES
First Israelite Victory in Canaan

GILGAL, 13TH CENTURY BC: Israelite forces under the command of Joshua today completely destroyed Jericho, the oldest city in Canaan.

The city's fortifications were said to have mysteriously collapsed before the city was stormed and burned. Virtually all inhabitants are reported killed.

From their base camp here at Gilgal, Joshua's forces had moved into the foothills and had been holding Jericho under siege for six days.

Before being burned, the city was looted for silver, gold, brass, and iron.

Rahab Spared

The Israelites had gained advance intelligence about Jericho from spies who contacted Rahab. She is variously described as a secret agent, harlot, and innkeeper, whose life was spared for her services to the Israelites. . . .

20th-Century Update: The site of ancient Jericho (one mile northwest of modern Jericho) has been excavated. The oldest settlement in the Holy Land, its springs had attracted hunters and gatherers since 7000 BC. It first had defensive walls about a thousand years later, and although destroyed several times, it was always rebuilt and always became a powerful and important city. It was especially prosperous during the Hyksos period before it was destroyed, probably by the Egyptians, about 1560 BC. Although pottery and other fragments show that it was inhabited at the time the Israelites came into Canaan, the site is unfortunately too eroded to provide support for the biblical account (Josh 2–6). Chances are its fortifications were more legendary than substantial at the time the Israelites attacked. Also, Jericho lies on a geological fault, so is frequently shaken by tremors and earthquakes, and archaeologists have found evidence that its walls collapsed at least once during an earthquake.

ISRAELITES CRUSH AI
Joshua Gains Foothold in Canaanite Hills

GILGAL, 13TH CENTURY BC: The city of Ai was razed today by Joshua's Israelite troops, who killed 12,000 warriors and civilians.

Joshua's strategy was to send a small decoy detachment that pretended to attack Ai and flee, luring the city defenders on a wild-goose chase. Thus the gates were open to Israel's main army contingent of 5000 men, who had been hiding west of the city. Ai's warriors were slaughtered, its wealth taken as spoils, and the city torched.

The king of Ai was hanged from a tree until sunset. His body has been tossed into the gate of the smoldering city for wild animals to devour.

Is Gibeon Next?

Informed observers here at Joshua's base camp near Gilgal believe that Joshua's next target will be Gibeon. Gibeon commands the entire mountain ridge just northwest of Jerusalem, and its capture would be strategically important. . . .

20th-Century Update: Archaeological remains show that the ancient walled city of Ai (Josh 2–8:29) was leveled by an earthquake about 2900 BC. It was then rebuilt while under Egyptian influence, but was destroyed again—this time in battle—about a thousand years before the time of Joshua. In Joshua's time, as Ai was beginning to be reoccupied, its buildings were crude and there were no fortifications. Because the name Ai means "ruin," some scholars suggest that biblical chroniclers writing at a later date might have confused Ai with another city, perhaps Bethel, which was very close to Ai and far more important in Joshua's time. Crushed and charred bricks, from fortifications covered with a deep layer of ashes, proved Bethel was burned in the 13th century BC.

FOREIGN AMBASSADORS AREN'T THAT FOREIGN
Treaty by Trick

GILGAL, 13TH CENTURY BC: Israelites were stunned today to learn that the foreign ambassadors with whom they signed a peace treaty three days ago were from a city only a few miles away: Gibeon.

The ambassadors had said that they came from "a very far country." As proof of their long journey they had pointed to their tattered clothes, worn shoes, moldy bread, dusty sacks, and torn wineskins. They now admit fear of annihilation by the Israelites made them engage in such deceit. They saw a peace treaty as the only way to save their city.

Joshua has announced that even though the treaty was made under false pretenses he will honor it. He has promised that the people of Gibeon will not be killed. Their only punishment, he said, would be condemnation to perpetual bondage. Gibeonites must from now on carry water and hew wood for the Israelites.

King of Jerusalem Incensed

King Adonizedec of Jerusalem is reported to be incensed with what he views as Gibeonite cowardice. He had hoped for an Israelite defeat at Gibeon. Rumors are that King Adonizedec will move quickly to prevent the Israelites from invading his territory. . . .

20th-Century Update: Gibeon is believed to be el-Jib (eight miles northwest of central Jerusalem). The settlement existed in Joshua's time (Josh 9), as it is mentioned in Arabic sources from the 13th century BC, but few remains uncovered by archaeologists date from before the 12th century BC.

JOSHUA ROUTS FIVE KINGS
Southern Highlands Under Israelite Control

GIBEON, 13TH CENTURY BC: Joshua's forces today overwhelmed armies of the five most powerful kings of southern Canaan, assuring the Israelites control of the Judean highlands.

Led by King Adonizedec of Jerusalem, the kings of Hebron, Jarmuth, Lachish, and Eglon had attempted to besiege Gibeon. But from Gilgal the Israelite guerrillas marched all night to Gibeon, surprising the southern forces.

Adonizedec tried to lead a retreat through the difficult pass at Beth-horon. As the southern armies negotiated the steep and treacherous slopes, a severe hailstorm inflicted heavy casualties.

The five kings, who attempted to hide in a cave at Makkedah, were found and killed. Their bodies were thrown into the cave and the cave sealed with a boulder.

Mopping-up Operations

Contingents of Israelite warriors are now moving through the Judean hills for mopping-up operations. Word is that they will not descend to the coastal cities, which are defended by iron chariots. . . .

20th-Century Update: The Bible's brief account of the Judean conquest makes it seem simple and rapid (Josh 10:27, 36–39; Judg 1:1–21). But archaeologists, who have not yet positively identified all the sites, believe the period of conquest was actually long and uneven. For instance, Eglon was an important city that was apparently damaged many times and continually rebuilt; after destruction in the 14th century BC it was unoccupied until the 10th century BC. Arad in the Negev, where evidence of extensive trade with Egypt has been found, was leveled and abandoned about 2700 BC. That Lachish was a wealthy city has been proven by the many imported objects and the ruins of great buildings from Joshua's time which have been found. Lachish also had a large temple where incense and animal sacrifices were offered. Pottery finds show the city was destroyed in 1221 BC.

NORTHERN CANAAN FALLS
Jabin's Forces Perish at Merom

MEROM, END OF 13TH CENTURY BC: Israelites under Joshua's command today surprised and smashed a northern coalition of forces led by King Jabin of Hazor.

The battle took place at the waters of Merom. At present Hazor is in flames.

Jabin had called upon his allies to amass a huge army of chariots and foot soldiers at the waters of Merom, northwest of Hazor. Troops began to converge from cities as distant as Achshaph and Shimron on the coast. These movements attracted the attention of Joshua, at his camp in Gilgal. Before Jabin's armies could be fully assembled, the Israelites unexpectedly attacked, sending the northern troops into such a panic they dispersed in all directions.

Hazor was besieged and is being demolished. The many chariots that the Israelites captured are being burned and their horses hamstrung.

Joshua's Last Battle?

Joshua, whose conquests have brought the Israelites control of the highlands of Canaan, is said to be frail and in poor health. He is 110 years old and many Israelites believe this may be his last battle. . . .

20th-Century Update: Hazor was the most prominent city in Palestine as early as the 19th century BC. Throughout its history it was both a major stopover for caravans traveling between Mesopotamia and Egypt, and a religious center. Hazor was consumed by fire toward the end of the 13th century BC (Josh 11:1–15), when the city was at its peak. It was so devastated that its site remained unoccupied until the 12th century BC, when a seminomadic people, probably Israelites, put up tents and huts on part of the ruins. A large but unfortified Israelite settlement continued to flourish in the 11th century BC, and Solomon finally rebuilt and fortified the city to make it prominent once again.

DEBORAH'S GUERRILLAS TRIUMPH
Sisera Dead, His Chariots Mired

MOUNT TABOR, END OF 13TH CENTURY BC: From this mountain overlooking the Plain of Esdraelon, Israelite guerrillas have gained an unexpected victory over Sisera's supposedly invincible Canaanite chariot forces. Sisera has been killed and his chariots decimated.

The Israelites in the north have long resented what they considered Canaanite oppression. This revolt was instigated by the prophet and judge Deborah. She massed her forces on Mount Tabor, whose slopes are too steep for chariots to negotiate.

Terrified Horses

To quell the revolt, Sisera brought 900 chariots to Megiddo and tried to cross the marshy Plain of Esdraelon to Mount Tabor. A thunderstorm hit, causing the Kishon River to rise and cut off retreat. As the cloudburst continued, the chariots bogged down. Shouting and trumpeting, Israelite warriors swarmed down the mountain slopes, terrifying the horses. The frightened beasts reared and plunged, miring the chariots so deeply that the Canaanites had to abandon them and flee on foot.

With ease, Israelite archers cut them down.

Tent Stake: A Deadly Weapon

Sisera escaped on foot into the hills, seeking sanctuary in the tent of Jael, wife of a Kenite. When Sisera collapsed into a deep sleep, she hammered a tent stake through his temples into the ground. . . .

20th-Century Update: The Bible is inconsistent in describing this important battle—possibly the last the Israelites fought against the Canaanites. Although Hazor was supposedly destroyed and its king Jabin killed after the battle at the waters of Merom, the city and its king reappear in Deborah's War as powers again (Judg 4, 5). Various theories have been proposed to explain this inconsistency. One is that biblical authors confused the order of events and that Deborah's War took place before the battle at Merom—it would therefore date to the late 13th century. Another theory is that the biblical sequence of events is correct and Deborah's War took place in the mid- or late 12th century. In this case, the Bible would have erred in mentioning Hazor or Jabin as still existing. Perhaps after Jabin's death his general, Sisera, had reorganized the defeated armies of the area under some other king or kings. Still another theory is that the battle of Hazor and Deborah's War are the same battle described by two different authors, one from the north and one from the south.

MIDIANITES DRIVEN INTO DESERT
Gideon Leads Israelite Ambush

MOUNT TABOR, 12TH CENTURY BC: Midianite camel corps allied with Amalekites and other "children of the east" were driven from Canaan, across the Jordan River, and far into the desert by an astonishingly small force of Israelite guerrillas led by Gideon.

The battle took place in the Valley of Jezreel. The Midianites have been terrorizing the Israelites for years, raiding livestock and crops. Until this sudden rebellion the Israelites had been hiding in mountain caves and dens to avoid conflict.

Trumpets and Torches

Apparently because the Midianites are so expert with cross and bow, and so adept at maneuvering their swift camels, Gideon did not risk a frontal charge. Although he had 22,000 men, he dismissed all but 300 chosen warriors.

Gideon attacked at night, his men divided to advance on the Midianite camp from three different directions. The Israelites crept up silently, each carrying a trumpet in one hand and in the other a torch hidden in a pitcher. At a signal, the Israelites smashed their pitchers, blew their trumpets, and shouted.

Startled out of sleep, the Midianites went into a panic. In the dark they began to stab each other as they raced to mount their camels and flee. . . .

20th-Century Update: There is as yet little archaeological evidence to support the vivid biblical account of this battle (Judg 6–8). From corroborating details, some historians believe that it took place in the 12th century BC.

SHECHEM IN FLAMES
Kingdom of Abimelech Smashed

SHECHEM, 12TH CENTURY BC: This city is today in flames and its population massacred or on the run after an attempted rebellion against its king, Abimelech. Abimelech, who had ruled Shechem for three years, is dead.

Shechem, with a population of Israelites and Canaanites, has been divided on the question of rule by Abimelech. The king, whose mother was from Shechem, is the son of the Israelite Gideon. The rebellion was led by the Canaanite part of Shechem's population, who objected to paying tribute from their temple to an Israelite.

Felled by a Millstone

After dealing with Shechem, Abimelech left to quell the surrounding countryside, which was also in revolt. He was trying to set fire to the tower at the Thebez town gate when a woman dropped a piece of millstone on his head, breaking his skull. To avoid the stigma of being killed by a woman, Abimelech ordered his armor-bearer to run him through with a sword.

Destruction Predicted

The destruction by fire of Shechem had been predicted by Jotham, brother of Abimelech. Jotham had been the only brother to escape when Abimelech had hired mercenaries to assassinate his seventy brothers so that his own inheritance would be uncontested. During Abimelech's coronation, Jotham had shouted from a hilltop that Shechem would burn for accepting a murderer as king . . .

20th-Century Update: Shechem is Tell al-Balata, a mile east of modern Nablus (also called Shechem). A city existed at the time of the patriarchs; during the Hyksos period it had a great temple (under which the graves of babies have been discovered) and was fortified with double walls. The site shows signs of damage around 1550 BC, probably by Egyptians driving out the Hyksos. Shechem probably had a Semitic population before Moses led his people to Canaan, and is believed to have been incorporated by treaty as it suffered no damage during the conquest of Canaan. Ruins of the Canaanite temple (Baal-Berith) and other landmarks mentioned in the Bible (Judg 8:30—9:57) have been excavated. The city is believed to have been abandoned in the 12th century BC, and may have been burned.

BROTHER VS. BROTHER
Jordan River Divides the Tribes

GILEAD, END OF 12TH CENTURY BC: Jephthah and his Gileadite forces have been assaulted by fellow Israelites from Ephraim.

Jephthah's counterattack has pushed the Ephraimites back east across the Jordan River, and Gileadites have taken possession of the Jordan fords. Jephthah has given orders that any Ephraimites who try to cross the Jordan are to be killed.

Previously a Hero

Before this unexpected development, Jephthah had been a hero among the Israelites for defending Gilead from the Ammonites, who were attacking it. He had gone on to a successful campaign in which he took twenty Ammonite cities in the area of Mizpeh. Observers believe the Ephraimites were angered that they were not consulted about this campaign. They may also distrust Jephthah because he has been a freebooter and employs large numbers of mercenaries.

Daughter Sacrificed

Jephthah has suffered personal tragedy. Before his war with the Ammonites he had vowed that he would offer as a burnt sacrifice the first person who came out of his house to greet him on his victorious return. When the campaign was over, his young daughter came dancing out to meet him. Though grief-stricken, Jephthah had to sacrifice her. . . .

20th-Century Update: The Bible (Judg 11; 12:1–7, 13–16, 19–20) uses this story—as well as Samson's lone and often vain confrontations with Philistines—to demonstrate the divisiveness that afflicted the tribes of Israel after they began to settle Canaan. Although excavations in the area of Mizpeh have not been extensive enough to support this biblical account, they provide evidence that tribal disunity, turbulence, and encroachment of Israel's boundaries did indeed occur toward the end of the 12th century BC.

PHILISTINES DESTROY SHILOH
Ark at Ebenezer Captured

EBENEZER, C. 1050 BC: The Philistines, who had invaded the Judean hills and camped at Aphek, today inflicted a stunning defeat on the Israelites. Today's death toll at Ebenezer is estimated at 30,000 Israelites. Previously the Israelites had lost 4000 men at Ebenezer. The Ark, which was taken from Shiloh to the battlefield, is now in Philistine hands. Shiloh is ablaze.

Corruption Charged

Israelites attributed their first defeat at Ebenezer to the absence of the Ark. This second defeat is blamed on the fact that when the warriors called for the Ark it was brought by the two corrupt sons of Eli, the high priest. Both are among the casualties. Israelite warriors are said to have been so totally demoralized that they hid in their tents instead of fighting.

Bad News, Broken Neck

Eli, the high priest, is dead.

When messengers brought news of the death of his sons and the capture of the Ark, he is said to have toppled over and broken his neck....

20th-Century Update: Shiloh, which had been settled by the 18th century BC and fortified since the 12th century BC, became an important center for Israelite worship after Joshua erected a tabernacle here. The old city site is Tell Seilun (twenty miles north of Jerusalem). Excavation tends to support the biblical story (1 Sam 4; Jer 7:12) that Shiloh suffered damage and a fire. Archaeologists disagree about the exact location of Ebenezer.

SURPRISE ATTACK
Philistine Setback Considered Temporary

MIZPEH, C. 1030 BC: Philistines, hearing that the Israelites had been summoned to Mizpeh by the prophet Samuel, made a surprise attack while the Israelites were at worship. A violent thunderstorm frustrated the charge, so that the Philistines fled.

Israelites, concerned by Philistine inroads into their territory, are said to be planning attacks at Ekron, Gath, and other coastal Philistine cities. But many observers do not believe they can hold their land against the Philistines ...

20th-Century Update: Because extensive rebuilding in later times has disturbed biblical sites (1 Sam 7), archaeological material on Philistine cities is sparse and subject to controversy. The battle of Mizpeh, however, may have taken place about 1030 BC. There is evidence that other Philistine sites also suffered disturbances at this time, and that Israelite occupation of this part of Canaan did not begin until at least 1000 BC.

---

10 Truths about Princes

1. Princes eat in the morning (Eccl 10:16).
2. Princes are roaring lions (Zeph 3:3).
3. Merchants are princes (Isa 23:8).
4. Princes shall be nothing (Isa 34:12).
5. Princes shall be drunk (Jer 51:57).
6. Princes are hanged (Lam 5:12).
7. Princes are not trustworthy (Psa 146:3).
8. It is not good to strike princes (Prov 17:26).

9. Princes are like wolves ravening (Ezek 22:27).
10. Princes are made glad with lies (Hos 7:3).

A Soldier's Prayer

One of the shortest prayers is reported to have been said by a soldier before the Battle of Blenheim:

"O God, if there be a God,
Save my soul, if I have a soul!"

—FRANCIS ATTERBURY, BISHOP OF ROCHESTER, 1662–1732

Onward Hebrew Soldiers

When War Began: Wars were governed by the seasons. When Palestine got cold and wet in winter, moving troops was difficult, so military campaigns began as soon as good weather set in. It was so common to think of spring as the season of warfare that the Bible defines spring simply as "the time when kings go forth to battle" (2 Sam 11:1; 1 Chr 20:1).

All verified dates of Assyrian and Egyptian campaigns show they began in spring—April or later. Israelite shepherds could go to war after the spring lambing and shearing, but until a professional full-time army was formed, combat was a hardship on farmers, as it coincided with the vital cycle from seeding to harvest. For fishermen, summer was the best season for their profession, and during Deborah's War the seashore tribes of Asher and Dan failed to volunteer for combat.

An unfinished war that ran into winter was simply suspended until the following spring. As late as 142 BC the Seleucid army ran into trouble trying to reach Jerusalem in winter, and when a snowstorm hit, they had to retreat to the warmer Jordan Valley. Even in Herod's time the Roman army deserted him when he had hoped to take Jerusalem in the winter—the army simply withdrew to its camp on the balmier coast right in the middle of a siege.

How War Began: In biblical times there was no formality about declaring war. The usual way to start a war was just to march your army in and pitch camp someplace where you didn't belong. When the inhabitants sent someone to find out what you were doing there, you outlined your conditions for withdrawal. This method was usually used by a strong aggressor who was willing to face armed conflict. However, it was hoped a battle would never ensue, and that the whole thing would be settled by negotiation.

Another method, favored by the Hebrews in their conquest of Canaan, was to take a foreign army or city by surprise. This involved sneaking up on the enemy, and often conquering by tricks or stratagems. The Hebrews used this method because it was best suited for an aggressor outnumbered by the defending population. The idea here was also to avoid a battle, or to engage in a minimum of hand-to-hand fighting.

Usually no excuse was needed to start a war, because kings who set out on conquests believed their wars had been ordained by their gods. However, occasionally kings did offer an additional reason. When David attacked the Ammonites, he said that it was because his ambassadors had been insulted. Sargon II explained in his annals regarding his southern conquests that the king of Ethiopia was so impolite that his ancestors had never sent messengers to inquire about the health of Sargon's forefathers.

Negotiated War: Many wars never got as far as an armed battle, and were settled by negotiation. The aggressor sized up the natives and calculated what could be gotten out of them; while the defenders juggled the costs of battle against the tribute demands—and tried to bargain the demands down. If the demands were not too onerous the residents agreed to the terms and the aggressor withdrew.

Even powerful armies stalled and argued in hopes of conserving resources by not engaging in battle. When Sennacherib wanted to take Jerusalem he first sent envoys to convince the city that resistance against Assyrian forces would be useless. Inside the city the defenders argued the point. First King Hezekiah was told that he shouldn't pin his hopes on Egyptian aid. Then one of the envoys shouted in Hebrew to the warriors defending Jerusalem's walls that a siege would reduce them to eating their own dung and drinking their own urine. They could avoid all this misery by surrendering to live pleasantly in Assyria—a land of corn, wine, bread, olive oil, and honey—where each man would have his own vine, fig tree, and water cistern. Although this tempting picture of what deportation to Assyria would be like failed to convince the Hebrews, all this talk took so long that the Assyrians finally had to withdraw to settle other matters (2 Kings 18:17–35).

Negotiating peace terms was often leisurely and the bargaining drawn out. When Ben-hadad laid siege to Samaria (1 Kings 20), quite a few messages passed between him and King Ahab of Israel about the amount of tribute, which Ahab was at first willing to pay. When Ben-hadad saw how easily Ahab gave in, he raised the price of peace, and only at this point did Ahab fight.

Sometimes, before a price was asked, tribute was offered by a weak power that assumed it would lose any confrontation. This happened when Judah watched Tiglath-pileser's Assyrian army advance on Israel in 734–732 BC. Without waiting for the Assyrian army to reach Judah, the king sent Tiglath-pileser tribute and a message saying "I am thy servant." Whereas Israel was severely punished for trying to fight back, Judah endured much longer by submitting.

If peace conditions were onerous—as when the Ammonites demanded the right to pluck out the right eye of every inhabitant of Jabesh—then the attacked peoples would decide not to give in. Yet this did not mean a battle necessarily followed. The enemy invasion was already a *fait accompli,* and the besieged population often just sat tight, hoping dwindling supplies, the coming of winter, or simple boredom would make the enemy go away.

Guerrilla Warfare: Because the Israelites had inferior weapons, and their early conquests had them fighting out in the open against enemies in fortified cities, Canaan was conquered through guerrilla tactics. When Israelites tried to fight pitched battles—as against the Philistines at Ebenezer and Saul's last battle at Gilboa—they usually lost (1 Sam 4:1–11; 31:1–7).

The first stage of a successful campaign would be an intelligence operation. Even Moses had sent spies into Canaan, and when the conquest began in earnest Joshua did the same. The job of spies was not merely to obtain information about vulnerable spots in a city's defenses, but also to try to convince some of the natives to become traitors. At Jericho, for example, Rahab befriended the spies and betrayed her city (Josh 2).

Spying, which continued to be characteristic of Israelite warfare, enabled the Israelites to launch surprise attacks. Bethel was taken when a friendly resident showed spies a secret entrance (Judg 1:23–25) and Jerusalem was taken through tunnels that ran from its spring to within the city walls—in both cases armed Israelites unexpectedly appeared among unprepared natives. Saul's first victory was a surprise attack before dawn.

Another feature of Israelite strategy was trickery. This practice began right after Jericho, when Joshua took Ai by having a small force pretend to attack the city and flee. This drew the warriors away from Ai in pursuit, and Joshua's main force simply walked in the open city gates. A similar ruse was used at Gibeah (Judg 20:29–43). A different sort of stratagem was Deborah's enticing of chariot forces to boggy ground.

While Israel's enemies depended on numbers, the secret of Hebrew guerrilla warfare was to hold the full army force in reserve for mopping-up or pursuit and to rely for the main operation on a small band of especially skilled and brave warriors. This had begun during the wandering in the desert, when the Amalekites attacked and Moses ordered Joshua to handpick a few men to defend all the people (Exod 17:9). Saul also, setting out to fight Philistines, used only 600 of the thousands of men who volunteered (1 Sam 13:2) and Gideon used only 300 of his 32,000 men (Judg 6). This policy of discarding halfhearted warriors meant the chosen were eager to prove themselves, and they were few enough to be used in stealth and easy to supervise.

Siege Warfare: If it was impossible to take a city by surprise, and peace negotiations failed, a siege was laid. The enemy settled its troops in tents outside the city walls. They blocked access roads and, if possible, took over the water supply. Often the enemy simply sat there, waiting for the city inhabitants to suffer enough thirst, hunger, or disease to surrender. Sometimes the attackers tried to demoralize the city population by haranguing them or shooting arrows at guards posted on the walls, and sometimes the city defenders tried to drive the enemy off. But sieges often went on for weeks or months with no action at all.

A critical factor for a besieged city was the water supply, since thirst became unbearable long before hunger did. Most ancient cities were built on natural hills on the rubble of preceding towns, and the springs were usually outside the city walls at the bottom of the hill, where the enemy could immediately take them over. Although almost all towns used cisterns to collect rainwater, there was little rainfall in the summer, when most wars were fought, and this standing water became foul. In Samaria, where archaeologists have thus far found only cisterns, the population managed to hold out against the Assyrians for two years (723–721 BC), but usually a town with such a limited water supply could not survive for long. At the battle of Bethulia, where the enemy occupied the springs outside the city, the cisterns went dry even though water was rationed; by the thirty-fourth day of siege even the young men were fainting from thirst in the streets (Judith 7:20–22).

Most lasting and powerful cities incorporated a water supply inside the fortifications by digging wells or cutting tunnels to springs. Gezer had a year-round water supply from springs and wells within its walls; one underground spring was reached through a 219-foot tunnel cut through solid rock. Hazor's water system extended 140 feet, and Megiddo's had a 75-foot shaft that led to a 210-foot tunnel. Jerusalem had a water tunnel reaching outside the city gates, which was undoubtedly one reason the early Israelites couldn't conquer the city, and the system was continually improved. Hezekiah, expecting an Assyrian siege, spent more than eight months building an elaborate tunnel to the spring at Gihon. Although Jerusalem suffered famine when besieged by Nebuchadnezzar, it did not suffer thirst, and held out a year and a half (2 Kings 25:1–3).

The army besieging the city also had problems because they seldom had a source of supplies and had to hold out on what stores they had brought with them plus what they could get from the land. Communicable diseases plagued the camps—as might have happened when the forces of Sennacherib besieging Jerusalem were suddenly found dead one morning. Bad weather or other factors could also demoralize the troops. Sieges could become boring too. At Samaria the powerful Assyrian army had taken to drink, and one morning they were all so drunk they couldn't get themselves together when the city population suddenly rushed out at them (1 Kings 20:16–20).

To avoid these problems and end the siege sooner, the enemy sometimes attacked. A simple early way of trying to breach a fortified city was to set fire to the gate—although when Abimelech tried this at Thebez a woman dropped a millstone on his head and broke his skull (Judg 9:52–53). Tomb reliefs show Egyptian troops setting ladders against city walls in an attempt to get warriors into the inner city, but this often resulted in heavy casualties. By the time of David the battering ram became a popular way of breaking down city walls with fewer casualties. Because fortified cities were usually built on mounds, a ramp of earth had to be constructed to bring the ram up to the height of the walls (2 Sam 20:15; 2 Kings 19:32; Jer 6:6). The Assyrians were especially adept at this. Sennacherib's annals also mention troops digging tunnels under city walls, and Assyrian illustrations show soldiers busily circling cities with mounds on which shelters were erected so that slingers and bowmen could shoot from heights equal to the defenders on the city's fortifications.

Once the ramps were constructed, the Assyrians brought up "machines"—shelters on wheels that could be drawn up the ramps to the city walls, protecting archers and the men operating battering rams (Ezek 4:2; 26:8–9). The Bible mentions shelters made by King Uzziah of Judah to protect archers and men throwing stones (2 Chr 26:15), but these were stationary structures on the city walls to protect defenders. The Hebrews probably did not acquire movable offensive machines until Greek times.

The Assyrian machines were frightening because there was not much defense against them. Warriors within the city could only try to ruin them by throwing rocks or to set them on fire by flinging torches. One Assyrian illustration shows city defenders trying to immobilize a battering ram by catching it with grappling hooks. Even though the men operating the machines were subject to arrows, rocks, and flaming torches, the main body of Assyrian troops could remain safely in the background, out of the line of fire. Once the advance troops broke a hole in the walls, the rested main force would rush in against the exhausted city defenders.

The Prophet Who Captured an Army

When the Syrians (Arameans) besieged Samaria, Elisha prayed to God to blind the besieging troops. God obliged, and the Syrians were so helpless that Elisha was able to lead them all by himself into the city.

81

There the blindness suddenly left the Syrians, and they found themselves surrounded by the people of Samaria. The king of Israel was so excited he asked Elisha eagerly, "Shall I smite them? Shall I smite them?"

But Elisha thought the Syrians had learned their lesson (he turned out to be wrong) and commanded they be set free (2 Kings 6:14-24).

How War Ended: Usually at the end of a war a peace treaty was drawn up—or, since many battles were between the same peoples over the same territory, an old treaty was renewed. The terms generally made the vanquished people vassals, having to pay tribute at the very least, and often having to provide forced labor.

In the early days the Mesopotamians sometimes left the native ruler on his throne. Or, if the king had been killed, the local population was allowed to replace him according to their own rules for succession. But this policy often led to later rebellion. The Assyrians improved on this system by deposing the native ruler and replacing him with an Assyrian governor who would remain permanently loyal to the conqueror.

Later the Assyrians elaborated this policy further by deporting not just the king but all people of wealth and influence (those most likely to cause trouble) to some far part of their empire. To replace them the conquered territory might get a new upper class drawn from people the Assyrians had vanquished elsewhere.

The end of a victorious war among the Israelites was celebrated with communal singing and dancing, in addition to thanksgiving (Ex 15:1; Judg 5:1; Sam 18:6-7; 2 Sam 22). Especially good spoils, such as the weapons of Goliath, might be put on display (1 Sam 21:9). Occasionally the Israelites erected a stone or pile of stones as a memorial, similar to those Joshua had left after crossing the Jordan (Joshua 4:5-9; 1 Sam 7:12).

Some of Israel's enemies had even more elaborate ceremonies and memorials. Foreign conquerors—especially the Egyptians—were fond of erecting stelae praising themselves and describing their exploits. And in both Egypt and Mesopotamia reliefs and paintings of battles were created, such as those in the temples of Karnak and Nineveh.

For the defeated, the end of a war meant that their city would be ransacked for anything of value and then burned. Occasionally only the fortifications were dismantled (2 Kings 14:33), but more usual was utter destruction of the entire city. This was done even when the conquerors intended to occupy the site. In conquering Canaan, the Israelites burned almost all the towns they vanquished, beginning with Jericho, yet later they restored fortifications on many of these same sites and rebuilt the cities for their own use. Sargon II (721-705 BC) destroyed Samaria and then proudly boasted that he rebuilt it better than it had been before.

In addition to booty, captives would be taken, varying numbers of the population killed, and tribute imposed.

How long a peace treaty remained in effect usually depended on when the vanquished felt they could safely stop paying the stipulated tribute. As subject people rebuilt their cities and their lives, they eagerly watched for any signs of weakness in the oppressor—such as a military defeat, internal strife, or evidence the oppressor was wearing itself thin over too large a territory—and then withheld tribute the next time it was due. Refusing to pay tribute was in itself a sign of revolt. Sometimes the subject people guessed right, and nothing happened. When Mesha of Moab revolted, Israel and Judah tried to send armies against Moab with little effect. Sometimes the subject people guessed wrong and the oppressor returned with an armed force; Judah was finally destroyed when King Zedekiah mistakenly thought it was safe to rebel against Babylonia.

Tribute: Tribute could be in whatever form of wealth the conquered people possessed. Mesha of Moab, who rebelled in 855 BC, complained bitterly on his stela of the tribute he had to pay Israel; the Bible explains that he was assessed 100,000 lambs and 100,000 rams, with the wool, because he was principally a sheepmaster (2 Kings 3:4). From Ammon, King Jotham of Judah (758–733 BC) annually collected 100 talents of silver, 10,000 measures of wheat, and 10,000 measures of barley (2 Chr 27:5).

Precious metals were usually preferred as tribute. The Bible says that Judah had to pay Assyria 300 talents of silver and 30 talents of gold under King Hezekiah (727-698 BC), but apparently Sennacherib did not consider this sufficient because his records show that Hezekiah also sent him gems, couches and chairs inlaid with ivory, ebony and boxwood, and concubines and musicians. Later, when Judah was less well off under King Jehoahaz (609 BC), Egypt demanded only 100 talents of silver and one talent of gold (2 Kings 18:14; 23:33).

Tribute also depended on what the conqueror needed. The Assyrian king Esarhaddon (680-669 BC), who collected tribute from twenty-two kings that included those of Tyre, Gaza, Edom, Ashkelon, Ekron, Byblos, and Ashdod, as well as King Manasseh of Judah, made them bring timber and quarry stones. Esarhaddon boasted that bringing such heavy tribute all the way to Nineveh was very difficult for these kings, especially since he demanded that the timber be big logs and long beams from trees that were old and had grown tall and strong.

Booty: In addition to any tribute they were forced to pay, a defeated people suffered pillage because it was customary for victorious troops to carry off whatever treasures they could find on the scene at the time the battle ended. Obviously, smart people often hid their private possessions before this could happen, but temple treasures that were public knowledge, livestock, and other things that were hard to hide were all confiscated.

Booty served two purposes—it punished rebellious people by reducing them to poverty and making insurrection unlikely, and it was a form of payment to fighting men, spurring them to victory. When David worked as a mercenary for the Philistines, he would take as pay the sheep, oxen, asses, and camels as well as the personal attire of people he defeated (1 Sam 27:9). Ezekiel (29:19) said God promised Nebuchadnezzar all the spoils of Egypt as wages for his army.

The custom of looting extended from Abraham's time (when the kings of the north carried off captives and treasures) to the end of biblical history.

In addition to getting booty from cities, armies overran the abandoned camps of defeated enemies. When the Assyrians were besieging Samaria and suddenly fled in panic because they thought they heard the noise of chariots in the night—and assumed Israel had hired Hittites and Egyptians to attack them—they ran so fast they left their camp intact. The people of Samaria came out and stripped it, taking everything from tents and livestock to food (2 Kings 7:7, 8, 15–16). In the 850 BC war against Moab, Israel and Judah won a victory because the Moabites were misled into thinking the enemy had fled. Moabite warriors were so eager to loot the camp that they apparently abandoned their weapons to be able to carry spoils, and were slaughtered when they found the camp fully occupied and ready for battle (2 Kings 3:23–24).

It was also customary to strip dead warriors of their arms (1 Sam 31:8), an important source of weapons for the Israelites, whose technology was not as advanced as that of many of their enemies. Even in Maccabean times the Jews had so few weapons that when Judas killed the Greek commander he took his sword to use thereafter (1 Macc 3:12).

Plundering was one of the great rewards of victory. The psalmist (Psa 119:162) even compared its joy to that of knowing God: "I rejoice at thy word, as one that findeth great spoil." People grabbed as much as they could carry. If they were able to store their booty, they returned again and again to loot. After one battle in the time of Jehoshaphat the people found so much wealth left by Ammonites and Moabites that it took them three days to strip the bodies and the camps, and since plunder came first they did not give thanksgiving until the fourth day after the battle (2 Chr 20:25).

On the other hand, there was danger that an army would be so distracted by booty that it would fail to complete its job. Saul had that problem when he routed the Philistines at Michmash and wanted to pursue them. He ordered his army not to stop for spoils, not even food; the army became resentful and finally so hungry that they slaughtered and ate sheep and oxen, a violation of the dietary laws (1 Sam 14:22–23). During the Maccabean wars, Judas had to warn his men not to risk defeat by being greedy and trying to take spoils too soon and urged them to delay plunder until victory was assured (1 Macc 4:17–18). After the conquest of Jerusalem, Herod feared that the population of Jerusalem would turn against him because the looting by the Roman army was so unrestrained; when the army refused to listen to his pleas, he had to pay them off to make them stop.

At first the custom among the Israelites was for everyone to help in collecting communal spoils and then to divide them up later (Judg 5:30). This sometimes led to argument, with some people demanding more than others thought they were entitled to (Prov 16:19). Moses said that half the spoils should go to the warriors and the other half should go to the priests and to support the tabernacle (Num 31:26-54). The people kept the livestock, while gold and other metals were given to the priests. Once a professional army began to evolve, new arguments arose. David stipulated that warriors should share the spoils with those who supplied the army (1 Sam 30:22-25).

Military leaders also shared in the spoils. After defeating the Midianites, Gideon asked for their golden earrings, which had a total weight of 1700 shekels of gold. The people not only gave him these, but voluntarily added the gold jewelry and purple clothing of the Midianite kings, and ornaments that had been hung on the camels (Judg 8:24-26). Before he was king, David was satisfied with taking just the livestock (1 Sam 30:20), but as the monarchy became more organized and costly to maintain, the gold and other more valuable parts of the spoils began to go automatically to him as king (2 Sam 8:2-11; 12:30).

Booty was such a source of pride that Sennacherib is pictured as sitting grandly on his throne as the spoils of Lachish are paraded before him. Kings in biblical times liked to leave for posterity itemized lists of what they got. The records of Tuthmosis III (1504-1450 BC) show that in his conquests at Megiddo and the Lake Huleh area of Palestine he collected not only the expected cache of weapons, precious metals, and livestock, but also seventeen knives, three walking sticks with human heads, six chairs and footstools, a decorated bed, kettles, jars, plates, and bowls. Tiglath-pileser III (745-727 BC) recorded his capture of wool that had been dyed the rare royal purple obtained only from shellfish on the coast of Palestine, and of mules trained to the yoke.

Death Tolls

1. The Israelites killed 25,000 Benjamites after they refused to surrender the Gibeans. The Gibeans had slaughtered a concubine and her master had called the other tribes together by sending parts of her body to the leaders (Judg 20).

2. Judah and the Israelite forces defeated and killed 10,000 Canaanites and Perizzites (Judg 1:40).

3. At the order of Moses, 3000 Israelites were slaughtered by the Levites. This was punishment for participation in the building of the golden calf (Ex 32).

4. In retribution for following Korach and his rebellion in the wilderness against the leadership of Moses, 250 people were swallowed by the earth (Num 16:35).

5. Another 14,700 Israelites died of a plague for rebelling against Moses in the wilderness (Num 16:49).

6. The Bible says 24,000 more Israelites died of a plague while they were encamped at Shittim because they had committed "whoredom with the daughters of Moab" (Num 25:1-9).

7. Ten thousand Edomite prisoners were thrown off the top of a cliff so that "they all were broken in pieces." Amaziah and the children of Judah had killed another 10,000 Edomites during the battle itself (2 Chr 25:11-12).

8. Samson's suicidal victory, destroying the Philistine temple, killed 3000 Philistines with falling debris. The Bible reports that perhaps another 3000, who had been on the roof during the ceremonies, also died (Judg 16:23, 29-30).

9. Because they could not pronounce the word "Shibboleth" as the Gileadites pronounced it, 42,000 Ephraimites were murdered. The Ephraimites were attempting to cross the Jordan River to escape. The men of Gilead caught them and made them say the word as a test of their origins. Because of a small difference in dialect, they could not pronounce it, bringing about their death (Judg 12:5-6).

10. A pestilence sent by God, angered by David's census of the people, killed 70,000 people within the boundaries of Dan and Beersheba (2 Sam 24:15).

11. The Lord killed 50,070 people of Beth-shemesh because they had looked into the Ark (1 Sam 6:19).

12. David slew 22,000 Syrians (Arameans) and another 40,000 Syrian horsemen (2 Sam 8:5; 10:18).

The Losers

Vanquished people were not treated very nicely in biblical times. In addition to warriors killed in combat, wars resulted in many civilian casualties during the looting and burning of cities. Entire populations were massacred. One pit excavated at Lachish, possibly from Nebuchadnezzar's 6th-century-BC campaigns, contained remains of some 2000 people. Some of the bones were charred.

The number of dead was a source of pride. Egyptian warriors, who were paid for each person killed, cut a hand off each corpse as proof of casualties. David took back to Saul a hundred foreskins as evidence he had killed a hundred Philistines. Assyrian warriors preferred to bring in enemy heads; these were recorded by scribes and then piled in putrid heaps or impaled on spikes for display.

Utterly Destroy Them: Under Mosaic law (Deut 7, 20) vanquished people were to be treated differently depending on whether they lived within the borders of the promised land or outside it:

Milder laws applied to enemies outside the promised land. They had to be given a chance to surrender. If they did so, they could be subjected to tribute or forced labor but could not be killed or otherwise punished. If they offered armed resistance, the warriors could be killed and the rest of the population enslaved, and spoils could be taken.

Harsher laws applied to Canaanites, Amorites, Hittites, and others in the promised land who posed an immediate threat to the Israelites. They were not to be given a chance to surrender and "thou shalt save alive nothing that breatheth: But thou shalt utterly destroy them."

Before entering Canaan, therefore, the Israelites recorded, "we took all his cities at that time, and utterly destroyed the men, and the women, and the little ones. . . . Only the cattle we took" (Deut 2:34–35; 3:6–7). But in Canaan, at Jericho; "they utterly destroyed all that was in the city, both man and woman, young and old, and ox, and sheep, and ass" (Josh 6:21).

In practice, these rules were hard to live by, and there was some confusion in interpretation. When the Israelites under Moses were victorious over the Midianites, they killed the men but took the women and children captive and kept the livestock as spoils. This angered Moses, who insisted that male children and women who were not virgins also had to be killed (Num 31:7–8). When Joshua began the conquest of Canaan at Jericho, the livestock was slaughtered, but by the second battle at Ai, and in succeeding battles at cities such as Hazor, the livestock was being taken alive (Josh 8:2, 27; 11:14). Obviously it was impractical for tired warriors to chase down every last sheep, and so animals began to be excluded from everything "that breatheth."

The prophet Samuel was a stickler for the old rules and condemned Saul for sparing the Amalekite king and livestock (1 Sam 15). But by the time of David the rules were relaxed again. When David fought Amalekites and others, he kept the livestock as spoil (1 Sam 27:8–9; 30:17–20). Moreover, beginning with his conquest of Jerusalem, all talk of annihilating native populations ceased—it was clear that David found it useful to keep vanquished people alive, as they were a source of slave labor and tribute (2 Sam 7–8).

By the time of the divided kingdoms, when Israel was suffering many defeats, in their few victories there was no longer any pretense of killing enemy populations. In fact, enemies now expected to be spared, saying, "We have heard that the kings of the house of Israel are merciful kings," and it was assumed live captives would be taken (1 Kings 20:31; 2 Kings 6:22).

Punish Their Kings: The enemy king came in for special abuse. Since the king was usually considered to be warring under the protection of the local god or gods, his death was taken as a sign that the troops had been deserted by their divinity. The death of the king in battle therefore frequently caused his troops to panic and flee. If the king survived the battle, he was usually killed by the victors because it was easier to control a conquered population if it was leaderless. Under Moses, five kings of Midian were among foreign leaders slain (Num 31:8), and the Bible claims Joshua killed a total of thirty-one kings (Josh 12:24).

The Bible even cites instances of disaster for *not* killing the king. When Saul spared the life of Agag, king of the Amalekites, Samuel declared him unfit for kingship. As an example of how things should be done, Samuel himself hacked Agag to pieces (1 Sam 15:8–33). Ahab of Israel not only declined to kill Ben-hadad, king of Syria, who had attacked Samaria, but declared, "He is my brother"! As a result, Ben-hadad lived to attack Samaria again, laying a cruel siege, and far from showing mercy on Ahab ordered his men to single him out and kill him (1 Kings 20:32; 22; 2 Kings 6:24; 13:3).

Often mere killing was not considered enough for a king—he also had to be humiliated or mutilated. Under Joshua, five Midianite kings were trampled before being hanged on trees (Josh 10:24–26) and Adoni-bezek had his thumbs and big toes cut off (Judg 1:6). However, the Israelites were mild compared to their neighbors. Adoni-bezek thought his punishment only just, since he himself had chopped the thumbs and big toes off seventy kings (Judg 1:7). Saul was so afraid of what the Philistines would do to him that he committed suicide to avoid falling into their hands. Frustrated, the Philistines chopped the head off the body and hung the corpse from the walls of Beth-shean.

Humiliation seemed to give most satisfaction to Tuthmosis III, because this pharaoh proudly recorded that when he had conquered Megiddo the princes groveled on their bellies before him, kissing the ground and begging for their lives.

The Assyrians were most cruel, making enemy kings part of the grand shows they liked to put on after victories. They enjoyed having foreign kings and nobles brought to them in chains or in cages so that they could make a public spectacle of torturing them, blinding them, and sometimes burning them alive. When Nebuchadnezzar defeated the last king of Judah, Zedekiah, he had Zedekiah watch the murder of his two sons and then blinded him. Zedekiah was then taken in chains to Babylon and left to die in prison (2 Kings 25:7; Jer 39:5–7; 52.9–11).

Ravish Their Women: When the women were not killed they were frequently raped (Isa 13:16; Lam 5:11). It was common for foreign warriors to be given women as slaves as part of their pay. Such captives could be kept as servants in the warrior's home or could be sold to the slave traders that followed victorious troops. Had Sisera's army triumphed, one or two women would have been doled out to each warrior (Judg 5:30). Job (4:3) speaks of lots being drawn for Israelite captives, and of women bartered for wine and boys for harlots.

Israelite warriors also took women captives. Moses ordered all the Midianites slaughtered except for the virgins, who were parceled out to his fighting men (Num 31:15–18). In the attack on Jabesh-gilead, the inhabitants were annihilated except for 400 virgins saved as wives for the Benjamites (Judg 21). Although Hebrews could also keep captives as servants or concubines or sell them on the slave market, the Law made provision for female slaves to be freed if the soldiers wanted to marry them (Deut 21:10–14).

Pregnant women came in for special cruelty. Elisha wept because he knew Ben-hadad of Syria would kill the Israelite men with swords "and rip up their women with child" (2 Kings 8:12). This was also done to the women of Gilead by the Ammonites (Amos 1:13). But it was not simply a foreign custom, because when King Menahem of Israel attacked Tiphsah in Mesopotamia he killed the men "and all the women therein that were with child he ripped up" (2 Kings 15:16).

Dash the Children: "Their eye," said Isaiah, speaking of enemies (Isa 13:18), "shall not spare children." Children were apparently not worth ruining swords on, and were bludgeoned to death or thrown from heights: "Their infants shall be dashed in pieces" (Hos 13:16); "her young children also were dashed in pieces at the top of all the streets" (Nah 3:10); "taketh and dasheth thy little ones against the stones" (Psa 137:9). Once a mother was said to have been "dashed in pieces upon her children" (Hos 10:14).

Children were sometimes spared for slavery. Tuthmosis III (1504–1450 BC) recorded 84 children among the 2503 captives he obtained in Palestine. A thousand years later, when Jerusalem fell, children were still a good catch for conquering armies. The young men of Jerusalem deported to Babylon had to carry millstones, while the small boys transported timber: "The young men have borne the mill, and the children have stumbled under the wood" (Lam 5:12).

---

20 Biblical Fears

1. After seeing the way Sodom and Gomorrah were destroyed, Lot was too terrified to stay on the plains and fled to the mountains (Gen 19:30).

2. Rebekah was so beautiful that Isaac was afraid he'd be killed if he let the Philistines know she was his wife, so he pretended she was his sister (Gen 26:7).

3. After Moses murdered an Egyptian, he feared his crime would be discovered (Ex 2:11–14).

4. Gideon was afraid to fight in daylight (Judg 6:27).

5. A poor man who owned only one talent was so afraid of losing it that he buried it instead of using it (Matt 25:25).

6. The children of Israel were frightened of Moses because "his face shone" (Ex 34:30).

7. Job was afraid of all his sorrows (Job 9:28).

8. Elihu was apprehensive about voicing his opinions before people older than he (Job 32:6).

9. The king of Israel, Ish-bosheth, was scared of his own general Abner (2 Sam 3:11).

10. Some Persians were so afraid of Jews that they adopted Judaism (Est 8:17; 9:2).

11. Adam was alarmed by God's voice and afraid of being caught naked (Gen 3:10). Fear of God is the most common fear in the Bible.

12. Moses feared seeing God's face: "And Moses hid his face; for he was afraid to look upon God" (Ex 3:6).

13. Many people became alarmed when they witnessed or heard about miracles (Mark 5:15; Luke 1:65; 7:16; 8:25, 35; Acts 2:43; 22:9). Peter was not afraid to walk on the sea until his faith faltered when the wind began to whip up the water (Matt 14:28–31).

14. Many people dreaded angels. Onan was so afraid of an angel that he sold David his threshing floor (1 Chr 21:18–23). Daniel and the shepherds were among others who trembled at visitations by angels (Dan 8:17; Luke 2:9).

15. After the prophet Urijah had painted a gloomy picture of the future for King Jehoiakim, he was so terrified the king would kill him that he fled to Egypt (Jer 26:20–21).

16. Jether, son of Gideon, was afraid to obey his father's command to murder two enemies (Judg 8:20).

17. People in power frequently feared the voice of the people. Saul let his subjects intimidate him (1 Sam 15:24). Herod was so nervous about public opinion that for a long time he dared not execute John the Baptist (Matt 14:5; Mark 6:20). Pontius Pilate continually tried to placate the Jews (John 19:8). Even the chief priests feared the reaction of the multitude in regard to Jesus (Matt 21:46; Mark 11:18; Luke 20:19; 22:2). Roman soldiers were afraid of mobs too (Acts 5:26).

18. On the other hand, people in power were generally feared. The Israelites feared Moses, Joshua, Samuel, and other leaders (Josh 4:14; 1 Sam 12:18). Persian officials were afraid of Mordecai (Est 9:3). Even Jesus was occasionally so intimidating that the disciples refrained from questioning him (Mark 9:32; Luke 9:45).

19. Because Paul had persecuted Christians, the disciples at first distrusted him after his conversion (Acts 9:26).

20. "All people, nations, and languages, trembled and feared" before the king of Babylon (Dan 5:19).

Three

I Looked over Jordan and What Did I See?

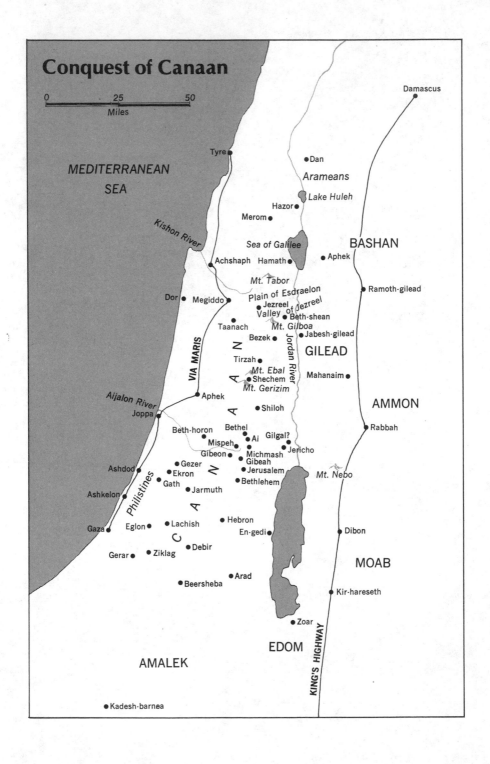

Conquest of Canaan

0   25   50
Miles

MEDITERRANEAN
SEA

Tyre

Dan

Arameans

Lake Huleh

Hazor
Merom

Sea of Galilee

BASHAN

Aphek

Kishon River

Achshaph Hamath

Mt. Tabor

Plain of Esdraelon

Ramoth-gilead

Dor   Megiddo

Jezreel   of Jezreel
Valley   Beth-shean

Mt. Gilboa
Taanach   Jabesh-gilead

Bezek   GILEAD

Jordan River

Tirzah

Mt. Ebal
Shechem   Mahanaim
Mt. Gerizim

VIA MARIS

Aijalon River

Aphek

Shiloh   AMMON

Joppa

Beth-horon   Bethel
Mispeh   Ai   Gilgal?
Gibeon   Rabbah
Michmash
Gezer   Gibeah
Ekron   Jerusalem   Mt. Nebo
Gath   Jarmuth
Bethlehem

Ashdod

Ashkelon

Philistines

Hebron

Gaza   Eglon   Lachish   En-gedi   Dibon

Debir

Gerar   Ziklag

Arad   MOAB

Beersheba

Kir-hareseth

Zoar

KING'S HIGHWAY

EDOM

AMALEK

Kadesh-barnea

Damascus

Land of Sand and Thorns

"I pity the man who can travel from Dan to Beersheba, and cry, 'Tis all barren,' " wrote Laurence Sterne *(A Sentimental Journey).* Indeed, the landscape of biblical Palestine ranged from coniferous forests to snow-covered peaks to salt deserts.

But a more narrow yet vivid picture is given by Mark Twain, who included the Holy Land in *The Innocents Abroad,* a memoir of his travels in 1867–1868: "Of all lands there are for dismal scenery, I think Palestine must be the prince."

Twain pointed out that our expectations of the Holy Land are colored by our Bible reading, which tells us how the ancient Israelites felt about it, and by our own veneration of and affection for events that took place on the landscape. While Twain acknowledged that "small shreds and patches of it must be very beautiful in the full flush of spring"—a season he did not see—he wrote that it was basically a "monotonous and uninviting" country. The Israelites saw it as a land of milk and honey only because they had been living in desert for forty years: "Their enthusiasm was at least warranted by the fact that they had never seen a country as good as this."

Mark Twain also noted that our images of the Holy Land are frequently distortions based on steel engravings, glossy colored illustrations in Bibles, or museum oil paintings. His own trip was on horseback, so that he had the opportunity to see what such pictures leave out—the dirt and fleas, the raw spots on the backs of donkeys, the flies on the sore eyes of children—all a part of what life must really have been like in biblical times.

What first impresses most visitors to the Holy Land—and Twain was no exception—is its small size. Again the Bible has colored our perceptions, because the land was a universe to the ancient Israelites. The entire area was only about 150 miles long and 80 miles wide, and would have been inconsequential if it had not been strategically situated on the main roads between Mesopotamia and Egypt. Yet in biblical days, if one traveled fast on asses, it took a good week to get from Dan to Beersheba, and an army with chariots needed at least two weeks. Anyone traveling such distances could have encountered 100° F. temperatures in the Negev, as well as snow in mountains that rise almost 4000 feet above sea level in Galilee. The land therefore seemed more formidable to the Israelites than it does today. Jesus never knew more of it than the hundred-odd miles between the Sea of Galilee and Jerusalem, and the expression "a far country" could refer to a place anywhere from 40 miles away across the Jordan to 300 miles away on the Euphrates.

The Coast—The Burden of Tyre

Stretching from the Brook of Egypt northward to Mount Carmel, the Mediterranean coast was the last area conquered by the Israelites. It consists of plains—the Plain of Philistia (north of Gaza), which the Philistines controlled, and the Plain of Sharon (north of Joppa), which David finally took from the Canaanites. In ancient times these plains were crisscrossed by sluggish rivers and swamps. Because the swamps bred disease and inhibited travel, they were drained—few remained by the time of Jesus.

Ancient sea trading bypassed Israel because the coast had no natural harbors. Only small boats could land, and larger ships had to berth south in Egypt or north at Tyre. At Tyre the coast turns mountainous, and has good ports that were developed by the Phoenicians. "The coast turneth . . . to the strong city of Tyre" (Josh 19:29) expressed how vital this link to the Mediterranean was to the Israelites. David and Solomon were careful to maintain good relations with King Hiram of Tyre, and later it was diplomacy that prompted Omri to marry his son Ahab to the Phoenician Jezebel. "The burden of Tyre" is how Isaiah referred to this constant thorn in Israel's side (Isa 23:1).

Herod tried to free Israel from dependence on northern ports by constructing an artificial harbor at the Plain of Sharon. He called it Caesarea, and it remained capital of the Roman province of Judea for about 600 years.

The Mountains—The Everlasting Hills

East of the coastal plain rise the mountains. Mark Twain called them "hills" and said they were barren, dull of color, and unpicturesque. The valleys, he said, were "unsightly deserts" fringed with feeble and despondent vegetation.

These highlands were the first part of Canaan conquered by Joshua, and they remained most consistently in Israelite hands even when other parts of the promised land were being chipped away by neighbors. From the high ranges of Lebanon the highlands run south like a backbone through Palestine to the hills and mesas of the Sinai wilderness.

Galilee: The highest point in Israel is Mount Meron (3692 feet), northwest of the Sea of Galilee, in the area called Galilee. The city of Dan in Galilee was traditionally spoken of as the northern boundary of the promised land (Judg 20:1; 1 Sam 3:20; 2 Sam 3:10; 17:11; 24:2; 24:15; 1 Kings 4:25; 1 Chr 21:2; 2 Chr 30:5). When the kingdoms were divided, King Jeroboam of Israel declared Dan a royal city and built one of his infamous shrines with a golden calf there. But Dan—in fact, all of Galilee—was hard to hold.

The plateau country of Galilee, which has elevations of between 1500 and 3000 feet above sea level, was heavily forested and sheltered the trade route that connected the Via Maris (coastal road) to Damascus. This route cut across Galilee via Megiddo and Hazor, which is why these cities were frequent battlegrounds. Megiddo was also on a route that cut through Galilee from Tyre to Jerusalem. Because it was a crossroads, Galilee was always subject to more pressure and influence from outside forces than were other areas of the promised land. As the old Kingdom of Israel disintegrated, it was the first major area to be permanently lost. Galilee comes into prominence in the New Testament because Jesus was born and preached there.

Galilee is separated from southern Israel by a wide valley that is a vital mountain pass. The valley extends inland from the Mediterranean (at Mount Carmel) along the Kishon River to the Plain of Esdraelon, and continues along the Valley of Jezreel to the Jordan River. This was one of the most bitterly contested areas—Deborah fought her war from Mount Tabor, which rises north of the valley, and Saul was killed at Mount Gilboa south of the valley. The kings of Israel kept a palace at the town of Jezreel, which is where Jezebel was killed. Some of the most important fortified towns of biblical times—Megiddo, Taanach, and Beth-shean—were built to guard this valley.

Mark Twain saw Galilee as "interminable hills and rocks," where he was sure the browsing goats and sheep were eating gravel because there was so little vegetation. But he was impressed by Mount Tabor. He found it green and grand compared to the "repulsive monotony" elsewhere, and wrote: "The view presented from its highest peak was almost beautiful."

As for the towns of Galilee, Twain called them dreary, melancholy, and stupid, and was astounded to find that some towns elsewhere in the Holy Land were even worse. However, he rather liked the oleanders at Capernaum: "If one is calm and resolute, he can look upon their comeliness and live."

97

Samaria: South of Galilee is Samaria, a fertile region of hills and valleys watered by numerous creeks. It was once forested, but was denuded in biblical times. Some scholars believe Samaria was settled by Hebrews before Joshua's conquest of Canaan, and that Shechem—on the main road linking Jerusalem to the north, and guarding the pass between Mount Ebal and Mount Gerezim—was one of their centers. Abraham built an altar at Shechem and Jacob bought land there (Gen 12:6-7; 33:18-19). The city remained so important that Rehoboam chose it for his coronation when he was hoping to keep the kingdom together (1 Kings 12:1).

Also in Samaria is Shiloh, the major religious center immediately after the conquest of Canaan (and until Jerusalem was conquered). Nearby Bethel was another city in which King Jeroboam built a religious shrine—to mark his southern boundary after Israel was divided.

A third important city was Samaria, built as the capital of the Kingdom of Israel by King Omri (1 Kings 16:24). A temple to Baal was built here under King Ahab (1 Kings 16:32-33), but the city did not acquire its bad reputation until it was conquered by Assyrians and repeopled with foreigners. The schism that developed between Samaritans and other Jews was a breach that troubled Jesus (Luke 10; John 4; etc.).

Judea: The southernmost region of Palestine contains fertile highlands that Mark Twain called "more stupid hills" and also two of the most forbidding areas of the Holy Land.

East, along the Dead Sea, is the inhospitable Wilderness of Judea, a region with sheer cliffs pocked with caves, and the famous springs of Engedi. Twain was unimpressed with this area, calling it a barren desert with rocky ridges and sterile gorges. Journeying to Bethlehem, he said it would take a miracle by angels to charm shrubs and flowers to life again and to restore the beauty he had imagined from the Bible.

To the south is the formidable Negev Desert (the name means "dryness" in Hebrew) with steep ravines that were skirted by the Via Maris and King's Highway. While Israel enjoys a Mediterranean climate north of the Negev—with long, hot, dry summers and short, cool winters that usually provide abundant rain—the Negev has less than ten inches of rainfall a year. Archaeologists have found evidence of scattered prehistoric settlements in the Negev, but in biblical days the Israelites used it chiefly for grazing livestock and also built fortresses there to make it a buffer against Egypt.

Because Judea contained Jerusalem, it was the core of Hebrew life and was the last area to fall to foreign conquerors. Although Mark Twain liked Jerusalem, he was stunned by the small size of the old city—a fast walker could go outside the walls and circle the city in an hour.

The Jordan Rift—Fire and Brimstone

The Great Rift Valley is an immense geological fault system that runs some 3000 miles from northern Syria down to Mozambique. Craters and other evidence of volcanic action have been found along the rift in Israel from the Transjordanean Hills to the Gulf of Akaba. In Israel, the fault line is marked by a series of waterways that begin with springs at Dan and continue south through Lake Huleh, the Sea of Galilee, the seventy-mile-long Jordan River, and the forty-five-mile-long Dead Sea.

Mark Twain was especially scathing about these waterways. Of the "puddle" at the springs of Dan he wrote: "The unutterable beauty of the spot will not throw a well-balanced man into convulsions."

Lake Huleh he called a shallow pond.

"Its history and its association are its chiefest charm," he wrote of the Sea of Galilee. It was not nearly as large as Lake Tahoe—and to compare their beauty was to compare a meridian of longitude to a rainbow. The waters of the Sea of Galilee he described as dim, neutral in color, and an "exceedingly mild" blue. The banks were unrelieved by shrubbery, there were unsightly rocks at one end, and the lake was surrounded by low desolate hills. In short, he was sorry he had ever seen it in "the rude glare of day" because one evening he discovered that, in darkness, "it has nothing repulsive about it."

For the Mississippi River pilot, the Jordan River was a huge disappointment. "When I was a boy I somehow got the impression that the river Jordan was four thousand miles long and thirty-five miles wide." All images from hymns and spirituals—"on Jordan's stormy banks" or "roll, Jordan, roll"—dissolved when he saw the shallow, twisting stream: "Many streets in America are double as wide as the Jordan."

The Jordan Valley has major earthquakes about four times a century, and more frequent minor tremors. Josephus recorded a violent earthquake in 31 BC, and archaeologists have found evidence of this quake in damaged walls in the Dead Sea area. The Church of the Holy Sepulcher in Jerusalem, the latest of a series of buildings at the site of Calvary rock and Jesus' tomb, has been damaged by earthquakes in the 20th century.

The area around the Dead Sea is believed to have been especially unstable in biblical times, and earthquakes there probably account for the destruction of Sodom and Gomorrah. South of the Dead Sea were copper and other resources that made the area economically and politically important. The mines were worked under King Solomon, and after the kingdom was divided the Kingdom of Judah fought several wars in a vain effort to keep them.

For Mark Twain the Dead Sea was not so much disappointing as depressing. The sea itself was small and smelly despite its clear water. "Nothing grows in the flat, burning desert around it but weeds and the Dead Sea apple. . . . barren hills gleam painfully in the sun." There was no pleasant thing to please the eye—it was all scorching, arid, repulsive: "It makes one think of funerals and death."

What's the Lowest Point on Earth?

The bottom of the Dead Sea drops to almost 3000 feet below sea level, making it the lowest place on the earth.

Transjordanean Hills—The King's Highway

East of the rift and running parallel to it is a chain of mountains that separated the Holy Land from the great deserts of Arabia. These mountains were often nominally part of ancient Israel, but in actuality remained pretty much autonomous. It was hard for Israel to keep a tight grip because there were not many places to cross the waterways of the rift. Bashan—the section east of the Sea of Galilee—was especially fickle; as a buffer between Galilee and the strong powers that kept arising to the northeast, it was often the first area taken by foreign conquerors. Gilead and Ammon, just across the Jordan, were easier to keep an eye on. But Moab and Edom, cut off by the Dead Sea, frequently rebelled.

These mountains offered rich grazing lands and forests, and also had the Yarmuk, Jabbok, and Arnon rivers, so that the tribes of Gad, Reuben, and half of Manasseh were willing to relinquish their inheritances in western Palestine to move there (Num 32).

Of prime importance was the King's Highway, which came south from Mesopotamia into these hills and ran all the way south to the Gulf of Akaba. At Ezion-geber at the head of the gulf a route branched across the Sinai Peninsula to Egypt. At several places along the King's Highway caravan routes cut in from the eastern desert. The road was therefore vital for economic and military power. Even before they had conquered Canaan, the Israelites were impressed by the importance of the road, because they were forced to take a long detour when the kings of Edom and Moab refused them access to it (Num 20:17-19; 21:22).

10 Great Views in the Bible

1. Sodom and Gomorrah: Lot missed seeing the destruction of Sodom and Gomorrah, which must have been a spectacular dis-

play of *son et lumière*. His wife, however, turned around to watch. Unfortunately, we don't know what she saw, since she turned to a pillar of salt (Gen 19:17, 24-26).

2. Mount Rephidim: Moses, on Mount Rephidim, was able to watch the battle between the Israelites and Amalekites, which he engineered by raising and lowering his arms to determine the victories and defeats (Ex 17:8).

3. Mount Peor: From Mount Peor, the prophet Balaam had a view of the entire desert where all the tribes of Israel were camped. Balaam had been called by the Moabite prince Balak to curse the children of Israel. In the first two sites where Balaam had been taken to view and curse the people, the only words he spoke were blessings. On the third try, at Peor, Balaam again uttered praises, which began with two lines still used whenever Jews gather to pray at a synagogue: "How goodly are thy tents, O Jacob, and thy tabernacles, O Israel!" (Num 23-24). In English, Balaam's name came to be used as a common noun meaning a worthless friend or ally or even rejected newspaper or magazine copy.

4. Mount Nebo: From here, Moses commanded probably the most extensive view in the Bible—all of the promised land from Dan to Zoar (Deut 34:1-4).

5. Mount Tabor: Deborah watched Barak lead her armies against Sisera while she remained on the crest of Mount Tabor (Judg 4:4-16).

6. Palace Roof: David, from the roof of his palace, had the most enticing view mentioned in the Bible—Bathsheba bathing in her courtyard (2 Sam 11:2).

7. Jerusalem: Ezekiel, in one of his visions, was carried to Jerusalem and shown the whole city as well as the goings-on of the inhabitants. At the time, Ezekiel lived in Babylon (Ezek 8).

8. Fish Belly: Jonah was the only person reported to have seen the inside of a belly of a great fish and to have lived. Perhaps it was not a large vista, but it certainly was unique (Jonah).

9. Painted Desert: South of the Dead Sea, a downpour during the night caused flash floods across the desert. When the sun rose in the morning and tinted the water, the desert was streaked with red as brilliant as fresh blood (2 Kings 3:22).

10. Moving Hills: When the Israelites left Egypt, "the mountains skipped like rams, and the little hills like lambs" (Psa 114:4).

Country Living

1. "We have treasures in the field" (Jer 41:8).
2. "The voice of the Lord . . . discovereth the forests" (Psa 29:9).

3. "The smell of my son is as the smell of a field which the Lord hath blessed" (Gen 27:27).

4. "Come, my beloved, let us go forth into the field" (S of S 7:11).

5. "The profit of the earth is for all: the king himself is served by the field" (Eccl 5:9).

6. "They shall dwell safely in the wilderness, and sleep in the woods" (Ezek 34:25).

7. "So the Lord shall make bright clouds, and give them showers of rain, to every one grass in the field" (Zech 10:1).

8. "The field is the world; the good seed are the children of the kingdom" (Matt 13:38).

Earthquakes

21st century BC(?): Sodom and Gomorrah were probably destroyed by earthquake (Gen 19:24–25).

13th century BC: When Moses assembled the Israelites at the foot of Mount Sinai, the mountain smoked like a furnace and "quaked greatly" (Ex 19:17–18).

13th century BC: During the Korah Rebellion, when 250 people rebelled against Moses, the "ground clave asunder," the earth "swallowed them up," "and the earth closed upon them" (Num 16:31–33).

11th century BC: During Saul's reign (before 1004 BC), when Jonathan attacked the Philistine garrison at Michmash, "the earth quaked" and there was "a very great trembling" (1 Sam 14:15).

9th century BC: During the reign of Ahab of Israel, (871–851 BC), the prophet Elijah fled because Jezebel had threatened to kill him. Elijah walked all the way to Mount Sinai, where he took shelter in a cave. Later, when he told God that the Israelites had forsaken the covenant and only he was still faithful, "a great and strong wind rent the mountains, and brake in pieces the rocks . . . and after the wind an earthquake . . . and after the earthquake a fire . . ." (1 Kings 19:9–12).

8th century BC: An earthquake during the reign of King Uzziah of Judah (769–758 BC) was so severe people fled (Zech 14:5). It was memorable enough so that Amos (1:1) uses it as a reference point—"two years before the earthquake."

1st century: When Jesus died on the cross, "behold, the veil of the temple was rent in twain from the top to the bottom; and the earth did quake, and the rocks rent" (Matt 27:51).

1st century: At the Resurrection, "behold, there was a great earthquake" (Matt 28:2).

1st century: When Paul was jailed in Philippi about AD 50, he and Silas prayed and sang praises at midnight: "And suddenly there was a great earthquake, so that the foundations of the prison were shaken" (Acts 1:25–26).

Other earthquakes in the Bible (often said to have been caused by God's anger) include Judg 5:4; 2 Sam 22:8; Psa 18:7; 60:2; Job 9:6; Isa 5:25; Nah 1:5. A few earthquakes were prophesied: Isa 29:6; Matt 24:7; Mark 13:8; Luke 21:11; Rev 6:12; 8:5; 11:13; 19; 16:18.

A Joke about Rocks

Jesus was traveling with the disciples and they all got hungry. Jesus told them each to pick up a stone and he would turn it into bread. All the disciples scurried around to find the largest stones they could, but Peter could find only a pebble. So, after they had eaten, Peter was still hungry. After they had walked farther down the road they came to a big boulder, and Jesus turned to Peter and said, "Upon this rock I will build my church."

"No, no!" yelled Peter. "Turn it into bread. I'm starving!"

Guide to Biblical Caves

Lot's Cave: This cave (Gen 19:30) was Lot's dwelling place after he fled from Zoar following the destruction of Sodom and Gomorrah. "And Lot went up out of Zoar, and dwelt in the mountain, and his two daughters with him; for he feared to dwell in Zoar: and he dwelt in a cave" (Gen 19:30). There he lived with his daughters, who, fearing they would never have children, made Lot drunk and then slept with him. The exact location of the cave is unknown.

Abraham's Cave: Abraham's Cave of Machpelah is where he buried his wife, Sarah, when she died in her 127th year. "And after this, Abraham buried Sarah, his wife, in the cave of the field of Machpelah before Mamre:

the same is Hebron in the land of Canaan" (Gen 23:19). The present structure at the alleged site of Abraham's cave has been through two thousand years of renovations and conversions. The original building was a Jewish shrine erected by Herod. In the 7th century it was converted to a mosque, in the 12th century to a church, and 150 years later it became a mosque again. Entry to the cave had been forbidden for many years when the mosque was captured by the Israelis in 1967.

The Cave of Makkedah: After the battle of Gibeon, during which the sun stood still until the Israelites defeated the Amorites, the five kings of the Amorites hid themselves in a cave at Makkedah (Josh 10:17–18). After pursuing other enemies, Joshua returned to the cave and slaughtered the kings as an example of the Lord's victory over all Israel's enemies. The site of the cave is unknown, though some believe it to be southwest of Ekron.

David's Cave of Adullam: David, fleeing Saul, escaped to the cave of Adullam. There he assembled various riffraff and malcontents into his army before he departed into Judah to begin his battle with Saul: "David, therefore, departed from there, and escaped to the cave of Adullam; and when his brethren and all his father's house heard it, they went down there to him" (1 Sam 22:1). Although the site of the cave is unknown, Moshe Dayan, in his book *Living with the Bible*, reports exploring a denlike cave filled with Canaanite pottery near Adullam.

---

11 of the Most Dangerous Places in the Bible

1. *The Entrance to Eden:* The entry to Eden, on the east, was guarded by cherubim and a flaming sword "which turned every way" (Gen 3:24).

2. *The City of Aphek:* During a battle between the Israelites and Syrians, the walls collapsed, killing 27,000 Syrians (1 Kings 20:30).

3. *Towers:* Fortified towers at city gates were the first target of enemy troops. Gideon demolished the tower of Penuel, near Succoth (Judg 8:8, 17). Other doomed towers included those of Tyre and of Syrene in Egypt (Ezek 26:4; 30:6).

4. *Temples of Pagan Gods:* About a thousand men and women who attempted to escape the Israelites by holing up in the temple of Baal-Berith in Shechem were slaughtered (Judg 9:46–49).

5. *City Houses:* In daylight, murderers, thieves, and adulterers take note of houses they intend to victimize and then attack at night (Job 24:14–16).

6. *Egypt:* Egypt was full of disease, suffered ten plagues, and continued to be threatened by God (Ex 3:20; Deut 7:15; 28:27,60; Jer 9:26; 46:25; Ezek 30:8, 16, etc.).

7. *Cave of Makkedah:* Five Canaanite kings fleeing from the Israelites believed the cave would provide sanctuary. But Joshua ordered the entrance sealed with boulders to imprison the kings until he had time to deal with them. After the battle, the kings were slaughtered and the cave resealed (Josh 10:16–27).

8. *Shiloh:* Shiloh proved rather dangerous for the virgins of Israel who came there to dance in a harvest festival. By agreement of the elders of the tribes, the Benjamites were permitted to kidnap them for wives (Judg 21).

9. *Jael's Tent:* The Canaanite general Sisera was killed by Jael when he took refuge in her tent. Pretending to be hospitable, Jael waited until Sisera fell asleep and then hammered a tent stake through his temples (Judg 4:11; 5:24–27).

10. *Highways:* In the time of Deborah, the Israelites feared to use the highways because of Canaanite oppression (Judg 5:6). Later the Benjamites killed people on the highways (Judg 20:31). People on the roads were beaten, robbed, and killed into New Testament times (Isa 33:8; Luke 10:30).

11. *Mount Sinai:* "There shall not an hand touch it, but he shall surely be stoned, or shot through; whether it be beast or man, it shall not live" (Ex 19:13).

Every Man under His Vine and Fig Tree

Algum (or Almug) Tree: The Book of Kings (1 Kings 10:11–12) calls this wood algum and says it was imported from Ophir, while the Book of Chronicles (2 Chr 2:8; 9:10–11) calls it almug and says it came from Lebanon. Since the books were written by different authors from politically divergent areas of ancient Israel, there is no telling which is more reliable.

According to the Bible, the algum or almug tree was used by Solomon to build pillars for the Temple and for musical instruments (1 Kings 10:11–12).

This tree is believed by some scholars, including the ancient rabbis, to be the red sandalwood. But there is much argument—while one source suggests that red sandalwood is not suited for making instruments such as harps, another source insists that it is still used in the Middle East for musical instruments. Possibly the algum was not a specific tree but a quality or variety of tree. Or perhaps it was another word for ebony (see below).

Almond Tree: *Sheked* ("to hasten") in Hebrew, the almond tree blossoms before it bears leaves. It is the first tree in Israel to blossom, with the fruit edible in two stages. The green pods, while still tender, are very tasty; the better-known nuts come later.

Because of confusion in Hebrew terminology and the common mistake of identifying biblical trees with those in Europe, trees are sometimes mis-named in the Bible. An example is "And Jacob took him rods of green poplar, and of the hazel and the chestnut tree" (Gen 30:37). The more accurate translation reads: "And Jacob took him rods of green poplar, and of the almond and plane tree."

When a rebellion broke out in the desert during the wandering of the children of Israel, an almond branch became the factor that decided which tribe should rule in the sanctuary. Each tribe's leader carved his name in a rod made from the almond tree, and all twelve rods were placed in the Tabernacle. On the following day, it was found that only Aaron's rod bore fruit: ". . . the rod of Aaron for the house of Levi was budded, and brought forth buds, and bloomed blossoms, and yielded almonds" (Num 17:1–10).

The shape of the bowls for the menorah in Jerusalem was copied from the almond blossoms ("bowls made like unto almonds, with a knop and a flower" [Ex 25:33]). The almond is held in such high esteem that a mishnaic story includes it among the ten things created on the eve of the Sabbath, another of which is the rod of Moses.

Aloe: The perfume of the aloe was a luxury in biblical days. Since it was not native to Israel the Bible mentions it as an import from, or as known from travels to, another land. Balaam, who came from a town near the Euphrates where the aloe undoubtedly grew, was supposed to have cursed Israel. Instead he pronounced a blessing, making use of the image of the aloe: "As the valleys are they spread forth, as gardens by the river's side, as the trees of lign aloes which the Lord hath planted" (Num 24:6).

Its pleasant scent made aloe a valuable ingredient, along with myrrh, in an embalming mixture, and Nicodemus brought a hundred-pound weight of myrrh and aloes to Jesus' body. Jesus was wound in linen cloths with the spices (John 19:39). The same mixture of aloe and myrrh, but with cinnamon added, was used by whores to perfume their beds (Prov 7:17), and the psalmist sings of the king's garments scented with myrrh, aloes, and cassia (Psa 45:8). The perfume, extracted from the tubular leaves rather than from the decorative red flowers, was valued throughout the ancient world.

Apple Tree: The legendary fruit of temptation is an item of hot debate among biblical botanists. The Hebrew *tappuach,* which today means "apple," is described in various places in the Bible as golden and sweet, hanging in a tree which offers a good deal of shade. But "apple" is only the traditional translation. Some scholars believe the fruit was an orange, a quince, or—with a few straggling supporters—even an apricot.

While the identity of the *tappuach* remains shady today, there was no uncertainty among the ancient Israelites when they heard the term. The tree was commonly used in similes of love, such as: "As the apple tree among the trees of the wood, so is my beloved among the sons. I sat down under his shadow with great delight, and his fruit was sweet to my taste" (S of S 2:3).

Unlike the apple of the Garden of Eden, which led man and woman to hiding and deception, the apple of Proverbs symbolizes truth: "A word fitly spoken is like apples of gold in pictures of silver" (Prov 15:11).

Balm: Known biblically as balm of Gilead, and botanically as *Mecca balsam,* this was a resin believed to have been produced from trees in the vicinity of Gilead, or to have been a major article of trade in the area.

Balm was sent by Jacob as a gift to Joseph in Egypt (Gen 43:11), but whether it was already a trade item in those early days or whether its mention is an editorial embellishment of an old story written at a much later date is uncertain. By Roman times, it did grow in Gilead.

Josephus wrote that balm was one of the herbs and spices brought to Palestine by the Queen of Sheba. Another tale is that Titus the Great counted it as part of his booty from Palestine and brought it to Rome in his victory procession.

The balm of Gilead has remained popular in folk medicine for a wide variety of ailments.

Bay Tree: Perhaps another mistake in translation. The one mention of bay tree in the Psalms, "like a green bay tree," could also be less poetically translated as "like a green tree native to the soil." Doubt has led botanists to suggest substitution of the rosebay or oleander, but the psalm may not be referring to a specific species at all.

Box Tree/Larch: Again under dispute as to its identity, the *teashur* tree is listed twice by Isaiah among various trees of Lebanon which he foresaw growing in the desert in the days to come and which he predicted would be used as wood for the construction of the Temple. The Hebrew comes from a root word signifying "straightness" or "uprightness," and whatever tree is meant is likely a tall, straight one. For this reason, the suggestion that *teashur* comes from the Arabic for the juniper or cypress is not plausible, since both grow so twisted and gnarled. Most scholars believe the box tree or larch is probably the correct translation.

The Burning Bush

The *sneh* of Moses' vision is one of the most mysterious plants in the Bible. As might be expected, much controversy exists over the identity of this reputedly miraculous bush (Ex 3:2). The Hebrew *sneh* signifies only a bush, perhaps bushes in general rather than a specific plant, and is probably the root for (Mount) *Sinai* and (Wilderness of) *Zin.*

The most plausible identification of the burning bush is proffered by the monks of the Convent of St. Catherine, located in the Sinai. They point to a common blackberry bush, which they call *Rubus sanctus*. It produces a roselike flower and red berries that slowly turn black. The bush grows thorns which curve inward, allowing a person to insert his hand but not to draw it back out unscathed. This plant fits talmudic tradition, which also describes the burning bush as having roselike flowers and thorns.

Those who dispute this theory suggest a number of other thorned bushes. The most startling suggestion is that the burning bush of Moses is *Dictamnus albus,* commonly called the gas plant. The bush is coated with oil from tiny glands on its leaves, and a lighted match placed near a stem will flare up briefly. Neither the leaves nor the stems are damaged.

Camphire: This widespread shrub is commonly called henna and is best known for the reddish dye extracted from its flowers. Today the dye is used by Arabs to dye their fingernails, the soles of their feet, and their palms for ritualistic purposes; however, there is no mention of this use in the Bible. The only reference to henna, in the Song of Songs, is as an allusion, comparing the beloved to a cluster of henna blossoms (S of S 1:14; 4:13). The blossoms, either cream-colored or red, have the fragrance of roses.

Caper: A small bush growing in clefts of rocks and cracks in walls, the caper is unusual in that the buds, flowers, and fruits all appear at the same time. The dry branches were used for firewood in biblical times and are still used today as fuel by the Bedouin.

The flower bud—used as a condiment to spur the appetite—is believed to be an aphrodisiac; indeed, one Hebrew word for caper has been translated as "desire" in some Bibles (Eccl 12:5). Capers are believed to have been an ingredient in various wines of biblical times, either as an aphrodisiac or for their pungent taste.

Carob Tree: Described in the tale of the prodigal son as food for the pigs (Luke 15:16) and otherwise known as Saint-John's-bread, carob pods have always provided food for the poor. The tree is known also as the locust bean tree, so that the pods may be the "locusts" on which John the Baptist subsisted in the wilderness (Mark 1:6). Some scholars suggest that Shakespeare referred to the carob pod in *Othello:* "The food that to him now is as luscious as locusts, shall be to him shortly as bitter as coloquintida."

The tree grows well in most places in Israel, and both the pods and the ripe seeds are edible. A sort of honey can be made from the seeds.

Both the Greek and German words for carob mean horn, as the pod is curved in the shape of a ram's horn, and has similar wrinkles.

Surprisingly, although the carob tree was common, it is not mentioned in the Old Testament. Scholars have therefore frequently tried to squeeze a hidden mention of it from various passages. For instance, the letters in the Hebrew words for "sword" and "carob" are the same—although they appear in different order—and the New English Bible reflects this in its translation of Isaiah 1:20: "But if ye refuse and rebel, locust beans shall be your food." Other Bibles read: "But if ye refuse and rebel, ye shall be devoured with the sword."

Carob was said to be a miraculous tree, which made bitter waters sweet (Ex 15:25), according to the medieval Arab philosopher Avicenna.

It has been claimed that carob seed was the original measure of gold and gems, and is, in fact, at the bottom of a complicated linguistic derivation of the word carat. If this is so, it gives the seed a history of 3500 years of use as a weight.

Cassia: The bark of the *Cinnamomum cassia* was powdered and used as cinnamon, because it has a flavor and odor similar to true cinnamon. This tree, however, is an evergreen of the laurel family and its bark is not as tasty as the authentic spice. Cassia is native to southeast Asia and so had to be imported into Israel. Solomon, it is believed, obtained the spice through the markets of Tyre (Ezek 27:19). It was included in the holy ointment that Moses was instructed to concoct (Ex 30:24). Cassia was one of the spices that scented the king's garment (Psa 45:8).

Cedar Tree: Most often the Hebrew *erez* refers to the cedars of Lebanon, grand trees that grow to 40 feet in diameter and over 100 feet high. It may, however, refer also to other evergreens, such as a small juniper of the Sinai. Where trees are described as growing by water (Num 24:6) they would not be cedars of Lebanon, as these do not flourish on the banks of waterways. In some passages (Ezek 31:8), the term *erez* is used generally for all non-fruit-bearing trees.

Cedars of Lebanon were used in building the Temple and Solomon's palace. They were popular for sacred architecture in the ancient world in general, and were chosen for the temple of Diana at Ephesus and the temple of Apollo at Utica. A grove of cedars at Bsherri, Lebanon, is called by the local inhabitants the "cedar grove of God."

Isaiah includes the *erez* as one of the trees that will spread to wasteland once the Messianic age arrives. Of the more imaginative and poetic references to cedars are "He moveth his tail like a cedar," referring to Behemoth (Job 40:17), and "Howl, fir tree; for the cedar is fallen" (Zech 11:2).

Interestingly, the numerous references to cedar all occur in the Old Testament; possibly the tree was rarely used during New Testament times, or its symbolic meaning had been exhausted.

Cinnamon: One of the rare uncontested species of plants in the Bible, its Hebrew name *(kinnamon)* bears a striking resemblance to both the Greek and English. It was used to perfume beds (Prov 7:17) as well as being an ingredient in the oil used in ritual (Ex 30:23). Revelation (18:13) says it is one of the trade items that shall no longer be available to merchants after the judgment and fall of Babylon. Both the inner layer of bark and the ripe fruit of the tree can be used to produce oil or the powdered spice.

Coriander: This spice is mentioned twice in the Old Testament as a comparison for manna (Ex 16:31; Num 11:7–8). Manna was said to be as white as coriander seed, and like the spice had to be ground in a mortar.

Cucumber: A highly prized vegetable in biblical times, the cucumber was abundant enough to be a favorite food of the poor. It was one of the foods the Israelites ate while in slavery in Egypt, and one that they missed during their march through the desert (Num 11:5). Two varieties are now known in Egypt and in irrigated areas of Israel. One grows with little water and is tougher and less tasty than the one that grows in well-irrigated gardens. Irrigated fields of cucumber are still guarded by watchmen as they were in the days of Isaiah, "as a lodge in a garden of cucumber" (Isa 1:8). The lodge is left to stand or fall on its own after the harvest.

Cumin: Mentioned three times by Isaiah and once by Matthew, cumin is one of the herbs subject to a tithe (Matt 23:23), along with dill and mint. Isaiah mentions it as being threshed with a rod, and the seeds are still separated from the plant in this manner (Isa 28:25, 27).

Cypress Tree: Whether the Hebrew word *tirzah* refers to the cypress, holm oak, evergreen oak, or any number of other trees remains under dispute. This tree is mentioned only once, along with other trees, both identifiable and unidentifiable (Isa 44:14). Some scholars have suggested the cypress as the questionable gopher wood of which Noah's ark was constructed (Gen 6:14), but most permit gopher wood to remain a mystery—perhaps a tree of which all traces were destroyed by the flood.

Date Palm: The requirements of the palm are explained by an Arab saying: The date's feet belong in water and its head in fire. The tree needs plenty of water and plenty of sun.

The date palm is an impressive tree, growing to 100 feet in a life-span that reaches maturity only after forty years. There are both male and female date trees—if both are not present in a palm orchard, the female will not bear fruit. Because the fruit ripens continuously rather than all at once, the tree provides food for a good part of the year.

In desert regions the sight of palm leaves meant the presence of an oasis— and water. The long branches and fronds were used to construct hasty but efficient shelters. Camels could eat the husks of the tree. Baskets and ropes were woven from the fibers. Little wonder that date-palm orchards were extensive in biblical times—Josephus recorded a palm forest outside Jericho that was seven miles long. The tree's usefulness is also why the psalmist predicted that "The righteous shall flourish like the palm tree" (Psa 92:13).

The date palm, appearing on an early coin from Palestine, was a symbol of Israelite victory. Revelation (7:9) describes born-again Christians wearing long robes and holding palm branches in their hands. The crest of the palm tree may have been the plant carved onto architectural elements, such as on the pillars in Solomon's Temple—although some experts believe the motif represented the water lily.

The dates of Israel are known as Nicholas dates. Nicholas of Damascus, a Greek philosopher and historian of Herod's time, learned that the Roman emperor Augustus had an insatiable taste for the fruit and thereafter kept the emperor's larder stocked with superior-quality dates from Israel. In gratitude, Augustus named the fruit after his supplier.

Dill: One of the three herbs mentioned by Matthew as subject to the tithe is *anethon,* a Greek word translated in the Authorized Version as anise, but an alternate translation appears in the margin: dill. The latter is probably correct, as the Greek is identical with the Latin *anethum,* which undoubtedly means dill. The aromatic leaves are used as flavoring and to make a carminative, and oil is extracted from the dill seeds.

Ebony: This highly valued wood was brought to Tyre by merchants from the Persian Gulf, and then traded from Tyre to places such as Israel. Ebony also came from Ethiopia, but there is no information as to which tree produced it; Virgil mentioned ebony as being traded from India. In the Bible, horns of ebony were traded along with horns of ivory (Ezek 27:15).

Fig Tree: By using its leaves to clothe themselves, Adam and Eve made the fig tree famous as the first identifiable tree mentioned in the Bible (Gen 3:7), and its leaves traditional for covering certain areas of nude statues. The tree, which can bear fruit for ten months of the year, grows as long as 400 years when the soil is cultivated around the base of the tree, as mentioned by Luke (13:6–9).

The fruit depends upon a burrowing insect, the fig wasp, which fertilizes the fig by entering it through a hole opposite the stalk.

The profusion of Hebrew terms—denoting such distinctions as early figs or bunches of figs dried for storage—shows the importance of the fruit in the everyday life of the people. The fig was thought to have medicinal properties and was used to cure boils (Isa 38:21). The wood from the fig tree was the only wood permitted to stoke the sacrificial fire. The fig, one of the seven foods that were the "glory of the land of Israel," was always an important article of trade.

A well-known image for the coming of the Messiah and a time of peace is that of each man sitting under his own vine and fig tree (Mic 4:4), symbols of prosperity. Another image uses the fig tree to symbolize the hypocrite (Mark 11:13): The distant promise of the fruit is not fulfilled upon close inspection.

Fir Tree: Although the cypress could apply to all the biblical passages that refer to fir trees, some authorities believe the translation should be a pine or juniper. Fir was used to make boards for ships (Ezek 27:5) and for musical instruments (2 Sam 6:5). The fir timber brought from Tyre for building the Temple was used mainly for the doors, floors, and ceilings (1 Kings 6:15; 2 Chr 3:5).

Frankincense/Galbanum: Although frankincense and galbanum are distinguished as two different resins in the Bible, they belong to the same family: the Burseraceae, commonly known as the incense tree. This family, which also includes myrrh and balm of Gilead, has so many genera and species defined in modern times that it is difficult to identify biblical equivalents. All shrubs and trees of the incense-tree family, however, secrete aromatic oils or resins from their stems.

Some of these resins can have rather unpleasant odors when burned, even though they are used as incense. When mixed with fragrant spices, however, the plant oils intensify the aroma. Used alone or in combination, these resins were used for incense, fumigation, perfume, embalming, and occasionally in medicines.

"Take unto thee sweet spices, stacte, and onycha, and galbanum; these sweet spices with pure frankincense" (Ex 30:34) is a recipe for the incense to be used for ritual purposes. Translators aren't sure whether galbanum here is classed as a sweet spice or whether it's simply another term for frankincense.

Frankincense is among the gifts brought by the wise men to the child Jesus (Matt 2:11) and was one of the trade items of Babylon (Rev 18:13).

A rabbinic story tells how, in the days of the Second Temple, only one family—the house of Avtinas—knew the recipe for the sacred incense, and they guarded it jealously. Temple authorities tried to break their monopoly by ousting them and having the recipe copied by the best perfumers of Alexandria, to no avail. Not only was the house of Avtinas reinstated as Temple perfumers, but the remuneration for their work was doubled. Women of the Avtinas family never used cosmetics or perfume, so that they could not be accused of using the sacred formula for common ends.

Gall: Some references to gall in the Bible evidently refer to the gall bladder or bile, but others refer to the poisonous juice of a plant. The exact plant is unknown. In Deuteronomy (29:18) it is coupled with wormwood (see below). The gall that Matthew (27:34) records as mixed with vinegar and given to Jesus on the cross was most likely myrrh (see below), although some scholars hold out for the poppy or the colocynth. The Hebrew word

113

for gall can also mean snake poison (Deut 32:33), which does nothing to clear up the mystery.

Gourd: Both gourd stories in the Bible leave botanists puzzled.

The first is the story of Jonah and the gourd tree, which grows, within hours, from a seed to a shade-giving tree. Although several varieties of gourds, such as the pumpkin, are fast-growing, nothing approaches this suggested speed.

In a lesser-known story (2 Kings 4:38–41), a wild gourd is shredded into the stew. Luckily, before the diners eat enough stew to become ill they realize the gourd is poisonous and dilute its effects by adding grain. About the best guess botanists have made is that it must have been a bitter-tasting gourd.

Hazel Tree: Jacob's streaked staffs (Gen 30:37) again offer a problem for botanists. The Hebrew *luz* has been translated as "hazel tree," but most recent scholars believe the almond tree was meant, and the Arabic word for almond supports this theory.

Holm Oak: The Hebrew *tirzah* (Isa 44:14), translated as "cypress" in some Bibles, may also be the holm oak. This evergreen is still planted near wilderness graves by Arabic peoples. A suggestion that *tirzah* is the carob tree may be a desperate attempt to identify *something* in the Bible with the carob, a common and useful tree never otherwise mentioned in the Old Testament.

Hyssop: Here again is a seemingly unidentifiable plant—in Hebrew the *ezob,* in Greek the *hussopos.* It may or may not be related to the aromatic herb of the mint family that is called hyssop today. The biblical plant apparently grew in bunches (Ex 12:22) and was used for medicinal and cleansing purposes (Lev 14:52), for the purification of those in contact with the dead (Num 19:6) and for the purification and curing of leprosy (Lev 14:4).

Cedar and hyssop are considered opposites in the plant world, the first being tall, straight, majestic, and the second being a lowly, clinging, and humble plant that hides among rocks and crevices.

Some Bibles translate as "hyssop" the branch on which the sponge soaked in vinegar was hoisted to Jesus on the cross (John 19:29). Other scholars suggest the caper bush, although its branches are crooked. Matthew and Mark's use of the term "reed" suggests the branch was straight.

Judas Tree: One tree in Palestine is now known as the Judas tree. It is a native tree that grows a long, red, narrow flower. Although Judas tree is not mentioned in the Bible, it may be the unidentified tree from which Judas hanged himself (Matt 27:5).

Juniper: Recent scholarship has reached agreement that the Hebrew *ar'ar* means "juniper"—not "heath" or "tamarisk." A deciding factor here, as in other translation disputes, is the similar Arabic word for juniper.

This translation renders certain images in the Bible more plausible. Jeremiah compares the juniper in the desert to the tree growing on a well-watered hill (17:6, 8)—the first being the cursed man who has no faith in God, and the second the blessed believer. The juniper growing in parched soil develops a twisted trunk and bent branches, and appears to be fighting a constant battle for survival. Translating the first verse as "heath" makes little sense environmentally, while junipers in the desert are a common sight.

The modern Hebrew translation for *ar'ar* is "to appeal." An image of the juniper constantly needing rain provides an apt metaphor for a man appealing to God for help, as expressed in Psalms: "He will regard the prayer of the *ar'ar* and not despise their prayer" (102:17)—translated in all versions of the Bible as "destitute."

Juniper not only provides excellent imagery but is an excellent fuel, available where little other wood grows.

While *ar'ar* is decidedly the juniper, confusion remains over another word, *retem,* translated by some scholars as "juniper" but most likely the broom tree.

Lily: In Palestine, the lily—probably the *Gladiolus segetum* or sword lily—grows in wheat fields. A talmudic story focuses on the beauty of this small flower. A king who has hired a new gardener finds that an entire area has been left with unmown weeds. In a rage he orders mowers to level the ground. Just in time he sees a lily—and spares the entire orchard to save the beautiful flower. Such exceptional beauty is expressed in "As the lily among thorns so is my love among the daughters" (S of S 2:2).

Lilies are among the most romantic flowers mentioned in the Bible. Although "lilies of the field" (Matt 6:28) probably meant any wild flower, the fragrant lily of the valley (S of S 2:1-2) contains toxins believed to cure heart ailments. Arum lilies were also used medicinally.

A Drop Becomes a Lily

Two non-biblical stories suggest the origin of the arum lily. In the first, Eve sheds tears when leaving the Garden of Eden. Her salt tears fall to the ground, where they grow into arum lilies. In the second story, the beads of sweat that fall from Jesus as he prays in the garden of Gethsemane (Matt 26:36–46) produce arum lilies, which are called Gethsemane lilies as well.

Mallow: Mentioned only once, by Job (30:4), mallows are bitter-tasting but edible plants that have little nutritional value. Mallows grow in salty areas, mainly around the Dead Sea, and are sometimes called sea purslane.

Mandrake: Twice in the Bible the mandrake is mentioned as an aphrodisiac. In addition, the mandrake's root can be imagined to resemble a human form, and the berries are believed to promote conception. In biblical times, when producing sons gave women status, the mandrake was highly prized. This is central to an episode in the story of Leah and Rachel, both of whom were married to Jacob:

Leah sent her son to gather mandrakes. When he returned, Rachel—who was still barren—begged her sister to give her the mandrakes. Leah refused, claiming that Jacob already loved Rachel more than he loved her, and that the mandrakes gave her the right to spend the night with him. She enticed Jacob into her tent: "Thou must come in unto me; for surely I have hired thee with my son's mandrakes. And he lay with her that night" (Gen 30:16).

In the Song of Songs (7:12–13) one lover entices the other with pomegranates, the smell of mandrakes, and numerous pleasant fruits.

Mangrove: In the Sinai desert, between Eilat and Sharm el-Sheik, is the oasis of Nabek, where a grove of mangrove trees surrounds the water. With aerial roots that grow upward, hugging the trunk, and leaves that are coated with salt, the mangrove is a fanciful-looking tree. As it grows, this unusual tree separates the salt from the water absorbed by its roots, and expels the mineral through the leaves. The crust produced on the leaves is sometimes used as a source for salt. This amazing tree might have produced the mysterious branch that Moses threw into the waters of Marah to make them sweet (Ex 15:25)—except that desalination does not occur with a severed branch.

Mint: One of the three herbs mentioned in the New Testament as tithed. It was this simple matter of paying tithes, Jesus said, that the Pharisees found so easy to fulfill, while the larger and more important matters of law went undone (Matt 23:23; Luke 11:42).

Mulberry Tree: The Hebrew for the tree which is commonly translated as "mulberry" is derived from the word for "crying"; when the Bible describes the tree as having willowy leaves, it is sometimes mistranslated as the "weeping willow tree." The Greek version of the Bible calls the tree the black mulberry (Luke 17:6), which is probably correct.

116

Mustard: The mustard is a large plant but its seeds are quite small. The New Testament refers to these attributes: Even faith the size of a mustard seed can move a mountain (Matt 17:20); the kingdom of heaven is compared to a mustard seed, planted when very small, which then grows into a large, spreading plant capable of supporting a bird at rest (Matt 13:31; Mark 4:32).

Myrrh: Myrrh, the gum resin produced from the *Commiphora myrrha* plant, is used as an oil for perfume and embalming and anointing compounds. As it was necessary for so many ritual purposes, it was a common and highly valued gift throughout biblical times—the most famous example being that which the Magi brought to the baby Jesus (Matt 2:11).

Stacte, mentioned as one of the ingredients for the perfume used in the Tabernacle (Ex 30:34), is believed to be the resin of the myrrh. In Job (36:27) the same word is translated as "drops of water."

Myrtle: The *Myrtus communis* is an evergreen tree producing white flowers. Its berries are white at first but turn a bluish-black as they ripen. Although edible, they taste rather bitter and were never used extensively as food.

Esther, whose Hebrew name was Hadassah ("myrtle"), had beauty comparable to that of the white myrtle flower—and it was her beauty that won her the title of queen in the court of Xerxes I (Book of Esther). The Arabic words *as* (myrtle) and *tur* (fresh) produced As-tur, or Esther—literally, "myrtle blossom," a direct translation of the Hebrew name into Arabic.

Nettle: Of the two words used in the Bible for nettle, one most likely refers to the specific plant and the other to any thorny plant or bush. "Nettle" is used throughout the Old Testament in descriptions of desolate places, or wild areas, giving the impression of destruction and abandonment (Job 30:7; Isa 34:13; Hos 9:6; Zeph 2:9).

Under the Oaks

1. Jacob hid the strange gods under an oak (Gen 35:4).
2. Deborah was buried under an oak (Gen 35:8).
3. Joshua wrote words in the book of the law of God, and took a great stone, and set it up under an oak (Josh 24:26).
4. An angel sat under an oak (Judg 6:11).
5. Absalom was hanged in an oak (2 Sam 18:9-10).
6. Man of God sat under an oak (1 Kings 13:14).

7. Saul and his sons were buried under an oak (1 Chr 10:12).

8. Sinners "shall be ashamed of the oaks which ye have desired, and ye shall be confounded for the gardens that ye have chosen. For ye shall be as an oak whose leaf fadeth, and as a garden that hath no water" (Isa 1:29–30).

9. Idols were put "under every thick oak" (Ezek 6:13).

10. Incense was burned under oaks (Hos 4:13).

Oak: Two different Hebrew words have been translated as "oak tree": *allon* and *elah.* The latter has been alternately translated as "pistachio" or "terebinth," causing more confusion.

Elah may derive from the Canaanite word *el,* which means "god," reflecting reverence for the oak. Idols were often placed under oak trees in Palestine. In areas barren of other trees it is still common to find either single oaks or an entire grove left standing, having been saved only by the belief in their sanctity.

The first mention of the oak is when Abraham leaves the place of his childhood and heads south, passing through Shechem into *eilon moreh*— either a plain or a grove of oak trees, depending on which version of the Bible you read. *Moreh* is derived from the word that means "to teach"; and the oak was a sacred tree to the people of Palestine, a tree under which oracles undoubtedly took place. Abraham's grove or plain would have been a well-known site to people of biblical times (Gen 12). Abraham and Lot set up their camps among oaks (Gen 13:18), which suggests that they remained in wooded areas rather than settling near the fields of the Canaanites. One old tree still standing in Palestine is known as "the oak of Abraham."

During Jacob's return to Canaan from Laban's land in Haran, Jacob was met by his mother's maidservant Deborah. The Bible version of the story says Deborah died on her way back home and was buried under a large oak tree called the Allon-bachuth ("oak of weeping"). However, *allon* may be translated as "another" rather than as "oak," in which case the phrase Allon-bachuth becomes "weeping for another." On the basis of this name, some scholars theorize that Deborah told Jacob of the death of his mother and that he was crying for her rather than for the maidservant (Gen 35). The "oak of weeping" is also believed to be the "palm tree" referred to in the story of the second Deborah, who "dwelt under the palm tree of Deborah" (Judg 4:5).

Oil Tree: The oil tree (a literal translation of the Hebrew) has been variously called the olive, the wild olive, the oleaster, and the pine. Descriptions suggest that the wood was used by idol worshipers to carve their images; the branches and leaves were used to build nomadic booths;

118

and the oil, which can be extracted manually, was used in curing (1 Kings 6:23-33; Neh 8:15; Isa 41:19).

Olive: Of the more than fifty-five times the Bible mentions the olive, not one suggests that the fruit was eaten. Instead, its oil as a staple item of diet is stressed. The olive tree produces two harvests each year, and an old tree, which may be up to 2000 years old, bears enough olives for twenty gallons of olive oil.

Olive oil was also used for sacred purposes, such as anointing the priests, and in the New Testament became the symbol of the Holy Spirit. It is attributed medicinal properties and was used by the Apostles and priests in curing the sick (Mark 6:13; Luke 10:34; James 5:14). Olive wood, which polishes to a beautiful light color, was used extensively in building. The posts and doors of the Temple as well as the cherubim in the Holy of Holies were made from olive wood.

The Bible also uses the olive metaphorically. The dove returned to the ark with an olive branch in its beak (Gen 8:11)—an image used to this day to denote serenity and peace. Though doves do not eat olives, they often nest in olive-tree branches.

An evil man is described as casting "off his flower as the olive" (Job 15:33). This refers to the flowers that fall from olive trees in abundance. Only one per hundred olive flowers actually produces an olive, and the fallen blossoms cover the orchard grounds like snow.

Onion: Mentioned explicitly only once in the Bible, onions are included along with cucumbers, leeks, melons, and garlic when the Israelites complained about the food from Egypt they missed while they wandered in the desert.

The onion was an important food for Egyptians. Apart from its nutritional value, it was believed to be endowed with supernatural qualities. Pliny suggested that it was worshiped. The concentric layers were seen by Egyptians as the universe, with successive layers representing the stars and planets.

Bezalel, the name of the man who constructed the sanctuary during the Exodus (Ex 36:1), may mean "divine onion"—*bezal*, "onion," and *el*, "god." The name of the man Bazluth in Ezra's time may have the same translation.

Plane Tree: Almost all biblical botanists agree on the two references to the plane tree. The few Bibles that substitute "chestnut tree" may be drawing on the translation of Rashi, an 11th-century scholar who identified all biblical plants and trees with those he knew from his country, France.

When Jacob streaked wands to change the appearance of the progeny of the flocks he tended (Gen 30:37), plane-tree branches were clearly meant. When scratched, these branches immediately develop white streaks.

The plane tree, growing to over a hundred feet tall, is one of the most striking trees native to Israel. One in Damascus was large enough to hold a shop inside its hollowed-out trunk. Plane trees can easily stand up to comparison with the cedars of Lebanon (Ezek 31:8), even though they tend to be slimmer.

Pomegranate Tree: The pomegranate tree, with thick thorny branches and dark-green leaves, produces bell-shaped flowers of a deep-red color. The fruit is round, about four inches in diameter, and changes from red to green as it ripens. The end of the fruit has a small crownlike projection. The rind produces a bitter acid used for tanning leather. A spiced wine was made from the juice (S of S 8:2), and parts of the plant were given credit for curing tapeworm.

The pomegranate is mentioned at least thirty times in the Bible. It was among the seven agricultural products exported from the Holy Land, and one of the items brought back to Moses by the spies (Num 13:23). The pomegranate motif decorated the hems of the priests' garments: "And they made upon the hems of the robe pomegranates of blue, and purple, and scarlet, and twined linen" (Num 39:24).

The Hebrew word for pomegranate, *rimmon,* may have a common origin with the name for the Syrian sun god, Hadad Rimmon. The fruit would have been a fitting symbol for this god of fertility, because its juicy red interior is filled with hundreds of small seeds.

Poplar Tree: Of the three kinds of branches used by Jacob to induce the birth of striped and speckled sheep in Laban's flock, poplar is the only one not disputed. The poplar is a white tree with darker-colored knots showing through the bark, giving the speckled effect Jacob was after (Gen 30:37). Both the Hebrew and Arabic words refer to the whiteness of the Mediterranean tree, which is similar to the North American flowering dogwood.

The beauty of the poplar enticed idol worshipers to set up their images under these trees as well as under oaks, and the Israelites were warned not to follow this example (Isa 65:3; Hos 4:13).

Basket Cases

1. The pharaoh's chief baker could balance three baskets on his head at one time, but it turned out this meant he would die in three days (Gen 40:16).

2. God showed Amos "a basket of summer fruit" and asked, "Amos, what seest thou?" Amos replied, "A basket of summer fruit" (Amos 8:1–2).

3. When Paul preached in Damascus, angry Jewish leaders planned to kill him and set guards at the city gates. His friends, learning of the plan, lowered Paul over the city wall in a basket (Acts 9:1–25).

4. Jehu ordered seventy members of the royal family executed and their heads sent to him in baskets (2 Kings 10:7).

5. God showed Jeremiah two baskets of figs. One basket had very good figs and represented the righteous. "The other basket had very naughty figs," which were so bad they couldn't be eaten. These represented the wicked, whom God was condemning to be "a taunt and a curse" (Jer 24:1–9).

Reeds: Several Hebrew words are translated as "reeds," "flags," and other types of grasses, but the most interesting is *ahu.*

The Hebrew *ahu,* meaning reeds, comes from the· Accadian word for riverbank. It would therefore refer to wetland species of grasses—rather than to the sorts of grasses found in drier pastures. Despite this it is sometimes translated as "meadow." An example is in the passage about the pharaoh's dream of fat cattle grazing by the river (Gen 41:2).

What is interesting about *ahu* is that this word also means brethren—as in "Though he be fruitful among his brethren . . ." (Hos 13:15). This conjures up a romantic vision that the tranquillity of true brotherhood is akin to that of well-fed cows lowing at pasture.

Rose: The rose, despite its beauty, is mentioned only twice in the Bible, once by Isaiah (35:1) and once in the Song of Songs (2:1). Some scholars suggest that the flower mentioned is not the rose at all but the autumn crocus or the narcissus.

Shittah (Shittim, plural): This is probably the acacia—the insect-resistant, hard, and heavy wood that was the only timber used in constructing the Ark and the Tabernacle. "And thou shalt make boards for the tabernacle of shittim wood standing up. Ten cubits shall be the length of a board, and a cubit and a half shall be the breadth of one board" (Ex 26:15–16). Since one cubit measured about 18 inches, each board had to be approximately 180 inches, or 15 feet, long. No provisions were made for fastening the wall boards together to attain such a height; therefore the trees providing the wood must have been straight and tall. Even though acacia grew in Palestine, it was a stunted tree, gnarled and twisted, found in the desert of Sinai and surrounding the Dead Sea. The wood for the Tabernacle may therefore have been imported from Egypt, where the acacia grew straighter in the damper soil.

Another suggestion is that the wood was not imported but came from the

Acacia albida species of Migdal Zevaya, in the Jordan Valley. This grove of trees was sacred, and in the 4th century the Talmud forbade their being cut for everyday use. As a result, these acacias still grow in the Jordan Valley area. Because this tree has a thick trunk and grows evenly to the required height, it may have been the species used for the construction of the Tabernacle.

Shittim is also the name of one of the campsites during the Exodus. Here the Israelites joined Moabites in sexual orgies linked with Moabite ritual, and here, says the Bible, 24,000 people died of the plague that God sent in retribution (Num 25:1–9). Whether these orgies were conducted under acacia trees, or any other trees, as Canaanite rituals were, is not known.

The acacia tree was used for mummy cases in Egypt, as a slow-burning fuel, and in the leather-tanning process.

Spikenard: This was fragrant imported oil from a plant known to have been grown in eastern India, and which may also have been native to the biblical area. The Song of Songs mentions it three times as a pleasant-smelling plant (S of S 1:12; 4:13–14). Oil of spikenard was in the ointment poured over Jesus' body at Bethany (Mark 14:3). It was also in the ointment Mary used to anoint Jesus' feet. This ointment was so expensive that Judas objected that the money should have been spent on the poor instead (John 12:3).

Sycamore/Fig Mulberry: Better known as the fig mulberry or the Turkish fig, the sycamore has always been common in Palestine. The modern city of Haifa was once known as Shikmonah (a name derived from the Hebrew for "sycamore"). The sycamore is confined to the lowland and coastal areas, and is extremely susceptible to frost, as the psalmist warns (Psa 78:47).

Among the uses to which it was put in biblical days were furniture, storage boxes, architectural elements, and fuel. The tree is large enough for climbing, and it is among the branches of the sycamore that Jesus found Zacchaeus (Luke 19:2–5). Because it is not affected by either moisture or heat the wood is extremely durable, and in Egypt was used for mummy cases.

Several times a year the sycamore produces a fig slightly sweeter than those from the fig tree itself. It was a common food for the poor, who gathered it a few days before the fig ripened. After taking it from the tree, they pierced the fig to induce artificial ripening. This was because, if they had left the fig to its natural ripening process on the tree, it would have been infested by insects and become inedible. The prophet Amos describes himself in some versions of the Bible as "a gatherer of sycamore fruit" but in other versions as "a dresser" of sycamore trees (Amos 7:14), referring to this piercing of the fruit.

Tamarisk: A bushlike tree, the tamarisk produces pink and white flowers. It is one of the possible translations for the "heath" mentioned by Jeremiah

(17:6), although most botanists prefer juniper. Some scholars have suggested it as the shrub under which Hagar placed her son when she thought they would die of thirst in the desert (Gen 21:15).

Thistle: A great number of thistle-type plants grow in the Holy Land. Most translators pick and choose at their own convenience, as there is no way of knowing which Hebrew word refers to which particular thorned plant. In any case, whether something is a bramble or a brier, a thorn or a thistle is inconsequential. What matters is the image of a plant that pierces the flesh and that grows in the wild rather than in cultivated fields.

One thorned plant that has been identified is the *galgal*—a biblical tumbleweed: "But God shall rebuke them, and they shall flee far off, and shall be chased as the chaff of the mountains before the wind, and like a rolling thing before the whirlwind" (Isa 17:13). The *galgal* (translated here as "chaff") is a very common plant. It grows to a large size and looks quite formidable. At its thorniest stage it is dry and the roots detach themselves from the stalk, so that the wind can blow it across the land.

Sayings about Thorns

1. "Thorns in your eyes" (Josh 23:13).
2. "Thorns in your sides" (Num 33:55. Judg 2:3).
3. "As a thorn goeth up into the hand of a drunkard, so is a parable in the mouths of fools" (Prov 26:9).
4. "As the lily among thorns, so is my love among the daughters" (S of S 2:2).
5. "The way of a slothful man is as an hedge of thorns" (Prov 15:19).
6. "As the crackling of thorns under a pot, so is the laughter of the fool" (Eccl 7:6).
7. "And thorns shall come up in her palaces, nettles and brambles in the fortresses thereof" (Isa 34:13).
8. "They have sown wheat, but shall reap thorns" (Jer 12:13).
9. "There shall be no more a pricking brier unto the house of Israel, nor any grieving thorn" (Ezek 28:24).
10. "Sow not among thorns" (Jer 4:3).
11. "Do men gather grapes of thorns?" (Matt 7:16).

The Vine: That vines and vineyards are mentioned approximately 500 times in the Old and New Testaments gives some idea of the extent to which grapevines were cultivated. Each vine has a potential production span of 300 years.

Keeping a vineyard required much work. The process included winter pruning and cultivation, dunging, spraying, watering, pruning in the spring, tying-in in the summer, and finally, the harvest. Ancient water towers have been found; these are believed to have led to ridges which divided the vineyards and supplied irrigation.

Wine or grape juice was pressed out from early times, and the Hebrew term for wine literally means "what is pressed out" from the fruit. However, not all the grapes were consumed by humans—they are a delicacy for wild animals such as the fox (S of S 2:15) and the boar (Psa 80:13).

Wine was stored in goatskins, or, for larger quantities, in ox skins. New wine was poured into newly prepared skins, as these expanded rather than split as the fermentation process took place.

A traditional image of the Holy Land is that of two of the men whom Moses sent to spy out Canaan returning with an oversized bunch of grapes carried on a pole between them: "And they came unto the brook of Eshcol, and cut down from thence a branch with one cluster of grapes, and they bare it between two upon a staff" (Num 13:23).

Vineyards are mentioned in the New Testament (Matt 20; 21:33; Luke 20:9), and Jesus once said: "I am the true vine, and my Father is the husbandman. Every branch in me that beareth not fruit he taketh away; and every branch that beareth fruit, he purgeth it, that it may bring forth more fruit" (John 15:1–2).

Vine of Sodom: The vine of Sodom (Deut 32:32) has been a puzzle to botanists. Ancient writers including Pliny and Josephus describe the vine of Sodom as bearing a fruit that appears edible but which turns to "smoke and ashes" when touched. Some believe that no plant in the Dead Sea area (probably the site of ancient Sodom) fits this description. Others point to the colocynth, an ornamental shrub still grown extensively there, as a perfect candidate. The colocynth falls off the vine when touched, squirting bitter juice as it tumbles.

A more recent and plausible suggestion is the Sodom apple. When touched it dissolves into a multitude of seeds and fibers, none of which is edible.

Walnut Tree: In the Song of Songs (6:11) a king goes down to the *egoz* garden—the only mention of this word in the Bible and a word which has confused scholars. It has been translated as "nuts," but modern translators propose "walnut." This suggestion is based upon the traditional Arab garden, which is designed around one central ornamental tree (reminiscent of the Garden of Eden), often a walnut tree.

Willow: Of the several varieties of willow tree found in Palestine, more than one probably grew there during biblical times. The willow was always described as growing on the banks of a river or brook (Lev 23:40; Job 40:22; Isa 15:7; 44:4; Ezek 17:5).

Wormwood: Mentioned along with gall, wormwood is a well-known bitter and perhaps poisonous herb, used in the Bible as a symbol of injustice and disaster. The loose and whorish woman shall come to a calamitous end "bitter as wormwood" (Prov 5:4); the evil man turns "justice to wormwood" (Amos 5:7); and among many disasters that would befall the earth at the time of Judgment was that "the third part of the waters became wormwood; and many men died on the waters, because they were made bitter" (Rev 9:11).

Then Said the Trees . . .

The trees once decided to choose a king and voted first for the olive. The olive declined, preferring to continue giving oil. The next choice, the fig, chose to retain its sweetness and fruit rather than gain a crown. Next, the vine refused because its wine was needed to cheer man and God. Finally the trees asked the bramble, which accepted the kingship and immediately became tyrannical. (Judg 9:15).

Hanging Harps on Willows

The popular folk song "There Is a Tavern in the Town," about the lover who hangs his harp on a weeping willow tree and promises to "never, never think of thee," was probably inspired by the psalm (Psa 137) about the Israelites who had been deported to Mesopotamia: "By the rivers of Babylon, there we sat down, yea, we wept, when we remembered Zion. We hanged our harps upon the willows. . . ."

Sayings about Trees

1. "The trees of the Lord are full of sap" (Psa 104:16).
2. "All the trees of the field shall clap their hands" (Isa 55:12).
3. "The voice of the Lord breaketh the cedars" (Psa 29:5).
4. "There is hope of a tree, if it be cut down, that it will sprout again" (Job 14:7).
5. "As an apple tree among the trees of the wood, so is my beloved among the sons. I sat down under his shadow with great delight, and his fruit was sweet to my taste" (S of S 2:3).

6. "And his heart was moved, and the heart of his people, as the trees of the wood are moved with the wind" (Isa 7:2).

7. "The tree of the field is man's life" (Deut 20:19).

8. "Wisdom is a tree of life" (Prov 3:18).

9. "The fruit of the righteous is a tree of life" (Prov 11:30).

10. "When desire cometh, it is a tree of life" (Prov 13:12).

11. "A wholesome tongue is a tree of life" (Prov 15:4).

12. "Shalt thou reign, because thou closest thyself in cedar?" (Jer 22:15).

13. "Howl, fir tree; for the cedar is fallen; because the mighty are spoiled: howl, O ye oaks of Bashan; for the forest of the vintage is come down" (Zech 11:2).

14. "I see men as trees, walking" (Mark 8:24).

Thou Shalt Not Plant a Tree

The Canaanites and other people surrounding the early Israelites used groves of trees for worship. To keep the children of Israel away from idol worship a law in the book of Deuteronomy forbids the planting of trees in the area surrounding any altar of God (16:21). During the time of the Second Temple a special prohibition was enforced that kept orchards, trees, and gardens at a distance from the building.

One rose garden, however, was permitted to remain—its origin attributed to the time of the prophets. Some commentators suggest that this exception was also made because the roses helped to sweeten the air—it seems that in the Jerusalem of biblical times, old vegetables, weeds, and the manure of animals all contributed a rather unpleasant odor to the streets.

Eating Books

Ezekiel claimed that God forced him to eat a book. According to Ezekiel, God gave him "a roll of a book" and then urged, "Eat this roll." Ezekiel obeyed and was surprised to find it "as honey for sweetness" (Ezek 2:8–10; 3:1–3).

Until paper was introduced in the 8th century, writing in the Near East was on papyrus, a water plant that was pressed and dried and then rolled into books. Papyrus, however, was also a food. Although the stem was tough and saved for products such as sandals or twine, the pith was tender enough to be eaten raw and was also commonly used in cooking.

However, papyrus may have had an aftertaste: "And I took the little book out of the angel's hand, and ate it up; and it was in my mouth sweet as honey: and as soon as I had eaten it, my belly was bitter" (Rev 10:10).

Biblical Bugs

Flies: While the Bible says flies were so annoying that they seemed able to "devour" people, the chief point of mentioning them was not to describe them as pests but to emphasize that God had power over them. This was important because a chief god among the Canaanites was Baal-zebub—Lord of the Flies—who was believed to be creator and controller of flies. Thus, when the Israelites went into the land of Canaan, where the power of their God was challenged by believers in the native gods, it was vital to show who actually controlled the flies. God is shown sending swarms of flies upon the pharaoh, upon his servants, and upon his people; flies also swarmed into the houses of Egyptians and all over the ground. In sending this plague, God spared only Goshen, where the Israelites lived. And later, when the pharaoh promised to let the Israelites go, God removed the flies (Ex 8:21–31).

In Isaiah (7:18) God calls for the flies, which swarm out of the rivers to alight in the desolate valleys, in the holes in the rocks, and upon all the bushes. Similar power to control flies is described in Psalms (78:45; 105:31).

The final biblical reference to flies (Eccl 10:1) does not mention Baal-zebub by name but describes a "stinking" ointment made with dead flies—apparently used in religious ceremonies dedicated to Baal-zebub or for some medical power it was believed to have had.

Locusts: No insect was more feared—or depicted more often in the Bible—than the locust. The Hebrew use of several words for locust has confused translators. For instance, in detailing the four edible flying insects that leaped (Lev 11:22), translators listed locust, bald locust, grasshopper; and—

stuck for a fourth term—some inserted beetle. However, as most beetles don't leap, other translators inserted "cricket" instead. Probably all the Hebrew words—whether translated as beetle, cankerworm, caterpillar, cricket, grasshopper, or palmerworm—refer to locusts in different stages of development.

Locusts pass through several distinct forms in their growth cycle. When the young (nymphs) hatch from eggs that have been laid in the ground, they have no wings and have to move about on their legs. Their hind legs, longer than the front ones, make them good jumpers. Normally locusts then develop long wings and a solitary lifestyle, and are no more bothersome than other crop-eating insects. This may be why in a few instances the Old Testament suggests that locusts are helpless and timid—Job (39:20) calls them "afraid"; in Numbers (13:33) some of the spies sent to Canaan report seeing giants who made them feel small as grasshoppers; and the psalmist (109:23) laments being "tossed up and down as the locust." New Testament authors apparently did not experience any plagues, because their only comment on these insects is that John the Baptist subsisted on them in the wilderness (Matt 3:4; Mark 1:6).

What changes locusts from relatively harmless grasshoppers to a horror is the migratory stage. Most locusts do not migrate regularly, as birds do, but at erratic, unpredictable intervals—at which times they develop a special, short-winged migratory form. This is the stage in which they become a plague, because simultaneously with the change to short wings locusts undergo a population explosion. Their metabolic rate rises, and the insects become nervous and restless. They cease their solitary life and become gregarious. Nymphs become more active and begin to wander about in bands. Adults congregate in large numbers and take flight in swarms, flying up to twelve miles per hour on the prevailing winds.

Why, since they have no leader to order them about, do locusts suddenly take it into their heads to go "forth all of them by bands"? The question, posed by Proverbs (30:27), has not yet been answered. Scientists trying to explain what triggers these sudden migrations and increases in numbers think unusually heavy rain is one factor.

Characteristic of migration is that the insects swarm, fly a leg of their journey, and then settle with voracious appetites to gather strength to fly on again. The Bible says they become a "burden" (Eccl 12:5), a "plague" (1 Kings 8:37), and an "evil" (2 Chr 6:28). As the enormous appetite of locusts on migration is recounted many times in the Bible, "devoured" is the word many writers chose to explain the sudden assault that strips bare gardens, vineyards, fig trees, olive trees, "all the herbs," fruit, even the grass (Deut 28:42; 2 Chr 7:13; Psa 78:46; 105:34–5; Amos 4:9; 7:12; Nah 3:15–17).

The most vivid descriptions of destruction by locusts are found in Exodus and Joel. Exodus (10:12–19) tells how the locusts suddenly flew into Egypt on an east wind, coming in such numbers that they blanketed the land and blotted out the sun, and laid such waste that no green thing was left in the land. Isaiah (40:22) says the insects stretched across the heavens like a curtain, spreading out over you so that you felt you were inside a dark tent. None of this is exaggerated. The migratory locust does fly in such swarms as to blacken the sky. One swarm in the Red Sea area in the late 19th century was estimated to extend over 2000 square miles. The largest swarm ever recorded was estimated at 40 billion locusts.

Once they settle on the landscape the swarm becomes a moving carpet, and Isaiah (33:4) conveys a certain horror with his complaint of their nervous "running to and fro." Nahum (3:15–17) explains the habit of these "great grasshoppers" of camping in the hedges as the sun goes down and it becomes cool, flying on their way the next day only after the sun has risen to warm and dry them. How far they fly depends on the temperature: They fly when the temperature goes over 60° F. in the sun or 75° F. on cloudy days, and descend when nightfall causes a drop in temperature. With such stopovers, swarms have been known to cover up to 3000 miles, so their descent in a new area—in an era without modern communications—came without warning.

The migratory phenomenon so impressed the ancients that the word locust became synonymous with an invasion of uncountable numbers. Thus Midianites overrunning the Israelites with their cattle and tents "came as grasshoppers for multitude" (Judg 6:5; 7:12); and in telling how Babylon would fall, God promises men and horses coming up "as caterpillars" (Jer 51:14, 27). Both comparisons evoke not only the image of total invasion, but also convey the astonishing noisiness of locust infestation. Locusts have sound-producing organs on their forewings and back legs, and since a single insect's song is audible to the human ear the collective vibration of a swarm becomes a roar. Even more eerie is that while the sound of a single grasshopper eating is inaudible, the working jaws of a swarm create a unique crackle that Joel (1:6) compared to the "teeth of a lion."

Joel's account of the descent of a swarm is chilling. He calls them a great army, leaping across the mountaintops, their wings making a terrible noise he can only compare to chariots or to the roar of a fire. They close out the sun, making the earth dark and gloomy. Men are helpless to stop them. They run like mighty soldiers, never breaking rank as they storm over walls, run to and fro in the city, climb up the houses and enter windows. They devour everything in their path—vineyards, apple and pomegranate trees, palms, wheat, barley, and other crops—so that while a Garden of Eden stretches before them, behind they leave only a desolate wilderness. They eat everything green, and strip bark from trees, so that branches are left white. Men lament, and even the cattle and sheep are perplexed and desolate at the disappearance of their pasture.

Moths: Disgust at finding clothes, rugs, and other woolen and fur possessions moth-eaten is vividly conveyed by biblical authors. Moths are unanimously judged to be destructive, not as the locust plague with all-consuming voracity, but in a slower, more insidious, and inevitable way. Thus, to punish Ephraim for iniquity, God promises to be as thoroughly destructive as a moth. Isaiah (50:9; 51:8) can find no choicer words for warning of what will happen to adversaries than to describe them as eaten up by moths like an old garment. That clothing will eventually be moth-eaten is taken for granted (Job 13:8; James 5:2).

Moths are frequently associated with something insubstantial. Job speaks disdainfully of building a house as a moth does (27:18) and of houses so flimsy they can be crushed by a moth (5:19); and in Psalms (39:11) beauty is said to be consumed like a moth. In the New Testament advice to store your treasures in heaven rather than on earth, the certain destruction of any earthly treasures you try to keep is attributed (Matt 6:19–20) to rust and moths or to theft and moths (Luke 12:33).

Scorpions: Although a species of scorpion inhabiting the Sahara Desert inflicts a sting that can kill a man within a few hours, the dozen or more species found in Palestine—which vary in size from less than an inch to six inches long—inflict painful though not lethal stings. Nevertheless, as they hide in crevices or under rocks during the day, they can be easily stumbled on by the unwary, and to the sandal-shod Israelites they represented a real danger (Deut 8:15; Ezek 2:6).

Scorpions played frightening roles in the mythologies of people surrounding the Israelites. In an Egyptian story, the evil god Set disguised himself as a scorpion to kill the good god Horus. In the *Epic of Gilgamesh,* the hero set out to find the world of the dead so that he could bring his friend Enkidu back to life. But Gilgamesh found that the way to the rising and setting sun was guarded by monsters that were half human and half scorpion. Only because Gilgamesh was two-thirds god did the scorpion people allow him to pass. Such traditions may have been in the mind of Jesus, who assured the disciples they could tread on scorpions without harm (Luke 10:19). In Revelation fear of scorpions persists (9:3, 5, 10); scorpions are said to "have power"; their method of stinging through their tails is described as dreadful; and to make torment meaningful it is equated with the "torment of a scorpion." In one image of particular horror, the loveless god is said to be like the father who gives a child asking for an egg a scorpion instead (Luke 11:12).

The sting of the scorpion is so painful that a special type of whip or scourge came to be given this name. The scorpion was probably more elaborate than a simple whip, with several cords or thongs tipped with metal knobs or spikes. King Rehoboam swore that though his father chastised the people with whips he was going to use the more dreaded scorpion (1 Kings 12:11, 14; 2 Chr 10:11, 14).

Every Creeping Thing

Chameleon: Chameleons of Palestine are small and agile, easily climbing trees and walls. Their skins change to various hues of green, gray, and brown—not depending on the background, as commonly believed, but on a combination of light, temperature, and emotional factors. They usually have a mottled appearance that camouflages them when they are among leaves or in shadows. Each eye moves independently, but when they see an insect they focus with both eyes to gauge distance and then flick out their tongues, which have a sticky tip that ensnares the prey. Whether they are really mentioned in the Bible is argued. In the listing of creeping things unclean to eat (Lev 11:30), some translations give chameleon as one of the three lizard-type of creatures.

Crocodile: The Nile crocodile, exterminated in much of Egypt and Palestine in the 19th century, was once known the length of Egypt; it swam in the Nile delta and Mediterranean, and inhabited coastal marshes and rivers in Israel.

In Egypt, crocodiles were sacred to Set, a god of evil. Ombos had a temple complex dedicated to a crocodile-headed god (Suchos), and at Crocodilopolis and other places where they were worshiped live crocodiles were kept in pools. Even crocodile mummies have been found in several Egyptian cemeteries. The Nile crocodile is more aggressive than many found elsewhere, and is known to be a man-eater. Incantations to keep crocodiles at a safe distance have been found in papyri. Egyptians domesticated the mongoose (ichneumon), which was said to protect man from crocodiles because it was fond of hunting their nests along the Nile and eating the eggs.

The Bible used no word specifically for crocodile but some of the references to dragons, monsters, or the Leviathan (Job 41) undoubtedly describe it, especially when the monster is used as a symbol of Egypt or the pharaoh: "Pharaoh king of Egypt, the great dragon that lieth in the midst of his rivers" (Ezek 29:3) and "Pharaoh king of Egypt . . . thou camest forth with thy rivers, and troubledst the waters with thy feet, and fouledst their rivers" (Ezek 32:2).

Distinctions between the crocodile and the snake were not always clear in ancient times. The Egyptian monster Apep was sometimes represented as a snake and at other times as a crocodile. In the story of Aaron's rod transforming itself into a "serpent" (Ex 7:9–13), a crocodile may have been meant, because the original Hebrew word was simply a general term for monster.

Frog: Frogs were not as hated as snakes were but there was some aversion to them—"unclean spirits like frogs" (Rev 16:13). When the Israelites were in bondage frogs were sent by God as a loathsome plague (Ex 8:2, 7; Psa 78:45, 105:30). So many frogs came out of the Nile that they poured into the houses, leaping into beds and ovens, and even jumping on the Egyptians themselves. When the frogs had covered the land, the pharaoh sent for Moses and asked that he have God return the frogs to the river. Instead, God killed the frogs so that they dropped dead all over the villages, houses, and fields; though the Egyptians tried to tidy up by tossing them into heaps, the stench of their rotting bodies remained.

Lizard: The Hebrew word for lizard was a general term for a number of species, and could have covered several or all of the following lizards found in Palestine:

Largest of all is the desert monitor *(Varanus),* a strong, rough-skinned creature that can grow over three and a half feet in length. It is fond of sandy terrain, prospering in the northern Negev, where it eats rodents as well as reptiles and amphibians. The related Nile monitor, which Israelites who had lived in Egypt might have known, is a good swimmer found in rivers and streams.

Harduns (agamids), which grow to only half the size of monitors, are more colorful; although they may be grayish or tannish when inactive in the cool of dawn or evening, some species when warmed by the sun (or during mating season) turn yellow, reddish, or even blue. Like monitors, harduns have rough skins and thick bodies, but because they prefer rocky terrain to sand they have longer legs to enable them to clamber over rocks. They are vegetarians and tend to be shy. While most species hide out in the Negev, one species *(Agama stellio)* is common in populated areas in central and northern Israel.

The smoother-skinned lizards (suborder Lacertilia) vary from tannish-hued desert dwellers to the green lizard of woodlands that can grow up to about a foot long. Especially interesting are the insect-eating geckos, which grow only up to two or three inches. Because their toes are covered with tiny bristles ending in suction cups (visible only under a microscope), they can climb walls with ease and hang upside down from the ceiling. Unlike other lizards, which seek the sun, geckos hunt at night. They are unique among lizards in being very vocal, and the name gecko derives from an Asian interpretation of the noise it makes, while its Hebrew name implies that its cry is a wail. Although some translators list "ferret" among the creeping things unclean to eat (Lev 11:29), "gecko" is probably correct here.

In other passages too, where snail, tortoise, land crocodile, mole, or other terms are used, some translators believe that one of the above lizards may have been meant.

SNAKES

The only good thing the Bible has to say about snakes is in Proverbs (30:19), where the serpent is admired—along with other wonders such as the flight of an eagle—for its beauty and grace of movement (or possibly just for the fact it can move about despite not having feet).

Everywhere else, the Bible reveals only loathing for snakes. Although Palestine has only about eight poisonous species, biblical authors are concerned mostly with these, holding the snake up as a symbol of evil.

Because Israel's neighbors associated the serpent with an earth mother, it is not surprising to find the serpent with Eve at the very beginning of Genesis (3). But while other peoples had the snake play a beneficent role in fertility cults, the biblical serpent is continually used to represent enemies, the wicked, and every other odious thing. Often there is the connotation that its attack is sneaky—as in "more subtle than any beast of the field" (Gen 3:1), or in the image of the way it hides in a wall (Eccl 10:8), or the contrast between the frontal assault of a lion as opposed to the quietness of the asp (Psa 91:13). Even when Jesus told his disciples to be wise as serpents (Matt 10:16), it probably wasn't a compliment on intelligence so much as a warning to be as cunning and subtle as Satan.

Biblical disparagement of snakes is probably due to the fact that snakes played a prominent role in the religions of virtually all the peoples with whom the Israelites had contact. In Egypt, Re was primary among several gods identified with the serpent, and pharaohs had the image of a cobra on their crown; Egyptians recorded on papyrus incantations to repulse snakes (and worms) and to ward off snakebite. One of the monsters of Egypt was the serpent fiend, Apep. Archaeologists have found votive models and serpentine decorative motifs in Egyptian temples, and live snakes may have been kept in the temples too. Because the snake sheds its skin and thus seems to renew itself, Mesopotamians and Semites believed it was immortal—or, as the Egyptian *Book of the Dead* says, the serpent dies and is born again, and grows young each day.

There is some evidence that some early Hebrews may have identified God with a serpent too, because while the Bible merely says that Moses was afraid to look upon God (Ex 3:6), a Midrash version has God appearing to Moses in the shape of a huge snake. In addition, after God sent fiery serpents that killed so many Israelites in the wilderness, Moses made the brazen serpent—a brass figure of a venomous snake that was set upon a pole. Anyone bitten by a snake had only to look at the brazen serpent to recover. The Israelites burned incense before this figure and revered it for hundreds of years, until King Hezekiah broke it to pieces about 700 BC (2 Kings 18:4). However, other metal serpents have been found by archaeologists; among those dated from the time of Moses (14th century BC) are an eight-inch snake from Gezer that seems to be a cobra, and a five-inch copper model with a gilded head from an Egyptian temple at Timna.

Because of the prevalence of snake worship, the Hebrews had to establish the supremacy of God by emphasizing that God had created snakes (Job 26:13) and their poison (Deut 32:24). Once having created snakes, God retained power over them (Psa 91:13). He used them to punish mankind, making the serpents appear and disappear at will (Num 21:6–7; Jer 8:17). Even if a man should try to hide in the bottom of the sea, God can command serpents to follow and strike him there (Amos 9:3). Isaiah's prediction (11:8) that snakes will become harmless to man after the restoration of Israel is reflected in the New Testament, where Jesus tells his disciples that they shall have the power to tread on serpents (Luke 10:19) and to handle serpents (Mark 16:18).

Perhaps God did not originally intend snakes to be evil, because the original serpent, in the Garden of Eden (Gen 3), is introduced simply as a snake, not as a viper or other venomous type. Eve is not afraid of it or of trusting its advice. In fact, this serpent differs from all others in the Bible in being able to speak. It also reasons intelligently enough to convince Eve, and it has a lot of self-confidence since it's not the least perturbed at disobeying God. Probably it even has charm, as Eve says it "beguiled" her. Far from suspecting this nice snake of evil, God first suspects Adam—it's not until Adam blames Eve that God is finally informed the snake is wicked. And it is only then that God curses the snake, decreeing perpetual enmity between snake and man—the snake would bruise (bite) man's heel and man would bruise the snake's head.

According to subsequent views of snakes in the Bible, snakes will bite you if you are on a path (Gen 49:17), if you disturb a hedge they're hiding in (Eccl 10:8), if they are not enchanted by snake charmers (Eccl 10:11), if God commands them to attack (Deut 32:24; Jer 8:17; Amos 9:3), or even if you just lean your hand against stones (Amos 5:19).

Their venom is "cruel" (Deut 32:33) and can kill you (Job 20:16; 1 Cor

135

10:9). Even the fact that snakes have no feet seemed to be held against them. In fact, some people have suggested that God's cursing of the snake "above every beast of the field" and commanding that "upon thy belly shalt thou go, and dust shalt thou eat all the days of thy life" (Gen 3:14) means that the snake once stood upright and was deprived of feet only after tempting Eve.

Everything evil in the Bible is compared to the venomous snake. Wicked men "suck the poison of asps" (Job 20:16) and contain "the gall of asps within" (Job 20:14), have the "poison of asps under their lips" (Rom 3:13), and hatch a cockatrice's egg that "breaketh out into a viper" (Isa 59:5). People whose speech offends have tongues "full of deadly poison" (James 3:8), slanderers "have sharpened their tongues like a serpent" and have adders' poison under their lips (Psa 140:3). Babblers are like snakes that will not be charmed (Eccl 10:11), and corrupt judges are "like the poison of a serpent" (Psa 58:4–5).

Entire populations who will not heed the word of God, such as Babylon (Isa 14) and Assyria (Isa 27), are compared to serpents. And Jeremiah (46:22–23) predicts that the voice of Egypt "shall go like a serpent." Finally, the New Testament sums up all sinners as a "generation of vipers" (Matt 3:7; 12:34; 23:33; Luke 3:7).

The only faintly amusing mention of snakes is the description of what happens when you drink too much wine—"at the last it biteth like a serpent and stingeth like a basilisk" (Prov 23:32).

Serpent: Although Israel has more than thirty-five species of snakes, the Bible has so few words for snakes that ancient translators and modern herpetologists have not been very successful at identifying particular species.

Of the Hebrew words used for snake one is a general term usually translated simply as "serpent." Theoretically serpent could mean any of the harmless snakes of the Middle East. The smallest of these is the blind snake (Typhlopidae)—so-called because its tiny eyes are overlapped with scales and hardly visible. This brownish burrowing snake, which could easily be mistaken for a big worm, seldom exceeds eight or nine inches in length and is almost toothless, feeding on larvae, ants, and other insects. The largest harmless snake is the sleek whip snake *(Coluber jugularis)*. However, because it grows over five feet long and is quick at pursuing birds, rodents, and other fast-moving prey, it looks formidable enough to be frightening, even though it belongs to the same family as the harmless garter snakes of North America. Israel's only aquatic serpent, the dice snake *(Natrix)*, named for the greenish-grayish mosaic pattern on its back, is common from Europe to Asia and North Africa. Usually no more than a couple of feet long, it feeds on fish and other cold-blooded water life.

Asps and Adders: Virtually all references to snakes imply they are venomous. This may reflect a sensible precaution, since early footwear would have made people vulnerable to snakebite, and under primitive living conditions even ordinary bacteria from the mouth of a nonpoisonous species could result in infection.

As snakes do not usually bite unless threatened, the trek via the Red Sea to the wilderness, where fiery serpents bit the people so that "much of the people died" (Num 21:6), sounds exaggerated. But as the Israelites were in unfamiliar desert, they probably met with new species whose habits were unfamiliar to them, and mass bites could have resulted from stumbling into an area favored for denning. Probably, too, the people would have been exploring—poking into caves, dislodging stones by climbing up hillsides to get an overview, and otherwise unwittingly disturbing snakes. Most dangerous of all was the necessity for camping near water, where the dampness would have attracted many species. At oases, the roots of palm trees dangle like long strands of spaghetti, making excellent hiding places for snakes, and a thirsty mob descending on a water hole would have terrified even docile snakes into defensive action. Snakes in the vicinity of water long remained a problem, because a well on the west side of Jerusalem was later called Dragon's Spring (Neh 2:13) and Zoheleth (a word for serpent) is the name given to rocks near springs at En-rogel (1 Kings 1:9). Another common way of being bitten, as happened to Paul (Acts 28:3), must have been the gathering of kindling and wood for fire. On Malta, Paul had either picked up a small snake while gathering branches or had built his fire over a hidden snake or den, because a viper came out of the fire and bit him.

Which poisonous species the Israelites encountered is not clear, not only because the Hebrews weren't specific but also because English usage is often almost as vague. While viper, cobra, asp, and adder usually designate poisonous snakes, all four are confused in popular usage (and, in fact, in some common names used by scientists). The venomous snakes of the Bible would either have been vipers (family Viperidae), which have long, movable fangs, or cobras (family Elapidae), which have short, stationary fangs as well as inflatable hoods. "Asps" and "adders"—not scientific designations—are usually vipers. Where confusion arises is in a few instances—such as that of the Egyptian asp—in which the snake commonly called an asp or adder is scientifically considered a cobra or may even be a totally harmless species of another family.

Vipers: Vipers have such long fangs that they cannot close their mouths with the fangs extended. The viper's unique characteristic is that its fangs swivel—they are kept folded against the roof of the mouth when the snake is at rest, but swing forward like hypodermic needles to inject venom when the snake bites. Vipers also have extra-wide heads to accommodate the two large poison glands, set either side of the jaw, that feed the fangs.

One reason vipers pose a hazard to humans is that although they hunt also at night, they are primarily daytime hunters. Today the most dangerous is the Palestine viper, because it seeks out rodents, and thus is most often encountered in settled areas where mice and rats thrive.

Another reason vipers are so dangerous to humans is that their efficient system of killing prey makes them rather sluggish. They are well camouflaged and tend to lie around in the open during the day, waiting for some small mammal or other victim to wander by; they strike like lightning and then drop the victim, not bothering to chase it because the toxin acts so fast (almost instantaneously). Between the camouflage and the reluctance to move, it's easy for a person to step on one unwittingly. "A serpent by the way, an adder in the path, that biteth the horse heels" (Gen 49:17) could describe a viper.

The "viper" that attacked Paul from his fire on Malta (Acts 28:3) is said to have fastened onto his hand so hard that he had to shake it off. When the locals saw his hand had not even swollen and he had not "fallen down dead," they decided he was a god. It is possible to be bitten by a poisonous snake without ill effects, because it has used up its venom on a previous strike or simply chose to bite and not inject poison. If this was a poisonous snake it is unlikely it was a true viper, because the fastening and holding on is contrary to typical viper behavior.

The vipers that live in the Negev include the nose-horned viper *(Vipera ammodytes)*—also called sand viper and other names. "Nose-horned" describes the characteristic soft "horn" covered with scales that protrudes from the snout. Seldom reaching three feet in length, and subsisting on small rodents and lizards, this snake is rather placid in disposition. It likes to bask in the sun and is slow to move away should a human approach.

The Palestinian horned viper or horned asp *(Cerastes),* sometimes used by snake charmers, is a special danger because it can see when almost completely buried in the sand. This snake, which can grow almost a yard long, is sandy-colored to match its desert surroundings. Its "horns" are two sharp spines, one above each eye. Its favorite method of hunting is to bury itself in the sand, hidden from view, with only its eyes and spines exposed. It is stubborn about budging from its hiding place, and will not move until it is almost stepped on. Sand vipers of the *Cerastes* genus move by sidewinding, a beautiful wavelike motion that makes them seem to skim over the sand and enables them to quickly sink from view.

Slightly different is the little carpet viper *(Echis carinatus),* which burrows rather than slithers into the sand. It too likes to lie in wait with only its head exposed, but is more excitable and quicker to bite than the *Cerastes* viper. At the approach of danger it will fling itself a foot or more into the air to attack. Although *Echis* is much smaller than *Cerastes,* the venom is extremely toxic and has caused fatalities.

Cobras: The cobra's fangs are so much shorter than a viper's that the cobra has no problem closing its mouth over them and therefore doesn't need the viper's fang-folding mechanism. Cobras behave quite differently and their strike is not nearly so fast as a viper's.

The Egyptian cobra *(Naja haje),* often called the asp, got its name

138

because it was so often chosen for exhibit by the snake charmers of Egypt. Charmers also use the horned *Cerastes* and other snakes, but as Jeremiah pointed out (8:17), there are some serpents "which will not be charmed, and they shall bite." The Egyptian cobra is a good choice for charmers as it grows to an impressive length—about six feet. Although it appears to follow the music, the Bible is correct in describing "the deaf adder that stoppeth her ear which will not hearken to the voice of charmers" (Psa 58:4–5). All snakes are deaf to airborne sounds (though sensitive to ground vibrations) and the cobras are in reality responding to movements of the snake charmer. Cobras are easily excited, blowing up their hoods, hissing, and repeatedly feigning strikes. However, whether they will "bite if not enchanted" (Eccl 10:11) is open to question. They tend to attack slowly, gliding forward with inflated hoods and moving their heads from side to side while hissing loudly. When they are confronted with humans this threatening display may satisfy them so that they do not bother to bite. Also, cobras appear not to strike accurately in daylight. This ability to put on a good show, and the ample warning before striking, make the Egyptian cobra good for exhibition. Charmers are in little danger if they remain alert to subtle changes in the snake's movements. There is some evidence that cobras are intelligent enough to play the game, having learned they have nothing to fear from the charmer.

Should the cobra bite, though, it doesn't favor the lightning injection and withdrawal of the viper but tends to sink its fangs deeply into its victim and to retain its hold. Snake charmers who don't trust their own skills frequently extract the fangs, which may be the meaning of "break their teeth" (Psa 58:3). Although the venom is effective on toads, birds, and other natural foods, few bites result in fatalities in humans.

Basilisk and Cockatrice: The use of "basilisk" and "cockatrice" in some versions of the Bible is confusing. Today, the basilisk—from the Greek, meaning "little king"—is the name of a crested lizard. But in the past the basilisk and cockatrice were legendary reptiles that hatched from a cock's egg and could kill with their breath or with a glance. In medieval bestiaries they were represented as having the head, wings, and legs of a cock but the tail of a serpent. A cock in medieval Europe was actually tried and executed for laying a cockatrice egg.

However, in the Bible the basilisk is apparently not a legendary monster but a real, venomous snake. Chances are the "little king" was a cobra, because this was a symbol of Lower Egypt and the pharaohs wore cobra motifs on their foreheads as well as headdresses that resembled the inflated cobra's hood. Isaiah's statement (59.5) that the cockatrice lays eggs would also point to a cobra, because many vipers are ovoviviparous (that is, they do not lay true eggs; the eggs develop fully inside the female and hatch as she ejects them). A good guess is that it was the Egyptian cobra—and the loud hisses this snake makes as it strikes might explain the basilisk's purported fatal breath. Another possibility is that it was a spitting cobra, which also hisses loudly but which sprays (instead of injecting) its venom. This snake, found in Egypt as well as other parts of Africa, grows as long as seven feet. Forcing its venom through the tips of its fangs in a jetlike stream, it attempts to hit its victim's eyes, causing blindness and intense pain. (The spitting cobra may also be the model for the serpent in Revelation 12:15, which "cast out of his mouth water as a flood.") Whatever snake was the basis for the basilisk legend, it was held in dread in biblical times, creating one of the most powerful images of the peaceable kingdom of the Messiah—"The suckling child shall play on the hole of the asp, and the weaned child shall put his hand on the cockatrice's den" (Isa 11:8).

Fiery Serpent: When "fiery serpent" was specified, a venomous species was meant. The Hebrew word for heat was used for venom because of the painful burning sensation resulting from some snakebites.

"Fiery serpents" would probably have meant vipers rather than cobras. Cobra venom works chiefly on the nervous system, causing gradual weakness and paralysis but little pain. Death would come as vital muscles—those of the heart or those connected with breathing—ceased to work.

In contrast, viper venom, though fast-acting on rodents and other small prey, is very painful in humans. This venom works primarily on the blood cells, breaking them down and inhibiting the blood from clotting. Within five minutes or even less, the area of the bite is painful—with a strong burning that "fiery" would aptly describe. In a few more minutes the area of the bite begins to swell and discolor rapidly, and swelling may involve the entire limb, doubling its size. Profuse perspiration and reflex vomiting are among the symptoms. Death is usually from internal hemorrhage or damage to the heart.

Flying Serpent: Although some snakes have loose belly scales that catch on bark, enabling them to climb trees, and such arboreal snakes are able to bridge gaps between branches, no snakes actually fly. The fiery "flying" serpent (Isa 30:6) might be a cobra, since—with a little imagination—the inflated hood might look like wings. However, "flying" would also appropriately describe the rapid strike vipers make, the carpet viper's ability to fling itself into the air, or the sand viper's way of skimming over sand as though not touching ground.

The Voice of the Turtle

Although Israel has turtles and tortoises, they are not mentioned in the Bible. One of the unclean animals that some Bibles translate as "tortoise" is probably a mistranslation for "lizard" (Lev 11:29). As for the turtles—such as "the voice of the turtle" that is heard in the spring (S of S 2:12)—these are not reptiles at all but turtledoves.

Creatures of Uncertainty

The Bible mentions about 130 animals—ranging from ants and flies to bears and lions—but many of the Bible's references to animals are controversial because:

1. Some animals have more than one name in Hebrew.

2. Some Hebrew words can mean more than one animal.

3. Hebrew occasionally had a different word for the male, the female, and the young of the same species.

4. Names of animals changed in popular speech.

5. Scientific animal classification was not widely adopted until the 18th century, long after major translations of the Bible had been made.

6. Some animals known in ancient times later became extinct.

7. Translators who lived in other times and in other environments used names of animals they knew instead of animals known to biblical authors.

8. The prohibition against graven images means that few illustrations have come down to us. Most pictures or sculptures are from Egypt and Assyria, where species might have been different from those in Israel and where animal depiction often was based on stylistic conventions.

9. Several animals mentioned in the Bible have never been identified. All of the above has resulted in some comic guesswork and startlingly different translations—one word has been translated both as "ferret" and "gecko," and another as "chameleon" and "mole."

All Creatures Great and Small

Except possibly for Solomon, who took enough scientific interest in animals to classify them loosely (as beasts, fowl, creeping things, and fish) and to lecture on them (1 Kings 4:33-34), the ancient Hebrews were not inquisitive when it came to wild animals.

The Hebrews took a very practical attitude, judging animals according to how beneficial or damaging they were to man. According to Mosaic law, most wild animals could not be used as food because they lacked cloven hooves or failed to meet other dietary strictures. Wild animals also could not be used in sacrifices because they did not represent wealth, and killing one would therefore not be a true loss. In addition, predators that lived by violence and animals that fed on carrion were considered inappropriate for the sanctuary. As a result, most wild animals were useless, if not a nuisance or outright danger. Unlike the Egyptians, who loved and revered wild animals, who tamed and kept many, and who had prohibitions against killing them, the Hebrews tended to dislike and fear wild animals and had few laws to protect them. Except for a hint that birds were caged (Jer 5:27), the Bible mentions no pets.

Ape: Apes were among the marvelous things brought back to Israel by Solomon's navy (1 Kings 10:22; 2 Chr 9:21). Monkeys too were imported as a curiosity. Although no illustrations exist of Solomon's fleet, an Egyptian relief shows one of Queen Hatshepsut's laden ships—less than 500 years after Solomon—returning with large apes, apparently unfettered, walking and sitting among the cargo.

Badger: It isn't clear whether badgers are mentioned in the Bible, because all references are to its pelt and give no hint of the animal's habits.

Israel does have a rock badger (see Coney), but the skin of this animal would not have made luxurious shoes (Ezek 6:10) or have been used to cover the Tabernacle (Ex 25:5; 26:14; 35:7, 23; 36:19; Num 4:10).

Because an Arabic cognate suggests a seal, some translators use "sealskin" instead of "badger skin." The "seal" might have been a dugong. The dugong, which grows over ten feet long, is a slow-moving mammal that is strictly vegetarian, feeding in the shallows of the Red Sea and other warm waters. Because it suckles its pup holding it upright between its fins, it is one of the animals that may have inspired mermaid stories.

Israel also has other small furbearers—such as otters and members of the weasel family such as the marbled polecat—which also would have yielded pelts.

Bat: Israel has more than a dozen species of bats, by modern definition, ranging from small insect-eaters to large fruit bats that can decimate groves of dates, figs, and other crops. In biblical times the bat was considered a bird. It is listed with storks and heron, and is one of the "fowls that creep, going on all four" that are prohibited as food (Lev 11:19; Deut 14:18).

The Israelites detested bats, as they detested owls and all other creatures of the night. In his vision of the day when God would be exalted and swords beaten into plowshares, Isaiah (2:20) sees idols cast to rodents and bats. In the Apocrypha (Baruch 6:22), Jeremy tells of bats sitting on the idols in the gloomy Babylonian temples.

Bear: The gray-colored Syrian bear *(Ursus syriacus)* that once inhabited the Holy Land became extinct in the early 20th century because of pleasure hunting, but in biblical times it inhabited forests and deserts throughout Palestine. Because it was unpredictable doing nothing at one meeting with man, and unexpectedly attacking at the next meeting—and because it made little effort to avoid man, the bear was feared more than the lion. In fact, Amos' remark (5:19) about a man fleeing from a lion only to meet a bear seems to be the Bible's equivalent of "out of the frying pan, into the fire."

Although the Bible (Lam 3:10) speaks of a bear "lying in wait," two she bears came boldly out of the woods to maul forty-two children who had taunted Elisha (2 Kings 2:24), and bears are also said to have been "ranging" and dangerous (Prov 28:15). Apparently they were a bother to shepherds; David killed one that was after his sheep.

Biblical authors knew quite a lot about bears, evidence that they frequently saw them. Daniel (7:5) describes the bear as a frightening beast, and Revelation (13:2) seems to find its huge feet especially horrible. Isaiah (59:11) was impressed by the roar and also used bears—contrasted feeding with cows—in an image of the Messiah's peaceable kingdom. Especially feared and dangerous was a sow robbed of, and sorrowing for, her cubs (2 Sam 17:18; Prov 17:12; Hos 13:8).

Boar: The wild boar, a forest dweller, is probably the ancestor of the modern pig. It was domesticated in Europe by 1500 BC, and was hunted in the wild for sport and game. Because a wild boar weighing up to 300 pounds could trample crops and root them up with tusks as long as nine inches, in the Bible boars are mentioned solely as a menace—"the wild boar out of the wood doth waste" the vine (Psa 80:13). Although neither Jews nor Muslims eat boar today, excavated caves on Mount Carmel show it was eaten in Old Testament times and that tools were made from its tusks.

Cat: Israel has a wild cat (probably related to the cat that has been domesticated in the Middle East for at least 5000 years) that lives in wooded ravines in the north. A slightly larger jungle cat frequents fishponds and the Jordan River, and there's a species of lynx that lives in the desert. But the Bible makes no mention of them.

This omission may have something to do with the cat's esteem and veneration among Israel's enemies. Egypt was especially fond of cats, which were kept around buildings to catch rodents and trained as retrievers in hunting. Only in the Apocrypha are cats mentioned briefly, and identified with idolatry: In Jeremy's epistle (Baruch 6:22) to captives being taken to Babylon, where he warns them not to be frightened by pagan practices, he explains that in the spooky foreign temples they can expect to see the faces of the idols blackened with smoke, and sitting on the images will be bats, swallows, and cats.

Chamois: This goatlike animal of European mountains is mentioned only once in some translations of the Bible (Deut 14:5), and probably the reference is to wild mountain sheep.

Coney: Although "coney" in England means a rabbit, in Palestine it refers to the common rock badger, or hyrax, a harmless little vegetarian that is widespread throughout the area. It's about the size of a rabbit, but has small round ears and a tail so short it's hidden by its fur. The Bible describes coneys as "a feeble folk," who make their homes in rocks and are "exceeding wise." Strangely enough, the coney's closest relative is probably the elephant.

The coney was considered by the Israelites to be an unclean animal, unsuitable for food (Lev 11:5; Deut 14:7) because its feet are not cloven. The other two mentions of the hyrax in the Bible also refer to its remarkable feet and rock-climbing ability (Psa 104:18; Prov 30:24, 26). Despite being chunky, it is agile, climbing with ease right up the face of smooth, steep surfaces. It can do this because of pads on the bottoms of its feet that, kept damp with special secretions, enable it to cling.

Deer: In Old Testament times, there were roe deer *(Capreolus capreolus)*, red deer *(Cervus elaphus)*, and fallow deer *(Dama dama)*, but confusions in terms and mistranslation have made them difficult to identify in biblical references. Also, "hart" and "roebuck" for male deer and "hind" for females occur in some Bibles and could mean any of these species.

Roe deer, sometimes called Carmel deer, survived until this century on Mount Carmel and at Huleh Lake. After they became extinct in the 1930s, new stock was imported from Poland to reestablish them in Israel.

Red deer, sometimes called Solomon's deer, became extinct during the Crusades and were reintroduced from Europe.

Fallow deer were taken to Great Britain in the Middle Ages by Crusaders, and from this stock breeding pairs were returned to Israel after they had become extinct there in the 20th century.

All ruminants that had cloven hooves and chewed cud were allowed to be eaten, and Isaac was said to have been especially fond of venison. Because of their generally gentle and "loving" nature (Prov 5:19), it's possible that deer were tamed and/or kept for food by others besides Solomon (1 Kings 4:23).

Deer were so well regarded that to compare the tribe of Naphtali to them was a compliment (Gen 49:21). Their fleetness was noted by Isaiah (35:6), in a vivid image of a lame man leaping like a hart, and is referred to in other passages regarding speed—"my feet like hinds' feet" (2 Sam 22:34; Psa 18:33; Hab 3:19). Their shyness gave them an air of mystery (Job 39:1; Psa 29:9), and their beauty and delicacy made them a favorite poetic image (Psa 5:19, 18:33; 29:9; 42:1; S of S 2:7; 3:5). Jeremiah (14:5) draws a pathetic picture of a doe having to abandon her fawn in drought because there is not enough grass to sustain them. And in depicting Zion's desolation, he says, "All her beauty is departed: her princes are become like harts that find no pasture, and they are gone without strength before the pursuer" (Lam 1:6).

Elephant: Although paleontologists have found fossil bones and tusks of prehistoric elephants in the Jordan Valley and elsewhere in Israel, these animals were extinct in Old Testament times. The early Israelites may have known of them only through carved ivories that came along the trade routes.

The Apocrypha has much to say of elephants trained for war. When Antiochus attacked Egypt and Elymois in Persia, he commanded a force of Indian elephants. To arouse them before battle, the elephants smelled or drank grape and mulberry wine. An Indian driver handled each elephant and 1000 foot soldiers and 500 soldiers on horseback escorted the beast. On its back the elephant carried a canopied towerlike structure which the Bible says held thirty-two soldiers; however, this number is an obvious error. Contemporary illustrations show only four archers per elephant.

One story concerns Eleazar the Maccabean, who noticed that one elephant's canopy was higher than any other and concluded that this animal must bear the king. During the battle he managed to dodge all the attendant cavalry and foot soldiers to reach this elephant, creep under it, and kill it. As it died, the elephant sank down upon Eleazar, crushing the hero to death (Macc 1:71; 6:34–37, 43–46).

Fox: Israel has several foxes, including the red fox, which spends most of its time stalking small mammals or digging up worms; and the tiny desert fox, which has oversize ears and is adept at pouncing on birds. When Jesus said, "Foxes have holes . . . but the Son of man hath not where to lay his head" (Matt 8:20; Luke 9:58), he was alluding to foxes' preference for dens rather than sleeping in the scrub as most of the large desert animals do. Lone foxes may curl up in thickets, but in mating season they den in underground burrows (often those dug by other animals). The desert fox is an especially good burrower, comically flinging mounds of sand behind it in a frenzy of digging.

Foxes were a nuisance in the vineyards, which they invaded from the time the grapes began to ripen in July: "Take us the foxes, the little foxes, that spoil our grapes: for our vines have tender grapes" (S of S 2:15). When Isaiah (5:2) describes someone planting a vineyard he notes that the farmer "built a tower in the midst of it." Guards were posted in such towers until the grapes were harvested in September, and also traps were set, not only to discourage foxes but jackals and perhaps lions too.

Yet even Solomon's scolding is affectionate in tone, because foxes were admired for their cunning. Tobiah said a fox could break down a stone wall (Neh 4:3), the prophets of Israel were compared to foxes in the desert (Ezek 13:4), and Jesus called Herod "that fox" (Luke 13:32).

Most mentions of foxes in the Old Testament are controversial, as the Hebrew term could also mean jackal. Although the little desert foxes tend to be more social than other types, most foxes are solitary except during mating season. Rather than running down prey with a pack, they stalk and hunt individually. Therefore, where the context of the biblical passage indicates a pack, some translators use "jackal" instead of "fox."

Gazelle: A symbol of love and gracefulness, this handsome and swift creature is much loved in Israel. One of the ancient names by which Israel was known, Eretz-Hatsvi, meant land of the gazelle. The gazelle was common along the Jordan River and in hilly country. Because it can go for weeks without water, obtaining moisture from vegetation, it thrives in desert too. When it became extinct, breeding pairs were brought from Iran, and today herds are found in the Issachar hills, in the Negev, and elsewhere. In some Bibles the gazelle is called a roe (see Deer).

An intriguing painting dated about 1900 BC from an Egyptian tomb at Beni Hasan shows seminomads with a pair of apparently tame gazelles, but there is no other evidence that gazelles were tamed and bred.

The gazelle's curiosity makes it bound away and then stop to look back, so that the Song of Solomon (2:9) uses it as a comparison for a lover hiding behind a wall and peering from behind a lattice. Because it is gentle, Proverbs (5:19) urges wives to be "as the loving hind and pleasant roe."

All other references are to its fleetness: David's mighty men were said to be "as swift as the roes upon the mountains" (1 Chr 12:8), and Asahel could run so fast he was "as light of foot as a wild roe" (2 Sam 12:18).

Horseleech: This common leech, which is aquatic, enters the mouths of animals while they are drinking. Its insatiability, and the way it attaches itself to its victims by means of suckers at either end of its wormlike body, are captured in Proverbs (30:15): "The horseleech hath two daughters, crying, Give, give."

Hyena: The spotted hyena—its Hebrew name means "speckled"—is no longer common in Israel but is still found in the Negev and elsewhere. Although commonly thought to be an ugly doglike creature that lives on carrion, it's actually more closely related to the cat and is an underrated predator. Hyenas are intelligent hunters, and the pack coordinates a kill of large prey every bit as expertly as lions do. Hyenas are feared in the Near East and have been known to attack humans. Like wolves, hyenas will pursue the sick or immature animals in a herd and raid livestock. They also eat garbage, which draws them to settled areas.

Because their small faces are set against powerful necks, and their short back legs make their backs slope and their bodies seem to slink, they have always been considered repulsive. But it's the terrible noise they make as they crunch bones with their massive jaws and strong teeth—and especially their chilling cries that sound like maniacal laughter—that make them truly loathsome.

Not all Bibles agree that "hyena" is the proper translation for the Hebrew word in the Bible. Some give "beast"—as in "that they might see that they themselves are beasts" (Eccl 3:18). Also, the word "monster" in Hebrew (often rendered as dragon) may have referred to hyenas.

Ibex: Ancient Israel probably had more than one species of wild goat (at least one species is known to have become extinct in this century), but the only one to survive today is the ibex. It is a handsome, deep-brown animal, and so graceful that it became a symbol of beauty—in Psalms (5:19) it is compared to a beautiful woman.

Ibex are still found—and are protected and increasing—from the north shore of the Dead Sea south along the ridges bordering the shore to Eilat. Herds are sprinkled also in the Negev highlands and the Sinai Peninsula. The En-gedi preserve (En-gedi means "springs of the kid"), a good place to see ibex in summer, is where David hid from Saul "upon the rocks of the wild goats" (1 Sam 24:1-2). This has been a favorite hideaway for goats and humans since ancient times, because the arid, desolate hills provide cover among caves and boulders.

147

Ibex herds graze continually in daylight, seeking shadows in which to rest at midday. At night they climb to safety among inaccessible rocks: "The high hills are a refuge for the wild goats" (Psa 104:18). Their spongelike hooves can grip sheer cliffs and they can jump at least three times their own height. Usually they escape to heights when threatened. Although females have short horns, the males have, in addition to a comical goatee, formidable backward-curving horns. In the wild these horns are seldom used, as lowering them to butting position is usually enough to frighten aggressors, but in Roman times contests between ibex were a popular spectator sport. These horns can look like a single horn in profile—the way they were depicted in ancient Near East art—and may be the origin of the unicorn myth. In Daniel's vision of the ram and the billygoat (8:5, 2), the goat had a big horn between his eyes, and was so agile he seemed not to touch the ground.

In discussing God's wisdom Job (39:1) remarked on the secretiveness of the ibex in bringing forth young. For protection from predators, the young are born (in March) at inaccessible rocky heights, but within a week are skilled enough at jumping to follow their mothers over the sheerest rocks.

Because they need to drink every few days, ibex stay in rocky cliffs near oases in summer, which makes them vulnerable to hunters. When rain fills wadis and water holes in winter and early spring, they wander farther afield.

An Egyptian tomb painting at Beni Hasan depicts a priest with an ibex, suggesting that the animal had religious significance as long ago as 1890 BC. The word ibex in Hebrew, *jael,* is still used to describe a beauty and is a popular girl's name. The most famous Jael was the intrepid woman who drove a tent stake through the head of the Canaanite general Sisera (Judg 4:17–21).

Magical qualities were attributed to the ibex as time went on, and long after biblical times amulets made of its horn were popularly believed to ward off disease. Other by-products of the ibex's body were also collected for medicinal purposes—the blood for curing calluses and the feces for tuberculosis. Such superstitions set the stage for its evolution from a real, if spectacularly wild and agile, creature to the mythical unicorn.

Jackal: Jackals are quite similar to American coyotes—they are about the same size and have the same habit of howling in the evenings. They tend to be nocturnal, hunting in small packs at night and sleeping in crevices or brush in daylight. Perhaps this secretiveness, coupled with their raids on farms for chickens or grapes or other crops, has something to do with the Hebrews' apparently using the same word for jackals that they used for foxes. This has created translation confusion in some passages. In other places the meaning is clear. For instance, the passage about men falling by the sword and being left for foxes to eat (Psa 63:10) is hard to imagine—unless a pack of jackals, who are fond of carrion, is being described.

In another instance, Samson was said to have caught 300 foxes and tied firebrands to their tails so they would race through the fields of the Philistines, setting the crops afire (Judg 15:4). Catching 300 foxes would have been quite a feat, because these solitary animals would have had to be snared individually and are wily enough to evade most traps. It has been suggested that rounding up 300 jackals by using baited defiles or man-made pens would have been easier, since they are less cunning and roam in packs.

Also, in describing the desolation of the mountains of Zion, some Bibles say "the foxes walk upon it" (Lam 5:18). Although foxes have been known to watch from heights, a group of foxes on a mountaintop is an unlikely sight. A more natural image is a pack of jackals, howling against the sky.

Another set of problems arises because the Hebrews apparently referred to jackals by their word for monster. Many passages using the word monster clearly mean a land creature, and some of the earlier translators rendered the word as "dragon." But when Hazor and Babylon are described as dwellings for dragons, or when Jerusalem and the cities of Judah are described as "dens" of dragons (Jer 9:11; 10:22; 49:33; 51:37), modern translators object that "packs of jackals"—or "wolves"—makes more sense. The verse "I will make a wailing like the dragon" (Mic 1:8) also could apply to the howl of the wolf or even hyena. Where some peculiarity of behavior is noted—as in swallowing up like a dragon (Jer 51:34) or "snuffed up the wind like dragons" (Jer 14:6)—there is too little to go on (in the last case one suggested translation is even "crocodile").

Leopard: The Hebrew word for leopard means "spotted" and probably also denotes the cheetah (often called the hunting leopard because it was tamed in India for game hunting). Both existed in Israel in biblical times, and though the cheetah is now believed to be extinct, the leopard is protected and a few survive in the forests of Galilee, En-gedi, and in the Negev Desert. Leopards were also found on the banks of the Jordan and on the heights of Mount Tabor.

Jeremiah (13:23) mentions the spotted pelt—"can the leopard change his spots?"—which was highly valued for rugs, saddle covers, and other ornamental purposes, and which camouflages the animal in the wild. Although the leopard is fond of easy prey and will take domestic livestock (especially goats) when it can, it seldom attacks humans unless attacked or cornered. There is evidence that leopards were sometimes tamed and bred in captivity, and the Talmud mentions them being trained for circus performances.

However, the Bible depicts them as ferocious. One sign of Isaiah's (11:6) peaceable kingdom of the Messiah is that the leopard will lie down with the kid. Jeremiah (5:6) gives an image of a leopard watching over a city, waiting to tear people to pieces, and Daniel (7:6) uses the word leopard to depict a four-headed, four-winged apocalyptic monster.

When Solomon (S of S 4:8) says, Come with me, my spouse, to look from

149

the top of mountains, "from the mountains of the leopards," he shows some understanding of leopards' habits. Leopards are solitary and somewhat lazy hunters who like to stalk their prey slowly and then spring at the last minute, and so prefer a habitat with forest or boulders or other good cover. They are good climbers who often drop unexpectedly from a tree or other height onto the victim. Hosea (13:7) used "as a leopard by the way" to describe a surprise appearance.

When Habakkuk (1:8) tells of horses "swifter than leopards," he may have had the cheetah in mind. It can spring at over sixty miles per hour and is the only predator that can run down a gazelle.

Lion: In biblical times lions roamed throughout Palestine. The pride of Jordan, they lived along the river when it was a shallow stream in spring and summer, and wandered farther afield when the fall rainy season provided water elsewhere and made the Jordan rise and become turbulent: "He shall come up like a lion from the swelling of the Jordan against the habitation of the strong" (Jer 49:19). Lions were also found in the mountains of Judah, in Moab, Bashan, Samaria, and elsewhere—in desert and wilderness, in woodland, in mountains, and even in settled areas.

These lions, which apparently became extinct around the time of the Crusades in the 2d century, looked much like the African lion of today. Lion hunting was a popular sport among Israel's neighbors, and Assyrian kings liked to have themselves depicted in reliefs as lion hunters. On a seal from Uruk dated to the 2d millennium BC, a king hunts with bow and arrow. A 7th-century-BC Assyrian king hunts from a chariot and in another relief he delivers the *coup de grâce* with a sword to a lion shot full of arrows.

The Bible doesn't mention lion hunting as a sport, nor does it describe the hunt as heroic. In the image used in Psalms (35:17), it is only the helpless woman who needs rescuing from the lion. And Proverbs (22:13; 26:13) says it is the lazy man who worries if "there is a lion without, I shall be slain in the streets." As a child David killed a lion merely by hitting it twice on the head with his shepherd's club (1 Sam 17:34–36); and Samson tore one apart with his bare hands, and didn't even bother mentioning the incident to his parents (Judg 14:5–6). Benaiah killed one in a pit in winter (2 Sam 23:20), because it tumbled into either a natural cavity or a trap. Voice alone must have been enough to deter many lions from livestock, because Isaiah (31:4) mentions as a rarity a young lion that is not turned back by shepherds doing no more than shouting and raising a ruckus. Dishonest men hired to guard flocks sometimes sold a sheep or two and then claimed they had been eaten by predators. The shepherd is thus warned to grab back from the lion's mouth at least "two legs or a piece of an ear" as proof of the attack (Amos 3:12).

The lion that killed and ate a man was probably rare. More common were lions who mauled people: "As a young lion . . . I will tear and go away, and none shall rescue him" (Hos 5:14). If Ezekiel (19:3–4) was not

150

speaking purely figuratively, he suggests that a man-killing lion was so rare it was talked about all over and was worth catching to put on exhibit.

That Daniel was cast into a den of lions (Dan 6:16-24) and not eaten is—apart from any miraculous explanation—entirely plausible given the unpredictable nature of these animals. Lions are notoriously lazy and kill only when driven to it by hunger. In between meals they loll peacefully near their natural prey and drink at the same water holes with them. Recent studies have even shown that they often prefer to drive another predator off a kill than to make their own. If Daniel's lions had not been especially hungry, and if he—trusting in his God and showing no nervousness—had simply lain down among them, it is conceivable they would have ignored him. Daniel was also in the den with them overnight, and lions tend to be daytime eaters. On the other hand, when Daniel's enemies were later tossed into the same den with their wives and children—all undoubtedly making a huge fuss—even if the lions hadn't been hungry they would have been unnerved enough to maul them until they were still (the Bible doesn't say these people were eaten, only that the lions pounced upon them and broke their bones).

Contact with lions came about partially because they were fond of taking livestock. Jeremiah (50:17) gives the image that a pride would first rush at a flock to scatter it, and then take a lamb or weakling. David killed his lion because it was after his sheep, and there are other references to problems shepherds had with lions.

Biblical language is very precise in describing the habits of lions. Clear distinctions are made among the various age groups. Cubs too young to hunt on their own are of less interest, and the pride leader that is too old to hunt and "perisheth for lack of prey" is pitied (Job 4:11).

It is the *young* lion—the one that has left the den and the pride, and is rambunctiously seeking to establish territory and take over a pride of its own—that strikes the imagination of biblical authors. In describing the peaceable kingdom of the Messiah, Isaiah (11:6) specifies that it is the young lion that will lie down with the calf; when God tramples a lion (Psa 91:13), it is a young lion. And those lions that "roar after their prey," bare their teeth, and have voracious appetites are almost always young lions (Judg 14:5; Job 4:10; 38:39; Psa 17:12; 58:6; 104:21; Isa 5:29; Jer 2:15).

Because the lion was less feared than admired, it is seldom used as a symbol of evil. Indeed, Proverbs states "the righteous are bold as a lion" (28:1). Sometimes the lion is used to represent strong enemies—"the sword shall devour the young lion" (Nah 2:13); "a voice of the roaring of young lions; for the pride of Jordan is spoiled" (Zech 11:3); or Jerusalem's "princes within her are roaring lions" (Zeph 3:3). But the lion is not even too lowly a symbol for God (Isa 31:4; Lam 3:10; Hos 5:14; 13:8). And Jesus, usually compared to a lamb, is a lion in Revelation (5:5).

In Babylonia, the lion-faced god Nergal was a leading figure in the pantheon. Cultic images of lions have been found at Hazor, Beth-shean,

151

and other sites, and they were popular on personal seals. The lion of Judah became the emblem of Jerusalem. And Lion of Judah was adopted as a title by the emperor of Ethiopia because of the legend that the queen of Sheba had an affair with Solomon that produced a son.

Solomon's Temple (1 Kings 7:29, 36; 10:19-20) had columns decorated with lions. Two lions flanked his throne and twelve lions the six steps leading to it. After the kingdom was split, Ahab of Israel may have had a similar throne, because the "ivory house which he made" (1 Kings 22:39) had wall decorations and furnishings of ivory on which lions were a prominent motif.

Mole: No true mole exists in Palestine. In Leviticus 11:30, where the mole is listed among unclean creeping things, a lizard is probably meant. Israel does have a mole rat, but this is an insectivore related to hedgehogs and shrews. The reference to moles in Isaiah (2:20) that describes the end of idolatry probably means rats and mice: "In that day a man shall cast his idols of silver, and his idols of gold . . . to the moles and to the bats."

Why You Should Never Touch the Hors d'oeuvres at a Canaanite Garden Party

In describing heathen rituals, Isaiah (66:17) says it was customary to assemble in gardens to perform rites. There the heathen would gather "behind one tree"—possibly a pole dedicated to the goddess Asherah—to eat things forbidden to the Hebrews, such as swine's flesh and "the mouse."

Oryx: This is a type of antelope that was known in biblical times and no longer survives in Palestine, though related species are now protected in Africa. Its horns—which sweep backward off its head across its back—can grow up to a yard long. In silhouette these, like the horns of the ibex, can seem to be a single horn, making this another possible candidate for the unicorn legends.

Porcupine: In describing the desolation of Assyria (Zeph 2:14), where cities will be inhabited only by animals, Bible translations often disagree. Is it "the pelican and the porcupine" or "the cormorant and the bittern" or "the pelican and the bittern" that are sitting on the lintels or capitals of buildings and singing in the windows?

Hedgehogs (genus *Erinaceus*) and porcupines *(Hystrix)* are often confused by casual observers. Both are found in Israel, but the hedgehog, an insectivore that also eats worms and small animals, is far more common. The porcupine is a rodent that eats plants and roots. Both live in burrows and have bristles or spines that can be erected as defense, but while the hedgehog likes to curl up in a ball when threatened, the porcupine is inclined to run backward into its attacker. Needless to say, neither one sings, though both make noises and the porcupine can rattle the quills in its tail.

Snail: Snails, of which there are several species in the Holy Land, are mentioned in Psalms (58:8), where the description of their melting probably refers to the slimy trail they leave behind. In some Bibles snails are listed among the unclean animals (Lev 11:30), but this is probably because of a mistranslation of a word which may mean lizard.

Whale: The Hebrew word translated as "whale" in some versions of the Bible really is a general word for monster. It has also been translated as "sea monster" or "crocodile" if the context makes it seem aquatic, and as "serpent" or "dragon" if it seems to live on land. In Genesis (1), where God created "great whales" in some Bibles, other translations give "sea monsters." Unfortunately, most mentions of monsters in the sea are too brief to discover if the word denotes a specific type of animal. Job (7:2) implies only that the monster is a large creature in the sea. An acute observer, the author of Lamentations (4:3) definitely describes a mammal, however. "Even the sea monsters draw out the breast, they give suck to the young." Seals, porpoises, and sea cows were all known in ancient Israel; but all are so inoffensive that it's hard to believe they would be conceived of as monsters. Ezekiel (32:2) first speaks of what might be a whale ("in the seas"), but then goes on to imply it came up the river, fouling the water, so some translators make it a crocodile.

Most controversial of all the passages are those involving Jonah, who was swallowed by "a great fish" that most people believe was a whale. (A minority believe it might have been a shark, and an ancient Egyptian story has a young man eaten by a crocodile and thrown up later, unharmed.)

Recounted in *The Year of the Whale,* by Victor B. Scheffer, are three purported swallowings by whales:

1. In 1771 a whale in the South Seas bit a boat in two and then dived with a crew member in its mouth, only to surface shortly and eject him—bruised but otherwise unhurt—on a piece of the wreckage.

2. In 1891, near the Falkland Islands, a small boat with two harpooners was launched by a whaler and was overturned by a lash of the whale's tail. One harpooner drowned and the other disappeared. When the whale was finally killed and hoisted on deck to be slaughtered, the missing harpooner was found in the stomach. Unconscious but alive, he soon recovered from his shock.

3. The third event, told by the ship's surgeon in 1947, occurred on a

fishing boat out of Newfoundland in 1893. When a seaman fell into the water and was swallowed by a whale, his comrades managed to kill the whale and rushed to open the stomach. In this case the seaman was dead, with a badly crushed chest and his extremities chewed and partly digested, but with the lice on his head still alive.

Scheffer, a world-renowned authority on marine mammals, points out that the second story was contradicted by the wife of the captain of the vessel involved. The third story was strangely not revealed by the ship's surgeon (or by anyone else) for over half a century, when it was too late to be confirmed by the ship's log. Although Scheffer doesn't commit himself, he implies that the story of Jonah and the whale must be taken on faith.

Wolf: In addition to the European wolf, which comes south into Israel, there is a smaller local species found in the Jordan and Mediterranean areas, and the even smaller steppe wolf that roams the Negev. In biblical times wolves were common enough to be a major threat to flocks. "Evening wolves" (Hab 1:8; Zeph 3:3) and "a wolf of the evening" accurately describe a wolf's habits. The animal is primarily nocturnal and often howls in the evening before the hunt. It's a good runner, maintaining a speed of twenty miles per hour so easily that eventually it exhausts most prey and runs them down. Wolves prefer to hunt in packs of a dozen or more, normally hunting ruminants or small mammals.

In the Bible, however, they prey only on sheep, leaping into a flock and scattering it so that the younger or weaker are left vulnerable (Gen 49:27; Hab 1:8; Matt 10:16; John 10:12; Acts 20:29). More than half of the Bible's references to wolves link them to sheep. There is the vivid picture of the hireling who—unlike the shepherd who owns the sheep—doesn't care for the herd as his own. Watching the wolf running relentlessly toward him, he turns and flees (John 10:12).

While the Bible mentions men killing bears and lions, nowhere does anyone kill a wolf. Not only that, but it seems to be taken for granted that the wolf is always going to get the lamb. Since the wolf is always represented as fierce and voracious (Hab 1:8; Matt 7:15)—as in "her princes are like wolves" or "her judges evening wolves"—it is a favorite symbol for corrupt rulers, enemies, the wicked, or Satan (Gen 49:27; Jer 5:6; Ezek 22:27; Hab 1:8; Zeph 3:3; Matt 7:15; 10:16; Luke 10:3; John 10:12; Acts 20:29).

Stories from the Talmud and Midrash give evidence that wolves sometimes attacked people—two children were supposedly eaten on the banks of the Jordan—and a wolf that inflicted a fatality could be sentenced to death. Wolves that took to hiding out near human settlements were trapped. However, a midrash also contains the legend of a wolf suckling infants, and wolves were trained for circus performances and were thought to be trustworthy once tamed. The wolf was often admired too—"more sharp-eyed than desert wolves" said Habakkuk (1:8)—and the name Zeev

154

(Hebrew for wolf) appears in the Bible (Judg 7:25) and is still given to boys today in Israel.

In a few places, the Hebrew word for monster may refer to wolves.

Worm: As in English usage today, the Hebrew word for worm in the Bible referred to insect larvae as well as to earthworms. Also, as today, the worm was used figuratively to mean the lowliest form of life: Thus man is said to be a worm (Job 25:6), God calls Jacob a worm (Isa 41:14), and in Psalms (22:6) there is the self-abasing "I am a worm."

Earthworms and moth grubs are each mentioned only once (Mic 7:17; Isa 51:8), although the damage done by moths is mentioned frequently. Jonah spoke of larvae that withered a gourd, and during the Exodus the bread and other food the Israelites prepared in advance for the Sabbath was remarkable because the next day it did not stink or have any maggots in it.

In all other cases worms are used in the Bible to describe the horror of larvae that feed on decaying human flesh. Herod's wounds were apparently infested by maggots because he is said to have been "eaten of worms" before he died (Acts 12:23). "Look upon the carcases of men," said Isaiah (66:24), "their worm shall not die"—a thought that so impressed Mark he repeated it three times (Mark 9:44, 46, 48). Job was so obsessed that he referred six times to the way maggots destroyed human bodies (Job 7:5; 17:14; 19:26; 21:26; 24:20) and went into detail about how once a body is placed "in the dust" the worms crawl all over it until the "flesh is clothed with worms," the skin is broken, and the flesh becomes loathsome. The result of the worm feeding "sweetly" on man is that man "shall be no more remembered." Isaiah (14:11) echoes the same idea, telling how the pompous are brought down by death, and maggots spread over the body. The devouring by worms thus becomes symbolic of the vanity and impermanence of earthly life and the need for belief in a spiritual life after the disintegration of the flesh.

The Pigs Who Committed Suicide

At the Sea of Galilee, Jesus met two men possessed by devils. The devils, fearing Jesus was going to cast them out of the human bodies they were inhabiting, asked to be transferred into a herd of pigs that was browsing nearby. Jesus granted this request, but when the devils entered the bodies of the pigs, the pigs ran headlong down the banks, threw themselves into the lake, and drowned (Matt 8:31–32; Luke 8:27–33).

Monsters

The Hebrew word for monster has created havoc with translators—one word seems to indicate any wild animal that avoids man and inhabits desert or other desolate areas, and a related word seems to mean a huge and unfriendly creature of land or sea. Baffled translators have used real and fabulous animals to describe the same creatures, so that the same word may be translated as *dragon, sea monster, jackal, snake* (especially *basilisk* and *cockatrice), crocodile, whale,* etc.

Behemoth: As Leviathan was a legendary monster of the sea, Behemoth (Job 40:15-24) was a monster of the land, and in some myths they were said to be mates.

Behemoth was nowhere near as frightening as Leviathan. In most legends it seems to be inspired by the hippopotamus, while in a few stories it is more like a wild ox. The hippopotamus was widespread in ancient times. In Egypt it was considered sacred and was associated with the goddess of pregnancy. It was hunted by Mesopotamian kings, and until the 4th millennium BC it was found along the coastal plains of Palestine and in the Jordan Valley.

Like the hippopotamus, Behemoth is a vegetarian. Although in a few legends it does eat animals, Job describes animals playing unconcernedly near it. Most stories agree with Job, saying Behemoth sheltered birds and other small creatures, and that annually at the summer solstice it reared up on its hind legs to roar a warning to wild beasts that they should not attack domestic livestock. Most of Behemoth's time was spent nibbling lotus leaves and reeds on the Nile—as the hippopotamus did—or grazing on the Thousand Mountains (at the source of the Nile).

Apparently what made Behemoth a monster was sheer size and strength. Job said it had a tail like a cedar and bones as strong as brass. "He eateth grass as an ox," said Job, and its belly was so huge that to fill it "he drinketh up a river . . . he can draw Jordan into its mouth." And it was, in fact, the damage this prodigious appetite did to crops that caused the hippos to be exterminated in the Lower Nile.

Otherwise Behemoth was rather inoffensive, and Job pictures it hiding in willows at riverbanks or lolling about under shady trees. Nevertheless, legends say that Behemoth will eventually be killed—either directly by God, or by angels, or in a duel with Leviathan.

Dragons: To us, dragons are fabulous monsters generally imagined as having the tail of a serpent, scaly skin, wings, and the claws of a lion. More simply viewed, the dragon might be called a gigantic winged crocodile.

By the time of Revelation the dragon is well established as Satan, identified with the serpent that tempted Eve and which is found throughout the Old Testament as a symbol of evil. Gradually the dragon's role was expanded to symbolize idolatry and finally simply sin, as it does in illustrations of Saint George and other heroes (often dressed in white) slaying dragons (often pictured in somber colors).

In Revelation (12) a "great red dragon" appears in the heavens. It has seven heads, with crowns upon each head, as well as ten horns and a huge tail. It menaces a woman about to give birth, threatening to eat her infant as soon as it is born, so that she flees into the wilderness. Michael and his angels fight the dragon, and though the dragon is "cast out into the earth" it then goes after the woman, who has borne a son in the meantime. Although the dragon casts "out of his mouth water as a flood," to wash the woman away in the waters, the earth helps her by swallowing the flood. This so enrages the dragon he decides to make war with the "remnant of her seed."

Revelation also describes a mighty dragon that speaks evil (13:11), and sends "unclean spirits like frogs" out of his mouth (16:13). Finally, the dragon is defined as "that old serpent, which is the Devil, and Satan" (20:2) and which is an object of worship for some (13:2, 4).

Before the dragon was this well defined and illustrated, a far murkier conception prevailed. In Egypt there was often no clear distinction among a dragon, sea monster, and snake. One Egyptian story tells of a shipwrecked sailor who manages to reach an island only to have a monster emerge from the sea with a noise like thunder. This huge serpent—over 500 feet long, with a 40-foot beard—draws its body into huge coils and settles down to talk to the terrified sailor. Its body is as blue as lapis lazuli and its scales overlaid with gold. Although the serpent says it can make the sailor vanish like a flame, it hasn't a mind to do so, and instead cares for him until he is rescued.

In Greek, Latin, and even archaic English the word used for dragon was also used for snake, and some translators of the Old Testament have used the word dragon as a synonym for serpent. This was sometimes done apparently only to avoid repetition, as in "wine is the poison of dragons and the cruel venom of asps" (Deut 32:33), or in "Thou shalt tread upon the lion and adder: the young lion and the dragon shalt thou trample" (Psa 91:13).

Sometimes, the dragon is obviously a creature of the sea: "Thou didst divide the sea by thy strength: thou brakest the heads of dragons in the waters" (Psa 74:13); "praise the Lord from earth, ye dragons, and all deeps" (Psa 148:7); and God "shall slay the dragon that is in the sea" (Isa 27:1). It's hard to say if this creature was a whale, man-eating shark, crocodile, some sea snake, a heathen god such as the Philistine fish-tailed god, Dagon, or one of the sea monsters such as Leviathan. At any rate it was disliked.

Ezekiel seems almost certainly to refer to crocodiles in describing the pharaoh as a monster in the river (see Crocodile), even though some translators render this dragon.

Sometimes the dragon was obviously a creature of the land (see Jackal).

Leviathan and Other Beasts of the Deep: Leviathan was an immense and terrifying sea creature which was respected and revered, in one form or another, by almost all the peoples of the Middle East. Scholars who have analyzed ancient Hebrew myths and tried to reconstruct the earliest levels of these stories—the myths behind the myths—identify Leviathan with the primeval sea monster Tehom, or Tiamet, as the creature is known in Babylonian tales. Tehom was probably the counterpart and antagonist of Beho—Behemoth—the land monster. The Hebrew word *tehom* appears in Genesis 1:2 and is translated by the Authorised Version as "the deep" in the line "darkness was upon the face of the deep."

The characteristics of this monster Tehom indicate that it is related to many sea monsters that appear in the Bible. For example, Tehom is thought to have symbolized the feminine principle. Some remnant of this belief may be seen in the biblical sea monster called Rahab—a feminine name it shares with a supposedly whorish woman (Josh 2:1-24; Heb 11:31). Rahab was a huge sea dragon that God destroyed while creating the world (Isa 51:9; Psa 89:10). In this respect Rahab not only resembles Tehom, but also the great dragon that Ezekiel describes. This aquatic monster, who boasts of creating the rivers and sea, is netted by God and killed (Ezek 29:3, 4).

Of all these monsters, the one mentioned most often and described in the most detail is Leviathan. The reason for the prominence of Leviathan, indeed for the name itself, lies in the influence of the Canaanite monster Lotan on the myths of the early Hebrews. Just as the word *tehom* of the Genesis story is connected to the Babylonian Tiamet, so the Leviathan of

Job is related to the Canaanite Lotan. But *tehom* survives from the ancient Mesopotamian sea-monster myths and "Leviathan" represents the influence from a later stage, when the Hebrews occupied Canaan. The root word behind both Lotan and Leviathan appears to mean "twisted" or "serpentine."

Lotan in Canaanite texts is described as a "tortuous serpent" with seven heads, much like, and probably the inspiration for, the seven-headed dragon of Revelation (17:9). In some stories Leviathan also has several heads. Psalms (74:14), for example, credits it with more than one head but doesn't specify the exact number. Archaeologists have turned up seals and other objects inscribed with a seven-headed monster at Babylon as well as at Sumerian and Hittite cities. Since most of the stories about these monsters state that each of the seven heads had to be killed separately, it was nearly impossible to kill such a beast.

In the stories about both Lotan and Leviathan it takes a deity to destroy the monster. In the case of Lotan, it is Baal, one of the chief Canaanite gods, that crushes the animal. In the book of Isaiah, God, of course, is the one who slays Leviathan (27:1); and a traditional story is that God has saved its skin to make a tent to cover Jerusalem in the Messianic age.

The Bible's most detailed description of Leviathan is in Job (41). Light shines from the monster's eyes, sparks and flames shoot from his mouth, and smoke pours from his nostrils as out of a seething caldron. His breath kindles coals and his heart is as firm as stone. Job notes that no one is so bold as to go fishing for Leviathan with a hook or to play with him "as with a bird." He is king over all the children of pride, the embodiment of evil.

Despite all the terror of Job's Leviathan, the beast sounds almost friendly in one place in the Bible. Psalms (104:26) says the monster plays in the sea. The image of Leviathan playing probably came to the author of Psalms from watching whales or dolphins sporting offshore. Indeed, many of the traits of Leviathan seem directly based on whale behavior. The smoke that Leviathan shoots from its nostrils is probably just the spout of water that the whale blows aloft when coming to the surface. And Leviathan's legendary stench might also have been based at least partially on the whale, which exudes an especially bad odor when slaughtered and an unbearable reek when beached and rotting.

Unicorn: The image of the unicorn as a handsome and gentle horselike animal with a single long horn jutting from the center of its forehead has been traditional since medieval times. Usually depicted as pure white, it has symbolized virginity and been associated with Jesus and the Virgin Mary. However, the animal translated as "unicorn" in some versions of the Bible was probably based on the much less romantic ibex or oryx, or some other wild ruminant of the time. The chief characteristics of the biblical unicorn are its strength and its inability to be tamed. Job (39:9–12) has the longest and most vivid description. To his mind the unicorn is not an animal you could trust or make use of even if it did have great strength, because you would not be able to train it to plow or to serve you. It is so wild you wouldn't be able to lock it in the barn or coax it to feed near you like a domestic animal.

In contrast to the gentleness of the mythical unicorn, the unicorn of the Bible represents power, and most often the power of God. For this reason some scholars believe it may be a counterpart of the bull that represented power in so many Near Eastern cults. God's strength in bringing the children of Israel out of Egypt is compared to that of the unicorn (Num 23:22; 24:8), and God's horns are said to be like the horns of unicorns (Deut 33:17). The animal could be dangerous, because the psalmist says God has saved him from the horns of the unicorn (Psa 22:21). The voice of God is said to break cedars and to make nations skip like young unicorns (Psa 29:6).

Four

All in the Family

The finding of Moses. "And when she [the daughter of Pharaoh] had opened it, she saw the child: and, behold, the babe wept. And she had compassion on him, and said, This one of the Hebrews' children. . ." Ex 2:6. FROM THE DORÉ BIBLE.

Keeping the Seed Alive

Children are as arrows in the hand of a mighty man, says Psalm 127:4; "happy is the man that hath his quiver full of them."

Possibly, bearing children was held in such high regard because God's promise to Abraham was that his seed would be multiplied and become as numerous as the stars in the heaven (Gen 15:5). Having children therefore meant helping to fulfill God's will.

Although exactly how "the bones grow" within the woman's womb was still a mystery to the author of Ecclesiastes (11:5), it was recognized that both men and women had "seed" which was combined for conception (Gen 3:15).

Nevertheless, it was commonly believed that God played a direct and active part in conception, barrenness, and fertility. God's control is made clear in statements such as "thy seed will I establish for ever" (Psa 89:4). This type of promise was made by God directly to Abraham and Jacob, and by an angel to Hagar (Gen 13:16; 16:10; 28:14). Jacob acknowledged that his children had been "graciously given" by God (Gen 33:5). God gave fertility not only to man but to beasts as well (Jer 31:27), and for this reason was entitled to the first fruits or firstborn (Num 8:16): "Lo, children are an heritage of the Lord: and the fruit of the womb is his reward" (Psa 127:3).

God "opened" and "shut up" the womb of women (Gen 29:31; 30:22; 1 Sam 1:5-6), and was also responsible for miscarriage: "Give them, O Lord ... a miscarrying womb" (Hos 9:14). He was responsible for bringing the fetus to term: "Shall I bring to the birth, and not cause to bring forth?" (Isa 66:9).

God also determined what the child would be like. Jeremiah said God

163

told him, "Before I formed thee in the belly I knew thee; and before thou camest forth out of the womb I sanctified thee, and I ordained thee a prophet unto the nations" (Jer 1:4-5).

The Seed of the Wicked: Children were a gift for the righteous, a reward for following God's commandments; and the woman who was clean and obedient to God would conceive (Ex 23:25-26; Num 5:28; Deut 7:14). One man denied children was King Abimelech, who took Sarah into his household after she had already married Abraham. As punishment, God closed up "all the wombs of the house of Abimelech." When Abimelech returned Sarah to Abraham, God restored fertility to the king's house so that his wife and maidservants bore children (Gen 20:17-18).

"For God loveth judgment . . . the seed of the wicked shall be cut off" (Psa 37:28). Saul's daughter Michal, who rebuked King David for shamelessly uncovering himself in public, is an illustration. She sarcastically told David, "How glorious was the king of Israel today!" David protested that he had danced before God, and God apparently agreed the rebuke was unmerited because Michal was punished by being deprived of children (2 Sam 6:16, 20-23). Among the specific sins for which barrenness is detailed is violating the marriage rules; men who do things like lying with an uncle's or a brother's wife "shall be childless" (Lev 20:20-21).

Nevertheless, being denied children was not always a sign of sinfulness. Sarah and other matriarchs were barren for years without any explanation of evildoing being offered. In the case of Elisabeth, the Bible is emphatic that both she and her husband, though childless, were "righteous" and "blameless" (Luke 1:5-13, 36-37). It may be significant that wherever in the Bible infants are born after years of barrenness and anticipation, they grew up to be extraordinary leaders. As with the later birth of Jesus, these conceptions had a miraculous quality.

Child of Adultery

David's grief at the death of his son by Bathsheba is a moving story. David had been told the child would die because he and Bathsheba had committed adultery. When the infant became ill, David prostrated himself before God and fasted. His friends could not press food on him or get him to rise. On the seventh day, when the infant died, everyone was afraid to tell David. Seeing people whispering, David guessed his son was dead. Instead of the outpouring of grief the household expected, David washed and dressed and sat down to eat. While the child was alive he had fasted and wept, he explained, hoping God would spare his son.

Now that the child was dead, "can I bring him back again?" (2 Sam 12:13-23).

Curing Barrenness: Barrenness in the Bible was curable by divine intervention. Because the Lord gives seed and "maketh the barren woman . . . to be a joyful mother of children" (Ruth 4:12-13; 1 Sam 2:5; Psa 113:9), an appeal was made to God. This was done directly, or through an angel, or through prayer at a temple or shrine. In keeping with the Bible's emphasis on men, the entreaty was usually on the part of the husband.

The first account is of Sarah and Abraham. Although God promised them a son, Sarah was barren and suffered greatly because of this. Yet it was Abraham who finally confronted God with the question of how a hundred-year-old man and ninety-year-old wife could possibly have a child. God's assurance satisfied Abraham. Sarah, having gone through the menopause, was not so easily convinced and even laughed at the idea. Despite the belief that divine intervention was normal in such circumstances, Sarah, like other biblical women, was surprised when God created the miraculous conception (Gen 11:30; 17:15-21; 18:10-15; 21:1-7).

Rebekah, wife of Isaac, was also barren, but became pregnant after Isaac "entreated the Lord" (Gen 25:21).

Rachel was so distraught she cried, "Give me children, or else I die," and blamed the barrenness on her husband Jacob—which infuriated him. Rachel apparently did her own praying, because "God hearkened to her" (Gen 30:1-2, 22-23).

Hannah "wept, and did not eat," even though her husband, Elkanah, tried to comfort her by asking, "Am not I better to thee than ten sons?" Hannah went to the temple to pray and did bear a son—the prophet Samuel—as well as other children (1 Sam 1:1-20; 2:21).

Manoah's wife was assured by an angel that she would have a son if she abstained from wine and strong drink, and obeyed the dietary laws. When she told Manoah, he begged God to send the angel back so that he could talk to him too. The angel returned and repeated what he had said before. In time Manoah's wife did have a son, Samson (Judg 13:3-7).

Elisabeth's husband, Zacharias, a priest, was the one who prayed for a child, and again it was an angel who conveyed the good news (Luke 1:7, 13). Their son was John the Baptist.

In one instance, a woman who had been childless for years consulted the prophet Elisha and was cured (2 Kings 4:14-17).

Children by Proxy: As a reward for obeying God, "thou shalt be blessed above all peoples, there shall not be male or female barren among you or your cattle" (Deut 7:14). This passage is surprising in that it acknowledges that males could also be infertile, yet the Bible cites no instances of this. If men failed to produce heirs it was ascribed to some cause other than infertility—such as dying too young. Barrenness always seemed to be the woman's fault, and the solution was frequently to take a second wife or a concubine.

When men had multiple wives, the women competed to produce children. In fact, giving birth to children—especially to male children—is the only conflict the Bible mentions among multiple wives. It always seemed to be the favorite wife who was barren. This was true of Jacob. Rachel, whom he'd courted and loved best, remained childless, while her sister, Leah, whom he was tricked into marrying first, had children. It was the same with Elkanah, who loved Hannah better even though his other wife, Peninnah, had borne him several children.

If a woman was barren, it was perfectly acceptable for her to have her slave sleep with her husband and have a child for her. Theoretically this meant she herself had given her husband the child. In practice, however, the conflict over children could be as keen between wife and slave as it was among multiple wives.

A prime example was the bitterness that developed between Sarah and her Egyptian handmaiden Hagar. It was Sarah who had pushed Abraham into Hagar's bed, yet contention broke out between the two women as soon as Hagar became pregnant.

Rachel and her sister, Leah, were locked into such fierce competition to produce sons for Jacob that their slaves were ultimately brought into the fray. As Leah had had four sons while Rachel remained barren, Rachel sent her handmaid Bilhah to Jacob to produce sons for her. Bilhah quickly had two sons. Fearing she was going to lose out, Leah countered by sending her own slave, who also had two sons (Gen 30:1–24; 35:22–26).

A Child Is Born: "I will greatly multiply thy sorrow and they conception," God told Eve, to punish her for letting the serpent tempt her. "In sorrow thou shalt bring forth children" (Gen 3:16).

Fear and pain experienced in childbirth are frequently used in the Bible to describe extreme anguish: "Fear took hold upon them there, and pain, as of a woman in travail" (Psa 48:6). The prophets Isaiah and Jeremiah were especially fond of ascribing "pangs" and "sorrows," "as of a woman in travail," to suffering nations and people, including the king of Babylon and the inhabitants of Lebanon and of Philistia (Ex 15:14; Isa 13:8; Jer 6:24; 13:21; 50:43). The extra-hard labor of a woman having a first child is also mentioned (Jer 4:31). When Isaiah experiences a "grievous vision," he says:

> Therefore are my loins filled with pain: pangs have taken
> hold upon me, as the pangs of a woman that travaileth. . . .
> My heart panted, fearfulness affrighted me: the night of my
> pleasure hath he turned into fear unto me [Isa 21:3–4].

166

The ultimate anguish is the woman who labors and is unable to give birth or who has a stillborn child, and the prophets again convey this desperation:

> Like as a woman with child, that draweth near the time of her delivery, is in pain, and crieth out in her pangs; so have we been in thy sight, O Lord. We have been with child, we have been in pain, we have as it were brought forth wind; we have not wrought any deliverance in the earth [Isa 26:17–18].

Despite this, the pangs of labor are described as "gracious" (Jer 22:23), and women rejoiced at birth: "A woman when she is in travail hath sorrow, because her hour is come: but as soon as she is delivered of the child, she remembereth no more the anguish, for joy that a man is born into the world" (John 17:21).

To give birth, women may have sat on two stones or stools (Ex 1:15), although the phrase "on the knees" is also used (Gen 30:3; Job 3:12). Later a chair of childbirth—mentioned in the Talmud and still found in the Middle East—was used.

The newborn was washed, rubbed with salt (to discourage demons), and wrapped in swaddling clothes. According to Ezekiel (16:4) the water made the baby "supple." Job (38:9) mentions a "swaddling band," probably an extra wrapping around the navel. Swaddling was still used in New Testament times (Luke 2:12).

Midwives assisted at births from the time of the matriarchs and were often the same women who later nursed the infants (Gen 35:17; 38:28). During the bondage in Egypt, women were also attended by professional midwives—and it was to these that the pharaoh gave instructions to destroy all male Hebrew infants. When the pharaoh discovered his command was not being obeyed, the midwives excused themselves with the unlikely story that the Hebrew women were so "lively" in giving birth that they all delivered before they could be attended (Ex 1:15).

A woman was considered unclean for only forty days after bearing a son but eighty days after giving birth to a daughter (Lev 12:1–8). During this time she was not allowed to touch sacred objects or to enter the sanctuary. At the end of this period she underwent purification by making an offering of a burnt lamb and a bird (or two birds if she could not afford a lamb).

Sorrow at Birth: Infant and maternal mortality rates are believed to have been high in biblical times. One scientist calculated that despite many births a woman was lucky to raise one or two children to adulthood. Rehoboam, for instance, with eighteen wives and sixty concubines, had only eighty-eight children, averaging slightly over one child per woman; Abijah's thirty-eight children from fourteen wives works out to almost three children per woman.

Indicative of this high mortality are the many descriptions of women grieving for their children—often used figuratively to describe the plight of nations or the people of Israel: "A voice was heard in Ramah, lamentation, and bitter weeping; Rahel weeping for her children refused to be comforted" (Jer 31:15).

It is therefore surprising that the Bible has only two stories about women who die in childbirth. Rachel died after going into a difficult labor while she and Jacob were traveling. The midwife tried to comfort her by saying, "Fear not; thou shalt have this son also," but Rachel was so bitter she wanted the child named Benoni ("child of my sorrow"). Jacob renamed the child Benjamin (Gen 35:16-20).

Phinehas, daughter-in-law of Eli the high priest, went into labor when she heard her husband had been killed by the Philistines—who had also captured the Ark—and that Eli had died on hearing the news. When it looked as though Phinehas would not survive the childbirth, the women with her tried to comfort her by telling her she had a son—but she would not reply or look at the child. Before Phinehas died, she named her son Ichabod ("inglorious") because "the glory is departed from Israel" (1 Sam 4:19-22).

Twins

Two good stories of twins appear in the Bible. When Rebekah conceived after years of barrenness, she realized that the amount of movement in her womb was unusual and asked God about it. He told her she was carrying twins—one would be stronger, but the elder twin would serve the younger. The first twin, Esau ("hairy" or "shaggy"), was born red "like an hairy garment" and became a cunning hunter. The second son, Jacob, lived a more placid life as herdsman; though he was the second son, he obtained the birthright. Because the Bible makes so much of their differences, Esau and Jacob may have been fraternal twins who did not look much alike. Only once were they confused with one another, and that was by their father, Isaac, at a time when Isaac was old and had "dim" sight. In fact, his sight was so dim that "he could not see," and when he called Esau to him, Esau had to announce his arrival by calling out, "Here am I" (Gen 25:21-34; 27).

When Tamar had twins, they were apparently identical. During birth the hand of one infant, Zarah, emerged first and the midwife immediately tied scarlet thread around the hand to identify the baby as the firstborn. However, Zarah withdrew his hand, and his twin was born first. The second twin was therefore named Pharez ("breach"), and was immediately scolded for having pushed himself out first (Gen 38:27-30).

Circumcision

That the rite of circumcision was practiced in the Middle East as early as the 23d century BC is known from a stela inscription describing an Egyptian ceremony in which 120 males were circumcised. Egyptian mortuary priests are shown performing circumcision on boys in a tomb painting dating about 2300–2000 BC. According to Herodotus, Egyptians performed the operation because they considered cleanliness more important than comeliness.

While it seems fairly certain that Egyptian priests were circumcised, contradictory statements in ancient records make it difficult to know how widespread the custom was among the general population. Joshua (5:7–9) calls lack of circumcision the "reproach of Egypt," and Ezekiel (32:18–32) says that neither the pharaoh nor his troops were circumcised. Yet Jeremiah (9:24–26) says Egyptians were physically circumcised, although not "in the heart." Archaeologists have not been able to clarify this contradiction because both circumcised and uncircumcised mummies have been found.

Among other neighbors of the Israelites there is also conflicting evidence. Edomites, Moabites, and Ammonites practiced at least some circumcision, and Jeremiah (9:24–26) lumps them with Egyptians and Arabs as having gone through the physical rite without being circumcised "in the heart." However, Ezekiel (32:18–32) says Edomites were not circumcised, and Josephus supports this by claiming that the Edomites were forced to go through this rite during Maccabean times, when John Hyrcanus made all subjected people adopt Hebrew customs. Arabs, Phoenicians, and at least some Assyrians were apparently circumcised.

Because only the Philistines totally rejected circumcision, the very term "uncircumcised" was used as a synonym for Philistines (Judg 14:3; 15:18; 1 Sam 14:6; 17:26, 36; 31:4). When David killed a hundred Philistines, the hundred foreskins he brought back to Saul (1 Sam 18:25) were proof of his kill because he could not have gotten these from any other peoples in the area.

Because circumcision in regard to Canaanites is not an issue in the Bible and because Philistines could be distinguished simply by being called "the uncircumcised," it is clear Canaanites practiced the rite.

For most of the neighbors of Israel, however, the operation was merely a custom that waxed or waned in popularity and that could readily be abandoned. This would account for the contradictions among early writers about which groups practiced the rite.

For the Hebrews circumcision was not merely a custom but a religious obligation. As many other peoples gave it up, it became a distinguishing mark of the Hebrews. This became even truer after the Greeks—who abhorred the practice—began to hellenize the Middle East. By the beginning of the Christian era, only the Jews practiced it in Palestine.

From the Old Testament, it is clear that circumcision among the Hebrews began long before the Exodus. Accounts of using a flint knife (Ex 4:25) show that it was an ancient custom dating to the Stone Age.

Abraham, when he was ninety-nine years old, adopted the practice as a symbol of the covenant between himself (and his descendants) and God (Gen 17:9–14). From then on, the soul of any male child not circumcised was to "be cut off from his people" as punishment for breaking the covenant. Not only to be circumcised were males born in the house, but also any males "bought with money." Abraham therefore circumcised himself, his thirteen-year-old son Ishmael, and all other males in his household, whether Hebrew or not (Gen 17:23–27).

After Abraham, the custom was kept by the Hebrews during their time of bondage in Egypt (Josh 5:4–5), although there were lapses. Moses, for instance, was not circumcised.

There was a lapse in the rite among Hebrews during the forty years of wandering in the wilderness after the Exodus. Therefore, after Joshua had led the Israelites across the Jordan River into Canaan to establish a camp at Gilgal, one of his first acts was to hold a mass circumcision of all males (Josh 5:2–9).

After this, the custom was so firmly established among the Hebrews that in Maccabean times they risked severe punishment—circumcised infants hanged (sometimes from their mothers' necks), their mothers and the people who had circumcised them killed (1 Macc 1:60–61; 2 Macc 6:10)—to continue the practice.

Among many primitive peoples in Africa, the Americas, and elsewhere who have practiced it, circumcision is usually done at puberty as a rite of passage into adulthood. It is therefore often a symbol of taking one's place in the community, a preparation for entering into adult work, marriage, and perhaps also of initiation into religious mysteries. In Egypt, where circumcision was performed at puberty, it might have been connected with certain religious cults. Among Arabs, where female circumcision is also practiced, the rite has a sexual connotation.

If Hebrews ever practiced circumcision at puberty, the custom was lost, because—apart from unusual instances of adult operations—the Bible mentions the rite as being performed in infancy. Beginning with Isaac, who was circumcised when he was eight days old, the operation was done on the eighth day after birth (Gen 17:12; 21:4; Lev 12:3). Because it was performed so early, its import was different from that of the circumcision in most other parts of the world. It did not signify passage into adulthood but into the Hebrew religious community. From the time of the Creation, seven had been an important unit of time in the Bible, and a child was not considered to have an independent existence until the eighth day. The infant's circumcision therefore signaled the beginning of a new cycle of life and his entering into the covenant with God. Later it also became customary to name the child on that day—Jesus, for instance, was circumcised and named on the same day (Luke 2:21).

That it was a purely religious observance is shown by the fact that uncircumcised foreigners were not allowed to share the Passover—"no uncircumcised person shall eat thereof" (Ex 12:48). Any foreigners who wished to participate in this ceremony had to be circumcised first. Anyone wishing to embrace the Jewish faith likewise had to be circumcised (Judith 14:10).

In the Bible, therefore, circumcision is not simply physical but is used metaphorically to connote faithfulness and righteousness: "Circumcise therefore the foreskin of your heart, and be no more stiffnecked" (Deut 10:16); "God will circumcise thine heart . . . to love the Lord thy God" (Deut 30:6); "Circumcise yourselves to the Lord, and take away the foreskins of your heart" (Jer 4:4). It is therefore possible to be physically circumcised yet be "uncircumcised in the heart" (Jer 9:24–25; Ezek 44:7). An uncircumcised ear is one that will not accept God's word: "Behold, their ear is uncircumcised, and they cannot hearken: behold, the word of the Lord is unto them a reproach; they have no delight in it" (Jer 6:10).

Circumcision is so intertwined with notions of cleanliness and purity that the Hebrew word for "uncircumcised" also means "forbidden." For example, the law that the first orchard fruits should not be eaten (Lev 19:23), is translated in some Bibles as "count the fruit therefore as uncircumcised."

Whether circumcision was necessary for salvation became a hot debate among early Christians. At the crux of the argument was the verse "Except ye be circumcised after the manner of Moses, ye cannot be saved" (Acts 15:1). Paul, Barnabas, and others gathered to consider the matter and decided it was unnecessary for Christians to be circumcised (Acts 15:6–24): "Circumcision is nothing, and uncircumcision is nothing, but the keeping of the commandments of God" (1 Cor 7:19). Nevertheless, the rite had been

172

such a strong tradition that Paul had to reassure people again and again about forgoing circumcision: "For in Jesus Christ neither circumcision availeth any thing, nor uncircumcision; but faith which worketh by love" (Gal 5:6); "ye are circumcised with the circumcision made without hands, in putting off the body of the sins of the flesh by the circumcision of Christ" (Col 2:11).

Dinah's Revenge

One of the most interesting stories of circumcision is that of Dinah, Jacob's daughter, who was raped by Shechem, a prince of the Hivites. Shechem then wanted to marry her, but Dinah's brothers replied that she could not marry an uncircumcised male. They suggested that if Shechem and his people wanted to marry Hebrew women all they had to do was to be circumcised. All the males of Shechem's city were promptly circumcised. Three days later, while the Shechemites were still disabled by pain from the operation, Dinah's brothers easily slaughtered them to revenge her rape (Gen 34).

A Good Name

According to anthropologists, naming is to some degree an act of power. To name someone or something is to know what it is, to have defined it, and thus to have limited it. Thus, to show that man had supremacy over other living things, God, after creating the animals and birds, "brought them unto Adam to see what he would call them: and whatsoever Adam called every living creature, that was the name thereof" (Gen 2:19–20).

Before this, God had already named Adam ("of the earth"), though no big fuss is made of this in the Bible. The name is dropped offhandedly, and apparently refers to the phrase "God formed man of the dust of the ground" (Gen 2:7; 19). Eve ("mother of all living") is not named until after the cattle, birds, and wild animals, and she is named by Adam: "And the man called his wife's name Eve; because she was the mother of all living" (Gen 3:20).

Power in Names: The issue of the power behind names is raised in the Bible in discussions between Moses and God. "I know thee by name," God tells Moses (Ex 33:17). But this creates a tricky problem for Moses: What should Moses call God? As Moses points out, when he goes to the children of Israel to say "The God of your fathers hath sent me unto you," the children of Israel will naturally reply, "What is his name?" So, Moses asks, "What shall I say unto them?"

God's reply is "I AM THAT I AM: And he said, Thus shalt thou say unto the children of Israel, I AM hath sent me unto you." God thus refuses to give Moses a name to use, stressing instead a generalized manifestation of spirituality. He further instructs Moses to use phrases descriptive of power instead of a specific name: "The Lord God of your fathers, the God of Abraham, the God of Isaac, and the God of Jacob ... this is my name for ever" (Ex 3:13–15). Thus, when Moses goes before the pharaoh, the term he uses for God is "the Lord," causing the pharaoh to reply that he has never heard of any such god (Ex 5:2). Rabbinic tradition elaborates this story and says the pharaoh had consulted his seventy scribes, who knew all the languages on earth, and they had advised him that no such god as "the Lord" existed. Elsewhere God explained: "And I appeared unto Abraham, unto Isaac, and unto Jacob, by the name of God Almighty, but by my name JEHOVAH was I not known to them" (Ex 6:3). At least, "Jehovah" is how the name is written in English translations of the Bible. In the original Hebrew the name Jehovah is only four letters—*YHVH*, known as the tetragrammaton. Orthodox Judaism prohibits the pronunciation of the tetragrammaton *YHVH*, substituting "the Lord" *(Adonai)*. The truly orthodox won't even use the term "the Lord" in any situation but prayer, and if they need to refer to God at other times they say *"HaShem"*—which simply means "the name"—instead. Mystical forms of Judaism teach that magical powers can be called upon by the proper use of the tetragrammaton, and that destructive powers will be unleashed by its improper use.

Hints of power in names remain in New Testament references to Jesus— "ye might find life through his name" (John 20:31) or "for there is none other name under heaven given among men, whereby we must be saved" (Acts 4:12).

The Longest Name

The longest name in the Bible, Maher-shalal-hash-baz, occurs in Isaiah 8.1 and belongs to the prophet's son.

Most Common Names in the Bible

Zechariah ("Jehovah remembers")—more than thirty times
Azariah ("helped by Jehovah")—more than twenty-five times
Meshullam ("rewarded")—more than twenty times

Who Named Children? Most of the time women named children. The Bible is contradictory about Seth, once saying he was named by Eve and later saying Adam named him (Gen 4:25; 5:3), but Samson, Samuel, and other later children were named by their mothers. Leah and Rachel named not only their own infants but also those of their slaves (Gen 30:4–24). About a third of the time, fathers named their children, but all of these instances involved men such as Abraham, Joseph, and David, who were unusually forceful leaders. Children of prophets were sometimes given symbolic names by their fathers (Job 42:14; Isa 8:3; Hos 1:4–9). Occasionally, when a child was to play a major religious role, its name was given by God or an angel: Isaac (Gen 17:19), Ishmael (Gen 16:11), Jesus (Matt 1:20–21).

What's in a Name? In an astounding number of cases, children had names indicating the role they were to play in life, leading to the suspicion that they changed their names once their careers were launched or that biblical authors gave appropriate names to the people they wrote about.

Even when names were not an indication of destiny, they were meaningful: A child might be named for the time of birth (Shaharaim, "dawn"); place of birth (Timna, "born in the town of Timnah"); some circumstance at the time of birth (Gershom, "sojourner," because Moses was "a stranger in a strange land" when he was born; Ex 2:22); or what the baby looked like (Korah, "bald"). Jacob ("supplants"; "one who grabs by the heel") was named because at birth he grabbed the heel of his twin, as though to hold him back and make himself firstborn (Gen 25:26). Names drawn from nature were also popular: Rimmon ("pomegranate"), Shapham ("rock badger"), Susanna ("lilies").

Names such as Peninnah ("pearl") or Haruz ("gold") were given to express the great value placed on the newborn. Samuel ("God has heard") had been born in answer to his parents' prayers (1 Sam 1:20).

Far sadder names were chosen by women wishing to commemorate their sufferings during labor. The most moving example is the story of Rachel, who, dying in childbirth, bitterly named her newborn Benoni ("child of my sorrow"). Jacob, apparently unwilling to have the child go through life under the burden of guilt for his mother's death, changed the infant's name to Benjamin ("son of my right hand"; Gen 35:18).

Another pitiful story involves Leah, who vainly tried to supplant her sister, Rachel, in Jacob's affections. Leah named her first son Reuben ("behold, a son") in the hope that when she showed the infant to Jacob he would love her. Her second son was Simon ("hearing"), because she thought "the Lord hath heard that I was hated" and had given her a second son as emotional leverage with Jacob. Her third son was called Levi ("joined"), from her conviction that "this time will my husband be joined unto me." When this hope also proved fruitless, she named her fourth son Judah ("may God be praised"), apparently giving up on Jacob and seeking solace from her God alone (Gen 29:32–35).

176

Names and Meanings

Abel—breath
Abimelech—father of the king
Abner—father of light
Abraham—father of multitudes
Amos—burden
Absalom—father of peace
Amos—burden
Barak—lightning
Bathsheba—daughter of oath
Benjamin—son of my right hand
Cain—a smith
Daniel—my judge is God
David—beloved
Elijah—God is my salvation
Elisha—God is my salvation
Elisabeth—God is my oath
Esau—hairy
Ezekiel—God gives strength
Gabriel—man of God
Gad—fortune
Gamaliel—reward of God
Habakkuk—basil planter
Hagar—one who has fled

Hosea—salvation
Ichabod—inglorious
Isaac—laughter
Isaiah—God saves
Jairus—enlightened by God
Jesus—God of salvation
Jonah—dove
Lazarus (Eleazar)—God has helped
Mahalaleel—praise God
Mary (Miriam)—stubbornness
Matthew (Mattathias)—gift of God
Michael—who is like God?
Noah—comfort
Peter—rock
Saul—asked for
Simeon—hearing
Solomon—peaceable
Stephen—(Greek) crown
Tabitha—gazelle
Tamar—date palm
Timothy—(Greek) honoring God
Zechariah—God remembers

Children of Prophets: Prophets were fond of saddling their children with names that had nothing to do with the child itself but which instead reflected the state of the nation. Shearjashub ("a remnant shall return") was the name Isaiah gave his son at the time the Hebrews knew they were threatened with deportation (Isa 7:3). Maher-shalal-hash-baz ("spoil speeds, prey hastens"), a name given to another son of Isaiah, also referred to the Assyrian threat to plunder Israel (Isa 8:1–4).

Jezreel ("God sows"), Hosea's first son, was named after the Valley of Jezreel; God told Hosea that the hated King Jehu could be destroyed there. Lo-ruhamah ("who hath not obtained mercy"), Hosea's daughter, was so named because God would no longer show mercy on Israel (Hos 1:6). Lo-ammi ("not my people"), Hosea's younger son, was named for God's anger at the rebellious nation. God had said, "For ye are not my people, and I will not be your God" (Hos 1:9).

In the Name of God

Incorporating the name of God in a person's name was popular, especially for prophets, kings, high priests, and others with sacred duties. Religious leaders such as Samuel and Jesus, destined from the start for religious careers, had from birth names symbolic of union with God. Others, for whom a career linked with religion might not have been predicted, took on new names as adults.

One form of the name of God was *El*—the root word meaning "God" that occurred in Semitic languages. Canaanites, Phoenicians, and others used *El* for gods, and names with "el" were also given to the children of the Edomites (Gen 36:41), Hittites (Gen 26:34), and others. Among the Hebrews the "el" usually occurred as a prefix or suffix, not only in names of people but in geographic sites such as Beth*el* ("house of God").

> *El*nathan (God the giver)
> *El*i (God is high)
> Bezale*el* (in the shadow of God)
> Nathana*el* (God has given)

More germane to the Hebrews was the prefix *Yah* (the Lord), usually written in English as "Jeh" (signifying Jehovah), but sometimes contracted as "Jo."

> *Jeh*oiada (Jehovah knows)
> *Jeh*oshaphat (Jehovah judged)
> *Jo*tham (Jehovah is upright)
> *Jo*nathan (Jehovah has given)

The name Jesus is a Greek version of the Hebrew name Yehoshua, or Joshua. This is a compound of *yah* (the Lord) and *shua* (to be freed), and thus means "the Lord of salvation" or "the Lord the saviour."

Surprisingly, Hebrews sometimes gave their children names that incorporated the names of forbidden gods. The name of the tribe of Gad ("fortune") is the name of an Aramean god of good luck. Especially popular were names incorporating that of Baal ("lord"), the son of El, an agricultural god whose widespread worship extended from Canaan to Mesopotamia. "Baal" occurs in geographic names—such as the Canaanite town of Baal-gad or the place called Baal-hamon where Solomon had a vineyard—as well as in personal names: Baalis was an Ammonite king (Jer 40:13),

178

Baal-hanan was an Edomite king (Gen 36:38); and Ethbaal, Jez-ebel's father, was king of Sidon (1 Kings 16:31).

Baal-hanan was also the name of the official, from the Canaanite town of Geder, who was overseer for David's olive trees (1 Chr 27:28). Foreigners, even when they were employed by Hebrews, apparently did not change their names. However, Hebrews whose names incorporated "baal" were compelled to change their names when they assumed prominent positions. Usually this was done by substituting the Hebrew word *bosheth* ("shame") for "baal." Jona-than's son Meribaal ("contender with Baal") was called Mephi-bosheth ("exterminator of shame") after he was favored by David (2 Sam 9:6; 1 Chr 8:34). Saul's fourth son had been called Eshbaal ("man of Baal"), but became Ish-bosheth ("man of shame") when he succeeded his father as king (2 Sam 2:8; 1 Chr 8:33).

Change of Life: Adults sometimes changed their names when they had undergone some experience that they felt made a profound change in their personalities.

Abram and Sarai changed their names to Abraham and Sarah to include the *h* symbolic of God after Abraham's renewal of the covenant and God's promise to multiply his seed (Gen 17:5, 15).

Jacob's name was changed to Israel ("prince") after he had won his struggle with the angel (Gen 32:28).

When Moses sent Oshea to spy out Canaan, he changed his name to Jehoshua—the "Jeh" prefix of Jehovah symbolizing that this was a sacred mission (Num 13:16).

Nathan called Solomon Jedidiah ("beloved by Jehovah") when he began to educate him, but this was either an intimate nickname between the two or was later abandoned, because it is not mentioned elsewhere (2 Sam 12:25).

This practice of name change at critical junctures in people's lives continued in New Testament times. Simon became Peter and Saul became Paul when they converted and became followers of Jesus (John 1:42; Acts 13:9).

Although the above examples indicated a new spiritual dimension, name changes were also made in secular life. Naomi ("pleasant") changed her name to Mara ("bitter") after her husband and sons had died, leaving her without means of support. She explained the change by saying, "The Almighty hath dealt very bitterly with me" (Ruth 1:20).

Changing a person's name was a way of demonstrating authority, so that when Joseph gained prominence in the Egyptian court the pharaoh changed his name to Zaphnath-paaneah (Gen 41:45). Daniel and his three

179

friends who were taken captive to Babylon were all renamed for Babylonian deities by the master of the eunuchs. Daniel, for example, was called Belteshazzar ("Bel protect his life") for the chief god of Babylon, while his friend Azariah had his name changed to Abed-nego ("servant of Nego") after the god of wisdom (Dan 1:6-7).

When Hebrew kings were made vassals by foreign powers, their names were often changed as a symbol of submission. Pharaoh Necho, who deposed Jehoahaz and made Eliakim the king of Judah, changed the latter's name to Jehoiakim (2 Kings 23;34). When Nebuchadnezzar allowed Mattaniah to rule Judah, he changed his name to Zedekiah (2 Kings 24:17).

In Mesopotamia and Egypt it was not uncommon for monarchs to change their names, often incorporating into the new name the name of a god to signify that they were ruling with divine dispensation. Because kings of Judah sometimes seem to have had more than one name in the Bible— one in the Book of Kings and another in the Book of Chronicles or in the books of the prophets—some scholars believe that the Hebrew princes might also have changed their names when they ascended the throne.

Argument over Naming John the Baptist

The angel Gabriel appeared to Zacharias and told him that his wife, Elisabeth, would bear a son, who was to be called John. Moreover, Zacharias was to be struck dumb until the prophecy was fulfilled.

Although he was speechless all during Elisabeth's pregnancy, Zacharias had managed to communicate this information to her. When the baby was born, friends and neighbors insisted the child should be named Zacharias after his father. Elisabeth protested her son had to be called John. Her friends and neighbors agreed that this was not a traditional name in the family. Finally Zacharias, undoubtedly worried he would never recover his speech, asked for a writing table and wrote: "His name is John." Zacharias immediately recovered his power of speech (Luke 1:5-25, 57-64).

The Children of Israel

Except for a prophetic vision that "the streets of the city shall be full of boys and girls playing" (Zech 8:5), the Bible never concerns itself with the joys of childhood. In fact, a typical view of children is "childhood and youth are vanity" (Eccl 11:10).

Most often children were cited as valuable for preserving the inheritance of the family, the tribe, or the people—and this meant sons. Daughters were less valued and far less frequently mentioned.

In fact, many times when "children" (or "sons" or "daughters") occurs in the Bible, adults are meant: "when Israel was a child" (Hos 11:1); "ye are children of the Lord" (Deut 14:1); "Abraham's children" (John 8:39); the many "children of God," "children of Israel," "children of Benjamin," or the New Testament's "children of light."

Occasionally it isn't clear whether a child or adult is intended, as when Jeremiah, speaking of his fury, chillingly threatened, "I will pour it out upon the children" (Jer 6:11).

Few examples of empathy for children exist in the Bible. Isaiah, who probably mentions children more often than any other author, comes closest: He draws the pathetic image of a child too innocent to know enough to cry when its parents and riches are "taken away before the king of Assyria" (Isa 8:4).

Suffer the Little Children: A general attitude of impatience with children is seen in the scenes where the disciples rebuked parents who tried to press their children on Jesus. Jesus' reply, "Suffer the little children to come unto me," would obviously not have been worth recording if his tolerance had

181

been a prevalent attitude (Matt 19:13–14; Mark 10:13–14; Luke 18:15–16).

Dalliance in childhood is a modern luxury. In biblical times people could not afford to be sentimental and lenient toward children. Children were expected to take their place in adult society as quickly as possible.

Almost nothing is said in the Bible about how children spent their time, and toys are never mentioned. However, in mounds at Gezer and elsewhere in Palestine, archaeologists have found small objects that may have been made for tombs or for ritualistic purposes but which probably also served as toys. Among these are pottery rattles, some in the shape of people or animals; whistles and musical instruments; and miniature houses and furniture. Clay horses and other animals, as well as dolls, have survived, and it is reasonable to assume that similar toys of wood or vegetable fibers existed.

Although many types of game boards have been found throughout the Fertile Crescent, the earliest dated to 5000 BC, relatively few have been unearthed in Palestine. The simplest of these are series of squares scratched into a rock at Mizpah and on paving in Jerusalem, for which the movable pieces could have been pebbles. Other gaming pieces were modeled of clay. The most elaborate were carved of ivory. Dice were sometimes used to determine the moves. These games—similar to checkers and skittles—were popular among adults as well as children.

Probably much of children's entertainment, like that of adults, was outdoors and consisted of interacting with others rather than depending on toys or equipment. Storytelling was an art in biblical days, and riddles are mentioned twice (Judg 14:12; Ezek 17:2). Matthew (11:16–17) suggests that children played at adult activities such as dancing and mourning when they got together at the markets. Children would also have taken part in the dancing and singing at festivals.

Playing time was undoubtedly limited once a child grew beyond the toddler stage, because the society offered little leisure. Much of childhood must have been spent doing tasks alongside working adults: In the domestic scene painted by Jeremiah (7:18) the mother kneads dough, the father kindles the fire, and "the children gather wood."

Sins of the Fathers: Among the few laws protecting children was one that orphans should not be "afflicted" (Ex 22:22). It was a sign of virtue to "save the children of the needy" (Psa 72:4).

The most important law specified that "every man shall be put to death for his own sin" and that children should therefore not be made to suffer for the sins of their fathers (Deut 24:16). Amaziah was singled out as a good king because he obeyed this commandment—when he revenged his father's death he killed adults only and spared the children (2 Chr 25:4). However, Amaziah seems to have been an exception, because battles for the crown usually resulted in the assassination of all royal contenders, even if they were mere infants. The execution of seven of Saul's sons because their father had sinned is only one example of children being punished for wrongdoing of which they were innocent (2 Sam 21:1-10).

This law of not visiting parental sin on children was not as effective as it might have been because of numerous exclusions. Children of slaves, for example, automatically became slaves at birth (Gen 14:14; 15:3; etc.) Children not born of the legitimate wife often did not share the inheritance, even if they were the firstborn (Gen 21:10; Judg 11:2). In fact, children born of an incestuous or adulterous union were excluded from the congregation for ten generations (Deut 23:2). Finally, if a child's father ran up debts and was unable to pay, his children could be enslaved by the creditors (2 Kings 4:1; Neh 5:5; Isa 50:1).

Out of the Mouths of Babes: The word "child" often meant someone dumb, or at least innocent. "Behold," said Jeremiah (1:6), "I cannot speak: for I am a child."

"I am but a little child," Solomon told God, "I know not how to go out or come in" (1 Kings 3:7)—a remark that pleased God so much that Solomon was given more than he had requested.

Because children represented ignorance—and therefore could not acknowledge God's word—it was possible for Isaiah to threaten Israel's humiliation in these terms: "And I will give children to be their princes, and babes shall rule over them" (Isa 3:4).

The frequent use of children as an image of ignorance once enabled Jesus to give a rather snappy rejoinder. The Temple priests were annoyed by the way people were following Jesus about, waiting to be cured and bringing their crying children into the Temple. But Psalms had made famous the line "Out of the mouths of babes and sucklings has thou ordained strength" (Psa 8:2). When the priests asked Jesus whether he heard how people were crying out to him "Hosanna to the son of David," Jesus replied with a riddling phrase: "Yea; have ye never read, Out of the mouths of babes and sucklings thou hast perfected praise?" (Matt 21:16).

Rebellious Children: Children were praised for being "goodly" and "pleasant" (Ex 2:2; Jer 31:20), and since "even a child is known by his doings" (Prov 20:11) being a child was no excuse for misbehavior. "Surely I have behaved and quieted myself, as a child that is weaned of his mother" (Psa 131:2) suggests that children were expected to conform and be somewhat independent soon after weaning.

"Better is a poor and a wise child than an old and foolish king," said Ecclesiastes (4:13) optimistically, on the theory you can't teach an old king new tricks. Biblical-age parents believed that if a child was properly trained, it would be good the rest of its life (Prov 22:6).

Because the Old Testament is a spiritual history of the Hebrews, it does not dwell on everything children were taught. The skills necessary for agriculture, trades, and crafts must have been part of a father's counsel,

183

while mothers must have instructed their daughters in the full range of home economics. Little of this is even hinted at, and the Bible devotes itself to religious instruction. God had said, "I will make them hear my words, that they may learn to fear me all the days that they shall live upon the earth, and that they may teach their children" (Deut 4:10). The stress on teaching children the commandments is repeated over and over again (Deut 6:7; 11:19; 32:46; Josh 4:6, 21, 22; Psa 78:4, 6).

That children were not always exemplary is evident in the frequent use prophets made of "backsliding," "sottish," "rebellious," "impudent," and even "lying" children (Isa 30:1, 9; Jer 3:14, 22; 4:22; Ezek 2:4).

"I nourished and brought up children," complained Isaiah (1:2), "and they have rebelled against me."

"Yea, young children despised me," said Job (19:18). "They spake against me." (However, he complained that his wife and friends disliked him too.)

And Elisha (2 Kings 2:23) was especially pained by the children of Bethel: "There came forth little children out of the city," he grumbled, and they taunted him with cries of "bald head."

Parent Power

Among the strongest and longest-lasting laws regarding children was the commandment that children were to honor and fear their parents (Lev 19:3; Deut 5:16). Jesus repeated, "Honour thy father and thy mother" (Mark 10:19; Luke 18:20). Children who failed to obey this commandment were cursed (Deut 27:16)—in fact, any child cursing its father or mother could be put to death: "Whoso curseth his father or his mother, His lamp shall be put out in the blackest darkness" (Ex 21:17; Lev 20:9; Prov 20:20). Children who were violent against their parents were also executed (Ex 21:15). "Stubborn" and "rebellious" sons who failed to obey their parents—as, for instance, any who were gluttons or drunkards—could be taken before the elders of the city and condemned to be stoned to death (Deut 21:18–21).

Spare the Rod: "Whom the Lord loveth he correcteth" is a frequent biblical thought (Deut 8:5; Prov 3:12; 13:24; etc.).

Parents were continually advised that correcting children was necessary and in their own interests. "Correct thy son and he will give thee rest"—such a child would "give delight," make a "glad father," and make the parents "greatly rejoice" (Prov 10:1; 15:20; 22:22, 24–25; 29:17). On the other hand, "He that begetteth a fool doeth it to his sorrow; and the father of a churl hath no joy." A foolish son "despiseth his mother" and "is the grief of his mother" (Prov 10:1; 15:20; 17:21).

Corporal punishment was enthusiastically recommended. Whips are mentioned (2 Sam 7:14), but usually rods are advised:

"He that spareth his rod hateth his son; but he that loveth him chasteneth him betimes" (Prov 13:24.)

"Foolishness is bound in the heart of a child; but the rod of correction shall drive it far from him" (Prov 22:15).

"Withhold not correction from the child: for if thou beatest him with the rod, he shall not die" (Prov 23:13).

"Thou shalt beat him with the rod, and shalt deliver his soul from hell" (Prov 23:14).

"The rod and reproof give wisdom: but a child left to himself bringeth his mother to shame" (Prov 29:15).

Finally, there was a warning against too-harsh corporal punishment: "Chasten thy son, for there is a hope; but set not thy heart on his destruction" (Prov 19:18).

The Apocrypha offers the most complete picture of bringing up a child:

> Cocker thy child, and he shall make thee afraid: play with him, and he will bring thee to heaviness. Laugh not with him, lest thou have sorrow with him, and lest thou gnash thy teeth in the end. Give him no liberty in his youth, and wink not at his follies. Bow down his neck while he is young, and beat him on the sides while he is a child, lest he wax stubborn, and be disobedient unto thee, and so bring sorrow to thine heart. Chastise thy son, and hold him to labour, lest his lewd behaviour be an offence unto thee [Ecclesiasticus 30:9–13].

Child Murder

In times of war or emergency, children were treated no differently from adults. There was no special mercy shown them during siege, they were slaughtered or enslaved if they were part of a defeated nation, and royal children were eliminated by usurpers of thrones.

Because children were valued and loved, threats of pending disasters and other calamities befalling Israel were often worded to include children: "Behold, I will punish them," said God, "the young men shall die by the sword; their sons and daughters shall die by famine" (Jer 11:22).

"And I will sell your sons and your daughters into the hands of the children of Judah, and they shall sell them to the Sabaeans, to a people far off" (Joel 3:8).

Instances of mass murder directed specifically at children also occur: the pharaoh had ordered the midwives to kill all infant boys at birth (Ex 1:15-17), God killed the eldest children of the Egyptians (Ex 11:5), and Herod ordered all children under the age of two slain (Matt 2:16).

Although it was decried by the Bible as a repugnant and desperate act, children in rare instances were killed as a source of food. This happened during the siege of Samaria (2 Kings 6:26-30). Lamentations (4:4, 9-10) suggests that mothers couldn't bear to hear their children beg for food during siege, and that quick, merciful killings were kinder than the prolonged suffering and painful death from thirst and hunger.

Child Sacrifice: The first story of child sacrifice in the Bible was when God tested Abraham by asking him to incinerate his son Isaac (Gen 22:1-10). Although in this case the sacrifice was not carried out, the incident shows that the custom of making a burnt offering of the firstborn child was known from very early times. Abraham was from Mesopotamia, where child sacrifice was still practiced when the Israelites were deported there after the fall of Jerusalem (2 Kings 17:17, 31). Among the Hebrews, child sacrifice was supposed to have been replaced by animal sacrifice, as illustrated in the story of Abraham and Isaac.

Even where the rite was practiced, child sacrifice was the ultimate offering, not an everyday affair. It was done in times of great distress, such as war or epidemic or drought. Since such misfortunes were believed to have been sent by God for some terrible sin committed by man, the offering had to be in proportion to the sin: "Shall I give my firstborn for my transgression, the fruit of my body for the sin of my soul?" (Mic 6:7).

Close neighbors of Israel such as the Phoenicians and Moabites, as well as the Canaanites among whom the Hebrews settled, all offered their children in emergencies. For instance, when the kingdoms of Israel and Judah attacked the Moabite capital, Kir-haraseth, the king of Moab "saw that the battle was too sore for him" and made a burnt offering of his son and heir on the besieged city walls (2 Kings 26-27). This particular sacrifice worked, as the Israelites withdrew without taking Kir-haraseth.

Usually a son was offered, since sons were more valued, and the oldest son was the extreme sacrifice. However, for a lesser sin, or when many victims were needed, younger sons and daughters were burned too. When Jephthah offered his daughter, it was not because she was a lesser offering, but because he had not named a specific victim in his vow—simply the first person to greet him on his triumphant return (Judg 11).

In the Bible, King Solomon is blamed for having revived child sacrifice in Israel because he erected a sanctuary to Molech in the Valley of Hinnom (Gehenna) and was said to have been influenced by his many foreign wives to engage in this worship himself (1 Kings 11:7). Molech was best known to the Hebrews as the Canaanite god of fire, but Molech was also an Assyrian god. He was known quite early to Hebrews because he is included in their laws: "Thou shalt not let any of thy seed pass through the fire to Molech" (Lev 18:21). "Whosoever he be of the children of Israel, or of the strangers that sojourn in Israel, that giveth any of his seed to Molech; he shall surely be put to death: the people of the land shall stone him with stones" (Lev 20:2).

Similar to Molech was an Ammonite god called Milcom, whom Solomon was also accused of worshiping. "For Solomon went after . . . Milcom, the abomination of the Ammonites" (1 Kings 11:5, 7, 33; 2 Kings 23:10, 13). These passages also accuse Solomon of worshiping Chemosh, the chief Moabite god—Moabites were called "the children of Chemosh" (Num 21:29)—to whom children were also burnt offerings. Chemosh is also mentioned earlier, in the time of Judges (Judg 11:24). A god named Malcham (Zeph 1:5) is believed to be a variant spelling or an error for Molech.

Thus the Hebrews were continually surrounded by people among whom child sacrifice was a popular ritual, and eventually many Hebrews, despite their laws, were drawn to this worship (Jer 32:35; Amos 5:26; Acts 7:43).

After Ahab of Israel married Jezebel, child sacrifice was blamed on her, as she popularized the Phoenician form of the cult among the Hebrews. Blaming foreigners was an easy excuse, but the prophets make clear that the Hebrews were just as guilty. Isaiah railed about "Enflaming yourselves with idols under every green tree, slaying the children in the valleys under the clifts of the rocks" (Isa 57:5). Ezekiel also accused Hebrews in his phrase "when they had slain their children to their idols" (Ezek 23:39). Two kings of Judah—Ahaz (733–727 BC) and Manasseh (698–642 BC)—are especially singled out for condemnation. Ahaz "made his son to pass through the fire, according to the abominations of the heathen" (2 Kings 16:3) and "burnt his children in the fire." Manasseh "burnt his children in the fire after the abominations of the heathen" (2 Kings 16:3; 2 Chron 28:3; 33:6).

Finally the reformer king, Josiah (639–609 BC), who had been brought up by the high priest in the Temple, reread old manuscripts in the Temple that plainly showed such worship was forbidden to the Hebrews—apparently by then the cult was so common that his subjects had completely forgotten the prohibitions against it. Heathen worship had even infiltrated the Temple in Jerusalem, which is where Josiah began his cleanup. Then he destroyed and burned images, sacred groves, and sanctuaries to foreign gods, and killed the priests—not only in Judah but even in Israel, where he did not rule. He made the Valley of Hinnom unfit for worship by spreading it with human bones and other loathsome materials (2 Kings 23:1–20; 2 Chr 34:1–7). Jeremiah wrote that the Valley of Hinnom should be called "the valley of slaughter," where bodies would be thrown as "meat for the fowls of the heaven, and for the beasts of the earth" (Jer 7:31–33). It became a place for garbage and filth to be collected and burned, and thus became the valley of fire and brimstone from which our concept of hell was drawn.

The Banished Child

One of the most touching stories in the Bible is the love of Hagar the Egyptian for her son, Ishmael, both of whom were banished by Abraham. Abraham gave them only bread and a bottle of water. Hagar and Ishmael wandered in the wilderness of Beersheba until the water gave out. Although she was certain they would soon die of thirst, Hagar pushed her son under a bush to keep him alive as long as possible. Then she sat a long distance from Ishmael, so she would not see him die. God heard her weeping and showed her a well, which enabled them to refill their water bottle and survive. God also promised Hagar that Ishmael would be father to "a great nation."

The Bible describes Ishmael as "wild," and he grew up in the wilderness of Paran (on the Sinai Peninsula), where he earned what must have been a precarious living as an archer. Possibly he was also a mercenary, because the angel's prediction—"his hand will be against every man, and every man's hand against him"—implies a violent career. He must have had a generous spirit, because he continued to love Abraham, and when the old man died, he returned to help Isaac bury him in the Cave of Machpelah.

Little else is known of Ishmael. He had at least one wife (an Egyptian) and at least twelve sons and one daughter, and he was greatly mourned by his household when he died at age 137 (Gen 16:12; 17:17–25; 21:1–21; 25:9–18; 28:9).

The Only Boy with Lunch

Of the thousands of people who had followed Jesus to the wilderness near the Sea of Galilee, the only one who had food was a

188

young boy. It was from this child's five barley loaves and two small fishes that Jesus fed the multitude (John 6:1-15).

Kids Who Got a Second Chance

1. Elijah prayed over the body of a widow's only son, and God revived the child (1 Kings 17:17-24).

2. When Elisha had promised a barren woman with an old husband that she would have a son, she could not believe him and begged, "Do not lie unto thine handmaiden." She did have a son, but one day when he was helping his father reap he began to cry, "My head, my head." The father had him carried back to the house, where the mother held him on her lap until he died at noon. The mother laid the child on his bed and then saddled an ass to ride to Elisha. She grabbed Elisha by the feet and cried accusingly, "Did I not say, Do not deceive me?" Elisha went to the dead boy and stretched himself upon the body "and put his mouth upon his mouth, and his eyes upon his eyes, and his hands upon his hands ... and the flesh of the child waxed warm." Suddenly the child sneezed seven times and opened his eyes (2 Kings 4:12-37).

3. A widow in Galilee had an only son that she had hoped would earn them both a living once he was grown, but the child died. The funeral procession was coming out of the city gates of Nain as Jesus was approaching with followers. Jesus, having compassion on the widow, said, "Weep not." Then Jesus called the dead son back to life by calling, "Arise" (Luke 7:11-17).

4. Jairus, the ruler of the synagogue at Capernaum, had a twelve-year-old daughter who had died, and he called on Jesus for help. The people wailing and weeping around the body laughed with scorn when Jesus entered and said, "The damsel is not dead, but sleepeth." However, when Jesus took the girl's hand and told her to arise, she got up and walked (Matt 9:18, 19, 23-26; Mark 5:22-24, 35-43; Luke 8:41-42, 49-56).

Holy Matrimony

Some of the most stirring imagery in the Bible compares man's relationship to God with a joyful marriage.

"Turn, O backsliding children, saith the Lord; for I am married unto you" (Jer 3:14) is typical of comparisons made between marriage and God's union with Israel. Others are "And I will betroth thee unto me for ever" (Hos 2:19-20); "and as the bridegroom rejoiceth over the bride, so shall thy God rejoice over thee" (Isa 62:4-5).

One of the most tender passages of all begins, "Behold, thy time was the time of love; and I spread my skirt over thee, and covered thy nakedness: Yea . . . and thou becamest mine" (Ezek 16:8-14).

The metaphor exuberantly continues as the groom washes his bride with water, anoints her with oil, then dresses her in embroidery, badgers' skin, fine linen, and silk. "And I put a jewel on thy forehead, and earrings in thine ears, and a beautiful crown upon thy head." Then the bride is fed with flour, honey, and oil, and her beauty is "perfect."

In the New Testament, similar imagery is found in "Behold, the bridegroom cometh" (Matt 25:6) and in many other passages where Jesus is compared to a bridegroom: "For the marriage of the Lamb is come, and his wife hath made herself ready" (Rev 19:7).

But honeymoons can end abruptly and some of these religiously romantic passages finish with a denunciation of man's failure to live up to God's expectations. Ezekiel's beautiful words turn suddenly from a joyful scene to the shocking "But thou didst trust in thine own beauty, and playedst the harlot" (Ezek 16:15), going on to list abominations and whoredoms. In the New Testament, the departure of the bridegroom turns future hopes to ashes: "Can the children of the bridechamber mourn, as long as the bridegroom is with them? but the days will come, when the bridegroom shall be taken from them" (Matt 9:15).

In the marriage of human and human, the course of love is often just as rocky and full of complication, and the Bible is the first to admit it.

Falling in Love: "Therefore shall a man leave his father and his mother, and shall cleave unto his wife, and they shall be one flesh" (Gen 2:24).

Although the first reference to marriage in the Bible suggests that a man leave his family to join his wife, the common practice throughout the Bible was that the woman left her family to join her husband. This often occurred at an early age; and only during talmudic times (4th to 5th centuries) was a minimum age limit defined for marriage: thirteen years for boys and twelve years for girls.

Quite often, the future wife of a man met the groom before her family did. Women worked outside the home, tending the flocks, drawing water from the community well, and doing other chores that brought them social contacts. Harvest festivals later offered a good opportunity for the young to meet, and many engagements were arranged soon thereafter. In patriarchal times, extending hospitality to strangers could result in a wedding. Rachel was watching her father's sheep when Jacob approached and kissed her; when he introduced himself as her cousin, he was invited into her home and she was soon promised to him as a wife (Gen 29:9–19). Moses too had been invited into the household of his future father-in-law after he helped Zipporah draw water (Ex 2:16–21).

Hebrews were supposed to try to find mates among their cousins, or at least within their tribe. Thus, when Abraham grew old, he worried that Isaac would marry a foreigner, and he sent a servant back to Mesopotamia to find a cousin (Gen 24:1–15). Isaac in turn encouraged his son Jacob to find a cousin, and he did twice as well as his father hoped, marrying two cousins, Leah and Rachel (Gen 28:1–2). Samson's parents were upset when he wanted to wed a Philistine, urging him to find a wife among his own people (Judg 14:2–3).

Even if an Israelite found a mate within the tribe, however, there were many restrictions. Any man "wounded in the stones" or having "his privy member cut off" was not a suitable husband (Deut 23:1). In addition, brothers and sisters, parents, step-parents, grandparents, grandchildren, aunts and uncles, nieces and nephews, and other blood relatives were illegal as spouses. Marriage with certain close in-laws or with a father's concubines was also prohibited. Remarriage to a previously divorced wife was not allowed if she had remarried—even if she had divorced her second husband or he had died. Women were also not supposed to marry men with whom they had committed adultery or men who were products of incestuous relationships.

191

Marriage with Captives: If a Hebrew man wanted to marry a woman captured in war, he had to allow her a full month of mourning for her family and her country before sleeping with her. During this time she had her head shaved and her nails cut as signs of mourning and cleansing. Presuming his ardor still remained at the end of the month, the couple could be married.

Marriage for a captive meant she lost her slave status. If her husband tired of her, he could divorce her but he could never sell her as a slave or servant (Deut 21:11–14).

Marriage of Hebrew Slaves: The Hebrew bachelor who indentured himself as a bondsman to another Israelite had to leave his servitude a single man. If a man was married when he entered servitude, his wife would be freed with him at the end of his service (Ex 21:3).

If a slave was given a wife by his master, this wife—and any children the couple might have had—remained the property of the master at the end of the period of service. Should the slave have become so attached to his wife and children that he preferred to remain voluntarily in service rather than leave them, his ear would be pierced with an awl as a sign he was indentured forever (Ex 21:4–6).

A Hebrew girl sold into slavery by her father would not be given her freedom in the seventh year the way a male slave was. She could, however, become the wife or concubine of either her master or her master's son, receiving full status and privileges in the family (Ex 21:7–11).

King Solomon Loved Many Strange Women: In addition to encouraging matches within the tribes, the Hebrews had many rules against marrying foreigners. Because Canaanites were idolatrous, they were off bounds for religious reasons (Ex 24:15; Deut 7:3, 4, 16). With the Ammonites and Moabites the main concern was economic; Jewish men could marry these foreign women because inheritance remained with the Israelites. But since Jewish women would have lost their inheritance they were not allowed to marry Ammonites or Moabites. Edomite and Egyptian men were allowed to marry Jewish women provided they had attained full citizenship in the Hebrew community—something that was not possible until the third generation after conversion (Deut 23:7, 8).

In the days of Nehemiah, Ezra revived old laws against intermarriage, partially because so many Hebrews had taken "strange wives" during the deportation to Babylonia. Ezra set up a divorce court that declared all intermarriages void. These included unions that had previously been allowed, such as to Ammonites and Moabites.

However, the laws against intermarriage were frequently violated. King Solomon was the most notorious example, having "loved many strange women," including at least one Egyptian, several Moabites, Ammonites,

Edomites, Sidonians, and Hittites (1 Kings 11:1; 14:21). Others who loved foreigners included:

Esau: two Hittites (Gen 26:34)
Joseph: an Egyptian woman (Gen 41:45)
Moses: a Midianite woman (Ex 2:21)
Naomi's two sons: Moabite women (Ruth 1:4)
David: Calebite, Aramean, Ammonite, and other foreign women (2 Sam 3:2–6)
Ahab: a Sidonian woman, Jezebel (1 Kings 16:31)
Bathsheba: a Hittite man, Uriah (2 Sam 11:30)
Hiram's mother: a Tyrian (1 Kings 7:13–14)

Battered Spouses

The prophet Nehemiah had little patience with Jews who had taken strange husbands or wives during the exile to Babylon: "I contended with them, and cursed them, and smote certain of them, and plucked off their hair" (Neh 13:25).

Many Wives: Multiple wives were common in the Middle East, and a strict hierarchy separated wives from the harem and concubines. One of the earliest laws found is the Assyrian Code of Law from the 2d millennium BC, which gives the wife the highest status, followed by harem members, with slave concubines at the bottom. It was possible for a woman from the harem to become a wife, but apparently a slave could not achieve this distinction unless she were first freed.

The Code of Hammurabi (c. 1700 BC) stipulated that only if a first wife was barren could a man take a second wife. However, he could have other women provided he considered them concubines rather than wives. But even for concubines there were laws. If a wife gave her husband her slave as a concubine, he had to take this woman in place of a concubine he might find on his own. Presumably this left some control in the hands of the wife—if she kept her husband supplied with unappealing slaves it would be easier to keep his affection. Even so, the number of concubines was restricted, because a second was allowed only if the first one proved barren. In at least some parts of the Assyrian Empire a barren wife was *obligated* to provide her husband with a concubine.

The influence of this thought on the patriarchs can be seen in the stories of Sarah (who provided Abraham with Hagar as a concubine when she herself proved barren) and Rachel (who did the same for Jacob when she was barren). However, Leah also gave Jacob a concubine even though she had had several children herself, so either the rules had been relaxed or they had never been as strict among the Hebrews.

Whatever rules had existed in earlier days seemed to have gone out the window by David's reign. Despite having at least six wives, David apparently allowed Bathsheba a prominent role in the household right to the end of his reign, and it was her son—rather than his firstborn—that he chose as his successor.

The first mention of polygamy in the Bible occurs early in Genesis, with Lamek and his two wives (Gen 4:19), and until the time of the New Testament polygamy was taken for granted (Deut 21:15-17). Of the patriarchs, Isaac alone had one wife, with no mention of concubines. From the time of David and Solomon, those who could afford to support a large household had as many wives and concubines as they desired. Most of the common people were probably monogamous simply because they couldn't afford to keep more than one woman.

While biblical law did not prohibit polygamy, it recognized its dangers: "Neither shall he [the king] multiply wives to himself, that his heart turn not away . . ." (Deut 17:17). The many wives of Solomon are blamed for causing him to stray from the God of Israel, turning this injunction into a prophecy: (1 Kings 11:4-8).

The Hebrew language reflects another danger of polygamy: The term for the many wives of one man is "rivals."

How Many Wives?

The unnamed king in Song of Songs (6:8) was said to have had sixty wives and eighty concubines and "virgins without number," but figures given for actual kings and leaders in the Bible vary greatly:

Abijah (2 Chr 13:21):	14 wives
Abraham (Gen 25:6):	1 wife, several concubines
David (1 Chr 14:3):	unspecified, but more than 6 wives and more than 10 concubines
Elkanah (1 Sam 1:2):	2 wives
Gideon (Judg 8:30–31):	many wives, plus 1 or more concubines
Isaac (Gen 25–28):	1 wife
Jacob (Gen 30):	2 wives and 2 concubines
King Joash (2 Chr 24:3):	2 or more wives

194

Josiah (2 Kings 23:31):	2 or more wives
Rehoboam (2 Chr 11:21):	18 wives, plus 60 concubines
Saul (2 Sam 3:7; 12:8):	"wives," plus at least one concubine
Solomon (2 Kings 11:3):	700 wives, plus 300 concubines

Bigamy?

The Bible has only a single instance of a woman being married to two husbands at one time.

King Saul's daughter Michal, who had been married to David while he was still in King Saul's favor, returned to her father's care when David was forced to flee for his life. While David was away, Saul gave Michal in marriage to another man, Phalti.

Much later, after Saul's death, and after David became king of Judah, David insisted that Michal was his. Probably he felt that having King Saul's daughter in his household would encourage the northerners to let him rule them too. The northerners agreed to return Michal. Phalti followed her for part of the trip south, weeping as he went, until he was sent back. Michal's feelings toward her two husbands were apparently not taken into consideration (2 Sam 3:13–16).

Giving in Marriage: Women were quite literally given in marriage. In almost all cases, the Old Testament father (sometimes in consultation with the mother) "gave" his daughter to a husband and "took" a wife for his son.

Rebellion against this custom seems to have been rare. One reason may have been that the participants were so young—boys apparently married by age fourteen or so, and girls even younger.

Another reason for compliance may have been that many fathers seemingly took the feelings of the young couple into account. Zelophehad allowed his daughters to marry "whom they think best" (Num 36:6), and when Saul's daughter Michal told her father she was in love with David, Saul arranged the match (1 Sam 18:20–28). Shechem asked for the wife he wanted (Gen 34:4), and even Samson's parents, who disapproved of his preference for a Philistine girl, gave in to his wishes (Judg 14:2–10).

This was unusual, however. Sons and especially daughters were often not consulted about their marriages. Rebecca was promised in marriage without her consent to a man she'd never seen (Gen 24:51), and Sarra was not called in to meet her future husband, Tobias, until her father had already made the arrangement (Tob 7:9–13). Occasionally, when women were promised as rewards, the choice of husband could be totally random.

Caleb, for instance, offered his daughter to whoever took the Canaanite city of Kirjath-sepher (Judg 1:12). In none of these cases did the girls object.

Even more bizarre was the story of Jacob, who worked for seven years to earn Rachel and then was tricked by her father into marrying Leah. Though Jacob was angry, he accepted the situation and agreed to work another seven years for Rachel (Gen 29:16–28).

The only instance of a man choosing a wife without consulting his parents was Esau, but he was forty years old when he did so. His marriage to two Canaanite women was "a grief of mind" to his parents, and Esau finally capitulated to their wishes by taking a Hebrew as a third wife (Gen 26:34; 28:8–9).

God as Matchmaker

1. Jeremiah said God told him not to take a wife at all (Jer 16:1–2).

2. Hosea claimed God told him to take "thee a wife of whoredoms," so that he chose Gomer, a loose woman who proved unfaithful (Hos 1–2).

Bride Payments: Dowry—a formal payment by the bride or her family to the groom or his family—was seldom mentioned in biblical accounts of engagements. Two other types of payment are mentioned, however: 1) fifty shekels of silver paid to the father of a raped virgin, and followed by compulsory marriage; and 2) *mohar*.

Mohar was the opposite of a dowry—an amount paid to the father of the bride by the bridegroom. The precise amount varied according to the social and economic status of the bridegroom. Although *mohar* appears identical to bride purchase, legally it was quite different. *Mohar* compensated the woman's family, but it did not make the bride a slave who could be resold. Some scholars feel that similarly to the practices of other peoples in the area, the *mohar* was held in trust for the woman by her father. The father could invest this money for himself, but would later return the original amount to the bride either as an inheritance or in the case of her becoming a widow. In fact, when Jacob took Laban's cattle, Leah and Rachel condoned this action on the grounds that Laban had not safeguarded their *mohar* (Gen 31:14–16).

Often the hopeful groom paid in labor rather than cash. Jacob worked as a shepherd for his wives (Gen 29:15–30); David fought the Philistines for the hand of Michal (1 Sam 18:26–27); Othniel destroyed a town for his wife (Josh 15:16).

Bride payments as a sort of insurance were common in the Middle East. Babylonia had a payment similar to the *mohar*—one to fifty shekels was paid by the groom to the bride or to her father for safekeeping in case she became a widow. If she died before her husband, the money went to her children.

Marriage Contract: Scholars disagree on the nature of the marriage ceremony, some believing it to have been a civil ceremony with little religious significance, and others holding that there was no formal contract and the only significance was religious. However, textual and archaeological evidence exists that some form of marriage contract was in use:

When Sarra married Tobias, her mother "took paper, and did write an instrument of covenants, and sealed it" (Tob 7:13–14). Among the Elephantine documents from a Jewish community of the 5th century BC, marriage contracts in the name of the husband have been found, along with the statement, "She is my wife and I am her husband, from this day forever." There was no parallel statement made by the bride.

Bridal covenants are also referred to allegorically (Prov 2:17; Ezek 16:8).

Most marriage contracts were probably less formal—merely verbal agreements.

Engagements: Some couples married as soon as an agreement was reached, while others had engagements that lasted for years. Longer engagements were characteristic when the man had agreed to perform labor in exchange for the girl. It is also possible—since the ages of children are seldom given in the Bible—that some children were engaged far in advance of marriageable age. During the engagement, the bride remained in her father's house and dependent on him, but was considered "saved" for her husband-to-be.

The engagement was usually sealed by gifts and/or a blessing. Such gifts were in addition to *mohar* or any other bride payments, and were given by both the bride and the groom's family. Achsah, for example, got land and springs from her father (Josh 15:18–19), and Laban gave his daughters slaves (Gen 29:22–24, 29).

Most of the gifts, however, were given by the groom's family to the bride or to her family—perhaps an assurance that the bride would be amply provided for in her new home. Rebekah was showered with silver, gold, and raiment, plus gifts for her brother and mother (Gen 24:53), and this show of wealth might have reassured her family about letting her go so far from home for her marriage to Isaac.

The practice of bestowing jewels on a bride and gifts on her father was also an Assyrian custom. The Code of Hammurabi (c. 1700 BC) stipulated that if the engagement was broken by the woman, she had to return to the groom double the value of the gifts he had given to her and to her family

Guaranteed Honeymoon

To encourage the development of love, certain safeguards for young couples were built into Hebrew law. A betrothed man who had not yet consummated his marriage was not sent to war "lest he die in the battle, and another man take" his intended (Deut 20:7). A man was not called to war for the first year of marriage, nor was he supposed to spend all his time on business. He was told to stay home the first year to "cheer up his wife" (Deut 24:5).

What Was the Biggest Wedding Present in the Bible?

The city of Gezer. The pharaoh gave the city to Solomon, when Solomon married the pharaoh's daughter (1 Kings 9:16). The gift was considered valuable even though the city was somewhat damaged—the pharaoh having burned it and killed its inhabitants—so that Solomon had to rebuild it.

The Wedding: The marriage ceremony consisted of an elaborate "taking" of the bride, accompanied by such "gladness and rejoicing" that "voice of gladness" and "voice of mirth" were almost synonymous with the bride and groom (Psa 45:15; Jer 7:34; 16:9; 25:10; John 3:29).

The bride and groom and their attendants were extravagantly dressed for the occasion. "I will greatly rejoice in the Lord ... for he hath clothed me with the garments of salvation ... as a bridegroom decketh himself with ornaments, and as a bride adorneth herself with her jewels" (1 Sam 61:10). The importance of clothes can be seen from the story of the king who invited people to a wedding and when one man came without proper attire the king had him bound hand and foot and "cast into outer darkness" (Matt 22:11). Because it was common to pretend a bridal couple was royalty, the mother of the groom might put a crown upon his head (S of S 3:11).

The groom and companions marched in a grand procession to the home of the bride's parents, where she and maidens waited; "and behold, there was much ado and great carriage: and the bridegroom came forth, and his friends and brethren, to meet them with drum, and instruments of musick" (1 Macc 9:39). Singers, musicians, and torchbearers might accompany the groom's party, and in the story of the wise and foolish virgins who went to meet the bridegroom the women carried oil lamps (Matt 25:1–3). The joy and eagerness are recounted in Psalms (19:5): "a bridegroom rejoiceth as a strong man to run a race." The men then escorted the women's party back to the groom's home, with onlookers joining the party along the way.

A large feast followed. When Laban rebuked Jacob for leaving secretly, he pointed out he would have sent him "away with mirth, with songs, with tabret, and with harp" (Gen 31:27). Nevertheless, he gave Leah a feast, and at Rachel's her people ate and drank all night (Gen 24:54; 29:22–24). At Samson's wedding feast he entertained guests with a riddle (Judg 14:10–12). And when Jesus turned the water into wine it was because there was no wine at a wedding feast (John 2:1–11).

The feast might last as long as seven or fourteen days. On the first night, the bride and groom retired to the bridal chamber. The bloodstained sheet, proving the bride had been a virgin, was retrieved in the morning, and kept as evidence in case the husband later accused her to the contrary (Deut 22:13–21).

Why Remove a Shoe?

Under the useful Hebrew law called the levirate, a childless widow was to be married by her dead husband's nearest male relative, usually his brother. If there was no brother, or if the brother died as well, the obligation passed on to other relatives. A man could refuse such a marriage, but had to do so before a court of elders; the woman then removed his shoe and spat at him, to show disgust. The community frowned on such a refusal, and called him "The house of him that had his shoe loosed" (Deut 25:5–10). Levirate marriage provided for the inheritance of the dead man to be carried on in his own name—the firstborn of the woman was to have the dead husband's name and inheritance. Any additional children the couple had were considered children of the second husband.

An example of a man who refused his obligation under the levirate is the unnamed "kinsman" in the story of Ruth. After Ruth's husband died, Boaz—a relative of her late husband—wanted to marry her. However, as the kinsman was closer to her under the levirate, the best Boaz could promise was to marry her if the kinsman did not. The kinsman appeared before the elders and removed his shoe, leaving the way clear for Boaz to marry Ruth (Ruth 3:12–13; 4:1–11).

An intriguing story illustrates the complications that could arise under the levirate:

Tamar had married Er, the oldest son of Judah. When Er died,

Judah gave Tamar to his second son, Onan, who was to "perform the duty of a husband's brother." Onan resented the fact a child born of this union would be considered Er's instead of his own. Therefore, when he slept with Tamar he spilled his seed on the ground to deprive his brother of a son. For this, God killed Onan.

Judah now promised Tamar that she would be married to his third son, Shelah, to fulfill the levirate law. But as Shelah was just a boy, she had to wait until he grew up. Tamar did wait, but once Shelah was grown he married another woman. Tamar tricked Judah into sleeping with her by disguising herself in veils like a prostitute. When Judah discovered Tamar's pregnancy, he wanted her burned for harlotry. But then he realized that since it should have been his duty to enforce the levirate, and that she had only deceived him into doing so, he decided he was more to blame than she. Tamar's life was spared and she gave birth to twins (Gen 38:6–30).

Onan II

Dorothy Parker (in a story that is probably apocryphal) claimed that she had a parakeet that she named Onan—because he always spilled his seed on the ground.

The Unpuritanical Bible

In sexual matters the Bible is both frank and explicit to a degree that often shocks even modern readers. And the range of sexual experience covered is, by almost any standard, virtually complete. From the tender and sensual Song of Solomon, to the unabridged liberties of Sodom and Gomorrah, the Bible omits nothing, censors no passage because its portrayal of sex is unacceptable. This is not to say that the Bible is for those over eighteen or should come in a plastic wrapper, but it is, in places, earthy, ribald, and lusty. It is quite simply the product of a culture in which morality, and honesty, were valued over prudery.

One whole book of the Bible is given over to love poetry. The Song of Solomon is an enraptured lyric about the beauty of love, of women and men, and of sex. This openly sexual lyricism, carried on for an entire book, did meet with disfavor by those who considered such frankness inappropriate to the Bible. From quite early on there grew up around the Song the interpretation that the author was not describing love between man and woman, but between God and the faithful.

At best such an interpretation is secondary. The Song of Solomon is primarily and obviously a dialogue between two very human lovers. Like the marriage songs which were, until recently, a tradition among peasants in Syria, the lover and the beloved in turn describe the beautiful and endearing qualities of the partner and the passion of their own love. In the Song of Solomon the lovers are a harem girl and the shepherd-king, probably Solomon. This could be an interracial love affair—the heroine is "black but comely" (S of S 1:5), the hero "white and ruddy, the chiefest among ten thousand" (5:10).

In imagery that is quaint and local, as befits the experience of a shepherd, and ornate and rich, as one would expect from the members of the royal household, the lovers pile metaphor upon simile to describe each other. To the woman Solomon says: "Thy teeth are as a flock of sheep which go up from the washing, whereof every one beareth twins, and there is not one barren among them" (6:6). She portrays him in regal terms:

> His hands are as gold rings set with the beryl: his belly is as bright ivory overlaid with sapphires [5:14].

Not only do they describe each other, but they enumerate the symptoms of love sickness with psychological and physiological honesty:

> By night on my bed I sought him whom my soul loveth: I sought him but found him not. I will rise now, and go about the city in the streets, and in the broad ways I will seek him whom my soul loveth: I sought him, but I found him not [3:1–2].

> My beloved put in his hand by the hole of the door, and my bowels were moved for him. I rose up to open to my beloved; and my hands dropped with myrrh, and my fingers with sweet smelling myrrh, upon the handles of the lock [5:4–5].

Song of Solomon is the most rhapsodic catalog of sexual attractiveness in the Old Testament. Though the wiles and attributes of the sexes are noted throughout the first books of the Bible, there is little to match the Song for sexual poetry. In Genesis, Sarah is called "very fair" (12:14) and her beauty is left at that. The distinction between the charms of the two sisters Leah and Rachel is summed up in a single sentence: "Leah was tender eyed; but Rachel was beautiful and well favoured" (Gen 29:17).

The later books of the Old Testament are somewhat more explicit, but in many of these passages the attractions of the opposite sex are represented as entrapments to be avoided. In one proverb, the author, perhaps Solomon himself, warns his son to keep away from "the flattery of the tongue of a strange woman. . . . Lust not after her beauty in thine heart; neither let her take thee with her eyelids" (6:24–25). Most of the danger to the naïve young man comes from the whorish woman. Proverb 7 is entirely given over to description of the harlot, "who hath cast down many wounded."

Almost every beautiful woman, no matter who she is or what her character may be, is potential trouble for the young man in the Old Testament. The story of David and Bathsheba is a case in point. One moonlit night, the king, restless and unable to sleep, walks upon the roof of the palace, and from there spies on the comely Bathsheba, washing herself. Falling in love, he inquires about her and learns she is married to Uriah. Undaunted, the king sends for her. They make love and before long she is pregnant. In hopes that he may not be discovered as the father, David tries to get Uriah, who has been away, to sleep with his wife, but the plan does not succeed. Taking a more brutal tack, David sends Uriah off to the "forefront of the hottest battle," where he is killed. After a period of mourning, Bathsheba becomes David's wife and bears his son. But here's the rub—God is displeased with David's behavior, and the child is struck dead. Even the most well-loved king in the Bible ends up paying for his romantic indiscretions.

Outside of the Song of Solomon, sexual playfulness is rare in the Bible, but the authors do seem to have a soft spot for sexual relationships in old age and can even rise to humor on the subject. There is hardly a scene more tragicomic than that of David's meeting with Abishag. Old, withered, his circulation so poor he continually shivers, King David is near the end. His servants, remembering his better days and a tried-and-true remedy for his royal blues, propose a solution:

> Let there be sought for my lord the king a young virgin: and let her stand before the king, and let her cherish him, and let her lie in thy bosom, that my lord the king may get heat [Kings 1:2].

A maiden is found and brought to the king. The old man obviously takes to her; for though he is too old to "know" her, he receives everyone, including his wife, Bathsheba, with the girl always on his lap (1 Kings 1:15).

Abraham and Sarah, too, get a big bang out of the idea of sex in old age. When God tells Abraham that he will get his wife with child, "Abraham fell upon his face, and laughed, and said in his heart, Shall a child be born unto him that is an hundred years old?" (Gen 17:17). When Sarah overhears this bit of news she breaks up, laughing: "After I am waxed old shall I have pleasure, my lord being old also?" (Gen 18:19).

Censored

The truth is, that when a library expels a book of mine and leaves an unexpurgated Bible around where unprotected youth and age can get hold of it, the deep unconscious irony of it delights me and doesn't anger me.

—MARK TWAIN

Before Oedipus: Though the Old Testament can be quite moralistic, as in the case of David and Bathsheba, it does not always censor practices that are sex taboos in modern society. For example, the early books of the Old

Testament mention incestuous acts with perfect aplomb. Lot's daughters get him drunk, then sleep with him? Interesting story (Gen 19:33). Abraham marries his stepsister? No kidding (Gen 20:12). And Amram marries his aunt? Yep, they were Moses' parents (Ex 6:20). Perhaps this laissez-faire attitude toward incest has something to do with the long sojourn in Egypt, where incest was permitted and even promoted among members of the royal court. And too, incest would have been almost inescapable in a society as small, and closed, as that of the patriarchs. With the laws of Leviticus 18, which Moses set down, unlawful marriages between relations were sharply defined and incest thus became prohibited.

More Instances of Incest

1. Cain and Seth, the sons of Adam and Eve, because they must have married their sisters (Gen 4:17; 5:4).
2. Nahor with Milcah, his niece (Gen 11:29).
3. Judah with his daughter-in-law, Tamar, when she seduced him (Gen 38:16–18).
4. Herod, when he married his sister-in-law (Mark 6:17–18).
5. Many in Palestine: "It is reported commonly that there is fornication among you . . . that one should have his father's wife" (1 Cor 5:1).
6. Reuben (Gen 35:22) and Absalom (2 Sam 16:22) also committed incest by sleeping with their fathers' concubines.
7. Jacob, because he married his first cousins, the sisters Leah and Rachel (Gen 29:10; 30:20–28).

Having a Gay Old Time: One practice the Bible has scant toleration for is homosexual behavior. Deuteronomy specifically prohibits transvestism (22:5), sodomy (23:17), and the use of the profit from male or female prostitution for a temple offering (23:18). Such earnings were called, in biblical slang, "the price of a dog."

It is Sodom, of course, which gave its name to the practice of sodomy and the threat of homosexual rape which led to the destruction of Sodom and Gomorrah. As Lot was entertaining two visitors, who the Bible tells us were angels, many men of Sodom "came round" the house, crying out that they wanted to "get to know" the two male guests (Gen 19:4–5). In one of the most bizarre gestures of hospitality ever recorded, Lot offered them his two virgin daughters instead, to do with as they thought best (19:8). This did not seem to satisfy them and in fact they became quite enraged at the proposal and directed their anger at Lot. The angels, having had enough of the whole business, struck the tumultuous crowd blind and soon destroyed both towns.

The practice of sodomy was perhaps encouraged by Canaanite religion, which ritualized both heterosexual and homosexual prostitution. The *kedeshim* were the boy prostitutes, the sodomites whose houses were located in groves, after the practice of Canaanite temples (2 Kings 23:7). These houses of prostitution were, together with idolatry, among the chief objects of reform for the kings of Judah (1 Kings 15:12; 22:46).

There has been some speculation that David and Jonathan had an ongoing homosexual relationship. Surely they were more than the best of friends. The Bible describes them as soulmates and lovers:

> The soul of Jonathan was knit with the soul of David, and
> Jonathan loved him as his own soul [1 Sam 18:1].

In David's eloquent tribute to Jonathan and Saul, he described Jonathan's love as "wonderful, passing the love of women" (2 Sam 1:26). Yet in almost every passage relating to the pair is the suggestion that Jonathan was much more enamored of David (1 Sam 19:2), and sacrificed much more for his friend, including his kingdom, than vice versa. That there was more than fraternal love between them is a distinct possibility, but in view of the incontestable evidence of David's vigorous heterosexuality, it seems more likely that it was Jonathan's infatuation with David and not any sexual involvement that gave their friendship its emotional intensity.

Five

Matters of the Mind

Winged gods of the Near East. *Upper left:* A female sphinx from Megiddo. The cherubim probably looked like this. *Upper right:* An Assyrian winged bull, possibly the inspiration for Hebrew cherubim. *Lower left:* A four-horned altar found at Megiddo. COURTESY OF THE ORIENTAL INSTITUTE, UNIVERSITY OF CHICAGO. *Lower right:* A fanciful rendering of Solomon's altar. COURTESY OF THE NEW YORK PUBLIC LIBRARY.

Biblical Covenants

The Rainbow Sign: Upon disembarking from the ark, Noah offered a burnt sacrifice to God. The smell pleased the deity. He decided to refrain from repeating the Flood ever again and to provide for the continuation of the natural cycles as long as the earth continued: "While the earth remaineth, seedtime and harvest, and cold and heat, and summer and winter, and day and night shall not cease" (Gen 8:22). Noah and his sons were summoned together and told to "be fruitful and multiply" with God's blessing. They were also given the go-ahead to eat meat—although stipulation was made that they were not to eat of flesh "with the life thereof, which is the blood thereof" (Gen 9:4). Only after all this was settled did God offer a covenant. Unlike those that followed, this first covenant was largely one-sided, with God contributing more than Noah. To seal the agreement, God gave the rainbow.

The most striking part of the covenant is that it was made not between God and man, but between God and man and the animals and the earth: "And I, behold, I establish my covenant with you, and with your seed after you; and with every living creature that is with you ... every beast of the earth. ... This is the token of the covenant which I make between me and you and every living creature that is with you, for perpetual generations: ... and it shall be for a token of a covenant between me and the earth" (Gen 9:9–10, 12–13).

Covenant of Flesh: The second covenant of the Bible was made between God and Abraham and consists of three parts.

In the first—which is introduced by the image of a smoking furnace through which a flaming torch passed—God promised that Abraham would have natural sons (rather than adopted, i.e., Eliezer) as numerous as the stars, who would inherit the land "from the river of Egypt unto the great river, the river Euphrates" (Gen 15:18). Solomon was the only Israelite king to rule this entire area, the "promised land."

The second part of the covenant occurred when Abraham was ninety-nine years old (Gen 17). At this time Abraham's name was changed (from Abram), as was Sarah's (from Sarai), and they were again promised descendants and a land for them to dwell in. The change of name adds the Hebrew letter for *h*, which symbolizes Jehovah's name.

More than Noah, Abraham was required to accept certain responsibilities and obligations. In the third part of the covenant Abraham agreed to observe the ritual of circumcision, a rite practiced by most of the ancient peoples in the surrounding area. "This is my covenant, which ye shall keep, between me and you and thy seed after thee; Every man child among you shall be circumcised ... [in] the flesh of your foreskin" (Gen 17:10–11). Circumcision thus became a requirement for the "people of the covenant," the Israelites. Failure to adhere to it is tantamount to excommunication: "And the uncircumcised man child ... that soul shall be cut off from his people; he hath broken my covenant" (Gen 17:14). (Nonobservance of Yom Kippur is the only other omission which leads to expulsion from the Jewish religious community.)

Who and What Was Cursed

"cursed shall be thy basket" (Deut 28:16)
"cursed be the man that trusteth" (Jer 17:5)
"cursed be he that giveth a wife to Benjamin" (Judg 21:18)
"cursed shall be the fruit of thy body" (Deut 28:18)
"cursed be he that doeth the work of the Lord deceitfully" (Jer 48:10)
"cursed be the day wherein I was born" (Jer 20:14)
"he that is hanged is accursed of God" (Deut 21:23)

A Gentleman's Agreement

It was the custom among the patriarchs, and still is the custom among Bedouin, to swear an oath to another by placing one's hand on the other's genitals. On his deathbed, Abraham has his eldest servant vow to carry out his last wish: "Put, I pray thee, thy hand under my thigh: And I will make thee swear by the Lord" (Gen

26:2). When Jacob makes Joseph swear to bury him in the land of his fathers, he says, "If now I have found grace in thy sight, put, I pray thee, thy hand under my thigh" (Gen 47:29).

Binding Arbitration: The third covenant, the giving of the Law at Sinai, was not an agreement between God and an individual, as it was in the case of Noah and Abraham, but a contract between a commanding and demanding God and an assenting and observing community.

God's part would be to supply the people with the continuation of the natural cycles of the creation: The rain would come in its season, the harvests would be full, the people would remain healthy, and the descendants of the people would be many. The land promised to the descendants of Abraham, Isaac, and Jacob was to become theirs as long as they obeyed the commandments given at Sinai.

The acceptance of the covenant came only after a long and protracted session in which Moses was the arbitrator, bringing messages back and forth between the two parties. God first appeared to Moses, told him the conditions of the agreement, and sent him off to secure consent from the leaders of the people. The people were told to prepare themselves—the "signing" of the agreement was to be a formal ceremony. Moses introduced the people to God: "Moses brought forth the people out of the camp to meet with God" (Ex 19:17). After a few more details were straightened out, God gave the children of Israel the Ten Commandments.

This, however, was only the beginning of the covenant. Moses returned to the mountain to receive the laws, which then became the book of the covenant (Ex 20:22—23:33), laws which he then placed before the people for ratification. "And he took the book of the covenant, and read in the audience of the people; and they said: All that the Lord hath said will we do, and be obedient" (Ex 24:7).

The final stage in the acceptance of the covenant was the ceremony that bound the two parties (God and the people) together by blood. The people sacrificed oxen, and Moses took the blood and sprinkled half on the altar and half on the people: "Behold the blood of the covenant, which the Lord hath made with you concerning all these words" (Ex 24:8).

The first breach of the Sinai covenant came close on the heels of its acceptance. After the people ratified it, Moses went up on the mountain to receive instructions from God about building objects to be used in rituals. When he came down, he found the people had broken the covenant by putting up the golden calf (Ex 32). After destroying the calf and killing those who had worshiped it, Moses apologized to God on behalf of those who were still willing to accept and observe God's laws. Forgiveness was granted and the covenant continued to be binding.

211

Cursed Curses

"thou shalt not . . . curse the ruler of thy people" (Ex 22:28)
"thou shalt not curse the deaf" (Lev 19:14)
"thou shalt not curse the people" (Num 22:12)
"curse not the king in thought" (Eccl 10:20)
"curse God and die" (Job 2:9)

Jeremiah Envisions a Covenant: In a vision, Jeremiah saw the coming of a new covenant that would amend the Sinaitic covenant slightly. This vision-ary covenant would be written on neither rock nor scrolls, but in the hearts of the people: "After those days, saith the Lord, I will put my law in their inward parts, and write it in their hearts; and will be their God, and they shall be my people" (Jer 31:33). None of the laws was replaced, no other description of the covenant itself was given: it was only asserted that the covenant would become an inwardly motivated force rather than imposed from without.

Covenant of Communion: According to the New Testament, the laws of the Old Testament covenant were superseded by the new covenant of commu-nion, where the wine symbolized the blood of the covenant: "This is the blood of the new testament, which is shed for many" (Mark 14:24). Basing his argument on the vision of Jeremiah, the author of Hebrews said that "if that first covenant had been faultless, then should no place have been sought for the second" (Heb 8:7), and continued with a restatement of God's words to Jeremiah about establishing a second covenant in the hearts of the people. Jesus was seen as "the mediator of the new testament, that by means of death, for the redemption of the transgressions that were under the first testament, they which are called might receive the promise of eternal inheritance" (Heb 9:15). Thus seen, Jesus replaced the sacrificial offering made at the time of previous covenants.

Does the Bible Forbid . . . ?

1. Eating lobster Newburg?
2. Wearing a sports coat made out of a blend of wool and linen?
3. Collecting interest on money lent to a friend?

4. Using profanity when talking about the President of the United States?

5. Flat roofs with no parapets?

6. A butcher putting his thumb on the scale?

7. Eating blood sausage or associating with Englishmen or Germans who do?

8. Painting a picture of a tree?

9. Having bacon and eggs for breakfast?

10. Women wearing ties?

11. Eating grasshoppers?

The Bible prohibits all of the above, except for the last item. See the following references:

1. "And all that have not fins and scales in the seas, and in the rivers of all that move in the waters, and of any living thing which is in the waters, they shall be an abomination unto you" (Lev 11:10). This law prohibits the eating of shellfish.

2. "Thou shalt not wear a garment of divers sorts, as of woollen and linen together" (Deut 22:11).

3. "Unto thy brother thou shalt not lend upon usury" (Deut 23:20).

4. "Thou shalt not . . . curse the ruler of thy people" (Ex 22:28).

5. "When thou buildest a new house, then thou shalt make a battlement for thy roof, that thou bring not blood upon thine house, if any man fall from thence" (Deut 22:8).

6. "Ye shall do not unrighteousness in judgment, in meteyard, in weight, or in measure" (Lev 19:35).

7. "No soul of you shall eat blood, neither shall any stranger that sojourneth among you eat blood" (Lev 17:12).

8. "Thou shalt not make . . . any likeness of any thing that is in heaven above, or that is in the earth beneath, or that is in the water under the earth" (Ex 20:4).

9. "And the swine, though he divide the hoof, and be cloven-footed, yet he cheweth not the cud; he is unclean to you" (Lev 11:7).

10. "The woman shall not wear that which pertaineth to a man, neither shall a man put on a woman's garment" (Deut 22:5).

11. "Even these of them ye may eat; the locust after his kind and the bald locust after his kind, and the beetle after his kind, and the grasshopper after his kind" (Lev 22:11).

Build Your Own Altar

The main thing to remember when building your altar is that it is a place on which to offer sacrifices. At least in the earlier models, functional stability is more important than beauty. If you want to lavish wealth and artistic talent on your altar, you'll have to build one of the later versions—in the Solomon or Ezekiel style.

When building an altar incorporating stone, do not hew the stone. This would pollute your altar and render it useless (Ex 20:25).

PATRIARCHAL ALTAR

For the simplest type of altar, which we can term the patriarchal altar, choose an open place, preferably on a hill or near a well (Gen 22:9; 31:25, 46–54, etc.). A rather large stone is all you need here—you don't have to prop it up on legs or do anything else to embellish it. This style is strictly *au naturel*. Simply pile kindling and wood on top, and it's ready for use.

If you cannot find a large stone, or if you have no one to help you roll it into place, a pile of small stones will suffice.

You can use earth, as God suggests (Ex 20:24), but then the altar will not last as long.

DO NOT use brick—brick altars are strictly Canaanite.

TABERNACLE ALTAR

Two types of altars are necessary for realistic construction of the Tabernacle that accompanied the children of Israel on their trek across the Sinai: the burnt-offering altar and the incense altar.

214

Burnt-Offering Altar (Ex 27:1–8): This was a portable, hollow box with a bronze grate on which animal sacrifices were made.

Materials: acacia wood (shittim wood); bronze; bronze net or grating; 4 bronze rings; various vessels.

Measurement: 1 cubit = 18 inches or 1½ feet.

Steps:

1. Cut the acacia wood to size and make a box. Each side should be 5 cubits wide and 3 cubits high. Plate all the wood with bronze.

2. Make 4 horns and cover each with bronze. Attach these to each corner of the wooden box. (These will become more colorful later, as they are daubed with blood during ceremonies.)

3. Build a rim all the way around the top of the box. (No one knows why.)

4. Put the bronze grating in the center of the altar.

5. Attach the bronze rings to the outside of the box, at the corners.

6. Make 2 staves of wood and cover each with bronze. These staves are to be inserted through the rings so that you can carry the altar without burning your hands.

7. For handling the ashes, blood, and sacrificial animal you will also need (all must be of bronze) ashpans, shovels, basins, fleshhooks, and firepans.

8. Place the entire thing in the courtyard of the Tabernacle, and burn your bird or animal on it.

Notes:

1. The altar is hollow because otherwise it would be too heavy to carry around the desert. When you want to use it, you can fill it with pebbles or dirt for stability, as was done in days of yore.

2. DO NOT use iron tools in building the altar, as this will pollute it (Deut 28:5).

3. If you find a wild-looking person grabbing the horns of your altar, it means he's in trouble and you must give him sanctuary (Ex 21:14; 1 Kings 2:28–34).

Incense Altar (Ex 30:1–10): This altar, although smaller than the preceding model, is more expensive because it is covered in gold. On this altar you burn fragrant incense—a far more pleasant odor than you get from the burnt-animal offerings!

Materials: acacia wood; gold for casting and overlaying.

Measurement: 1 cubit = 18 inches or 1½ feet.

Steps:

1. Cut acacia wood to size and make a box. Each side should be 1 cubit long and 2 cubits high.

2. Make 4 horns (see Burnt-Offering Altar, above).

3. Overlay all the above with gold.

4. Make a crown of gold and fit it along the top rim of the altar.

5. Make 2 staves of acacia wood and overlay them with gold.

6. Make 2 gold rings, large enough to fit around the staves, and attach these to opposite sides of the altar.

7. Loop the staves through the gold rings to lift the completed altar.

Notes:

1. On this altar you may NOT offer flesh or drink, but once a year the horns should be coated with blood.

2. For the correct ambiance, you should house this altar in a Tent of Congregation, before the curtain of an Ark of the Covenant; accouterments should include 2 golden candelabra, a burnt-offering altar, and a golden table.

3. Be sure you use the proper incense, as "strange incense" is not allowed. God suggests stacte, onycha, galbanum, and frankincense (Ex 30:9, 34).

SOLOMON'S ALTAR

This is the most mysterious altar in the Bible, as no specifications are given (some scholars suggest Solomon used altars built by David). The Bible does, however, offer some handy hints:

1. The incense altar can be built of cedar rather than acacia wood, and no one will know the difference if you are careful to hide it with lots of gold overlay (1 Kings 6:20).

2. Don't invite too many friends to the first sacrificial burning. Solomon made this mistake and his bronze altar proved too small to accommodate all the animals. The fat made quite a mess of the courtyard (1 Kings 8:64).

EZEKIEL'S ALTAR

This altar, for burnt sacrifices, is named for Ezekiel because God gave him the measurements. But it is also known as the Ahaz or Damascus-style altar, because King Ahaz had it copied from one he saw in Damascus (2 Kings 16:10–16). For self-styled visionaries, prophets, or dreamers, this altar is highly recommended even though it's complicated to build. It uses the same hollow-box principle as the simpler altars, but it piles box upon box so that it resembles a square wedding cake (or a Mesopotamian ziggurat), and of course it is not portable (Ezek 43:13–17).

Notes:

1. You'll have to build a ramp or set of steps—preferably on the eastern side. This runs contrary to the prohibition against altar steps ("that thy nakedness be not discovered thereon" [Ex 20:26]), but you do need a way to reach the top to carry out your sacrifice.

2. You might want to build a walkway 2 cubits wide all the way around the upper level to keep the priests from falling in (Israelite tradition does not approve of human sacrifice).

Cornerstone Kids

The custom of laying the cornerstone for a new building with ceremony, and of embedding something in it, was known in biblical days. Children may have been sacrificed for this purpose. When Hiel rebuilt Jericho during the reign of King Ahab, "he laid the foundation thereof in Abiram his firstborn, and set up the gates thereof in his youngest son Segub, according to the word of the Lord" (1 Kings 16:34).

How to Act When You Meet God

1. SHOUT AND FALL FLAT ON YOUR FACE: Shouting isn't essential, although this is what the Israelites did when God appeared to them during the wanderings in the desert, but you must fall flat on your face (Lev 9:24; Num 16:22, 45; etc.).

2. IF ORDERED TO, STAND UP: Often, when prophets and others were lying prostrate, God might say, "Son of man, stand upon thy feet and I will speak unto thee" (Ezek 2:1).

3. TAKE OFF YOUR SHOES: When Moses approached the burning bush, God warned him, "Put off thy shoes from off thy feet, for the place whereon thou standest is holy ground" (Ex 3:5).

4. BUILD AN ALTAR: After meeting God, always build an altar and offer some sort of sacrifice. Noah's burnt offerings were one of every "clean beast, and of every clean fowl" (Gen 8:20). After Jacob erected his altar he "poured a drink offering ... and he poured oil" (Gen 35:14).

When God Calls You

1. When God calls you, the proper response is "Here am I" or "Here I am." This is what Abraham, Jacob, Moses, and others replied (Gen 22:1, 11; 31:11; 46:2; Ex 3:4; Isa 6:8), and it is also a proper response if an angel should happen to call you.

2. Learn to recognize God's voice so that you don't make a fool of yourself as Samuel did. When Samuel was young, being educated by the high priest Eli, God called him for the first time in the middle of the night. Samuel thought it was Eli calling and ran to wake the poor old man, yelling "Here am I." Eli said he hadn't called and told Samuel to go back to sleep. This happened three times, until Eli figured out what was going on. In this case, to put an end to the confusion, Eli advised Samuel to reply by calling out, "Speak, Lord; for thy servant heareth" (1 Sam 3:1–9).

3. It's okay to ask God questions (Num 16:22). God also doesn't seem to mind argument, because both Abraham and Jonah argued without being castigated (Gen 18:23–32; Jonah 4).

4. If God should ask *you* a question, answer as briefly as possible. God usually asks very easy questions. He might show you a basket of figs or a plumb line and ask you what it is, so you shouldn't have difficulty thinking up an answer (Jer 24:1–9; Amos 7:8; 8:1–2).

5. Don't be disappointed if you don't get a chance to say too much. Prophets often recorded that God spoke at length without interruptions or questions. Sometimes, too, God or angels asked a series of questions without pausing for replies. Don't worry about these—they are simply rhetorical questions and you are not expected to reply (1 Sam 2:27–29).

6. Don't think you can flatter God by using a lot of fancy phrases and compliments. People whom God liked to talk to a lot, such as Abraham and Moses, always spoke simply and directly. Phrases like "Holy, holy, holy, is the Lord of hosts; the whole earth is full of his glory" are for seraphim to cry out (Isa 6:3).

Build Your Own Solomon-style Cherubim

The cherub of the Bible was not the plump, winged toddler pictured in paintings by Raphael and other Christian artists. Exactly what the Hebrew cherub looked like is not positively known, but most scholars believe it had a lion's body, a human face, and huge pointed wings.

Cherubim were embroidered on tabernacle hangings from the time of the Exodus, but Solomon used them also as decorative elements in friezes and elsewhere in his Temple. The two described here were special—carved, overlaid with gold, and balanced above the Ark of the Covenant in the Holy of Holies (Ex 3:24; 26; 1 Kings 6:23–29; 2 Chr 3:10–14).

Materials: very large chunks of olive wood; gold for overlay; a Holy of Holies room 30 feet across and at least 15 feet long.

Steps:

1. From the olive wood carve 2 cherubim, each 15 feet high. The cherubim should be identical except that they should face in opposite directions. Overlay with gold.

2. Make 2 wings for each cherub; each wing should be 7½ feet long, so that each cherub's wingspan totals 15 feet.

3. Hang the cherubim so that they stand "on their feet" over the Ark. Their outstretched wings will then cover the 30-foot width of the room—that is, their outer wings will touch the walls and their inner wings will meet in the center over the Ark. The cherubim's "faces were inward," meaning that they faced each other.

Notes:

1. Do not give the cherubim innocent, Raphaelite faces. Hebrew cherubim were probably somewhat fierce, because they are first mentioned as guarding the entrance to Eden (Gen 3:24) and later continued to inspire awe.

2. Several types of sphinxes found in Palestine from Israelite times resemble the famous Great Sphinx of Egypt in that the lion-body is lying down while the man-head is held erect. Do not use these as a model for the stance, as the Bible clearly says that Solomon's cherubim "stood on their feet." Also, the sphinx of Egypt was male and symbolized the god Horus; the sphinxes of Palestine were frequently female, symbols of the goddess Astarte.

3. A minority of scholars believe Solomon's cherubim may have resembled the winged boys and girls found in Egypt, the winged bulls found in Mesopotamia, or even the griffins (with lions' bodies and eagles' heads) of the Hittites.

4. Most archaeologists believe the best likeness of the Hebrew cherub is a lion with four paws firmly planted in a rather rigid stance. Huge pointed wings tower above the body. A pair of such cherubim that supported the throne of King Hiram of Byblos (c. 1200 BC) were excavated at Megiddo. The likelihood that Solomon's cherubim looked like these is increased because the Bible tells us that Solomon was friendly with Hiram (sometimes spelled Huram), received Temple gifts from him, and hired Phoenicians to work on the Temple (2 Sam 5:11; 1 Kings 5-6; 7:13-45; 10; 2 Chr 2; 4:11-22; 8-9).

5. Ezekiel's cherubim were a rare breed that scholars believe may have been inspired by statues he saw in Babylon. In one chapter (Ezek 10) he says they had humanlike hands, four noisy wings, and four faces (of a cherub, a man, a lion, and an eagle). In another passage, where he probably described the same "living creatures," he said that "they had the likeness of a man" except that they sparkled like burnished brass, flashed like lightning, and had feet "like the sole of a calf's foot" (Ezek 1:5-14).

How Do the Cherubim Serve God?

In giving instructions for the construction of the cherubim, God said, "And there I will meet with thee from above the mercy seat, from between the two cherubims" (Ex 25:22).

Later, Moses "heard the voice of one speaking unto him from off the mercy seat that was upon the ark . . . from between the two cherubims" (Num 7:89).

Elsewhere, too, biblical authors agree the God "dwelleth between the cherubims" (1 Sam 4:4; 2 Sam 6:2; 2 Kings 19:15; Psa 99:1; Isa 37:16).

Also God was known to jet-set about by riding on cherubim. "And he rode upon a cherub, and did fly" (2 Sam 22:11; Psa 18:10; Ezek 9:3; 10:4).

Poor Construction

1. The walls of Jericho fell (Josh 6:20).
2. The walls of Aphek fell on 27,000 Syrians (1 Kings 20:30).
3. Joash broke down the walls of Jerusalem (2 Chr 25:23).
4. Nebuchadnezzar broke down the walls of Jerusalem (2 Chr 36:19).
5. Walls built with untempered mortar collapsed (Ezek 14:10-14).
6. A house built on sand fell (Matt 7:27).
7. A house fell in a windstorm (Job 1:19).
8. The temple fell on Samson and the Philistines (Judg 16:30).
9. A lattice gave way under King Ahaziah (2 Kings 1:2).
10. A house was "broken up" by a thief (Matt 24:43; Luke 12:39).

---

12 Broken Things in the Bible

1. bows (1 Sam 2:4; Psa 37:15; Jer 51:56; Lam 3:4)
2. gates of brass (Psa 107:16)
3. crown (Jer 2:16)
4. idols (Jer 22:28)
5. the arm of the pharaoh (Ezek 30:21)
6. skin (Job 7:5)
7. heart (Psa 69:20; 147:3; Jer 23:9)
8. the Sabbath (John 5:18)
9. horse hooves (Judg 5:22)
10. ships (1 Kings 22:48)
11. lions' teeth (Job 4:10)
12. roof (Mark 2:4)

Urban Decay

1. "Succour us out of the city" (2 Sam 18:3).
2. "The city is full of lies and robbery" (Nah 3:1).
3. "He that is in the city, famine and pestilence shall devour him" (Ezek 7:15).
4. "This city is the caldron" (Ezek 11:3, 7, 11).
5. "Shall a trumpet be blown in the city, and the people not be afraid?" (Amos 3:6).
6. The wicked "were forgotten in the city" (Eccl 8:10).
7. "The city is full of violence" (Ezek 7:23).
8. "Him that dieth . . . in the city the dogs shall eat" (1 Kings 21:24).
9. "Blessed shalt thou be in the city" (Deut 28:3).
10. "Cursed shalt thou be in the city" (Deut 28:16).
11. "Men groan from out of the city" (Job 24:12).
12. "Thy wife shall be an harlot in the city" (Amos 7:17).
13. "The city is full of perverseness" (Ezek 9:9).
14. "Peradventure there be fifty righteous within the city" (Gen 18:24).
15. "I have seen violence and strife in the city" (Psa 55:9).
16. "They of the city shall flourish like grass of the earth" (Psa 72:16).
17. "Men . . . give wicked counsel in this city" (Ezek 11:2).
18. "The rich man's wealth is his strong city" (Prov 10:15).
19. "When it goeth well with the righteous, the city rejoiceth: and when the wicked perish, there is shouting" (Prov 11:10).
20. "For thou hast made of a city an heap; of a fenced city a ruin: a palace of strangers to be no city" (Isa 25:2).
21. "For this city hath been to me as a provocation of mine anger and of my fury from the day that they built it . . . I should remove it" (Jer 32:31).
22. "He hath prepared for them a city" (Heb 11:16; 12:22).
23. "I have hid my face from this city" (Jer 33:5).
24. "And the spoiler shall come upon every city, and no city shall escape" (Jer 48:8).
25. "The city of my joy!" (Jer 49:25).
26. "Every city . . . divided against itself shall not stand" (Matt 12:25).
27. "Every city shall be forsaken" (Jer 4:29).

Solomon's Temple

A great deal of mystery surrounds Solomon's Temple (1 Kings 6–8; 2 Chr 3; 5; Ezek 40–41), because even though the Books of Kings and Chronicles, two relatively early sources, give many details of the building's specifications, they often disagree. The Book of Chronicles seems to have based its description on the account given in First Kings and a second unknown account, perhaps the Book of Ezekiel, which predated Kings by approximately twenty years. Ezekiel's vision itself is cited by scholars as an attempt of a highly emotional man to reconstruct the details of a structure he had seen standing during his childhood, compounded, undoubtedly, by remembrances of older compatriots around him. Josephus based his own description of the First Temple (Solomon's) on common rabbinic belief of his time, which attempted to reconcile the three biblical accounts. No archaeological remains have been found of this Temple, for some very good reasons: the Temple Mount, the hill which it crowned, was repeatedly razed during antiquity and now has had so many sacred buildings that excavation is impossible.

King David not only dreamed of building a temple in Jerusalem to unify the religious expressions of the Israelites, but began to amass fortunes of gold and silver for its construction (2 Sam 7:2; 1 Kings 8:17; 1 Chr 22:1–9, 28, 29). As tradition tells it, he was prohibited from overseeing its actual building because he shed blood unjustly in winning Bathsheba for a wife (2 Sam 11). However, Bathsheba's child Solomon, the favored son of David, inherited his father's vision as well as his throne.

With the help of foreign craftsmen and builders from Phoenicia, and the use of innumerable slaves as well as the labor tax (corvée) of Israelites, the

223

Temple was built over a period of seven and a half years (from about 960 BC to 952 BC). The building was used for religious purposes until it fell in flames to the Babylonians in 586 BC.

From what scholars can piece together, Solomon's Temple was of simple but majestic lines. It stood on a stone platform raised about nine feet above the courtyard. The twenty-cubit (thirty-foot) width of the main building is believed to be the structural limit of wood beam before supporting pillars were required. Including the side buildings, but not the platform, the structure measured 150 by 75 feet, and all the buildings probably had flat roofs. Along the back and sides, the Temple was surrounded by a three-level tier of rooms built for storing the Temple treasures and objects used in ritual. The flat roof over these was lower than the level of the Temple roof.

The front of the Temple faced east and had a short flight of stairs. Two bronze pillars, about forty feet high and measuring nearly eighteen feet in circumference, flanked the stairs. These were freestanding pillars, decorated at the top with carved lilies and pomegranates. It is said the right pillar was named Jachin and the left one Boaz. Between them was a gate about twenty feet wide. This entrance led one to the porch *(ulam)*, a reception area 30 by 15 feet, its height still under dispute.

Between the porch and main hall was a fifteen-foot-wide gate which held two cypress doors. Olive-wood doorposts made up the frame. The doors were elaborately carved, according to some accounts. A nine-foot-thick wall separated the porch from the main hall *(hechal)*, where most of the ritual was performed.

The main hall was 60 by 30 feet, its ceiling towering about forty-five feet above the floor. Latticed windows, wider on the outside than on the inside, stretched across the long sides of the room and provided light as well as air. The walls were paneled in cedar. Pillars with palm-tree designs alternated with Solomon's gold candelabra along the length of the hall. Furnishings would have included tables for shewbread, an incense altar, and various shovels, basins, spoons, and other objects needed for ritual.

At the rear of the main hall a flight of steps led up to olive-wood doors which opened (at least to the high priest) into the Holy of Holies *(debir)*, a cubical room of about 30 by 30 by 30 feet. The fifteen-foot difference in height between this and the main room has been explained in various ways—the most popular theory being that a raised floor was accompanied by a false lowered roof. The two carved cherubim spread their wings over the platform which held the gold-topped Ark of the Covenant.

All in all, the completion of the Temple served to centralize worship of the Israelite God in Jerusalem to such an extent that after the fall of the Second Temple orthodox Jews ceased both incense and burnt offerings. These are not to be resumed until the Temple is rebuilt a third time after the coming of the Messiah.

What Was the Most Gruesome Temple Decoration in the Bible?

After King Saul was killed, the Philistines chopped off his head and hung it in the temple of Dagon (a god with a man's torso and a fish tail) at Beth-shean (1 Chr 10:10).

What God Didn't Know

1. God didn't know where Adam was. One day, walking in the Garden of Eden, God had to call out, "Where art thou?" (Gen 3:9).

2. When Sarah laughed at having a child in her old age, God asked Abraham, "Wherefore did Sarah laugh?" (Gen 18:13).

3. Sometimes God, undecided about what to do, wondered out loud. "Shall I hide from Abraham that thing which I do?" (Gen 18:17).

4. God didn't know how many wicked and good people were in Sodom and Gomorrah (Gen 18:28–32).

5. God didn't know Moses was holding a rod. "What is that in thine hand?" God asked (Ex 4:2).

6. Wondering about someone to tell the wicked of their iniquity, the Lord asked, "Whom shall I send, and who will go for us?" (Isa 6:8).

7. God didn't know why Cain was upset. God had to ask him, "Why art thou wroth? and why is thy countenance fallen?" (Gen 4:6).

8. God didn't know where Abel was. It was God who asked Cain, "Where is Abel thy brother?"—enabling Cain to give his famous reply, "Am I my brother's keeper?" (Gen 4:9).

9. God didn't know what happened to Abel. God also asked Cain, "What hast thou done?" (Gen 4:10).

NOTE: Sometimes God used questions to scold: "What hast thou here?" (Isa 22:16). And sometimes God posed rhetorical questions purely for effect: "Is anything too hard for the Lord?" (Gen 18:14).

Articles of Faith

Ark of the Covenant: An acacia-wood chest with dimensions of 2½ by 1½ by 1½ cubits (1 cubit = 1½ feet) was covered both inside and out with gold. It was carried by means of two gold-overlaid poles, each of which passed through two gold rings that were attached to the corners of the chest. Inside the chest were said to be the Tablets of the Law brought to the people by Moses at Sinai (Ex 25:10–22). Two golden cherubim, with wings spread and faces set toward each other, stood upon the gold cover (the "mercy seat") of the Ark of the Covenant.

The Ark was carried through the desert, across the Jordan River, and—as the Bible tells it—seven times around Jericho until the city walls fell. After settling the land, the Israelites constructed a central sanctuary in Shiloh where the Ark was housed and which served as a religious gathering point.

At the battle of Ebenezer, the Israelites were suffering defeat and called for the Ark, hoping it would reverse their luck. Instead, the Ark was carried off in triumph by the Philistines. However, it brought the Philistines such bad luck that after about seven months it was returned willingly to the Israelites at Kiryath Jearim (1 Sam 4–6).

It remained at Kiryath Jearim for twenty years, until David decided to house it in Jerusalem (1 Sam 7). For many years it was housed in its own tent.

At the time of the completion of the Temple built by Solomon, the Ark was placed inside the innermost chamber, in the Holy of Holies, where only the high priest might enter on special occasions. Whether it was destroyed during the devastation of the Temple and Jerusalem, whether it was carried off as a spoil of war by the Babylonians, or whether it was successfully sequestered in some corner of the land is still unknown.

Holy but Lethal

On pain of death, the *Holy of Holies* could not be entered by anyone except the high priest, who first had to perform an elaborate ritual of preparation (Num 4:19–20).

The *altar* was lethal if one offered "strange fire before the Lord." Aaron's two sons did this and died instantly (Lev 10:1–2).

The *Ark of the Covenant* was especially dangerous. When the Philistines captured it and put it in the temple of their fish-tailed god, Dagon, the statue of Dagon fell on its face. After the idol was righted, it fell on its face again, and this time "the head of Dagon and both the palms of his hands were cut off." Moreover, the Philistines were afflicted with emerods and decided the Ark brought such bad luck they should return it (1 Sam 5:1–6).

The Ark of the Covenant was so sacred it could not be touched even for the best of motives. When it was being taken toward Jerusalem during David's reign, it was carried in a cart drawn by oxen. The oxen stumbled, and a man named Uzzah put out his hand to steady the Ark so no harm should come to it. Despite his good intentions, it had been an "error" for Uzzah to touch it, and God therefore killed him on the spot. This so frightened David that he was afraid to take the Ark into Jerusalem and left it in the home of a Gittite for three months. When the Gittite received only blessings from God during this time, David was finally convinced it would be safe to complete the Ark's journey to Jerusalem (2 Sam 6:4–12; 1 Chr 13:7–14).

In fact, the Ark was so holy that 50,070 men of Beth-shemesh were killed by God for having presumed to look into it (1 Sam 6:19).

The Shofar: A trumpetlike instrument made of a hollow ram's horn is sounded at certain Jewish festivals to this day (Rosh Hashanah, Yom Kippur). In the days of the Temple, the shofar was blown at all festivals, including the New Moon celebrations, at the times of burnt offerings, and during the sacrifices accompanying peace offerings (Num 19:10). Philo (lst century) suggested that the shofar, an instrument of war (for example, the trumpets used by Joshua were shofroth, while he was conquering the land of Canaan), symbolized an appeal to peace and to the cessation of all problems that face people. The sound of the shofar ushered in the Jubilee Year, and the faithful believe that it shall usher in the Messianic age as well.

What God Does

God "fainteth not, neither is weary" (Isa 40:28).

Sometimes God winks (Acts 17:30).

In the past God has preached to the Gentiles (1 Tim 3:16).

In the future God "shall wipe away all tears" (Rev 21:4).

The word of God is "sharper than any two-edged sword, piercing even to the dividing asunder of soul and spirit, joints and marrow" (Heb 4:12).

"The Lord himself shall descend from heaven with a shout" (1 Thes 4:16) and "God is gone up with a shout" (Psa 47:5).

"And the Lord put a word in Balaam's mouth" (Num 23:5).

"The Lord do that which seemeth him good" (2 Sam 10:12).

The Menorah: The seven-branched candelabrum, the menorah, has been symbol of the Jewish people since the days of their wandering in the desert of Sinai (Ex 25:31–36), and today the menorah is the symbol of the State of Israel.

In the Tabernacle, the menorah stood opposite the table of shewbread, on the south side of the building (1 Kings 7:49). Dimensions of Solomon's menorah were about 5 by 3½ feet.

The biblical description of the menorah (Ex 25) reads like a botanical almanac. Made of pure gold, it had a main shaft or stem, branches, bowls, knops, and flowers. It is compared to almonds: "three bowls made like unto almonds . . ." Scholars, however, compare the menorah to wild sage, the moriah, that grows throughout Israel. Some species have seven branches growing out from the main stem, with small flowers (the knops) spaced on each branch.

The Arch of Titus in the Roman Forum depicts the Jerusalem menorah. When Rome destroyed Jerusalem, a special base decorated with Roman mythological figures was formed to carry the menorah in triumphal procession back to Rome. To this day, many Jews refuse to walk under the Arch of Titus.

Other early representations of the menorah can be found etched on Jason's tomb wall and engraved on a measuring cup of Herod's time.

Christologists believe that the menorah represents Jesus as the Light. Noting that the Tabernacle had no natural light entering it, they suggest that the menorah illuminates and reveals all things in the divine, spiritual light of Jesus.

Old Testament Miracles

The Wrath of God

The flood	Gen 7:17
The confusion of tongues	Gen 11:19
Destruction of Sodom and Gomorrah	Gen 19:24
The ten plagues	
Water made blood	Ex 7:20
Frogs	Ex 8:5
Lice	Ex 8:16
Flies	Ex 8:20
Murrain	Ex 9:3
Boils and blains	Ex 9:8
Hail	Ex 9:22
Locusts	Ex 10:12
Darkness	Ex 10:21
Death of the firstborn	Ex 12:29
Destruction of Nadab and Abihu	Lev 10:1
People at Taberah consumed by fire	Num 11:1
Death of Korah, Dathan, and Abiram	Num 16:31
Destruction of Jericho	Josh 6:6
Philistines slain	1 Sam 5:11
Uzzah slain	2 Sam 6:7
Jeroboam's hand withered	1 Kings 13:4
Ahaziah's troops consumed by fire	2 Kings 1:10
Mocking children destroyed by bears	2 Kings 2:24
The Syrian army blinded	2 Kings 6:18
Sennacherib's army destroyed	2 Kings 19:35
Uzziah smitten with leprosy	2 Chr 26:13

The Love of God

Passage of the Reed Sea	Ex 14:21
Sweetening the waters of Marah	Ex 15:23
Manna sent from heaven	Ex 16:14

Water drawn from a rock	Ex 17:5
Water drawn from a rock	Num 20:7
The serpent of brass heals	Num 21:8
Passage of the Jordan	Josh 3:14
The widow's meal increased	1 Kings 17:14
The widow's son raised	1 Kings 17:17
Elijah obtains rain	1 Kings 18:41
Passage of the Jordan	2 Kings 2:8, 14
Sweetening of the waters of Jericho	2 Kings 2:21
Jehoshaphat's army given water	2 Kings 3:16–20
The widow's oil increased	2 Kings 4:2
The Shunammite's son raised	2 Kings 4:34
Poisonous pottage made edible	2 Kings 4:40
Naaman's leprosy healed	2 Kings 5:10
Revival of a dead man by Elisha's bones	2 Kings 13:21
The furnace rendered harmless	Dan 3:20
Daniel unhurt by the lions	Dan 6:16
Jonah survives the whale	Jonah 2:1

The Signs of God

The burning bush	Ex 3:2
Aaron's rod becomes a serpent	Ex 7:10
Aaron's rod budding	Num 17:8
The ass speaks	Num 22:28
The sun and moon stayed	Josh 10:12
Elijah's sacrifice consumed by heavenly fire	1 Kings 18:30
Elijah drawn into heaven	2 Kings 2:11
The axhead floated	2 Kings 6:5
Shadow on the sundial goes back	2 Kings 20:9

Top: Maurice Bardin's rendering of Babylon. The procession is entering the Ishtar Gate. The Hanging Gardens and the Ziggurat are in the upper right. *Bottom:* Shalmaneser's obelisk, 841 BC. King Jehu of Israel (or his ambassador) kneels in tribute before the Assyrian king. COURTESY OF THE ORIENTAL INSTITUTE, UNIVERSITY OF CHICAGO.

Top: Dead Sea, showing pillars of salt. *Bottom:* An oasis in the Sinai wilderness. COURTESY OF THE ISRAEL GOVERNMENT TOURIST OFFICE.

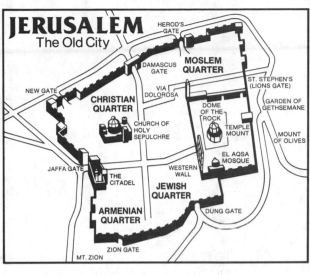

Upper left: The Wailing Wall. The larger blocks date from the time of Herod. "Master, see what manner of stones and buildings are here!" Mark 13:1. *Upper right:* Jerusalem, the Old City. *Bottom:* Jerusalem from the summit of the Mount of Olives. COURTESY OF THE ISRAEL GOVERNMENT TOURIST OFFICE.

Upper left: Sea of Galilee. The fortifications date from the Crusades. *Upper right:* The Jordan River. Note how shallow it is. *Bottom:* Capernaum. The ruins of this 2d-century synagogue are on the site where Jesus preached. Mark 1:21. COURTESY OF THE ISRAEL GOVERNMENT TOURIST OFFICE.

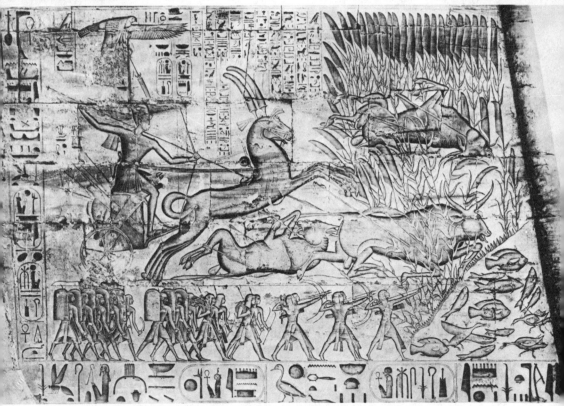

Top: Egyptian animal fable. The magistrate mouse orders the bailiff cat to chastise the bad boy. C. 1200 BC. *Bottom:* Rameses III (1198–1166 BC) hunting wild bulls. COURTESY OF THE ORIENTAL INSTITUTE, UNIVERSITY OF CHICAGO.

Top: Egyptian relief from Temple of Rameses III. Prisoners from the pharaoh's foreign conquests, left to right, a Libyan, Semite, Hittite, Philistine, and Semite. COURTESY OF THE ORIENTAL INSTITUTE, UNIVERSITY OF CHICAGO. *Bottom:* War elephant like those used in Maccabean Wars.

Left: The stela inscribed with Hammurabi's Code of Law. Seated on his throne, the sun god Shamash presents Hammurabi with the law. *Upper right:* King Darius hearing a petition. Xerxes his son stands behind him. Note the footstool; every throne had one (Isa 66:1). *Lower right:* Restored Dead Sea Scroll jar. COURTESY OF THE ORIENTAL INSTITUTE, UNIVERSITY OF CHICAGO.

Dürer woodcut showing the whore of Babylon enticing the inhabitants of earth with her cup of abominations. She is seated on a scarlet-colored beast with seven heads and ten horns. Babylon burns in the upper right. Faithful and True, followed by the armies of heaven, rides a white charger in the upper left. Rev 17–19.

Miracles

Science and the Miracle: Some events which seemed wondrously strange to the people of biblical times do not seem miraculous at all to us. The rainbow, for all its wonderful, majestic beauty, is well understood by scientists as the result of sunlight passing through water vapor. But water vapor and sunlight didn't figure in the biblical explanation—the rainbow was simply a sign that mankind will never again be destroyed by flood (Gen 9:13).

Examples like the rainbow—miracles or signs of God for which there is a thorough scientific explanation—are rare. Hardly any miracles in the Bible have been "explained away" by science; indeed, scientific theories about biblical miracles are often little more than guesses because the accounts usually give the scientist very little information to work with.

The miracles recorded in the first books of the Old Testament are an exception, because many scientific theories have been advanced to explain them, more so than for any other group of miracles in the Bible.

Of Snakes and Crocodiles: One miracle story in the Bible is intriguing, for it has been given three explanations—it was a miracle, magic, or merely a curiosity of nature. It is the story of the rods that became serpents. The Bible implies that this can be accomplished with mere magic, since the Egyptian sorcerers are also able to perform this feat (Ex 7:11). Naturalists point out that several kinds of snakes, including young cobras, will play dead when threatened, and other types can be temporarily paralyzed by pinching the snake on the neck or merely turning it on its back.

Perhaps Aaron's rod was really just one of these snakes immobilized momentarily. It could even have been a crocodile, for the Hebrew word translated as "serpent" really means "monster"—a term most people think

239

appropriate to the crocodile. Crocodiles react much as snakes do; they too can be paralyzed by flipping them onto their backs. This puts them in a trance of sorts during which they can be held or otherwise handled. But only with care. The length of the trance is unpredictable and the crocodile springs back to life without warning.

There is another qualification that snakes and crocodiles fulfill. In the story of Aaron's rod it is reported that when his staff turned to a serpent, it ate up all the serpents that the Egyptian sorcerers had produced with their staffs. Crocodiles and many snakes are cannibalistic. Thus if Aaron's serpent were a snake or crocodile it could have eaten up the serpents of the Egyptians—if it were hungry enough.

The Wonders of the Nile: The ten plagues of Egypt have also been given a scientific explanation. The plague of "water made blood" (Ex 7:20) is probably a description of the Nile in flood stage when the silt-bearing water takes on a reddish tinge. During this stage insects multiply so quickly that they often congregate in swarms of immense size. The plagues of lice, flies, locusts, and even frogs that the Bible describes aren't much worse than the plagues that have vexed Egypt for thousands of years.

Indeed, the size and density of some swarms are so great that large areas of the countryside are thrown into shadow as if suffering a "plague of darkness" like the one in the Bible (Ex 10:21–22). Since the biblical description is not very detailed, many other explanations of the plague of darkness are possible. The most likely one is a sandstorm. The siroccos of Egypt whip up dust clouds for days at a time, and these clouds can shade the entire land in twilight.

As the insects multiply during the Nile floods, disease often grows rampant. It is likely that the plagues of boils, blains, and murrains (Ex 9:3–8) was an epidemic of skin disease spread by the insects. Cattle murrain, which also affects humans, and is spread by flies, is probably the particular disease of these plagues.

The plague of hail is difficult to account for since such weather is very rare in Egypt. But most inexplicable of all is the death of the firstborn of Egypt the night the angel of death passed over the houses of the Hebrews (Ex 12:29). No contagion known to science can account for that night.

Free Food: A miracle which seemed for many years to be one of the most amazing and wonderful has now been "explained" by science. Most authorities now agree that manna, the sweet, honey-colored granules that God provided the hungry Israelites on their trek through Sinai (Ex 16:31), is a carbohydrate secretion left by a plant louse that feeds on the tamarisk tree. As the Bible reports, the tiny deposits, resembling frost, will disappear if not collected soon after dawn—however, they do not melt in the hot sun, as the Bible says, but are consumed by foraging ants (Ex 16:21). Arab nomads still collect and eat the sweet, resinous excretion; they call it "the bread of heaven."

Pillar of the Church: Another riddle is the "pillar" of smoke or fire that hovered over the Israelites during their wanderings in the wilderness. During the day the pillar seemed to be a cloud; during the night it appeared to be of fire. Since the pillar always remained at the head of the caravan it was thought to be leading the Israelites (Ex 13:21–22), and was either God himself or a sign of his presence.

Naturalists and scientists have arrived at various theories to account for the pillar, none of them very convincing. One theory, favored for many years, was that the pillar was a brazier or torch, used to lead the caravan at night. But since these fires were not used during the day, the pillar of cloud cannot be explained as smoke.

Some contend that the pillar was a volcano erupting to the east of the Israelites. During the day the smoke spewing from its cone would be seen, while at night the molten lava alone was visible. There's one drawback to this theory and it's very considerable. No active volcanoes existed along the route of the Exodus.

Trees and Branches: It would be going too far to suggest that all the Old Testament miracles involving trees or wood are a remnant of tree worship or druidism, but wood certainly possesses more wonderful properties than any other class of matter. The burning bush, Moses' and Aaron's rods, and the branch that sweetened the waters of Marah are a few of the wooden objects that were the instruments of miracles.

The rods used by Moses and Aaron were modeled after the staff used by a shepherd as a walking stick and prod and as a defense against wild animals. In the hands of these leaders the staff was primarily a symbol of authority over the "flock" of Israelites. It was also the "magic wand" of miracles.

Aaron's rod, in addition to being transformed into a serpent, miraculously bloomed with flowers and bore almonds after being placed in the Tabernacle for one night (Ex 17:8). It is not uncommon for a freshly cut branch, when placed in damp soil, gradually to develop roots and leaves, but no branch can sprout leaves and fruit overnight.

Magic Wands: A branch is even less likely to part the Reed ("Red") Sea, but the Bible (Ex 14:16) says that Moses' rod did. As the Bible describes it, the opening of the waters was a miracle, pure and simple, and science has yet to come up with any explanation that would account for the staff's power over the sea.

In the Bible it's clear that God is the force behind Moses' staff; there is, in fact, one scene in which God bestows power on the wand. It is one of the few passages in the Bible with a good deal of tongue-in-cheek humor. God asks Moses, "What is in thine hand? And he said, a rod. And he said, Cast it on the ground. And he cast it on the ground, and it became a serpent; and Moses fled before it" (Ex 4:2–3).

Besides opening the Reed Sea, this magic wand had other powers over water. Like some super-duper divining rod, it brought forth water from rocks on two occasions (Ex 17:6; Num 20:7). Indeed, it would be convenient to offer the "scientific" interpretation of Moses' rod as a divining rod—if only scientists thought divining rods worked. Even though they have been in use since antiquity, by the Greeks, Romans, and Persians, and are still toyed with in rural America, divining rods, or dowsers, are ineffective in locating water, metal, or anything else underground. The only reason they seem to work is that water and metal will be found at the bottom of almost any hole dug deep enough.

Another miraculous happening which was the result of a sacred stick was the transformation of Laban's livestock. Laban had agreed to give Jacob all the animals with speckled and streaked markings. Jacob cut saplings of hazel, poplar, and chestnut and grooved the bark so that white streaks showed where the scratches had been made. Jacob set the cuttings in the animals' water trough, and behold, the animals conceived speckled and streaked offspring (Gen 30:37–39).

There is still another connection between wondrous woods and water. When the Israelites found that the waters of the oasis at Marah were foul, God told Moses that he could sweeten them by throwing in a certain tree. The tree was plunked in and the waters were indeed freshened (Ex 15:23–25). The prophet Elisha did the same trick later at Jericho and elsewhere, but he used salt (perhaps a bit of chlorine) to make the water potable (2 Kings 2:16–21).

Finally, there is one magic wand that did not work. Elisha gave his staff to a man named Gehazi and told him to lay the staff against the face of a dead child to revive the boy. Gehazi did as told, "but there was neither voice, nor hearing." Elisha had to come in and give the boy mouth-to-mouth resuscitation to bring him back to life (2 Kings 4:29–31).

In the Heavens: Celestial miracles are favorites with biblical authors. As the "home" of God the heavens were the appropriate place for him to exercise power and he did it with flair. Heavenly fire incinerated people all the time (2 Kings 1:10; Num 11:1) and once it consumed a sacrifice Elijah had set out (1 Kings 18:30). The sun and moon were made to stop one day (Josh 10:12), on another the shadow on a sundial went backward (2 Kings 20:9), and on the day of Jesus' Crucifixion the "sun was darkened" (Luke 23:45).

There is no way to explain the heavenly fire in "scientific" terms. Meteor showers do not often penetrate the earth's atmosphere. It is even more difficult to explain how the sun and moon could have stood still, although one scientist, Immanuel Velikovsky, has tried. In his book *Worlds in Collision,* Velikovsky argued that a comet passing extremely close to the earth could produce such effects, but his book has not been well received by astronomers. The darkening of the sun could have been an eclipse. This eclipse, however, has not been established for a date that would correspond to the Crucifixion.

Miracle Genealogies: As the Bible evolved, the later miracles began to echo earlier ones. One reason for the similarity among miracles is that some of the later prophets wanted to be capable of the same feats as their predecessors. Jesus' miracles of healing and reviving are much like those of Elijah and Elisha. Some of Jesus' miracles can be traced as far back as Moses. For example, the walk on the Sea of Galilee owes its ancestry to Elijah and Elisha's passage of the Jordan, which in turn has Moses' crossing of the Reed ("Red") Sea as its ancestor. Also, the feeding of the multitudes is of the same stock as the story of Elijah's increasing the widow's flour.

Jesus' Miracles

	Matthew	Mark	Luke	John
Healing:				
The nobleman's son				4:53
The impotent (lame) man				5:9
Peter's mother-in-law	8:16	1:30	4:38	
The leper	8:3	1:44	5:15	
The paralytic	9:7	2:14	5:25	
The withered hand	12:13	3:4	6:10	
The centurion's servant	8:12	7:9		
The blind-and-dumb demoniac	12:22		11:14	
The woman with the issue of blood	9:21	5:33	8:47	
The two blind men	9:30			
The dumb demoniac	9:32			
The demon-possessed girl	15:27	7:29		
The deafmute		7:36		
The synagogue demoniac		1:27		
Raising From the Dead:				
The widow's son			7:13	
Jairus' daughter	9:25	5:42	8:55	
Lazarus				11:44
Feeding Multitudes:				
The 5000	14:20	6:43	9:16	6:12
The 4000	15:38	8:9		
Signs:				
Turning water into wine				2:10
Catch of fish			5:6	
Stilling the storm	8:26	4:40	8:24	
The devils entering the swine	8:33	5:19	8:38	
Walking on water	14:32	6:51		6:20

Endless Food

1. When Elijah entered the gates of the city of Zarephath, he met a widow and asked her for a bit of bread. She informed him, "I have not a cake, but an handful of meal in a barrel, and a little oil in a cruse: and, behold, I am gathering two sticks, that I may go in and dress it for me and my son, that we may eat it, and die." Elijah, however, pressed her to do his bidding, and promised that "The barrel of meal shall not waste, neither shall the cruse of oil fail, until the day that the Lord sendeth rain upon the earth" (1 Kings 17:9–16).

2. A widow with two sons approached the prophet Elisha, begging for his help. She was poor, and feared that the creditor would take her two sons as slaves. In response to Elisha's question, "What shall I do for thee? tell me, what hast thou in the house?" she answered that she had only a pot of oil. Elisha commanded her to gather all the empty containers she could find, including those of her neighbors, and to pour her oil into them. She filled all these vessels, and found that even more oil was left. With this proliferation of oil she was able to sell enough to pay the creditor and to support herself as well as her two sons (2 Kings 4:1–7).

3. In a rare instance of accord, all four Gospels describe the multiplication of the five loaves and two fishes. Jesus and his disciples had crossed the Sea of Galilee to escape from the crowds who gathered to hear Jesus preach. On the other side, however, they were met by even more people, about 5000 men (not counting the women and children). Jesus preached to them all day, and when evening came, the only food they had was "five loaves and two fishes." Jesus blessed the food, giving it to the disciples to disperse. After all 5000 had eaten to their satisfaction, twelve baskets of leftover crumbs were collected (Matt 14:13–21; Mark 6:31–44; Luke 9:10–17; John 6:1–14).

Dreams

For the authors of the Bible there was no middle ground regarding dreams—no natural, scientific, or psychological explanation. Dreams were either religious experiences, which were more than real, or they were less than real, mere fantasy, illusion, and "vanity." The distinction between the religious, prophetic dream and the illusory dream was the agency of God. In those dreams that God sent to men, what the Lord commanded had to be accomplished on risk of punishment. Sometimes God appeared in person to deliver a message (Gen 20:3; Num 1:25; 1 Kings 3:5-10) and sometimes an angel appeared in his place (Gen 31:11; Matt 1:20-21).

The First Dream: The first dream reported in the Bible is a rather straightforward instance of God's will being accomplished through a dream. God appeared to Abimelech, who was living with Sarah, Abraham's wife, to tell him to return Sarah to Abraham. The order puzzled the good Abimelech, for he had not touched Sarah but had taken her in as a sister—an act, he said, done in the "innocency of my hands" (Gen 20:5). As a reward for heeding the dream and dutifully restoring Sarah to Abraham, Abimelech acquired a large and fruitful family.

Do's and Don'ts in Dreams: Some biblical characters tended to receive prophetic or symbolic dreams frequently. Jacob received two from God. In the first, which came upon him as he slept in the wilderness with "stones for his pillows," he saw a ladder whose footings were on the earth and whose top reached to heaven. "And behold the angels of God ascending and descending on it. And, behold, the Lord stood above it, and said, I am the

245

Lord God of Abraham, thy father, and the God of Isaac: the land whereon thou liest, to thee will I give it, and to thy seed" (Gen 28:12-13).

Jacob awoke immediately, saying to himself, "How dreadful is this place!" (Gen 28:17). Despite the celestial land deed he was just granted, Jacob did not stick around to homestead. He took the rocks he had used for pillows, piled them up, and poured a little oil over them to consecrate the spot. He named it Beth-el ("the house of God") and left immediately.

But God wasn't about to let Jacob get away that easily and soon came to Jacob again in a dream. Jacob had made a deal with his uncle Laban to take all Laban's livestock with "ringstraked, speckled, and grisled" markings. Miraculously, all Laban's cattle begin to bear only streaked and speckled calves. About the time the cattle began to conceive, Jacob had the second dream: "And the angel of God spake unto me in a dream, saying, Jacob: And I said, Here am I. And he said, Lift up now thine eyes, and see, all the rams which leap upon the cattle are ringstraked, speckled, and grisled.... I am the God of Beth-el, where thou anointedst the pillar ... now arise, get thee out from this land, and return unto the land of thy kindred" (Gen 31:11-13).

This time Jacob listened to the dream and made ready to leave. Laban, who normally would have done everything to stop Jacob from leaving now that he had nearly all his herd, also had a dream from God telling him what to do: "God came to Laban the Syrian in a dream by night, and said unto him, Take heed that thou speak not to Jacob either good or bad" (Gen 31:24). Laban did not follow the commandment to the letter, for he pursued Jacob to talk with him. But Laban was mindful of the order: "It is in the power of my hand to do you hurt: but the God of your fathers spake unto me yesternight, saying, Take thou heed that thou speak not to Jacob either good or bad" (Gen 31:29). Laban chided Jacob for leaving so secretly, but wisely did not try to stop him.

Doubting Dreams: In most cases where God appeared in a dream the outcome is direct and simple. But when God is not the cause of a dream or an angel does not attend the dreamer, complications arise even for people in God's favor. Joseph, for example, is one of the most able dreamers and interpreters of dreams in the Bible, but for years his talent did nothing but get him into hot water.

As a youth Joseph had a dream about ruling the Hebrews. Joseph's family didn't regard the dream as prophetic and was not about to let Joseph start ruling them. Joseph's father thought he was putting on airs and lording it over the family by having such a dream: "What is this dream that thou hast dreamed? Shall I and thy mother and thy brethren come to bow down ourselves to thee to the earth?" (Gen 37:10). Joseph's brothers were so envious of his dream they decided to kill him: "Behold the dreamer cometh, come now therefore, and let us slay him" (Gen 37:19-20). After considering this plan a little more they finally decided it would be more profitable and just as final to sell him into slavery. As a slave, Joseph ended up in Egypt.

Prison Dreams: In Egypt Joseph continued to use his troublesome knack for interpreting dreams. He had been unjustly thrown into prison and one day heard two new prisoners, the pharaoh's former butler and baker, lament that there was no one to interpret the dreams they had had the night before. Like most ancient Egyptians, they believed that dreams were prophetic and that a holy man was necessary for their interpretation. Joseph spoke up: "Do not interpretations belong to God? tell me them I pray you" (Gen 40:8).

The butler's dream was this: "In my dream, behold, a vine was before me; and in the vine were three branches: and it was as though it budded, and her blossoms shot forth; and the clusters thereof brought forth ripe grapes, and pressed them into Pharaoh's cup, and I gave the cup into Pharaoh's hand."

Joseph answered with a specificity that Freud would have envied. The three branches were three days. The butler would be restored to his former position after three days and hand the pharaoh his cup.

The baker, happy to hear the promising interpretation of his friend's dream, told Joseph his: "I had three white baskets on my head: and in the uppermost basket there was of all manner of bakemeats for Pharaoh; and the birds did eat them out of the basket upon my head."

The baker also had three days to wait. But at the end of his three days he would hang on a tree and the birds would eat all the flesh off of him.

Even though everything Joseph said came true, his talent went unnoticed and unacknowledged. "Yet did not the chief butler remember Joseph, but forgat him" (Gen 40:23).

The Pharaoh's Dream: For two years Joseph languished in the prison. Only when the pharaoh was beset with a puzzling dream that the Egyptian sorcerers could not interpret did the butler finally send for him. The pharaoh had dreamt that seven fat cattle came up from the Nile, followed by seven lean cattle that devoured them. The second half of the dream was just as ominous: Seven full ears of corn were overgrown by seven thin ears.

The imagery of this dream is not very subtle. Seven years of plenty would be followed by seven years of famine, of plenty, and of famine again. The pharaoh considered this interpretation and concluded that no one would be better than Joseph to oversee the country's entire harvest. Thus Joseph's dreams finally paid off and he came to rule Hebrews, though only over those who were in Egypt.

False Prophets: With Jacob and Abimelech as a precedent, the case for God appearing to someone in a dream had already been set. In Numbers, the first book after Genesis in which dreams are mentioned, a prophet is defined as someone to whom God appears in a dream: "And the Lord came down in the pillar of the cloud, and stood in the door of the tabernacle, and called Aaron and Miriam: and they both came forth. And he said, Hear now my words: If there be a prophet among you, I the Lord will make myself known unto him in a vision, and will speak unto him in a dream." As the religion of the Israelites developed and the office of the prophet became more important, it became necessary to distinguish the inspired prophet, who had heaven-sent dreams, from the false prophets, who had only empty dreams.

Since only the dreamer really knows the substance of his dream, external signs to distinguish the false prophet from the true prophet had to be devised. Deuteronomy sets forth one definition of the false prophet: "If there arise among you a prophet, or a dreamer of dreams, and giveth thee a sign or wonder, and the sign or wonder come to pass, whereof he spake unto thee, saying, Let us go after other gods, which thou hast not known . . . thou shalt not hearken unto the words of that prophet, or that dreamer of dreams. . . . And that prophet, or that dreamer of dreams, shall be put to death" (Deut 13:1–5).

Despite the handiness of this definition, the difficulty in knowing whether or not a dream was worthwhile remained. Jeremiah realized that most people's dreams were not prophetic. But he also thought that anyone who thought he had a prophetic dream should tell it: "I have heard what the prophets said, that prophesy lies in my name, saying, I have dreamed, I have dreamed. . . . they are the prophets of deceit of their own heart; which think to cause my people to forget my name by their dreams which they tell every man to his neighbor. . . . The prophet that hath a dream, let him tell a dream. . . . Behold, I am against them that prophesy false dreams, saith the Lord" (Jer 23:25–32).

False Dreams

"How are they brought into desolation, as in a moment! they are utterly consumed with terrors. As a dream when one awaketh; so, O Lord, when thou awakest, thou shalt despise their image" (Psa 73:19–20).

"For a dream cometh through the multitude of business; and a fool's voice is known by multitude of words" (Eccl 5:3).

"And the multitude of all the nations that fight against Ariel [Jerusalem], even all that fight against her and her munition, and that distress her, shall be as a dream of a night vision. It shall even be as when an hungry man dreameth, and behold, he eateth; but

248

he awaketh, and his soul is empty; or as when a thirsty man dreameth, and, behold, he drinketh; but he awaketh, and, behold, he is faint, and his soul hath appetite: so shall the multitude of all the nations be that fight against Zion" (Isa 29:7–8).

"He shall fly away as a dream, and shall not be found: yea, he shall be chased away as a vision of the night" (Job 20:8).

"For thus saith the Lord of hosts, the God of Israel; Let not your prophets and your diviners, that be in the midst of you, deceive you, neither hearken to your dreams which ye cause to be dreamed. For they prophesy falsely unto you in my name: I have not sent them, saith the Lord" (Jer 29:8–9).

"When I say, My bed shall comfort me, my couch shall ease my complaint; Then thou scarest me with dreams, and terrifiest me through visions" (Job 7:13–14).

"For the idols have spoken vanity, and the diviners have seen a lie, and have told false dreams; they comfort in vain" (Zech 10:2).

". . . these filthy dreamers defile the flesh, despise dominion, and speak evil of dignities" (Jude 8).

The Tent Dream: Despite all the Bible's cautions about false dreams, quite a few kings, prophets, and citizens of the realm received significant and even prophetic dreams. The victory over the Midianites was foreseen in a strange and comical dream that came to one of Gideon's soldiers: ". . . there was a man that told a dream unto his fellow, and said, Behold, I dreamed a dream, and, lo, a cake of barley bread tumbled into the host of Midian, and came unto a tent, and smote it that it fell, and overturned it, that the tent lay along" (Judg 7:13).

Solomon's Dream: Soon after taking the throne, King Solomon, like Abimelech and Jacob, had a dream in which God appeared to him—at least that's how the story goes. It is such a sweet tale, it sounds like someone made it up just to explain how Solomon got his legendary wisdom: ". . . the Lord appeared to Solomon in a dream by night: and God said, Ask what I shall give thee. And Solomon said. . . . I am but a little child: I know not how to go out or come in. . . . Give therefore thy servant an understanding heart to judge thy people, that I may discern between good and bad: for who is able to judge this thy so great a people? And the speech pleased the Lord, that Solomon had asked this thing" (1 Kings 3:5–10). God was so happy that Solomon had not asked for long life, or money, or the death of his enemies—all the usual requests He got—God bestowed exceptional wisdom on Solomon: "so that there was none like thee before thee, neither after thee shall any arise like unto thee" (3:12).

Solomon was unique among the kings of the monarchy period in receiving a dream from God. His father, David, never saw God in a dream; he tended to rely on prophets to transmit messages to him. Solomon's predecessor Saul had begged God to answer his prayers, but as the Bible notes: "the Lord answered him not, neither by dreams, nor by Urim [one of a set of oracular dice], nor by prophets" (1 Sam 28:6).

Nebuchadnezzar's Statue Dream: Outside of Joseph, the greatest interpreter of dreams in the Bible is Daniel. His talents would be even greater than Joseph's—for Daniel interpreted King Nebuchadnezzar's dream before the king told it to him—if Daniel hadn't had direct help from God.

The dream that troubled Nebuchadnezzar is one of the most bizarre in the Bible. The king saw the image of a man who had a head of gold, an upper torso of silver, and a lower torso of brass. "His legs were of iron, his feet part of iron and part of clay." The statue was broken to pieces by a stone "cut out without hands," and like "the chaff of the summer threshing floors" the pieces were carried away by the wind. The stone that destroyed the image became a great mountain that "filled the whole earth" (Dan 2:31–35).

Pretending he had forgotten this spectacular dream, Nebuchadnezzar challenged his court astrologers and sorcerers to tell him what it was and to interpret it. His wise men could not perform so prodigious a feat of mind reading, of course, so Nebuchadnezzar decreed that all the wise men in Babylon be slain. As a scribe at the court, Daniel too would be put to death.

Telling the king's captain that he would interpret the dream, Daniel retired to his home and prayed for assistance. During the night help came in a vision and when Daniel went before the king the next morning he gave the king both the dream and the interpretation:

The statue represented the kingdom of Babylon. Nebuchadnezzar, as the most glorious and splendid king, was the head of gold. After his rule would come a lesser king (silver), followed by one which would rule everywhere (brass) and one of great strength (iron). Finally the people in the kingdom of iron would "mingle themselves with the seed of men," that is, they would mix with a foreign population. This would harm the kingdom, for the two peoples would not become one: "they shall not cleave one to another, even as iron is not mixed with clay." This kingdom would be destroyed by one created by God (the stone). And God's kingdom "will consume these kingdoms, and it shall stand forever" (the mountain).

When he heard the dream and the analysis, Nebuchadnezzar fell to his knees before Daniel and praised Daniel's God. As a reward Daniel was promoted to "chief of the governors over all the wise men of Babylon" (Dan 2:48).

Nebuchadnezzar's Tree Dream: The next episode in Daniel's career as a dream analyst came soon after. Nebuchadnezzar had erected an enormous golden statue before which everyone in the kingdom was to kneel in worship. When the king heard that a group of Hebrews, Daniel's friends, had refused to venerate this idol, Nebuchadnezzar ordered them to be incinerated in the royal furnace. Miraculously they survived, saved by an angel.

Immediately after this miracle Nebuchadnezzar had a puzzling dream. He saw a huge tree which reached to heaven. In its branches birds made their nests and under it beasts of the field found shade. But a "holy one" came down from heaven to fell the tree, leaving its stump in the grass, at the same level as the common beasts (Dan 4:5-17).

Daniel saw that the tree was Nebuchadnezzar himself. For setting up the idol and not worshiping God, Nebuchadnezzar was to be "cut down," reduced from the power and glory of his dominion to the subhuman level of a "beast." Despite Daniel's warnings, Nebuchadnezzar did not repent and within a year was overcome with a fit of madness. He wandered from the palace and took to eating grass; his hair became like "eagles' feathers" and his nails grew like birds' claws. Only when he praised heaven, lifting up his eyes like a man, was Nebuchadnezzar's humanity restored (Dan 3-4).

Daniel's Dreams: Daniel's last reported dealings with dreams introduce some new twists—for once he had the dreams himself and he had a series of them, "visions of his head upon his bed" (Dan 7:1). Basically, all that happened in Daniel's dream was that he saw four wondrous beasts rise out of the sea. But the wild creativity and complexity of the creatures in these dreams made them more than passing strange.

The Bible says that the beasts represent "four kings [kingdoms] which shall rise out of the earth" (Dan 7:17). But since it doesn't say which kingdoms they are, these four beasts have been the object of an incredible amount of speculation. The beasts and the nations they are sometimes thought to represent are given below.

The Four Beasts of Daniel

The First Beast: "The first was like a lion, and had eagle's wings: I beheld till the wings therefore were plucked, and it was lifted up from the earth, and made stand upon the feet as a man, and a man's heart was given to it" (Dan 7:4).

This beast is usually thought to be Babylon under Nebuchadnezzar. In painting and sculpture the king of Babylon was often represented as a winged lion. The wings, an artistic device inherited from earlier Mesopotamian culture, symbolized the rapidity of the king's conquests. In Jeremiah (7:4) Nebuchadnezzar is alluded to

251

as the lion "come up from his thicket, and the destroyer of the Gentiles." Nebuchadnezzar becomes a man, losing the "eagle's wings" and the claws he has grown during his madness (Dan 4:33) when he extols Daniel's god. Thus he stands upright and is given the heart of a man.

The Second Beast: "And behold another beast, a second, like to a bear, raised up itself on one side, and it had three ribs in the mouth of it between the teeth of it: and they said thus unto it, Arise, devour much flesh."

The bear is usually thought to symbolize the coalition of Persians and Medes. Many scholars, including Isaac Newton, have conjectured on the meaning of the three ribs. Newton thought they were Babylon, Lydia, and Egypt, three nations which the Persians overran.

The Third Beast: "After this I beheld, and lo another, like a leopard, which had upon the back of it four wings of a fowl; the beast had also four heads; and dominion was given unto it."

The leopard may represent the empire founded by the military genius Alexander the Great. With an army of modest size, Alexander swiftly conquered all of Asia Minor and Egypt. The four wings symbolize the speed of his conquest, the four heads the all-devouring rapacity with which he seized territory, and the body of the leopard—one of the smallest of the wild cats—the relative compactness of his army.

The Fourth Beast: "After this I saw in the night visions, and behold a fourth beast, dreadful and terrible, and strong exceedingly; and it had great iron teeth: it devoured and brake in pieces, and stamped the residue with the feet of it: and it was diverse from all the beasts that were before it; and it had ten horns. I considered the horns, and, behold, there came up among them another little horn: and, behold, in this horn were eyes like the eyes of man, and a mouth speaking great things."

No one is sure what nation the fourth beast symbolizes; some speculate that it is the Roman Empire. The "little horn" is the most perplexing part of the image. Many Christian scholars think it represents some sort of Antichrist figure. Various candidates for the little horn have been proposed, among them Antiochus IV, the hated Syrian ruler of Palestine; Julius and Augustus Caesar; several popes; Charlemagne; and Napoleon.

Joseph's Dreams: In the New Testament, no one shows as much aptitude for interpreting dreams as Joseph and Daniel did in the Old Testament, but

252

Joseph, Mary's husband, receives a few important ones. In the first instance, an angel comes to him to assure him that he should wed Mary even though she is pregnant: "for that which is conceived in her is of the Holy Ghost. And she shall bring forth a son, and thou shalt call his name Jesus" (Matt 1:20–21).

After this introduction, Joseph is frequently visited by his guardian angel. Both Joseph and Mary are warned in a dream not to take the same route out of Bethlehem that they took into the city (Matt 2:12). Once on the road, Joseph is told to take mother and child into Egypt (Matt 2:13).

After Herod's death, the angel comes again to Joseph in a dream, telling him to backtrack: "Arise ... and go into the land of Israel: for they are dead which sought the young child's life" (Matt 2:20). Once again the family hits the road, only to be given a change of course en route. This time they are warned not to go into Judea, the southern part of Palestine, because Archelaus, Herod's son, is ruling there (Matt 2:22). They divert as ordered and settle in Nazareth, in Galilee.

Prophetic Dreams: Only one other prophetic dream occurs in the New Testament. Pontius Pilate's wife was troubled by a dream concerning Jesus. According to the Gospel of Matthew, as Pilate sat down in his "judgment seat" he was handed a note from her which read: "Have thou nothing to do with that just man: for I have suffered many things this day in a dream because of him" (27:19).

Perhaps the scarcity of prophetic dreams in the New Testament—in comparison with the Old—has something to do with the belief that prophecy and dreams shall in the future (at the time of the Second Coming) be common to every believer. After the Crucifixion Peter states this belief, repeating the words of the prophet Joel: "And it shall come to pass in the last days, saith God, I will pour out of my spirit upon all flesh: and your sons and your daughters shall prophecy, and your young men shall see visions, and your old men shall dream dreams" (Joel 2:28; Acts 2:17).

Festivals of the Hebrews

Passover

Passover is an eight-day festival commemorating the Hebrew escape from bondage in Egypt. Not only a celebration of the symbolic rebirth of the Hebrew people, Passover also marks the coming of spring and the rebirth of the earth.

The story of the first Passover is told in Exodus (1–13). After the pharaoh refused Moses permission to take the Israelites from Egypt, the Egyptians suffered ten plagues, the last of which was the slaying of the firstborn. To protect the Israelites from the plague, Moses instructed each family to slaughter a lamb and daub their doorposts with its blood so that the angel of death would "pass over" the household. As they readied for their flight, the Israelites had no time to let their bread rise, so throughout their journey they ate unleavened bread.

In remembrance of these days of preparation and hardship, observers of Passover eat nothing with leaven during the holiday (Ex 12:14–20). Today the unleavened bread, "matzo," is still made especially for the festival. Deuteronomy (16) states that a sacrifice—a symbol of the slaughtered lamb, the "paschal"—should also be made. Because the holiday takes place at the beginning of the calving season and at the time of the harvest of the first grains, calves and grains were also offered at the Temple (Lev 23:9–14).

The observance of Passover has been long and virtually continuous. A papyrus letter from the Jewish community at Elephantine in Egypt gives written evidence that Passover was practiced in 419 BC. The Bible records several instances of its occurrence after the night of the Exodus: upon entering Canaan (Ex 13:5-6; Josh 5:10), during Solomon's monarchy (2 Chr 8:13), Hezekiah's celebration (2 Chr 30:13-22), Josiah's reinstitution of the observance (2 Kings 23:21-23; 2 Chr 35), the "Last Supper" that Jesus celebrated with his disciples (Matt 26:17).

The Bible's description of the Last Supper records in some detail the practices of the Passover meal as it was held in the 1st century. It was the habit of Roman citizens to recline while eating; only slaves sat during meals. Thus one of the disciples, probably John, is said to "lean on Jesus' bosom" and "lie on Jesus' breast" when turning to speak with him (John 13:23, 25). Passover, as one of the most important holidays of the Jewish year and as a celebration of freedom, seems to have been an occasion when one or more prisoners were released by the Romans: "for of necessity he must release one unto them at the feast" (Luke 23:17; Matt 27:15; Mark 15:16; John 18:38).

Today observance begins by cleaning the entire house of old food and bringing in specially prepared foods and matzo. The first two nights of the holiday, the family and guests sit at the dining table and read from the Haggadah, a book containing a history of the Exodus and lessons drawn from the period of the slavery. At the dinner service, the Seder, symbolic foods other than the matzo are also set out: the bitter herbs (representing the harshness of slavery [Ex 12:8]), salt water (the tears of hard labor), the haroseth (a mixture of nuts, wine, cinnamon, and apples that represents the mortar that the Israelites made while in captivity), a shank bone (the lamb offering), a hard-boiled egg (symbolizing new birth), and greens (spring). Following a late tradition most families also place a large glass of wine in the center of the table—in hope that the Messiah, Elijah, will come and take a place at the table.

The second night of Passover begins the "counting of the Omer" as commanded in Leviticus (23:9-14). Fifty days are counted from that night until the Festival of Weeks, otherwise known as Shavuot or Pentecost (Lev 23:15). The fifty days of Omer traditionally symbolize the fifty days from the night of Exodus to the time Moses received the Law on the mount.

Parties and Feasts in the Bible

Abraham gave a great feast the day his son Isaac was weaned (Gen 21:8).

When Elisha decided to follow the prophet Elijah, he gave his people a good-bye party at which he served boiled ox (1 Kings 19:21).

Laban gave a wedding party for his daughter Leah's marriage to Jacob (Gen 29:22).

When Samson married a Philistine girl, he gave a party for more than thirty people that lasted seven days. His idea of entertainment was to pose a riddle (Judge 14:10-14).

After Solomon was anointed king, the trumpet was blown and "the people piped with pipes, and rejoiced with great joy, so that the earth rent with the sound of them" (1 Kings 1:39-40).

Solomon also gave a party "for all his servants" after he had a dream in which God spoke to him (1 Kings 3:15), and he gave a fourteen-day feast after building the Temple (1 Kings 8:65).

Having settled his disagreement over the wells with the Philistines, Isaac celebrated with a feast for the Philistine king, the king's friend, and his army captain (Gen 26:30).

For reasons not mentioned, Nabal held a feast, "like the feast of a king," with much drinking (1 Sam 25:36).

David gave a party for Abner and his twenty men at which Abner promised to add the north of Israel to David's southern kingdom (2 Sam 3:20).

In Song of Solomon (5:1), the menu for a great feast is honeycomb with honey and wine with milk, which one should "drink, yea, drink abundantly."

Four lepers who discovered the Syrian army had suddenly abandoned its camp hid treasures for themselves and sat in a tent to "eat and drink" before telling anyone else of the spoils left behind (2 Kings 7:8).

When the prodigal son returned home, his father dressed him in "the best robe" with "a ring on his hand, put shoes on his feet," and held a party with music and dancing at which he served a fatted calf (Luke 15:22-23).

"He that is of merry heart hath a continual feast" (Prov 15:15).

Birthday Parties in the Bible

1. The pharaoh of Egypt celebrated his birthday by making a feast "unto all his servants," freeing his chief butler from jail and restoring him to his former post, and hanging his chief baker (Gen 40:20-22).

2. Herod "made a supper to his lords, high captains, and chief estates," and to reward Salome for dancing before the guests

Herod had John the Baptist's head brought in on a platter for her (Matt 14:6-11; Mark 6:21-28).

The Day of Atonement (Yom Kippur)

The Day of Atonement, the most solemn day of the Jewish year, is the occasion ritually to purify the individual and the community. The first practice of Yom Kippur was by Aaron, to atone for the sin of his sons who offered "strange fire"—some improper sacrifice—on the altar (Lev 10:1-2). On this day Aaron, and later each high priest, had to ritually purify himself by bathing and putting on clean white linens. He would then enter the Holy of Holies, the most sacred part of the Tabernacle, to present a sacrifice. Next he would make the "goat offering." Two goats were chosen, and lots would be cast to see which would be slaughtered and sacrificed to God and which would be the "scapegoat." The scapegoat was sent into the wilderness after the priest had placed his hands on the animal, symbolically setting the "sins of the people" on it. The man who led it out remained "unclean" until the end of the feast.

Scholars see two strains of ritual in the observance of the Day of Atonement. The first is the Levitical strain, the cleansing of the body to represent the cleansing of the soul before God and the offering of the sacrifice in the Holy of Holies. The second strain, the goat offering, is evidently much older. There is some similarity between this ritual and the Babylonians' rite of *kippuru,* which took place on the fifth day of their New Year feast. The Babylonians sacrificed a ram and spread its blood on the temple. Then the head of the ram and its trunk were carried to the Euphrates. In this rite the priest and the slaughterer were ritually unclean until the end of the feast.

Some scholars also speculate that the scapegoat may have had its origins in devil worship, since the goat is sent out into the wilderness where the devil was thought to lurk. In the Syriac version of the Old Testament, an early Christian translation, the goat is sent out to a demon.

Yom Kippur is mentioned by neither Ezra nor Nehemiah, when he relates the festivals reinstituted by the Israelites on their return from Babylonian captivity in 458 BC. This has led many to conclude that it was introduced relatively late and was originally tied to the Babylonian feast of *kippuru.*

Today the observance of Yom Kippur resembles the festival as it was described in Leviticus, with the exception that no sacrifices have been made since the destruction of the Temple in AD 70. The rabbi, acting as priest, undergoes elaborate preparation and dons white robes for the holiday. The congregation fasts and prays in the local sanctuaries throughout the day.

Yom Kippur is the last day of the year to attain forgiveness; it is the time when one's fate is sealed for the year to come. At the end of the fast, the shofar (the ram's horn) is blown. By tradition, the first thing eaten should be sweet, to usher in a sweet year.

The Party's Over

1. After the Amalekites burned and sacked David's city, Ziklag, they got so much booty that they held a celebration. They were just in the middle of "eating and drinking and dancing" when David and his men descended on them. Only 400 Amalekites managed to reach their camels and flee—the rest were massacred (1 Sam 30:16–17).

2. On David's death, his oldest son, Adonijah, hoped to inherit the throne. Adonijah had slaughtered sheep, oxen, and fatted cattle for a fine feast of celebration of his kingship. Just as Adonijah and his friends got through eating, they learned that Bathsheba had convinced David to name her own son Solomon as king and that Solomon had been anointed. Adonijah's party came to an abrupt end. His friends crept away. Adonijah himself was so scared he ran to the sanctuary and grabbed the horns of the altar until Solomon took pity and told him he was free to go despite his presumption (1 Kings 1).

3. On Mount Carmel, Elijah and 450 priests of Baal had made prophecies in a competition before King Ahab to prove whose god was stronger. Elijah's prophecies came true while those of the priests of Baal were unfulfilled. Elijah's final prophecy was that there would be an "abundance of rain." King Ahab, apparently not yet convinced, went off to eat and drink as the sky remained cloudless. Elijah, climbing to the top of the mountain, threw himself to the ground and "put his face between his knees" to await the rain. Soon a cloud appeared, and then the king's feast was interrupted as the heavens became "black with clouds and wind." As a "great rain" poured down, Ahab jumped into his chariot and returned to his wife, Jezebel, to inform her that Baal had lost against the power of the Israelite God (1 Kings 18:41–45).

4. After Elisha had captured Syrian warriors, he advised the king of Israel not to kill them. So the king "prepared great provision for them: and when they had eaten and drunk" he set

258

them free. They returned home, regrouped, and returned to besiege Samaria (2 Kings 6:21-24).

5. To show off the riches and power of Persia, King Ahasuerus
threw a bash in honor of himself. Important and unimportant
people were invited to the palace. Queen Vashti hosted the women
indoors. Ahasuerus gave the men's party in the palace gardens,
which were decorated with white, green, and blue hangings. The
couches on which guests lay while they ate were of gold and silver.
Wine was poured into golden cups, each of different design, and
everyone was given as much wine as he wanted. The party lasted a
week.

It was too much of a good thing. After a fight between
Ahasuerus and his queen because she refused to be shown off
before the drunken men, they were divorced (Est 1).

6. Esther invited the king of Persia and Haman, the prime
minister, to a "banquet of wine." When the king had been softened
up on the second day of drinking, Esther announced Haman's
plans to annihilate the Jews. The king was so angry he went to pace
in the garden. The frightened Haman collapsed on Esther's bed, so
that when the king suddenly returned, he thought Haman was
trying to seduce Esther. This was too much for the king, who
ordered Haman dragged out and hanged (Est 7).

The Sabbath Holidays

Although many holidays have some relation to the number seven, as the
seven weeks counted between Passover and the Festival of Weeks, four
holidays are directly based on the number seven: *the Sabbath*—the seventh
day of the week; *Rosh Hashanah*—the seventh month; *the Sabbatical Year*—
the seventh year; and *the Jubilee Year*—the Sabbath of the Sabbatical
Years, the fiftieth year.

One might well wonder what the addiction to the number seven is all
about. Many ancient Middle Eastern cultures ascribed mystical value to the
seventh day. In Babylonia the seventh, fourteenth, twenty-first, and twenty-
eighth days of the month were considered evil. The king was not allowed to
act as sovereign and had to follow a ritual diet, which prohibited cooked
meats and baked breads. The Accadians regarded the fourteenth day of the
lunar month, the *shapattu,* as a day of good omen. And the Canaanites also
gave some weight to the seventh day in their religious texts although they
did not endow it with any special significance.

Amid these cultures and no doubt influenced by them, the Hebrews

259

made their seventh day special and distinctive, and carrying the Sabbath beyond the week made the seventh week, month, and year occasions for holiday.

The Sabbath Month: The first two references to the holiday which became known as Rosh Hashanah make it clear that it is a celebration of the coming of the seventh month:

> In the seventh month, in the first day of the month, shall ye have a sabbath, a memorial of blowing of trumpets, an holy convocation [Lev 23;24].

> And in the seventh month, on the first day of the month, ye shall have an holy convocation; ye shall do no servile work: it is a day of blowing the trumpets unto you [Num 29:1].

Since the celebration of the seventh month was not a major holiday, it probably had little significance before the days of the Second Temple. It came into its own, as did many other festivals, with the reforms instituted after the return from exile. And, as with many other festivals, its nature changed after its return.

The religious calendar that the Hebrews kept before the Exile was gradually forgotten during the Babylonian captivity. In this old system the first month (Nisan) was the beginning of the new year because it was the month of the Exodus, and Tishri was the seventh month.

Ezra was the first to institute Rosh Hashanah as a New Year's celebration, when on that day in 458 BC he gathered the returned exiles and read the Law to them. It was a dramatic beginning for the new version of the holiday. After Ezra's reading, Nehemiah proclaimed that from that day on Rosh Hashanah would be a holy day observed by festivity and feasts (Neh 8:9–10). By reinterpreting Rosh Hashanah as a New Year's festival Ezra and Nehemiah adapted a Babylonian festival at the same time that they purged it of its pagan influences. Yet they also lost the original sense of the holiday as a Sabbath.

Even though sacrificial rites were probably reinstated on the return from Babylon, Rosh Hashanah remained a "stay-at-home" holiday. The sacrifices were confined to the Temple and witnessed by few of the population. Undoubtedly the shofar (the trumpet) was sounded during the holiday as it is today.

By the time of the return from Babylon, Rosh Hashanah had become associated with the idea that God's judgment came on this day, possibly because of the shofar, the instrument that many believed would announce the last days. The reason for considering the New Year celebration a day of judgment may also have something to do with the Babylonian custom of casting lots on New Year's Day to seal one's fate.

This traditional view of the holiday has been carried down to the present.

In the liturgy read on the holiday it is often repeated that of one's fate "on Rosh Hashanah it is written and on Yom Kippur it is sealed." However some nonrabbinic sects, such as the Samaritans, Falahim, Karaites, Sadducees, and others, never celebrated the first of Tishri as anything more than a trumpet sounding for the new moon.

The Sabbath: According to the Bible the origins of the Sabbath are as old as the world itself: And God blessed the seventh day, and sanctified it; because that in it he had rested from all his work which God created and made" (Gen 2:3). The next mention of the Sabbath (Ex 16:13–29) gives the first hint that man should do no work on this day. On this occasion the Israelites were told not to collect manna on the Sabbath, but to gather two portions of it on the preceding day. Shortly thereafter, when Moses brings the Ten Commandments down to the Israelites, the observance of the Sabbath is spelled out:

> Remember the Sabbath day to keep it holy. Six days shalt thou labor and do thy work: But the seventh day is the Sabbath of the Lord thy God: in it thou shalt not do any work [Ex 20:8–11].

In later laws, the Sabbath was observed by additional sacrifices (Num 28:9), and by bread baked especially for the Sabbath (Lev 24:8).

Throughout the period of the captivity Sabbath was the only holiday which could be easily observed in the home and so became a unifying force. But with the return from exile and the recognition of the Sabbath's importance came the stricter laws: All business was prohibited, even the loading of a beast with goods. During the Maccabean period (c. 160 BC) observance was so rigorous that many Jews were murdered by Seleucid troops because they refused to fight on the Sabbath.

Today the Sabbath is the most important Jewish holiday except for Yom Kippur. Talmudic and biblical laws pertaining to the Sabbath, such as the prohibition against kindling fires (Lev 35:3) and against traveling more than a certain distance away from one's home, are extended by orthodox observers to include abstention from the use of electricity and the avoidance of motor travel. An elevator already programmed to stop at every floor of a building is usable on the Sabbath; it is prohibited to push a button to have an elevator make a special stop not previously arranged.

The Christian Sunday is not the heir of the Jewish Sabbath. Although Jesus did observe the Jewish Sabbath (Luke 4:16), he preached that one should not refrain from doing good works just because it was the Sabbath (Mark 3:4; Luke 13:15–16). He declared that the "sabbath was made of man, and not man for the sabbath" (Mark 2:27), a reaction to the strict laws which had grown up around its observance. As the Christian Church developed, the Saturday Sabbath was observed less and less, and gradually

Sunday, the day of the Resurrection, became the holy day of the week in Christianity.

Sabbatical Year: The biblical injunction for the observance of the Sabbatical Year occurs four times in the first five books of the Old Testament. In various references it is called the Sabbath of Sabbaths, the year of rest, the year of release, and the seventh year (Ex 23:10–11; Lev 25:1–7; Deut 15:1–18; 31:10–13).

The laws state that the seventh year should be a year of rest for the vineyards, the olive groves, and the soil. During the year the natural growth in the fields should be left for the poor, the stranger, the widow, the orphan, and others without means. Even the beasts of the field are allowed to pick over the land after humans have taken what they need.

The Sabbatical Year also provided a time for the remission of debts—though only of the Israelites, not of foreigners. Hebrew bond servants were to be freed from service in the seventh year and to be free thereafter. The calculation of this seventh year seems to be from the beginning of their service, so it does not always coincide with the generally observed Sabbatical Year. Slaves who were freed in the seventh year were to be given part of the employer's flocks, harvest, and wine in order that they might start their freedom with some capital (Deut 15:9–14).

It was never reported that people went hungry during this year—indeed, part of the rationale for the Sabbatical Year was to feed the poor. Landowners stored food during the previous harvests (Lev 25:20–22) and some edible wild foods were available to all. The reasoning behind the Sabbatical Year was sound: The land benefited from the year it lay fallow, the freed slaves could contribute more directly to the economy and of course got their freedom, and landowners could pursue occupations other than farming.

Nevertheless the Sabbatical Year, being a hardship for those who could not produce enough to get them through, was practiced only sporadically.

Jubilee Year: The year of Jubilee, also called the year of liberty (Lev 25:8–55; 27:16–25; Num 36:4), occurred after every seven Sabbatical Years. Proclaimed by the blasting of ram's horns, on the tenth day of Tishri, the Jubilee Year followed the forty-ninth year, a Sabbatical Year. Thus every fifty years the land would lie fallow for two years, since all Sabbatical Year restrictions held for the Jubilee Year as well.

Jubilee Year ensured an equalization, a return to origins, about once every lifetime. Fields and all houses that were outside walled cities were returned to their original owners. In effect, all families regained whatever part of the inheritance of Canaan they had been granted upon entry into the land with Joshua (Num 26). All Hebrew slaves, including those who had previously been refused release, were set free. Family members returned to their families, if for any reason except marriage they had left them during the previous forty-nine years.

According to tradition, the first Jubilee Year was celebrated during the sixty-fourth year after entry into the land of Canaan. The Jubilee seems to have been only rarely practiced and it has not been reinstituted.

Hosting Strangers

The Hebrews were warned not to eat "any thing that dieth of itself." However, it was okay to feed such food to strangers or to sell it to an alien (Deut 14:21).

Hannukah

Hannukah is not a biblical holiday in the sense of being ordained or recorded in the Old Testament. Its story is recorded in the apocryphal Books of the Maccabees and in the Talmud. According to the Talmud, when Jewish rebel forces took Jerusalem and the Temple from the Syrians in 164 BC, they found only one small container of the sacred oil used to fuel the eternal light in the Temple. Nevertheless they lit the light with this oil, only a day's supply, and it lasted for eight days—the miracle that Hannukah celebrates. Though it is not mentioned in the Bible itself, Hannukah seems well founded in history. One biblical scholar, Roland de Vaux, in his book *Ancient Israel,* noted that "Hannukah is the only Jewish feast whose institution is recorded in a late text, and which is also connected with an undeniable historical event."

Of the texts that record Hannukah, the Second Book of the Maccabees stressed the involvement of God in the victory and the miracles associated with the holiday. One part of the book may have been written by Judas Maccabeus himself, the leader of the rebel forces. It is a letter addressed to the Egyptian Jewish community, urging them to celebrate Hannukah. Another early source, the historian Josephus, called the holiday "the Festival of Lights." The term Hannukah comes from the Greek word meaning dedicated, inauguration, or renewal. In the New Testament this is the name used in John (10:22), and this is the term that the talmudic sages employed.

Some scholars contend that Hannukah is a reinterpretation of the pagan celebration of the winter solstice, the shortest period of daylight in the year. The main objection to this theory is that the winter solstice is based upon the solar calendar, while the Jewish holidays, such as Hannukah, are fixed by the lunar calendar. Yet it was not uncommon for ancient peoples to identify with each other two occurrences that took place at about the same time. Therefore the tradition of lighting fires on hilltops, a practice continued in the modern State of Israel with torch races, may be a vestige of pagan solstice celebrations.

Today Hannukah is celebrated by the lighting of an eight-stemmed candelabrum, or menorah, with a ninth candle used to light the others. One candle is lit the first night of the holiday, and each evening an additional candle is lit, to celebrate the eight days that the light in the Temple miraculously stayed lit. Hallel (a psalm of thanksgiving) is recited, and a betting game called "dreidel" is played. The dreidel is a four-sided top, each side bearing the initial letters of the words in the saying *Nas gadol hayah shom,* "A great miracle happened there."

Purim

The story of Purim is found in the Book of Esther, a tale about the nobles of the Persian court at Babylon. The story begins when King Ahasuerus divorces his Persian wife, Vashti, and chooses Esther, from all the maidens in his kingdom, to be his wife. The king is not aware that his new bride is Jewish. Esther's guardian and uncle, Mordecai, advises her against telling the king about her heritage, apparently because he fears Ahasuerus will be influenced by the anti-Semitism rampant in the kingdom and divorce Esther. As long as Esther is queen, Mordecai can monitor the court gossip and keep tabs on impending dangers for the Jewish community.

Not too long after the marriage, the king decrees that everyone should bow before his new second in command, Haman. When Mordecai refuses to bow, Haman becomes so incensed at the elderly Jew he begins to take out his hatred on the Jewish population and even sets a date to begin executions. Esther learns of the slaughter to come and has the king remove Haman from office. But by Persian law the king cannot revoke decrees once they are made. Therefore he issues a counterdecree which allows the Jews to take up arms to defend themselves against attackers. On the thirteenth of Adar the Jews successfully fight off the troops sent by Haman's order, and on the fourteenth of Adar they celebrate their victory.

The Book of Esther is easily recognized as unique among the books of the Bible. Even the casual reader senses it is closer to the moralistic story than to a factual history. Scholars note that no king with a name like Ahasuerus ruled during the period in which the story is set, and in any case it would have been impossible for a Persian king to marry a Jewish woman since the lineage of a prospective queen was closely inspected to ensure that she was of the Persian aristocracy.

As a further argument for the story's being fictional, it has been pointed out that the names of the characters correspond to gods in Babylonian myths: Mordecai = Marduk, Esther = Ishtar, Haman = Uman, Vashti = Mashti. The conclusion generally reached is that the story of Purim was written to justify the adoption by Jews of a Babylonian feast day, perhaps an ancient New Year's festival during which stories about these gods were told.

Today Purim is celebrated by reading the Book of Esther (the *Megillah*). Every time the name Haman is read, adults and children stamp and whirl noisemakers. Children often dress up in costumes. In the past they came as characters from the story; nowadays they wear any costume they choose. It is a holiday of celebration, and the only holiday on which drunkenness is countenanced.

Great Hosts

When the three messengers approached Abraham's tent they were offered water to wash their feet, seats under a shade tree, and a meal of bread and calf meat with butter and milk (Gen 18:3-8).

Two messengers traveled to Lot's home to warn him of the destruction of Sodom. When the men of Sodom demanded the two men for their sexual pleasure, Lot offered his virgin daughters for the orgy instead. Luckily for Lot's daughters, the messengers were angels and prevented the rape by blinding the men of Sodom (Gen 19:1-11).

When Gideon entertained an angel, he gave him meat from a kid, broth, and unleavened cakes. The angel didn't eat it, though. He told Gideon to put the food on a rock, and "there rose a fire out of the rock" that consumed the food—at which point the angel disappeared (Judg 6:19-21).

Jethro, hearing that Moses had helped his daughters at the well, offered Moses not only hospitality but his daughter Zipporah to wed (Ex 2:15-21).

The rich woman of Shunem invited Elisha to a meal at her home when he traveled through her town, and then suggested to her husband that they provide Elisha with a fully furnished guest room for future visits (2 Kings 4:8-17).

When Elijah fled to the wilderness to escape King Ahab and Jezebel, "ravens brought him bread and flesh in the morning" and in the evening (1 Kings 17:6).

Obadiah hid a hundred prophets, who were also fleeing Ahab and Jezebel, in a cave and fed them bread and water (1 Kings 18:4).

When the king of Babylon heard that King Hezekiah had been ill but was recovered, he sent messengers with letters and a present. Hezekiah responded by showing them "all the house of his precious things, the silver, and the gold, and the spices, and the precious ointment, and all the house of his armour, and all that was found in his treasures: there was nothing in his house, nor in all his domain, that Hezekiah shewed them not." When he learned of this, Isaiah was furious that the king had revealed the nation's treasures to enemies, and he prophesied the fall of Israel to Babylon: "all that is in thine house . . . shall be carried into Babylon. . . . And of thy sons . . . they shall be eunuchs in the palace of the king of Babylon" (2 Kings 20:13–18).

When Solomon gave feasts for the queen of Sheba, she was so astounded by the food on the table, the cupbearers, and the way the courtiers dressed that "there was no more spirit left in her" (1 Kings 10:5).

While Nehemiah was rebuilding Jerusalem after the Exile to Babylon, he fed at his table 150 "Jews and rulers" as well as heathens. Each day they consumed an ox, six choice sheep, and many fowl, and once every ten days they got "all sorts of wine" (Neh 5:17–18).

Christmas

In Western churches the birth of Jesus is celebrated on December 25, and the Epiphany (commemorating the appearance of the wise men) twelve days later, on January 6. Because the Roman emperor Aurelian fixed December 25 as the date for the winter solstice holiday in AD 274, it is thought that the early Christians adopted this day for their Christ-mass so that they would be less conspicuous in the observance of their holiday. Also, since the solstice holiday celebrates the increase of light per day until summer, the holiday could be easily adapted by the Christians to express the parallel notion that Jesus was the light of the world growing stronger from birth. Most scholars believe the birthday of Jesus was never known and that the December date was chosen solely for convenience. Still, astronomical analyses demonstrate that a highly unusual occurrence, which might be construed as the Star of Bethlehem, did take place in December of 7 BC, a year appropriate for the birth of Jesus.

The earliest known observance of Christmas on December 25 was in the year 336 in Rome, as recorded in a Christian calendar of the period. There are many references to the December date before this time, but they are thought to be untrustworthy or later insertions.

The earliest Christians seem to have celebrated January 6 as the day of the Christ-mass, but that day commemorated the baptism of Jesus, not his birth or the Epiphany. Indeed there has long been some confusion within Christianity over what Epiphany (Greek, "appearance") did celebrate. Some hold that it was the occasion of the appearance of God in the infant Jesus, others, more recently, that it was the appearance of the wise men.

Throughout antiquity other dates for the birth were advanced—March

25, April 19, November 17, among others—but there is no evidence, literary or historical, that supports any of these dates.

Almost everywhere in Europe, in both Roman and Teutonic countries, the period around the winter solstice was celebrated with lights, to symbolize the increase of sunlight to come, and with greenery, usually evergreens, to represent the coming of spring and eternal cycles of growth. At the Saturnalia festival (December 17–24), Romans would present each other with sprigs of holly as gifts for the holiday. When Teutonic tribes began to usurp power from the Romans in Europe, they brought their Yule, or winter feast, traditions with them. The Yule log and wassailing are two of these traditions.

The origin of the Christmas tree is usually traced to Saint Boniface, who in the 8th century persuaded the Teutonic tribes to abandon worship of the sacred oak of Odin, a remnant of Druidism, and to confer it instead on the fir, a more appropriate symbol of Jesus and eternal life. Martin Luther may have been the first to decorate a Christmas tree when he fixed candles to a fir. The Christmas tree (or *Tannenbaum,* as it is known in Germany) was brought to the United States by Hessian troops during the Revolutionary War and also by the Germans who settled in Pennsylvania. These first trees were decorated with strings of popcorn and cookies, candies, and apples.

Surprisingly, Christmas was not celebrated in New England until a hundred years ago. The Puritans, like Charles II, who abandoned the practice of Christmas in England in 1644, were suspicious of its pagan origins.

For We Have Seen His Star in the East

The Star of Bethlehem, mentioned only by Matthew, has been explained as a meteor, a comet, and a nova, but the most likely explanation is that it was an unusual conjunction of the planets. Once every twenty years, the orbits of Jupiter and Saturn cause them to appear aligned close together along a north–south axis—a conjunction. But late in the year 7 BC, this happened three times within six months, and each time the alignment took place in the constellation Pisces (called the "House of the Hebrews" by ancient astrologers). This triple conjunction occurs only once every 120 years.

The Magi, who were astrologers in Mesopotamia, undoubtedly noticed the first conjunction in June, 7 BC, with some interest. Because it happened in the constellation of Pisces, a constellation long associated with Israel, they probably wondered what bearing the conjunction had on the affairs of that nation. The Bible implies (Matt 2:2) they had heard the biblical prophecy: "I shall behold him, but not nigh: there shall come a Star out of Jacob, and a Sceptre shall rise out of Israel" (Num 24:17). When, on September 27, the conjunction happened again, they may have begun preparations to go westward to Jerusalem. At first they moved *away* from the conjunction, for it had appeared in the eastern sky. This agrees with their statement to Herod: "we have seen his star in the east" (Matt 2:1-2). As the seasons changed, however, the planets moved toward the west. If the Magi arrived in Jerusalem around December 10 they would have seen the conjunction a third time, but now it would be in the south-southwest, toward Bethlehem. This movement may be linked to the line from Matthew: "and lo, the star which they saw in the east, went before them, till it came and stood over where the young child was" (2:9). According to Matthew they knew which town to go to anyway, for Herod's priests quoted them the prophecy from Micah: "But thou, Bethlehem Ephratah, though thou be little among the thousands of Judah, yet out of thee shall he come forth unto me that is to be ruler of Israel" (5:2).

Shortly after the third conjunction in December, the planet Mars began moving closer to the pair of Jupiter and Saturn. By this time the planets had also moved close to the western horizon and all of them except for Jupiter were obscured by the setting sun. The Magi may have thought that this final grouping of planets was a sign they had reached their destination. This accords more closely with the time of year implied by Luke's statement that "the shepherds were guarding their flocks by night." During early spring the lambing season begins and the sheep are especially vulnerable to attacks by wild animals.

Longer than the Bible:
The Book of Life

"Let them be blotted out of the book of the living, and not be written with the righteous" (Psa 69:28).

"He that overcometh ... I will not blot out his name out of the book of life" (Rev 3:5).

"And all that dwell upon the earth shall worship him, whose names are not written in the book of life of the lamb slain from the foundation of the world" (Rev 13:8).

"And I saw the dead, small and great, stand before God; and the books were opened: and another book was opened, which is the book of life: and the dead were judged out of those things which were written in the books, according to their works" (Rev 20:12).

"Whosoever was not found written in the book of life was cast into the lake of fire" (Rev 20:15).

"And I saw a new heaven and a new earth. . . . And there shall in no wise enter into it any thing that defileth, neither whatsoever worketh abomination, or maketh a lie: but they which are written in the Lamb's book of life" (Rev 21:27).

Astronomy and Astrology

Astronomical observations were carried out by Chaldean priests for thousands of years. These observations, which probably began before 2300 BC, recorded the shape and relative brilliance of the constellations, their rising and setting, and the motions of the planets. Like all astronomers before the time of Kepler, the Chaldeans were also astrologers. In fact, to the Hebrews the name Chaldean was synonymous with "astrologer" (Dan 2:2, 10). As scientists the Chaldeans certainly deserved their reputation for accuracy. They were able to predict eclipses of the sun with some frequency, and their calculation of the length of the solar year was within thirty minutes of that determined by modern instruments.

Because of their knowledge of celestial reckoning and their occasional success with divination, the Chaldean priesthood gained political power in Babylon, and by 650 BC they had great influence throughout the city-state. Chaldean astrologers belonged to the highest caste, a fact which helps explain their ability to maintain the longest stretch of continuous astronomical data-gathering known in the ancient world—360 years. The Magi that Nebuchadnezzar sent to Herod were Chaldeans.

The early Hebrews were familiar with some aspects of astronomy, probably because of the need to be familiar with celestial navigation while in the desert and because their calendar was based on the lunar month. In Job, the constellations Orion, the Pleiades, and Arcturus are named (9:9; 38:32). Throughout the Bible, however, astrology and divination are treated with suspicion or outlawed altogether. To resort to divination or to be an "observer of times, or an enchanter," was to partake of the "abominations" of other nations (Deut 18:12). In Isaiah, those who do not believe in God are scornfully told: "Let now the astrologers, the stargazers, and the monthly prognosticators, stand up, and save thee from these things that shall come upon thee" (47:13).

Nevertheless, there is a long tradition of astrological lore in the Talmud and Midrash and in Judaic mystical and apocalyptic writings. Much of this lore is based on the correspondence perceived between the twelve sons of Jacob and the twelve signs of the Zodiac (or Mazzaroth [Job 38:32]).

Tribe	Zodiac	Tribe	Zodiac
Joseph	Pisces	Zebulun	Virgo
Benjamin	Aries	Issachar	Libra
Reuben	Taurus	Dan	Scorpio
Simeon	Gemini	Gad	Sagittarius
Levi	Cancer	Asher	Capricorn
Judah	Leo	Naphtali	Aquarius

To each sun-sign pair, Hebrew astrologers assigned a general character based on scriptural evidence. For instance, Reuben, the spiritual ruler of Taurus, is mentioned as having slept with his father's concubine Bilhah (Gen 35:22). Thus all Taurians are thought to be susceptible to impulsive acts of lust and passion in the style of their biblical predecessor. For a more detailed and elaborate presentation of this astrological theory, see *To Rule Both Day and Night: Astrology in the Bible, Midrash and Talmud,* by Joel Dobin.

Twelve Tribes

The Hebrew tribes were founded by the twelve sons of Jacob: Reuben, Issachar, Dan, Simeon, Zebulun, Naphtali, Levi, Joseph, Gad, Judah, Benjamin, and Asher. In addition, two grandsons— children of Joseph adopted by Jacob and elevated to tribal heads— Ephraim and Manasseh, are counted as one tribe.

This would seem to make thirteen tribes. However, the Levites were entrusted with worship and instead of being given land they were scattered among the other tribes and supported by them. They are thus often not counted as one of the twelve tribes in the Scriptures; if they are counted, then Ephraim and Manasseh are subtracted as a tribe and lumped with Jacob to retain the number twelve.

Numbers

Most numbers in the Old Testament are probably not intended to be accurate. The Hebrews were not much interested in mathematics and they sometimes used numbers more for their symbolic meaning than for designating exact amounts. That some numbers (nine, for example) occur infrequently, while other numbers (such as seven) are used over and over, is clear evidence that numbers in the Bible have some mystical significance.

One, Two, Three: The most primitive numbers were based on finger counting, and the earliest mathematical systems in the Middle East had symbols for one, two, and three. The earliest counting systems did not have symbols for numbers above three. A four was designated with two symbols for two, a five combined the symbols for two and three, an eight was made of four of the symbols for two or of two symbols each for three and one, and so on. Counting was thus cumbersome until a decimal system was invented, but even after this invention the first three numbers retained special importance.

One and two are symbolic numbers in the Middle East. They defined the concept of odds and evens, which formed the basis of Middle Eastern divination systems and moves on gaming boards.

Three was a sacred number in Mesopotamia, with a trinity of gods (Anu, Bel, Ea), and in Egypt, with a similar trinity (Isis, Osiris, Horus). Among the Hebrews, as with other peoples in the Middle East, the universe was seen as tripartite—heaven, earth, and underworld. In the Bible three frequently occurs as a sacred number in the Old Testament (as in a three-cubit measurement for an altar) but it took on greater significance in the New

Testament: three crosses on Calvary, three days in the tomb, and the trinity of Father, Son, and Holy Ghost.

Four: For the Hebrews an important number was four. One explanation for its significance is that the name of their god, Yahweh, is spelled in Hebrew with four letters. Four is also a significant number among people who believe the earth to be flat and that it has four corners. Hebrews believed the earth had four "quarters" from which four winds emanated (Jer 49:36) and that the river of Eden branched into four streams (Gen 2:10). Altars had four horns, one at each corner, and many instructions for objects of religious use were measured or counted by fours (Ex 25:26, 34; 26:2, 8; 27:16; 37:20; etc.).

Multiples of four are frequent in the Bible. Forty years was considered the length of a generation. Forty was the number of years the Israelites wandered after the Exodus, the number of days that Moses spent on Mount Sinai and that Jesus spent in the wilderness of temptation. Forty also occurs frequently as the number of years kings ruled or before they took some important step.

Five: The meaning of five is unknown. It seems to have been important especially in sacred literature, where it occurs as a frequent division—such as the five books of Moses or the five chapters of Lamentations. Yet occasionally it seems to be a bad number—five was the number of Midianite kings that Gideon fought and the number of Philistine princes who ordered Samson caught.

Six: Six seems sometimes to have been a favored number—being half of a "good" number, twelve—and twelve occurs in counts used in religious items. But 666 is special. In the early Christian era 666 was a runic number used to designate anti-Christian officials, and in Revelation (13:18) there is an interesting mention: "Here is wisdom. Let him that hath understanding count the number of the beast: for it is the number of a man, and his number is Six hundred threescore and six."

Seven: In Mesopotamia, seven was an ominous number. The seventh, fourteenth, twenty-first, and twenty-eighth days of each month were unlucky, and every forty-ninth day (seven times seven) was called the day of wrath.

Of all numbers, seven was the most significant to the Hebrews. Probably it was associated with the "seven stars" (Amos 5:8; Rev 1:16, 20; 2:1; 3:1)—the sun, the moon, and the five planets recognized in biblical times (Mercury, Venus, Mars, Jupiter, and Saturn).

Because Creation had required seven days, seven symbolized completion and perfection. Much of ritual life hinged on this number—unclean people were isolated seven days, and priests sprinkled sacrificial blood or holy oil seven times. Seven days was the period of mourning. Because a new cycle of life began after seven days, a child was circumcised on the eighth day.

Not only was every seventh day the Sabbath and a day of rest, but every seventh year was a Sabbath Year, when the fields and vineyards were to lie fallow (Lev 25:2-7). And some religious festivals, such as Passover, lasted seven days.

Among the many examples of this number: Jacob bowed before Esau seven times; the Israelites paraded around Jericho seven times; Naaman had to wash in the Jordan seven times to be cured of leprosy; and Jesus cast out seven devils. The menorah—the seven branched candlestick—is still the symbol of the State of Israel.

Multiples of seven were also sacred. At the end of every forty-ninth year the trumpet was sounded to announce the Jubilee Year in which property was to be returned to its original tribe, Israelite slaves were to be freed, and other customs observed. Seventy years is cited as the length of the Babylonian Exile and the length of time Tyre deserved to be forgotten. In addition to the apostles, Jesus appointed another seventy helpers, and said that "seventy times seven" was the number of times one should forgive a brother.

Ten: Because of finger counting, ten (all fingers) became significant, and symbols were invented for it as early as 3400 BC in Egypt and by 3000 BC in Mesopotamia. For the Hebrews the number was significant in itself—Ten Commandments, ten curtains of the Tabernacle, ten virgins—as well as for multiplication. Multiplying ten with a favorite number made the result significant too. Many biblical counts are multiples of sevens or threes with ten: Noah's ark was 30 cubits high and 300 cubits long; Jesus was sold for thirty pieces of silver.

Twelve: Many symbolic numbers in the Middle East were derived from astrological calculations based on sun and moon worship in Mesopotamia and Egypt. A zodiac of twelve signs, for instance, was invented in Mesopotamia before 2000 BC, and the year was divided into twelve lunar months in both Mesopotamia and Palestine.

Because of its astrological significance, twelve became an important number. Jacob had twelve sons who founded the twelve tribes of Israel. Ishmael also had twelve sons. Joshua used twelve stones to commemorate crossing the Jordan into the promised land. Elijah built an altar of twelve stones and Elisha plowed with twelve yoke of oxen. Solomon had a dozen chief officers. Jesus had twelve Apostles, and when one proved to be a traitor, another was substituted to keep the count the same. Jesus may have chosen twelve as the number of Apostles in connection with the belief that there were twelve thrones of heaven to judge the twelve tribes of Israel (Matt 19:28).

Twenty: Like ten, twenty (all fingers and toes) was a favorite multiplication factor among the Hebrews, constituting the basis of most counts up to a hundred: Fourscore years is given as an age, four hundred and fourscore years is given as a passage of time, fourscore thousand hewers were in the mountains, and one hundred fourscore and five thousand Assyrians were slain by an angel.

How Many Israelites?

Although the Bible purports to give population figures, demographers have calculated that these are largely inaccurate and are based on symbolic numbers rather than on realistic counts.

For example, the Bible claims that 600,000 warriors, together with their wives and children and the old and servants, left Egypt during the Exodus (Ex 12:37–38). Such a "mixed multitude" would have meant a total population of several million (whom the pharaoh tried to stop with a mere 600 chariots!). Not only is the idea of Moses trying to lead such a horde out of Egypt in one night preposterous, but such a population could never have survived on the meager resources of the Sinai Peninsula—even if they had spread out across it. Equally preposterous is the idea that these millions camped for years around the limited springs at Kadesh-barnea. The size of the Israelite band during the Exodus is impossible to gauge, but even a total in tens of thousands would be too large.

The famous census taken during the reign of David claimed that 1,300,000 men were of military age (2 Sam 24:1–9), but demographers strongly doubt that the Israelites in biblical times, even at peak power and prosperity, ever exceeded a million people.

How Large Were Armies?

In the Old Testament, the numbers of men in armies are not intended to be exact—only to indicate large, impressive assemblages. The army was referred to vaguely as the "thousands of Israel" because each tribe was theoretically supposed to contribute a thousand warriors. No matter how many men a tribe actually offered in wartime, the military leader of each tribe was called the "leader of a thousand," and when he divided his men into smaller units these were called a "hundred" (Num 31:5; Josh 22:21; Judg 7:16; 1 Sam 17:18; 18:13; 22:7). Such free and easy approximations satisfied most biblical authors.

276

Even when biblical authors felt they should be more precise they did not strive for accuracy but picked a nice round figure based on multiples of symbolic numbers. For instance, multiples of four were favored for the calculation of armies. So the Bible reports that 40,000 men of Israel fought in Deborah's War (Judg 5:8), 40,000 warriors attacked Jericho (Jos 4:13), Israel sent 400,000 warriors against Benjamin (Judg 20:17), and David had 400 mighty men (1 Sam 22:2).

The careless way exaggerated numbers were tossed about can be seen in the size of armies Saul was said to muster. At his first call, to defend Jabesh against the Ammonites, 300,000 men of Israel and 30,000 men of Judah supposedly responded; when Saul marched against the Amalekites, 200,000 men of Israel and 10,000 men of Judah followed him (1 Sam 11:8; 15:4). Yet when Israel countered the serious threat of the Assyrians under Shalmaneser III in 853 BC—when figures were more realistic— it mustered only 10,000 infantrymen.

Similarly, the Philistines were said to have amassed 30,000 chariots against Saul at Michmash (1 Sam 13–15). However, the records of Sargon II show that he captured only 200 chariots at Hamath and 50 at Samaria. And when virtually all the states of the Near East from Damascus to Egypt allied against Assyria in 853 BC, the grand total of chariots from a dozen nations came to only 3940.

Funny Figures

1. God has 20,000 chariots (Psa 68:17).
2. The neck of the lover is like David's armory—hung with a thousand shields (S of S 4:4).
3. Solomon offered 22,000 oxen and 120,000 sheep at one gigantic sacrifice (1 Kings 8:63).
4. Solomon had 70,000 porters (1 Kings 5:15).
5. The Lord usually appears with 10,000 saints (Deut 33:2; Jude 14), but heaven actually had "ten thousand times ten thousand, and thousands of thousands" saints (Rev 5:11).

The Almighty Shekel

SHEKELS

The denomination of money most frequently mentioned in the Bible, the shekel ("weight"), was, properly speaking, not a unit of currency but a unit of weight (Ex 30:23). Unfortunately, its value is confusing because it was used to designate more than one weight in the various systems of measures that appeared in the Near East at different times.

In addition, the two common systems of weight—the Babylonian and the Phoenician—had two different weights to which the word shekel applied, a light weight and a heavy weight, the light being half of the heavy.

The first system used in Palestine and throughout the Near East was the Babylonian. At first both gold and silver were weighed with the light and the heavy shekel. Around the time that the Israelites entered Canaan, the second system, the Phoenician, came into use for weighing silver, perhaps because the Phoenicians began minting silver. Even though the Israelites adopted the Phoenician shekel for silver, they continued to use the Babylonian shekel for gold. Most of the archaeological evidence, such as shekel weights and coins that have been found, indicates that the heavy Phoenician silver shekel weighed about 224 grains, or about six ounces, and the light silver shekel weighed 112 grains. The heavy Babylonian gold shekel may have weighed about 336 grains, and the light about 168.

Trade was first carried out by barter or the exchange of unminted precious metals for goods, services, or land. When they were to be used in exchanges, gold and silver were often formed into rings (Judg 8:26)—a practice borrowed from the Egyptians and Babylonians—or were cut from a bar, giving the metal a wedge shape (Josh 7:21, 24; Isa 13:12). As many

Bible passages indicate, gold was rarely used in ordinary transactions. This was because of its high relative value: Fifteen heavy Phoenician shekels of silver were considered equivalent to one heavy Babylonian shekel of gold. Coins were not minted in Palestine until the time of Alexander Jannaeus (103–76 BC).

There are many difficulties in determining the worth of a shekel. Very often Bibles will use a phrase such as "piece of silver" where "shekels of silver" would have been a more accurate translation. In the original Hebrew neither the word "shekel" nor "piece" is present but it is likely that a shekel is the measure implied—just as we might say, "Lend me twenty," with the word "dollars" implied.

Just what a shekel is worth in modern currency is a thorny question. The values assigned to the heavy silver shekel by modern authorities range from 64 cents to $2.50. Obviously many biblical mentions of money are completely out of line with these figures. A field for $42.50 is too good a deal to be true, but that's what seventeen shekels is worth according to the highest of these rates of exchange (Jer 32:9). The idea of assigning an absolute value to the shekel becomes even more absurd when one considers that yearly salaries mentioned in the Bible, even though they included food, ranged from ten to forty shekels (Neh 5:15; Judg 17:10). That would be a lot of years of saving if one wanted to buy a couple of statues for 200 shekels, as Micah's mother did. Here's what shekels bought:

Shekels of Silver

(1 silver shekel = anywhere from 64 cents to $2.50, depending on the scholar you believe)

¼ *shekel* was the payment offered a man who gave travelers directions (1 Sam 9:8).

½ *shekel* was what rich and poor alike were to offer to God (Ex 30:15).

1 shekel bought a measure of fine flour or two measures of barley when these were plentiful (2 Kings 7:1, 16, 18).

3 shekels was the value of a female Israelite aged one month to five years (Lev 27:6).

5 shekels was the value of a male Israelite aged one month to five years (Lev 27:6).

5 shekels was what about a pint of dove's dung was sold for when Samaria was under siege (2 Kings 6:25).

10 shekels of silver a year, plus food and a suit of clothes, is what Micah paid when he hired a private priest (Judg 17:10–13).

10 shekels of silver was the value of female Israelites aged five to twenty and of women over sixty years old (Lev 27:5, 7).

10 shekels of silver and a girdle is what Joab said he would pay a man to kill Absalom (2 Sam 18:11).

15 shekels, plus about 16 bushels of barley, is what Hosea paid a harlot to live with him (Hos 3:2).

15 shekels was the value of a male Israelite over sixty years old (Lev 3:7).

17 shekels was the value of a field (Jer 32:9).

20 shekels was the value of a male Israelite aged five to twenty (Lev 3:5).

20 shekels is what Joseph's brothers got for selling him as a slave (Gen 37:28).

20 shekels a day was the value of the meat Ezekiel was to eat (Ezek 4:10).

30 shekels was the value of a woman Israelite aged twenty to sixty (Lev 3:4)

30 shekels was the value of an adult heathen male slave (Ex 21:32).

30 shekels was what the shepherd was offered for his annual wages (Zech 11:12–13).

30 shekels is what Judas was paid for betraying Jesus (Matt 27:6, 9).

40 shekels of silver, plus bread and wine, is what governors took as pay in the postexilic period (Neh 5:15).

50 shekels of silver was the value of a male Israelite aged twenty to sixty (Lev 3:3).

50 shekels of silver was to be paid by a rapist to the father of the abused woman (Deut 22:29).

50 shekels of silver or 600 shekels of gold is what David paid for oxen and a threshing floor (2 Sam 24:24; 1 Chr 21:25).

50 shekels of silver each is what the wealthy men of Samaria had to pay the king of Assyria to keep the city from being taken (2 Kings 15:20).

50 shekels of silver is what a homer (11 bushels) of barley seed was worth (Lev 27:16).

70 shekels was the measure of the silver bowl of flour and oil princes offered, along with a charger of 130 shekels, in the time of Moses (Num 7:13).

70 shekels was what Abimelech was paid from the temple of Baal-Berith to be king of Shechem (Judg 9:4).

80 shekels is what an ass's head sold for when Samaria was under siege (2 Kings 6:25).

100 shekels of silver was to be paid to the father of a bride whose groom falsely accused her of not being a virgin (Deut 22:19).

100 shekels is what Jacob paid for a piece of a field at Shechem (Gen 33:19).

150 shekels was the price of an Egyptian horse trained to pull chariots (2 Chr 1:17).

200 shekels was the weight of Absalom's splendid hair (2 Sam 14:26).

200 shekels was what Micah's mother paid for one graven image and one molten image (Judg 17:2).

300 shekels and five changes of clothes is what Joseph gave his brother Benjamin (Gen 45:22).

400 shekels of silver is what Abraham paid for the Cave of Machpelah and the field around it (Gen 23:15-16).

600 shekels is the price Solomon got for the Egyptian chariots he sold to Hittites and Syrians (2 Chr 1:17).

1000 shekels was the rent Solomon got for his vineyard (S of S 8:11-12).

1000 shekels of silver is what a loyal subject said was not enough payment for killing King David's son (1 Sam 18:12).

1000 shekels was gift Abimelech gave Abraham (Gen 20:16).

1100 shekels was what Delilah was paid for revealing the secrets of Samson's strength to the Philistine leaders (Judg 16:4-18).

50,000 shekels of silver was the value of the books on magic that were burned by Paul in Ephesus (Acts 19:19).

Shekels of Gold

(1 gold shekel = anywhere from $9.60 to $37.50)

½ shekel was the weight of Rebekah's golden earring (Gen 24:22).

10 shekels was the weight of Rebekah's two gold bracelets (Gen 24:22).

10 shekels was the measure of the gold spoon of incense to be offered to God (Num 7:14).

600 shekels of gold went into each of the 200 shields that Solomon ordered made (1 Kings 10:16).

1700 shekels was the weight of the gold earrings of the Midianites given to Gideon as his part of the spoils for leading the war (Judg 8:26).

TALENTS

After shekels, talents are the most frequently mentioned units of weight in the Bible. Only one thing is truly certain about the talent: It was worth far more than a shekel. Most authorities fix a talent at 3000 times the weight of the shekel, the value it had in the Canaanite system.

The talent could be of gold or silver. As with the shekel, the talent of gold was heavier than the talent of silver because it was weighed in accordance with the Babylonian system. The word "talent," actually a Greek word, is a translation of the Hebrew *kikar. Kikar* ("loaf" or "cake") suggests that the shape of the talent was circular like the bread of the area. Here's what some people with many talents got:

Talents of Silver

(1 silver talent = anywhere from $1920 to $7500—take your pick)

1 talent of silver, or his life, was the fine imposed on a guard for failing to keep watch over a prisoner (1 Kings 20:39).

1 to 5 talents of silver was what the man "travelling into a far country" gave his servants to keep them until his return (Matt 25:15).

2 talents of silver is what King Omri of Israel paid for the hill on which he built his capital, Samaria (1 Kings 16:24).

100 talents of silver was used to cast sockets for the sanctuary (Ex 38:27).

100 talents of silver is what it cost King Amaziah of Israel to hire 100,000 warriors for a battle (2 Chr 25:6, 9).

100 talents of silver, plus wheat and barley, was the tribute paid by the Ammonites to King Jotham of Judah (2 Chr 27:5).

100 talents of silver was what the Persian local treasurers were ordered to give Ezra, if he asked for it, when the Jews were preparing to return from Babylon to Jerusalem (Ezra 7:22).

1000 talents of silver was paid by the Ammonites to hire 32,000 chariots and their horsemen from Mesopotamia, Syria, and Zobah to help them fight the Israelites (1 Chr 19:6).

1000 talents of silver is the tribute King Menahem of Israel paid Assyria (2 Kings 15:19).

Talents of Gold

(1 gold talent = anywhere from about $14,000 to $30,000 or more)

1 talent of gold made a snuff dish for the Temple (Ex 25:39; 37:24).

1 talent of gold made a king's crown—for a petty king (2 Sam 12:30; 1 Chr 20:2).

120 talents of gold is what King Hiram of Tyre sent Solomon as a friendship offering (1 Kings 9:14).

120 talents of gold is what the queen of Sheba gave Solomon as a gift (1 Kings 10:10; 2 Chr 9:9).

420 or 450 talents or gold is what Solomon's fleet brought back from Ophir (1 Kings 9:28; 2 Chr 8:18).

666 talents of gold is what Solomon collected annually (1 Kings 10:14).

High Finance

100 talents of silver and 1 talent of gold is what the Egyptian pharaoh demanded as tribute from the Kingdom of Judah (1 Kings 23:33; 2 Chr 36:3).

1,000,000 talents of silver and 100,000 talents of gold is what David collected to build the Temple in Jerusalem. He said he was not going to count the brass and iron "for it is in abundance." Later, however, he said 3000 talents of gold and 7000 talents of silver were to overlay the walls of the Temple, while for the "service of the house of God" he left 5000 talents of gold, 10,000 talents of silver, 18,000 talents of brass, and 100,000 talents of iron (1 Chr 22:14; 29:4, 7).

100 talents of gold and 650 talents of silver, plus 100 talents of silver vessels, were among the treasures Ezra turned over to the priests on the return from Babylon (Ezra 8:26).

10,000 talents of silver is a debt that the creditor wanted to collect by selling the debtor and his wife and children and "all that he had" (Matt 18:24).

10,000 talents of silver is what Haman intended to pay to have the Jewish wealth brought to the treasury of the Persian king (Esther 3:9).

300 talents of silver and 30 talents of gold is what Hezekiah of Judah had to pay the Assyrians as tribute (2 Kings 18:14).

10 talents of silver and 6000 shekels of gold (plus ten changes of clothes) is what Naaman took with him for his journey from Damascus to Samaria (2 Kings 5:5).

PENCE

In New Testament times the most-used coin was the silver denarius, worth about 16 cents or the equivalent of a day's wage for an unskilled laborer. It is often translated as "pence."

The good Samaritan left *2 pence* with an innkeeper to take care of the needs of a man who had been beaten by bandits (Luke 10:35).

A debt of *100 pence* was enough to make the creditor grab the debtor by the throat to demand payment (Matt 18:28).

The spikenard ointment poured on Jesus cost *300 pence,* which Judas considered a waste (Mark 14:5; John 12:5).

Unemployment Compensation

After King Amaziah of Israel had agreed to hire 100,000 warriors for 100 talents of silver, a man of God told him that only God gave victory or defeat. "But," asked Amaziah, "what shall we do for the hundred talents which I have given to the army of Israel?" The man of God assured him that "God is able to give thee much more than this." Satisfied, Amaziah dismissed the men he'd hired. Enraged, the dismissed warriors went on a rampage from Samaria to Beth-horon, killing 3000 people and looting the cities (2 Chr 25:6–12).

Six

The Dark Side

Ezekiel's vision of the valley of the dry bones. "And he said unto me, Son of man, can these bones live? And I answered, O Lord God, thou knowest. . . ." Ezek 37:3. FROM THE DORÉ BIBLE.

Cheering God and Men

Wine not only "maketh glad the heart of man," but also "cheereth God" (Judg 9:13; Psa 104:15).

Wine, one of the blessings of God and one of the riches of Israel, is mentioned well over a hundred times in the Bible, not counting more than thirty references to drinking it and many mentions of vines, vineyards, grapes, "the blood of the grape," and various aspects of drunkenness.

In the original Hebrew, several different words were used for wine to indicate its quality, the region of origin—such as "wine of Helbon" (Ezek 27:18)—and whether it was new or old wine. Yet archaeologists have discovered that these were only a few of the names used in biblical times. Many others have turned up in other ancient records and on the seals of wine jugs in Palestinian digs.

Most wine was made from grapes, but dates, pomegranates, apples, and other fruits were also used. Herbs and spices were added for color, taste, or medicinal properties (pomegranate wine was especially popular as medicine). Ordinarily wine was diluted with water for drinking, although Isaiah (1:22) obviously disapproved of this—he compared it to silver reduced to dross.

Drinking wine gave one a "merry heart" (Gen 43:34; Judg 9:27; Ruth 3:7; 1 Sam 25:36; 2 Sam 13:28; Zech 10:7; etc.). Solomon, who said the roof of a lover's mouth was like the best wine "that goeth down sweetly," twice implied that the only thing to top wine was love (S of S 1:2; 4:10; 7:9).

The importance of wine in Hebrew life is seen in its frequent listing, with food and oil, as a necessity. To have no wine was a great deprivation. Lack of preservation methods for most foods meant that wine was vital in travel, during siege, or during any emergency that deprived people of milk or water (Deut 28:8; Josh 9:13; 2 Chr 22:28; Jer 50:26; etc.).

Why Drink?

Wine was perceived to have a certain amount of self-revelatory benefit. The Bible speaks of giving oneself "unto wine" to acquire wisdom (Eccl 2:3) and says, "Thou hast made us to drink the wine of astonishment" (Psa 60:3; Ezek 23:33).

Wine was also useful for forgetting. The poor and the bitter were urged to drink to forget poverty and misery (Prov 31:7).

THE VINEYARD OF THE LORD

From the earliest books of the Bible, wine was prominent in pictures of the happy life. When God promised the chosen people they would have money to spend on whatever they desired, the order of the first four items Hebrews were thought to desire was oxen, sheep, wine, and strong drink (Deut 14:26).

God would make "a feast of wines," promised Isaiah in his messianic vision. "In that day sing ye unto her, a vineyard of red wine" (Isa 25:6; 27:2). Even people without money would be able to buy wine; "the stranger shall not drink thy wine," God promised, but the Hebrews would drink their own wine "in the courts of my holiness" (Isa 55:1; 62:8-9). In fact, Israel was "the vineyard of the Lord" (Isa 5:1-7).

No party was complete without wine: "A feast is made for laughter, and wine maketh merry" (Eccl 10:19). A good party consisted of harp, viol, and other music—plus wine—said Isaiah: "let us eat and drink; for tomorrow we shall die" (Isa 5:12; 22:13).

"They have no wine," Mary pointed out to Jesus, when they attended a wedding at Cana, and Jesus promptly performed the first miracle—turning water into wine to make the festivities complete. One of the few amusing passages in the Bible follows—the bridegroom is chastised because everyone knows you should put out your good wine first and then when everyone is drunk serve the rotgut, yet here the bridegroom had served the good wine last (John 2:1-9).

Wine (often with bread) was a symbol of hospitality that was routinely offered guests, and was imperative when one wanted to do honor (Gen 14:18; Judg 19:19). When Abigail wanted to placate David, she included wine among her gifts (1 Sam 25:18). Ziba, wishing to impress David after the king had been driven from Jerusalem, brought him bread, fresh fruit, and wine (2 Sam 16:2).

To own your own vineyard was symbolic of prosperity. Thus, when the Assyrians were trying to convince Jerusalem to surrender, they pictured the ideal life that awaited Jews in Mesopotamia as "every man under his own vine" (1 Kings 4:25; 2 Kings 18:31).

The kings of Israel and Judah had large vineyards and they also collected wine as a form of taxation (1 Chr 12:40; 27:27; 2 Chr 11:11). Before then, Solomon had used wine as part of the payment given to the workers who built his Temple (2 Chr 2:10).

An Old Southern Story

A revenue officer caught a bootlegger with a lot of jugs in his truck and asked what was in them.

"Water," said the bootlegger.

The officer didn't believe him and opened one of the jugs to taste it.

"Looks like wine," he said, "and tastes exactly like wine."

"Lord, Lord," cried the bootlegger. "Jesus has done it again!"

A SWEET SAVOUR UNTO THE LORD

Throughout the Middle East, wine was an important part of cultic worship, and among the Hebrews it also had sacred uses.

Because wine was said to have "a sweet savour unto the Lord," it was part of the offering made during animal sacrifice and was offered during daily, monthly, and holy-day ceremonies (Ex 29:40; Lev 23:13; Num 15:5–7; 28:14). The amount of wine offered varied with the animal being sacrificed. Wine was measured by the hin (about a gallon), and half a hin was offered with a bullock, a third with a ram, and a quarter of a hin with a lamb. Unlike wine for ordinary drinking, which was frequently watered down, sacrificial wine was not to be diluted. Priests obtained wine as part of the regular payments of first fruits the people had to make to sustain the priests (Deut 18:4).

Wine was also used during blessings. Bread and wine were produced for the blessing of Abraham by the high priest (Gen 14:18–19). Isaac brought out wine when he blessed Jacob, and his blessing included "plenty of corn and wine" (Gen 27:24–28). Jacob, in turn, blessed Judah with a hope for so

289

much wine that he would wash "his garments in wine, and his clothes in the blood of grapes: His eyes shall be red with wine" (Gen 49:11-12).

In the New Testament wine became symbolic of the blood of Jesus (Matt 26:27-29; Luke 22:17-20).

Because of its sacred aspect, wine made by pagans was sometimes disapproved of in the Bible (Deut 32:33; Rev 17:2; 18:3), although imported wines became popular, especially under Greek rule, and many foreign wine jugs have been found in excavations in Israel.

Cold Sober

"Only her lips moved" when Hannah went to the temple to pray for a son, but since no sound came out, the high priest accused her of being drunk. "Put away thy wine from thee," he ordered. Hannah protested she had had neither wine nor strong drink, and was only sorrowing. The high priest did not exactly apologize for his error but he did promise that her petition would be granted (1 Sam 1:13-16).

On the day of Pentecost, when the Apostles were gathered to pray, "they were all filled with the Holy Ghost, and began to speak with other tongues." People in Jerusalem hearing this were amazed and mocked them, saying, "These men are full of new wine." Peter pointed out it was too early in the day to be drunk, and that it was only the prophecies of Joel being fulfilled (Acts 2:1-16).

FIREWATER

Wine was pleasant enough, and one could even get thoroughly drunk on it, but in addition the Hebrews felt a need for "strong drink." As Proverbs (31:6) described the distinction, wine was good enough for men "of heavy hearts," but strong drink was needed for those that were "ready to perish."

The ingredients of strong drink have not yet been identified. It might have been a drink distilled from grain and possibly borrowed from the Egyptians, who made an intoxicating beverage from barley. It might have been a pomegranate wine fortified with drugs, because the Song of Solomon (8:2) speaks of a special "drink of spiced wine of the juice of my pomegranate." Wines made from palm and honey have also been suggested.

Heavy drinkers had a choice of wines laced with drugs. At least some of these drugs were derived from the incense-tree family, as the New Testament mentions gall and myrrh being added as sedatives for those undergoing crucifixion (Matt 27:34; Mark 15:23). Wormwood may have also been used: "He hath filled me with bitterness, he hath made me drunken with wormwood" (Luke 3:15).

Drugged wine—sometimes called "mingled" or "mixed" wine in the Bible—was not consistently approved (Prov 9:1-2, 5; 23:30-32). However, in one passage, God is described as dispensing it: "For in the hand of the Lord there is a cup, and the wine is red; it is full of mixture" (Psa 75:8). This was the drink God poured for the righteous, while the dregs were left for "the wicked of the earth." Some of the wine jugs found by archaeologists in the Holy Land had strainers in the spout, indicating there was plenty of sediment to remove before drinking.

There's a Tavern in the Town

The joyful description of being taken by one's lover into the "banqueting house" (S of S 2:4) is mistranslated from the original Hebrew; the phrase meant a wine house or tavern. Isaiah's description of a tavern is not as exuberant—he speaks of people throwing up all over the tables (Isa 28:8). The corner bar was one of the earliest public establishments in the Holy Land, and excavations at Tell en-Nasbeh—one of the few Israelite towns preserved *in toto*—show that many homes had their own winepresses.

SONG OF THE DRUNKARDS

"Winebibbers" were classed with gluttons and condemned in both Old and New Testaments (Deut 21:20; Prov 23:20; Matt 11:19; 24:49; Luke 7:34; 12:45; 21:34): "For the drunkard and glutton shall come to poverty" (Prov 23:21). Wicked women were said to "love flagons of wine," drinking it by the jugful (Hos 3:1).

"I was the song of the drunkards" (Psa 69:12), meaning that even drunks derided the psalmist, indicates the contempt in which overimbibers were held.

Addiction to wine was naturally a danger. "Woe unto them," said Isaiah (5:11), that started with strong drink in the morning and continued drinking until night. Such a man "transgresseth by wine," never staying home, "enlarging his desire as hell, and is as death; and cannot be satisfied" (Hab 2:5).

291

Paul was especially hard on drunks. He not only repeatedly warned, "Be not drunk with wine," but classed drunkards with thieves, extortioners, fornicators, and murderers. He spoke of walking "in lasciviousness, lusts, excess of wine, revellings, banquetings, and abominable idolatries." Not only were drunkards barred from entry into the kingdom of God, but Paul warned members of the Corinthian church to refrain even from sharing a meal with them. However, he had nothing against wine in general and even recommended it "for thy stomach's sake" (1 Cor 5:11; 6:10; 11:21; Gal 5:21; Eph 5:18; 1 Tim 3:3, 8; 5:23; 1 Pet 4:3).

Tottering in Judgment: Because alcohol clouds judgment, it was not good for kings and other authorities to drink wine while on duty. They would then forget the Law and pervert justice, "reel in vision" and "totter in judgment" (Prov 31:4; Isa 28:1-8). A king "sick with bottles of wine" associated with the wicked (Hos 7:5).

Power in the hands of drunks was dangerous, as proved by Babylon, which had been "a golden cup in the Lord's hand" and made all the earth drunk so that every nation ended up "mad" (Jer 51:7).

As a result, one of God's curses was that "Every bottle shall be filled with wine," so that all of a nation's princes, wise men, prophets, mighty men, priests—even the entire population—would get drunk. Then they would "sleep a perpetual sleep, and not wake," because "while they are drunken as drunkards, they shall be devoured" (Jer 13:12-14; 51:39, 57; Nah 1:10).

Boozing It Up

Wine did not give everyone a "merry heart." It made some people languish and feel mournful, so that even "the merryhearted do sigh"—and strong drink made one bitter (Isa 24:6-7, 9, 11). One could even be filled with such sorrow as to suck the empty cup and finally smash it (Ezek 23:33-34). Among other bad reactions:

1. People became shameless, lost modesty, and were seen naked (Gen 9:21; Lam 4:21; Hab 2:15-16).

2. Wine gave people red eyes and made them "behold strange women" (Prov 23:29, 33).

3. Drinkers babbled and uttered "perverse things" (Prov 23:29, 33).

4. Drinkers became careless and got thorns in their hands (Prov 26:9).

5. New wine and, worst of all, strong drink could make men lose heart and sap their strength (Isa 5:22; 63:6; Hos 4:11).

6. Wine made people so dizzy it was like lying down "in the

midst of the sea" or swinging from "the top of a mast" (Prov 23:34). "The earth shall reel to and fro like a drunkard" said Isaiah (24:20), and staggering like a drunken man was a popular image applied to being at sea in a storm (Job 12:25; Psa 107:27; Isa 19:14; 28:1-8; 29:9).

7. The shakes are mentioned as "trembling" (Isa 17:20). Most vivid was Jeremiah (23:9), who, describing himself as a drunken man, said, "All my bones shake."

8. Drunks who passed beyond the stage of derision became disgusting and wallowed in their vomit: "For all tables are full of filthy vomit, and no place is clean" (Isa 19:14; 28:1-8; Jer 48:26). A man at this point was hardly redeemable: "Drink ye, and be drunken, and spue, and fall, and rise no more" (Jer 25:27).

Raging Drunk: Violence was one of the less attractive results of drink, and it was especially liable to occur with strong drink: "Wine is a mocker, strong drink is raging" (Prov 20:1). Wine and strong drink inflamed people, caused violence, and even led to rioting (Prov 4:17; Isa 5:11; Rom 13:13).

As a result, the fury of God and man was equated with drink: "Then the Lord awakened as one out of sleep, and like a mighty man that shouteth by reason of wine" (Psa 78:65). In such a state, God said, "Take this cup of this fury at my hand, and cause all the nations . . . to drink it" (Jer 25:15).

"I will make mine arrows drunk with blood," said Moses (Deut 32:42). Swords could also be made drunk, and people could be drunk with blood "as with sweet wine" (Isa 49:26; Jer 46:10; Ezek 39:19).

Teetotalers

In the Old Testament, abstention from wine and strong drink was occasionally required for religious reasons. Priests who were officiating at the Tabernacle were supposed to abstain from wine or strong drink (Lev 10:9).

Nazarites—men or women who consecrated their lives or a period of their lives to the service of God—not only refrained from wine but even from eating fresh or dried grapes (Num 6:3).

Rechabites also were teetotalers. The Rechabites, descendants of Rechab, were a group that believed in the return to the austerity of nomadic life. They lived in tents rather than houses, and would not plant crops or vineyards or drink wine (Jer 35).

Manoah's wife, who was to give birth to Samson, was told by an angel to refrain from wine and strong drink during her pregnancy, as both she and her child were to take the vow of the Nazarite (Judg 13:4–14).

Apparently also as a sign of consecrating his life to God, John the Baptist did not drink intoxicating beverages: "For he shall be great in the sight of the Lord, and shall drink neither wine nor strong drink" (Luke 1:15; 7:33).

The custom of abstention as a sign of a godly life lapsed in New Testament times. Because abstention was unusual, and the Bible remarks on it for John but not for Jesus, it is probably safe to assume Jesus drank wine. He certainly had nothing against it, as he turned water into wine. Other evidence that bread and wine were probably a routine part of meals is that the disciples were not surprised to see these at the Last Supper and the Bible does not describe them as special. In fact, it was probably because they were so ordinary that Jesus made them symbols.

At the Last Supper, Jesus held out the cup of wine and said, "Take this, and divide it among yourselves." Jesus drank none: "I will not drink of the fruit of the vine, until the Kingdom of God shall come." This was because Jesus was using wine, like bread, as a sacred symbol: "For this is my blood of the new testament, which is shed for many for the remission of sins"—"This cup is the new testament in my blood, which is shed for you." His abstention at this meal therefore was not intended as disapproval of wine, because Jesus promised "to drink it new with you in my Father's Kingdom" (Matt 26:27–29; Luke 22:17–20).

Awake Ye Drunkards, and Weep!

1. Lot was raped by his daughters after he let them get him drunk two nights running. They did this because they were hiding out in a cave in the mountains, with no one else around, and they feared Lot's seed would not be preserved. Lot was so soused he never noticed them lie down or get up, and the Bible doesn't record his reaction when he discovered they were pregnant (Gen 19:30–36).

2. Boaz was more or less trapped into marriage by getting drunk. Ruth waited until "his heart was merry" and he finally passed out on a heap of corn, and then she crept up softly and lay down beside him. In the middle of the night, when he turned over and found her, his groggy mind decided he should be flattered she had not chosen a younger man, and he called her "a virtuous woman" and promised to marry her. Obviously he was too drunk

for any sexual overtures, and she outfoxed him by getting up before he came to in the morning (Ruth 3:7–14).

3. After Abigail had given away a generous part of her husband's provisions, she wanted to tell him what she had done. But Nabal's heart was "merry within him"—in fact, "he was very drunken"—and she wasn't able to tell him until morning. By then "the wine was gone out of Nabal," and the news was too much on top of a hangover, so he dropped dead "as a stone" (1 Sam 25:36–37).

4. When Absalom wanted to avenge the rape of his sister Tamar by Amnon, he had his men wait until Amnon had lost his caution by drinking. As soon as Amnon's heart was "merry with wine," Absalom's men slew him (2 Sam 13:28).

5. Uriah let David get him drunk and David got Bathsheba (2 Sam 11:13).

6. King Elah of Israel ruled barely two years, because he was assassinated while getting drunk (1 Kings 16:9).

7. "Ben-hadad was drinking himself drunk in the pavilions" when he and thirty-two allied kings were supposed to be besieging Samaria. They started drinking so early in the day that one day when the Samaritans charged them at noon they were too drunk to resist and had to flee (1 Kings 20:12–19).

8. When Nehemiah wanted to leave Babylon and return to Jerusalem, he waited until King Artaxerxes had been softened up with a little wine before making his request—and it was granted (Neh 2:1).

9. The heart of Ahasuerus, king of Persia, was so "merry with wine" after seven days of drinking at a celebration he was giving himself that he ordered the queen brought in. Men and women were supposed to drink separately, but he got it into his head he should show the queen off to all his drunken male guests. The queen refused to come. Ahasuerus was "very wroth, and his anger burned in him" so that he banished her and got a new queen (Est 1:3–12).

10. Job's sons and daughters were so busy "eating and drinking wine" that they failed to notice a great wind storm coming up, and they were all killed (Job 1:13–18).

11. King Bel-shazzar of Babylon gave a huge feast for a thousand of his lords along with his wives and concubines. After they'd been drinking awhile, the king got the idea they should drink out

of the gold and silver vessels his father had taken from the Temple of Jerusalem. They drank some more, drinking long enough to praise the gods of gold, of silver, of brass, of iron, of wood, and finally the gods of stone. It was at this point the king saw a man's hand writing on the palace wall (Dan 5:1-5).

Slavery

Slavery was common throughout the Middle East. Pyramids and temples in Egypt were built by slaves, and the Hebrews had helped to construct a new capital for Rameses II during their bondage there. In Mesopotamia slavery was also common and was regulated by the Code of Hammurabi.

Israelite laws on slavery were somewhat complicated because they distinguished between Hebrew slaves and non-Hebrew slaves. Basically the difference was that foreigners were enslaved for life. Hebrews were supposed to be enslaved only temporarily, although they could voluntarily agree to lifetime bondage. In the case of either foreigners or Hebrews, however, children born in bondage remained the property of the master rather than of the parents.

A slave was defined as "a possession" that could be bought and sold (Ex 12:44; Lev 25:44–46; Eccl 2:7), but there were many laws that attempted to ensure that slaves were well treated. The Hebrew words for slaves (translated as "servants") meant "to serve" or "to attend," and were the same words use for a king's subjects, tributary nations, and in expressions such as "servants of God."

The proportion of slaves in the population can only be guessed at—in part because so many slaves were theoretically only temporarily in bondage, and in part because figures are seldom given. In the Bible exact numbers are given only from the time of Nehemiah; when the Israelites returned to Jerusalem after the Exile in Babylon, there were 42,360 free people and 7337 slaves (Neh 7:66). Earlier, most women of substance had at least one handmaid (Gen 16:1; 30:3, 9).

THE SLAVE TRADE

Foreign slaves were obtained through capture in war or bought on the slave market.

Enslaving foreign captives was known from the time of Moses. At first male captives were slain and only virgins were kept (Num 15:18; 31:25–35), but later male adults and children were enslaved too (2 Sam 8:2). However, kidnapping someone to be a slave in time of peace was outlawed (Ex 21:16; Deut 24:7).

After the wars of conquest, slaves had to be bought. Some came along the trade routes: Joseph was sold by his brothers for twenty pieces of silver to traveling merchants who took him to Egypt for resale (Gen 37:28). But the largest trading was carried on at Tyre by the Phoenicians, who imported people from Asia Minor and elsewhere (Ezek 27:13; Amos 1:6, 9). Although Amos says Gaza also had slave traffic, Tyre remained the major port, and when the people of Judah were themselves enslaved they were exported from Tyre (Joel 4:6).

Value of Life

A slave was probably worth thirty shekels, as this is the compensation you had to pay a slave owner if his slave was gored by your bull (Ex 21:32), and this is also the price Judas got for betraying Jesus (Matt 26:15).

How Hebrews Became Slaves

1. A man unable to support himself could sell himself to another Hebrew or to a non-Hebrew (Ex 21:2; Lev 25:39, 47).

2. A man who ran up debts could be enslaved by his creditors to work off the debt in labor (Lev 25:39; Deut 15:2–3; Job 24:9).

3. A thief who was caught and who was unable to make the restitution required by law could be enslaved until he had paid off in labor the equivalent amount owed (Ex 22:1–7).

4. Children whose parents ran up debts could be enslaved by creditors (2 Kings 4:1; Neh 5:5; Isa 50:1).

5. Children born while their parents were slaves were the property of the owner (Ex 21:4).

6. A woman could be sold as a slave by her father (Ex 21:7).

State Slaves: From the earliest days, foreigners were put into bondage to care for the Temple. The first mention of this is when Joshua enslaved the Gibeonites in retaliation for their having deceived him (Josh 9:23, 27). Temple slaves existed up to the Exile, and even returned from Babylon to take up their duties again in the days of Nehemiah (Neh 7:57-60; 11:3). It was probably King David who expanded state slavery to secular work, because the Bible indicates that he forced the Ammonites to make bricks and do construction work (2 Sam 12:31). However, it was Solomon who established state slavery on a large scale, using Canaanite descendants and other non-Hebrews for his building projects at Jerusalem, Megiddo, and elsewhere, for his fleet, and for his mining operations (1 Kings 9:15-27; 2 Chr 8:18).

TREATMENT OF SLAVES

Slaves were treated as members of the family and therefore had to be circumcised, whether they were Hebrews or foreigners (Gen 17:12-13). Slaves rested on the Sabbath and took part in rituals and festivals (Ex 12:44; 20:10; 23:12; Deut 5:14; 12:12, 18; 16:11, 14).

Job (31:13) implies that slaves could be contentious, and Proverbs (29:19) advises: "A servant will not be corrected by words: for though he understand he will not answer." That slaves were beaten is plain from references to "rods" and from the law requiring them to be set free if they lost a tooth or an eye (Ex 21:26-27). A master who killed a slave was to be punished; however, it was assumed that a master would not do this deliberately—because the slave "is his money"—and if the slave lived several days before dying of the beating the master was not punished (Ex 21:20-21).

Although adultery was usually punishable by death, a female slave was only whipped for this offense, on the supposition she had had little choice in the matter (Lev 19:20). A female slave could be married off by her master, but she and his children remained his property (Ex 21:4).

Female slaves worked in the house as attendants to the wife, as nurses to the children, or as concubines. Men apparently helped with agricultural chores. They were naturally assigned the lowest form of work, so that a form of humility for nonslaves was to propose to do a slave's job. When Abigail was asked to be the wife of David, she replied, "Behold, let thine handmaid be a servant to wash the feet of the servants of my lord" (1 Sam 25:41). For this reason, Peter was stunned when Jesus washed the feet of the disciples (John 13:5-8).

Slaves that were born in the house were apparently treated much better than other slaves—Proverbs (29:21) suggests they became almost like the master's own sons. Jeremiah also implies that homeborn slaves were "spoiled" (Jer 2:14).

Hebrew slaves were to be treated better than foreign slaves, and were to be considered on a level with wage earners and free foreign residents (Lev 25:39-40). Some scholars believe Hebrew slaves may have been allowed to own property. Evidence for this is that Saul's slave had a bit of money (1 Sam 9:7-8). The issue is more confusing in the case of Ziba, a slave who served as steward to Saul's family. The Bible says Ziba had twenty slaves of his own, yet "all that dwelt in the house of Ziba were servants unto Mephibosheth" (2 Sam 9:10, 12). This may mean that slaves were allowed to control slaves and other property but that true ownership remained with the slave owner.

When Elisha's slave Gehazi managed to come by money and clothes through deceit, he tried to hide these from Elisha. Here it is unclear whether he didn't want Elisha to know of the goods themselves, or whether he was concerned only about Elisha discovering the deceit involved, but in either case there is no doubt Gehazi thought he could own property. However, when Elisha found out, he punished Gehazi severely, indicating that rights of slaves were at the pleasure of their masters (2 Kings 5:20-27).

Although slaves were treated more kindly in Israel than in many other places where slavery existed, runaway slaves were a problem. Two servants were runaways in the time of Solomon (1 Kings 2:39-40), and in the time of David "many servants" were said to flee (1 Sam 25:10).

Branding Slaves

In Mesopotamia, slaves were sometimes branded with a hot iron or tattoo or other symbol of ownership. This practice may have been limited to those who had tried to run away. Among the Hebrews branding is not mentioned. Slaves who volunteered to remain slaves for life had their ears pierced against the doorway of the master's house; this was not branding, but symbolic of the fact they belonged to the house forever (Ex 21:6; Deut 15:17).

Bondsmen Forever: Foreign slaves were "bondsmen forever," and were handed down with other property as part of a man's inheritance to his children (Lev 25:46). As time went on, the number of foreign slaves increased, because their children automatically became slaves at birth.

A female prisoner of war had a chance of emancipation if she could get her master or her master's son to marry her. Such a marriage made her a free woman, and even if she were later divorced she remained free (Deut 21:10-14). However, she could also be kept as a concubine, in which case she remained a slave.

The only other way a foreign slave could be emancipated was if he was badly enough injured to lose an eye or a tooth (Ex 21:26-27)—a law apparently made to prevent physical mistreatment.

A master could, of course, voluntarily free a slave, but the only instance of this in the Bible was when Abraham reluctantly "freed" Hagar because Sarah didn't want her around (Gen 21:1–14).

There is one case of a Hebrew who had no sons and who therefore married his daughter to his Egyptian slave, apparently freeing him (1 Chr 2:34–35). Abraham also indicated that had he had no son, his heir would have been his child born of a foreign slave (Gen 15:3).

EMANCIPATION

With the exceptions noted under Bondsmen Forever, foreign slaves could not be freed. Hebrew slaves, however, had several ways of being emancipated:

Jubilee Year: In the Jubilee Year, which came every fifty years, all Hebrew slaves were supposed to be freed (Lev 25:40 41). However, this was apparently an ideal law and scholars can find no evidence that it was ever applied.

Seventh Year: The law said that a Hebrew slave who had been bought was to serve six years and be freed in the seventh year (Ex 21:1; Deut 15). The only exception to this was a woman who had been sold as a concubine (Ex 21:7). If a slave declined to be set free in the seventh year, he became a slave for life (Ex 21:6; Deut 15:16–17).

Redeemed: A slave put in bondage for debt was redeemed when his debt was paid. He could work off the debt in time and labor or in money (in the unlikely case he had a sudden windfall), or a relative could redeem him by paying his debt for him. The woman whose two children were threatened by a creditor kept them from slavery after Elisha helped her raise the money to pay off the debt (2 Kings 4:1–7). This law supposedly applied whether the slave was owned by a Hebrew or a non-Hebrew, but of course there was no way to enforce it outside the kingdom's boundaries (Lev 25:47–53). The price of redemption was figured on the yearly wages of a hired hand.

Set Free: A woman who had been bought as a concubine could demand to be set free if the master tired of her and, after replacing her with another woman, failed to treat her properly (Ex 21:7–11).

Despite the above rules for redemption, scholars believe few slaves did go free again. Most of them had been enslaved because of poverty, so their chances of being self-sustaining again were not very good. The provision that a slave could voluntarily agree to stay for life suggests that many slaves were afraid to go out again on their own, or were reluctant to leave their wives and children.

In addition, Jeremiah (34) says that masters did not obey the law to liberate their slaves after seven years. When a Hebrew slave was freed, he was not to "go away empty" but furnished "liberally out of thy flock, and out of thy floor, and out of thy winepress," because Hebrews were to remember their bondage in Egypt (Deut 15:13–15). This may have been an ideal, but apparently it was seldom lived up to. When Abraham released Hagar, he gave her only bread and a bottle of water, though this stinginess may have been because she was a foreigner. The Old Testament provides no other instances of anyone freeing a slave. Jeremiah suggests that far from providing well for freed slaves, masters only pretended to release them at the end of seven years. Then they went right out after them and forced them back to servitude (Jer 34:10–16).

By the Skin of My Teeth

1. The king of Sodom escaped attackers by hiding in slime pits (Gen 14:9–11).

2. Moses made an escape after he had killed an Egyptian taskmaster who had been beating Israelites. The story got around, and Moses realized it would be only a matter of time before he was caught for this murder, so he fled to safety in Midian (Ex 2).

3. David had several close calls. When King Saul became so jealous of David's popularity that he wanted to kill him, he threw a spear at David. David neatly sidestepped the javelin so that it went harmlessly into the wall, and he made his escape (1 Sam 19:10).

The next day, Saul sent messengers to fetch David. Michal, David's wife, lowered him out of a window. Then, to give him time to get away, she put a large idol in his bed and befuddled the messengers by pretending David was too sick to go to Saul. When the messengers returned to Saul, he refused to take illness as an excuse and demanded David be brought to him—bed and all. David was far away by the time Saul discovered the figure in the bed was only an idol (1 Sam 19:11–18).

Still in flight from Saul, David found himself at Gath, where the king was none too pleased to have such a popular folk hero around. To get out of this jam, David pretended to be crazy (1 Sam 21:10–15).

4. Later, when David was king and Absalom was trying to depose him, two of David's messengers, Jonathan and Ahimaaz, pursued by Absalom's men, were hidden in a well by a woman who

sympathized with David. To be sure that they would not be found by Absalom's search party, the woman "spread a covering over the well's mouth" and then spread ground corn on top of it to disguise it. When Absalom's men arrived, she sent them off in the wrong direction, enabling David's men to escape (2 Sam 17:17-21).

5. After Ehud stabbed the Moabite king Eglon while they were alone together, Ehud slipped out and locked the door to the king's chamber behind him. Eglon's servants were afraid to open the door, thinking the king "covereth his feet" (a euphemism meaning he was on the toilet). By the time they got up the nerve to unlock the door, the king was dead and Ehud was long gone (Judg 3:23-26).

6. When calamities began to befall Job's household, four men had narrow escapes, First, the Sabeans attacked the herdsmen, and one man escaped. Then God sent a fire from heaven, consuming all the shepherds except one. Then the Chaldeans arrived on camels to carry off all but one of the servants. Finally a storm destroyed the house, and again only one person escaped (Job 1:14-19).

7. When Nebuchadnezzar breached the walls of Jerusalem, the king and many of the warriors escaped through a secret gate next to the king's garden. The king pursued and captured them, but many of the army got away (2 Kings 25:1-5).

8. To escape Herod's edict—that all male children under two years of age were to be killed—Joseph took Mary and the baby Jesus to Egypt (Matt 2:13).

9. One winter in Jerusalem, Jesus was threatened with stoning by people gathered for the Feast of Dedication. Although the Bible does not explain how, it does report that Jesus "escaped out of their hand" (John 10:22-39).

10. "A certain young man" who was following Jesus at the time of the betrayal by Judas was dressed in a "linen cloth cast about his naked body." When the men who had grabbed Jesus tried also to take hold of this young man (some the scholars believe this was Mark), "he left the linen cloth, and fled from them naked" (Mark 14:51-52).

Prisons

Even though at least eleven Hebrew words have been translated as "prison" in the Bible, no biblical laws specify any crime for which imprisonment is the punishment.

Locking people up appears to be an idea that grew gradually among the Hebrews and that may have been borrowed from neighbors. Although temporary detention of people awaiting trial occurred as early as the Exodus, a jail is not mentioned until the reign of King Ahab of Israel (871–852 BC).

Under the early laws, crimes were defined as defiance against God's authority. Since crimes were violations of God's commandments, they were punishable either by death or just recompense, as set out in the Books of the Law. After the laws were written, a new authority came into existence—the monarchy. The old laws did not cover violations of the king's will. The early kings resolved the problem of crimes against the state by killing opponents. But by the time of Ahab a new compromise had been reached: Opponents of the monarchy were subject to death, banishment, confiscation of goods, or imprisonment for disobeying the law of God *or* "the law of the king" (Ezra 7:26).

An analysis of who was imprisoned demonstrates that in every case the crime was not against God's commandments but against those of the king and the state.

Who Was Jailed and Why

Joseph: (falsely) accused of raping the wife of an official (Gen 39:7–19).

Joseph's brothers: (falsely) accused of being spies in Egypt (Gen 42).

Samson: political enemey of Philistines (Judg 16:24).

Hanani: prophesied doom for King Asa (2 Chr 16:10).

Macaiah: prophesied defeat and death for King Ahab (1 Kings 22:26–27).

King Hoshea: defied Assyrian authority (2 Kings 17:4).

King Jehoiachin: defied Babylonian authority (2 Kings 25:27–30).

King Zedekiah: defied Babylonian authority (2 Kings 25:6 7).

Jeremiah: prophesied destruction of kingdom (Jer 37–38).

John the Baptist: denounced Herod's marriage to Herodias (Matt 14:3–5; Mark 6:17–20; Luke 3:19–20).

Peter: preached the gospel (Acts 4:3; 12:3–10).

Paul: preached the gospel (Acts 16:16–24; 23:10 ff.).

In Jail Abroad: Evidently the Egyptians had a form of jail, because Joseph was locked up in one (Gen 39:20–41:45). But they were so rare that the author of Genesis feels called on to define a prison as "a place where the king's prisoners are bound." This jail is called a dungeon, probably meaning that it was underground. However, it was not a special building but a reserved area "in the house of the captain of the guard."

Joseph was not alone there, and in fact was put in charge of his fellow prisoners. Whether they were chained or shackled is not clear, because the word "bound" may only have referred to being locked up. There must have been some freedom of movement, because Joseph was made responsible for whatever the prisoners did.

When Joseph's brothers, who had mocked him as a youth, arrived in Egypt, he accused them of being spies and put them all "into ward" three days. Then he released all but his brother Simeon, whom he kept as a hostage until the others proved themselves trustworthy. This jail, again, does not seem to have been a separate penal institution but was in or near the home of Joseph's steward (Gen 42–43:24).

Egyptian prisoners of war were apparently also kept in dungeons, because when God smote the firstborn of Egypt this included even "the firstborn of the captive that was in the dungeon" (Ex 12:29).

Among the Mesopotamians, Shalmaneser of Assyria had prisons, one of which contained King Hosea of Israel (2 Kings 17:4). And Nebuchadnezzar had a prison in Babylon where King Jehoiachin of Judah was kept captive for thirty-seven years (2 Kings 24:12, 15; 25:27-30; Jer 52:31-33). His successor, King Zedekiah, was blinded after attempting to rebel against Nebuchadnezzar, and languished in a Babylonian jail until his death (Jer 52:11).

Guard Duty: The first recorded instances of imprisonment among the Hebrews are described as putting a person "in ward" (Lev 24:12-23; Num 15:32-36). This was done to a man who blasphemed and to another who had gathered sticks on the Sabbath, and both were cases of temporary detainment until they were executed. To be put "in ward" may have meant only that the offender was bound or somehow restrained from escaping. Possibly he was kept in a cave since at this time the Israelites were in the wilderness. Because the word "ward" is also used in the Bible to mean guard (1 Chr 12:29; Neh 12:25; Isa 21:8; Jer 37:13), it is likely that "in ward" meant simply "under guard."

King David kept ten of his concubines "in ward." As the Bible describes it, this meant they were kept in the palace and fed, but were confined to some isolated area of the palace where they saw no one.

What the Fool Does

1. uttereth slander (Prov 10:18)
2. foldeth his hands (Eccl 4:5)
3. does mischief and thinks it sport (Prov 10:23)
4. rageth and is confident (Prov 14:16)
5. hath no delight in understanding (Prov 18:2)
6. despiseth his father's instructions (Prov 15:5)
7. is contentious (Prov 18:6)
8. meddles (Prov 20:3)
9. walketh in darkness (Eccl 2:14)
10. uttereth all his mind (Prov 29:11)

Prophets without Honor: The first mention of a prison in Canaan is the Philistine jail in which Samson was confined (Judg 16:21, 25): "The Philistines took him, and put out his eyes, and brought him down to Gaza, and bound him with fetters of brass; and he did grind in the prison house." This seems to have been a separate building near the temple he later demolished, or possibly a lockup in the temple itself.

King Ahab of Israel had the first Hebrew prison we know of. Its tenant was the prophet Micaiah (1 Kings 22:27; 2 Chr 18:26). For predicting Ahab's defeat and death, Micaiah was slapped across the face and then thrown in jail, where he was to be given only bread and water. Another prophet, Hanani, shared a similar fate when he told King Asa of Judah that he had acted "foolishly." Hanani too was thrown into "a prison house" (2 Chr 16:10).

Further evidence that prisons of some sort existed is also shown by the plea "Bring my soul out of prison" (Psa 142:7) and the phrase "out of prison he cometh" (Eccl 4:14). These jails were apparently underground chambers, because Isaiah speaks of prisoners being shut up "in a pit" and of sitting in darkness in a prison house; he also said people in prison were bound (Isa 24:22; 42:7, 22; 53:8; 61:1).

Nehemiah mentions a "prison gate" in Jerusalem and describes the court of the prison as being near the tower of the king's palace (Neh 3:25; 12:39). Jeremiah, who was confined in the Jerusalem prison, says it was in the palace, and provides the most extensive description (Jer 29:26; 32:2, 12; 33:1; 37:16, 21; 38:6-14, 26-28; 39:14): This prison had two levels. At first Jeremiah was held only in the "court" of the jail, apparently a ground-level area where the proceedings took place and the witnesses appeared. It had some sort of cells which the Bible calls "cabins." In the court Jeremiah did not suffer enough to remark on it, and he was given a fresh piece of bread daily.

However, Jeremiah was also put into a dungeon. The dungeon was also in the palace, at the court, but it was a private possession the king must have rented because its owner is named. It was some sort of pit in the ground into which Jeremiah was lowered with ropes, and which had a bottom of ooze. Jeremiah records it had no water, implying there had been water in the court. Because the king's eunuchs were afraid Jeremiah would die there, they obtained the king's permission to haul him out and lodge him in the court again. In the court he was allowed to have visitors, and various princes came to see him. But he was not released until Jerusalem fell and Nebuchadnezzar ordered him free.

Most people put into dungeons apparently did not survive. Lamentations (3:53) speaks of life being cut off in the dungeon, a stone being cast on the prisoner, and water flowing over the prisoner's head.

In New Testament times prison was no longer a rarity. John the Baptist was imprisoned by Herod and later beheaded there (Matt 4:12; 11:2; 14:3, 10; Mark 1:14; 6:17; Luke 3:20; John 3:24). It is unclear if this prison was in Herod's palace, but it was close enough for John's head to be brought in during Herod's party. Peter, John, Paul, Silas, and others were jailed, and putting Christians in prison soon became a "frequent" occurrence (Acts 5:18-22; 12:4-7; 16:23-27; 26:10; 2 Cor 11:23). The Bible doesn't usually make clear where these prisons were. Paul was once imprisoned in Herod's palace at Caesarea, and a "common prison" is mentioned (Acts 5:18).

People were also "bound unto the chief priests" (Acts 9:21) and some detention cells for those awaiting trial may have been in the temples. Casting people into prison is mentioned in passing and Jesus spoke of visiting people in prison (Matt 25:36; Luke 12:58; 21:12; 22:33).

In the New Testament, such crimes as sedition and murder were punished by imprisonment (Luke 23:19, 25), but confinement was probably temporary—until they came up for trial. For the first time imprisonment for debt is mentioned, and debtors were to remain in jail until their debt was paid (Matt 18:30).

Great Prison Breaks

1. Some of the Apostles were locked in prison by the high priest. During the night an angel let them out. Next day, the prison was found still locked and the guards still posted, but there was "no man within" (Acts 5:17–20, 22–23, 25).

2. Herod put Peter in jail, and for good measure bound him with chains to two soldiers so that he had to sleep between them. During the night an angel woke Peter and "his chains fell off his hands." The angel told Peter to put on his sandals, which he did, and then they got past two guard posts to the iron gate. These opened, and they passed out into the street—at which point the angel disappeared (Acts 12:4–8, 10).

3. Paul and Silas were beaten and thrown into prison. To make sure they were safely locked up, the jailer was warned to keep an eye on them, they were put in maximum security, and their feet were bound into stocks. Paul and Silas prayed and sang praises unto God. Suddenly there was a great earthquake that shook the foundations of the prison. All the prisoners' bonds were loosened and all the jail doors flew open. The jailer was about to commit suicide with his sword, assuming his charges had all escaped, when Paul stopped him by explaining that the prisoners were still there. The jailer converted on the spot and even fed the Apostles and urged them to flee. But Paul refused to go until the magistrates, obviously shaken by all this, also urged they leave the city (Acts 16:22–39).

Fit to Be Tied: Binding prisoners with cord or metal fetters was common in Old Testament times (Job 36:8). This was done routinely for prisoners of war. After Abner died, David's lamentation pointed out that he had not died "as a fool"—with his hands bound or his feet in fetters like the common captive (2 Sam 3:34).

Brass fetters were used on King Zedekiah when he was taken captive to Babylon, not because he was as strong as Samson but probably to show his importance or because cords could have been filed through on such a long journey. The same type of fetters were probably used on Kings Manasseh and Jehoiakim when they were taken to Babylon, and possible on Hoshea when he was taken captive by Assyrians (2 Kings 17:4; 25:7; 2 Chr 33:11; 36:6). Apparently fetters of iron were good enough for nobles below the rank of king (Psa 149:8).

Another way of displaying captive kings was to bind them in chains (Psa 149:8). Chains were apparently first extensively used after the fall of Jerusalem, when all of the captives taken to Babylon were chained, including Zedekiah and Jeremiah (Jer 39:7; 40:1; 52:11; Nah 3:10). However, they had been used on a limited scale earlier for prisoners of war, even by the Israelites (Psa 68:6; Isa 45:14). They were used on the hands (Jer 40:4) and on criminals as well as on kings: "Make a chain: for the land is full of bloody crimes, and the city is full of violence" (Ezek 7:23).

During Jesus' time it was customary to bind the violently insane in fetters and chains (Mark 5:4; Luke 8:29). Binding had become so common by the time of the New Testament that almost eveyone arrested, including Jesus, was bound (Matt 14:3; 27:2; Mark 6:17; 15:1; John 18:2; Acts 9:2, 21; 22:5, 25, 29). Most prisoners were subdued with rope, but Peter had been bound in two chains between two soldiers (Acts 12:7).

Stocks were another form of restraint used in Old and New Testament times, sometimes on people in prison (Job 13:27; 33:11; Jer 29:26; Acts 16:24). However, stocks were often put where crowds of people congregated so that offenders would suffer publicly. Jeremiah, for example, was humiliated by being exhibited in stocks at the city gate (Jer 20:2-3). Fools were said to go "to the correction of the stocks" (Prov 7:22).

A novel way of binding prisoners was invented by Nebuchadnezzar, who cast Daniel's friends into the fiery furnace bound in their coats and hats (Dan 3:21).

---

10 Signs of the Wicked

1. They borrow, and do not pay back (Psa 37:21).
2. They plot (Psa 37:12).
3. They walk on every side (Psa 12:8).
4. They oppress (Psa 17:9).
5. They boast (Psa 10:3).

6. They are estranged from the womb (Psa 58:3).
7. They are filled with mischief (Prov 12:21).
8. They have drawn out the sword (Psa 37:14).
9. They lay snares (Psa 119:110).
10. They have hearts like potsherds (Prov 26:23).

Cities of Refuge

In the Old Testament, one type of crime—an unintentional murder—was punishable by a unique form of imprisonment: The unwitting murderer was permitted to escape the "avenger of blood" (a member of the deceased's family responsible in common law for such revenge) by entering one of the six "cities of refuge."

These cities were set up not as asylums for people convicted of murder but for the unlucky who murdered by accident. The Law gives the example of a man who goes into the woods with a friend to cut wood. Suddenly his axhead flies off the handle and strikes his friend dead (Deut 19:5). This man could then flee to a city of refuge.

The six cities of refuge—three east and three west of the Jordan River—were to be:

1. Hebron in southern Judah (Josh 21:11; 2 Sam 5:5; 1 Chr 6:55)
2. Shechem on Mount Ephraim (Josh 21:21; 1 Chr 6:67)
3. Kedesh in Galilee (1 Chr 6:76)
4. Bezer in Moab (Deut 4:43; Josh 20:8)
5. Ramoth-gilead (Deut 4:43; Josh 21:38; 1 Kings 22:3)
6. Golan in Bashan (Deut 4:43; Josh 21:27; 1 Chr 6:71)

The cities of refuge were sprinkled around the Holy Land so that one would be easily accessible to anyone who had committed manslaughter, no matter where he lived. Special rules required that good roads and bridges had to be kept clear to these cities and that at every crossroads there had to be signs pointing to them. The Talmud says that two scholars accompanied the refugee to help him get to safety and fight off the avenger if the latter turned up on the road.

311

All this was necessary because one of the rules was that the perpetrator of manslaughter could be killed by the avengers if they overtook him before he reached the city of refuge (Num 35).

Upon reaching the gate of a city of refuge, the person who had committed manslaughter formally requested asylum from the elders. Later he was brought before the community for a trial in which he had to prove his innocence. Various passages in the Old Testament recommend specific topics and evidence that the elders were to consider before establishing innocence or guilt: premeditation; the implement of death; any previous history of malice toward the victim; etc. (Deut 19; Josh 20:1–7; Num 35:9–15). If acquitted, the refugee remained within the walls of the city of refuge until the death of the high priest. If he strayed from the refuge he could be killed by the avenger. But if the avenger turned up at the city of refuge, the population was not to hand the refugee over. This time limit assumed that grief over the death of the high priest would quell the desire for revenge, and the refugee could then return home. If, however, the refugee was found guilty of murder, not even the Temple in Jerusalem would afford asylum.

Later, the names of the six cities of refuge were applied to the characteristics of Jesus, who was seen as the final refuge of those who repented:

Hebron ("brotherhood")—referring to the brotherhood of followers.

Shechem ("shoulder")—from the passage "and the government shall be upon his shoulder" (Isa 9:6).

Kedesh ("holy")—sanctity of Jesus.

Bezer ("fortress")—Jesus seen as fortress of strength.

Ramoth ("high")—Jesus is exalted.

Golan ("joy")—Jesus brings joy.

Disease

Abhorrence of the "unclean"—according to the Law, a dead body should not be touched, and certainly not cut open for anatomical study—meant that scientific knowledge of disease was impeded in Israelite culture. Descriptions of disease in the Bible are therefore vague. Medical experts attempting to identify the diseases mentioned in the Bible have turned up between twenty-six and thirty-six illnesses, ranging from congenital blindness to leprosy to malnutrition.

Health and disease were viewed as expressions of the divinity's grace or anger—as reward or punishment. Sinners who did not obey the commandments were to be struck by God with consumption, fever, failing eyesight, inflammation, plagues, emerods, scabs, itches, incurable boils "from the sole of thy foot unto the crown of thy head," madness, bowel diseases, and other afflictions (Lev 26:14-16; Deut 28:22, 27-29, 35, 58-61).

Many examples of individuals who were diseased because of their sins are given. Moses' sister, Miriam, who had spoken against him was afflicted with leprosy (Num 12:1-15). When King Jehoram failed to follow the commandments, God promised to strike him with a bowel disease "until thy bowels fall out." Jehoram grew increasingly ill, and after two years his bowels did indeed fall out and he died (2 Chr 21:14-15, 18-19). When King Jeroboam attacked the man of God at the altar, God withered Jeroboam's hand (1 Kings 13:2-4).

God also struck entire populations with disease. The fifth and sixth plagues of Egypt were murrain (a contagious disease not yet identified) and boils (Ex 9:1-12). When the Ark was captured and taken to Ashdod, God smote the Philistines with "emerods in their secret parts" (1 Sam 5:6, 9, 12).

The Israelites themselves were punished for sin with incurable bruises and "grievous" wounds (Jer 30:12).

Usually disease was sent on God's initiative, but sometimes God acted at the request of man. When the Syrians attacked Samaria, the prophet Elisha asked that the Syrian troops be blinded, which enabled him to capture them single-handedly (2 Kings 6:14–20). Prophets apparently had the ability to inflict disease too, because Elisha struck his slave Gehazi with leprosy (2 Kings 5:27).

My Friends Stand Aloof: Because the sick were sinners, they were not looked on with sympathy. The abhorrence of the sick and dead may also have been a reaction against contagion. The idea was that contact spread "evil." Here, in vivid detail, is the plight of a syphilitic man, whose loved ones keep their distance from him:

> "For my loins are filled with a loathsome disease. . . . I am
> feeble and sore broken. . . . My lovers and my friends stand
> aloof . . . and my kinsmen stand afar off" [Psa 38:7–11].

No one with a blemish or handicap—blindness, lameness, a flat nose, with "any thing superfluous," broken hands, a hunchback, dwarfism, eye problems, scurvy, scabs, "broken stones," or with any other impairment—could go near the high altar (Lev 21:16–23). It did not matter whether these infirmities were the results of birth defects or later accidents.

The two blemishes mentioned most often are blindness (mentioned more than sixty times) and lameness. These were apparently the most common afflictions, because they are often cited together as symbolic of disease in general: "I was eyes to the blind, and feet to the lame" (Job 29:15).

Thorns in the Flesh: Because the Hebrews were for the most part uninterested in medicine, their language was imprecise. Often the Bible simply says people were weak or sick and lets it go at that. This was true into New Testament times. John (5:3) spoke vaguely of "impotent" folk (meaning disabled), and Paul was so obscure about the "thorn in the flesh" that buffeted him all his life (2 Cor 12:7) that guesses have ranged from earaches to malaria to hypochondria.

Even when the Bible attempted to define an illness, it was usually in terms of some obvious symptom. Fever, for instance, is mentioned in Old and New Testaments. But since the cause was sin, there was little interest in whether the fever was acute or recurrent, and no attempt was made to identify patterns of accompanying symptoms that might have distinguished one fever from another.

One common ailment, especially in old age, was swelling of the feet: "their clothes waxed not old, and their feet swelled not" (Neh 9:21). Such fluid accumulations are now known to be associated with heart disease and disturbances of other sorts, but the biblical world considered them simply a problem of the feet. King Asa, for example, was said to have a disease "in his feet" that became so "exceedingly great" that he died (1 Kings 15:23; 2 Chr 16:12).

Any body discharge was considered unclean, to be treated with ceremonial cleansing. It made no difference from which orifice the discharge came or whether the discharge was normal, such as menstruation (Lev 12:7; 15:19–28), or abnormal, such as the all-encompassing "a running issue out of his flesh" (Lev 15:2). In fact, if you were spit on by someone with "the issue," that made you unclean too (Lev 15:8).

Skin Deep: The most common illnesses of biblical times were skin diseases—variously translated as boils (or blains), botch, scab, scall, itch, leprosy, sores, wens, and cysts. Figuring out modern equivalents for these terms is almost impossible, because even today skin diseases continue to be reclassified; many are not diseases in themselves but symptoms of internal disorders.

Boils were nodules containing fluid. The first time they are mentioned they are the result of a divine blight. After Moses flung ashes into the air as God instructed, the Egyptians received such terrible boils that they could no longer stand (Ex 9:9–11). When Satan smote Job with boils "from the sole of his foot unto his crown," Job scraped them with a potsherd and sat in ashes to cure himself (Job 2:7–8). And when King Hezekiah got boils they were so bad he "wept sore" and was "sick unto death," but Isaiah cured them with "a lump of figs" (2 Kings 20:1–7; Isa 38:21).

Scabs were probably scaly skin diseases. Isaiah mentions such a disease attacking "the crown of the head" of women as well as "their secret parts" (Isa 3:17). It is also mentioned in the laws (Lev 13:1–8; 14:56; 21:20; 22:22), where it is explained that if the disease did not clear up in seven days it was rediagnosed as leprosy.

Leprosy was a word thrown about pretty freely by biblical authors, but the long description of the illness (Lev 13) portrays an affliction with little resemblance to what we call leprosy today. Moreover, the Bible says it was possible for houses and clothing and articles of daily use to get this leprosy too, since the Hebrew word for leprosy applied to the various sorts of molds and mildew that grew on walls, leather, and fabric (Lev 13–14).

The chronic disease known as leprosy today is believed to have existed in Egypt by at least 4000 BC. Early symptoms include numbness in the extremities or lesions on mucous membranes. However, in diagnosing biblical leprosy, the priests looked for white splotches and hairs on the skin, and loss of hair and beard. Biblical lepers often turned "white as snow" (Ex 4:6; Num 12:10; 2 Kings 5:27).

If untreated, the disease we know as leprosy results in deformities the Bible never mentions. The so-called lepers were always well enough to be walking about. The leper Naaman even headed the armies of Damascus.

Biblical leprosy could be stubborn but was curable without treatment, or with mere washing. Naaman was cured by bathing seven times in the Jordan River (2 Kings 5:1-23). Part of the purification ceremony for all lepers (Lev 14) was washing. The disease was probably some sort of skin rash or scaling—or possibly the word leprosy covered a number of such disorders.

Although leprosy is known to be mildly infectious today, the biblical variety was not considered contagious. The law did call for temporary isolation until the disorder cleared up, and this was adhered to in Old Testament times (Lev 13:46; 2 Kings 7:3, 8; 2 Chr 26:19-23). However, the banishment was for uncleanliness, and included restrictions—such as not entering the sanctuary—that also applied to blemishes considered noninfectious. Even in New Testament times lepers were not permanently segregated as they were later in history, and they mingled freely in the crowds following Jesus.

She Should Have Sued for Malpractice

One woman had been ill twelve years and "had suffered many things of many physicians, and had spent all she had, and was nothing bettered, but rather grew worse" (Mark 5:26).

CURING

No Balm in Gilead? Because disease was believed to be caused by sin, the remedy was sought in God, or in representatives of God such as priests and prophets. Although the Hebrews were well aware of physicians—they are mentioned very early in connection with Egyptians (Gen 50:2)—they apparently never attempted to develop a science of medicine for themselves. Except for midwives, neither the study of medicine nor a medical profession is ever mentioned among Hebrews until New Testament times.

Foreign physicians undoubtedly came into the courts after Solomon, when having foreigners about was an affectation of kings, but they were roundly denounced: "Forgers of lies, ye are all physicians of no value" (Job 13:4). King Asa (908–867 BC) was criticized because when he became ill "he sought not to the Lord, but to the physicians" (2 Chr 16:12).

Jeremiah remained firm in the belief that medicine was worthless—"thou hast no healing medicines" (Jer 30:13)—and that cures were with God. His famous question—"Is there no balm in Gilead; is there no physician there?"—follows passages about false teachers provoking God with graven images and "strange vanities" and is meant to show the uselessness of such foreign remedies (Jer 8:1–22). Later, Jeremiah also spoke scornfully of "the daughter of Egypt: in vain shalt thou use many medicines; for thou shalt not be cured" (Jer 46:11).

Even in the New Testament, where medicine was an acknowledged profession, physicians were an object of distrust. Two Gospels (Matt 9:12; Mark 2:17) quote Jesus as connecting disease with sin and saying, "They that be whole need not a physician." Luke, despite being called the "beloved physician," recorded the memorable line "Physician, heal thyself" (Luke 4:23).

Herbal remedies concocted by apothecaries were apparently popular in ancient Israel. Although these would have been useless for tuberculosis, poliomyelitis, and other serious illnesses known from Egyptian mummies and Palestinian skeletons to have existed in the Middle East in biblical times, they may have offered much relief for lesser afflictions.

Because unguents, oils, and other cosmetic and medicinal mixtures were one of the few items the Israelites could export to their more technologically advanced neighbors, Hebrew apothecaries became highly skilled. Their craft was called an "art" (Ex 30:25, 35; 37:29; Eccl 10:1), and there is no reason to suppose they had not discovered antiseptic and pain-killing qualities among the various vegetable substances they used. "Balm"—possibly the balm of Gilead (Jer 8:22)—was valued on the trade routes from the time of the patriarchs to the Babylonian Exile, and unless the Hebrews were exceptionally glib salesmen it must have had some merit (Gen 43:11; Ezek 27:17).

Isaiah (1:4, 5–6) speaks of wounds, bruises, and putrefying sores being "mollified with ointment" and bandaged. This method was still used in New Testament times, as the good Samaritan who found the wounded man "bound up his wounds, pouring in oil and wine" (Luke 10:33–34).

Drilling for Devils

Skulls have been found showing evidence of a rudimentary type of surgery called trepanning. Trepanning consisted of boring a hole or cutting a disk in the skull. In cases where the brain had been injured, it relieved pressure. The practitioners of this method of surgery believed it to let out any evil spirit that might have been tormenting the victim. One of three trepanned skulls found at Lachish attests to the success of this operation—the patient lived long enough for the skull to heal.

Despite the success of some herbal cures, most diseases continued to be treated with superstition. Many small cultic objects and amulets have been found by archaeologists in Palestine. Hebrews were not supposed to make or to use them, but they were popular with Canaanites, Philistines, Phoenicians, and other neighbors. Some were imported from Egypt and other countries, but many were produced locally. Among the purposes these served were warding off disease or effecting cures. The Bible records that when God punished the Philistines with emerods for stealing the Ark, they hoped for a cure by fashioning five golden mice (perhaps evidence that the Israelites knew or suspected that mice carry plague) and five golden emerods as offerings to the God of Israel (1 Sam 6:4–5).

Healing: Because of the Israelite distrust of medicine, almost all cures in the Bible are miraculous.

In the Old Testament, it is promised "the Lord will take away from thee all sickness" (Deut 7:15). This theme is often repeated: "Bless the Lord . . . who healeth all thy diseases" (Psa 103:2–3); "The Lord . . . healeth" and bindeth up wounds (Psa 147:2–3; Isa 30:26; Jer 17:14).

Often the sick did not dare ask for a cure and merely inquired of prophets whether a cure was possible. Not only Hebrews did this, but also foreigners who apparently distrusted their own gods or hoped for a reversal of opinion from the Hebrew God. Thus Ben-hadad of Damascus sent a messenger to Elisha to ask: "Shall I recover of this disease?" In this case the messenger, being told the king could recover, killed Ben-hadad (2 Kings 8:7–15).

Some Israelites struck down by sickness or injured appealed to foreign gods for salvation. When King Ahaziah of Judah fell from a second story, he sent messengers to the god of Ekron to find out if he would recover. Elijah assured him that people who consulted strange gods had no hope of cure, and Ahaziah never left his bed again until his death (2 Kings 1:2, 16–17).

Old Testament prophets were capable of healing as well as of inflicting illness. When King Jeroboam's hand was withered, he did not pray to God directly but asked the "man of God" to restore it for him (1 Kings 13:4–6). Elisha revived a dead child by stretching himself over the corpse and praying (2 Kings 4:18–37). Elisha's power did not end with his death, as a corpse put into his tomb "revived, and stood up on his feet" as soon as it touched Elisha's bones (2 Kings 13:20–21).

In the New Testament, healing is prominent among the miracles of Jesus. He healed "every sickness and every disease" (Matt 4:23–24; 9:35). Most of the diseases were those that had also been common in Old Testament times—blindness, lameness, leprosy, fever. He also cured a withered hand, paralysis, a speech impediment, and deafness; and cast out devils.

When Jesus raised the dead, it was usually by a simple verbal command—"Arise" or "Lazarus, come forth" (Luke 7:11–15; John 11:14–44). His word also cured leprosy (Luke 17:12–14) and exorcised devils (Matt 8:16, 28–32; etc.).

More common were cures by touch. Often a cure was accomplished by just a touch of the hand or a laying-on of hands, but in the case of two blind men Jesus touched their eyes (Matt 8:3, 14–15; 9:18, 24–25; 12–13; 20:30–34). Touching the hem of Jesus' garments also worked cures on people who managed to reach him through the crowds (Matt 9:20–22; 14:36). Occasionally the sick person was nowhere near Jesus, but would be cured when a relative spoke to Jesus (Matt 8:6–13; John 4:46–52).

Great Expectorations

Never was Jesus described as having used medication, but in three instances he used spit. For one blind man, Jesus spat one day and then applied the moistened clay to the eyes; the man later washed his face off in the pool of Siloam and was able to see again (John 9:6–7). Mark (8:22–25) also mentions a blind man being cured by having Jesus "spit on his eyes." For a man who was deaf and who also had a speech impediment, Jesus "put his fingers into his ears, and he spit, and touched his tongue" (Mark 7:32–35).

DEVILS AND LUNATICS

Though the Bible is replete with examples of strange behavior, much of it seems to have been tolerated and not even regarded as abnormal. If behavior became significantly aberrant, it usually ran afoul of one law or another and so tended to be classified as deliberate evildoing rather than as illness.

Nevertheless, the Bible did recognize mental illness and distinguished between depressive and manic behavior.

The Hebrew word for madman comes from a root meaning "raving," and the term was applied only to people who were noisy and violent. Among David's antics, when he pretended to be insane, were that he "scrabbled on the doors of the gate, and let his spittle fall down on his beard" (1 Sam 21:13). Proverbs (26:18) also expected a wild display: "As a mad man who casteth firebrands, arrows, and death." Jeremiah (48:2) also equated madness with violence, though Ecclesiastes (1:17; 2:12; 7:25; 9:3; 10:13) seems to limit its definition to irrationality. Madness was one of the punishments God decreed for those who failed to obey the commandments, yet the Old Testament laws do not provide any purification rites or other instruction for dealing with it (Deut 28:28).

In the New Testament the word "lunatic" occurs (Matt 17:15–18), reflecting the belief that exposure to the full moon caused insanity. Worship of the moon, as ruler of the night, was common from Mesopotamia to Egypt and was frequently condemned in the Old Testament (Deut 4:19; 2 Kings 21:3–5; 23:5; Jer 7:18; 8:2; 44:17), even though it was believed the moon could "smite" one at night (Psa 121:6). However, Matthew (4:24) hints that lunatics and those possessed by devils might be slightly different, as he lists them separately.

Depressive behavior was more tolerable. King Ahab went into a deep depression—taking to his bed, turning his face to the wall, and refusing to eat—just because Naboth wouldn't sell him a vineyard, yet the Bible never calls him mad (1 Kings 21:4).

However, King Saul, whose moods alternated between moroseness and unpredictable violent outbursts, was judged abnormal. The Bible never calls him mad, either, but explains that he was troubled by "an evil spirit" sent by God (1 Sam 16:14–15). No religious prescription was considered, and no priest called in. Instead, each time the evil spirit descended upon Saul, David was summoned to play the harp. This playing "refreshed" Saul, "and the evil spirit departed from him" (1 Sam 16:16–23; 18:10; 19:9).

In the Old Testament the word "devil" was limited to a foreign god (Lev 17:7; Deut 32:17; 2 Chr 11:15; Psa 106:37), but in the New Testament it was applied to the evil spirits that caused mental illness. Some confusion arises, however, because devils were also used as personifications of evil having nothing to do with illness (Luke 4:2–6, 13 ff.).

In the New Testament, people "possessed" by devils, demons, or "unclean spirits" continued to be distinguished from those who were merely physically ill (Matt 4:24; 8:16; Luke 4:40–41; 9:1).

One girl with demons was described as "grievously vexed," and two men possessed with devils were so "exceedingly fierce" that no one dared go near them (Matt 8:28–32; 15:22–28). The New Testament extended the signs of possession by spirits beyond purely emotional symptoms to cover people who were so severely ill that their behavior ceased to be normal. A child "sore vexed" by a devil, and defined as a "lunatic" by his father, might have been an epileptic or suffering some ailment affecting his balance, because he was said to fall into the fire or into water (Matt 17:15–18). Luke (9:39–42) says a boy is possessed by demons when he suffers convulsions and other violent outbursts—crying out, foaming at the mouth, and bruising himself. A woman possessed by Satan for eighteen years "could in no wise lift herself up" (Luke 13:11–16), and a man who was blind and dumb (Matt 12:22; Luke 11:14) was also "possessed."

The New Testament also extends the concept of possession to multiple spirits: Mary Magdalene had seven, although there is no implication she was insane (Luke 8:2), and other people are described as having more than one. In addition, Luke seemed to feel possession was not uncommon, saying "many" people had devils (Luke 4:41).

The plight of the mentally ill was best described by Luke, who told of a man called Legion because so "many devils were entered into him" (Luke 8:27–33). Legion was said to have had devils a long time. Apparently banished beyond the city limits, he had no home and had to live in the tombs. He wore no clothes. Often he was so violent that he was restrained in chains and fetters.

What clearly differentiated possession from other illnesses was that the devils were spirits that had to be exorcised from their victims' bodies and that devils had the power of speech. While Jesus often cured by touch, in the cases of demon possession Jesus usually "rebuked" or otherwise spoke to the devils. Often the devils talked back. In one case they bargained with Jesus about where they were to go after being cast out of their present victim (Matt 8:31). In another case devils, at the mere sight of Jesus, "fell down before him, and cried, saying, Thou art the Son of God"—at which Jesus cautioned them that this information should not be made public (Mark 3:11). Devils were thus intelligent, possessed of more knowledge than men, and able to hold men as their helpless victims unless challenged by a superior spiritual force.

Capital Crimes

The following were crimes for which the Bible demanded the death penalty.

Cursing your father or mother (Ex 21:17).

Smiting your father or mother (Ex 21:15).

Rape (Deut 22:25).

Sodomy (Ex 22:19; Lev 20:15).

Kidnapping and selling a man (Ex 21:16; Deut 24:7).

Murder (Ex 21:12).

Working on the Sabbath (Ex 31:15; 35:2; Num 15:32–36).

Adultery (Lev 20:10; Deut 22:22).

Worshiping foreign gods (Lev 20:2; Num 25:1–9; Deut 13:6–15; 17:2–5).

Blasphemy (Lev 24:14–16).

Being a witch or wizard or having a familiar spirit (Ex 22:18; Lev 20:27).

321

Presuming to be a prophet (Deut 13:5; 18:20).
Incest (Lev 20:11, 14).
Lying about being a virgin (Deut 22:17–21).
Whoring, if you are a priest's daughter (Lev 21:9).
Being a stubborn and rebellious son (Deut 21:18–21).

Cruel and Unusual Punishment

Beheading: In the biblical world beheading was known but was not a common form of execution. Usually heads of the executed or slain were cut off for display or for identification. The Assyrians did this with enemies and criminals, making a show of the heads on poles or in piles. Some scholars believe that even though the pharaoh's baker was hanged, the phrase "lift up thy head from off thee" may mean he was later decapitated (Gen 40:17–22). Saul was posthumously beheaded by the Philistines because they wanted to send his head and armor around to the Philistine population as proof he was dead (1 Sam 31:8–9).

Among the Hebrews, Ish-bosheth's head was cut off his corpse by his murderers, who wanted evidence to show David (2 Sam 4:8). When Jehu wanted to exterminate the house of Omri, he sent a letter as king that his subjects send the seventy royal heads to him at Jezreel. The heads were necessary for identification, but he also used them for display, heaping them in two piles at the city gate (2 Kings 10:6–9).

In the Old Testament the only person who may have been executed by decapitation was Sheba. Sheba, who had hoped to keep alive Absalom's rebellion against David, had barricaded himself inside the fortified city of Abel-Beth-maachah. To save themselves, the city residents, who were sympathetic to David, threw Sheba's head over the city walls to the Israelite army camped outside. The biblical narrative does not make clear whether Sheba was dead or alive when his head was cut off (2 Sam 20:21–22).

More direct proof that people were executed by decapitation is the plea Abishai made to David, when David was being insulted by Shimei, "Let me go over, I pray thee, and take off his head' (2 Sam 16:9).

323

In the New Testament, beheadings are ascribed to Romans (Matt 14:8–12; Rev 20:4).

Crucifixion: Crucifixion was an elaborate variation on hanging (see below), and in ancient records the distinction between hanging and crucifixion is not always clear. This torture was known in the Middle East before Roman times, and in 519 BC Darius of Persia put down a revolt in Babylon by crucifying 3000 rebels. The first Jews known to have been crucified were from Jerusalem, a group who rebelled against Antiochus IV in 175 BC, shortly before the start of the Maccabean Wars. However, these are not mentioned in the Bible. Nor are there details on the several Jews, as well as early Christians such as Peter, who were crucified after Jesus. The only clear and detailed crucifixion in the Bible is that of Jesus (Matt 27; Mark 15; Luke 23; John 19).

Death by crucifixion was so painful that under the Romans it was usually reserved for slaves and pirates and others without full civil rights, but it was also used for political agitators. Unlike hanging by the neck, in which death came very quickly, the horror of hanging by the arms was that it took so long for the victim to die—two days or longer was not unusual. Death came gradually as the blood failed to circulate properly to the heart.

A ledge was often nailed to the upright shaft of the cross to serve as a sort of seat on which the victim could support himself to ease the pressure on his arms. (Paintings showing a ledge to support the feet of Jesus are inaccurate, as this was a flourish added after biblical times.) At some point the Romans would decide that the victim had had enough and would club his legs until they broke, thus hastening his death. This was done to the two thieves who were hanged with Jesus, "But when they came to Jesus, and saw that he was dead already, they brake not his legs." A Roman soldier did, however, thrust a spear into Jesus' side to ensure death.

During the 1st century, the cross used most often for Roman crucifixion was X-shaped—called St. Andrew's cross. The Bible does not describe the cross of Jesus, but scholars have assumed it was not a St. Andrew's because a superscription reading "the King of the Jews" was "set up over his head." If this is accurate, the cross must have had an upright shaft; an inscription on a St. Andrew's cross would not have been directly over Jesus' head but to one side or the other.

The two crosses with upright shafts that were also used for crucifixion were St. Anthony's cross—which resembles a capital T, with the crossbeam across the top—and the more familiar Latin cross, where the crossbeam is affixed below the top of the shaft. The latter has been pictured traditionally as the cross of the Crucifixion, but there is no proof it was the type used. Between the time the Roman emperor Constantine abolished crucifixion and the time the Crucifixion of Jesus began to be depicted in works of art, the exact shape of the cross was forgotten, and no crosses have been found by archaeologists.

The only archaeological evidence for crucifixion is the skeleton of a young man found in a cave at Jerusalem and dated to about the time of Jesus. He had been crucified in a crouching position. The outstretched arms had been nailed to either arm of the cross through the forearms, not through the palms of the hands. The body and legs had not hung straight—the legs were drawn up, with the knees flexed, and had been bent to one side, twisting the torso. This twisted position resulted from the feet being nailed sideways to the upright shaft of the cross. A single spike had been hammered through the sides of both ankles, just above the heels.

Nails through the feet of Jesus are not mentioned in any of the Gospels.

Nails through the arms or hands are not mentioned in the first three Gospels, but John makes much of the hands when Thomas doubts the Resurrection. Thomas said he would not believe, "Except I shall see in his hands the print of the nails, and put my finger into the print of the nails." Jesus swept away his doubt by saying, "Behold my hands." Thomas was not exaggerating about putting his finger into the holes of the nails. Roman nails of the type that must have been used have been found by archaeologists. They are of iron, thick as a finger, topped with bulky heads, and are up to nine inches long.

Before being placed on the cross, the condemned were whipped. Josephus and other writers indicate that this was a severe scourging that left the body bloody.

Although the Bible says that a Simon ("a Cyrenian") was appointed to carry Jesus' cross, the usual custom was to leave the upright shafts in place for numerous executions and to make the condemned carry his own crossbeam to the site. The victim was stripped and offered a sedative of wine and myrrh.

In the case of Jesus, the Gospels vary as to what drink was offered, when it was offered, and whether Jesus drank any of it. Matthew and Mark say a drink was offered before crucifixion: Mark called it wine and myrrh and said Jesus refused it; Matthew called it vinegar and gall and said Jesus tasted it before refusing it. Luke describes vinegar being offered merely as a mocking gesture after Jesus was already on the cross. John places the drink much later, recording that just before Jesus gave up the ghost he "received" vinegar hoisted to his mouth on a sponge (Matt 27:34; Mark 15:23; Luke 23:36; John 19:29–30).

After the drink the victim's arms were fastened to the crossbeam with either thongs or nails, and the crossbeam was hoisted to the upright shaft and attached. Lastly the feet were fastened.

Usually crosses were placed near a road, not only for convenience in transporting criminals but also as a public warning. When Jesus was on the cross, with the two thieves beside him, "they that passed by reviled him, wagging their heads."

After death, the bodies were normally left to rot and to be devoured by vultures and animals. However, in the case of Jesus, the Romans bowed to

325

Hebrew law that decreed that corpses had to be taken down by sunset. This was especially important since the Passover Sabbath began that evening. As a result, Pilate had given Joseph of Arimathea permission to claim the body of Jesus.

Bow and Arrow: In giving instructions on execution, the Bible offers shooting with arrows as an alternative to stoning—"he shall surely be stoned, or shot through" (Ex 19:13). This option was apparently necessary for cases where the victim could not be approached closely for stoning.

Burning Alive: The Code of Hammurabi lists burning alive as a means of capital punishment. One law decreed that if a nun—one of the women dedicated to the gods—entered a wineshop to drink, she was to be burned. Another law, and a brutally practical one, stipulated that anyone who tried to steal from a home while pretending to help extinguish a fire was to be thrown into the fire.

In the days of the patriarchs incineration as a means of execution was known, because Tamar was threatened with it for playing the harlot (Gen 38:24). Under the later Mosaic law burning alive was specified for such crimes as lack of chastity in a priest's daughter or for illicit sexual unions (Lev 20:14; 21:9).

The Bible, however, does not give any instances of this punishment being carried out. Achan was burned, but this was only after he had been stoned to death (Josh 7:25). Possibly the custom of burning alive had lapsed by the time the Bible was written or possibly biblical authors did not approve of it because it smacked of human sacrifice to foreign gods and they therefore avoided any reference to it. Whatever the reason, burning alive is depicted as a foreign custom. The Philistines were said to burn people alive (Judg 15:6), and the punishment is shown to have persisted in Mesopotamia: Nebuchadnezzar had a "burning fiery furnace" into which he threw people who annoyed him (Dan 3:20). Jeremiah confirms the Babylonian custom of having captives "roasted in the fire" (Jer 29:22).

Dismemberment: This form of execution was practiced in Egypt and Mesopotamia, but the first mention among the Israelites was when Samuel hacked the Amalekite king Agag to pieces with his sword (1 Sam 15:33). David apparently sawed and axed Ammonite prisoners of war (2 Sam 12:31; 1 Chr 20:3), and sawing enemies "asunder" is also mentioned in the New Testament (Heb 11:37).

Drowning: Drowning was a common form of execution in Mesopotamia, and the Code of Hammurabi listed this as punishment for wanton women. In some cases, such as the man who slept with his son's bride, the offender was tossed in bound, with no chance of surviving. However, if there was a question of guilt—as with a man charged with sorcery—the offender was not bound and was to jump into the Euphrates River, which became the final judge: If the man was able to scramble to safety, it was believed the river threw him back because he was innocent; if the river swept him away, his guilt was proved.

Possibly because Israel has so few rivers, and even these are shallow, drowning as a punishment was either rare or nonexistent.

The New Testament mentions that people had millstones tied to their necks and were then cast into the sea to drown (Matt 18:6; Mark 9:42).

Hangings in the Bible

1. The pharaoh hanged his chief baker (Gen 40:22).

2. Because a severe famine during the reign of David was blamed on Saul's sins, seven of Saul's sons were hanged (2 Sam 21:1–10).

3. The kings of Ai, Jerusalem, Hebron, Jarmuth, Lachish, and Eglon were hanged during the conquest of Canaan (Josh 8:29; 10:26).

4. Rechab and Baanah were hanged for killing Saul's son Ishbosheth (2 Sam 4:12).

5. Two eunuchs who plotted to murder King Ahasuerus of Persia were hanged. Haman, the king's chief minister, was hanged on gallows he had intended for Mordecai for having ordered the extermination of the Jews, and his ten sons were also hanged later (Est 2:23; 7:9–10; 9:14).

6. The Assyrians were said to have hanged the princes of Judah (Lam 5:12).

7. Judas hanged himself after betraying Jesus (Matt 27:4–5).

Hanging: Hanging was a common form of execution in the Middle East. The Bible implies that hanging "on a tree" could be used in place of stoning for any "sin worthy of death" (Deut 21:22). The terminology is not always clear on whether simple hanging or crucifixion was meant, because "on a tree" could mean on a cross made of wood. For example, "Jesus, whom ye slew and hanged on a tree" occurs in the New Testament (Acts 5:30; 10:39), even though scholars agree this was a crucifixion.

Except among the Hebrews the bodies were left to rot and to be devoured by vultures and wild animals. Among the Hebrews the corpses had to be taken down the same day because "he that is hanged on a tree is accursed of God" and defiles the land (Deut 21:23).

When Moses encountered idolatry among the Israelites he was ordered to

"Take all the heads of the people, and hang them up before the Lord." The first man was run through with a javelin, and the first woman had the spear thrust "through her belly," so it is possible that all 24,000 Israelites were killed with weapons first (Num 25:3–9). Some scholars believe the Hebrews hanged only the corpses of those who had already been executed by some other means.

Biblical evidence is not clear. When Joshua hanged the king of Ai, there is no mention of killing him first. However, when Joshua captured five other kings of Canaan, he had his army captains stand on their necks, and then he slew them before hanging them from trees.

Rechab and Baanah, who had murdered Saul's son Ish-bosheth, were also killed before hanging. In this case their hands and feet were cut off before the rest of the corpses were suspended over the pool at Hebron (2 Sam 4:12).

When a three-year famine in Israel was blamed on Saul's sins, seven of his sons were hanged, but the Bible gives no details about whether they were strung up dead or alive (2 Sam 21:1–9). The hilltop setting suggests that instead of the Israelites' using trees growing naturally, poles or a form of cross had been erected at a place chosen to be conspicuous. This hanging was also unusual in that it violated the rule about cutting the bodies down the same day, as the Bible says they were left for months.

When Cyrus of Persia (559–530 BC) ordered freedom for the Jews to worship in Jerusalem he stipulated that anyone interfering with Hebrew worship was to be hanged on timber taken from his own home (Ezra 6:11). Cyrus' specifications that "timber be pulled down from his house" and "set up" for the hanging make the device sound more complex than a mere pole, and it is possible crucifixion was meant. Another possibility was that the culprit was impaled, as this was also a common punishment in Mesopotamia.

People Who Were Stoned to Death

1. Adoram, the royal tax collector in the time of King Rehoboam, was stoned to death for trying to make people pay their taxes (1 Kings 12:18; 2 Chr 10:18).

2. A man who gathered sticks on the Sabbath in the time of Moses was stoned by the congregation (Num 15:32–36).

3. A man whose mother was an Israelite but whose father was Egyptian was stoned by the children of Israel for blaspheming (Lev 24:10–23).

4. Achan, who took a garment, 200 shekels of silver, and gold

weighing 50 shekels from Jericho, was stoned because Joshua had commanded that the spoils be given to God (Josh 7).

5. Naboth was stoned after an unfair trial ordered by Jezebel because King Ahab wanted Naboth's vineyard (1 Kings 21:9-14).

6. Zechariah, son of the high priest in Jerusalem, was stoned to death for trying to warn people away from idolatry (2 Chr 24:20-21).

7. Stephen was stoned to death for teaching Christianity (Acts 7:58-59).

8. Paul was stoned and left for dead, but he recovered and fled to preach again, and tradition has it that his eventual death was by beheading (Acts 14:19-20; 2 Cor 11:25).

NOTE: David tried to kill Goliath with a single stone, but the stone did not kill him. David then ran him through with a sword (1 Sam 17:49-50).

Stoning: Stoning was the usual means of capital punishment among the Hebrews and is mentioned specifically as the method of execution for such crimes as idolatry, rebelliousness in children, witchcraft, child sacrifice, blasphemy, breaking the Sabbath, and adultery (Lev 20:2, 27; 24:14, 16, 23; Num 15:35; Deut 13:10; 17:5; 21:21; 22:24). Not only men were executed this way, but animals too (Ex 21:28; Heb 12:20). Stoning was also practiced by the Egyptians in the time of Moses (Ex 8:26), and was still in common use after the time of Jesus (Acts 14:5).

Stoning was done by the congregation, all the inhabitants of a city, or "all Israel," acting on orders from God, a leader, or after a trial before elders (Num 14:10; 15:35; Deut 21:21; etc.). If witnesses had been involved in condemning someone of a crime, two or three witnesses were necessary for capital punishment to be imposed; the testimony of a single witness was considered too unreliable for the death penalty (Deut 17:6). The witnesses were to cast the first stones (Deut 17:7; John 8:7; Acts 7:58). Stoning of the entire populations of Jerusalem and Samaria was threatened in Ezekiel (16:40; 23:47).

Although leaders usually imposed stoning on others, they were not immune to the penalty themselves. In the wilderness Moses complained to God that the Israelites "be almost ready to stone me" (Ex 17:4). When Ziklag was invaded by the Amalekites, "David was greatly distressed; for the people spake of stoning him" (1 Sam 30:6). Shimei threw stones at David to show contempt for the king, leading to the assumption that an unpopular monarch risked the possibility of being deposed in this manner if enough of his subjects took part (2 Sam 16:6). In this way, stoning could be viewed as a somewhat democratic institution, in which the common

329

people were able to express their will; but it naturally ran the danger of being indistinguishable from mob violence.

Theoretically, stoning someone to death was a crime if the stoning had not been sanctioned by a higher authority (Num 35:17, 23). In practice, though, miscarriage of justice was not unknown. Jezebel managed to have Naboth stoned to death on trumped-up charges even though he had committed no crime in refusing to sell his vineyard to King Ahab (1 Kings 21:9-14).

Strangling: Although some scholars believe strangling was a common form of execution in biblical times, the only mention is by Job (7:15), who refers to his soul strangling.

Swording: Because of Hebrew attitudes toward blood, swords, javelins, and other blood-producing weapons were favored for killing idolators and for blood vengeance. Although individual idolators were to be stoned to death, groups of idolators were slain "with the edge of the sword" (Ex 32:27; Lev 26:25; Num 25:7-8; Deut 13:15). Thus the sword figures prominently in the extermination of Canaanites, Philistines, the priests of Baal, and other idolators.

Blood revenge, widespread in biblical times and practiced in the Middle East into modern days, also called for a death in which the victim shed blood (1 Sam 18:25; 25:26, 33). Thus in stories such as the avenging of Dinah, her brothers "took each man his sword" and slew "with the edge of his sword" (Gen 34:25-26). When Joab killed Abner to avenge his brother he stabbed him under the ribs, possibly with a dagger (2 Sam 3:27). And when Abner wanted to call for cessation of killing between the brethren of Israel and Judah, he asked, "Shall the sword devour for ever?"

Throwing off Cliffs: Although individuals could be punished by being thrown off precipices, the method was especially handy when large groups of people had to be disposed of. When Amaziah of Judah was faced with an army exhausted from killing 10,000 enemies in Seir and he still had to get rid of another 10,000 captives, the second group was marched to the top of precipices and forced over to rocks below (2 Chr 25:12). Psalms (141:6-7) mentions judges "overthrown in stony places," and the practice was still current in New Testament times (Luke 4:29).

Wild Animals: Although the Hebrews sometimes tossed the corpses of enemies outside city walls to be devoured by animals, other peoples in biblical times used wild animals as a form of execution. Daniel was thrown into a lion den on the assumption he would be killed, and although he was unharmed the men who had accused him were later killed when they (with their wives and children) were also thrown to the lions (Dan 6:16-24).

330

Among the Romans the popular spectator sport of throwing people to wild animals was a form of execution; the humans usually lost these battles but a few survived (1 Cor 15:32).

Most Tasteless Moments—Cannibalism in the Bible

1. God twice threatened the Israelites with curses of cannibalism: "And ye shall eat the flesh of your sons, and the flesh of your daughters shall ye eat" (Lev 26:29); and "thou shalt eat the fruit of thine own body, the flesh of thy sons and daughters" (Deut 28:53).

2. When the Assyrians besieged Samaria about 850 BC, hunger became acute. The king was stopped by a woman who cried out, "Help!" She told the king that the previous day she had killed and cooked her son, sharing the meal with another woman. In return, the other woman had promised to cook and share her son. Instead, she had hidden him. The stunned king, rather than get involved in the argument, rent his clothes and put on sackcloth to show grief (2 Kings 6:26–30).

3. Isaiah envisions the day on which each man "shall snatch on the right hand, and be hungry; and he shall eat on the left hand, and they shall not be satisfied: they shall eat every man the flesh of his own arm" (Isa 9:20).

4. Ezekiel also had a vision of cannibalism: "Therefore the fathers shall eat the sons ... and the sons shall eat their fathers" (Ezek 5:10).

5. The author of Lamentations complains to God about the destruction and poverty of his people, asking, "Shall the women eat their fruit, and children of a span long?" (Lam 2:20).

6. In another lament over the destruction of Jerusalem, the prophet makes the following comparison: "They that be slain with the sword are better than they that be slain with hunger.... The hands of the pitiful women have sodden their own children: they were their meat in the destruction of the daughter of my people" (Lam 4:9–10).

7. The vision in Revelation is also of cannibalism: "Ye may eat the flesh of kings, and the flesh of captains, and the flesh of mighty

men, and the flesh of horses, and of them that sit on them, and the flesh of all men, both free and bond, both small and great" (Rev 19:18).

The Depths of Hell

Three words in the Bible have been loosely translated into English as "hell." In their original languages these three words had vastly different meanings:

Hell #1—Sheol: *Sheol,* a Hebrew word occurring sixty-five times in the Old Testament, designates a gloomy subterranean place where the souls of the dead went. It was quite literally underground, in "the lowest parts of the earth," "in the deeps," in a "pit" or in "the lowest pit" (Job 11:8; 33:24, 28; Psa 9:15; 28:1; 30:3, 9; 55:15; 63:9; 88:4, 6; 139:15; Prov 9:18; Isa 14:9, 15; 44:23; Ezek 31:16–17; 32:21). Amos spoke of digging into hell (9:2); and expressions such as "down into the chambers of death" (Prov 7:27) and "her feet go down to death; her steps take hold on hell" (Prov 5:5) demonstrate that biblical writers conceived of Sheol as a place deep inside the earth. As one proverb has it, "the way of life is above" (15:24).

Locating Sheol under the earth may have been the natural outgrowth of the tendency to see the grave as the "home" or "abode" of the dead. The Bible's translators clearly thought of burial in connection with Sheol, for they translated the Hebrew word as "grave" thirty-one times and as "pit" three times.

In fact, the Bible's translators tried to avoid rendering Sheol as "hell" and stressed the burial connotations of the word, because the Sheol of the Old Testament is quite different from the Christian hell. First of all, Sheol was not a place for the punishment of the wicked because the righteous went there too. Sheol contained "all the chief ones of the earth" and "all the kings of the nations" as well as the lowly and corrupt (Isa 14:9). "The Lord killeth, and ... bringeth down to the grave" people of all walks of life and all degrees of righteousness (1 Sam 2:6–8).

Despite its varied and diverse population, Sheol was not a festive place. "The sorrows of hell compassed me about," lamented David (2 Sam 22:6). One of Sheol's chief drawbacks was that it was "in darkness" (Psa 88:6). And people were confused and forgetful there. One psalmist asks God, "Shall thy wonders be known in the dark? and thy righteousness in the land of forgetfulness?" (Psa 88:12). Thus cut off from the living, the souls of the dead could not expect to receive God's comfort: "Shall thy lovingkindness be declared in the grave?" is an important question for one psalmist (88:11). It was bad enough that the dead should wander in darkness,

332

confused and weak (Isa 14:9–10), but that God should be indifferent to those who had left this world was the worst punishment for the believer:

> They are dead, they shall not live; they are deceased, they
> shall not rise: therefore hast thou visited and destroyed them,
> and made all their memory to perish [Isa 26:14].

Hell #2—Hades: Hades, a Greek word occurring eleven times in the New Testament, is translated as "grave" or as "hell" in some Bibles but left as "Hades" in others. Hades was the Greek version of the underworld, ruled by Pluto and Persephone. The dead had to be ferried across the River Styx by the avaricious ferryman Charon, and so the Greeks buried their dead with a coin in the mouth to pay for the passage. Once in Hades, the dead were judged. The righteous and courageous went on to the Elysian Fields, a not unpleasant meadow at the edge of the western world. The very wicked were doomed to eternal suffering in Tartarus, the lowest region of the netherworld.

Hell #3—Gehenna: Gehenna is the Greek name for the Valley of Hinnom, a deep ravine southwest of Jerusalem. The name occurs over twelve times in the New Testament, where it is translated as "hell." Early in biblical history this valley had no special significance except as a dividing line between Israelite tribal territories, but it became infamous beginning in the time of Solomon (965–928 BC).

Despite Hebrew laws forbidding child sacrifice, Solomon established a sanctuary above the Valley of Hinnom where children became burnt offerings to a heathen god (1 Kings 11:7). These sacrifices continued into the 7th century BC, so that the valley became known as a place of heathen fires, of evil and "abominations." Finally the pious King Josiah of Judah (639–609 BC) destroyed the sanctuary and used the valley for burning corpses. From then on, the valley was a dumping ground for human waste, corpses, and other rotting matter. As much of this was burned, fire was incessant, and the valley became known as the "lake of fire and brimstone."

By the time of Jesus, Gehenna—the cesspool of Jerusalem—was a popular expression for a place of ever-burning fire, abomination, and loathsomeness. In short, hell. Jesus thus used the word Gehenna to describe "the fire that never shall be quenched" (Mark 9:43–48), and Gehenna is translated as "hell" in passages such as "Fear him, which after he hath killed hath power to cast into hell" (Luke 12:5); and "Ye serpents, ye generation of vipers, how can ye escape the damnation of hell?" (Matt 23:33).

The Wages of Sin Is Death

In the Garden of Eden, Adam and Eve had been warned that if they ate from the tree of good and evil "thou shalt surely die" (Gen 2:17). When they did eat from it, therefore, God cursed Adam with death: "unto dust shalt thou return" (Gen 3:19).

Exactly when a man died was up to God. Job (14:14) assumed each man had an "appointed time." Psalms allows seventy years of life for the average man and eighty years for the exceptionally strong man (90:10). However, a person's life was cut short if he or she angered God: Er "was evil in the sight of the Lord; and he slew him" (1 Chr 2:3). Many of the kings—such as Amaziah (2 Chr 25:15-27)—who "did that which was evil in the sight of the Lord" were punished with early deaths.

The concept that "the wages of sin is death" (Rom 6:23) remained constant into New Testament times. Death was said to have entered the world through sin, and since all men sin, all men die: "sin, when it is finished, bringeth forth death" (Rom 6:23; James 1:15).

---

10 Punishments for the Wicked

1. The wicked shall be burnt up in flames (Psa 106:18).
2. The wicked shall fall in their own nets (Psa 141:10).
3. The wicked shall be ashamed (Psa 31:17).
4. The wicked shall be shaken (Job 38:13).

5. The wicked shall be silent (1 Sam 2:9).
6. The wicked shall be condemned (Deut 25:1).
7. The wicked shall be turned into hell (Psa 9:17).
8. The wicked shall not inhabit the earth (Prov 10:30).
9. The wicked shall perish (Psa 37:20).
10. The wicked shall drink the dregs of the wine (Psa 75:8).

FUNERALS

Israelite funerals were rather simple, consisting of the preparation of the body, lamentations and other expressions of mourning, a funeral oration, carrying the body to the grave, and a feast for the mourners.

All of this probably took place on the day of death, although the Bible doesn't say so. The only references to time elapsed between death and burial are those concerning the law that bodies of hanged criminals had to be taken down by sunset of the day they were hanged (Deut 21:22–23). However, when people died on journeys, as Rachel and Rebekah did, they were buried on the spot (Gen 35:8, 19–20). Because Hebrews did not practice embalming or cremation or any other form of hygienic treatment of corpses that would have allowed delay, it is inconceivable that burial did not take place as quickly as possible.

Preparing the Body: When someone died, the first thing that was done was to close the eyes (Gen 46:4). Then the body was hugged and kissed by a close relative or friend (Gen 50:1). The body was washed (Acts 9:37) and then wrapped in clothing. Apparently, in early Old Testament times the dead person was buried in his own clothing, because the Bible says Samuel returned from Sheol in his cloak (1 Sam 28:14), and archaeologists have found bodies that were fully clothed and wearing jewelry. This practice was derived from the belief that the dead needed much the same things in the afterlife that they had used on earth. As beliefs about death became more sophisticated, the burial paraphernalia decreased. By New Testament times bodies were merely wrapped in a shroud (Matt 27:59; John 11:44).

The New Testament also mentions that the body was anointed with oils and perfumes, and that spices were wound in the linen used to wrap the body, "as the manner of the Jews is to bury" (John 12:7; 19:39–40). This had long been customary in Old Testament times—at least for kings or others who could afford the aromatic substances. When King Asa of Judah died, in 867 BC, he was laid in a bed "filled with sweet odours and divers kinds of spices prepared by the apothecaries' art," and incense was burned (2 Chr 16:14). The Bible carefully notes that Jehoram, who died in 843 BC, was so unpopular that no incense was burned for him (2 Chr 21:19).

In the case of Jesus, anointing and preparing the body became a problem because of the time of his death—3 P.M. Friday. By the time Jesus' friends had claimed the body and wrapped it in a shroud, sundown was approaching. Biblical law forbade handling the dead on the Sabbath, which started at sundown on Friday, and so the body was laid in a tomb without the customary application of ointments and spices. For this reason the women returned to the sepulcher at dawn on Sunday, their first opportunity to anoint the body.

Orations and Lamentations: Lamentations, often including an elegy, were customary at death. These were usually performed by family and friends, often with men and women separate (Zech 12:11-14). Led by paid professionals, the lamentations varied in quality according to what the family of the deceased could afford.

For poor people, sharp cries—such as "Alas! alas!"—or "a wailing like the dragons, and mourning as the owls," with perhaps a reference to the deceased having been noble as a lion, might suffice (Amos 8:10; Mic 1:8). For the wealthy and famous, long "songs" could go on for days after the burial and include speeches praising the qualities of the deceased (2 Chr 35:25).

It is perhaps significant that the greatest funeral oration recorded in the Bible was not by a professional mourner but was a heartfelt composition by David to memorialize Saul and Jonathan (2 Sam 1:19-27). It begins with the famous line "The beauty of Israel is slain upon thy high places: how are the mighty fallen!" The entire Book of Lamentations, which bewails the fall of Jerusalem to the Babylonians, is written in imitation of such funerary laments. Many of the professionals undoubtedly used tired and hackneyed phrases that they had learned from others and carried over from funeral to funeral. David's dirge was still being copied in Maccabean times, even for so important a person as Judas Maccabeus (1 Macc 9:21).

In calling for mourners, Jeremiah (9:17-18) specified that they should be "cunning" so "that our eyes may run down with tears, and our eyelids gush out with waters." This implies that many were not adept enough to create the impression of genuine grief.

Funeral Procession: In the time of the patriarchs the dead seem to have been carried to the grave whatever way was handiest. Moses ordered the corpses of the sons of Aaron to be carried in the coats of their brethren (Lev 10:4-5). But by the time of David a bier was in use, with a retinue of mourners following (2 Sam 3:31). Biers (or at most open coffins) were used into New Testament times (Luke 7:12-14).

Because virtually all of the dead were buried outside the city, a lengthy funeral procession of friends and relatives sometimes accompanied the bier to the grave (Judg 16:31). In the case of important people, the procession might be huge. "All the Israelites" were said to have gathered for Samuel's

336

funeral (1 Sam 25:1), and King Hezekiah was seen off by "all Judah and the inhabitants of Jerusalem" (2 Chr 32:33).

The grandest procession—and possibly the most ragtag—may have been Jacob's. It was also the longest-lasting, since they marched from Egypt to Hebron. Led by Joseph, the procession included Jacob's relatives, numerous representatives of the pharaoh, chariots and horsemen, as well as all the flocks and herds belonging to Jacob's huge family—altogether "a very great company" (Gen 50:7-9).

Funeral Feast: After the burial a meal was served. In the case of wealthy people this could be an elaborate feast, as David's was said to have been after Abner's funeral (2 Sam 3:35). The meal included wine—"the cup of consolation to drink" (Jer 16:7; Hos 9:4). Because the dead and the house of the dead were unclean, no food could be prepared during mourning. The feast was therefore held at someone else's home, or friends or relatives brought bread and wine to the home of the deceased.

Funeral for a Head

When Saul's son Ish-bosheth was murdered by his officers, they decapitated the body and took the head to David. David was outraged at this murder and had the assassins executed, but then also wanted to honor Ish-bosheth with a decent funeral. David therefore ordered Ish-bosheth's head buried at Hebron, where Ish-bosheth's army commander Abner had been buried (2 Sam 4:12).

MOURNING

Mourning was a convention formalized with many do's and don'ts. The rules applied not only to grief over individual deaths, but to displays of sorrow at personal and national calamities. Ezra (9:2-3) went into mourning because the Israelites began to marry foreign wives.

Crying and lamenting were only part of the rituals. Mourning also involved making oneself unattractive and even uncomfortable. Symbols of mourning were similar to those of penitence, and in a word mourning was an exhibition of repentance because the Israelites thought death was the result of sin. It is also possible that mourning was connected with uncleanliness, because the instructions for a leper include rending clothes and other signs of mourning (Lev 13:45).

337

Mourning for the dead usually lasted seven days (Gen 50:10). For a great leader, such as Moses, it lasted thirty days (Deut 34:8). The only variations from this practice mentioned in the Bible were the extra times allowed for Jacob and Joseph, who had died in Egypt and had been embalmed (Gen 50:2-3, 10, 26).

Weeping and Lamenting: Because weeping was always part of mourning, it is sometimes used as a synonym for mourning. Weeping in the Middle East was—and is—more than shedding tears. It involved loud wailing, even howling and shrieking. When God killed the firstborn of Egypt, the people responded with "a great cry" (Ex 12:30). In the wilderness, the Israelites not only wept but "lifted up their voice, and cried" (Ex 14:1), and when David wept for Abner he also "lifted up his voice" (2 Sam 3:32).

A Season for Weeping

1. Hagar wept when she thought that her son, Ishmael, would die of thirst in the desert (Gen 21:16).

2. At Sarah's death, Abraham wept (Gen 23:2).

3. After Isaac had mistakenly given Jacob the blessing (and therefore the inheritance) instead of to his firstborn, Esau, Esau cried as he begged Isaac for his own blessing (Gen 27:38). After years of separation due to this dispute over the inheritance, Esau and Jacob met again, embraced, and wept (Gen 33:4).

4. Jacob wept with joy and love when he first met Rachel (Gen 29:11).

5. Jacob cried again when he thought that his son Joseph was dead (Gen 37:35).

6. Joseph shed tears when his brothers appeared in Egypt, begging for food. They did not recognize him, and he cried in private. When he identified himself to them, he cried again. Joseph also shed tears over his brother Benjamin, when he saw his father again, and when his father died (Gen 42:24; 43:30; 45:2, 14-15; 46:29; 50:1, 17).

7. As a baby, Moses cried when the pharaoh's daughter opened up his basket (Ex 2:6).

8. Because her husband's second wife taunted her for being barren, Hannah "wept, and did not eat" (1 Sam 1:7).

9. King Saul wept when he realized that David had had a chance to kill him but had refrained from doing so (1 Sam 24:16).

10. Job speaks of himself as a man whose "eye poureth out

tears" and whose face is "foul with weeping" (Job 16:16, 20). Job wept not only for himself but also for those in trouble and for the poor (Job 30:25).

11. The prophet Jeremiah, sorrowing over the sins of the people, wrote, "Oh that my head were waters, and mine eyes a fountain of tears, that I might weep day and night" (Jer 9:1). Not only did his eyes cry, but "my soul shall weep in secret places" (Jer 13:17).

12. Nehemiah wept when he heard that the walls of Jerusalem were in ruins (Neh 1:4).

13. When Michal was forced to return to her first husband, David, her second husband, Phalti, wept as he followed her part of the way (2 Sam 3:16).

14. The author(s) of Psalms, who wept a number of times (Psa 6:8; 30:5; 69:10; 102:9), wrote, "Weeping may endure for a night, but joy cometh in the morning."

15. Old Israelite men who remembered how grand the Temple had been in Jerusalem cried when they saw the shabby new one built after the return from Babylon (Ezra 3:12).

16. "Rachel weeping for her children refused to be comforted" (Jer 31:15; Matt 2:18).

17. David wept more than anyone else in the Bible. Among his reasons were love for Jonathan; seeing the ruins of his city, Ziklag; the fatal illness of his child by Bathsheba; the attempted coup by his son Absalom; the deaths of Saul, Jonathan, Abner, and of his sons Amnon and Absalom (1 Sam 30:4; 20:41; 2 Sam 1:12; 3:32; 12:22; 13:36; 15:30; 18:33).

Crocodile Tears?

1. After her first few attempts to trick and betray Samson had failed, Delilah wept for seven days until he finally gave in and told her the answer to the riddle he had posed to the Philistines (Judg 14:16–17).

2. The prophet Elisha wept when he prophesied the death of the enemy king Ben-hadad (2 Kings 8:11).

3. Joash, king of Israel, may have been distressed when Elisha fell deathly ill, but when he went to the prophet's bedside and "wept over his face" it was also to get one last prophecy and blessing (2 Kings 13:14–19).

4. When King Hezekiah fell ill, it is unclear whether he "wept sore" because his boils hurt him so much, or because Isaiah told him he would die, or because he believed himself to be a great

sinner. God judged him to be truly repentant and granted him an extra fifteen years of life (2 Kings 20:3; Isa 38:3).

Ripping Clothes: Mourning is described in Ecclesiastes as "a time to rend" (3:7), because the first act of the mourner was to rip his clothes. When news of the deaths of Saul and Jonathan reached David, he and his men immediately rent their clothes (2 Sam 1:11). In the New Testament, the high priest ripped his clothes after hearing Jesus speak what he considered blasphemy (Matt 26:65). Many scholars believe this was a more civilized form of the ancient practice of cutting the flesh.

Shaving and Cutting: Cutting some part of the body as a manifestation of grief was widespread among Egyptians, Canaanites, and others in the Middle East. The Israelites, however, were prohibited from engaging in these practices: "They shall not make baldness upon their head, neither shall they shave off the corner of their beard" and "Ye shall not cut yourselves, nor make any baldness between your eyes for the dead" were among the prohibitions (Lev 19:27; 21:5; Deut 14:1).

The only exception was for female captives who were brought home as wives; they were allowed to follow their foreign customs of shaving their heads and paring their nails (Deut 21:12).

Despite these laws Israelites in mourning often shaved their heads or cut their hair, plucked or cut their beards, and occasionally made cuts on their bodies. All of these practices were so common that they were taken for granted even by prophets who normally railed at heathen customs. In fact, the prophets themselves sometimes advocated and engaged in these signs of mourning. "For every head shall be bald, and every beard clipped," said Jeremiah. And phrases such as "cut off thine hair, O Jerusalem" (Jer 7:29; 48:37), "Baldness upon every head," and "Baldness is come upon Gaza" are frequent among the prophets (Isa 22:12; Jer 16:6; 41:5; 47:5; Ezek 7:18; Amos 8:10). When Ezra (9:3) heard that Israelites had married foreign women, he said he "plucked off the hair of my head and of my beard." Job (1:20) shaved his head at the loss of his property and family.

Despite "Ye shall not make any cuttings in your flesh for the dead" and similar prohibitions (Lev 19:28), Jeremiah mentions people "having cut themselves" (41:5; 48:37).

Wearing Sackcloth: Sackcloth was the coarsest and most base material, used for carrying corn and other agricultural products (Gen 42:25; Lev 11:32). It was made of goat's hair sometimes mixed with camel's hair, and was somber in color—possibly black, since Jeremiah (8:21), speaking of his mourning clothes, says, "I am black."

Usually sackcloth was draped around the lower part of the torso. Jacob

340

"put sackcloth upon his loins" when he mourned Joseph (Gen 37:34). Women wore sackcloth too, for Isaiah (32:11) tells women, "Gird sackcloth upon your loins" and Joel (1:8) speaks of lamenting "like a virgin girded with sackcloth."

Most of the time sackcloth was probably worn over underclothing, but an extreme form of mourning was to wear it against the skin. "I have sewed sackcloth upon my skin," said Job (16:15). Also, when the king of Israel learned that famine had reduced his people to eating their own children during the siege of Samaria, he donned "sackcloth within upon his flesh" (2 Kings 6:30).

Another extreme form of grief was to "lie all night in sackcloth" (Joel 1:13).

Removing Ornaments: Even if sackcloth was not worn, people in mourning were expected to dress austerely, with less show than usual. Kings were to "lay away their robes, and put off their embroidered garments" (Ezek 26:16). The dress of commoners is vaguely described as "mourning apparel" (2 Sam 14:2), which apparently included not wearing a headdress (Ezek 24:17, 23) and not putting on "ornaments" (Ex 33:4).

Nakedness: Since nakedness was considered a disgrace and humiliation it was sometimes a sign of mourning. It was not used in mourning individuals but only by prophets mourning the sins of all of Israel (Jer 13:22, 26; Nah 3:5): "Therefore I will wail and howl, I will go stripped and naked," said Micah (1:8). Isaiah mentioned that prisoners of war were humiliated by having to walk barefoot and naked, "even with their buttocks uncovered," and that he himself went naked this way for three years (Isa 20:2-4).

Going Barefoot: Many references to removing shoes as a sign of mourning include "Thy heels made bare" (Jer 13:22) and Ezekiel's instruction for ending mourning: "put on thy shoes upon thy feet" (Ezek 24:17, 23).

Applying Ashes: Apart from rending clothing, smearing the body with ashes or earth was the most common mourning practice. After the early defeat at Ai, Joshua and the elders "put dust upon their heads" (Josh 7:6); Tamar put ashes on her head (2 Sam 13:19); Hushai mourned Absalom with "earth upon his head" (2 Sam 15:32); and in later days the elders of Zion "cast dust upon their heads" (Lam 2:10). When Job was afflicted with misfortunes his friends merely sprinkled dust on their heads, but Job himself repented "in dust and ashes" and appears to have rolled his head in dirt (Job 2:12; 16:15; 42:6).

In extreme circumstances, people rolled about in ashes to coat their entire bodies. "Wallowing" in ashes is mentioned (Jer 6:26; Ezek 27:30), and Micah (1:10) advises, "roll thyself in the dust."

341

Covering Face or Head: Men sometimes draped their heads and faces. When Ezekiel (24:17, 22) says, "Cover not thy lips," he is speaking of putting an end to mourning. When Israel suffered a drought, the men "covered their heads" to show grief (Jer 14:4). David, fleeing from his usurper son Absalom, "had his head covered," and "all the people that was with him covered every man his head" (2 Sam 15:30).

Not Washing: Among the most common forms of mourning was to wash neither clothes nor body, and to refrain from using body oils or perfumes: "Anoint not thyself with oil" (2 Sam 14:2).

"Neither did I anoint myself at all," said Daniel of his three-week mourning (Dan 10:3). Mephibosheth also observed this custom for a long period when David was driven from Jerusalem. Mephibosheth "had neither dressed his feet, nor trimmed his beard, nor washed his clothes, from the day the king departed until the day he came again in peace" (2 Sam 19:24).

Matthew (6:16–17) indicates that Jesus may have disapproved of not washing, because he quotes, "When thou fastest, anoint thy head, and wash thy face."

Fasting: Although the law did not dictate fasting during mourning, Israelites often fasted in times of distress, and fasting was apparently often a voluntary act by the bereaved. "I ate no pleasant bread, neither came flesh nor wine to my mouth," said Daniel of his three weeks of mourning (Dan 10:3). Ezra too, on hearing that the Hebrews had married foreign women, "did eat no bread, nor drink water" (Ezra 10:6). David was joined by his companions in a day of fasting when Saul and Jonathan died, and fasted alone when Abner died. When Saul and his sons died, the people of Jabesh fasted the full seven-day mourning period (1 Sam 31:13).

Assuming Abject Postures: In addition to formalized mourning rituals, people in the Bible are described as assuming a number of body postures. These may have evolved from natural reactions to grief, but they seem so standardized that they may also have become conventions of mourning. These include:

Trembling: "They shall clothe themselves with trembling . . . they shall tremble at every moment," said Ezekiel (26:16), and Isaiah (32:11) commanded, "Tremble, ye women."

Falling Face Down: This may have been a sign of throwing oneself on God's mercy. Joshua "fell to the earth upon his face" when he was defeated at Ai (Josh 7:6), Job fell to the ground to worship (Job 1:20), and David lay prostrate when his son was dying (2 Sam 12:16).

Bowing the Head: "To bow down his head as a bulrush" (Isa 58:5) describes this attitude of sorrow, which is also vividly pictured in Lamentations (2:10): "The virgins of Jerusalem bow down their heads to the ground."

342

Lifting Hands: Two variations of hand movements are described in the Bible as signs of sorrow. One—"laying hands upon the head" (2 Sam 13:19; Jer 2:37)—may have been a conventional sign of mourning in the Middle East, for it is pictured in Egyptian tombs. The other is spreading the hands wide in supplication or despair: "I fell upon my knees, and spread out my hands to the Lord" (Ezra 9:5). "Zion spreadeth forth her hands, and there is none to comfort her" (Lam 1:17).

Sitting in Silence: Sitting or lying on the ground without a sound was an expression of deep, drawn-out distress and weary suffering. It probably followed the loud outbursts of emotion that went with initial weeping. Princes would descend from thrones they were about to lose and "sit upon the ground" (Ezek 26:16), commoners sat "astonied" (Ezra 9:3), and the elders of Zion faced with the magnitude of their loss sat upon the ground and kept silence (Lam 2:10).

Famous Last Words

Jacob: After blessing Ephraim and Manasseh, Joseph's sons, Jacob blessed his own sons, one by one, then asked to be buried in Israel: "I am to be gathered unto my people: bury me with my fathers in the cave that is in the field of Ephron the Hittite ... which Abraham bought ... for a possession of a buryingplace" (Gen 49:29–30).

Moses: The last words that the Bible records Moses speaking to the children of Israel are those which come after his blessing them tribe by tribe: "Happy art thou, O Israel: who is like unto thee, O people saved by the Lord, the shield of thy help, and who is the sword of thy excellency! and thine enemies shall be found liars unto thee; and thou shalt tread upon their high places" (Deut 33:29).

Wife of Phinehas: When Phinehas' wife heard that the Ark had been captured by the Philistines and that her father-in-law and her husband had died, she went into labor and was soon moribund. Her last words were to name her child Ichabod, saying, "The glory is departed from Israel: for the ark of God is taken" (1 Sam 4:22).

David: David's last words were spoken to Solomon: "I go the way of all the earth: be thou strong therefore, and shew thyself a man; And keep the charge of the Lord thy God, to walk in his ways, to keep his statutes, and his commandments, and his judgments, and his testimonies, as it is written in the law of Moses, that thou mayest prosper in all that thou doest, and whithersoever thou turnest thyself: That the Lord may continue his word which he spake concerning me, saying, If thy children take heed to their way, to walk before me in truth with all their heart and with all their soul, there shall not fail thee (said he) a man on the throne of Israel." David ended with the request that Solomon exact vengeance on some of his enemies (1 Kings 2:1–9).

Elijah: While they were waiting for the whirlwind that was to carry Elijah to heaven, Elisha begged him for "a double portion of thy spirit." Elijah's last words, just before the chariot of fire appeared, were "If thou see me when I am taken from thee, it shall be so unto thee; but if not, it shall not be so" (2 Kings 2:9–10).

Elisha: Elisha's last words were angry ones. When he was dying, King Joash arrived for a last blessing and counsel. Ordering the king to take up his bow and arrows, Elisha explained that the arrow was "the arrow of the Lord's deliverance, and the arrow of deliverance from Syria." Then he told Joash to take his arrows and "Smite upon the ground." Joash smote three times and waited for Elisha's reaction. Elisha went into a fury and stormed at the king: "Thou shouldest have smitten five or six times; then hadst thou smitten Syria till thou hadst consumed it: whereas now thou shalt smite Syria but thrice" (2 Kings 13:14–19).

Jehoram: When King Jehoram of Israel realized he was betrayed and was about to die at the hands of his general Jehu, his last thought was for his kinsman Ahaziah, the king of Judah. Jehoram shouted the warning, "There is treachery, O Ahaziah." Ahaziah did flee but was soon overtaken by Jehu, who killed him too (2 Kings 9:23).

Jezebel: Jezebel's last words were defiant. When Jehu entered the palace gates to kill her, she reminded him of Zimri, a former usurper who had taken the throne by murder and who ended up committing suicide: "Had Zimri peace, who slew his master?" (2 Kings 9:31).

What Jesus Said on the Cross

The four Gospels record different sayings, and only once do any two agree:

1. Luke (23:34) says that Jesus prayed for his executioners, "Father, forgive them; for they know not what they do."

2. Luke (23:42–43) also records that Jesus promised one of the thieves hanged with him, "To day shalt thou be with me in paradise."

3. John (19:26–27) says Jesus entrusted Mary to him, saying to her, "Woman, behold thy son!" and saying to him, "Behold thy mother!"

4. Matthew and Mark record that Jesus quoted Psalm 22:1: "My God, my God, why hast thou forsaken me?"—"*Eli, Eli, lama sabachthani?*" However, the Roman soldiers thought Jesus was calling for Elias (the Greek word for Elijah) to save him (Matt 27:46–49; Mark 15:34–36).

5. John (19:28) says that vinegar was given because Jesus had said, "I thirst," in order to fulfill the prophecy: "They gave me also gall for my meat; and in my thirst they gave me vinegar to drink" (Psa 69:21).

6. Luke (23:46) records Jesus' last words as "Father, into thy hands I commend my spirit."

7. John (19:28) records Jesus' last words as "It is finished."

8. Matthew (27:50) and Mark (15:37) say that Jesus "cried again with a loud voice" before dying, but record no final words.

KEEPING BODY AND SOUL TOGETHER

Great care was taken to protect the bodies of the dead in the ancient Middle East because most people believed that the soul remained in the corpse after death. The Bible often uses the word "sleep" to describe death, since the Israelites believed that so long as the body or at least the bones were preserved their dead maintained some sort of semiconscious existence in the underworld.

For this reason the Israelites never cremated their dead. And although they did not practice embalming, they were horrified by the prospect that their flesh and bones might be destroyed. One of the worst curses was "thy carcase shall be meat unto all the fowls of the air, and unto the beasts of the earth" (Deut 28:26; Jer 7:33; 16:4). When the sons of Rizpah were hanged, she kept a long vigil to keep the birds off the corpses by day and the animals away at night (2 Sam 21:10).

Only the very wicked deserved such a fate: Jezebel was eaten by dogs (2 Kings 9:35). Others who practiced idolatry were not buried so that they too might be eaten by dogs, if they died in the city, or by vultures, if they died in the country (1 Kings 14:11; 16:4). The body of King Jehoiakim, an

345

idolater, was to be cast out of the gates of Jerusalem for wild animals to eat (Jer 22:19).

Usually a proper burial was performed by the children or other close family member, and it was such a sacred duty that when Abraham died even the banished Ishmael returned to help Isaac bury him (Gen 25:9). The remark by Jesus, when a disciple wished leave to go bury his father, was therefore shocking for the time: "Follow me, and let the dead bury their dead" (Matt 8:21).

Monuments to the Dead: The dead were considered unclean and "He that toucheth the dead body of any man shall be unclean seven days" (Lev 21:1-4, 11; 22:4; Num 6:6; 19:11-6). By extension, entering the tent in which a person died, or touching a grave or tomb, also made one unclean for a week (Num 19:14-16).

Erecting a funerary monument—even if this was no more than a heap of stones—was not only a memorial but also a way of marking a grave so that people could avoid it. The custom of erecting monuments, common throughout the Middle East, reached its zenith in Egypt with the development of the pyramid. Rectangular structures of brick or stone were placed over Egyptian graves, and as new monuments were erected over old, the pyramid evolved.

Among the Israelites monuments never got that far out of hand, because they were usually not placed on top of each other but side by side. In Palestine the custom of heaping stones over burial pits was in existence before 10,000 BC, and before the days of the patriarchs the dolmen—a tablelike structure also found in prehistoric Europe—was in use. The dolmen was constructed of four boulders that served as legs, topped by a huge slab of rock. Hundreds of these structures have been found in Galilee and thousands east of the Jordan River. Often burials were grouped to form cemeteries, so that several hundred to a thousand monuments might be found at one site—the largest cemetery ever found is at Bab-edh-Dhra (a few miles east of the Dead Sea), where there are at least 20,000 pit burials.

The first monument mentioned in the Bible is the "pillar" that Jacob erected over Rachel's grave. Monuments were still in use during David's reign because Absalom—having no son and afraid his tomb would be forgotten—erected one for himself (Gen 35:20; 2 Sam 18:18). However, as tombs in caves became more common—especially in Judah—monuments ceased to be erected. Except where tombs were disguised, to discourage grave robbers, whitewashing the tomb entrance served as a warning to passersby that a tomb existed. The idea that burials were unclean persisted into New Testament times, when Jesus was met by "two possessed with devils, coming out of the tombs" (Matt 8:28).

Back from the Dead

The prophet Samuel is the only person in the Bible that came up from the underworld and returned there immediately. He was brought back by a medium—the Witch of Endor—at Saul's insistence. Saul was in such despair over a coming battle with the Philistines that he demanded, "Bring me up Samuel"—even though in life Samuel had told him he was not fit to be king. The medium described Samuel: "An old man cometh up; and he is covered with a mantle."

Samuel was none too pleased to be called up from the dead and said to Saul, "Why hast thou disquieted me, to bring me up?" Even when Saul explained his distress, Samuel was far from comforting, reminding Saul he was not fit to be king and predicting defeat and death in battle.

Because Saul fell to the ground in shock, ending the interview, no questions were ever asked about what life was like in the underworld (1 Sam 28:7-15).

Taking It with You: In the earliest burials found in Palestine (before 10,000 BC), skeletons (sometimes painted red) are surrounded with everyday utensils and often with ornaments.

Placing objects for use in the next world near the body reached its greatest elaboration in Egypt and in Mesopotamia. In Egypt, the wealthy and powerful were buried with all the comforts of home, including games, embalmed pets (in turn buried with their toys and saucers of food), and paintings or reliefs of happy scenes from the deceased's life on earth. Even the poorest, buried naked in the sand, had food and water.

The royal tombs at Ur, dating from about 2500 BC, show similar concern. The tombs of the wealthy often consisted of several vaults. Chariots heaped with luxuries were driven in, and the draft animals interred. Servants—from five to eighty—were apparently poisoned and their corpses were placed in a crouched position, ready for service. The corpse of Lady Shub-ad, in one of the grandest tombs discovered, was decked out in elaborate jewelry set with precious stones and an ornate headdress; she lay on a bier, a golden cup within her reach. Males had their helmets and daggers for war, as well as everyday necessities, buried with them. The tombs of the poor were naturally simpler, but even they had personal belongings and food, and often their hands were folded around a cup.

In Palestine, the greatest number of objects are found in tombs that date

347

from about the time of the conquest of Canaan. Toilet articles, such as combs, were placed close to the body, and many pottery vessels surrounded it. In areas occupied by the Hyksos, warriors were buried with their horses and their armor, and even in later tombs weapons were frequent. Ezekiel (32:27) mentions soldiers buried with their shields under their torsos and their swords under their heads.

At Jericho, tombs jammed with jewelry, wooden objects, baskets, bronze implements, and luxury items of alabaster have been unearthed. Corpses were buried fully clothed and laid on reed mats (one had a wooden bed). At Bab-edh-Dhra many figurines of goddesses were found in tombs. Food and drink were common—one tomb at Affuleh contained the remains of a lamb's head on a platter.

Israelites were not supposed to give food or offerings to the dead (Deut 26:14), and the idea is mocked in the Apocrypha (Baruch 6:26). But this referred to the Canaanite custom of placing food at grave sites rather than to objects placed within the tomb.

As ideas of the afterlife became more sophisticated, fewer objects were left. By the time of the deportation to Babylon, only a few lamps and pottery jugs were entombed. By the time of Jesus, no mention is made of objects placed with the body in the tomb.

Sleeping with One's Fathers: Because of the belief that the dead person retained feelings after death, it was important to be buried with loved ones. In fact, an Assyrian curse was to wish a person would never enjoy burial with his family.

Those who could afford to therefore maintained communal tombs where all family members could be buried together. When Sarah died, Abraham bought the Cave of Machpelah in Hebron, where later Abraham, Isaac, Rebekah, Leah, and Jacob were also buried (Gen 23:1-20; 25:9; 49:31; 50:13). Because this site is a shrine, it has never been excavated, but archaeologists have found many examples of communal tombs in natural and man-made caves at Megiddo, Jericho, and elsewhere.

At one of the best preserved sites, Bab-edh-Dhra, a shaft about four feet wide would be dug vertically through soft stone to a depth of about nine feet. Domed chambers would then be excavated around the central shaft, each with an entrance large enough for a body to be squeezed through. The chambers were small—only about six feet in diameter and three feet high—each containing several skeletons.

At Jericho, some of the older tombs were pits dug under the living quarters in which only the skulls were buried. These skulls were often plastered with clay that was molded to represent lifelike features. The later burials at Jericho were in caves outside the city walls, where there was more room and the entire skeleton could be preserved.

By about 4000 BC, a new form of burial was invented. Instead of being scattered in the tomb, the bones, once the flesh had disintegrated, were placed in ossuaries (containers for bones) that were stored in caves. Ossuaries had been in use earlier, to contain the skeletons of infants. As time went on, these ossuaries became very elaborate and were molded into the shape of houses, animals, or human faces. The houses, which had doors that opened for inserting the bones, were probably exact replicas of the deceased's homes. Sometimes the ossuaries were painted or had designs in relief.

The tomb at the bottom of a shaft continued to be common, but walk-in tombs began to be adopted too. At first these were natural caves enlarged by excavation. Often there was an antechamber where the bier was placed on a ledge until the body dried out. Then the bones were placed in niches in a rear or subterranean chamber.

The use of family tombs was such a strong tradition among the Israelites that the phrases "he slept with his fathers" or "he was gathered to his people" occur throughout the Bible to mean "he died." Because Jacob expressed the wish to be buried with his fathers, his body was brought all the way back from Egypt to Canaan (Gen 49:29; 50:2–13). After the return from Babylon the urge to be buried with one's ancestors was still strong, and Nehemiah begged the king of Persia to allow him to return to "the place of my fathers' sepulchres."

Unfortunately, although many biblical tomb sites are identified by tradition—Samuel's on Nabi-Samwil, Absalom's in the Kidron River valley, Jesus' in Jerusalem, those of the kings of Judah—none have been verified by archaeologists. In 1978 monks at St. Makarios Monastery in Egypt announced that they had found fourteen bodies and thirteen skulls, leading them to believe that the extra body was that of John the Baptist; however, the bones had been found two years before the announcement, and had been moved for public exhibit, so that scientific verification may not be possible.

Coffins: In Egypt, elaborate coffins of durable, rot-resistant woods, made in the shape of a human body, were part of the tradition of preserving the body. The coffins of pharaohs and other important people had additional safeguards. They might be overlaid with nonperishable precious metals, or a series of coffins of many different nonperishable materials might encase the one containing the body.

In Palestine an effort was occasionally made to imitate the splendor of Egyptian practice. The Philistines, for instance, made tombs that were many-chambered, as was the custom in the area, but the way to the tomb was terraced in imitation of the steps used in Egypt rather than being through a shaft as was usually common in Palestine. Most extraordinary of all, the dead were placed in elaborate clay coffins that were made in human form like those of Egypt. The body was slipped inside the coffin through a lidded opening at the top. As in Egypt, the surface of the coffin was worked to resemble the occupant, with a face in high relief.

349

Because they were embalmed in Egypt, Jacob and Joseph probably had Egyptian-style coffins. This is not certain for Jacob, but the Bible mentions Joseph's coffin (Gen 50:26).

The Hebrews did not use coffins regularly, however. The dead were carried to the sepulcher on a bier. This is evident in the story of the man carried into the sepulcher of Elisha—the minute his body was let down and touched Elisha's sacred bones he revived and stood up, obviously unencumbered by a coffin (2 Kings 13:21). Biers are mentioned not only in the Old Testament—when David followed the bier of Abner (2 Sam 3:31)—but into New Testament times: When Jesus was approaching Nain, a funeral procession was coming out of the city with the bier of a widow's son; Jesus had only to touch the bier for the young man to rise (Luke 7:11–14).

City Burial: Being buried in a city was an honor accorded only to the elite. In Paleolithic times (before 10,000 BC) it was common for people in Palestine to be buried in pits sunk below the more elaborate pit that served as living quarters. This type of burial, which enabled the living to keep their dead close by, survived for centuries. But at populous sites such as Jericho, an alternate method had to be developed. By 7000 BC the citizens of Jericho were burying their dead in caves outside of the city. As towns grew larger, cemeteries outside of the city became a practical necessity.

By the time of the conquest of Canaan, burial inside the city was reserved only for important people, such as kings and prophets, and was worthy of special mention in the Bible. David "was buried in the city of David," inaugurating a tradition that made interment in Jerusalem an honor. After David, Kings Solomon, Rehoboam, Abijam, Jehoshaphat, Ahaziah, Amaziah, Jotham, and Ahaz were all buried in the city of David.

Not all kings were allowed into the royal tombs. Joash, for instance, became so unpopular toward the end of his reign that he was murdered; "they buried him in the city of David, but they buried him not in the sepulchres of the kings." Other monarchs were denied royal burial because of idolatry or disease (1 Kings 2:10; 11:43; 14:31; 15:8; 22:50; 2 Kings 8:24; 9:28; 12:21; 14:20; 15:7, 38; 16:20; 2 Chr 9:31; 12:16; 14:1; 21:1, 20; 24:16, 25; 27:9).

Extensive but futile searches have been conducted for the royal tombs of Judah. David's tomb (which Josephus claimed contained silver, gold furniture, and other treasures) is believed to have been on Mount Zion, and after the return from Babylon the exact site was still known (Neh 3:16). One theory is that it was destroyed by vengeful Romans during the Bar Kokhba Rebellion of AD 135. Other royal tombs are believed to have been south of Jerusalem at Ophel, but none of the tombs thus far found in this area has been positively identified.

King Uzziah was not buried in the royal tombs because he was a leper (2 Chr 26:23). However, a plaque dated from the time of the return from

Babylon has been found in a monastery on the Mount of Olives. The plaque, which says Uzziah's bones were transported to the Mount of Olives for reburial, warns that his ossuary should not be opened—but the ossuary to which the plaque was attached has unfortunately never been found.

Almost certainly the Kingdom of Israel also had royal tombs, because Baasha was said to have been buried at the old capital of Tirzah (1 Kings 16:6). A new site was apparently inaugurated after Omri reestablished the capital at Samaria, because he, his son Ahab, and other kings such as Jehu were entombed there (1 Kings 22:37; 2 Kings 10:35). But the Bible is always less detailed on the northern kingdom and none of Israel's royal tombs have been found either.

Besides kings, prophets were accorded the privilege of city burial. Samuel, for instance, was buried at Ramah, his birthplace and official residence (1 Sam 25:1; 28:3). Occasionally other dignitaries were also buried in cities—Jehoiada, for example, the high priest who had raised Joash, was not only buried in Jerusalem but "among the kings, because he had done good in Israel" (2 Chr 24:16).

Pauper's Fields: In many areas of Palestine, burial in a family tomb was possible only for the rich. Abraham had had to pay 400 shekels of silver for the Cave of Machpelah (Gen 23:1-20), and even if this was an especially fine cave, buying and maintaining a tomb was an expensive undertaking.

From the earliest times, therefore, most of the poor were buried in public graves—"graves of the children of the people." For the people of Jerusalem the public burial ground was along the brook of Kidron, in the valley between the city and the Mount of Olives (2 Kings 23:6). Here the bodies were laid in simple trenches and covered with earth. That this was an undesirable means of burial is clear from references that foreigners and criminals were also cast "into the graves of the common people" (Jer 26:23).

Public graves for the poor continued into New Testament times. After Judas had betrayed Jesus and killed himself, his body too was thrown into "the potter's field, to bury strangers in" (Matt 27:7). This potter's field, called Aceldama ("field of blood"), was in the infamous Valley of Hinnom. It was bought by priests (or by Judas himself) with the thirty pieces of silver Judas received for betraying Jesus, and is the origin of the term "potter's field" to describe a pauper burial ground (Acts 1:18-19). Possibly potters had once owned this land (Zech 11:13) or used its soil for clay. Pottery, being cheap and easily shattered, was used as a term of contempt in the Bible and the term "potter's field" may therefore have meant only that the land was worthless, good for no more than discarding potsherds. In medieval times the soil of this tract was believed to have miraculous power to devour corpses and was therefore carted off during the time of the Crusades to be spread on European cemeteries.

The Lock on Heaven's Door

An epitaph for a locksmith, dated 1637, reads:

> A zealous locksmith died of late,
> And did arrive at heaven gate,
> He stood without and would not knock,
> Because he meant to pick the lock.

AWAKE AND SING

Although the pots and household implements buried with the dead clearly show that Israelites from earliest times believed in life after death, the early books of the Bible do not specify the nature of immortality. Not until the Psalms were written do the Scriptures begin to discuss the issue, and the concept of immortality was then refined by the prophets.

With the Psalms, Sheol clearly emerges as only a temporary resting place and God as a final refuge: "Yea, though I walk through the valley of the shadow of death . . . I will dwell in the house of the Lord for ever" (Psa 23).

"Shall the dead arise?" (Psa 88:10) is answered by numerous passages where God "delivers" or "redeems" man from the grave (Psa 49:15; 86:13; Prov 23:14). Yet because the Hebrew word for soul meant a breathing creature, and was applicable to animals as well as to men, the Psalms seem to offer hope that the body will be revived as well. One exceptional passage makes a distinction between flesh and spirit: "then shall the dust return to the earth as it was: and the spirit shall return unto God who gave it" (Eccl 12:17). But the more common and lasting notion seemed to be that the dead soul would breathe again in its body: "My flesh also shall rest in hope. For thou wilt not leave my soul in hell . . . thou wilt shew me the path of life" (Psa 16:9–11).

"If a man die, shall he live again?" asked Job, who struggled not only with the question of whether God was unjust but also with the question of what happens to man after he "giveth up the ghost." In passages that are disputed and may have been later emendations, God's voice from the whirlwind counseled Job that this cannot be understood any more than creation or the annual budding of spring. Job acknowledged that man cannot fully comprehend the "thunder" of God's power, and in a dramatic passage expressed his faith: "For I know that my redeemer liveth, and that he shall stand at the latter day upon the earth: And though after my skin

352

worms destroy this body, yet in my flesh shall I see God" (Job 14:10–14; 19:25–26; 25:6; 26:14; 38:4, 27).

Of all the prophets, Isaiah created the most beautiful images of God's kingdom. It would be established "in the top of the mountains ... exalted above the hills." A great light would shine "in the land of the shadow of death," and God would "swallow up death in victory." Plows would be beaten into plowshares, war would be learned no more, and a Prince of Peace would be born so that none would "hurt nor destroy in all my holy mountain." There would be wisdom, understanding, justice, and such joy that the people "shall mount up with wings as eagles" (Isa 2:1–4; 9:2, 6–7; 11:1–9; 25:8; 26:14; 40:31).

Ezekiel was far less poetic, but his visions were precise: "The soul that sinneth, it shall die," said Ezekiel, but he held out the promise that the repentent person who turned away from sin "shall surely live, he shall not die" (Ezek 18:20–21).

Ezekiel (37:1–14) offers a detailed and elaborate picture of God's ability to infuse life into the dead. He set the scene in a valley full of bones that were so old "they were very dry." God asked Ezekiel, "Can these bones live?" Soon "there was a noise, and behold a shaking, and the bones came together," and "lo, the sinews and the flesh came upon them, and the skin covered them above." At first, despite being reconstituted in the body, the dead did not breathe, but finally they received breath and stood. To the "whole house of Israel," it is emphasized, God has promised, "Behold, O my people, I will open your graves, and cause you to come up out of your graves.... And shall put my spirit in you, and ye shall live." Ezekiel's vision thus included a rebirth in flesh as well as in spirit.

Daniel, like Ezekiel, lived during the Exile in Babylon, when salvation was a relevant question to Jews removed from their homeland. Despite the alien environment, Daniel was faithful to God's commandments, and his interpretation of life after death was similar to Ezekiel's visionary experience: "And many of them that sleep in the dust of the earth shall awake, some to everlasting life, and some to shame and everlasting contempt. And they that be wise shall shine ... as the stars for ever and ever" (Dan 12:2–3).

This is the promise also found in the New Testament. The wicked "shall go away into everlasting punishment: but the righteous into life eternal" (Matt 25:46). The Resurrection of Jesus included the reunion of body and spirit (Matt 28; Mark 16; Luke 24; John 20).

Jesus' own words on the subject of resurrection were few, given in reply to the case posed by the Sadducees (a sect which did not believe in life after death) of a woman who had had seven husbands. They asked Jesus which husband she would have after the resurrection. He replied, "In the resurrection they neither marry, nor are given in marriage, but are as the angels of God in heaven" (Matt 22:25–30; Luke 20:27–36).

The lengthiest statement in the New Testament concerning resurrection was made by Paul, who addressed the question directly—"How are the dead raised up? and with what body do they come?" He rejected the notion that "flesh and blood" could inherit the kingdom of God and explained that there was a "natural body" and a "spiritual body." The resurrection of the dead is "sown a natural body; it is raised a spiritual body" (1 Cor 15:35–56).

Who Went to Heaven?

1. Enoch: The Old Testament said that "Enoch walked with God ... three hundred years" and that after he had lived a total of 365 years "he was not; for God took him" (Gen 5:22–24). In the New Testament Paul makes a statement that some scholars interpret to mean Enoch had been transported to heaven: "By faith Enoch was translated that he should not see death; and was not found, because God had translated him" (Heb 11:5).

2. Elijah: Elijah was taken "into heaven by a whirlwind" (2 Kings 2:1, 11).

3. Jesus: Forty days after the Resurrection, Jesus "was received up into heaven, and sat on the right hand of God" (Mark 16:19; Luke 24:51). Matthew and John do not mention this, ending their Gospels with appearances after the Resurrection, but it is mentioned again in Acts (1:9–11).

4 and 5. Depending on how the passages are interpreted, the Apostles Paul and John went to heaven or at least had visions of it (2 Cor 12:1–9; Rev 4; etc.).

NOTE: The Assumption of Mary is not mentioned in the Bible. The Roman Catholic Church announced by an 1854 papal decree and a 1950 papal bull that she "was taken up, body and soul, into the glory of heaven."

HEAVEN

"God made the firmament.... And God called the firmament Heaven" (Gen 1:1, 6–7). Heaven in the Bible often meant only the sky (from a Hebrew word meaning lofty), but it could also be the abode of God and angels. "I have talked with you from heaven," God told Moses (Ex 20:22; Deut 4:39). Whenever God called out to men, and frequently when angels

354

did, it was from heaven (Gen 19:24; 21:17; 22:11, 15; 1 Chr 21:26; Neh 9:13; Matt 3:17). Heaven was occasionally used as a synonym for God, as in the expression to "sin against heaven" (Luke 15:18, 21).

Because God was conceived of as looking down from heaven to watch the doings of men, the afflicted sometimes begged God to look their way: "Look down from thy holy habitation, from heaven" (Deut 26:15); "Look down from heaven, and behold from the habitation of thy holiness" (Isa 63:15); "The Lord looked down from heaven upon the children of men" (Psa 14:2; 33:13; 53:2).

Heaven was a place of "precious things" and "wonder" (Deut 33: 13; Joel 2:30). From heaven God "cast great stones" (Josh 10:11), sent fire (Gen 19:24; 2 Kings 1:10, 12, 14; 2 Chr 7:1; Luke 9:54) or sometimes fire and brimstone (Luke 17:29), lightning and thunder (1 Sam 2:10; 2 Sam 22:14; Luke 10:18), rain (Gen 8:2; Deut 11:11; Jer 10:13; 51:16), and manna (Ex 16:4). Men therefore looked to the heavens for a "sign" from God that could be used as divine guidance (Matt 6:1; Mark 8:11; Luke 11:16; 21:11).

To emphasize divinity, Jesus said, "I am the bread which came down from heaven," and distinguished this bread from manna: "I am the living bread which came down from heaven: if any man eat of this bread, he shall live for ever. . . . not as your fathers did eat manna, and are dead: he that eateth of this bread shall live for ever" (John 6:38-58).

What Heaven Was Like: Heaven was originally envisioned as an arch above the earth that was supported by pillars (Job 26:11). These "foundations of heaven moved and shook" when God was angry (2 Sam 22:8; Isa 13:13).

Heaven was apparently believed to be solid, because it had ends or sides, and God was able to walk "in the circuit of heaven" (Deut 4:32; Job 22:14; Isa 13:5). Also it seems to have been thought of as square, because Jeremiah (49:36) speaks of the "four quarters of heaven."

More specifically, there were windows that God opened to let out rain upon the earth, and closed when the people were being punished with drought (Gen 7:11; 8:2; Deut 11:17; 28:12; 1 Kings 8:35; 2 Kings 7:2, 19; 2 Chr 6:26; 7:13; Luke 4:25). Sometimes the heavens were opened so that chosen people could see God or a sign from God (Ezek 1:1; Matt 3:16; Acts 10:11). Heaven also had a gate or doors (Gen 28:17; Psa 78:23) that could be opened for similar reasons.

Possibly the material of heaven was thought to be somewhat flexible, because the psalmist begs, "Bow thy heaven, O Lord, and come down" (Psa 144:5).

The Bible notes that heaven is located, quite simply, "above thy head" (Deut 28:23). But it apparently had three levels because Paul speaks of "the third heaven" (2 Cor 12:2). It was a complicated structure with "outmost" or "uttermost" parts (Deut 30:4; Neh 1:19; Mark 13:27), and a "heaven of heavens" (Deut 10:14; 1 Kings 8:27; 2 Chr 2:6; 6:18). The level closest to earth was the height at which birds flew (Jer 4:25; 8:7; 9:10; Rev 19:17). This lowest level was also meant when the cities of Canaan were described as "great and walled up to heaven" (Deut 1:28; 9:1).

Above this was probably an intermediate heaven that contained the stars and planets: "God said, Let there be lights in the firmament of the heaven" (Gen 1:14–18).

Perhaps clouds were also in this intermediate level, because Job poses the question of how God is able to judge man if dark clouds shroud the earth from God's sight (22:13).

The Bible emphasizes that God was in "the height of heaven" which was a level above the stars. In trying to explain how high this was, Job says, "Behold the height of the stars, how high they are!"—yet the heaven of God was above them (Job 22:12), in an area referred to as "on high" (Psa 68:18; 93:4).

God, as the ultimate being, could rise above even this level, as suggested by the frequent theme of "Be thou exalted, O God, above the heavens" (Psa 57:5, 11; 108:5; 148:4). God rides "upon the heavens" (Psa 68:4, 33) on the highest plane, a place of glory: "The Lord is high above all nations, and his glory above the heavens" (Psa 8:1; 113:4; 148:13).

Exactly where the angels lived is not quite clear, but they were probably in the intermediate level. Jacob dreamed of a ladder that reached to heaven on which angels ascended and descended, and David saw an angel "stand between the earth and the heaven" (Gen 28:12; 1 Chr 21:16). These and other accounts hint that angels lived at a level accessible to earth, somewhere between where the birds flew and the place where God lived.

However, this is not certain because of the ambiguous phrase "the host of heaven." In earliest days this host may have referred to celestial bodies such as the moon, sun, and stars (Deut 4:19; 17:3; 2 Kings 17:16; 21:3, 5; 2 Chr 33:3, 5; Jer 8:2; 37:22; Dan 8:10). Later, however, when the Israelites developed a monarchy, they began to picture God as sitting on a throne and overseeing a kingdom (Psa 11:4; 103:19; 145:11–13; Matt 5:34): "The heaven is my throne, and the earth is my footstool" (Isa 66:1; Acts 7:49). The host then appeared as attendant angels: "I saw the Lord sitting on his throne, and all the host of heaven standing by him on his right hand and on his left" (1 Kings 22:19; 2 Chr 18:18).

Visions of a resplendent heaven came late in the Bible. In the early books, people assumed they would go to Sheol and did not aspire to heaven, which they considered solely God's domain.

By the time of the kings, however, Elijah was swept up into heaven by a whirlwind (2 Kings 2:1, 11). The idea of man going to heaven or to glory began to be probed tentatively: "If I ascend into heaven" (Psa 139:8); "Who hath ascended into heaven?" (Prov 30:4).

Isaiah denounced this hope as one of the pretensions of Lucifer (Isa 14:13). Instead of heaven, he offered magnificent visions of the day when "the glory of the Lord shall be revealed." His visionary city had foundations of sapphires, windows of agate, "borders of pleasant stones," and gold and silver in place of baser metals. His emphasis was not on material riches, however, but on the peace and justice that would bring rejoicing (Isa 40, 54, 60–61, 65).

It was Jesus who first characterized the kingdom of God as "paradise" (Luke 23:43). Nevertheless, Jesus avoided any description of material splendor. He told the parable of the beggar who "was carried by angels into Abraham's bosom," where he was comforted, while the rich man who "also died, and was buried," was tormented (Luke 16:22–25). His promise, "in my Father's house are many mansions. . . . I go to prepare a place for you" (14:2), offered a heaven for man, but in the teaching of Jesus it was called a "mystery" and divorced from materiality (Matt 19:24; Mark 4:10; 10:23–25; Luke 8:10; 18:24–25; etc.).

The popular images of pearly gates and other magnificence are based on neither Isaiah nor Jesus but on the Book of Revelation. Here a heavenly city, the new Jerusalem, is described as lavish with gems, paved with gold, and shining without need of the sun.

Seven

Winners and Sinners

Dürer's portraits of five Apostles. *Upper left:* Bartholomew (Nathanael). Because legend says he was flayed alive, he is depicted holding a knife. *Upper right:* Simon. He is holding a saw, the traditional instrument of his martyrdom. *Lower left:* Thomas. He, too, is holding the traditional instrument with which he was martyred. *Lower right:* Peter and John healing the cripple.

Angels

The Bible is heavily populated with angels: They appear in almost every book and their presence is crucial in many of the most important scenes in both the Old and New Testaments. As Saint Augustine suggests, the word angel comes from the Greek word *angelos,* meaning "messenger," as does the Hebrew, *malakh.* Indeed, their terrestrial visits are restricted solely to those occasions when they are upon the work of God or communicating his will.

Among the hosts of angels that God supervises (1 Sam 1:3) there appear to be many subdivisions. There are archangels (1 Thes 4:16; Jude 9), principalities, powers, and dominions (Col 1:16), cherubim and seraphim (Ex 15:18; Isa 6:2), yet there is little in the Bible to indicate the relative positions of each of these offices in the celestial hierarchy. Apparently, the cherubim and seraphim are of a superior order of angels, the seraphim a little above the cherubim, for they sit beside the throne of God and there sing their antiphonal songs. Below these, most commentators agree, are the principalities, powers, thrones, and dominions, though the order of these offices is often disputed. Still lower are the archangels, followed by the angels. Almost all authorities would agree on this arrangement. The noted exception is Dante, who in partial dispute with this positioning puts principalities beneath archangels and angels. (For a more extensive presentation of angelic offices see *A Dictionary of Angels,* by Gustav Davidson.)

In form, angels are as men and usually are indistinguishable from them— so much so that many biblical characters find out they have been talking to an angel only after the celestial being has revealed his identity with some supernatural sign. Gideon, for example, realizes he has been questioning an angel only when the angel sets a rock ablaze by tapping it with his cane (Judg 6:10–22).

Unlike the average angel, the seraphim and cherubim frequently appear in spectacularly supernatural form. The seraphim that Isaac sees have six wings each: two to cover their faces, two to cover their feet and two to fly with. In Ezekiel's vision the cherubim are even more fantastic:

> And there appeared in the cherubims the form of a man's hand under their wings. . . . And every one had four faces: the first face was the face of a cherub, and the second face was the face of a man, and the third the face of a lion, and the fourth the face of an eagle [Ezek 10:8–14].

One common element worth noting in the description of both the cherubim and seraphim is the wings of these angels. Traditionally, cherubim have always been depicted with wings, probably because of the influence upon the Israelite arts of the winged lions and bulls of the Assyrians and the griffins of the Hittites. Moses is instructed to have the cherubim that are mounted above the Ark of the Covenant guard it with their wings: "And the cherubims shall stretch forth their wings on high, covering the mercy seat with their wings, and their faces shall look one to another" (Ex 25:20). It was only toward the end of the 4th century, in Christian iconography, that all angels, from seraphim to the rank and file, began to be distinguished from mortals by their wings.

Although there has been a long tradition among the commentators of naming angels, there is little information about particular angels in the Bible itself: Michael (Dan 10:13–21) and Gabriel (Dan 8:16), as well as Belial and Satan, who have often been called "fallen angels," are mentioned by name, but only rarely.

One of these "fallen angels," indeed, one of the best-known of this demonic crew, is not an angel at all in the Bible. The line in Isaiah, "How thou art fallen from heaven, O Lucifer, son of the morning!" (14:12), gave rise to the notion, first advanced among the early Church fathers, that Lucifer was simply Satan by another name. The name Lucifer, which means "light giver" or "day star," here actually refers to Nebuchadnezzar. Through the passage in Revelation (22:16) in which Christ calls himself the "bright and morning star," the fallen "bright star," Lucifer, became associated with the Antichrist and hence Satan.

About the personalities and nature of angels the Bible again offers scant information. In the Old Testament, angels appear to be perfectly sinless, for there is no mention of any angel being punished or rebuked. It is clear that the author of Second Samuel also thought them to be omniscient. David is said to be wise "according to the wisdom of an angel of God, to know all things that are on the earth" (14:20).

It is only in the New Testament that angels are represented as having any independence and freedom of will—demonstrated by the freedom to fall: "God spared not the angels that sinned, but cast them down to hell, and delivered them into chains of darkness, to be reserved unto judgment" (2 Pet 2:4).

The reason for their expulsion is not clear. All that is said is that Satan "deceiveth the world." Traditionally, Satan is cast out of heaven for the sin of pride. Some commentators point to Genesis, which implies that angels, the "sons of God," were guilty of coveting mortal women: "That the sons of God saw the daughters of men that they were fair; and they took them wives of all which they chose" (Gen 6:2).

Naked Came I

To "wail and howl" over the fate of Jerusalem, the prophet Micah went "stripped and naked" (Mic 1:7).

When David brought the Ark into Jerusalem he danced in public; in the words of his wife, Michal, he "shamelessly uncovereth himself" (Sam 6:20).

Simon Peter was caught naked by Jesus: "Now when Simon Peter heard that it was the Lord, he girt his fisher's coat unto him (for he was naked), and did cast himself into the sea" (John 21:7).

Isaiah walked naked three years as "a sign and wonder upon Egypt and upon Ethiopia" (Isa 20:3).

When Noah got drunk he lay about naked in his tent, which disturbed his sons so that they covered him (Gen 9:21–23).

In one of his attempts to capture David, King Saul and his men were struck with the power to prophesy. This halted their pursuit for quite a while. Saul "stripped off his clothes also, and prophesied ... and lay down naked all that day and all that night" (1 Sam 19:24).

Captives were humiliated by being stripped of clothes (2 Chr 28:15).

The symbolic woman who doted on Assyrians and committed whoredoms was naked (Ezek 23:10, 29).

Hosea threatened to take away the flax that covered his wife's nakedness (Hos 2:3, 9).

NOTE: The word naked, as the Bible uses it, means only with the outer garments off, not necessarily nude.

Antichrists

The term "antichrist," from the Greek word *antichristos,* meaning "one who opposes or is an antagonist to Christ," is used only by John (1 John 2:18, 22; 4:3). Early Christians associated the word with any false teacher preaching non-Christian or anti-Christian beliefs. Only later did the idea of a single Antichrist, an apocalyptic embodiment of Satan opposed to God and attempting to assume the offices and position of Jesus, supplant this original notion.

However, the concept of a supremely evil individual attempting to overthrow the dominion of God has its origins in Judaic apocalyptic thought and probably owes a good deal to the religious myths of many other Near Eastern cultures. The program for apocalypse, as conceived by Judaism, begins with powers of evil holding sway over all the nations of the earth. The kingdom of God and the powers of good vanquish evil only after a terrible battle with some diabolical adversary who is finally and completely defeated. In Daniel this adversary is represented as being a horn "with the eyes of a man and a mouth speaking great things." This is a mighty ruler heading vast armies, persecuting saints and changing times and laws (Dan 7:8, 27). When Jesus refers to this figure, "the abomination of desolation, spoken of by Daniel the prophet," he is thinking also of an imposter or usurping force "standing where it ought not" (Mark 13:14).

The identification of this evil incarnation with some political figure is an early tendency. It is probable that Antiochus IV Epiphanes, a Jewish persecutor contemporary with the composition of the Book of Daniel, was considered to be a prototype for such an embodiment of evil. Indeed, it may have been Antiochus' decision to convert the Temple into a Greek shrine that introduced the conception of an adversary of God as being one "who stands where [he] ought not," i.e., one who occupies and thus desecrates a holy place. Hundreds of years later, the Roman emperor Caligula (37–41), cast as the Antichrist for his persecution of the Christians, would also be an archfiend to the Jews because he gave the order, never executed, to have his statue erected in the Temple at Jerusalem.

That the adversary of the "last days" would be a desecrater and pretender to the throne of God is made most clear in Paul's description:

> Let no man deceive you by any means: for that day shall not
> come, except there come a falling away first, and that man of
> sin be revealed, the son of perdition; who opposeth and
> exalteth himself above all that is called God, or that is
> worshipped; so that he as God sitteth in the temple of God,
> shewing himself that he is God [2 Thes 2:3, 4].

As in Isaiah (11:4), where it is said the Lord will destroy the wicked "with the breath of his lips," this imposter "the Lord shall consume with the spirit of his mouth"—imagery which suggests that this adversary, who speaks "lying wonders" (much as the speaker of "great things" in Daniel), will be refuted as if in debate. What is most novel about Paul's description, however, is that it bridges the gap between the Antichrists of John, who are mortal teachers of false gospels, and the visionary, supernatural being of Daniel and other apocalyptic writings. In Revelation (12), for example, it is a dragon, much like the dragon of chaos that battles the supreme god Marduk in Babylonian epic, that is the avatar of Satan and adversary of God.

It is an Antichrist like the final adversary described by Paul, that early Christians began to identify with political leaders such as the oppressive Roman emperors Titus, Nero, and Caligula. Over the years, the practice of naming the Antichrist grew until no one seemed immune from the charge. In 1213, Pope Innocent III declared that Mohammed was the Antichrist, but within a hundred years the imperious Boniface VIII and the wealthy John XXII would be among those popes so accused. By the 14th and 15th centuries there were so many false alarms called in on the Apocalypse and so many purported Antichrists on earth that the Fifth Lateran Council (1516) prohibited prophecy of the imminent coming of the Antichrist.

The Apostles

Twelve Apostles were selected from the disciples, the followers or "students" of Jesus. In Greek an apostle was "someone sent on behalf of another," in short, an ambassador. The word gained in meaning and use as the history of Christianity evolved. In the Gospels the word is used sparingly; in fact, in Mark and Matthew it is used only once per Gospel.

Jesus may have chosen twelve as the number of Apostles to correspond with the twelve tribes of Israel or with the twelve kingdoms of heaven (Matt 19:28). The number had some significance because after Judas betrayed Jesus and committed suicide, an election was held to bring in one Apostle (Matthias) to replace him (Acts 1:15–26). Lists of the twelve Apostles appear in four places (Matt 10:2–4; Mark 3:16–19; Luke 6:14–16; Acts 1:13).

The duties and privileges of the Apostles were simple. The Apostle was a preeminent disciple who traveled with Jesus and received private teachings apart from the public sermons. Sometimes Jesus would send the Apostles off in pairs to preach repentance. He required that they carry no provisions or money on these missions, only a staff, and that they outfit themselves simply in a single cloak and sandals. They were given "power over unclean spirits" and thus were able to "cast out many devils" and to heal people (Mark 6:7–13; Luke 9:1–6).

Among the Apostles, Peter and the brothers John and James constituted a kind of inner ring of those closest to Jesus. Only these three saw the raising of Jairus' daughter (Mark 5:37; Luke 8:51), the Transfiguration (Matt 17:1; Mark 9:2; Luke 9:28), and the prayers in the garden of Gethsemane (Matt 26:37; Mark 14:33). Once, when Jesus went up on the

Mount of Olives to foretell the coming of the false prophets, Andrew was admitted to this circle (Mark 13:3).

After Jesus' death the Apostles continued to preach Christianity in Jerusalem and throughout the Mediterranean world. It is nearly certain that the two best-known of the Apostles, Peter and Paul, went to Rome, but by and large the traditional and apocryphal stories recording the wanderings of the other Apostles should be read with some skepticism since there is no mention in the Bible of their traveling extensively.

The life-span of the average Apostle was short; the most common form of death, if we can believe tradition, was martyrdom. The need for others to spread Christianity made it imperative that the original twelve devise some qualifications for the appointment of new Apostles. Peter set out the first qualification when he directed that the replacement for Judas be someone who had seen Jesus after his death—"a witness with us of his resurrection" (Acts 1:22). Paul, who was not one of the original twelve, alleges that his commission as an Apostle came directly from Jesus (1 Cor 15:10; Gal 1:1) in a vision (Acts 9:1-19). Paul himself is very cautious about admitting novitiates because of the many "false apostles" who took the title for themselves without having it bestowed on them by Jesus (2 Cor 11:13).

Peter: Because he was their leader and often their spokesman, Peter is always first in the lists of the Apostles (Matt 10:2-4; Mark 3:16-19; Luke 6:14-16; Acts 1:13). He enjoyed the special consideration of Jesus and together with the two sons of Zebedee, John and James, formed the intimate core of the Apostles surrounding Jesus.

Before following Jesus, Peter was living with his wife, mother-in-law, and brother Andrew in Capernaum, along the shore of the Sea of Galilee. There he and Andrew were fishermen, in partnership with Zebedee and his sons (Luke 5:10). After Peter had joined Jesus, Peter's house, near the synagogue where Jesus preached, was a meeting place for the Christians at Capernaum. Recent excavations beneath the Byzantine chapel over the supposed site of Peter's house have indeed uncovered foundations of residences from the 1st century.

Peter's given name was Simon, which sometimes occurs in the Gospels in its Semitic form, Simeon. The name Peter means "rock" in Greek, and is a translation of the Semitic nickname "Cephas" that Jesus gave him.

The Gospels differ on the story of how he got his nickname. According to John, he received it when he was first introduced to Jesus (1:41). But Matthew says he was named Peter at Caesarea Philippi, when he asserted that Jesus was the Christ (16:16-18). Jesus therefore praised him as the "rock" on which the Church would be founded. Mark and Luke, however, imply that he was dubbed "the rock" at the time Jesus was appointing his twelve disciples.

Peter did have a vein of rock-hard stubbornness in him, for better and for worse. When he denied knowing Jesus (Matt 26:69-74), he denied him not once but three times. To his credit, he was equally steadfast in his repentance of this betrayal and pledged his love for Jesus three times (John 21:15-17).

As a man of large expressive passions, he was the most outspoken and robustly active of the Apostles. Although Peter was often rebuked for the things he said (Mark 8:33), Jesus valued him highly because he always spoke his mind when asked the hard question (Matt 17:24; Luke 7:43). He was a man with a simple heart, "unlearned" in the complexities of religious law (Acts 4:13). His failings—from his denial of Jesus to his failure to stay awake while on watch in the garden of Gethsemane—can be traced to the quite human tendency toward self-interest.

Still, the Gospels represent him as the Apostle most like Jesus. He walked on water, as briefly as his faith would sustain him (Matt 14:28-29). And traditionally, his martyrdom by crucifixion has been compared to Jesus'. Because of his virtues and his forthright leadership Jesus called on him to "feed my sheep" (John 21:17), to "strengthen your brethren" (Luke 21:17), and to keep "the keys to the kingdom of heaven" (Matt 16:19)—all clear signs that he was chosen to be foremost among the Apostles after Jesus' death. The honor is again confirmed when he becomes the first Apostle to see Jesus after the Resurrection.

His first act as administrator of the Apostles was to organize the election of a twelfth Apostle to replace Judas. As their spokesman, he explained to the multitudes the meaning of the visions and the ability to speak in tongues that possessed the Apostles on Pentecost. And as religious leader he was the first of the Apostles to perform a miracle in Jesus' name when he healed the lame man at the Beautiful Gate of Jerusalem (Acts 1-3).

While on his travels throughout Palestine, preaching and performing miracles, he received an enigmatic vision telling him "what God hath cleansed, that call not thou common." Immediately afterward he was summoned by men on behalf of Cornelius, a Roman centurion who had just had a vision from God commanding him to seek out Peter. Interpreting this vision as a sign that gentiles were considered "clean" by God, Peter preached to Cornelius and baptized him. Peter's decision to admit gentiles to the Church displeased many of the Apostles in Jerusalem, particularly James the brother of Jesus, and became the main cause of factionalism among them.

It appears that Peter remained the undisputed head of the Jerusalem Church for only a short while. Paul reports that on his second visit to Jerusalem, James (the brother of Jesus), John, and Peter were the "pillars" of the Church, suggesting they shared duties on some sort of apostolic council. And he mentions that later, in Antioch, Peter defers to James' request that he not eat with gentiles.

The New Testament has little to say of the later life of Peter. Sometime after the death of James (the son of Zebedee), Peter was imprisoned by Herod and miraculously escaped. Acts then says he "departed and went to

368

another place" (12:17), but it does not specify if he went to another country, a section of Palestine, or a neighborhood in Jerusalem. Perhaps he went to Corinth, for Paul indicates there is a party in the Church there which claims allegiance to "Cephas," Peter (1 Cor 1:12). Dionysius, a bishop at Corinth (c. 170), boasted in a letter to the Roman Church that both Peter and Paul preached in Corinth. Eusebius, who wrote a history of the Christian Church, published in 326, says the Apostle may have done missionary work in what is now Turkey and Asia Minor.

Eusebius goes on to say, in agreement with tradition, that Peter came to Rome to preach and was crucified—head downward at his own request, undoubtedly to avoid an exact parallel to Jesus' crucifixion. The *Annals* of the Latin historian Tacitus (c. 55–117) provides an interesting perspective on the martyrdom of Peter. He records that the emperor Nero was suspected of setting the great fire that destroyed much of Rome (64) and that the emperor—who legendarily fiddled in the flames—blamed the fire on the Christians. The accused Christians suffered cruelly. In Tacitus' words, "they were dressed in the hides of wild animals and were set upon by dogs or put on crosses to be set afire," all while Nero held a play in his circus (stadium) or walked about in his charioteer's costume.

Tacitus' account of the horrors of Nero accords remarkably well with the tradition that Peter died in Nero's circus and was buried nearby. Caius, an elder in the early Roman Church, promised in a letter (c. 200) to point out to the visitor the tombs of Peter and Paul. Modern visitors are told that Peter's death took place near the present site of the obelisk in St. Peter's Square. As for the tomb itself, Pope Pius XII authorized excavations in the 1940s and 1950s which uncovered, beneath the high altar at St. Peter's, a tomb from 160, with 3d-century graffiti relating to Peter. Even though this may not be his tomb, other evidence supports the tradition that Peter died in Rome, probably in 64, with the Christians persecuted by Nero.

Andrew: In comparison to his brother (Simon) Peter, Andrew is a diminutive figure in the Gospels. Although he is mentioned in all the lists of Apostles and always among the first four, he is always in the background. Most of the bits of information given about him—that he was originally from Bethsaida (John 1:44), that he was living in Peter's house at the time of Jesus' Galilean ministry—are those he shares with Peter.

But because of his relation to Peter he does appear in some significant scenes. According to the Gospel of John, Andrew is one of the first followers of Jesus. Originally a disciple of John the Baptist, Andrew adopted John's view that Jesus was the Messiah and introduced his brother Simon (Peter) to Jesus (John 1:35–42). Mark and Matthew have a slightly different, though not necessarily incompatible, slant to the story of how Andrew and Peter came to be disciples. Both say that the brothers were at their nets fishing when Jesus called on them to leave their work and become fishers of men (Matt 1:18–19; Mark 1:16–17). Luke elaborates on this story by adding the details of the miraculous catch of fish (5:1–10), but does not mention Andrew's presence.

Most of the remaining information about Andrew comes from John. He notes that Andrew was the one who found the boy with the basket of bread when Jesus fed the multitude (John 6:8–9). And he tells of Andrew and Philip introducing some Greek believers to Jesus (12:21–22), an incident which echoes Andrew's introduction of Peter to Jesus.

That the Gospel of John has the most references to Andrew and gives the most details about Andrew may have some significance. John (the son of Zebedee), disputed author of the fourth Gospel, was Peter and Andrew's fishing partner. He would therefore know Andrew intimately and be likely to mention him more than the other Gospels would.

John, however, omits one very important episode in Andrew's life which is mentioned in Mark. Mark includes Andrew among the inner circle of Apostles on the Mount of Olives when Jesus is describing the coming of the false prophets (13:3).

After that Andrew turns up only once more in the Bible. He is present in the "upper room," the second-story chamber in the Jerusalem house where Jesus appeared after the Crucifixion (Acts 1:13).

There are several apocryphal books about him—including one called the Acts of Saint Andrew—but these date from the 3d or 4th century and are probably unreliable. Eusebius, a fairly solid source, recounts Andrew's ministry in what is now southern Russia, around the Black Sea. One account has him on Patras, a city in the northwest of Greece's Peloponnesian peninsula. There he was reputedly martyred in AD 60 on an X-shaped cross—from which comes St. Andrew's cross, the symbol of Scotland that can be seen on the flag of Great Britain.

John and James: Unlike Peter and Andrew, the brothers John and James are almost indistinguishable in style and in character. Besides their similarity, they were virtually inseparable, and therefore are recognized as a pair throughout the Gospels. Jesus apparently thought of them as a kind of dynamic duo, giving them the nickname "Boanerges" ("sons of thunder" [Mark 3:17]). The moniker presumably refers to their booming voices or volatile tempers, but may also have something to do with a taste for flashy miracles: When a village refused to admit Jesus, the brothers wanted to "command a fire to come down from heaven and consume" the villagers (Luke 9:52–54).

The two were the sons of Zebedee and, possibly, a woman named Salome. (This was not the dancer who carried John the Baptist's head on a plate, but another who has been the subject of some conjecture. In Mark [15:40], she and two other women, Mary Magdalene and Mary "the mother of James and Joses," attend Jesus during the Crucifixion. But the Crucifixion scene in Matthew [27:56] lists only the two Marys by name and calls the third woman "the mother of Zebedee's children," thus giving rise to the inference that she and Salome are the same—a quite sensible inference because Mark [15:41] also notes that Salome was a follower of Jesus in Galilee [see Matt 20:20], the area where John and James grew up.) Their father, Zebedee, must have done quite well in his fishing business because he was able to afford hired servants (Mark 1:20).

They are among the first disciples of Jesus, leaving their fishing nets and father behind to become "fishers of men" (Matt 4:21; Mark 1:19). There are no remarkable incidents that set them apart from the other disciples until Mark (10:35–40), where they impetuously ask Jesus if they might sit beside him in heaven. The account in Matthew (20:20–23) differs slightly, in that it is their mother who makes the request for them. In both versions Jesus rebukes the brothers, telling them, "Ye know not what ye ask." He does say that they will indeed "drink of the cup I shall drink of and be baptised with the baptism that I am baptised," veiled words which have been construed as a prediction of their martyrdom—a baptism of pain like Jesus' Crucifixion.

Evidently they were often reproved, since the next we hear of the pair, John is being scolded for forbidding a man from exorcising devils in Jesus' name. Jesus tells him he should not forbid such practices, "for he that is not against us is for us" (Luke 9:49–50).

It is worth noting that in the fourth Gospel, supposedly written by John, they lose this bad image—in fact, they are mentioned only once (21:2), as being present at the Sea of Galilee when Jesus appeared after his Resurrection. One wonders how these members of Jesus' inner circle could have been virtually omitted from a Gospel unless the writer was John, trying to be modest—or trying to avoid self-incrimination.

Some scholars believe that the character in the fourth Gospel referred to as the "disciple Jesus loved" is John, speaking of himself (19:26). Thus he would be the disciple whom Jesus entrusted with the care of his mother, Mary (19:26).

In Acts the brothers begin to come into view again. Both are present at the election of Judas' replacement (1:13). James turns up only once more in the New Testament: He is the first Apostle martyred, killed by the sword of Herod Antipas (AD 44 [Acts 12:2]). John, however, assists Peter in healing a crippled man (3:1–11) and journeys to Samaria with him on a mission (8:14). In Galatians, Paul calls John one of the pillars of the Church (2:9).

Both brothers have been the subject of some apocryphal stories. A 17th-century source reports that James visited Spain before his martyrdom and his bones eventually came to rest in a shrine in Santiago de Compostela, in northwest Spain.

John supposedly went to Ephesus (on the Aegean coast of Turkey), where he wrote his Gospel, and then to the Greek isle of Patmos, where he composed his Revelation. Tradition has it that he was martyred and buried at Ephesus.

Thomas: Though named in all four Apostle lists, Thomas (from the Aramaic, meaning "twin") does not put in any significant appearances except in John. There, however, he is prominent enough to allow some analysis of his character. He is certainly skeptical, questioning, and sometimes grim: The phrase "doubting Thomas" aptly summarizes his character. Nevertheless, he can be resolute when he knows the answers and his doubts have been allayed.

The first time we hear of him is after Jesus has made the decision to return to Judea to heal Lazarus. Jesus has been driven from Jerusalem under the threat of stoning and his decision to return could well mean his death. Facing off with reality, Thomas encourages the others to go with Jesus, saying, "Let us go, that we may die with him" (11:16).

The next time he comes forward he is querying Jesus. Jesus has been enigmatically speaking to his disciples about his coming departure, and says, "And if I go and prepare a place for you, I will come again, and receive you unto myself; that where I am, there ye may be also. And whither I go ye know, and the way ye know." But Thomas, not one to allow uncertainty, says, "We know not whither thou goest; and how can we know the way?" (14:5).

A few days after this, Thomas hears from the other Apostles that Jesus has been resurrected and has appeared before several of them. He declares himself doubtful, saying, "Except I shall see in his hands the print of the nails, and thrust my hand into his side, I will not believe" (20:25).

About a week later, when Jesus returns to his disciples, Thomas is among them. Jesus implores him not to be "faithless, but believing." And Thomas, seeing the wound in Jesus' side and holding his hands, does indeed believe. He then addresses Jesus as "my Lord and my God" (20:26–28).

The last time that Thomas turns up in John is at the Sea of Galilee when Jesus makes the miraculous catch of fish. We know that he is present at the election of Judas' replacement (Acts 1:13), but the remainder of his life must be reconstructed from sources outside of the Bible.

There is a long tradition, supported by Eusebius, the early Christian historian, of Thomas' having preached in Edessa (modern Urfa, in Turkey near the Syrian border). An apocryphal work, the Acts of Thomas, also tells of his evangelical journey to India and of his martyrdom there. An Indian branch of Christianity still holds the belief that these Acts record historical fact. Some of the narrative—for example, the meeting with King Gondaphares, a king recorded nowhere else in early Western literature—does indeed corroborate their belief.

The Acts of Thomas also opens up an intriguing possibility. Thomas' full name may have been Judas Thomas, in other words, "Judas the twin," since that is how the name is given in John's Gospel in the Syriac version of the Bible, one of the oldest (2d century) versions. The Acts of Thomas—on the basis of Matt (13:55) and Mark (6:3), where Jesus is said to have a brother named Judas—states that Thomas is Jesus' twin.

In 1945 a papyrus manuscript was discovered in Egypt that contained more than a hundred sayings attributed to Jesus. The heading on the manuscript credited "Judas Thomas" as the editor. Although these sayings resemble many of Jesus' parables, the authenticity of "Thomas' Gospel" is doubtful.

Matthew: Like Peter, Andrew, John, and James, Matthew came from Capernaum in Galilee (Mark 2:1, 14), where he was a tax collector in Roman service. As was common among the Apostles, he had both a Greek name and a Hebrew name: his Hebrew name was Levi, as he is known in Mark and Luke. He is the son of one Alphaeus (Mark 2:14), and thus may be the brother of the Apostle James (the Younger).

Matthew received his call from Jesus while sitting at his desk in the customshouse. Jesus simply said, "Come with me," and Matthew did, "leaving all" (Luke 5:28). Luke reports that they then adjourned to Matthew's house for a meal with "publicans and sinners." To the oppressed Jews, a tax collector for the Romans, a publican, wasn't much different from the sinner, and Matthew undoubtedly suffered much scorn for holding this office.

Little else is said about Matthew. The lists of Apostles (Matt 10:2-4; Mark 3:16-19; Luke 6:14-16; Acts 1:13) all mention him. In Matthew and Luke he seems to be paired with Thomas, a sign that they went together when Jesus sent the Apostles off two by two on their missions (Mark 6:7-13; Luke 9:1-6). Mark and Acts, however, imply that Bartholomew was his partner.

Eusebius, the 4th-century Christian historian, reports that Matthew preached to the Hebrews in the years following the death of Jesus. This would accord with the style of his Gospel, which directs itself to a Jewish audience by representing Jesus as "the son of David," the fulfillment of Jewish messianic hopes. Eusebius' history also dovetails nicely with reports that Matthew made a collection of Jesus' sayings in Hebrew.

So many traditions of Matthew's martyrdom exist that the only certainty is that he died—in Ethiopia, in Persia, or in Pontus (on the Black Sea).

Bartholomew: This Apostle is mentioned only in the four lists of the Apostles (Matt 10:2-4; Mark 3:16-19; Luke 6:14-16; Acts 1:13) and nowhere else. Since Bartholomew literally means "son of Tholmai" in Hebrew, it is probably a surname. In the 9th century someone conjectured that Bartholomew was the last name of Nathanael, the Apostle whose call is recounted in John (1:43-51). The conjecture is supported by some circumstantial evidence. First, Bartholomew is not mentioned in John, and Nathanael is mentioned nowhere else. Second, Bartholomew is paired with Philip in the Apostle lists and it was Philip who introduced Nathanael to Jesus.

The story of the introduction is told with some humor. When Philip mentions that Jesus is from Nazareth, the dusty little town next to Nathanael's own town of Cana, Nathanael asks, "Can anything good come of Nazareth?" Jesus evidently appreciates Nathanael's puncturing wit, for on the first meeting he hails Nathanael as "an Israelite indeed, in whom there is no guile." When Nathanael asks Jesus how he knows this much about him, Jesus replies that he's seen Nathanael before, sitting under a fig tree. Hearing this, Nathanael spouts out that Jesus is truly the "Son of God and King of Israel." Jesus then returns with a jibe, "Because I said unto thee I saw thee under the fig tree, believest thou?"

After this brief story Nathanael's name crops up only once more; he is present among those who witness the appearance of Jesus at the Sea of Galilee after his Resurrection (John 21:12).

According to tradition he did missionary work throughout Mesopotamia and was martyred—flayed alive by the orders of the king of Armenia.

Philip: Philip was a native of Bethsaida, the hometown of Peter and Andrew. Like Andrew, Philip was probably a disciple of John the Baptist before following Jesus (John 1:29–43). He was called in Galilee and soon afterward introduced Nathanael (Bartholomew) to Jesus (1:45–51).

His main function seems to have been as a liaison or public-relations man. He and Andrew introduced Jesus to some Greeks who were interested in meeting this new preacher (John 12:21–22), and they were the ones put in charge of supplying bread (John 6:5–8).

At the Last Supper, after Jesus says, "If ye had known me, ye should have known my Father also," Philip is obviously not satisfied that he knows the "Father" and tells Jesus, "Lord, shew us the Father, and it sufficeth us." Rebuking him, Jesus replies, "Have I been so long time with you, and yet hast thou not known me, Philip? he that hath seen me hath seen the Father" (John 14:9).

Tradition puts the later ministry of Philip in Scythia (along the northeast Black Sea) and Hierapolis (in southwest Turkey), where he may have been crucified.

Simon: Though he is on all the Apostle lists, Simon does not do anything of note in the New Testament. The Authorized Version mistranslates his name in Mark and Matthew, calling him Simon the Canaanite. A better translation would be "Simon the Zealot," the name he is known by in Luke and in Acts.

Since he is always in the last four names on the Apostle lists it can be safely assumed that he did little to distinguish himself from the others and that the Bible's representation of him as a background character is correct. Despite his relative anonymity, postbiblical legends have grown up around him. Some say he preached in Egypt and Persia, where he was martyred with Saint Jude.

Judas: One of the more obscure Apostles, he is scarcely noted in the Gospels except to distinguish him from Judas Iscariot. To add even more uncertainty to his identity, the Bible is not clear whether he is "the brother of James" or "the son of James," who this James is, or whether Judas is to be identified with Thaddeus, the Apostle whose name appears in place of his in the Apostle list in Mark. He might be the author of the Epistle of Jude, and might even be Jesus' brother James, though both possibilities are less than likely.

James (the son of Alphaeus): Another of the shadowy Apostles, James is sometimes alleged to have been the brother of Jesus, though this seems doubtful if Alphaeus was his father. It is more certain that James was the brother of Matthew, since Mark (2:14) notes that Levi (Matthew) is also the son of Alphaeus.

Judas Iscariot: There is some dispute over Judas' surname. Some scholars allege that Iscariot means "man of Kerioth," others that it is a corrupt form of the Latin *sicarius* ("assassin," or "murderer"), a word that became the name of a Jewish nationalist group, the Sicarii.

Because the New Testament was written long after the Crucifixion, the authors always wrote their Gospels with the awareness that Judas was a traitor, making any attempt to reconstruct his position and esteem among the Apostles before the betrayal almost impossible.

Every incident in his life, no matter how minor, is darkly colored in retrospect. In John (12:6), when Judas asks Jesus why some precious ointment was not sold and the money given to the poor, the Gospel's author says, in an editorial aside, that Judas asked "not that he cared for the poor; but because he was a thief, and had the bag." "Having the bag" means that he carried the money of the Apostles and acted as their treasurer (John 13:29).

The only other details about him come in connection with the betrayal. At the Passover meal, the Last Supper, Jesus says he will be betrayed by one of the Apostles in the room. Each asks, "Lord, is it I?" According to Matthew (26:25), Jesus answers Judas' question with the words, "Thou hast said."

There have been many explanations offered for Judas' betrayal. The one put forth most strongly by the Bible is that Judas was possessed by Satan (Luke 22:3). Whether or not greed played a part is open to debate. Matthew says that Judas went to the authorities, seeking money in return for bringing in Jesus (26:14-16), while Mark's account reports that Judas went on his own initiative to give information on Jesus' whereabouts and was then offered money in return (14:10-11).

One theory, with no biblical support, is that Judas was the most loyal of the Apostles, and was thus chosen by God to betray Jesus, so that he might end his ministry on earth and be resurrected.

Also among the explanations without biblical evidence is the suggestion that Judas was forcing the issue, hoping that in crisis Jesus would prove himself the political messiah by overthrowing the Roman procurate. This view depends on the derivation of Judas' surname, Iscariot, from Sicarii, the zealous nationalists who were active at the time in usurping Roman rule in Palestine. It is generally believed that their conception of the Messiah was as "the son of David," the political and military leader. Judas may have been a member of this party and thought that Jesus, as the Messiah, could call the powers of God into battle against the Romans.

The Gospels agree that Judas took thirty pieces of silver as pay. (If, as some scholars believe, the value of this amount was only about twenty dollars, then greed might be discounted as one of Judas' motives.) The gospels also agree on the manner of betrayal. In the garden of Gethsemane, Judas approached Jesus and kissed him on the cheek to signify to the guards who his master was.

Where there is conflict in the New Testament is over the end of Judas' life. Matthew (27:9) seems to be interpreting Judas' final acts before he hanged himself as a fulfillment of a passage in Zechariah (11:12–13) in which the prophet casts thirty pieces of silver to "the potter in the house of the Lord"—even though Matthew seems to be confused about the origin of the passage, attributing it to Jeremiah (Jer 18:1–4). Thus, Matthew says that Judas, regretting what he had done, threw the silver into the Temple and the priests bought a potter's field with the money, since they could not put "the price of blood" in the Temple treasury.

Acts says that Judas himself purchased the field and that he died there by "falling headlong . . . and all his bowels gushed out," perhaps by throwing himself from a precipice (Acts 1:18).

Mark: After Jesus' death the Apostles would meet at Mark's mother's house (Acts 12:12). Tradition has it that the second-story guest chamber of this house was the "upper room," the site of the Last Supper (Mark 14:15; Luke 22:12), and the place Jesus met his disciples after the Resurrection.

At the time of Jesus' ministry Mark was in his early teens. Though he does not appear in the Gospels, legend links him to the young man who was arrested in the garden of Gethsemane with Jesus. This quick-thinking youth managed to escape the clutches of his abductors by slipping out of his robe and running naked from the garden (Mark 14:51–52).

Acts contains the only reference to Mark by name. There he is called "John whose surname was Mark," or simply John.

He was an assistant to Barnabas and Paul on their missionary journey to Antioch (Acts 12:25). But when they got to Perga (on the Aegean coast of Turkey), he left the party and returned to Jerusalem (13:13). Evidently Paul was angered at Mark's lack of endurance or missionary zeal, so angry that when Barnabas took Mark on as an assistant for his second mission, Paul broke with Barnabas (15:37–39). Paul must have repented of his anger and reconciled with Mark in the next ten years, for at the time he wrote the Second Epistle to Timothy he wanted Mark to come to him and praised him as "profitable to me for the ministry" (2 Tim 4:11).

The other epistles imply that Mark may have visited Colossae (in present-day Turkey) and been in Rome with Peter (Col 4:10; 1 Pet 5:13). Mark's connection with Peter is confirmed by Papias, the 2d-century Christian bishop, who relates that Mark was the interpreter—the ghost-writer—of Peter's memoirs, which form the Gospel of Mark.

The remainder of Mark's life is obscured by a still more nebulous haze of speculation and legend. Various traditions make him the founder of churches as far distant as Egypt and northern Italy.

Paul: The best-known and perhaps the most revered of the Apostles, Paul was not among the original twelve. He was born in Tarsus, a hellenized city in Asia Minor. Tarsus was one of the lights of the ancient Middle East; the learning of the citizens had impressed the Greek philosopher Strabo, and the city's vital and prosperous economy was widely renowned. Paul himself was quite proud of his hometown, boasting that it was "no mean city" (Acts 21:39).

He was born into a family of Pharisees whose lineage had been traced back to the tribe of Benjamin (Phil 3:5). His given name was Saul, as he is known in Acts. The Roman version of this, Paul, was the name he used exclusively after starting on his first mission. Undoubtedly he adopted the Latinized form of his name to make himself and his mission more germane to a Roman audience. Acts notes that he prided himself on his Roman citizenship (22:28) and that he used the citizen's prerogative of appealing to Caesar (25:11) to redress his grievances.

It is not known how his family came to possess citizenship, though historical sources report that Jewish tradesmen were brought to Tarsus in 171 BC to stimulate the economy and that they were given Roman citizenship in exchange. Perhaps Paul's ancestors were among this group. There is some evidence that Paul was adept at tentmaking, and this could have been the craft of his forefathers and father (Acts 18:3).

As a youth he trained to be a rabbi and went to Jerusalem to study with Gamaliel, the foremost teacher of the day (Acts 5:34–39; 22:3). There he joined a faction of religious fanatics that became committed to extinguishing Christianity (Acts 26:9–11; Gal 1:13). He was present at the stoning of Stephen, the first Christian martyr, and though he cast no stones himself he was "consenting unto his death" (Acts 7:58; 8:1). He took a more active part by desecrating Christian churches, dragging the parishioners off to prison, and witnessing against them (Acts 8:3; 26:10).

His conversion to Christianity was sudden and traumatic. He was on the road to Damascus, with letters of marque from the Jerusalem high priests giving him the authority to bring Damascus Christians back to Jerusalem for trial, when he saw a blinding vision of Jesus. There are three detailed accounts of the vision in Acts (9:1–19; 22:6–21; 26:12–18) which allow us to reconstruct the scene.

It was about noon, as Paul was nearing Damascus, when he was dazzled by the brilliant light in the sky. As he fell to his knees in astonishment, Paul heard a voice saying, "Saul, Saul, why persecutest thou me?" It was the voice of Jesus, and it called on him to stop hounding Christians. The voice told Paul to continue to Damascus, where he would receive instructions. Paul, completely blinded by the vision, had to be led to the town by his companions, who had not seen the light but had heard the voice. Paul lay in bed for three days, eating and drinking nothing. Then Ananias, a disciple to whom Jesus had appeared with instructions for finding Paul, came to the house where the stricken man was laid up, and restored his sight.

Paul's conversion was immediate. He stayed a few days with the Damascan disciples and then began to preach in the synagogues. Everyone in Damascus was aghast, for Paul's reputation as a Christian persecutor had preceded him. So powerful was the story of Paul's conversion that those who opposed the Christian movement plotted to kill him. The disciples got wind of the plot and smuggled Paul out of Damascus by lowering him over the city wall in a basket.

He returned to Jerusalem, but was not well received by the disciples there. His conversion was too sudden and his notoriety too dark for him to be immediately admitted to their circle. Barnabas, having heard Paul preach in Damascus, vouched for him, however, and Paul's sermons in Jerusalem convinced the disciples of his sincerity.

For the next thirteen years Paul dropped virtually out of sight. He spent about three years in Damascus and Arabia (Gal 1:17), then went to Tarsus and did missionary work there, in Syria, and in Cilicia (the area around Tarsus). Before he went to Tarsus he met with Peter and James in Jerusalem. For some reason he saw only these two disciples while he was there (Gal 18:19). For ten years following this meeting he stayed away from Jerusalem, apparently as penance for his misdeeds, and worked and studied so hard his reputation spread to the city without his presence (Gal 1:20–24).

After this period he joined Barnabas: first to preach in Antioch for a year, then to go on an extended mission. On this trip, known as the first mission, they went from Antioch (on the Syrian coast) to the island of Cyprus, to Perga (on the southern Mediterranean coast of Turkey), to the *other* Antioch (in central Turkey) and neighboring cities, and finally turned back, taking the same route on their return, but skipping Cyprus.

Their routine was to go directly to the synagogue in each town and preach there, adjourning afterward to a private house to answer questions. Generally they were treated kindly (Gal 4:14), but on occasion they met with violent opposition; once Paul was nearly stoned to death at Lystra (Acts 14:19), ironically suffering the same punishment he had once condoned for Stephen.

On their return trip they checked the progress of the Christian churches their sermons had inspired, and they appointed elders to report to them by letter.

When they arrived in Syrian Antioch they were disturbed to hear that the Jerusalem Church was imposing Mosaic law on all converts, including gentiles. They went to a convocation of early Church leaders at Jerusalem and there Paul's liberal views won out: It was agreed that gentile Christians should keep only a few of the laws, mostly those which prohibited idolatrous practices (Acts 15:29).

Paul's next mission took him even farther afield, and with new companions. He had dropped Barnabas because Barnabas had wanted to take Mark, their assistant on the previous mission who had abruptly left them at Perga. Paul picked Silas to make the journey with him, and he was later joined by Timothy, a young Greek Christian, and Luke, the author of the Gospel and Paul's physician.

The second mission became an overland journey, for the most part. Sticking to the coast, they walked north to Syrian Antioch, then northeast and inland to Tarsus, Antioch in Pisidia, and finally toward Greece and Athens. On this mission Paul brought Christianity to Europe. Despite the noble-sounding accomplishment of this journey, it was more troubled than the first, especially as Paul reached Europe. In Philippi, one of the first stops on the Greek coast, Paul and Silas were flogged and thrown into prison. At Thessalonica, just down the road, they barely eluded an angry mob.

Paul went alone into Athens. He met with no mistreatment here; indeed, the Athenians were ever ready to "hear some new thing" and to dispute over it (Acts 17:21). But Paul's concept of a single God, omnipotent and omniscient, bounced off the idolatrous Greeks, and the idea of resurrection did not sit well with an audience as self-consciously rational and philosophy-filled as the Athenians.

In Corinth he was far more successful and he stayed there eighteen months. He moved on only because the Roman governor, Gallio, pressured him to stop preaching (Acts 18:12–17). He left for Jerusalem, stopping at Ephesus (on the Aegean coast of Turkey) and Caesarea (on the northern coast of Palestine), and finally Jerusalem.

Paul must have quickly gotten restless or been very worried about the fate of the churches he had set in motion, for he apparently began his third mission soon after he got to Jerusalem.

Essentially he stuck to the route of the second mission. Besides revisiting many of the cities where he had preached on previous trips, he stopped at many new cities, several of these along Turkey's Aegean coast, and at the islands nearby. During this mission he also wrote many of the letters, the epistles, that are preserved in the Bible.

Although the return to Jerusalem was triumphant in many ways and he was warmly greeted by the heads of the Jerusalem Church, there was much suspicion, among both the Christians and the Jews, that he had been loose with the laws. He tried to appease his critics by spending a week in observance of the rituals and making sacrifices in the Temple, but there he was recognized and set upon by a mob. Saved from the crowd by the Roman authorities and from imprisonment by his Roman citizenship, Paul was taken in protective custody to Caesarea. He demanded to be heard by the emperor, as was his right as a citizen, so he sailed for Rome, no doubt with the conviction he could spread Christianity there as well.

For the two years he was in the capital of the empire he was provided with a house by the government and was free to receive guests and preach as his case awaited hearing.

No one knows what became of Paul after this. He wanted to go to Spain to carry his mission even farther—and perhaps he did, since Pope Clement I (AD 95) implied such was the case. Many scholars believe that he died in Rome.

What a Way to Go!

Pan-fried: In Maccabean times, under Antiochus, eight Jews— seven brothers and their mother—were forced to eat swine's flesh and were whipped and scourged. One of the brothers told the king it was useless to torment them, as they were prepared to die rather than transgress the Jewish laws. This made the king so mad he ordered pans and caldrons heated. While the mother and brothers looked on, the tongue and "utmost parts" were cut off the brother who had spoken. Still alive, he was then fried in a pan.

When he was dead, the second brother's torture began. His skin, with the hair still attached, was pulled off his head, and then he was treated as the first brother had been. The other five sons were killed in the same way, and the mother was killed last of all (2 Macc 7:1–4).

Beaned: Abimelech, who had tried to build himself a little king- dom at Shechem, found himself faced with revolt. After setting fire to Shechem, he marched on the outlying town of Thebez, where the inhabitants had gathered in the tower. As he was trying to set fire to the tower, a woman dropped a piece of a millstone on his head, breaking his skull. Wanting to avoid the indignity of having been slain by a woman, Abimelech ordered his armor-bearer to pierce him with a sword (Judg 9:50–54).

Trampled Underfoot: When the Assyrians suddenly broke off their siege of Samaria and fled, they left their camp full of spoils. The king appointed a guard for the city gate, but the Samaritans were so eager for the booty that they stomped the guard to death as they raced out of the city (2 Kings 7:20).

Suffocated: Hazael, wanting the Syrian throne for himself, murdered King Ben-hadad of Damascus by dipping a thick cloth in water and spreading it over Ben-hadad's face (2 Kings 8:15).

Gutted: Razis, an elder of Jerusalem in Maccabean times, decided to kill himself when 500 soldiers sent to murder him broke through his door and prepared to set fire to the building. Razis fell upon his sword, but in his haste he botched the job. He then flung himself from the wall onto the warriors. However, the soldiers stepped aside so that Razis crashed to the ground. By now "his blood gushed out like spouts of water, and his wounds were grievous." Nevertheless, he managed to scramble onto a steep rock. As a final gesture of defiance, Razis pulled his intestines out with both hands and threw them on the soldiers before he died (2 Macc 14:41–46).

Broken Neck: The chief priest Eli was ninety-eight years old and rather heavyset at the time the Philistines captured the Ark. He was sitting on a chair in the gate of the city when a messenger brought him the news, and he "fell from off the seat backward by the side of the gate, and his neck brake, and he died: for he was an old man, and heavy" (1 Sam 4:18).

Tangled: After Absalom's unsuccessful battle to take his father's throne, he rode off on a mule. The mule walked under a thick oak, where Absalom's head got caught between the branches. Then "the mule that was under him went away" and left Absalom hanging there. David's general Joab thrust three darts into the heart of the helpless Absalom and then had his men deliver the death blow (2 Sam 18:9–15).

Left-handed Stab: During the period of judges, the Moabites invaded Israel and their king, Eglon, made Jericho his headquarters. For eighteen years he exacted tribute from the Israelites until Ehud determined to deliver his people. Ehud hid a dagger under his clothes and went to see Eglon. By saying he had a secret message for the king, he gained a private audience. Eglon did not know that Ehud was left-handed, and so he did not take alarm in time when Ehud suddenly withdrew the dagger with his left hand. The king was fat, and when Ehud thrust the dagger into his belly, "The haft also went in after the blade; and the fat closed upon the blade, so that he could not draw the dagger out of his belly" (Judg 3:14–22).

Eunuchs

Although using eunuchs as especially trusted servants in royal and wealthy households was widespread in the Middle East, it is unlikely that the Israelites castrated any of their own people because castrated men were not allowed to enter the congregation (Deut 23:1).

Eunuchs are not mentioned during the period of the patriarchs, during the united monarchy, or during the early days of the divided kingdoms. Their first appearance in a position of importance in Israel is under King Ahab (871–852 BC), who had a eunuch among his court officials. Possibly having a eunuch at court was one of the foreign pretensions adopted by Ahab's Phoenician wife, Jezebel.

Jezebel was described as being attended by eunuchs. When Jehu went to kill her, he looked up at her window "and there looked out two or three eunuchs." Jehu ordered them to throw her down, which they did (2 Kings 9:32–33). Eunuchs continued to be associated with foreign religions into the time of Josiah of Judah (639–609 BC), when one is said to have guarded a temple to Baal (2 Kings 23:11). In Isaiah's time, when they seemed to have been thoroughly accepted in Israel, they were still called "the sons of the stranger" (Isa 56:3).

Eunuchs were an important commodity in the African trade, and several biblical eunuchs are described as Ethiopian.

Eunuchs were also obtained in war. It was not uncommon for conquering enemies to castrate young males and take young girls for their harems. Darius is said to have done this to entire populations (as at Chios and Lesbos). But the Hebrews seemed to fear this only for children of the royal household. When Jerusalem was about to fall to Nebuchadnezzar, Isaiah warned King Hezekiah that its population would be deported to Babylon and "thy sons . . . shall be eunuchs in the palace of the king of Babylon" (2 Kings 20:18; Isa 25:19; 39:7). Because of this, some scholars believe Daniel and his companions, who were entrusted by Nebuchadnezzar to "the master of his eunuchs," must have been castrated (Dan 1:3-7).

The Greek *eunuch* means "keeper of the bed" (sometimes translated as "chamberlain" in the Bible), and castrates are best known as guardians of harems. Esther mentions that one had charge of the concubines and that another one had charge of the girls being considered for queen (Est 2). In Israel they may also have been used to guard women and children (Jer 41:16).

In practice, eunuchs gained such an intimate knowledge of the workings of royal households that they were able to achieve great power. There seemed to be a common misconception about them—that they were somehow harmless and trustworthy—so that they often attended the king or headed the palace guard. The Book of Esther (1:10) said Xerxes I had seven eunuchs as personal attendants, and similar figures are given for kings of Judah (2 Kings 25:19-21). Esther, as queen, had a eunuch who waited on her and carried her confidential messages to Mordecai (Est 4:5-6, 9-10).

Eunuchs were often given sensitive assignments. In Assyria, for instance, they had the delicate job of recording spoils of war, and a eunuch is mentioned as treasurer of Ethiopia (Acts 8:27). Contrarily, they were also thought to be especially good military leaders, and often headed elite troops. Monuments to warrior eunuchs have been found in Assyria. The Bible mentions that in Judah a eunuch had "charge of the men of war" (Jer 52:25).

During Hezekiah's reign (727-698 BC), at least one of the ambassadors whom Sennacherib entrusted with the mission of trying to convince Jerusalem to surrender was a eunuch. This officer is listed in the Bible as Rabsaris, which is not a proper name but a title meaning "chief eunuch" (2 Kings 18:17). Rabsaris is again mentioned as one of the chief Assyrian officials who took over the city (Jer 39:3) and as one who, later in Babylonia, was entrusted with freeing Jeremiah and making sure the prophet got back to Judah (Jer 39:11-14).

When Jerusalem fell, the captain of its warriors was a castrate and five to seven eunuchs were attendants to the king of Judah—and all were deported to Babylon and executed (2 Kings 25:19-21; Jer 52:25-27). In listing captives taken to Babylonia by Nebuchadnezzar, Jeremiah indicates the high position eunuchs had achieved in Israel by enumerating the royal household in this order: the king, the queen, the eunuchs, the princes (Jer 29:2). Elsewhere Jeremiah again lists castrates with the princes and priests of Judah (Jer 34:19).

The Book of Esther (2:21; 6:2) describes two eunuchs in the Persian court who plotted to overthrow Xerxes I; although Mordecai foiled this plot, Xerxes was later assassinated and a subsequent Persian monarch was simply a puppet whose kingdom was ruled by his eunuchs.

While eunuchs never seemed to attain the power in Israel that they did elsewhere, Israelite attitudes toward them changed from distaste to approval. Jeremiah (38:7–13) described an Ethiopian eunuch, Ebed-melech, as playing a heroic role. When King Zedekiah imprisoned Jeremiah, Ebed-melech pleaded with the king for the prophet's release. His standing was such that the king granted the request. The Bible details the solicitude the eunuch showed the prophet: Ebed-melech even threw rags down to Jeremiah in the dungeon and instructed him to pad his armpits so that the ropes would not cut or burn him as he was hoisted to the surface (Jer 38:7–13).

In an interesting passage, Isaiah counts eunuchs among those whom God will bless. In discussing people who keep the Sabbath holy, Isaiah (56:3–5) wrote: "Neither let the son of the stranger, that hath joined himself to the Lord, speak, saying, The Lord hath utterly separated me from his people: neither let the eunuch say, Behold, I am a dry tree.

"For thus saith the Lord unto the eunuchs that keep my sabbaths . . . and take hold of my covenant; Even unto them will I give in mine house and within my walls a place and a name better than of sons and of daughters: I will give them an everlasting name, that shall not be cut off."

An echo of this is seen much later, when Jesus, replying to a question from the disciples about whether "it is not good to marry," said: "For there are some eunuchs, which were so born from their mother's womb: and there are some eunuchs, which were made eunuchs of men: and there be eunuchs, which have made themselves eunuchs for the kingdom of heaven's sake. He that is able to receive it, let him receive it" (Matt 19:11–12).

Best-dressed List

Joseph's coat of many colors, given to him by his father, Jacob, made him the envy of his brothers. But the coat may have been a symbol that Jacob considered Joseph—who was not the firstborn—his heir (Gen 37:3).

The Israelites had such good clothes that their garments never got old, nor did their shoes wear out, despite forty years of tramping around the wilderness (Deut 29:5).

The high priest may have been the best-dressed man in the Bible. His ephod (the main garment) was of fine linen of gold, blue, scarlet, and purple; embroidered, multicolored pomegranates and golden bells decorated the hem. Over the ephod the high priest wore a breastplate of fine linen. The breastplate was fastened with gold rings and chains that held twelve gems carved with the names of the twelve tribes. Around his head he wore a miter with a gold plate bearing the words "Holiness to the Lord" (Ex 28).

David was apparently a clotheshorse, because his clothing is frequently mentioned in the Bible. He had good clothes of his own, such as a robe of fine linen (1 Chr 15:27), yet he never disdained castoffs: He willingly took Jonathan's robe and other garments and girdle (1 Sam 18:4), and the Amalekite's crown and bracelet (2 Sam 1:10); and he put the crown of the king of Rabbah on his own head (2 Sam 12:30).

Job's idea of fine dress was being decked with majesty, excellency, glory, and beauty (Job 40:10), but he himself wore "an earring of gold" (Job 42:11).

Jeremiah's idea of being well dressed was being clothed in crimson with golden ornaments and a painted face (Jer 4:30).

Isaiah's best-dressed person is clothed with righteousness as a breastplate, a helmet of salvation, garments of vengeance, and a cloak of zeal (Isa 59:17).

Ezekiel's ideal outfit included shoes of badger's skin, embroidery, silk, bracelets, a necklace, earrings, a jewel on the forehead, and a beautiful crown (Ezek 16:10–13).

In the Song of Solomon, beautiful dress included "cheeks comely with rows of jewels, thy neck with chains of gold" (S of S 1:10).

The "princes of the sea" (Phoenicians) wore embroidered garments of fine Egyptian linen and blue or purple robes (Ezek 26:16).

King Saul wore a crown and a bracelet (2 Sam 1:10).

The Midianite warriors wore golden earrings, and their kings wore purple robes with ornaments and collars—even their camels wore necklaces (Judg 8:24–26).

John the Baptist wore what was then considered common dress but is now considered stylish: a camel's hair robe (Matt 3:4).

When Joseph was given a high post in Egypt, he wore fine linen, a gold chain around his neck, and the pharaoh's ring (Gen 41:42).

Jacob is the only person mentioned in the Bible as having gloves, and they were kidskin: Rebekah "put the skins of the kids of the goats upon his hands" (Gen 27:16).

God decked out Jerusalem as a beautiful woman with embroidered clothing, linen, and silk, a crown, bracelets, earrings, necklace, and a jewel on her forehead (Isa 16:10–13).

The Unpopular Queen

Athaliah of Judah (842–836 BC) was the only queen either kingdom ever had. Her father was Ahab of Israel. Her mother, Jezebel, daughter of the king of Tyre, had been married to Ahab to cement friendship between Tyre and Israel, and Athaliah in turn had been married to King Jehoram of Judah to strengthen the alliance between Judah and Israel.

Jezebel had been condemned for fostering the worship of Baal in Israel, and Athaliah was hated for doing the same in Judah.

When Athaliah was widowed, her twenty-two-year-old son, Ahaziah, took the throne, but Athaliah remained a hidden power, encouraging him in pagan worship. After ruling only a year, Ahaziah was murdered, and Athaliah tried to butcher all remaining royal males in Judah so that she could claim the throne for herself.

Ahaziah's sister, however, hid his infant son, Joash, during this massacre. Then she and her husband, the priest Jehoiada, secretly raised Joash in the Temple until he was seven. With the palace guard and army officers surrounding him with spears and shields, Joash was crowned king of Judah. The crowd applauded and yelled, "God save the king," and people began to rejoice, singing and blowing trumpets.

Hearing the noise, Athaliah dashed into the Temple and saw the crowned child. Tearing her clothes, she cried, "Treason, treason!"

Guards dragged Athaliah from the Temple to the Horse Gate of the palace, where they ran her through with swords. Smashing the altar and images in the temple of Baal and killing its priest, the crowd then took Joash into the palace and sat him on the throne (2 Kings 8:26; 11:1–20; 2 Chr 22–23; 24:7).

Kings

UNITED MONARCHY

Saul (before 1004 BC): A handsome and humble Benjamite whom the prophet Samuel anointed Israel's first king, Saul came into his own when he rallied the nation to defend Jabesh. He united the tribes for the first time since Joshua and scored impressive victories over the Philistines and other enemies pressing on Israel's borders. But his achievements were over-shadowed by his personal torment and possible insanity, his clashes with Samuel, and his love/hate relationship with David. After a reign of twenty years, he killed himself after being wounded at the battle of Gilboa (1 Sam 9–31; 2 Sam; 1 Chr 5:10; 8:33; 9:39; 10; 15:29; 26:28).

David (1004–965 BC): Anointed king by Samuel when he was a child, David was an outlaw and womanizer by the time he came to the throne at age thirty. A charismatic and brilliant leader, he made Israel a major power. He conquered Jerusalem and made it the national capital, secured territory between Dan and the Brook of Egypt that included the major trade routes, strengthened his borders with treaties and vassal states, and gave Israel an army. His later years were saddened by an attempted coup by his son Absalom, famine, pestilence, and other problems. Before he died, he made Solomon, his son by Bathsheba, his successor (1 Sam 16–31; 1 Kings 1–2).

Solomon (965–928 BC): Famed for his wisdom, Solomon built on the foundations laid by David, organizing the kingdom for tax and administra-tive purposes, developing commerce and shipping, launching a lavish building program to embellish the kingdom, and establishing an extravagant court life. Although his subjects were proud of him, his splendid court and building projects drained much of the new wealth, and he was accused of falling under too much foreign influence—even to the point of worshiping foreign gods. Toward the end of his reign there was discontent over taxation and forced labor, as well as unrest at the borders of the kingdom, and the united kingdom failed to survive after his death.

KINGS OF JUDAH (928–586 BC)

Rehoboam (928–911): Son of Solomon, Rehoboam was unable to hold his father's kingdom together and ruled only in Judah. He wasted Judah in wars with Israel. When Pharaoh Sheshonq I invaded, Rehoboam lost his Red Sea outlet and had to pay heavy tribute to save Jerusalem. He built fifteen border fortifications, leaving only the north open in hopes of reconciliation with Israel. He was accused of idolatry, a sin attributed to the influence of his many foreign wives (1 Kings 11:43; 12; 2 Chr 9:31; 13:7).

Abijam (911–908): Attempted to conquer Israel but advanced only a few miles, to Bethel (1 Kings 14:31; 15:1–8; 2 Chr 11:20, 22; 12:16; 13).

Asa (908–867): Israel tried to invade Judah, and Asa asked help of Benhadad of Aram-damascus, who attacked Israel. As soon as Israel withdrew, Asa fortified the border between them. Later he repelled an invasion by Zerah the Ethiopian. Asa was a religious reformer who tried to stamp out idolatry, but was accused of relying too heavily on doctors instead of on God for curing his own ills (1 Kings 15, 16; 2 Chr 14—17:2; Jer 41:9).

Jehoshaphat (867–846): Toured the kingdom to institute religious and judicial reform, strengthened fortifications and army, revived commerce. Renewed friendship with Israel by marrying his son to their royal family and by joining in common wars (1 Kings 15:24; 22; 2 Kings 1:17; 3; 8:16; 12:18; 2 Chr 17–21).

Jehoram (846–843): Jehoshaphat bequeathed shares in his wealth and reign to seven sons, so Jehoram killed his six brothers. Was accused of idolatry after he married daughter of Ahab and Jezebel of Israel to seal friendship between the two nations. Lost Edom. His family—except for youngest son, Ahaziah—was wiped out in a Philistine invasion that reached Jerusalem. The Bible says he died of bowel disease, but as he was not mourned, or buried in royal tombs, he may have been murdered (2 Kings 1:17; 8:16–29; 12:18; 2 Chr 21:1–16; 22:1–11).

Ahaziah (843): Trying to aid Israel's war with Aram-damascus, Ahaziah was caught in Jehu's coup and was killed as part of Jehu's program to wipe out Jezebel's descendants (2 Kings 8:24–29; 9:16–29; 10:13–14; 11:1–2; 12:18; 14:13–14; 2 Chr 22).

Athaliah (842–836): Daughter of Jezebel, she was the only queen either kingdom ever had. Promoted worship of Baal. She seized power after her son Ahaziah's death by massacring heirs to the throne—only Ahaziah's infant son, Joash, escaped when he was hidden in the Temple by the priest Jehoiada. When he was seven Joash was crowned king in the Temple under armed guard. Athaliah, hearing the singing and trumpeting, dashed in, yelling, "Treason, treason." She was dragged from the Temple and killed (2 Kings 8:26; 11:1–20; 2 Chr 22–23).

Joash (836–798): Although he had been saved and enthroned by Jehoiada, the priests lost influence because Joash knew they were taking the Temple funds and instituted reform that included executing Jehoiada's son. Joash lost the Temple treasures anyway when King Hazael of Aram-damascus threatened Jerusalem. For the murder and the heavy ransom, he was killed by his own officers (2 Kings 11–13:1; 2 Chr 22:11, 24).

Amaziah (798–769): Amaziah, aged twenty-five, took a census to conscript an army. In a successful war against Edomites he recovered trade routes to the Gulf of Akaba. Then he erred by challenging Israel. He was defeated by King Jehoash of Israel, who destroyed part of Jerusalem's walls and took hostages and spoils. His people rose against him, killing him at the fortress of Lachish (2 Kings 12:21; 13:12; 14:1–23; 15:3; 2 Chr 24:27; 25; 26:1).

Uzziah (769–758): Taking the throne at age sixteen, Uzziah made Judah more prosperous than it had been since Solomon. He repaired relations with Israel and reorganized Judah's army to reconquer all lost territory. Uzziah recovered Edom and repaired the port of Ezion-geber, annexed Philistine cities on the coast, and built fortifications along highways and borders. Jerusalem was refortified and became a busy commercial center. But after Uzziah developed leprosy he lived in seclusion in the palace, having his son Jotham execute his orders. Because of his leprosy he was not buried in the royal tomb (2 Kings 14:21–22; 15:1–8; 2 Chr 26; Amos 1:1).

Jotham (758–733): Well trained by his father, Jotham maintained Judah's prosperity and military advantage (2 Kings 15:5, 7, 30–38; 16:1; 2 Chr 26:21–23; 27).

Ahaz (733–727): A weak king who inherited the throne at age twenty, Ahaz indulged in pagan cults that involved child sacrifice and burned his son as an offering. He was unable to control Edom or the Philistine coast, both of which broke away. When he was invaded by a coalition of Israel and Aram-damascus, he appealed to Tiglath-pileser, saying "I am thy servant." The

Assyrians obliged by crushing Damascus and most of Israel, but in return Ahaz had to pay Tiglath-pileser heavy tribute. He too was denied burial in the royal tombs (2 Kings 15:38; 16:1–20; 23:12; 2 Chr 27:9; 28:1–27; 29:19; Isa 7:1–12, 14–28).

Hezekiah (727–698): Judah was no more than an Assyrian vassal when the able Hezekiah came to the throne at age twenty-five. As Assyrian power was declining, he risked restoring Israelite worship in Jerusalem and inviting the people of Israel to participate, acts that gave him strong backing from the prophet Isaiah. Knowing war was inevitable, Hezekiah produced large numbers of weapons, constructed storehouses for staples, and improved the capacity of Jerusalem's water supply to withstand siege. Against Isaiah's advice, he joined an anti-Assyrian coalition that resulted in the destruction of Lachish and heavy tribute being imposed on Jerusalem. Despite a siege, Jerusalem was spared (2 Kings 16:20; 18–20; 2 Chr 28:27, 29–32; Isa 36–39; Jer 26:18–19).

Manasseh (698–642): Made king at age twelve, he is noted only for the restoration of pagan cults and continued tribute to Assyria (2 Kings 20–21; 2 Chr 32:33; 33; Jer 15:4).

Amon (641–640): Continued idolatrous practices. Was assassinated by his own officers (2 Kings 21:18–26; 2 Chr 33:20–25).

Josiah (639–609): Became king at age eight. Instituted religious reform. Was killed in battle when he foolishly tried to prevent the Egyptian army from crossing his land to get to Assyria (2 Kings 21:24–26; 22–23; 2 Chr 33:25; 34–35).

Jehoahaz (609): Tried to be king after his father's death, but Pharaoh Necho II sent him in chains to Egypt, where he died (2 Kings 23:30–40; 2 Chr 36:1–4).

Jehoiakim (608–598): His name was Eliakim, but it was changed by Pharaoh Necho, who appointed him puppet ruler of Judah. Jeremiah said he deserved the burial of an ass because he built himself a palace when his people were heavily taxed to pay Egyptian tribute. In 605 Babylonia won Judah from Egypt. After three years of their rule Jehoiakim rebelled and then promptly died, leaving his son to cope with Babylonian revenge (2 Kings 23:34–37; 24:1–6; 2 Chr 36:4–8; Jer 22:18–24; 26:21–23; 36:1, 9, 20–32; 46:2; Dan 1:1–2).

Jehoiachin (597): Succeeded to throne just as Nebuchadnezzar arrived at Jerusalem, and after a three-month siege was taken captive to Babylonia. Judah kept hoping for his return. After thirty-seven years in prison, he was freed, but never did return to Jerusalem (2 Kings 24:6–17; 25; 27–30; 2 Chr 36:8–9; Est 2:6; Jer 24:1; 52:31–34).

Zedekiah (596–586): Appointed to the throne by Nebuchadnezzar, who changed his name from Mattaniah, Zedekiah ruled under a handicap: His subjects considered Jehoiachin their king. Moreover, the land was desolate, and most skilled laborers had been deported to Babylonia. Nevertheless, he rebuilt Jerusalem's defenses and saved the city from the Edomites. Unbelievably, though, he then conspired against Babylon so that Nebuchadnezzar laid siege and destroyed Jerusalem. Zedekiah was taken in chains to Nebuchadnezzar, who forced him to watch the execution of his sons and then blinded him and sent him in chains to Babylon, where he died (2 Kings 24; 2 Chr 36:11–20; Jer 34; 37–39; 52; Ezek 17:15–20).

KINGS OF ISRAEL (928–723 BC)

Jeroboam (928–907): After an unsuccessful plot to overthrow Solomon, he had taken asylum with Pharaoh Sheshonq I. He returned to rule Israel on Solomon's death, built a new capital at Tirzah, and was condemned for setting up gold calves at new sanctuaries in Bethel and Dan to keep his people from worshiping in Jerusalem. He reigned only four years before Pharaoh Sheshonq overran Israel. Border wars with Judah began (1 Kings 11:26–40; 12–14; 15:6, 9; 2 Kings 3:3; 9:9; 10:29, 31; 13:2, 11; 14:24; 15:9, 28; 17:21, 22; 23:15; 2 Chr 10:2–16; 11:1–4, 14; 12:15; 13:1–20).

Nadab (907–906): He battled Judah over the border. While he was warring with Philistines, Baasha killed him and seized the throne (1 Kings 14:20; 15:25–31).

Baasha (906–883): He unsuccessfully invaded Judah and was in turn invaded by Damascus, which took much of Galilee. Tolerated idolatry (1 Kings 15–16; 21:22; 2 Kings 9:9; Jer 41:9).

Elah (883–882): He ruled only until, "drinking himself drunk," he was murdered by Zimri, one of his officers (1 Kings 16:8–10).

Zimri (882): Ruled seven days. The army, angered by his treason, proclaimed Omri king and surrounded the capital. Zimri set fire to the palace and let it collapse on him (1 Kings 16:9–20).

Omri (882–871): A great and wise king, Omri made peace with Judah and won back Moab and other lost territories. To cement ties with Tyre, he married his son Ahab to Jezebel, daughter of Tyre's king. Since Jezebel encouraged her own cults in Israel, Omri was denounced by the prophets and is slighted in the Bible. He brought his nation peace and prosperity and established a strategically sited new capital, Samaria, to guard the Via Maris and to rival Jerusalem. Although Omri died after only twelve years on the throne, he so impressed contemporaries that Israel was afterward known as the Land of Omri (1 Kings 16:21–28).

Ahab (871–852): Also a good ruler. Continued Omri's peaceable foreign policy and domestic prosperity. Completed construction in Samaria, rebuilt Jericho. His wife, Jezebel's, promotion of Phoenician cults (Ahab was accused of taking part) brought the wrath of the prophet Elijah on him. Ben-hadad of Aram-damascus launched two attacks that Ahab repelled, but Ahab was criticized for sparing Ben-hadad's life. Meanwhile, Moab revolted. Ahab was killed in a final battle against Ben-hadad (1 Kings 16–22; 2 Chr 18).

Ahaziah (852–851): Son of Ahab and Jezebel, Ahaziah's first act as king was to injure himself by falling from a second story. He lived only long enough to fail twice: He tried to kill Elijah, who had predicted his death; and he tried to start a navy, which apparently sank (1 Kings 22:51; 2 Kings 1; 2 Chr 20:35–37).

Jehoram (851–842): Also a son of Ahab and Jezebel, Jehoram made an abortive attempt to recover Moab. Samaria was besieged by Arameans but survived. In a new Aramean battle Jehoram was wounded, and while he recuperated turned the army over to his general Jehu. The prophet Elisha instigated a revolt against Jehoram, anointing Jehu king and urging him to kill the descendants of Jezebel, starting with Jehoram (2 Kings 3; 8:28–29; 9; 2 Chr 22:5–7).

Jehu (842–814): Jehu, busy butchering Jezebel and her family and stamping out the worship of Baal, was oblivious of the fact that his kingdom was meanwhile falling apart—the economy crumbling, foreign alliances deteriorating. Territory east of the Jordan was lost to Damascus (1 Kings 19:16–17; 2 Kings 9–10; 12:1; 13:1; 14:8; 15:12; 2 Chr 22:7–9; 25:17; Hos 1:4).

Jehoahaz (814–800): Jehu's son managed to lose even more territory. Israel became a dependency of Damascus (2 Kings 10:35; 13:1–10, 22–25; 14:1, 8, 17; 2 Chr 25: 17, 25).

Jehoash (800–784): Recovered territory lost by his father. Judah attacked, so Jehoash punished Jerusalem by breaching the walls and taking captives and treasures (2 Kings 13:9–25; 14:1–27; 2 Chr 25:17–25).

Jeroboam II (784–748): A strong ruler, he made peace with Judah and recovered territory until Israel was the size it had been in David's time. His rule was prosperous, with new building at Samaria (2 Kings 13:13; 14:16–29; 15:1, 8; Amos 1:1; 7:9–11).

Zechariah (748/7): Reigned six months before being assassinated by Shallum (2 Kings 14:29; 15:8–9).

Shallum (748/7): Reigned a month and was murdered by Menahem (2 Kings 15:10–15).

Menahem (747/6–737/6): Went on a killing spree in which he "ripped up" pregnant women and otherwise suppressed opposition to his reign. Became even more unpopular by imposing heavy taxation to pay tribute to Tiglath-pileser to keep Assyrian forces at bay (2 Kings 15:14–22).

Pekahiah (737/6–735/4): Continued to collect tribute for Assyria until murdered by one of his army officers, Pekah (2 Kings 15:22–26).

Pekah (735/4–733/2): Tried to get Judah to join a coalition of Israel and Aram-damascus against Assyria. When Judah refused, Pekah attacked Judah and carried off captives. Judah called on Assyria for aid, and Tiglath-pileser responded by conquering all of Israel and deporting much of its population to Assyria, leaving Pekah only the hill country of Samaria. Pekah was murdered by Hoshea (2 Kings 15:25–32, 37; 16:1, 5; 2 Chr 28:6; Isa 7:1).

Hoshea (733/2–724/3): A puppet king who collected tribute for Assyria until Tiglath-pileser died. Then he tried to rebel. This brought Shalmaneser V of Assyria down to capture Samaria and deport its population, ending the kingdom of Israel (2 Kings 15:30; 17:1–6; 18:1, 9–10).

The Seven-year-old King, Joash (836–798 BC)

When Joash was an infant, his father, King Ahaziah of Judah, was killed in a coup. His grandmother Athaliah seized the throne, and to prevent any other heirs from contesting her rule she tried to wipe out the rest of the family.

But Ahaziah's sister, Jehosheba, chose to save Joash. She hid him with his nurse in a bedroom so that Athaliah could not find him as she went about her slaughter in the palace. When the bloodbath was over, Jehosheba took the baby to the Temple, where she and her husband, the high priest Jehoiada, raised him.

Joash must have had a strange childhood. For six years he was tended in total secrecy in the Temple. He grew as a nobody in the shadow of the palace, under the nose of his unsuspecting grandmother Queen Athaliah. Then, suddenly, when he was seven years old, Jehoiada showed him off to the palace guard and the army, who were dissatisfied with Queen Athaliah's pagan cults. A pact was made to declare Joash king immediately.

Little Joash was hustled into the Temple and placed next to a large pillar, while men armed with swords and shields—including the weapons of King David—surrounded him. The guards ranged along the altar and spread out to each corner of the temple. Others kept watch over the Temple entrance and the palace.

A crown was put on Joash's head, and he was declared king and anointed. Spectators clapped and cried, "God save the king!" People began to rejoice, sing, and blow trumpets.

All this noise brought Queen Athaliah running, but she was dragged away and killed. The crowds then rushed to destroy the temple of Baal that she had sponsored and to kill its priests. Joash was taken to the palace and put on the throne.

Because Joash was so young, at first he did everything Jehoiada instructed him to, agreeing to the high priest's campaign to wipe out Baalism. Yet the campaign seemed to have little effect— Baalism still flourished in the kingdom. Moreover, as Joash grew he noticed that the money people gave to the Temple was being confiscated by the priests and that the Temple was falling apart. Joash rebelled, calling Jehoiada and the other priests to account. Jehoiada agreed to bore a hole in the lid of a chest, which was placed beside the altar to keep the Temple money safe. When enough money had been collected, Joash had the Temple repaired, and added bowls and vessels of gold and silver, trumpets, and other treasures.

But these Temple treasures, which earned him praise, proved Joash's downfall. When King Hazael of Syria threatened to invade Jerusalem, Joash stopped him by sending him all the Temple's treasures. This made Joash's subjects so angry that they killed him one day when he was lying in bed ill, and did not give him the honor of burial in the kings' tombs. Joash was forty years old when he died (2 Kings 11-12; 2 Chr 23-24).

The Eight-year-old King, Josiah (639–609 BC)

Josiah was only eight when he was crowned—after his father, King Amon of Judah, had been murdered by his servants for worshiping foreign gods. As a child king, Josiah easily fell under the influence of the high priest and learned piety rather than statesmanship.

When he was sixteen Josiah "began to seek after the God of David," and when he was twenty he launched a campaign to cleanse his kingdom of idolatry. This campaign carried him not only throughout Judah but even into the kingdom of Israel. Wherever he went he sought out altars and high places dedicated to Baal, where he had the tombs of idolatrous priests opened. The bones were removed and burned on the altars, which were then destroyed. He had the sacred groves cut down and the images broken and ground into dust.

This work took him six years, and then he returned to Jerusalem to begin repairs on the Temple. While this was under way an ancient manuscript was discovered—"a book of the law"—which was read to Josiah by his scribe. The king was so frightened by the punishments threatened for idolatry that he called the people to Jerusalem, read the manuscript aloud to them, and made a covenant with God. For the next Passover, Josiah donated 3000 bullocks and 30,000 lambs and kids, and with his subjects donating just as generously it was the greatest Passover the nation had seen since the time of Samuel.

Unfortunately Josiah's diplomacy fell far short of his religious zeal: when Pharaoh Necho wanted to bring his army through Judah on his way to war on the Euphrates, Josiah sent troops to stop him. Necho was amazed. "What have I to do with thee, thou king of Judah?" he asked. "I come not against thee." Josiah wouldn't listen. Disguising himself as a soldier, he went into battle against Necho near Megiddo, and was quickly hit with a random arrow. He was taken in his chariot to Jerusalem, where he died (2 Kings 21–22; 2 Chr 34–35).

Another Eight-year-old King?

King Jehoiachin of Judah ruled only three months and ten days in 597 BC before "he did that which was evil in the sight of the Lord" and was carried off as a prisoner to Babylon by Nebuchadnezzar. He survived in prison for thirty-seven years and was released by Nebuchadnezzar's successor, but he never returned to Jerusalem.

The Bible gives two different ages for Jehoiachin at the time of his accession to the throne: eight (2 Kings 24:8) and eighteen (2 Chr 36:9). Apart from the fact that it is hard to imagine that an eight-year-old could have done so much evil as to be blamed for the deportation, one passage mentions that he had wives (2 Kings 24:15), and many scholars believe he must have been eighteen.

The Lame Prince

Mephibosheth was the son of Jonathan. He was only five years old when his father was killed along with his grandfather King Saul in battle against the Philistines. Because of the danger that the child might be killed in a fight for succession of the throne, Mephibosheth's nurse rushed to take him into hiding. In the panic the frightened child fell and was so badly injured he became permanently lame in both legs.

Despite his deformity, Mephibosheth married and had a son. Finally King David remembered that he had an obligation to the son of his good friend Jonathan. He looked up Mephibosheth and befriended him, bringing him and his son to Jerusalem to eat daily at the royal table, restoring his lands, and ordering Zibah to cultivate these lands for him.

During Absalom's rebellion, when David fled Jerusalem, Mephibosheth did not accompany him. Zibah denounced Mephibosheth, telling David that Mephibosheth was siding with Absalom. In anger, David gave Zibah all of Mephibosheth's lands.

Later Mephibosheth told David this was not true. He claimed he could not flee because he was lame. He had, however, ordered an ass, intending to join the king later. Apparently King David did not wholly swallow this excuse, because he restored only half the land to Mephibosheth and let Zibah keep the other half (1 Sam 20:15; 2 Sam 4:4; 9; 19:24–30; 1 Chr 9:40).

The Magi

According to Matthew (2:1–12), when Jesus was born "there came wise men from the east" who believed an important king had been born among the Jews.

This was not the first mention of the Magi in the Bible. At least by the time of Isaiah, the Hebrews had known of the "astrologers" and "star-gazers" and men who could cast "enchantments" in Babylon (Isa 47:9, 13). Jeremiah called them diviners, dreamers, enchanters, and sorcerers, and he mentioned that among the officials Nebuchadnezzar sent to Jerusalem was Rab-mag—which some scholars interpret as "chief of the Magi" (Jer 27:9; 39:3, 13). Daniel, who had considerable contact with them, called the Magi wise, and to their other skills he added that they were magicians, soothsayers, and interpreters of dreams and signs (Dan 1:20; 2:2, 5, 10, 27; 4:6–7; 5:7, 11).

The Magi were a priestly caste or fraternity of ancient Persia whose powers—including their supposed ability to control demons—became so famous that their name gave rise to our word "magic."

Little is known of the Magi, despite diligent research by scholars, but their mystique and the awe in which they were held caused Christian legend to embroider Matthew's few words into elaborate fantasies with little basis in fact and little relation to what the Bible really says.

The most popular legend is that there were three Magi who visited the infant Jesus. Actually, Matthew didn't say how many there were, but because there were three gifts listed—gold, frankincense, and myrrh—legend assumed three Magi. In fact, there might have been only two, or there might have been twelve (as Eastern tradition contends) or even more.

Popular legend also calls the Magi kings. Matthew never said they were kings—he called them "wise men"—and the first reference to them as kings does not seem to have occurred until the 3d century. Describing them as monarchs may have been an attempt to reconcile Old Testament prophecies that have been interpreted to apply to a Messiah with Matthew's account of the birth of Jesus. Psalms (72:10–11) mentioned that "kings shall fall down before him" and that the "kings of Tarshish and of the isles shall bring presents" and "the kings of Sheba and Seba shall offer gifts." Sheba and Seba were in the area of modern Yemen, and Tarshish was a Phoenician word meaning refinery that probably referred to Solomon's metalworks at Ezion-geber on the Persian Gulf. All of these sites are south of Jerusalem and would not fit Matthew's description of Magi coming from the east.

The names Gaspar or Caspar ("white"), Melchior ("light"), and Balthazar ("lord of the treasury") that have become traditional for these supposed kings were apparently not bestowed until the 6th century. Moreover, these are all names derived from the names of ancient Mesopotamian gods and adopted by historical Magi.

The myth of the three kings has persisted in the West because Saint Helena, mother of Constantine, was fond of collecting Christian relics. She claimed to have found the bones of the three Magi who had visited Jesus, and took them to the Church of St. Sophia in Constantinople. Later they were transferred to Milan, and they now rest in a golden shrine in the cathedral of Cologne.

The Magi probably originated among the Medes, and they developed a religion that influenced the great Persian prophet Zoroaster (c. 628–551 BC). Whether Zoroaster was a Magus is still not certain, but after the prophet's death Zoroastrianism was controlled by the Magi.

One reason myths may have circulated that the Magi were kings is that they were aristocrats. They never aspired to create a popular, mass religion. Instead, they guarded their secrets so jealously that they permitted the marriage of blood relatives to keep their circle as closed as possible. They also tended to form intimate, isolated communities that could pass the secrets on without fear of betrayal to the outside world.

The Magi did many things to set themselves apart and to preserve their image of being special and even forbidding. For instance, in an area and time when the loving preservation of human remains was in vogue, they exposed their own corpses on mountains or "towers of silence" so that they would be eaten by vultures and wild animals. To other Middle Easterners this was the ultimate horror, an end they inflicted only on the worst criminals. The Magi also specialized in making—and profiting handsomely from—an intoxicating vegetable drink used during Persian religious festivals. As with most intoxicating substances, people attached endless powers to this beverage.

Many functions of the Magi were religious. For example, no sacrifices could be performed without the presence of a Magus. In time of war the Magi marched with the warriors to carry the sacred fire and offer sacrifices for victory. Other functions were quasi-religious and dealt with matters such as dream interpretation that are not well understood even today. But two characteristics stand out as important in their visit to Jesus.

One is that the Magi were astronomers and astrologers. They were well versed in the movements and configurations of stars and planets, and unusual events in the heavens were usually announced as accompanying some significant event on earth, such as the birth of a major leader. For this reason, when they saw the unusual "star" (see "For We Have Seen His Star in the East," page 268), the Magi assumed a new king had been born.

The second characteristic of the Magi was their talent for hovering about the center of power. While the height of their political control in Persia came in the 6th century BC, for centuries they remained the hidden power behind the emperor. Royal children were educated by the Magi. The coronation of kings was not held in the Persian capital of Susa but in a temple at Pasargadae, where the Magi had two open-air altars on which cattle, horses, and occasional humans were sacrificed. The Magi were also proficient at the complicated Persian script. One of their functions was to keep and to interpret the sacred scriptures, but they are also believed to have been court scribes and registrars who retained control of Persia's legal and state documents. When the kings of Persia died, it was the Magi who were entrusted with guarding the royal tombs.

It was therefore natural, when they thought a powerful king had been born among the Jews, that the Magi took presents and prostrated themselves before the infant Jesus. Their stay was brief, however. When they left they were canny enough not to report to Herod but "departed into their own country another way"—probably going even farther from Jerusalem by taking the coastal road north. There is no record that the Magi were ever sufficiently impressed with Jesus' career to return later for additional adulation or that their visit had any impact on religious belief in Mesopotamia.

Coming out of the Closet (Unexpected Appearances)

1. God appeared to Abraham many times, beginning when Abraham was seventy-five years old, and came at night as well as in the day (Gen 26:24). Abraham never seemed surprised except once, when he did not see God, and God had to call out, "Behold, here I am" (Gen 22:1).

2. When the Israelites made a burnt offering during the wanderings "there came a fire out from before the Lord, and consumed upon the altar the burnt offering and the fat" (Lev 9:24).

3. When two Israelites offered "strange fire" before the Lord, "there went out fire from the Lord, and devoured them, and they died" (Lev 10:1–2).

4. When God first appeared to Moses, Moses was surprised at God's disguise as a burning bush (Ex 3:2–4).

5. When Miriam and Aaron grumbled to each other about the power Moses had over the people, God appeared to them "in the pillar of the cloud" and stood at the door of the Tabernacle (Num 12:5). God appeared in a cloud up to New Testament times (Luke 9:31–35).

6. Isaiah described God sitting on a throne surrounded by seraphim. As God began to speak to Isaiah, the doorposts moved and the house filled with smoke (Isa 6:1–4).

7. Ezekiel also described God seated on a sapphire throne with an amber aura around it and fire forming the body. "As the appearance of the bow that is in the cloud in the day of rain, so was the appearance of the likeness of the glory of the Lord" (Ezek 1:26–28).
Before seeing God, Ezekiel had seen a vision commemorated in the spiritual: "Ezekiel saw the wheel, way up in the middle of the sky." This was during the Babylonian captivity, and Ezekiel saw a whirlwind, a great cloud, "a fire enfolding itself," and a brightness on the banks of the Chebar River. Out of the fire came four living creatures that looked like men except that each had four faces and four wings. Each had a wheel with eyes around the rim. The living creatures flew about on noisy wings and the wheels whirled before Ezekiel saw and heard God (Ezek 1–2).

8. Amos experienced a singular appearance of God: "The Lord stood upon a wall made by a plumbline, with a plumbline in his hand" (Amos 7:7).

9. On the top of an unspecified mountain, Jesus, Peter, John, and James saw Moses and Elias appear before them as they prayed. Moses and Elias spoke with Jesus of "his decease . . . at Jerusalem" (Luke 9:28–31).

Mary the Mother of Jesus

On the subject of Jesus' birth, about the only thing confirmed by all the gospels is that a woman named Mary bore Jesus. Of her origins we know little. She had one sister (John 19:25) and at least one cousin, Elisabeth, the wife of the priest Zacharias (Luke 1:5, 36). Thus Mary was probably from a strongly religious or even priestly family. There is a tradition, possibly originating in the apocryphal Gospel of James (2d century), that she was born in Jerusalem to elderly parents, Joachim and Anna. The site of her birth in Jerusalem is supposedly beneath the Church of St. Anne. Another tradition, however, locates her birthplace in Sepphoris in Galilee, a town about five miles from Nazareth.

Luke gives the most detailed account of the birth of Jesus. The angel Gabriel comes to tell Mary that she will conceive a son, whom she will name Jesus, and this son will be "the Son of the Highest: and Lord God shall give unto him the throne of his father David." Rather practically Mary—who at this time is betrothed but not wed to Joseph—asks, "How shall this be, seeing I know not a man?" The angel replies that "The Holy Ghost shall come upon thee, and the power of the Highest shall over-shadow thee" (Luke 1:26–35).

It is interesting that Matthew, the only other Gospel that mentions the virgin birth, presents Joseph's view of the affair. In that Gospel, Mary and Joseph are espoused and he is called her husband, but they have not slept together. He finds out that Mary is pregnant, however. As he is considering a course of action, the angel comes to him to tell him not to be outraged. The angel explains to Joseph that the Holy Ghost conceived the child in Mary and that *Joseph* should name the child "Jesus" (Matt 1:18–25).

The apocryphal Gospel of James says that the angel's announcement, the Annunciation, took place beside the town well in Nazareth. This well, which survives today, has been the site of shrines to Mary since the 2d century.

To avoid wagging tongues, Mary goes to her cousin Elisabeth's house "in a city of Judah." Elisabeth is unusually sympathetic with the young girl's plight, for though Elisabeth is old and has been barren a long time, she too is about to have a miraculous birth. Mary lives with her about three months and then returns home, though her child is not yet born. Shortly after Mary's departure, Elisabeth gives birth to the child who becomes John the Baptist (Luke 1:39–60).

According to Luke, Mary and Joseph travel to Bethlehem because of Augustus Caesar's edict requiring that all citizens return to their place of birth to be taxed. Luke and Matthew agree that Jesus is born in Bethlehem, but Luke says that the wise men find the child in a manger (Matt 2:11; Luke 2:15, 16).

On the eighth day after birth, in accordance with Jewish custom, the child is circumcised and christened. After the forty days of purification, during which the mother was considered unclean, Mary and Joseph travel the ten miles or so to Jerusalem to "present him to the Lord" (Luke 2:22). All firstborn males of a family were so presented and it was normal to pay a "redemption price" of five shekels to the Temple. Mary and Joseph must have been quite poor, for they give the alternate offering of "two pigeons or two turtle doves" reserved for those without enough money for the lamb sacrifice that was also given (Lev 5:7; Luke 2:24). While they are there Mary and Joseph "marvel" at the things told them by Simeon, a "just and devout" man, and by Anna, an aged prophetess. They say the child is to be the salvation and redemption of Jerusalem (Luke 2:34–38).

Matthew, however, does not mention that the family brings the infant Jesus to Jerusalem. The story given there, and nowhere else, is that Joseph is told by an angel to take the family to Egypt until Herod dies, when it will be safe to bring the child back. Ever since the wise men came to Herod speaking about the king who had just been born, Herod has been hunting the infant (Matt 13:16).

The Bible records only a few incidents from Jesus' childhood and youth, but almost all of these incidents involve Mary. According to Luke (2:42–51), the family travels to Jerusalem every year for the "feast," a common pilgrimage by the faithful. The year when Jesus is twelve, the family begin to return from the celebration in a company of friends and relatives when Mary and Joseph notice Jesus is missing. At first they assume the boy is playing with some relatives, but after a while they begin to worry about his absence. Finding Jesus nowhere in the company, they turn back toward Jerusalem and search the city. He has been talking with the priests.

The words that mother and child exchange at this point are significant, for they represent in miniature Jesus and Mary's relationship throughout Jesus' life. Mary asks Jesus, "Son, why hast thou thus dealt with us? behold, thy father and I have sought thee sorrowing." Where most parents would be at least a little angry, Mary is puzzled, grieving, and even respectful. She would never quite understand her son's behavior and it hurt her that she did not. But even though she could not comprehend Jesus, she believed he was to be great. On this occasion, as on others, she remembered all the things he said, and what was said about him, and "kept all these things, and pondered them in her heart" (Luke 2:19, 51).

Jesus' reply here also represents him well. He says, "How is it that ye sought me? wist ye not that I must be about my Father's business?" Even in youth Jesus displays his tendency to refer to his metaphorical family, the "family" of God and the disciples, as his true family. Although Jesus returns to Nazareth with his parents and is "subject unto them" he will always stand apart from them thereafter.

John relates a later incident in which Jesus demonstrates his full independence from his mother. He and Mary are attending a marriage at Cana, and she remarks to Jesus that the marriage party has no wine. Jesus' reply, though often said to be affectionate, has more than a hint of irritation in it. He answers her with "Woman, what have I to do with thee? mine hour is not yet come." Evidently she is implying that Jesus should go get wine. Jesus' testy reply is a clear sign that she should abandon her idea and let him do what he wants. She therefore tells the servants, "Whatsoever he saith unto you, do it." Jesus has them draw six stone vats of water and in secret changes the water to wine, his first miracle (John 2:1-11). At this stage in his career he begins to obey God's will and not his mother's.

Since Mary moved to Capernaum with Jesus (John 2:12) after he had begun preaching it is assumed that she traveled with him on other journeys down to the Crucifixion. It is also assumed that Mary was a believer in Jesus' divinity. Indeed, it is almost certain that she was a believer after the Crucifixion, because Acts (1:14) states of the early Christians: "These all continued with one accord in prayer and supplication, with the women, and Mary the mother of Jesus, and with his brethren."

But there are, in fact, many questions about Mary's faith before the Crucifixion and they happen to be tied up with an even more controversial question—did Mary have other children? In spite of some strong arguments for Mary's perpetual virginity, there is plenty of evidence that Jesus had siblings and that they, and their mother, may have had their doubts about Jesus at first.

The reason that passages referring to Jesus' mother, brothers, and sisters also happen to involve the question of their faith in him as a messiah has to do with a bit of logic something like this: If Jesus had brothers and sisters, wouldn't they be the first to recognize him as the messiah and wouldn't they be divine themselves? Thus Mark (6:3)—in the passage that gives the most powerful support to the contention that Mary had "other children"—questions Jesus' divinity by asking if he isn't really an ordinary fellow with an ordinary job and "normal" brothers, sisters, and mother. The passage reads, "Is not this the carpenter, the son of Mary, the brother of James, and Joses, and of Juda, and Simon? and are not his sisters here with us?" A similar passage occurs in Matthew (13:55), where the same four brothers are named.

The main argument against Mary's having had other children is the claim that the terms "brothers" and "sisters" are used metaphorically, to describe Jesus' cousins or friends. This is a common usage in many languages including the two known to Jesus, ancient Aramaic and Koine Greek, and even occurs in modern English.

But if "brother" is used metaphorically for those close to Jesus, what would be the sense of saying of Jesus, as the Gospel of John does, that "neither did his brethren believe in him?" (John 7:5). Indeed, one story virtually proves that such language is not figurative when used by the gospel writers. It is a story that the gospel writer considered important, for Matthew (12:46–50), Mark (3:31), and Luke all report it. Here is the version from Matthew:

> While he yet talked to the people, behold, his mother and his brethren stood without, desiring to speak with him. The one said unto him, Behold, thy mother and thy brethren stand without, desiring to speak with thee. But he answered and said unto him that told him, Who is my mother? and who are my brethren? And he stretched forth his hand toward his disciples, and said, Behold my mother and my brethren! For whosoever shall do the will of my Father who is in heaven, the same is my brother, and sister, and mother.

It is hardly likely that Jesus would evoke the figurative meanings of "mother" and "brethren" if his actual mother and brethren weren't standing outside. As he did when a boy at the Temple, Jesus consciously plays on the difference between his real family, his mother and brothers, and his metaphorical family, the disciples of God.

Another point to note is that Jesus' mother and brethren are not listening to him preach; they are calling him from it. Evidently they do not believe in him. They may have even thought he was insane and said among themselves, as Jesus' friends did, "He is beside himself" (Mark 3:21).

In contrast to passages like these, where the "normalcy" of Jesus' family and their doubts about him are cited, there is one that gives the other side of the coin. One of his believers thought that Mary, as the mother of the messiah, should be worshiped. After preaching one day, Jesus was addressed by a woman who declared, "Blessed is the womb that bare thee, and the paps which thou hast sucked." To this Jesus replied, "Yea rather, blessed are they that hear the word of God, and keep it" (Luke 11:27–28).

There is reason to think that Mary may have begun to believe in Jesus just before his death and that his brothers believed in him only after the Resurrection. The argument for Mary's faith before the Crucifixion depends on John's version of Jesus' death (19:26–27). While on the cross, Jesus said to his "beloved disciple," probably John, "Behold thy mother!" thus suggesting that John should look after Mary in her old age, which he did: "From that hour that disciple took her unto his own home." It is argued that Jesus would not have done this unless Mary had someone else to look after her. If Jesus had siblings they must have had some reason to reject their mother in old age. One plausible explanation is this: If Jesus had blood brothers who did not share Mary's faith in Jesus—and John (7:5) states they did not—then entrusting her to the believer John was a sensible and compassionate act, designed to save her faith and give her one comfort in old age that her sons could not provide.

Evidently, Jesus' brothers had a change of heart after the Crucifixion and Resurrection. James, a brother mentioned as Mary's son in Matthew (13:55) and Mark (6:3), became a powerful leader in the early Christian Church (Gal 1:19). And one passage from Acts already mentioned (1:14) states that among the Christian prayer group after Jesus' death was "Mary the mother of Jesus, and with his brethren." But for some reason they became believers only after Jesus' death.

It should be noted that there is much room for various interpretations of these and other passages regarding Mary's life, and that it has been and is still argued that she did not have any other children. Although many Christians accept the notion that Jesus had brothers and sisters, the Greek Orthodox and Roman Catholic churches hold that Mary was a perpetual virgin. Where the Crucifixion scene in John may be cited as evidence that Mary's children did not support her in her faith, it has also been used to argue that she did not have children at all.

One particularly strong argument against Mary's having other children points out the confusion among the Gospels regarding the women at the Crucifixion and at the tomb. Below is a table summarizing who the Gospels say was there:

Matthew (27:56)	*Mark* (15:40)
Mary Magdalene	Mary Magdalene
Mary the mother of James and Joses	Mary the mother of James the less and of Joses
the mother of Zebedee's children	Salome
	John (19:25)
Luke (23:49)	Jesus' mother
the women	Jesus' mother's sister
	Mary the wife of Cleophas
	Mary Magdalene

After comparing these lists only one thing is sure: Mary Magdalene, who is definitely not Jesus' mother, was present at the Crucifixion. Another conclusion is usually reached: Salome was the mother of Zebedee's children (see Apostles, John and James).

Now the problems begin. Let's take the passage from John first. It says "there stood by the cross of Jesus his mother, and his mother's sister, Mary the wife of Cleophas, and Mary Magdalene." Because of the phrasing of the sentence, particularly the placement of the "and's," it seems that three people, not four, are being named. If so, then Jesus' mother would have a sister married to a man named Cleophas, but her sister would also be named Mary. This would be likely only if they were stepsisters.

But there is a puzzle here if we compare all the lists. Is Mary the wife of Cleophas also the mother of James and Joses? One argument says she is. It is based on Matthew (10:3), which mentions a James the son of Alphaeus. Many people in the New Testament have two names, one Greek, one Aramaic, and these names often mean the same thing, as Cephas/Peter's names mean "stone." Alphaeus is from the same root as Cleophas, therefore Mary wife of Cleophas might be Mary mother of James and Joses.

The case would seem to be closed. Not so. Mary the mother of Jesus could be identified with Mary the mother of James and Joses. Mark (6:3) and Matthew (13:55) both say that among Jesus' four "brothers" are a James and a Joses. Yet why don't Mark and Matthew simply say "Mary the mother of Jesus" if that's the woman they are identifying?

Those who contend that Jesus' mother didn't have "other children" clear up the confusion by coming to the following conclusions: Mary's stepsister had two children by Cleophas/Alphaeus, James and Joses, and Mark and Matthew figuratively refer to these two as Jesus' "brothers" even though they are truly his cousins.

There is no solution to the puzzle of the women at the Crucifixion. The problem of who was there must have been recognized early, for Luke, who usually gives the most detailed accounts of Mary's doings, avoids the problem altogether by saying simply "the women" were there.

Acts (1:14) contains the last biblical mention of Jesus' mother. In Romans (16:6), Paul sends greetings to a Mary who "bestowed much labor on us," but this is probably not Jesus' mother despite the attention given to the birth/labor pun.

The traditions of her Immaculate Conception and Assumption into heaven are quite late. Immaculate Conception became official Roman Catholic dogma in 1854 and her Assumption into heaven was made official in 1950 by Pope Pius XII.

Worst Dressed

Adam and Eve sewed themselves aprons of fig leaves (Gen 3:7). These must have looked pretty bad, because later God made them fur coats (Gen 3:21).

The prophet Ahijah tore his new clothes into twelve pieces and gave ten of the shreds to King Jeroboam (1 Kings 11:30).

False prophets wore "rough garments to deceive" (Zech 13:4).

When Jonah was in the belly of the big fish he wore weeds wrapped around his head (Jonah 2:5).

Everyone in Jacob's household had worn earrings until Jacob took them away and buried them under an oak (Gen 35:4).

When the Gibeonite ambassadors wanted to trick Joshua into thinking they had traveled a long way, they wore old shoes and old clothes (Josh 9:5).

To draw pity from King Ahab of Israel, the Assyrians "girded sackcloth on their loins, and put ropes on their heads" (1 Kings 20:32).

Elijah was described as a "hairy man, and girt with a girdle of leather about his loins" (2 Kings 1:8).

Zechariah saw Joshua in a vision "clothed with filthy garments" (Zech 3:3–5).

Someday the rich will go about with their gold and silver "cankered" and their garments motheaten (James 5:2).

Jonathan stripped himself of his girdle, robe, and other garments to give them all to David (2 Sam 18: 4).

To poke fun at David's messengers, the Ammonite king shaved off half their beards and "cut off their garments in the middle, even to their buttocks" (2 Sam 10:4).

What Not to Wear

The Lord promised to punish (Isa 3:16–24) the "daughters of Zion" who walked haughtily about wearing changeable suits of apparel, mantles, wimples, crisping pins, glasses, fine linen, hoods, and veils. Other items of clothing the Lord found especially disgusting:

1. tinkling ornaments about their feet
2. cauls
3. round headdresses like the moon
4. chains, bracelets, and mufflers
5. bonnets
6. leg ornaments
7. headbands
8. earrings
9. rings
10. nose jewels

To punish these women, God commanded that instead of smelling sweet they would stink; instead of having well-set hair they would be bald; instead of a stomacher they would be girdled in sackcloth. In short, God would give them "burning instead of beauty."

God also frowned on foreign clothing of any type and once promised to punish any king's children who wore any such "strange apparel" (Zeph 1:8).

The Mystery Man

Melchizedek ("king of righteousness") first appears in the time of Abraham as the priest-king of Salem (Gen 14:18–20). Salem—or Uru-salim ("city of peace"), as it appears in the Amarna Letters—is believed to be the ancient name of Jerusalem. In the New Testament (Heb 7), Melchizedek is called a king of righteousness and peace—"Without father, without mother, without descent, having neither beginning of days, nor end of life; but made like unto the Son of God; abideth a priest continually."

This can be interpreted to mean he was never born and never died, and that he had neither parents nor children, although some scholars claim it merely means that his name was nowhere recorded in the priesthood registers. In any case, he became a symbol of the ideal priest-king, so that the Messiah was predicted to be "a priest for ever after the order of Melchizedek," who was identified with peace and righteousness (Psa 110:4; Isa 11:4–9; Zech 6:9–15). Jesus was therefore called "a priest for ever after the order of Melchizedek" (Heb 7).

Messiah

The word messiah, from the Hebrew *mashiah*, literally means "the anointed one," as does the New Testament version of the word, "christ," from the Greek *christos*. In the Old Testament, kings, priests, and prophets are sometimes called messiah because part of the ritual of assuming such offices was receiving a dab of unguent on the forehead (Ex 29:7). The term "messiah" could even be applied to inanimate objects, as for the shield of Saul (2 Sam 1:21), and in this usage simply meant "anointed."

A messiah was, in most cases in the Old Testament, someone selected by God (1 Sam 26:11), and only rarely meant a future redeemer. One exception occurs in Daniel, one of the later books, where a messiah is predicted who will rebuild Jerusalem (Dan 9:25–26). Because he is referred to as a "prince," this figure may owe something to the hoped-for Davidic king that Isaiah (9:6) and Ezekiel (34:24) predict.

This belief in a political messiah, someone from the line of David who would reunite the kingdoms of Israel and rebuild the Temple, became popular only after the Exile, when foreign oppressors in Palestine made the former glories of the united kingdom more attractive than ever. Since messianic belief developed relatively late in Hebrew religion, it was not uniformly accepted or interpreted, and is not as extensive in the Old Testament as in the Apocrypha. Among the various sects who advocated different beliefs about a messiah during the postexilic years, the Zealots stressed the nationalistic aspect of the Messiah's coming, the Pharisees the adherence to the Law that his advent would bring, and so on, each faction advancing an interpretation that fit with their own theology. The Qumran sect, those who probably wrote the Dead Sea Scrolls, evidently believed in a royal messiah, a "son of David," and a second, priestly messiah, "a son of

Aaron," a notion that parallels a popular belief in a messiah from the house of Joseph who would precede the Davidic messiah and fall in the battle of Gog and Magog (Rev 20:8).

A great deal of such doomsaying became prominent at this time. For instance, the Dead Sea Scrolls from the 1st century BC describe an apocalyptic battle between the forces of good and evil, a battle that will be decided by God. Some of this literature portrays the Messiah as coming at the time of the Apocalypse, but only one of these books, Daniel, is included in the Old Testament. Another work, the Book of Enoch, which survives only in the Pseudepigrapha, a collection of diverse writings which forms a peripheral body of scripture, explicitly links the coming of a Messiah, a mysterious "Son of Man," with the last days.

Around AD 70 messianic and apocalyptic works such as Enoch began to be shunted from the mainstream of Judaic religious thought, possibly because the books precipitated much rebellious activity against the Romans, who reciprocated with vengeance. Also, these books were being adopted by the early Christians, who used them for their own purposes.

The relationship between Jewish messianic traditions—in both the Old Testament and the later noncanonical works—and Christian theology has been hotly and extensively debated: proof of the arguments' insolubility as well as their importance. One thing, however, is clear—the Christian concept of the Messiah differs radically from the earlier versions, which, as we have seen, often differed from each other.

One approach to understanding the Christian Messiah can be made through a brief analysis of the names given to Jesus. Besides Messiah, which is used only twice (John 1:41; 4:25), Jesus is referred to by the Greek equivalent, Christ, over one hundred times in the New Testament, indicating that the early Christians were more familiar with the Greek translations of the Bible than with the original Hebrew. Nevertheless, in some respects Jesus is portrayed as being in the mainstream of the Hebrew messianic tradition. In Revelation he is referred to as the "root and offspring of David," a phrase that alludes to Isaiah (11:10), in which a deliverer is predicted from "the root of Jesse," the father of David. And in Acts (3:22), Jesus is linked to the passage from Deuteronomy that begins "I will raise them up a prophet from among their brethren. . . ." Still, Jesus was not the political or military leader that was expected by most Jewish sects.

410

The Patriarchs (2000–1250 BC)

Abraham ("father of multitudes" or "father is exalted"): Born in Ur of the Chaldees (Babylonia), he traveled with his flocks and entourage to Egypt and Canaan, searching for a land good for both his flocks and his newly developing faith. He bargained with God to save the righteous people of Sodom and Gomorrah, but it turned out that the only one worth saving was his nephew Lot. He sired two sons: Ishmael (both Jews and Arabs believe Ishmael is the forerunner of modern Arab peoples), whom he was forced to turn out of his house (Gen 21); and in his old age, Isaac, whom he almost sacrificed at the request of God (Gen 22). Abraham died at the age of 175 (Gen 25), after being promised that his descendants would be as numerous as the stars in the heavens and the grains of sand by the sea (Gen 22:17) and that they would inherit the land of Canaan.

Isaac ("he laughed"): His name reflects the laughter of his parents, Abraham and Sarah, when they were told they would have a son in their old age (Gen 17–18). As a child he had a close call when Abraham almost offered him as a human sacrifice. Remaining most of his life in and near Beersheba, Isaac and entourage traveled once to Gezer during a famine. God renewed the covenant with Isaac, who married Rebekah, a close relative, and produced two sons: the twins Esau and Jacob. When Isaac was old and blind, he was tricked into blessing his younger son, Jacob, as his heir (Gen 27). Isaac lived to be 180 years old.

Jacob ("he who supplants"): The second of the twins born to Isaac and Rebekah, Jacob became the stay-at-home shepherd. When his brother,

Esau, returned from a hunt hungry, he sold Jacob his birthright for a bowl of lentil stew (Gen 25). Convinced by his mother to dress in an animal skin so that Isaac would take him for Esau, Jacob received the blessing of the firstborn and the inheritance of God's covenant. Afraid of Esau's anger over losing the inheritance, Jacob fled to the house of Rebekah's brother Laban, where he indentured himself as shepherd and fell in love with his cousin Rachel. The custom of Laban's people, however, was to have the eldest daughter married first, and through a masquerade as underhanded as his own against his brother, Jacob was married to Leah first. Finally, with both wives, children, and flocks, Jacob returned to Canaan, successfully wrestling with the angel of God on the way (Gen 32) and meeting and appeasing his brother, Esau (Gen 33). Jacob fathered twelve sons, each of whom became the forefather of a tribe of Israel. Jacob went to Egypt during a famine to see his son Joseph honored as second-in-command to the pharaoh. Jacob died there at age 147.

Sarah ("princess"): As the wife of Abraham, she traveled with him to Canaan. Finding she could not bear children, she gave him her handmaid Hagar as a concubine. Sarah was such a beauty that Abraham feared he might be killed by a jealous rival, so he passed her off as his sister to the pharaoh and to the king of Gerar; although she entered both of their harems, she was returned to Abraham when they learned she was his wife (Gen 12, 20). Sarah bore Isaac in her old age, and when Hagar and Ishmael mocked her, she forced Abraham to send them away. Either while her husband and son were on Mount Moriah, or on their return, she died at age 127. Abraham bought the Cave of Machpelah in Hebron to bury her in.

Rebekah ("noose"): Wife of Isaac, she was in pain while carrying twins. She went into the wilderness to pray and received a vision that the younger should inherit rather than the older (Gen 25). When she overheard Isaac telling Esau to prepare for the blessing, Rebekah realized that the chance for her vision to be fulfilled was at hand. She forced Jacob to deceive his father so that he obtained the inheritance, and then sent him away to hide with her family (Gen 27).

Leah (disputed: "gazelle" or "exhausted"): Disguised as Rachel in wedding garb and veil by her father, Laban, Leah remained the unloved and unwanted first bride of Jacob (Gen 29), yet she and her handmaid bore many children. She was buried in the Cave of Machpelah.

Rachel ("ewe"): The second, much-loved wife of Jacob, she was anguished at remaining childless while her sister bore sons. Finally she had Joseph and then died in childbirth when Benjamin—whom she called Benoni ("child of my sorrow")—was born. Rachel also played a part in the dramatic confrontation between Laban and Jacob during Jacob's flight back to Canaan, since her theft of her father's idols caused Laban to follow them (Gen 31). She is the only one of the matriarchs or patriarchs not buried in the Hebron cave.

The Prophets

Enoch (c. ?): He foretold the coming of thousands of saints at the Last Judgment (Jude 14).

Noah (c. 2000 BC): He predicted the victory of the Lord, in the person of the Israelites, over the Canaanites and others (Gen 9:27).

Deborah (c. 1700 BC): A judge and prophetess, possessing a moral authority that was inspired by God, she was a Joan of Arc figure, successfully leading the Israelites against the Canaanites (Judg 4–5).

Moses (c. 1300 BC): He was considered to be a prophet because he gave the Israelites a code of living inspired by God and rebuked those who had taken up idolatry (Ex 19–34).

Samuel (c. 1100 BC): A message from God allowed him to predict the death of Eli's sons (1 Sam 3:13). He warned the Israelites against backsliding into idolatry and called forth a storm to stop the advancing Philistine army (1 Sam 7:9–10). He cautioned the people against taking a king, since God had been leading them, and was continually feuding with King Saul. He produced another storm as a sign of the power of the Lord (1 Sam 12:18–19). After Samuel died, Saul summoned up his spirit, and the ghost of the prophet foretold Saul's death on the following day (1 Sam 28:19).

Gad (c. 970 BC): He warned David against hiding in the cave of Adullam where Saul might catch him (1 Sam 22:5). He told David that God was

414

angered by his taking of a census (1 Chr 21). He advised David to build an altar on Araunah's threshing floor to propitiate God (2 Sam 24:18).

Nathan (c. 970 BC): He told David that Solomon was to build the Temple, not he (2 Sam 7:4–17), and that God was displeased that he took Bathsheba for his wife (2 Sam 12). He advised Bathsheba, near the time of David's death, that Solomon should become king soon (1 Kings 1:11–27).

Ahijah (c. 910 BC): He encouraged Jeroboam in his plot against Solomon and declared that Jeroboam would rule, as he did, after Solomon's death (1 Kings 11:31). He foretold the death of Jeroboam's infant son and the end of Jeroboam's line (1 Kings 14:5–16).

Elijah (c. 870, 850 BC): He predicted drought to King Ahab (1 Kings 17:1). He fed a widow, her son, and himself by miraculously multiplying her food, and also revived her son (1 Kings 17:18). As signs of God's power he called down a heavenly fire to consume a sacrifice and summoned a storm (1 Kings 18:20–44). While fleeing Ahab by traveling through a desert, he was fed by an angel, and later appeared to Ahab and prophesied the end of his line (1 Kings 21:21, 29). He invoked a heavenly fire against those sent by King Ahaziah to capture him and predicted the death of Ahaziah (2 Kings 1:9–18). He parted the waters of the Jordan so that he might cross and then ascended to heaven in a chariot of fire (2 Kings 2:1–11).

Elisha (c. 850 BC): A disciple and successor of Elijah, his first display of prophetic powers was the parting of the Jordan, as Elijah had done on the way across, when he was returning from the spot where Elijah had ascended to heaven (2 Kings 2:14). He miraculously purified a spring near Jericho, and in what appears to have been a fit of temper, he called forth two bears upon a crowd of children who had been mocking his baldness (2 Kings 2:19–24). The list of his predictions and miracles in Second Kings is long: He foretold the coming of water that would appear on the land without the presence of cloud or rain (3:17), multiplied a widow's oil (4:5), revived a dead boy (4:18–37), made a poisonous soup edible (4:38–41), healed leprosy (5:8–14), caused an axhead lost in a river to float (6:1–7), temporarily blinded some Syrians who attempted to capture him (6:8–23), predicted the end of a famine in Samaria (7:1) and the death of King Ben-hadad (8:10), and on his deathbed predicted that Joash would defeat the Syrians three times (13:14–19). Even after Elisha's death his powers continued unabated: A dead man placed in Elisha's tomb was revived by touching the prophet's body (2 Kings 13:21).

Micaiah (c. 850 BC): Hated by King Ahab because he always predicted evil for the king, he did indeed predict the defeat of Ahab's army (1 Kings 22:8–28).

Zedekiah (c. 850 BC): Spokesman for the prophets consulted by Ahab, he threatened Micaiah after he made his prediction of Ahab's death (1 Kings 22:11, 24).

The Twelve Minor Prophets

The twelve minor prophets were a group of literary prophets each the presumed author of the Old Testament book bearing his name.

Amos (c. 785–760 BC): He denounced the impiety of Judah, Israel, and surrounding nations, foretold the punishment of idolatrous nations by fire and plague, and related a number of visions in which the Lord appeared to him.

Hosea (c. 750–690 BC): In the first section of the book he told of his marriage to, his divorce from, and reconciliation with Gomer, his adulterous wife. This story is often taken as a parable symbolizing God's dissolution and restoration of the covenant with an idolatrous, unfaithful Israel. In the remainder of the book Hosea related the punishments God would visit upon nonbelievers and finally predicted the restoration of the nation.

Micah (c. 720 BC): Micah was particularly harsh on the cities, for he believed that their inhabitants were the oppressors of the rural poor. He denounced greedy, dishonest merchants, hypocrites, and the rich.

Zephaniah (c. 625 BC): Zephaniah railed against idolatry, astrology, and other cult practices in Jerusalem. He predicted dark destruction for many neighboring nations, including the Ethiopians, Ammonites, Assyrians, and Philistines.

Nahum (c. 615 BC): Unlike the other literary prophets, whose chief object was the denunciation of impiety in Israel, Nahum lashed out at Nineveh, the capital of the Assyrian Empire, and vividly described the battle that would destroy the city.

Habakkuk (c. 600 BC): He asked God why the righteous often suffered more than the wicked, and briefly described the terrible supernatural majesty of the presence of God.

Haggai (c. 520 BC): This postexilic prophet encouraged the Israelites to rebuild the Temple, and to make it more glorious than the original.

Zechariah (c. 520 BC): With Haggai, Zechariah urged the reconstruction of the Temple. The last six chapters of Zechariah have been given various interpretations: Some believe they foretell Alexander's expedition to Egypt, others believe they prefigure the age of the Messiah. There seem to be two authors of the book: Chapters 1–8 suggest a young man of the Persian period; chapters 9–14, someone of the Greek age.

Malachi (c. 460 BC): Malachi denounced those priests who despised God's name and offered crippled animals for sacrifice. He also took the Jewish people to task for neglecting to pay their tithes, for taking foreign wives, and for doubting that there was any profit in fulfilling the will of God.

Obadiah (c. 400–350 BC): Obadiah related a vision in which God denounced the Edomites and gave his reasons for their destruction and for the salvation of the Israelites. The book shows evidence of two authors: one whose style is historic and factual (1–14), and another who is given to apocalyptic language (15–21).

Joel (c. 350 BC? dates as early as 9th century given): In the first part of the book the prophet described a plague of insects and a drought, which he interpreted as God's judgment on Judah. He called on the people to repent and make offerings to the Lord. In the second part of the book, he foretold the Judgment Day, after which Jerusalem would be a holy city and the land of Judah fruitful.

Jonah (c. 350 BC? dates as early as 9th century given): The first part of the book relates how Jonah was swallowed by "a great fish" as a consequence of his refusal to prophesy against Nineveh. After three prayerful days in the belly of the great fish Jonah was spewn forth and called again to prophesy. Knowing better than to refuse, he went into Nineveh doomsaying, and everyone there repented. This upset Jonah because God wouldn't destroy the city as Jonah had predicted. God had to explain to Jonah that it was better that thousands of lives be saved than Jonah's prophecy be fulfilled.

The Major Prophets

Isaiah (c. 740–700 BC): The author of chapters 1–39 of the Book of Isaiah. He served as the counselor of three Judean kings and the moral conscience of his nation for over forty years. He was called to prophecy at twenty-five when he received a vision of God attended by all his angels. He censured Judah and Jerusalem for rebellion against the Lord, for religious hypocrisy, for callousness toward the oppressed, and for pride, greed, and idolatry. In the eighth chapter he tells of the coming of a messianic figure often taken to be Jesus. He predicts doom for the Assyrians, Babylonians, Ethiopians, Egyptians, Phoenicians, and Moabites.

"Second Isaiah," "Third Isaiah": It has been generally assumed by modern critics that chapters 40–66 were written by one or several authors other than the author of the first part of Isaiah. Chapters 40–55 have often been attributed to a "Second Isaiah" because the theology, mood, style, and historical background of these chapters suggest that they were composed during or shortly after the Exile. Chapters 55–66 appear to have been written at a still later period, after the return from Babylonia and the reconstruction of the Temple. These chapters have been ascribed variously to a "Third Isaiah" or to a group of prophetic disciples.

The second part of Isaiah (chapters 40–55) is much more joyful than the first; the deliverance of the Israelites is at hand and Zion is about to be restored. Cyrus is celebrated as the agent who will do God's will in setting free the Israelites and destroying the Babylonians.

The third section of the book returns to admonitory prophecy, and once again the Hebrews are reproved for backsliding into idolatry.

Jeremiah (c. 640–587 BC): Like all the prophets, Jeremiah spoke out against the moral degradation of the unfaithful among the Hebrews and predicted the destruction of infidel nations. The distinctive trait of his prophecy is the personal tenor of his relation to the deity. His prophecies and "confessions" show him to have been a private and retiring man who was nevertheless invested with an urgent sense of mission and with the courage to speak out despite hostility.

He predicted the fall of Jerusalem and the deportation of Hebrews to Babylon (Jer 20:5; 25:11), the deaths of Jehoiakim (22:19) and of Hananiah, a false prophet (28:16), and the capture of King Zedekiah (37:17). The book was written by Jeremiah or dictated to his secretary, Baruch.

Ezekiel (c. 588–571 BC): Unlike Jeremiah, Ezekiel was deported to Babylon, where he began to prophesy five years after his exile began (c. 593 BC). His first vision, in which God appeared to him, is one of the most vivid and bizarre in the Bible (Ezek 1:4–3:15) and its imagery undoubtedly influenced John's Revelation. From a blazing and whirling cloud God is borne forth on a chariotlike apparatus drawn by creatures with many heads and wings, and Ezekiel receives a scroll which he eats, symbolizing the complete ingestion of prophetic power. Among the prophet's more amazing visions are God's transporting him, by grabbing a hank of his hair and taking him in tow, to Jerusalem—where he peeps into the Temple and sees the abominations within (8:1–16); the dry bones which come together, have living flesh come upon them, and thus assemble into a great army (37:7–11); and the vision of the restoration of the Temple (40–43).

What Were Job's Strangest Eccentricities?

1. "I washed my steps with butter" (Job 29:6).
2. "I prepared my seat in the street!" (Job 29:7).

Who Had Twenty-four Fingers and Toes?

The Philistine giant from Gath, a relative of Goliath, had six fingers on each hand and six toes on each foot (2 Sam 21:20).

Who Was a Road Menace?

The head of the Israelite forces, Jehu, left the battlefield in his chariot to go to the summer palace at Jezreel, because the prophet Elisha had convinced him he should be king. His mission was therefore to kill King Jehoram of Israel, who was recuperating from battle wounds, and King Ahaziah of Judah, who was visiting the sickbed. As Jehu's chariot approached Jezreel, the watchman in the city tower could not see the occupant, but he recognized the wild way of driving. "The driving is like the driving of Jehu," said the watchman, "for he driveth furiously" (2 Kings 9:20). In England, a reckless coach or cab driver used to be called a jehu.

17 Famous Women in the Bible

Abigail: Before David was king, he supported himself and his band with what was the biblical equivalent of protection money. One of the wealthy men his band solicited—Nabal—refused to pay, saying "Who is David?"

Nabal's wife, Abigail, realized this had been a stupid thing to do because David would surely come to kill them. Without telling Nabal, she loaded up their asses with bread, wine, dressed sheep, raisins, and figs, and started out to look for David and his band. She met them on the road, all armed with swords. Abigail prostrated herself and pressed the gifts on David. He relented and turned back.

When Abigail got home Nabal was so drunk she had to wait until he sobered up next morning to tell him about it. Nabal immediately had a heart attack, and he died about ten days later. When David heard this he said, "Blessed be the Lord," and married Abigail.

Later, at the battle of Ziklag, Abigail, who accompanied David on his exploits, was captured by the Amalekites. David went through great hardship and fierce battles to free her. After David became king they moved to Hebron and Abigail bore him a son. By then, though, David had acquired many wives, and the Bible never mentions Abigail again (1 Sam 25; 30:1–18; 2 Sam 2:2; 3:3; 1 Chr 3:1).

Anna: Widowed after only seven years of marriage, Anna became a prophetess and devoted the rest of her days and nights to prayer and fasting, never again leaving the Temple in Jerusalem. When she was eighty-four years old Jesus was presented at the Temple. Her fame rests on her thanking God and telling people looking for redemption to turn to Jesus (Luke 2:36–38).

Deborah: One of the most remarkable women in the Bible, Deborah (who lived before 1000 BC) was a judge of Israel. She judged the tribes under a palm tree on Mount Ephraim, and not from a city, as most judges did.

She is remembered primarily for masterminding the defeat of Canaanite forces under the supposedly invincible chariot forces of Sisera. It was her battle all the way:

Deborah chose the time for the battle.

Deborah chose Barak as leader for the Israelite forces. But she remained the leader in reality, because Barak would take command only if Deborah promised to be present at the battle. Otherwise, "I will not go," he said.

Deborah chose the troops.

Deborah chose the battlefield. The Israelites would assemble on Mount Tabor, leaving the Canaanite chariots the hopeless task of trying to reach them over the boggy ground around the Kishon River at the foot of the mountain.

Deborah rallied the troops by predicting they would be victorious.

Deborah told Barak to forget about killing Sisera—Sisera would fall "into the hand of a woman."

Finally, everything Deborah had predicted came true—the Canaanites were defeated and Sisera was killed by Jael, a woman. Afterward Deborah sang her beautiful song of victory. Although the Bible says Barak sang it with her, it is popularly called "Deborah's Song"—possibly because the entire story clearly shows who was boss. In addition, the song chastises Israelites who did not respond to the call of battle—a prerogative of judges rather than of military leaders.

Finally, the song is obviously that of a woman because it pays great attention to women's achievements and suffering. Jael is much praised in beautiful language for killing Sisera: "At her feet he bowed, he fell, he lay down; at her feet he bowed, he fell." Sisera's death is passed over as inconsequential in comparison with the sorrow of his mother, who is pictured standing at a window awaiting her son and crying, "Why is his chariot so long in coming?" Her "wise ladies" tried to comfort her, but she would not be pacified in her grief because she knew there had been plenty of time to win and even to divide the spoils.

After building to a climax in describing Jael and Sisera's mother, the song ends abruptly. There is no doubt its author was a woman who felt most keenly the impact of war on women (Judg 4–5).

Elisabeth: Elisabeth holds a special place in the Bible not only because she was the mother of John the Baptist but also because she appears to have been a great comfort to her cousin Mary, the mother of Jesus.

After years of childlessness, Elisabeth's husband learned from an angel that she would conceive. Her age is not given, but the Bible says she was "well stricken in years." For five months, Elisabeth concealed her pregnancy. Finally, the angel Gabriel, announcing to Mary that she would conceive, mentioned that Elisabeth was in her sixth month. Mary immediately left home and went to the older woman. Mary and Elisabeth lived together for three months before Mary returned home and Elisabeth had her child (Luke 1:5-25; 36-60).

Queen Esther: Esther was the Persian name given Hadassah when she married Ahasuerus and became queen of Persia.

An orphan, Esther had been brought up by her cousin Mordecai, who was an officer in Ahasuerus' court. When Ahasuerus divorced his first wife, Vashti, Esther was chosen from among the most beautiful virgins in Persia and made queen. On Mordecai's advice, she never revealed that she was Jewish.

Conflict arose when Haman was appointed minister. By Ahasuerus' order all other officials had to prostrate themselves before Haman. Mordecai refused. Seeking revenge, Haman convinced the king the Jews were a menace and should be destroyed. Ahasuerus told Haman to do whatever he thought best, and Haman issued a decree in the name of the king, saying the Jews were to be killed and their property seized.

Before the decree became effective, Mordecai sent a copy to Esther, warned her that she was in danger too, and asked her to intercede with the king on behalf of the Jews.

This put Esther on the spot. She had not seen the king in a month, and she was not supposed to try to see him unless he called for her. Since anyone who tried to see the king unbidden could be executed, Esther risked her life by going before the king. Luckily the king allowed her the interview. Esther denounced Haman's plan to annihilate the Jews, and the king became so angry he had Haman hanged on the gallows he had prepared for Mordecai. Mordecai thus became chief minister and the Jewish community was saved.

Huldah: A prophetess during the reign of Josiah, Huldah was living in Jerusalem when repairs on the Temple turned up a book of the law. This book, recalling the lapsed laws, was to start a movement for religious reform in Judah in which Huldah played an important role.

When the book was found, the priests consulted Huldah, who prophesied that God would bring evil on Judah because the inhabitants had angered God by burning incense to foreign gods. But because King Josiah had a tender heart and was so humble that he wept before God, Huldah said that he would be spared the agony of seeing his nation desolate. He would go in peace to his grave so that his eyes would not see the evil God would wreak.

One of the first true diplomats in history, Huldah managed to chastise the people while showing mercy to their pious king (2 Kings 22:14–20; 2 Chr 34:22–28).

Jael: Jael is one of the most controversial women in the Bible because she violated the nomadic code of hospitality by killing a guest who took refuge in her tent.

Her guest was Sisera, captain of the Canaanite forces, who had fled ignominiously on foot after the Israelites under Barak and Deborah had defeated him. He was exhausted by the time he reached Jael's tent, and she came out to greet him, saying, "Fear not." She gave him milk and covered him with a mantle. Sisera asked her to stand in the door of the tent so that if anyone came looking for him, she could deny having seen him.

But the minute he had fallen into a heavy sleep, Jael took a tent stake and hammered it through his temples into the ground.

Jael has been condemned because she lied and pretended to give refuge and then murdered her guest. Some scholars have tried to explain her behavior by saying she was sincere in her offer of hospitality and was later moved to treachery by fear of Barak or by an order from God—but the Bible makes no excuses for her.

In the Bible, Jael was lauded by Deborah, who sang, "Blessed above women shall Jael . . . be, blessed shall she be above women in the tent"—a phrasing strangely similar to words used by Gabriel when he told Mary, "Blessed art thou among women" (Judg 4:17–22; 5:24–27; Luke 1:28).

Jezebel: One of the most magnetic and influential women of the Bible, Jezebel was a Phoenician, daughter of the king of Tyre, and was married to King Ahab of Israel to strengthen political alliances. It was her religion for which she was condemned throughout the Bible, and for which she is accorded more space than any other woman. So powerful is the Bible's condemnation of Jezebel, her name lives on to slander her still: A jezebel is a painted, brazen woman.

Jezebel's form of worship centered on Baal and Asherat, fertility gods worshiped by Canaanites in their temples, in high places, and groves. Asherat, who appears under several names in the Middle East, was also worshiped by the Philistines. In Palestine, thousands of clay figurines and other images of her have been found. In most of these she is naked, has long hair, and may cup her breasts in her hands or may hold a lily and/or a serpent. Rituals were exuberant, including burnt offerings, incense burning, and feasting. Some sort of lewd dancing and male or female prostitutes were also involved. Although she was a stranger in Israel with its austere worship, Jezebel was not intimidated and determinedly set out to introduce the Israelites to her own gods. Ahab seems to have been her first convert, and their court soon supported 450 priests of Baal and 400 of Asherat, establishing the new religion throughout Israel.

Jezebel then ordered the Israelite priests killed. They survived on bread

423

and water in caves that Elijah found to hide them in. Elijah was the only person to oppose Jezebel. He led a rebellion, in which Jezebel's 850 priests were killed on Mount Carmel. Elijah also so terrified Ahab with displays of God's strength that Ahab rode back from Mount Carmel to the palace at Jezreel to tell Jezebel. Jezebel didn't lose her cool. She sent word to Elijah that she would have him dead within twenty-four hours.

The net result of this rebellion was that Elijah went into hiding for about six years, leaving Jezebel triumphantly propagating her religion, with Ahab completely under her domination. When Ahab wanted a vineyard and the owner, Naboth, refused to sell, Ahab refused to get out of bed or to eat. He sulked with his face turned toward the wall. Jezebel took over, had Naboth killed, and then told Ahab to get out of bed and take over his vineyard. In effect, Jezebel had become the queen.

Elijah finally got to Ahab again, scaring him with prophecies about how Jezebel would be eaten by dogs. The moody and depressed Ahab rent his clothes, fasted, and lay in sackcloth. Jezebel again kept her cool, and did not let Ahab influence her. She married her daughter off to the house of Judah, spreading her religion to the southern kingdom. She outlived both Ahab (who died in battle) and Elijah by several years. Her power continued undiminished as her sons Ahaziah and Jehoram ruled Israel.

Jezebel did not meet her doom until Elijah's successor, Elisha, made it his personal mission to end her influence. Her age is unknown, but she could not have been young since she had been in power for thirty years. Elisha masterminded a coup by the general Jehu, who killed the kings of Israel and Judah and most of the royal family and retinue. When Jehu came for Jezebel she did not cringe. She put on an elaborate headdress and painted her face, and with eunuchs on either side she stood majestically at a palace window, watching Jehu's chariot approach. "Had Zimri peace?" she asked Jehu, referring to a former army officer who had usurped the throne but held it only seven days. Jehu ordered the eunuchs to throw her down. Her blood spattered the palace walls and the horses, and Jehu ran over her with his chariot. Her corpse was left for the scavenging dogs.

But Jezebel must have gotten to Jehu too, because later, when he got drunk, he decided she should have a decent burial—"for she is a king's daughter," he said. All they could find of her, however, were the skull, feet, and palms of her hands.

Yet Jezebel's influence did not end with her death. Jehu's attempts to wipe out Baalism failed, and her religion continued to be a potent force until the Kingdom of Israel collapsed. In Judah, Baalism continued strong for 250 years after her death. Even then her name survived into New Testament times as a symbol of pagan license. She is the last woman mentioned by name in the Bible (1 Kings 16:31–32; 18; 19:1–3; 21; 2 Kings 9:7–37; Rev 2:20).

Martha and Mary: Martha, sister of Lazarus, is shown in the Bible to have been an energetic, impatient, and questioning person—in contrast to her

424

quieter and more trusting sister, Mary. All three were friends of Jesus, who obviously felt comfortable with them, but Martha's dominant position is evident by the description of their house in Bethany as hers.

Once, when Jesus was a guest, Martha—who was bustling about while Mary just sat adoringly at Jesus' feet—impatiently burst out, "Lord, dost thou not care that my sister hath left me to serve alone? bid her therefore that she help me." Jesus good-naturedly reproved Martha, pointing out that she was "troubled about many things," but emphasizing that Mary's "good part" should not be belittled.

In one scene, when Lazarus died, Jesus insisted on going to Bethany even though the disciples feared he would be stoned. It was Martha who came out of the city to greet Jesus, while Mary "sat still in the house." Martha immediately told Jesus that Lazarus would not have died if Jesus had been there. Jesus reassured her that Lazarus would rise, but Martha countered that that was in the resurrection "at the last day." Jesus chided her that "he that believeth in me, though he were dead, yet shall he live." Thus chastened, Martha replied that she believed Jesus was the Christ.

Martha then called Mary to greet Jesus, and Mary fell at his feet and sobbed. Jesus also was moved to tears and went to the tomb. Lazarus had been buried in a cave, with a stone rolled up to the door, and Jesus ordered that the stone be rolled away.

Martha objected right away, pointing out that Lazarus had been dead four days and "by this time he stinketh." Perhaps Martha was so disgusted that she left, because only Mary is mentioned at the scene after Lazarus was raised.

The last time Jesus visited, Martha again did all the serving, while Mary wiped the feet of Jesus with her hair and anointed them with a spikenard ointment so powerful its odor filled the whole house. Judas Iscariot criticized her, saying that she should have given the money she paid for this ointment to the poor, but Jesus again defended Mary (Luke 10:38-42; John 11:1-39; 12:1-8).

Miriam: The older sister of Moses and Aaron, Miriam was a prophetess. She first appears in the Bible standing on the banks of the Nile to guard the basket containing her baby brother. When the pharaoh's daughter rescued the basket, it was Miriam who offered to find a wet nurse and who arranged for Moses' mother to be hired to nurse her own infant. After the Israelites had escaped the pharaoh's chariots, she led the women in a dance of celebration and a song about how the horses and riders fell into the sea.

Later, however, Miriam and Aaron became annoyed at Moses' Ethiopian wife, for some reason not explained, and began to resent Moses' leadership. They questioned Moses' being the only prophet, saying, Hadn't the Lord "spoken also by us?" This angered God, but only Miriam was punished: God turned her "white as snow"—a condition the Bible calls leprosy. As a leper she was unclean for seven days and Moses had to call a halt in the journey for this week.

Apparently Miriam never regained either her health or her prestige because she is not mentioned as playing a major role again. She died, apparently young, at Kadesh-barnea and was buried near the springs (Ex 2:4–8, 15:20–21; Num 12:1–16; 20:1).

Rahab: Rahab, a harlot, was the heroine of Jericho. When Joshua sent spies into Jericho before attacking the city, Rahab gave them hospitality and information, hid them, and later helped them to escape. As a reward the Israelites spared her life and that of her family when they wiped out the other residents.

Rahab later married an Israelite, and her descendants included David and Jesus.

Rahab was unusual in that she had her own home—on or against the city walls—while her family lived elsewhere. Some scholars believe—because flax and scarlet thread were stored in her house—that she may have made linen and been a dyer or that she traded in these products (Josh 2; 6:22–23; Matt 1:15).

Rizpah: After Israel had suffered three years of famine during David's reign, God told David it was because Saul had killed the Gibeonites. Seven of Saul's sons were therefore hanged in expiation, to end the famine. Despite Hebrew belief that the body should be preserved, these corpses were to be left for vultures and wild animals to devour.

Two of these children belonged to Saul's concubine, Rizpah, who climbed the hill where the corpses of her sons and five other of Saul's children hung. She spread sackcloth on a rock and began a day-and-night vigil to keep the bodies from being desecrated. She "suffered neither the birds of the air to rest on them by day, nor the beasts of the field by night."

Her children had been killed at the beginning of the barley harvest—the earliest of the harvests in the spring—and Rizpah kept her watch for months, until the winter rains began (2 Sam 21:1–10).

Salome the Dancer: One of the most famous women in biblical stories, Salome is not named in the Bible and her identification comes from the writings of Josephus.

Salome's role in biblical history is due to her mother, Herodias, who had a sexual relationship with her uncle Herod Antipas that John the Baptist denounced as "not lawful." Infuriated, Herodias wanted John the Baptist killed, but Antipas feared public reaction and would only jail him.

Salome and her mother were not so lily-livered. On Antipas' birthday, which was celebrated with extravagant festivities, Salome made an unusual offer to dance before the men. Parties then were segregated by sex, and women of noble birth were secluded from the supposedly wilder carryings-on of the male guests. The novelty of such a performance, and Salome's mastery of dance, charmed Antipas. He rashly asked her to name her own reward.

Salome left the men's party to consult with her mother about the reward. "The head of John the Baptist," said Herodias.

Antipas was not too happy about this grisly request but could not go back on his word, so he ordered Salome's wishes followed. Salome triumphantly carried the platter with the head back to the women's party and presented it to Herodias (Matt 14:1-11; Mark 6:17-28).

The Other Salome: The Salome named in the Bible is not the dancer who asked for John the Baptist's head but the wife of Zebedee. Some scholars believe she may have been a sister of Mary, the mother of Jesus.

Salome appears only three times in the Bible. Once, she enraged the disciples by asking Jesus to allow her two sons seats of honor in the kingdom of heaven—a request not granted. Despite this, she remained a devoted follower, for she was present at the Crucifixion and later took spices to the tomb (Matt 20:20-23; Mark 15:40; 16:1).

Queen Vashti: According to the Book of Esther, Vashti was the independent-minded wife of Ahasuerus, king of Persia. Ahasuerus is believed to have been Xerxes I (486–465 BC), but Persian records list another woman as his queen.

The biblical story relates that Ahasuerus held a week-long celebration of his reign. He partied with the men in the decorated gardens while Vashti entertained the women inside the palace. Wine flowed freely, and by the seventh day Ahasuerus was feeling no pain and sent his eunuchs to fetch the queen so he could show her off to the male guests. Vashti had no stomach for being paraded before that drunken crowd and refused to go.

Ahasuerus was furious. He consulted about what could be done, within the law, to punish Vashti. At meetings possibly marred by hangovers, the princes read fury in the king's face and quickly decided Vashti had done great harm not only to Ahasuerus but to the entire kingdom. Soon all women in the land would know Vashti had disobeyed her husband, and all the women of Persia would begin to disobey their husbands. Persia would be torn apart; the women would be contemptuous and the men angry.

To prevent this calamity, Vashti was made an example. She was divorced and banished, and another queen (Esther) was chosen. A royal decree was sent to every province in the land, warning men to rule their wives firmly and warning women to honor their husbands (Est 1).

The Witch of Endor: Intelligent and competent, the Witch, the only one mentioned in the Bible, was rich by biblical standards, because she had both a bed and a fatted calf. She lived at Endor, only a few miles from Mount Tabor, possibly hiding in a cave in the foothills to escape King Saul's persecution.

Saul, despite having ordered that everyone with a "familiar spirit" should be killed, finally decided to resort to a witch when he needed advice the night before battle. When he arrived at night and in disguise, the Witch didn't recognize him at first. She was reluctant to use her powers in the face of the death penalty but finally asked Saul whom he would like brought up from the underworld.

As soon as Saul said he wanted to see Samuel, the Witch guessed that her client was the king. Instead of being afraid, she scolded, "Why hast thou deceived me?"

Saul reassured her there was nothing to fear, and she began the séance, bringing Samuel up so that Saul could converse with him. Samuel did most of the talking, predicting defeat for Saul and promising that by the next day Saul and his sons would be joining him in the underworld.

Saul was so shaken he fell flat on the ground. The Witch felt sorry for him and urged him to eat to gain strength before facing the ordeal Samuel had outlined. "I will not eat," said Saul stubbornly. Finally the Witch got Saul's aides on her side and together they coaxed Saul to get up off the floor and sit on the Witch's bed.

The Witch of Endor turned out to have a fatted calf in the house and to be adept at butchering and cooking. She slaughtered the calf quickly and put it on to cook. Meanwhile she kneaded flour and began to bake bread. Before the night was over she had spread a fine feast before the doomed king and his aides (1 Sam 28).

Seven Forgotten Women

The Ethiopian Woman: The Ethiopian woman is mentioned only once, as the wife of Moses and as the reason his brother and sister—Aaron and Miriam—rebelled against him (Num 12:1).

Elsewhere, however, Moses' wife is said to be Zipporah, a Midianite (Ex 2:15-22).

Scholars offer various explanations for the contradiction: Moses had two wives; Moses married the Ethiopian woman after Zipporah died; Zipporah was the Ethiopian woman and the passage which describes her as a Midianite is in error.

Jephthah's Daughter: The only daughter of Jephthah remains unnamed in the Bible even though her tragic story is told in detail. Jephthah, on going to war against the Ammonites, had vowed that if God gave him victory he would offer as a burnt sacrifice the first living creature that greeted him on his return home.

When he defeated the Ammonites and returned home, "his daughter came out to meet him with timbrels and with dances." Aghast, Jephthah tore his clothes and cried "Alas," and told his daughter of his vow. She agreed he had to carry out his vow but she begged him for two months of life, "that I may go up and down the mountains, and bewail my virginity."

Jephthah agreed. For two months, with her friends, she mourned her early death. Then she returned to her father, who carried out his vow.

The women of Israel were so touched that it became a custom for them to go annually to spend four days mourning the sacrifice of Jephthah's daughter (Judg 11:30–40).

The Pharaoh's Daughter: The pharaoh's daughter who found the basket in the bulrushes is unnamed in the Bible. When she found the basket containing the baby Moses, she knew at once it was one of the Hebrew infant boys her father had ordered killed. When the baby cried she decided to flout her father's command and saved it. Even more ironic, she hired as a wet nurse Moses' own mother. Then she adopted the child and brazenly brought Moses up under the pharaoh's nose—possibly she had a sense of humor in addition to compassion. Undoubtedly, the easy access Moses had to the pharaoh when he wanted to argue the Israelites' case owed much to this woman (Ex 2:5–10).

Serah: Serah, the daughter of Asher, is a truly forgotten woman because the Bible fails to tell us why she was important. Yet that she was extraordinary is incontestable—she is not merely the only woman the Bible lists in the naming of the tribes, but she is listed three times (Gen 46:17; Num 26:46; 1 Chr 7:30).

Sherah: Sherah is mentioned only once in the Bible, yet she must have been a formidable woman because this verse credits her with founding upper and lower Beth-horon, two fortified towns guarding the treacherous and important pass northwest of Jerusalem. She is also credited with building Uzzen-sherah, a city of fortifications that has not yet been identified (1 Chr 7:24).

The Wise Woman of Abel-Beth-maachah: The Bible describes the woman who saved the fortified city of Abel-Beth-maachah as wise but does not name her. Her city was endangered when Sheba, who had attempted to carry on Absalom's rebellion against King David, had taken refuge there. David sent his army under the command of Joab to lay siege to the city. Joab's army had dug in around the city walls and had made earth banks to bring up the battering rams. The wise woman called out from the walls for Joab and asked him to approach. She told him she and others of the town were peaceful and were faithful to David, "but thou seekest to destroy a city and a mother in Israel." Joab replied that he was not bent on destruction, he only wanted Sheba. The woman proposed that the city residents would throw Sheba's head over the wall to Joab, and Joab agreed he would then withdraw. Over the wall came Sheba's head, and Joab blew the trumpet and called off his troops (2 Sam 20:15-22).

The Woman at the Well: This saucy, unnamed woman was from Sychar, a small village just northeast of Shechem in Samaria. She was important because she illustrated Jesus' attitudes toward Samaritans.

When the old Israelite kingdom had been divided, new shrines had been established in the north (at Dan and Bethel) to keep the population from worshiping in Jerusalem. The split was intensified after Jezebel made Samaria a center for idolatry. When the northern kingdom fell, two hundred years before the south, its population was deported, and foreigners were brought in to repopulate the area. Even though many Jews later resettled in Samaria, they did not worship in Jerusalem and they were distrusted by the devout.

Against this background the woman at the well became an important symbol. Jesus, returning from Jerusalem, had stopped to rest at a well Jacob had dug hundreds of years before. The woman came to fill her jug, and Jesus asked her for a drink, which started a spirited conversation.

She was stunned that a Jew would talk to her, for Jews usually had nothing to do with Samaritans. Jesus replied that if she knew who he was she would ask for "living water." She asked if he thought he was greater than Jacob, but Jesus said only that his water would give her "everlasting life." Impressed, she asked if she could have some so she wouldn't have to keep coming to the well.

Jesus asked her to get her husband and she said she had none. Jesus replied, "Thou hast well said.... For thou hast had five husbands; and he whom thou now hast is not thy husband" (John 4:17-18).

"I perceive that thou art a prophet," she said, and changed the subject to ask why men should worship in Jerusalem when their forefathers had worshiped at the mountain above them. This got them into a discussion of the messiah that convinced her Jesus was the Christ.

She ran back to Sychar and got the townspeople to come out to see Jesus, and the townspeople prevailed upon Jesus to stay two days. Samaritans thus became among the first to accept Jesus as the "Saviour of the world" (John 4:1-42).

Whores and Harlots

Throughout the Old Testament, prostitution and promiscuity in women are portrayed as vile and abhorrent, as types of behavior that corrupt the society and the individual. Much of the Hebrews' abhorrence probably developed from the association of prostitution with the cultic rites of the Babylonians and the Canaanites. In Babylon, every woman of every social station was required to spend one night in the temple of the goddess of love, and during the night she had to give herself to anyone who offered any sum of money to her. Among the Canaanites belonging to some cults, celebrations of fertility and reproduction sometimes involved orgiastic festivals in the groves and precincts surrounding the shrines. The Hebrew word for temple prostitute, *kedayshah,* often applies to any prostitute, and it is used as a term of derision.

Although references to harlots are not extensive, there are enough to piece together a rather telling portrait of a "typical" biblical prostitute. It seems that a veil was one of the signs by which a prostitute indicated her profession:

> And she put her widow's garments off from her, and covered
> her with a veil, and wrapped herself, and sat in an open
> place, which is by the way to Timnath; for she saw that
> Shelah was grown, and she was not given unto him to wife.
> When Judah saw her, he thought her to be an harlot; because
> she had covered her face (Gen 38:14–15).

The prostitute is typically portrayed as being brazen:

> And, behold, there met him a woman with the attire of an
> harlot, and subtil of heart. (She is loud and stubborn; her feet

abide not in her house: Now is she without, now in the
streets, and lieth in wait at every corner.) So she caught him,
and kissed him, and with an impudent face said unto him . . .
Come, let us take our fill of love until the morning: let us
solace ourselves with loves [Prov 7:10–18].

Yet occasionally the Old Testament thumbnail sketches of prostitutes have
truly poetic poignancy: "Take an harp, go about the city, thou harlot that
hast been forgotten; make sweet melody, sing many songs, that thou mayest
be remembered" (Isa 23:16).

And there are passages where the sharp and critical eye of the author
picks out the most minute details of character: ". . . and thou hadst a
whore's forehead, thou refusedst to be ashamed" (Jer 3:3).

In the Book of Ezekiel prostitutes are seen to be like unfaithful Israelites
in danger of breaking the covenant. In that book God says to all Jerusalem:
"But thou didst trust in thine own beauty, and playedst the harlot because
of thy renown. . . . Thou hast also taken thy fair jewels of my gold and my
silver, which I had given thee, and madest to thyself images of men, and
didst commit whoredom with them" (Ezek 16:15, 17).

The author of Ezekiel makes it clear that he considers the prostitute to be
in no way a product of her environment or society. She is, quite simply, an
oversexed woman: "Thou hast played the whore also with the Assyrians,
because thou wast unsatiable; yea, thou hast played the harlot with them,
and yet couldest not be satisfied" (Ezek 16:28).

Yet for all the vehemence in the Old Testament's denunciation of
prostitutes there is no prohibition against the profession itself. Instead there
are commandments which imply that the responsibility for eradicating the
social ills of prostitution lies with the family. God says to the Israelites:

I will not punish your daughters when they commit whoredom, nor your spouses when they commit adultery: for
themselves are separated with whores, and they sacrifice with
harlots: therefore the people that doth not understand shall
fall [Hos 4:14].

And in Leviticus, the Lord exhorts all fathers:

Do not prostitute thy daughter, to cause her to be a whore;
lest the land fall to whoredom, and the land become full of
wickedness [Lev 19:29].

In addition to the commandments there are stringent punishments in the
Old Testament which would effectively curb the spread of prostitution.
Against any woman who married without being a virgin there was the
strictest of penalties:

Then they shall bring out the damsel to the door of her
father's house, and the men of her city shall stone her with

stones that she die: because she hath wrought folly in Israel, to play the whore in her father's house: so shalt thou put evil away from among you [Deut 22:21].

For the prostitute who was with child the punishment was just as final:

And it came to pass about three months after, that it was told Judah, saying, Tamar thy daughter in law hath played the harlot; and also, behold, she is with child by whoredom. And Judah said, Bring her forth and let her be burnt. [Gen 38:24].

In the New Testament prostitution is treated with more toleration though it is not condoned. Jesus allows that the woman of the streets may pass into heaven before many of the more self-righteous: "Verily I say unto you, That the publicans and the harlots go into the kingdom of God before you" (Matt 21:31). In Luke, Jesus forgives a woman who has been a sinner, i.e., has led a profligate life, after she has demonstrated her faith by washing his feet (7:39–50).

In Revelation, the prostitute is again used as a symbol of a nation's infidelity, but there the nation so portrayed is Babylon, not Israel:

I saw a woman sit upon a scarlet coloured beast, full of names of blasphemy, having seven heads and ten horns. And the woman was arrayed in purple and scarlet colour, and decked with gold and precious stones and pearls, having a golden cup in her hand full of abominations and filthiness of her fornication: And upon her forehead was a name written, MYSTERY, BABYLON THE GREAT, THE MOTHER OF HARLOTS AND ABOMINATIONS OF THE EARTH [Rev 17:3–5].

Biblical Suicides

When Samson pulled the pillars of the Philistine temple down onto his enemies he knew that he would die with them: "And Samson said, Let me die with the Philistines. . . . So the dead which he slew at his death were more than they which he slew in his life" (Judg 16:30).

Saul, seeing that he was losing the battle against the Philistines at Mount Gilboa, commanded his armor-bearer to kill him. The man, however, refused. "Therefore Saul took a sword, and fell upon it."

The armor-bearer did the same "and died with him" (1 Sam 31:4–5).

Ahithophel counseled Absalom to pursue his father, King David, to slay him and his armies. When Absalom refused Ahithophel's counsel, the latter "saddled his ass, and arose, and gat him home to his house . . . and hanged himself, and died" (2 Sam 17:1–23).

King Zimri reigned for seven days as king of Israel. The people then turned against him and elected Omri as king, who immediately besieged the city of Tirzah, where Zimri held court. "When Zimri saw that the city was taken, that he went into the palace of the king's house, and burnt the king's house over him with fire, and died" (1 Kings 16:15–18).

There are two versions of the death of Judas Iscariot. In the first he throws his reward for the betrayal of Jesus at the feet of the priests "and went and hanged himself" (Matt 27:5). In the second version, he dies in the field which he bought with the money. "Falling headlong, he burst asunder in the midst, and all his bowels gushed out" (Acts 1:18).

Eight

About the Good Book

THE LITERARY TRADITIONS IN THE BIBLE

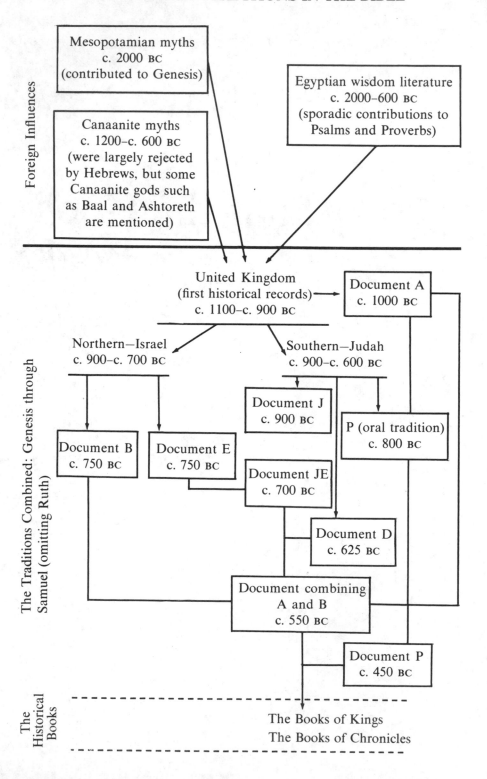

Who Wrote the Bible?

The Bible is a book with many authors; it is, in fact, a book comprising many books, and a book written in many places—in Palestine, perhaps in Babylonia, on the roads that lead from the Middle East to Rome. No one knows when the Bible first began to be composed, but most authorities date the Bible's beginnings as a *written* work at about 1300 BC. No doubt many of the stories in Genesis are much older, being part of the oral tradition of the early Hebrews and Mesopotamian world in general. The account of the flood, for instance, resembles one part of the ancient Babylonian *Epic of Gilgamesh* so closely that it is almost certain that the biblical story derives from the earlier tale.

How Did God Write?

God wrote with his finger on tables of Stone (Ex 31:18: 34:1; Deut 10:1–2).

THE OLD TESTAMENT

The Pentateuch: Traditionally, Moses is said to have authored the first five books of the Bible—Genesis, Exodus, Leviticus, Numbers, and Deuteronomy—collectively called the Pentateuch. Although the Bible itself never states he wrote these five books, and the style suggests an author living later than Moses, many people still hold to the belief. Mosaic authorship of the Pentateuch has, however, been challenged since antiquity, by pagan critics such as Porphyry, and by later philosophers and scholars such as Abelard and Hobbes.

437

The first major critic of Mosaic authorship was the Frenchman Jean Astruc. In 1753 Astruc published a book suggesting that Moses wrote the final draft of Genesis after consulting two other sources. Astruc had made a very astute observation: In Genesis, two names are used to denote God. In some places God is called Jehovah, while in other places God is called Elohim. Astruc also noticed that the style of the passages where Jehovah is used are strikingly different from those where Elohim is employed. Astruc therefore concluded that two authors must have originated Genesis—he tagged these the Jehovistic source and the Elohistic source. Although Astruc was careful to retain Moses as the ultimate author of Genesis, he feared his work might be construed as heresy so he had it published anonymously.

J and E: Astruc's tag names—Jehovistic and Elohistic, usually shortened to J and E—have been retained by biblical commentators, but his methods and critical techniques have been refined. Later scholars not only discovered more sources than the J and the E, but also decided that the Book of Joshua formed a unit with the first five books.

In its simplest form, the "documentary hypothesis"—as the revised and established version of Astruc's initial theory has come to be called—alleges that two main literary traditions can be discerned in the first six books of the Old Testament. The J source reflects the language and preoccupations of someone from the southern part of Palestine, the Kingdom of Judah. The E source suggests a writer from the northern part of Palestine, the Kingdom of Israel. It is believed that the two authors composed their epics, the spiritual and historic record of each nation, by drawing on stories and folk histories of their respective locales—and that these two epics were edited and combined into one, long after their original composition.

The detail with which some scholars have reconstructed the characters of the J and the E authors is remarkably fine, and, to those conservative theologians who still opt for Mosaic authorship, remarkably conjectural. For example, it is now generally believed that the author of the J document was a Judean who lived in Jerusalem around 900 BC. This was a period of great power and prosperity for the Kingdom of Judah, and this sense of national well-being permeates the J narrative, making it particularly optimistic. J's passages express faith in the providence of Jehovah and in the continuation of the covenant, and portray the patriarchs complete with all the human foibles.

Unlike the J author, whose style is usually described as simple and noble, the E author possesses a refined and theologically cautious style, suggesting he was probably a priest. He is thought by many to have lived in Bethel and to have composed his epic there sometime around 750 BC.

Besides their literary style, the authors are distinguished by the materials they draw upon. Though both are writing from the more or less common tradition of early Hebrew oral literature, undoubtedly many versions of the same story circulated, and probably each of the two kingdoms had its favorite. Moreover, many ancient myths and tales from other cultures, particularly from Canaan and Mesopotamia, were incorporated—and which of these stories were used often gives a clue as to whether J or E is responsible for a particular section. For example, J liked to borrow from Canaanite tradition. Since Abraham, Isaac, and Jacob have their roots in ancient traditions in which they are cited as the founders of various Canaanite sanctuaries, most of the material on these patriarchs belongs to the J document. On the other hand, E emphasized the cultic aspect of the early Hebrews. and so he is assumed to have included the story of the sacrifice of Isaac.

P and D and Others: In addition to the J and E authors, the narratives of several others have been trailed through the Old Testament. The two most important of these, the P (for the Priestly Code) and the D (for the Deuteronomic Code), are alike in that they seem designed to give written form to the laws of the Hebrews, but they are otherwise radically different. The style of the Priestly Code is dry and legalistic; its accounts of geneologies and ritual practices are little enlivened by detail or anecdote. The Deuteronomic Code, however, has the high rhetoric and oratory of the Mosaic sermon. Also, P and D were undoubtedly from different eras; D dates from c. 625 BC, about two hundred years earlier than P. It is the D document to which the Bible itself probably refers in the story of the discovery of the scroll of the law (2 Kings 22:8–11).

Besides the original narrators there are a number of editors or redactors who probably condensed and integrated the original documents. They are usually referred to by the names of the documents they combined. Thus the JE redactor is the editor who spliced the epics of J and E together.

The entire process of the authorship of the first six books of the Bible, according to the documentary hypothesis, is easily represented on a schematic chart (see page 436). This is of course only an outline of what was a complex process, and one whose history is at best uncertain. For a more complete listing of the various documents thought to make up the original sources and a detailed inventory of which chapter and verse are from a particular document, see the *Harper Bible Dictionary,* under Sources.

Where to Keep Your Bible

"Take this book of the law, and put it in the side of the ark of the covenant" (Deut 31:26).

The Book of Joshua: Traditionally the Pentateuch, or Torah, has been thought to form a distinct literary work. Most modern scholars, however, believe that the first six books of the Old Testament—which would include the Book of Joshua—form a literary entity. The Book of Joshua fulfills promises made in the earlier books, and its style is similar. The early, though postbiblical, view was that Joshua wrote the book bearing his name. Those who hold to the documentary hypothesis credit the majority of the Book of Joshua to the E document (chapters 1-12, 24) and to the P document (chapters 13-20).

Still another theory, advanced by Martin Noth, proposes that Joshua is part of a connected work by a single author. Noth believes that this work, which he labels the "deuteronomic history," is composed of the present books of Deuteronomy, Joshua, Judges, First and Second Samuel, and First and Second Kings. These books can be seen as the history of Israel from the death of Moses to the period of Babylonian Exile, and Noth contends that this history was composed by a Judean in Jerusalem sometime after the city's fall to the Babylonians in 586 BC. Noth's theory is widely accepted, though perhaps not as widely held as the documentary hypothesis.

Book of Judges: Conservative and modern theories on the composition of the Book of Judges differ radically. The conservative position is that the book is very early, from the time of Saul (c. 1020 BC), and may have been written by Samuel himself. Modern critics contend that the book is a fusion based on J's account of the conquest of Canaan and E's version of the conquest (in which Joshua is portrayed as the hero). This theory accounts for obviously ancient material, such as "Deborah's Song" by suggesting that such stories were added from other sources. The fusion of J, E, and other sources is usually dated sometime during the 8th century BC, but as late as the 4th century.

Book of Ruth: No one knows who wrote the Book of Ruth and few authors have been conjectured. Jewish tradition credits Samuel with composition, but modern scholarship usually places it much later than the time of Samuel. The language of the book, and its implied protest against the condemnation of mixed marriages, suggest a date of about 400 BC—the postexilic period of Nehemiah and Ezra, when mixed marriages were coming under censure. As with the books that follow it, the Book of Ruth is certainly too late to have been part of the J, P, D, and E documents which make up the sources of the earlier books. A recent theory is that the book may be as early as the 9th century BC.

Books of Samuel: In the Books of Samuel, the sources are more apparent since little editing seems to have been done. That two main strands have been incorporated in the Books of Samuel becomes quite clear when one notices two different and sometimes contradictory versions of the same story. For example, there are two accounts of David's introduction to Saul (1 Sam 16:14-23; 17:55-58). There are even two versions of the death of Goliath: the familiar story of David and the sling, and a second version in which the soldier Elhanan kills Goliath (2 Sam 21:19). The editors of the Authorized Version eliminated the latter contradiction by adding words not in the Hebrew, thus having Elhanan kill "the brother of" Goliath.

The two sources in Samuel are often designated A and B. A is characterized by its optimistic view of the incipient monarchy and its portrayal of Samuel as a relatively unknown, local seer. The later B source depicts Samuel as the reigning prophet of all Israel, ridiculing and harassing the monarchy. The A source probably drew on writings contemporary with the reign of David, perhaps even on the court annals of the time. The author of these annals may have been one of David's court priests—Abiathar, Ahimaaz, or Zadok. Not only is the A source the oldest extended historical record known, but the author also shows an appreciation for detail and a tolerance for the complexities of character unrivaled by any other historian before Herodotus.

The B strand, dated about 750 BC, appears to be derived from histories and sources in northern Israel, as suggested by the author's antimonarchical stance. It was fused with the A source sometime around 550 BC, perhaps by the editor of the "deuteronomic history" mentioned above.

Books of Kings: In the Books of Kings we have for the first time an editor who cites sources. He mentions a "book of the acts of Solomon" (1 Kings 11:41), the "book of the chronicles of the Kings of Israel" (1 Kings 14:19), and a "book of chronicles of the kings of Judah" (1 Kings 14:29), and though he does not say that he used these books, he does indeed cover the history of Solomon and the kings of Israel and Judah. The first editor of the Books of Kings may have been a scribe, an office known to exist from numerous references in the historical books (1 Kings 4:3; 2 Kings 18:18; 2 Sam 8:17). It seems that this first editor had attempted to write a history which would establish Josiah as the ideal Hebrew king, the consummation of the royal line, the protector of the worship of Jehovah. The final form of the books may be the work of the deuteronomic revisionist (c. 550 BC).

Books of Chronicles: With the Chronicles we have the Bible beginning to use itself as a source. Except for the first nine chapters, Chronicles is adapted from Second Samuel through Second Kings and from the earlier books of the Bible. The manuscript of these books that the chronicler had before him was close to that used in making the early Greek translation of the Old Testament, the Septuagint, and thus differs slightly from the traditional Jewish (Masoretic) text that lies behind most modern Old Testament translations. Evidently the Chronicles were written in a period (c. 350 BC) when the Bible was beginning to be canonized—that is, the ancient writings were treated with respect, but were not yet considered so sacred and immutable that no new scriptures could be added to them.

The author is intensely interested in Levitical matters and shows a fascination with the music of the temple (1 Chr 15:16; 25;1). Most people believe that the author also wrote the Books of Ezra and Nehemiah, and may have been Ezra himself.

Ezra, Nehemiah, Esther: The chronicler, whoever he was, is thought to have written the books of Ezra and Nehemiah around 350 BC. Scholars disagree about the authenticity of the sources the chronicler depended on. Some consider the books to be merely propagandist fictions slanted toward the priesthood; most believe parts of the books to be founded on genuine records, including Nehemiah's personal memoirs and various temple and royal records.

One work that is surely more fiction than fact, and more a patriotic than religious story, is the Book of Esther. Written by someone with an intimate knowledge of the Persian court, perhaps an exiled Jew, the book reached final form around 450 BC, though it may be based on a tale centuries older. The author's set purpose, beyond presenting an entertaining story, is to promote the Feast of Purim, a festival which is probably of Persian origin.

Book of Job: Although the author of the Book of Job must be listed among the world's greatest writers, his identity is unknown and rarely conjectured. His vocabulary—the widest of the Old Testament authors—employs many words of Edomite origin and shows a heavy Aramaic influence, suggesting he was a learned man from the southern part of Palestine. The ethnic flavor of his language may, however, indicate only the origins of the folktales from which the final version was derived. Dating of the book is difficult because of the many sources which seem to be involved in its composition. The dialogue of the book seems to show the influence of the Book of Jeremiah and to have influenced Isaiah, suggesting a date between 580 and 540 BC, but the dates that scholars have assigned it range from 700 to 200 BC.

Some Same Psalms

In Psalm 107, the following verses are alike: 8, 15, 21, 31: "Oh that men would praise the Lord for his goodness, and for his wonderful works to the children of men!"

All twenty-six verses of Psalm 136 end with the phrase "For his mercy endureth forever."

Book of Psalms: Two thirds of the psalms have had authors assigned to them, but most of this is guesswork. Among those named as the hymns' authors—Moses, Solomon, and others—David is possibly the only one who wrote any of the psalms ascribed to him. His reputation as a psalmist is too widespread to be a complete fiction. Nevertheless, he did not write every one of the seventy-three psalms reputed to be his—and certainly not the ones that mention the Temple (Psa 5:7; 27:4; 29:9; etc.), as the Temple was built after his death.

Proverbs: Proverbs, the literary legacy of Hebrew wisdom literature, is supposedly the work of Solomon, but there are too many disparaging remarks made about the monarchy and too many words from the postexilic period for the entire work to have been his alone. The commonly held belief is that Proverbs is a collection of aphorisms, many of which were derived from ancient Egyptian or Canaanite originals, gradually accumulated over the years. Solomon was undoubtedly the author, perhaps the first anthologist, of some of the proverbs. He is too often characterized as being wise, and too often said to be the author, not to have had some part in their conception.

Bible Statistics

The Bible has more than 773,000 words and 3½ million letters. The following divisions also occur:

	Old Testament	New Testament	Total
Books	39	27	66
Chapters	929	260	1,189
Verses	23,214	7,959	31,173

The word "and" occurs more often than any other word in the English versions of the Bible; however, "and" is not a word, but a prefix in the Hebrew.

Did You Know People Wrote . . . ?

on a plate of pure gold (Ex 39:30)
on great stones plastered with plaster (Deut 27:3, 8)
in the earth (Jer 17:13)
on a rod (Num 17:3)

on houseposts and on gates (Deut 6:9; 11:20)

upon the table of thine heart (Prov 3:3; 7:3; Jer 17:1; 2 Cor 3:3; Heb 8:10)

on the horns of altars (Jer 17:1)

on sticks (Ezek 37:16–20)

on a woman's forehead (Rev 17:5)

on the thigh of Faithful and True (Rev 19:12, 16)

on the gates of heaven (Rev 21:12)

Ecclesiastes: More uniform than Proverbs, Ecclesiastes is the work of a single author who calls himself *koheleth,* or "preacher," and says, in the first verse, that he is "son of David, king in Jerusalem." All but a few scholars believe that the writer is impersonating Solomon to give his work authority. The conjectures surrounding the author's identity all begin with internal evidence. The vocabulary and syntax are late Hebrew, implying a date of about 250–200 BC, and the use of "Elohim" exclusively for the name of God (instead of "Jehovah") implies that the author was a less than passionately devout Hebrew.

Song of Solomon: The third and last of the books traditionally ascribed to Solomon, the Song of Solomon is also probably not his work entirely. The king is mentioned in the third person, and the Aramaic influence on the language is generally thought to be a sign of the postexilic period. Still, the Book of Kings does say that Solomon wrote "a thousand and five" songs (1 Kings 4:32) and the author of the songs did have the extensive knowledge of nature that Solomon was reputed to have (4:33).

The songs are closely related to other Middle Eastern wedding songs. In Sumeria and Canaan, a ritual wedding between the king and the goddess of fertility—probably portrayed by a priestess—was enacted through the exchange of such songs. And as recently as the 19th century, weddings in Syria were celebrated by the bride and groom, in the roles of queen and king, singing love songs to each other.

What the Bible Says about Itself

"This is the book of the generations of Adam" (Gen 5:1).

"Do all the words of the law that are written in this book" (Deut 28:58).

"Great is the wrath of the Lord that is kindled against us, because our fathers have not hearkened unto the words of this book" (2 Kings 22:13).

"I will bring upon that land all my words which I have pronounced against it, even all that is written in this book" (Jer 25:13).

"Blessed is he that keepeth the sayings of the prophecy of this book" (Rev 22:7).

"All the curses of the covenant . . . are written in this book of the law" (Deut 29: 20–21, 27).

"His commandments and his statutes . . . are written in this book of the law" (Deut 30:10).

"Then the Lord will make thy plagues wonderful . . . and of long continuance. . . . Moreover he will bring upon thee all the diseases of Egypt. . . . Also every sickness, and every plague, which is not written in the book of this law" (Deut 28:59–61).

"On that day they read in the book of Moses . . . that the Ammonite and the Moabite shall not come into the congregation of God for ever" (Neh 13:1).

Lamentations: Before the 18th century there had been no question that Jeremiah was the author of Lamentations, the collection of elegies for the fallen Jerusalem. The Bible's assertion (2 Chr 35:25) that the prophet was the author of "the book of lamentations" was often cited as proof. But Jeremiah's authorship came to be doubted when it was noticed that many of the ideas and sentiments expressed in Lamentations did not agree with those in the Book of Jeremiah. For example, in the Book of Jeremiah, Egypt is always portrayed as a land of bondage, whereas in Lamentations Egypt holds the promise of delivering Jerusalem from the Babylonians. Also, the Bible (2 Chr 35:25) reports that Jeremiah lamented Josiah's death (c. 610 BC) and not the destruction of Jerusalem, which fell in 587 BC. But some element of truth usually underlies the traditions. Here the descriptions of the destruction of Jerusalem show all the signs of being eyewitness accounts, and it is known that Jeremiah was such a witness.

Book of Daniel: The story of Daniel is set during the period of the Exile; the question of whether or not it was written then has generated much controversy and substantial arguments on both sides. Modern critics argue that the book is sometimes historically inaccurate for the period it purports to describe, making errors such as mixing up the reigns of the Babylonian kings. Another sign of late composition is the large number of Greek loan words, implying that the book was written after Alexander the Great's conquest of Palestine (332 BC). Those who take the conservative view maintain that the Greek words are merely evidence of how worldly Nebuchadnezzar's court was. One strong point in the conservative argument is the mention of a Daniel in the Book of Ezekiel (14:14, 20; 28:3)—a book that is generally believed to have been written c. 593–571 BC by the prophet while he was in Babylonia. Modern criticism counters by saying that the Daniel mentioned is identical with Danel, a hero of Canaanite legend.

The Prophetic Books: For almost every prophetic book, critical consensus is that the prophet was the original author of the book that bears his name, but that all of these books show signs of later editing. Except for the Books of Samuel (see above), information on the authorship of the prophetic books is contained in the section on Prophets.

THE NEW TESTAMENT

The Gospels: Mark: Almost all authorities agree that Mark is the earliest of the Gospels, since all the others borrow stories and phrases from it. Mark may have been composed around AD 75. The basis for this date comes from the assumption that Mark 13:2, 14 refers to the destruction of the Temple of Jerusalem and is a prophecy after the fact. Some scholars argue that it could have been written before the destruction, however. At any rate, it is likely that Mark, or whoever the author was, wrote his work sometime after the Great Fire of Rome (AD 64–65), a time of terror for the early Christians. They were persecuted as if they were responsible for the fire, and the author's purpose may have been to supply a written record of the life of Jesus to those whose faith was shaken. And he probably was aware that as eyewitnesses to the life of Jesus became fewer and fewer, a reliable biography was more urgently needed.

From internal evidence it seems that the author of Mark was brought up in a Jewish family in Jerusalem, since he is familiar with the geography of the city and with Jewish customs and the offices of the priesthood. The author also shows a familiarity with Aramaic, but a preference for Greek as his literary, and probably as his spoken, language. These meager indications of the author's personality and origins accord with the little that is known of Mark. Acts (12:12) mentions Mark's family's house in Jerusalem as the gathering place for prayer and worship of the new church, and part of such an upbringing could well be a knowledge of Greek and Aramaic and certainly a knowledge of the terrain around Jerusalem.

If this were all that scholars had to go on, nearly everyone living in Jerusalem at that time could be a contender for the authorship of Mark. But further evidence that Mark wrote the first Gospel comes from a 2d-century source, Papias the bishop of Hierapolis (60–130), who states that Mark was the "interpreter" of Peter, setting down "the things said or done by the Lord" as Peter remembered them.

The Gospels: Matthew: Although it is the first of the Gospels in the Bible, Matthew was the second to be written. Besides Mark, of which Matthew reproduces 90 percent, the author used a collection of Jesus' sayings—often designated as the Q source—in the composition of Matthew. That he polishes up the Greek of Mark, changing the wording of a sentence to make it more fluent and supplying idioms or transitional phrases to smooth out clumsy prose, points to an author whose native language was Greek, which is what one would expect, considering that Greek was the lingua franca of the hellenized Middle East.

The case for Matthew's authorship of the Gospel bearing his name is no less strong than that for Mark. Papias (mentioned above) names Matthew as the author; and without any direct refutation, there seems little reason to doubt Papias' statement.

The Gospels: Luke: It is now generally agreed that after the author of Luke wrote his Gospel he composed Acts as the sequel. The Gospel was written from the same sources as Matthew and employs one other source unknown to the authors of Matthew and Mark. The author's Greek is the most literary of all the Gospels and his use of foreign loan words is common, suggesting a man of education and worldliness.

Of Luke, the reputed author, little is known, because he is mentioned only twice in the New Testament. According to biblical tradition he was a physician (Col 4:14) and the traveling companion of Paul (2 Tim 4:11). It is his very obscurity, however, that lends credence to the traditional view that he is the author—there is no danger here, as there is almost everywhere else in the Bible, that the name of a prominent personage has been linked to a book merely to give it authority. Most authorities date this Gospel as well as Acts to the last quarter of the 1st century AD.

The Gospels: John: John is the most troublesome of the Gospels. Although its style suggests that it could be the work of a single author, the chronology of the events is so jumbled that it is possible the book was written or edited by more than one person. To top off confusion with chaos, there is no consensus, even among the earliest commentators, that the John reputed to have written the fourth Gospel is the same John credited with writing Revelation and the Epistles. The arguments over authorship of these books generally lead to the following tentative conclusions: John, the Apostle and disciple, is the authority for, if not the author of, the fourth Gospel and the First Epistle; the author may have been the man Papias names as "John the Elder"; it is probable that "John the Elder" wrote the Second and Third Epistles; the John who wrote Revelation probably did not write the fourth

Gospel. Nowhere else in the Bible is the question of authorship so knotted and so difficult as it is with the books ascribed to "John."

Other New Testament Books: As a refreshing surprise, some of the books attributed to Paul are undoubtedly his. Ephesians, Colossians, First and Second Timothy, Titus, and Hebrews are disputed. All the rest—Romans, Corinthians, Galatians, Philippians, Thessalonians, and Philemon—were probably written by Paul.

The books of Timothy and Titus—the "pastoral Epistles"—appear to have been written by someone using Paul's name to give these works authority. The Epistle to the Hebrews has been credited to Clement of Rome, an early pope, and to Luke. These are the candidates of early commentators; no internal evidence points to Clement, Luke, or anyone else as the author.

Of the remaining books of the Bible it can also be said that with one exception the authors traditionally ascribed to these books have been disputed even from the earliest times. In the case of the Epistle attributed to James, scholars have noted that it ignores the ritual requirements of the Law, an aspect of theology in which James is known to have been interested, and the Epistle displays a knowledge of Greek that is far beyond what one would expect of a hellenized speaker such as James. The two Books of Peter are usually considered to be the work of someone with an extensive knowledge of Greek and an appreciation of certain Greek philosophical ideas, particularly gnosticism—an improbable body of knowledge for a Galilean fisherman such as Peter. The Epistle of Jude is so short, there is little to confirm or deny Jude's authorship. Jude, together with James, was supposedly Jesus' brother—younger, of course (Matt 13:55; Mark 6:3)— and so the case for Jude as the author would have to allow for a date of composition no later than c. 90 BC, a figure which scholars have determined is acceptable basing their opinion on the literary style of the letter.

Five Inconsistencies and Contradictions

In some places the Bible shows signs of being poorly edited:
   1. Goliath is killed by David (1 Sam 17:50) but also by Elhanan: "the son of Jaare-oregin, a Beth-lehemite, slew *the brother of* Goliath the Gittite" (2 Sam 21:19). The italics that appear in the King James Version indicate that the words are not in the original and have been supplied by the translators.

   2. There are two stories of Saul's death. He commits suicide in First Samuel (31:4-6) by falling on his sword. In Second Samuel (1:9-10) he asks an Amalekite soldier to slay him because he is

wounded and his army has been defeated. The soldier reports to David that he does slay him.

3. It is not clear who Jesus' paternal grandfather was. Matthew (1:16) says that Joseph's father was Jacob, but Luke (3:23) says Joseph's father was Heli.

4. When he began to rule, Jehoiachin was eight years old, says Second Kings (24:8), but eighteen years old, says Second Chronicles (36:9).

5. Judas committed suicide either by hanging himself (Matt 27:5) or by throwing himself off a precipice (Acts 1:18).

A Few Words about Words

1. "I will make my words in thy mouth fire, and this people wood, and it shall devour them" (Jer 5:14).
2. "Thy words were found, and I did eat them" (Jer 15:16).
3. A "gift blindeth the wise, and perverteth the words of the righteous" (Ex 23:8).
4. "How long will ye . . . break me in pieces with words?" (Job 19:2).
5. "My God, my God, why hast thou forsaken me? Why art thou so far from helping me, and from the words of my roaring?" (Psa 22:1).
6. "The words of his mouth were smoother than butter, but war was in his heart: his words were softer than oil, yet they were drawn swords" (Psa 55:21).
7. "The words of the wicked are to lie in wait for blood" (Prov 12:6).

The Dead Sea Scrolls

Mummies are eternally fascinating whether they are human or literary. They bespeak permanence. Things seem a little more stable when one notices that Rameses II doesn't look all that different from someone who might be running a hardware store. And not a few people find it reassuring to know that the Book of Isaiah, read in churches and synagogues everywhere, is, but for translation, virtually identical to that known by Jesus and his contemporaries in Jerusalem during the lst century AD.

Until the discovery of the Dead Sea Scrolls, no one had this assurance. For about 3000 years, from the time the first books of the Old Testament are assumed to have been composed until the time when the printing press was invented, the books of the Bible were entirely handwritten. The oldest complete manuscripts of books of the Old Testament date from about the 10th century AD, and the oldest extant biblical fragment of Hebrew, the Nash Papyrus in the British Museum, was written in the 2d century AD. With the discovery of the Isaiah Scroll in 1947—the first of the Dead Sea Scrolls—scholars had the opportunity to study an entire book of the Bible 300 years older than the Nash Papyrus and 300 years closer to the original manuscript.

The Discovery of the Scrolls: The story of the discovery of the scrolls in caves near the Dead Sea is fairly well known in its broadest outlines, but it is a tale which by now perhaps consists more of imaginative embellishments than truth. One source says that it was a lone goat that the young Bedouin herdsman was chasing that day, another says it was a flock; one book says he spotted two openings in the craggy cliff above, another says there was a single hole. At any rate, all the stories agree on what happened next. The herdsman, Mohammed, tossed a rock into the cave opening and heard pottery shatter. Hoping there was treasure inside, he scrambled up the rocks and peered into the cave. That day (or the next), alone (or with one or two companions), Mohammed took out of the cave several ceramic jars containing parchment scrolls. The scrolls traveled with the Bedouin tribe for a time, perhaps as long as two years, and eventually came into the possession of one Kando, a cobbler in Bethlehem who also dealt in antiquities. (The remarkably good condition of the scrolls is attested to by one story which if untrue is at least plausible—that Kando at first considered using the supple parchment of the Isaiah Scroll for shoe leather.)

From the point that the scrolls go up for sale the tale becomes more convoluted and uncertain. There are many reasons the trail is so unclear. In all of his dealings Kando was suspicious and evasive. He had good reason to be wary. In Israel unauthorized excavations were, and are, illegal. And both he and the Bedouin wanted to keep the site of the cave a secret in case selling scrolls should prove to be a profitable enterprise.

Among the tangles of uncertainty surrounding the sale of the scrolls a few things are certain. Kando first contacted Father Samuel of the Syrian Orthodox Church in Jerusalem, and the priest in turn contacted other religious and scholarly institutions about buying them. Eventually Father Samuel managed to bring four scrolls to the United States, including the Isaiah Scroll, the commentary on Habakkuk, and *The Manual of Discipline.* These scrolls were sold at an exorbitant price, through a classified ad in the *Wall Street Journal,* to someone acting for the newly established Israeli government. Back in Jerusalem, these scrolls joined others which Kando had sold to Professor Sukenik at the Hebrew University. Among these were a second copy of Isaiah, *The War of the Sons of Light and the Sons of Darkness,* and *The Scroll of Thanksgiving Psalms.* All of these scrolls are now on display in the Shrine of the Book in Jerusalem, a building designed to house the scrolls in a controlled environment and architecturally inspired by the elegant curves of a scroll jar lid.

The Manual of Discipline

The Manual of Discipline is one of the most important nonbiblical books found with the Dead Sea Scrolls. It was a code of conduct for the members of a monastic sect. The rigorous code governs the individual's behavior by a series of fines meted out for forbidden acts. Such a "fine" might be an exclusion from privileges, perhaps even a reduction in the food ration, for a number of days. The work opens with a brief introduction to the philosophy of the sect—

451

that there are two completely antithetical forces which govern men's acts, the force of goodness and light and the force of evil and darkness. On comparing the code of the *Manual* with the institutions of the Essene sect described by Philo and Josephus, many scholars have concluded that the members of the Qumran community were the Essenes or their forerunners.

Here are some sample excerpts (after Theodor Gaster's *The Dead Sea Scriptures*):

"Anyone who interrupts his neighbor in a public session is to be fined for ten days."

"If a man bring out his hand from under his cloak, and so expose himself that his private parts become visible, he shall be fined for thirty days."

"He [the member] is to bear unremitting hatred toward all men of ill repute, and to be minded to keep in seclusion from them."

"The general members of the community are to keep awake for a third of all the nights of the year studying books, studying the Law and worshipping together."

Cave Two: In the years following the discovery of the first cave, more than ten caves within two miles of the original site have been found to contain scrolls or scroll fragments. In the latter part of 1951, the Bedouin had come upon a second cave (eventually to be called Cave Two) containing the remains of many scrolls. By that time, after the first scrolls had become a popular curiosity with international fans and frenzy, fragments were being sold by the square centimeter to any and all comers. Thus it was imperative that careful excavation of this and any remaining caves be carried out immediately if scroll fragments were to be properly reconstructed, translated, and preserved—if, indeed, fragments were to be had at all for a reasonable cost.

Archaeologists trying to locate Cave Two arrived hours too late to salvage anything; all they found were the debris and settling dust of a hasty but extensive Bedouin dig. Later they would sift out two fragments. Beginning in the spring of 1952, soon after this incident, a team of French and American archaeologists began systematically to comb the cliffs for additional caves.

The Monastery: The search began in the vicinity of Khirbet Qumran, the ruins of a monastery which was being excavated at the time. From the rubble archaeologists were removing jars identical to those found in Cave Two, inkwells stained with the residue of carbon ink identical to that used on the scrolls, and long rows of writing tables. It was becoming more than apparent to them that the monastery was the place where the scrolls were written. During the search in the surrounding hills for further scroll sites, over 230 crevices and caves were explored and found empty. Twenty-five others, however, contained pottery similar to that found in Cave One and Khirbet Qumran. On March 14, 1952, the expedition discovered what would be its only scroll cave. Besides fragments of about a dozen manuscripts and remains of about forty jars, the cave, later designated Cave Three, produced one of the most unusual of all the finds.

The Zadokite Document

This is a caustic commentary on those who broke the covenant, mixed in with brief explications of biblical passages, a code of ethics for life in the city and camp, and a little prophecy. The book is so named because the faithful are called "the sons of Zadok." Zadok was a priest in the time of David and the forebear of a line of high priests.

Sample excerpts:

"Now listen, all right-minded men, and take note how God acts: He has a case against all flesh and exacts satisfaction from all who spurn Him."

"Now concerning purification by water, No one is to bathe in dirty water or in water which is too scant to fill a pail."

A Hoax? Near the entrance were two scrolls made of copper and clearly showing on the outside the imprint of lettering stamped on the inner face. The crumbling scrolls were too corroded to be unrolled, and the problem of reading them was solved only when they were cut open three years later.

The two scrolls originally formed a single plaque over eight feet long. The inscription gives the location of more than sixty sites of buried treasure, most of which are pools and cisterns around Jerusalem and the area northwest of the Dead Sea, and lists in detail the items found at each location. Most of the treasure consists of gold and silver, in the form of ingots or artifacts, and the total weight of the loot has been estimated at over 130 *tons!* Although none of these purported treasure troves has yielded up any pay dirt, the plaque is usually assumed to be genuine, or at least not the work of a prankster.

Those who suggest that the inscription is not a hoax have a number of theories which would account for the Qumran community's knowledge of such wealth. One theory holds that the treasure could be the private monies of individuals in the monastery, secreted away so that it could be collected in some emergency, but not available for day-to-day use, since material wealth would be inappropriate for the communal and ascetic life of those who lived at Qumran. Of course, it may be objected that it is unlikely that those who entered the order would have or could have given up as much gold and silver as is listed, or that the sect could accumulate such wealth on its own.

Another theory is that the treasure was removed from the Second Temple and hidden before the Romans could seize it as booty in the siege of AD 70. But evidence from historical commentators and from the excavation at Qumran indicates that the monastery fell in AD 68, when the treasure was still in the Temple. Furthermore, many of the secular scrolls show that the men at Qumran considered Jerusalem to be a hotbed of sin, had little sympathy for its inhabitants, and thus were unlikely to help them in any crisis.

In his book *The Dead Sea Scriptures* Theodor Gaster gives some credence to the theory that the scroll may be part of a fraud. He cites an ancient Jewish legend about a copper tablet said to list the location, in Babylon, of vessels from the First Temple. Gaster suggests that this legendary tablet may be the foundation of a hoax that Josephus (AD 37?–100) reports as having taken place during the administration of Pontius Pilate (AD 26–36). Someone professing to be a deliverer of the people would rally large crowds by promising to reveal where the Temple treasure lay. Gaster speculates that the copper scrolls found in Cave Three may have something to do with this or a similar fraud, in which the hoaxter would extort money from the naïve, perhaps by offering his "authentic" copper tablet for sale.

The Scroll of Thanksgiving Psalms

This document consists of a number of hymns beginning with the formulaic opening, "I give thanks unto Thee, O Lord." For image and diction the hymns rely heavily on Bible allusions.

Sample excerpts:

"The spirit that lies in man's speech, Thou didst create."

"Thou has known all the words of man's tongue and determined the fruit of his lips, ere those lips themselves had being. It is Thou disposeth all words in due sequence and giveth to the spirit of the lips ordered mode of expression; that bringeth forth their secrets in measured utterances, and granteth unto spirits means to express their thoughts. . . ."

Who's Winning? Shortly after Cave Three was excavated, there came a report of new sales in scroll fragments. Clearly the Bedouin had found another cave, and it was rumored to be in the area of the original discovery.

The Bedouin had done a few days of digging before they were found out by archaeologists who spotted the cloud of dust the frantic excavation had raised. Very few of the tens of thousands of manuscript fragments that had once been in the cave remained for the scientists—the fragments would have to be bought if they were to be obtained at all. As it turned out, this cave, Cave Four, had held more scroll fragments than any other cave and it would take years to buy all the pieces and fit them together.

The Bedouin said they had learned of the cave's existence from one of the tribe's elders who, upon hearing talk of scrolls and the prices they were bringing, remembered once trailing a wounded partridge into a cave that contained many ancient jars. Following his directions, some younger members of the tribe had rediscovered this cave and two other less productive sites, caves Five and Six, nearby.

Over the years it became clear who the winners were in this earnest game of find-the-scrolls. Although archaeologists could claim caves Seven through Ten as theirs, none of these sites produced more than a few fragments. It was the Bedouin who made all the major finds but one, Cave Three.

The last of the scroll caves discovered, Cave Eleven in 1956, was another Bedouin victory and one which showed up the archaeologists: The cave had almost certainly been searched during the French-American expedition in 1952, but somehow no one had noticed that the roof in the back of the cave had collapsed. Behind the rockfall a niche held a neatly piled group of manuscripts, again the work of the Qumran monastery.

The War of the Sons of Light and the Sons of Darkness

This scroll is a plan for the apocalyptic battle between the forces of good and evil. *The War of the Sons of Light and the Sons of Darkness* is laden with details of strategy that owe much to Roman military tactics and goes into particulars so minute that it prescribes which is the correct spear for each stage of the battle and what is to be written on the blade of each spear.

Sample excerpts:

"On the third dart they shall write: *Flame of the sword devouring the evil-doing slain by the judgment of God.*"

". . . out of the center gap in the ranks there shall come into the lines seven priests of the descendants of Aaron, clothed in robes of white silk, wearing the linen tunic and the linen breeches, girt with the linen girdle of silk twined artistically with blue and purple and deep scarlet thread, after the model of broidery, and with mitred turbans on their heads—garments of war which they are not to bring into the sanctuary."

"All the cavalry . . . shall consist of stallions swift of foot, non-biters, long in the wind, full-grown and mature, trained for battle and used to hearing all kinds of sounds and facing all kinds of sights."

The Ruins of Qumran: The combination of archaeological evidence from the excavation of the Qumran monastery, the translation of the scrolls themselves, and the reports of ancient historians has given scientists a detailed picture of the life of those at Qumran. The people who wrote the scrolls appear to have been members of an extraordinarily devout, austere, and self-righteous sect. They were probably the Essenes, a group of religious zealots mentioned in the works of three ancient historians: Pliny, Josephus, and Philo.

Pliny describes the Essenes as a "solitary tribe" located on the "west side of the Dead Sea." He goes on to say, all too ambiguously, that "lying below the Essenes was the town of En-gedi then comes Masada." The Qumran ruins are indeed on the western shore of the Dead Sea, and are north (above?) En-gedi, which in turn is north of Masada.

Philo says members of the sect lead a simple communal life, sharing meals and studying ethical laws. *The Manual of Discipline,* one of the secular books found in Cave One, prescribes a code of behavior for members of such a religious sect and does in fact mention communal meals. That meals were considered a community function at Qumran has been confirmed, as best as archaeology can confirm something of this nature. A large dining hall, with benches along the wall, and doorways leading to kitchen areas containing hundreds of plates, has been excavated there.

Finally, Josephus mentions, among other things, that the Essenes had various baptismal and purification rituals. Unearthed at Qumran was a complex water system including what seems to be baptismal or bathing pools. Moreover, Josephus reports that the Essenes were greatly interested in ancient writings!

Verse Facts

The shortest verse in the Bible is "Jesus wept" (John 11:35).

The longest verse in the Bible is in Esther (8:9). It consists of ninety words describing the Persian Empire as consisting of 127 provinces from India to Ethiopia, to whom the decree concerning new rights for Jews was being sent.

The middle verse of the Bible is Psalm 118:8: "It is better to trust in the Lord than to put confidence in princes."

Have You Copied Any Good Books Lately?

The Old Testament was written in Hebrew, with occasional parts in Aramaic, over a period of 1200 years, from about the 13th century to the 1st century BC (see "Who Wrote the Bible?" page 437). There is no way to tell when the books of the Bible began to be canonized—that is, accepted as sacred and thus preserved without change.

Books Before the Bible: From mention of "books" that lace the Old Testament—the books of laws (Deut 17:18; 31:24), the book of Jasher (Josh 10:13), the book of the Kings of Israel and Judah (1 Chr 9:1), and others—it is clear that as early as Deuteronomy a group of standard religious and historical works existed that had enough of a circulation that people recognized them by title alone. The group of scribes who copied these works must have taken great professional care in transcribing the books, especially those said to be dictated from God to Moses. On the other hand, many books, such as the book of Jasher, have apparently not survived.

In trying to reconstruct what the books of the Bible looked like as they left the hand of the author, scholars cannot rely on the Dead Sea Scrolls alone, since only fragments of some Old Testament books have been recovered from the scrolls. They must also use the oldest manuscripts from the literary traditions that have grown up around the Bible.

The Samaritan Version: One important source used to check the early history of the Bible is the Samaritan version of the Pentateuch. In the 4th century BC, Samaria, once the capital of Israel, broke off relations with the surrounding cities. Thus, after the 4th century BC, its version of the

Pentateuch had an entirely independent development from the traditional Jewish version. Indeed, the two renderings differ significantly in about a thousand different places. Comparison has shown that in some places the Samaritan Pentateuch is closer to the Dead Sea Scrolls than to the traditional version, indicating it is more true to the earlier copies. In other places the traditional Bible is closer to the scrolls, indicating it is truer to older versions.

The Greek Version: Fortunately there is another way to investigate the development of the Bible. In the 3d century BC seventy Greek-speaking Jewish scholars are said to have translated the Old Testament into Greek, the lingua franca of the Jewish Diaspora during that period. It was the first scholarly translation of the Bible and in one way the best: It was the earliest that we know of. There is, however, one drawback. The oldest copies we have are from the 4th century AD and are not completely reliable. Nevertheless it is important for several reasons unrelated to its antiquity: It was partially the basis of the Latin Vulgate Bible, which in turn was the basis for many other versions—including the King James and more directly the Douay—and it was the Bible in use in Jerusalem at the time of Jesus.

The Masoretic Tradition: Jerome, the Latin scholar who translated the Vulgate, also based his work on the Hebrew text commonly called the Masoretic. Strictly speaking, the Masoretes (from the Hebrew word meaning "to hand down") were an order of religious scribes that flourished in Babylonia during the 7th century AD. However, "Masoretic" is loosely used for the traditional Hebrew Bible as developed in the mainstream of early Judaism.

The name has stuck to the early text of the Hebrew Bible because the work of the early scribes was much like that of the Masoretes. While taking utmost care to add or subtract nothing to the substance of the manuscripts they were transcribing, copyists took the liberty of inventing and inserting punctuation marks and some vowels. Early Hebrew, like the advertisements that ask if you "cn rd ths msg," had no vowels, and though this convention was clear enough to regular readers of the Bible, it was a hindrance to those who were beginning to read Hebrew for the first time. Under the influence of the scribes, about AD 70 the Masoretic text was established—"frozen"—into the Hebrew text as it is known today.

A Good Line Is Hard to Find

Patrick Henry quoted the Bible three times in a speech given before the Virginia Convention at Richmond on March 23, 1775:
1. "Are we disposed to be the number of those who, having eyes,

459

see not, and having ears, hear not, the things which so nearly concern their temporal salvation?" From:

"Hear now this, O foolish people, and without understanding; which have eyes, and see not; which have ears, and hear not" (Jer 5:21).

2. "The battle, sir, is not to the strong alone." From:

"The race is not to the swift, nor the battle to the strong" (Eccl 9:11).

3. "The gentlemen may cry, Peace, peace! but there is no peace." From:

"They have healed also the hurt of the daughter of my people slightly, saying, Peace, peace; when there is no peace." (Jer 6:14).

Daniel Webster alludes to Moses bringing forth water from a rock and Elisha's bones reviving the dead man (Num 20:11; 2 Kings 13:21) in a speech about Alexander Hamilton, March 10, 1831:

"He smote the rock of the national resources, and abundant streams of revenue gushed forth. He touched the dead corpse of Public Credit, and it sprung upon its feet."

Lincoln quoted the Bible three times in his Second Inaugural Address, March 4, 1865:

1 and 2. "It may seem strange that any men should dare to ask a just God's assistance in wringing their bread from the sweat of other men's faces, but let us judge not, that we be not judged." From:

"In the sweat of thy face shalt thou eat bread" (Gen 3:19); "Judge not, that ye be not judged" (Matt 7:1).

3. "The judgments of the Lord are true and righteous altogether" (Psa 19:9).

Lincoln's speech at the Republican State Convention in Springfield, Illinois, in 1858, included the famous statement that "a house divided against itself cannot stand." It is taken from Matthew (12:25): "Every kingdom divided against itself is brought to desolation; and every city or house divided against itself shall not stand."

Franklin Roosevelt's First Inaugural Address, March 4, 1933, alludes to Jesus' expulsion of the moneylenders from the Temple (Matt 21:12–13): "The money changers have fled from their high seats in the temple of our civilization."

John Kennedy's Inaugural Address, Jan. 20, 1961, contains a near quote from Luke: "For of those to whom much is given, much is required." From:

"For unto whomever much is given, of him shall be much required" (Luke 12:48).

Clichés in Everyday Speech

I am escaped with the *skin of my teeth* (Job 19:20).

Am I *my brother's keeper?* (Gen 4:9).

And ye shall eat *the fat of the land* (Gen 45:18).

But man dieth, and wasteth away: yea, man *giveth up the ghost,* and where is he? (Job 14:10).

He that *spareth the rod hateth his son* (Prov 13:24).

Pride goeth before destruction, and an haughty spirit before a fall (Prov 16:18).

A man hath no better thing under the sun, than to *eat,* and to *drink and* to *be merry* (Eccl 8:15).

Woe is me! (Isa 6:5).

The nations are as *a drop of a bucket* (Isa 40:15).

He is brought as a *lamb to the slaughter* (Isa 53:7).

I am *holier than thou* (Isa 65:5).

Can the Ethiopian change his skin or *the leopard change his spots?* (Jer 13:23).

Ye are the *salt of the earth* (Matt 5:13).

Beware of false prophets, which come to you *in sheep's clothing,* but inwardly they are ravening *wolves* (Matt 7:15).

461

In Other Words—
The Bible in English

The first "modern" English translation of the Bible was made under the supervision of John Wycliffe around 1380. Working from the Latin Vulgate, Wycliffe and his assistants tried to present the English people with a complete edition of the Old and New Testaments they could understand without the aid of the clergy. They accomplished their aim all too well. Such a translation was a politically dangerous act, for it eroded one of the power bases of the Church.

Bible Reading Banned: In 1408 Canterbury decreed that no one could translate the Bible into English without Church approval and that public reading of any English translation would be a criminal offense. Despite persecution, manuscripts were widely circulated and read. Indeed, for 150 years handwritten copies of Wycliffe's translation and that of Purvey, his friend and revisionist, were transcribed and read throughout England.

Wycliffe's translation is, to our ears, strikingly vernacular, even vulgar. But to the Englishman of the time it was vulgar in the true and original sense of being "common" and "ordinary"—its language is the language of the common man. For "children" Wycliffe has "brat"; for "father" he has "dad"; for "chariot," "cart." Such a vocabulary made the translation accessible in one way, if not in every way. Handwritten copies were of course expensive and only a few could afford them. It is reported that people would pay quite a bit to study the book for an hour, and that farmers would pay for their hour with a load of produce.

Burning the Bible: Though Wycliffe's version remained popular, with printed editions coming out as late as 1850, it was superseded by the new translations that came at the beginning of the Reformation, the Protestant rebellion from the Catholic Church. The first of these translations, indeed the first English translation of the New Testament to be printed and not handwritten, was John Tyndale's. Tyndale was a student of classical languages at Oxford and Cambridge. After graduation, he became committed to the idea of an English translation, undoubtedly under the influence of Luther, who had published his German New Testament in 1522. Finding no support in England for his project, Tyndale left for the Continent in 1524 and enrolled at Wittenberg to become Luther's student. But Tyndale had arrived at a bad time. Luther had already been condemned for heresy, declared an outlaw, and excommunicated. In 1524 the Peasants' War broke out, and this revolt was blamed in part on the new printing industry that was making the writings of the Reformation—and Bibles—widely available. Printers were being closely watched by ecclesiastical authorities.

By the summer of 1525 Tyndale had completed a manuscript of the New Testament and submitted it to printers in Cologne. One of Luther's foes had been tipped off about publication and plied the printers with drink to get them to talk. Learning all, he brought the authorities down on the shop and Tyndale barely made good his escape to Worms, where 3000 copies were completed in secrecy. The editions were smuggled across the Channel in bags of flour, and by other contrivances arrived in London. When the authorities got wind of the book an attempt was made to round up all copies. Those confiscated were burned at St. Paul's Cross. Over the next three years around 18,000 copies were produced. Of these, only three remain, one of these a mere fragment—testimony to the effectiveness of the censors. As with Wycliffe's translation 150 years earlier, Tyndale's evoked an edict, this time by Henry VIII, decreeing it "be clerely extermynated and exiled out of the realme of Englande for ever."

Though Tyndale managed to publish only the Pentateuch and New Testament in his lifetime, his translations stand among the best in English. His prose is smooth, rhythmical, and clear, so much so that perhaps three quarters of his phrases are retained in the Authorized Version. And his work is founded on good scholarship—he was the first to translate into English directly from the original languages of Hebrew and Greek.

Like Wycliffe, who suffered censure and scorn in his lifetime and even in the grave—for his bones were disinterred and scattered forty years after his death—Tyndale led a martyr's life. Exiled and impoverished for most of his days, he was finally betrayed by a supposed friend and imprisoned in Belgium. He died in prison, by strangulation, and his body was burned at the stake.

Thou Shalt Read Proof Carefully

In 1631, the king's printers Robert Barker and Martin Lucas printed an edition of 1000 copies of the Bible with the word "not" left out of the seventh commandment, rendering it "Thou shalt commit adultery." For this they were fined 3000 pounds.

The Bible Becomes Approved Reading: It is one of history's most vicious ironies that in 1534, one year before Tyndale's death, Henry VIII, the man who wrote the edict forbidding dissemination of Tyndale's work, ordered the publication of a new English Bible at the request of a convocation at Canterbury. Henry had joined the Protestant cause, begun in Germany with Luther, and such a translation was important as a sign of England's breach with Rome. The task fell to Miles Coverdale, who was competent in Latin but who had no extensive training in Hebrew or Greek. Coverdale was a friend of Tyndale's and did, in fact, pick up some Hebrew while helping Tyndale translate the Pentateuch, but he had to take a step backward in his translation and rely on the Latin Vulgate, Luther's German, and Tyndale's English for his edition. The work was completed in 1535 and dedicated to Henry VIII. It was the first complete English Bible to be printed.

Matthews Bible: With the Reformation gaining momentum in England, the Bible could now be safely translated with royal sanction and even favor. In 1537 the "Matthews" Bible appeared. It was the work of another of Tyndale's friends, John Rogers, operating under the pseudonym "Thomas Matthews." Taking Tyndale's manuscripts of the books from Joshua to Second Chronicles, unpublished at the time of Tyndale's death, and Tyndale's published books, Rogers added the remaining books from Coverdale's work to make up his Bible.

The Great Bible: This Bible was reworked into the version which has become known as the "Great Bible"—a nickname that at the time reflected its bulky size, but could well indicate its importance. Coverdale was again behind this Bible and took as his guides and checks Latin Old and New Testaments. By royal decree it was placed in every church in England. But even without this mandate it would have been a successful work. In fact, the psalter from this Bible, generally known as the Book of Common Prayer, is still used because it is more adaptable for singing than the Psalms of the later Authorized Version.

The "Breeches Bible": For Bible scholars things were reversed once again in England when Queen Mary took the throne. She did not accept the Reformation, its Bibles, or its translators. She had John Rogers burned at the stake, and Coverdale was put on probation. Coverdale had nothing to look forward to but an end like Rogers' or Tyndale's when he received permission to emigrate to Denmark. From there he moved to Switzerland in 1557 to begin work with a group of English exiles on a Bible that would be the first attempt since Tyndale's to translate the Bible from the original languages into English. This book, the Geneva Bible, became the most successful Bible of the age and the standard until the publication of the Authorized Version in 1611. It was the version Shakespeare would have known, though he probably referred to it, as many did, as the "Breeches Bible." The name comes from Genesis (3:6), where Adam and Eve are said, in this version, to have made themselves "breeches" of fig leaves.

The Geneva Bible achieved a number of firsts among English Bibles: It was the first to use italics for words not in the original language but necessary to make a sensible translation, it was the first to omit the Apocrypha, the first to divide the Bible into verses, and the first to be printed in Roman and not "Old English" type. This is the edition the Pilgrims carried on the *Mayflower* and preferred over the Authorized Version.

Douay and Bishop's Bibles: With so many translations reaching the layman, the clergy, both Anglican and Roman Catholic, felt the need to supply their own. The Catholics produced the Douay, a literal translation of the Latin Vulgate. It was called Douay because the Old Testament section was made at the College of the Divines at Douay in Flanders. The Anglican clergy during Queen Elizabeth's rule brought out the "Bishop's Bible," a revision of the Great Bible that included theological margin notes. The Douay remains the standard work for Catholic believers; the Bishop's Bible, however, has fallen into disuse.

Authorized Version: Influenced by the Puritans who objected to the Anglican marginalia in the Bishop's Bible, King James, something of a biblical scholar himself, appointed fifty-four scholars to prepare a new translation. Forty-seven of them survived to complete the work in 1611. From 1604 to 1607 they prepared themselves individually by reading and research, and from 1607 to 1611 they did the translating or, more accurately, the comparing, revising, and editing. Their real job was to synthesize one hundred years of Bible translation. Though they were supposed to stay close to the Bishop's Bible, they borrowed most from Tyndale. The Bible they made is known as the King James version, or the Authorized Version (AV)—even though it was not the first version authorized by royalty and there is no proof that King James authorized the final manuscript.

Hands Off!

Biblical warnings not to add to or subtract from the Bible include:

1. "What thing soever I command you, observe to do it: thou shalt not add thereto, nor diminish from it" (Deut 12:32).

2. "If any man shall add unto these things, God shall add unto him the plagues that are written in this book" (Rev 22:18).

3. "If any man shall take away from the words of the book of this prophecy, God shall take away his part out of the book of life, and out of the holy city" (Rev 22:19).

And it shall be, when thou hast made an end of reading this book, that thou shalt bind a stone to it, and cast it into the midst of Euphrates [Jer 51:63].

Index

470

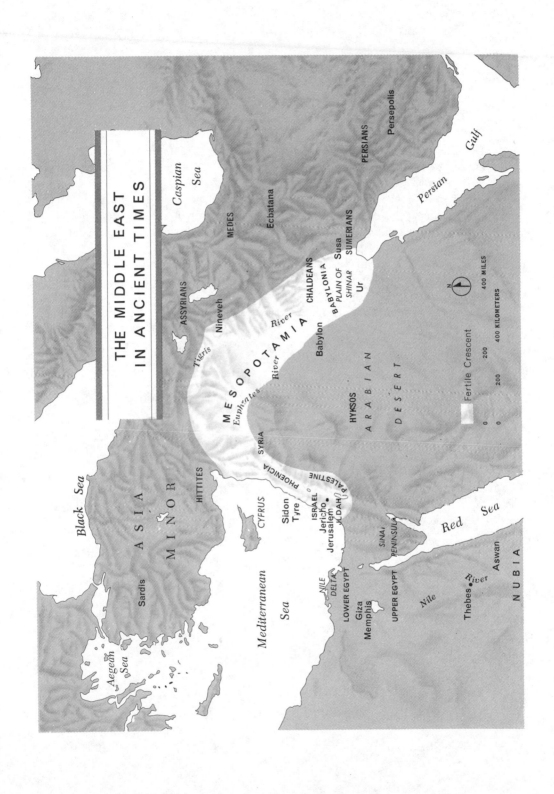

THE MIDDLE EAST
IN ANCIENT TIMES

Black Sea

Caspian Sea

ASIA MINOR

HITTITES

Sardis

MEDES

ASSYRIANS

Nineveh

Ecbatana

PERSIANS

Persepolis

Persian Gulf

Tigris River

MESOPOTAMIA

Euphrates River

CHALDEANS

BABYLONIA

PLAIN OF SHINAR

SUSA

SUMERIANS

Ur

Babylon

SYRIA

PHOENICIA

ARABIAN DESERT

HYKSOS

Aegean Sea

Mediterranean Sea

CYPRUS

Sidon

Tyre

ISRAEL

Jericho

Jerusalem

JUDAH

PALESTINE

NILE DELTA

LOWER EGYPT

Giza

Memphis

SINAI PENINSULA

Red Sea

UPPER EGYPT

Nile

Thebes

Nile River

Aswan

NUBIA

N

Fertile Crescent

0   200   400 MILES

0   200   400 KILOMETERS

About the Authors

This book was prepared under the editorship of Eunice Riedel, Project Director, with the assistance of Thomas Tracy, Senior Project Editor, and Barbra D. Moskowitz, Assistant Project Editor.

Eunice Riedel is a graduate of Barnard College, where she majored in anthropology. Before becoming an editor at Morrow she worked at the American Museum of Natural History. She has traveled widely and has lived and worked in Amsterdam, Berlin, and Madrid.

Thomas Tracy is an honors graduate of Wesleyan University, where he majored in English literature and classics. He received the Ingram Prize for excellence in the study of New Testament and classical Greek. He has traveled widely in Europe and America, and is a luthier (guitar maker).

Barbra D. Moskowitz has a master's degree in anthropology from SUNY and is especially interested in sociolinguistics. She has studied Judaism intensively, is fluent in Hebrew, and has lived in Israel.

Temple Israel

Minneapolis, Minnesota

IN HONOR OF THE SPECIAL BIRTHDAY OF
JIMMY SEGAL
FROM
FRED & MARGO BERDASS